*All Clever Men, Who Make Their Way*

# ALL CLEVER MEN, WHO MAKE THEIR WAY
## *Critical Discourse in the Old South*

Edited with an introduction
by Michael O'Brien

The University of Georgia Press
Athens and London

Published in 1992 as a Brown Thrasher Book
by the University of Georgia Press, Athens, Georgia 30602
© 1982 by Michael O'Brien
Preface to the Brown Thrasher Edition and
"Suggestions for Further Reading"
© 1992 by Michael O'Brien
Published by The University of Georgia Press
Athens, Georgia 30602
www.ugapress.org
All rights reserved
Printed digitally in the United States of America

The Library of Congress has cataloged the hardcover edition of
this book as follows:
Library of Congress Cataloging-in-Publication Data

All clever men, who make their way : critical discourse in the
Old South / edited, with an introduction, by Michael O'Brien.
   xv, 466 p. ; 24 cm.
   ISBN 0-8203-1490-0 (pbk. : alk. paper)
   Originally published: Fayetteville : University of Arkansas
Press, 1982.
   "Brown thrasher books."
   Includes bibliographical references (p. 443-451) and index.
   1. Criticism—Southern States—History—19th century.
2. Southern States—Intellectual life. 3. Southern States—
Civilization—1775–1865. I. O'Brien, Michael, 1948– . II. Title.
F213 .A44                                           1992
975'.03 20                                       92-17539

Paperback reissue 2008 ISBN-13: 978-0-8203-3201-7
ISBN-10: 0-8203-3201-1

British Library Cataloging-in-Publication Data available

*Laborum Periculorum Meorum*
*Socio*
*Virium Elegantiae Subiectarum*
*Explicatori et Exemplo*

# Contents

Preface to the Paperback Edition, *ix*

Introduction:
On the Mind of the Old South and Its Accessibility, *1*

Editorial Note, *26*

1.
James Hervey Smith,
"Sismondi's Political Economy," *29*

2.
Jesse Burton Harrison,
"English Civilization," *55*

3.
Hugh Swinton Legaré,
"German Diaries," *89*

4.
Thomas Roderick Dew,
"Republicanism and Literature," *125*

5.
George Frederick Holmes,
"Schlegel's Philosophy of History," *177*

6.
Henry Augustine Washington,
"The Social System of Virginia," *228*

7.
James Warley Miles,
"The Possibility and Nature of Theology," *263*

8.
*Charles E. A. Gayarré,*
"The Rise and Fall of John Law," *280*

9.
*Frederick Adolphus Porcher,*
"Modern Art," *310*

10.
*Louisa Susanna McCord,*
"Enfranchisement of Woman," *337*

11.
*John Holmes Bocock,*
"Emerson on History," *357*

12.
*Richard Henry Nisbet,*
"American Authorship and Nathaniel Hawthorne," *376*

13.
*Basil Lanneau Gildersleeve,*
"The Necessity of the Classics," *398*

14.
*James Henley Thornwell,*
"Memoir of Dr. Henry," *420*

Acknowledgments, *441*

Suggestions for Further Reading, *443*

Index, *453*

# Preface to the Paperback Edition

In 1977 or so, I finished a book on the conception of Southern identity in the 1920s and 1930s. There I had asserted that the dispersal of Romanticism in the South during the early nineteenth century had been peculiarly influential in forming the conception of Southern culture. But a book on the twentieth century was a place ill-adapted to demonstrate a claim about the nineteenth century. Assertion was not proof. So I decided to go backwards and write a second work on Romanticism and the Old South, to be called something like *The Intellectual Origins of Southern Identity*. It was going to be a brisk book, which would sketch the best modern scholarship on Romanticism and demonstrate the influence that movement had on Southern thinkers. The secondary literature pertaining to Romanticism was ample, growing, thoughtful. Secondary works about Southern thinkers were thin, which was a nuisance for the want of guidance but also an opportunity. Take a little M. H. Abrams, add a dash of Morse Peckham, read some Schlegel—this was my plan. Then trot through Poe, Simms, and . . . Who else? There were names in the secondary literature: Legaré, Grayson, others. I was firmly told by everything I read that these antebellum Southerners were sorry, dull, rigid people. But I sat down to read them anyway, holding my nose in the approved attitude of disdain, looking at old editions and at periodicals thick with dust, untouched, I fancied, since Ulrich Phillips had been in the same stacks in Ann Arbor.

Gradually my nose tilted downward, the disdain ebbed away, the interest grew, the puzzlement compounded. "This," I said to myself, indicating the secondary literature, "bears no relationship to that," pointing to the original sources; the one asserted sterility, the other evidenced vitality. I read on. Coming to know more, I observed this contradiction widening to the point where it became intolerable, where I was left with no alternative but to throw over the orthodoxy. I set aside my copies of Rollin Osterweis, Clement Eaton, even William R. Taylor, let alone Perry Miller and Merle Curti, and placed before myself a sheet of paper headed "The Mind of the Old South," which I left blank. Matters were such that knowledge of ignorance was an advance over knowledge in error.

Gradually I tried to fill the sheet. The experience was exhilarating, though a little disturbing. It is hard to navigate if you cannot heed familiar landmarks. I *thought* Hugh Legaré was a first-rate mind, but no one else seemed to think so. Who was I to say it? Reading on, I discovered that Lord Acton thought so too, which was some consolation.[1] And then there was the question of slavery. For the orthodoxy assumed that a slaveholder could not be intelligent or erudite or write well. This perspective was intended out of respect for the sufferings of slaves or the energies of abolitionists. This was amiable morality, but bad history. Jefferson contradicted it, Cicero and Sophocles made it absurd. Yet I knew that a historian who addressed himself to a modern American audience and said that Southern slaveholders had a developed intellectual culture was a historian who brought news that no one wanted to hear, that few needed except those whom I had little desire to encourage—those who wanted to play the game of competing with Yankees.[2] Still, I felt it was true.

But how to say it? The long-range answer was to do further research and begin to write essays, biographies, works of synthesis. This I set about doing. But in the short-run? I could have written an article, sent it to the *American Historical Review* or the *Journal of Southern History*, and made my case. But the case rested upon a reading of texts that, I could safely assume, none of my readers would have known. It would not be possible, under such circumstances, to be persuasive. Interpretation and text had to be made simultaneously available. So I designed this book, a "reader" of sorts that presents fourteen substantial works by antebellum Southern intellectuals, prefaced by an essay that formally makes the case I have just informally described. This was an odd venture. Such

---

1. Lord Acton, "Political Causes of the American Revolution," in *Essays on Freedom and Power*, ed. Gertrude Himmelfarb (New York, 1948), p. 203. This is quoted at the beginning of my Legaré biography, as a talisman to ward off evil spirits: see Michael O'Brien, *A Character of Hugh Legaré* (Knoxville, 1985), p. xii.

2. Some have been encouraged, despite my desires: see, for example, John C. Guilds, ed., *"Long Years of Neglect": The Work and Reputation of William Gilmore Simms* (Fayetteville, Ark., 1988), pp. 3–19.

readers usually embody orthodoxies by summing up an established perspective. Seldom do they attempt to initiate a heresy. Understandably, publishers were reluctant. One dismissed the venture out of hand; another hinted that he *might* do it if I signed simultaneously a contract for a more conventional book; a third sat on the manuscript for nearly a year before returning a cryptic refusal that spoke grimly of marketing problems, a diffuseness of focus, and so forth. Fortunately in 1980 I went to teach at the University of Arkansas, which was then founding a press anxious to lay its hands quickly upon manuscripts. The Arkansas Endowment for the Humanities was persuaded to subvent the venture. So *All Clever Men* was published in 1982, but as a very expensive book that few could buy. Indeed it was ironic that a book intended to diminish the inaccessibility of antebellum Southern thought was itself so inaccessible. It is, therefore, peculiarly welcome now to be able to preface a paperback edition.

In the introduction, the reader will find these ironic remarks, first written in about 1979: "The picture is gloomy. It is only justice to add, however, that in very recent years a few books have trickled forth to hint at the emergence of a Southern intellectual history. It is not a self-conscious trickle. There are no bands of malcontents that gather at historical conventions and declaim the virtues of their subject, foundations are not besieged to finance conferences in agreeable spots, newsletters are not issued to eager Young Turks steeped in the lesser writings of Albert Taylor Bledsoe." Irony dates very quickly. There is now a small annual meeting of those interested in the history of Southern thought, the Southern Intellectual History Circle. There is now a Southern Texts Society, which is doing on a larger scale what this reader was intended to do on a small scale: identify, edit, and publish a series of book-length collections of manuscript or rare printed materials important to understanding the culture of the American South and its expressive life.[3] These ventures are still small, as they should be. In the great market square of American history, the intellectual culture of the South deserves only a few modest booths, for those who like that sort of thing.

It would overtax the resources of a brief preface to offer a summary of what historians and literary critics have done since 1982 to rewrite accounts of the Old South and its cultural life. But the argu-

3. Of the intellectuals anthologized in *All Clever Men*, there are editions in progress for Louisa McCord, Thomas R. Dew, and Basil Gildersleeve.

ment of *All Clever Men* seems to have made its way in the world and found a response. Within the confines of Southern history, my standpoint seems widely accepted.[4] Among American intellectual historians, the old orthodoxy is moribund without having been supplanted by a new one. That is, historians in Boston are somewhat less likely to greet the phrase "Southern intellectual history" with a stale joke about oxymorons but would be hard pressed to specify the content of that history. And partly, that is our fault, not theirs. The history of Southern thought has as yet been written piecemeal—a monograph here, a text there—and we still lack the Southern Perry Miller whom I invoked in 1982 as a *deus ex machina*. But the subject is young, there is no hurry, and there is much basic work yet to be done. And it is important to stress that, though I did this book out of a marked sense of heterodoxy, even in 1982 I saw ventures— by Drew Faust, Robert Brugger, and others—on which to build and with which partially to sympathize. If the standpoint of this book has proved persuasive, it is because people were prepared to be persuaded and listened to many voices other than my own. The large number of those voices, speaking since the early 1980s, will be evident from the Suggestions for Further Reading, which the reader will find appended to this edition.

My sheet of paper has more scribbles on it now than in 1982, which would lead me to change things, if I were to begin anew. I might make some different selections. I chose to print Hugh Legaré's German diaries because I wished forcibly to counter the argument that only New Englanders like George Ticknor were open to German thought. Yet the scope of Legaré's thought might have been better represented by the intellectual manifesto, "Classical Learning," with which he initiated the *Southern Review* in 1828.[5] For an example of an antebellum Southern historian, I would be more likely now to choose William Henry Trescot over Charles Gayarré, whose importance I accepted from Clement Eaton but whose ac-

---

4. For example, in Eugene D. Genovese, *The Slaveholders' Dilemma: Freedom and Progress in Southern Conservative Thought, 1820–1860* (Columbia, S.C., 1992), pp. 1–3; Richard J. Calhoun, ed., *Witness to Sorrow: The Antebellum Autobiography of William J. Grayson* (Columbia, S.C., 1990), p. 12; James Oscar Farmer, Jr., *The Metaphysical Confederacy: James Henley Thornwell and the Synthesis of Southern Values* (Macon, Ga., 1986), p. 4.

5. Hugh Swinton Legaré, "Classical Learning," *Southern Review* 1 (February 1828): 1–49.

complishment, I notice now, I doubted even in 1982. Or I might select Mitchell King's *Discourse on the Qualifications and Duties of an Historian* (1843).⁶ I might now choose for a sample of James Henley Thornwell, not his memoir of Robert Henry, but something like his "Theology, Its Proper Method and Its Central Principle" (1858) or perhaps the *Letter to His Excellency Governor Manning on Public Instruction in South Carolina* (1853).⁷ I would find now more space for women's voices; though my selection from Louisa McCord was not, I think, ill-judged and seems to have been of interest to scholars of women's history.⁸ And I would drastically rewrite that part of the biographical sketch of McCord that falls back upon stale caricatures about sentimental female verse. In truth, I had not read her *Caius Gracchus* with sufficient care and so deserved Richard Lounsbury's rejoinder: "In the biographical introduction to a recent edition of one of her essays, Mrs. McCord's play is explained in an impulse toward 'sentimental verse and fiction,' and is consigned to the level of a Beerbohm parody, but with 'the disadvantage of seriousness' (a stage direction is usefully provided as evidence)."⁹

In the Editorial Note, I observed that "the anthology concentrates upon the reception and understanding of new ideas, since I take it that the open or closed quality of Southern thought is a, if not the, leading issue." My selections were much directed towards Southern reactions to European thought: Smith on Sismondi, Harrison on Hegel, Dew on Madame de Staël, Holmes on Friedrich von Schlegel, Miles on David Strauss. Here the anthology was most a quarrel with William R. Taylor's *Cavalier and Yankee*, whose argument that antebellum Southern culture had "lost touch with Europe" is discussed in the introduction and which most exercised me as an error. I do not repent of this emphasis. It was necessary in its day. Now, when the notion that European ideas significantly influ-

---

6. Mitchell King, *A Discourse on the Qualifications and Duties of an Historian; Delivered before the Georgia Historical Society, on the Occasion of its Fourth Anniversary, on Monday, 13th February, 1843* (Savannah, 1843).
7. John B. Adger et al, eds., *The Collected Writings of James Henley Thornwell*, 4 vols. (1871; Edinburgh, 1974), 1:445–88; James Henley Thornwell, *Letter to His Excellency Governor Manning on Public Instruction in South Carolina* (Columbia, S.C., 1853).
8. See Elizabeth Fox-Genovese, *Within the Plantation Household: Black and White Women in the Old South* (Chapel Hill, 1988).
9. Richard C. Lounsbury, "*Ludibria Rerum Mortalium:* Charlestonian Intellectuals and Their Classics," in Michael O'Brien and David Moltke-Hansen, eds., *Intellectual Life in Antebellum Charleston* (Knoxville, 1986), p. 445.

enced the South is better established, the point may seem overly labored.[10] I probably made more of the influence of German thought than I would now. I would emphasize a dialogue of Southerners with other Americans, more than is managed in my selection of Nisbet's discussion of Hawthorne and Bocock's of Emerson.

Among those other Americans were other Southerners. My subtitle for this book, *Critical Discourse in the Old South*, had been intended as the title, until my publisher requested something livelier. In some haste, I foraged around in Byron and rediscovered his splendid parody of periodical reviewing. Even then, I was aware that *All Clever Men* was inapt for an anthology that included a woman, even if Louisa McCord was a woman whom many modern feminists would elect to banish from their sex. Not for the first or last time, I was tempted more by wit than by virtue—not the priority of our age—and let Byron stand. In fact, the subtitle is as problematical as the title, as one reviewer sensibly noticed.[11] "Discourse" implies a conversation. In my anxiety to stress that Southerners knew the world beyond the South, I paid too little attention to their internal debates. And there were plenty of these debates available for anthology. Legaré's "Classical Learning" would have shown him arguing with Thomas Grimké of South Carolina over the utility of the classics. Thornwell's "Theology, Its Proper Method and Its Central Principle" is a critical review of the differing theology of Robert J. Breckinridge of Virginia. I might have used the texts of Henry Timrod's quarrel with William J. Grayson over the value of Wordsworth. The opportunities were there. However aware of European or Northern thought, Southerners were most aware of themselves. Any culture is finally about the quarrel with itself.

I have taken the opportunity of this new edition to correct the odd misprint and a few errors. In 1982 I seem to have been under the impression that Daniel Raymond was French, not American; that the common French phrase *vogue la galère* could be found only in the letters of Madame de Sévigné; that the story of Cornelia referring to her sons, the Gracchi, as her jewels could best be found in

---

10. See, for example, Elizabeth Fox-Genovese, "The Fettered Mind: Time, Place, and the Literary Imagination of the Old South," *Georgia Historical Quarterly* 74 (Winter 1990): 629.

11. Robert Brugger, review of *All Clever Men, Who Make Their Way: Critical Discourse in the Old South*, edited by Michael O'Brien, *Journal of Southern History* 49 (November 1983): 614.

# Preface to the Paperback Edition

Richard Burton's *The Anatomy of Melancholy* (1621). These delusions have passed, though doubtless they kept few awake with outrage. Two errors of transcription in Louisa McCord's essay need, however, especial notice, since they materially affected her meaning. The first occurs on the second line of page 351. The 1982 edition reads: "Man, generally, uses it to subdue his inferior, the negro. Both are right, for both are according to God's law." This, alas, makes no sense and should have read: "Man, generally, uses it to subdue his inferior, the beast. The white man uses it to subdue his inferior, the negro. Both are right, for both are according to God's law." The second is at the bottom of page 353. I contrived to transcribe this: "In the field of literature, how many women have enjoyed all the advantages which men can command, and yet how far behind are even those few from the great and burning lights of letters!" It should have been: "In the field of literature, how many women have enjoyed all the advantages which men can command, and yet how very few have distinguished themselves; and how far behind are even those few from the great and burning lights of letters!"

*All Clever Men, Who Make Their Way*

"The Quarterly—Ah, sir, if you
Had but the genius to review!—
A smart critique upon St. Helena,
Or if you only would but tell in a
Short compass what—but to resume:
As I was saying, sir, the room—
The room's so full of wits and bards,
Crabbes, Campbells, Crokers, Freres, and
    Wards,
And others, neither bards nor wits:
My humble tenement admits
All persons in the name of gent.,
From Mr. Hammond to Dog Dent.

A party dines with me to-day,
All clever men, who make their way;
Crabbe, Malcolm, Hamilton, and Chantrey,
Are all partakers of my pantry.
They're at this moment in discussion
On poor De Staël's late dissolution.
Her book, they say, was in advance—
Pray Heaven, she tell the truth of France!
Thus run our time and tongues away . . . "

    Byron, "Epistle from Mr. Murray
        to Dr. Polidori"

# Introduction: On the Mind of the Old South and Its Accessibility

Very few are disposed to grant any vitality to the mind of the Old South. That it was superficial, unintellectual, obsessed with race and slavery, enfeebled by polemic is a ruling assumption of American scholarship. The explanation for this is well-worn. The humane eclecticism of the Enlightenment, it is said, was displaced by the focused narrowness of a Calhoun. The planter class, which dominated the region, withdrew from its former cosmopolitanism, grew out of touch with modern intellectual developments when once it had led them, became frantic with worry or guilt over the place of slavery in the Union, was isolated on remote and supine plantations far from the invigoration of urban life. Skepticism became displaced by the emotionalism of evangelical religion. Thought had become prejudice.

Wilbur Cash, on this as on many things, dashingly summed it up. "Leaving Mr. Jefferson aside, the whole South produced, not only no original philosopher but no derivative one to set beside Emerson and Thoreau; no novelist but poor Simms to measure against the Northern galaxy headed by Hawthorne and Melville and Cooper; no painter but Allston to stand in the company of Ryder and a dozen Yankees; no poet deserving the name save Poe—only half a Southerner. . . . In general, the intellectual and aesthetic culture of the Old South was a superficial and jejune thing, borrowed from without and worn as a political armor and a badge of rank; and hence (I call the authority of old Matthew Arnold to bear me witness) not a true culture at all."[1]

Now I suspect that this judgment is seriously mistaken and that

1. Wilbur J. Cash, *The Mind of the South* (New York, 1941), pp. 96–97.

we stand in our understanding of antebellum Southern thought where the study of colonial New England stood when Perry Miller came to revise the orthodoxy of Brooks Adams. That is a large claim, I am aware, probably beyond the scope of a book like this to substantiate. But beginnings are being made elsewhere, in books by the likes of Drew Faust, Robert Brugger, and E. Brooks Holifield, that make the claim begin to seem plausible.[2] This book is intended to provide texts for the claim, and this introduction the structure of an explanation of why Cash's judgment came to be stated, is still believed, and should no longer be believed. The mind of the Old South has come to seem uninteresting and inaccessible, come to be worth studying only for the proslavery argument or for picking out from its literary dross the solitary gold of Poe or the tarnished silver of Simms. Why?

It helps to begin with a brief social portrait of the antebellum Southern intellectual and the institutional structure of his discourse, although only part of the explanation is intrinsic to the Old South itself. The term *intellectual* must, of course, be used with reluctant caution for it has acquired in our century an air of professionalism. We have come to see the intellectual as someone who lives by and for ideas, their understanding, dissemination, and judgment. By this modern and anachronistic definition, there were few antebellum Southern intellectuals in the period between Jefferson's decline and the Civil War. Instead there were a great many men, and a very few women, who were interested in ideas and might be described by Coleridge's term, the clerisy. A very few, like Simms, lived by the pen, but most read and wrote in the midst of lives otherwise engaged. They were lawyers, politicians, clergymen, planters, diplomats, teachers, newspaper editors: sometimes several of these simultaneously or serially. Most lived in cities and small towns, rather than on plantations. Some owned plantations, it is true, but most moved within the penumbra of urban life. They might live part of the year in the country, but the house in Charleston or the visit to Richmond usually offered the impulse to set thought to paper. Editors were vigilant for literate visitors who could turn their reading of Eugène Sue's latest novel into an essay for a periodical

2. Drew Gilpin Faust, *A Sacred Circle: The Dilemma of the Intellectual in the Old South, 1840–1860* (Baltimore, 1978); Robert J. Brugger, *Beverley Tucker: Heart Over Head in the Old South* (Baltimore, 1978); E. Brooks Holifield, *The Gentlemen Theologians: American Theology in Southern Culture, 1795–1860* (Durham, 1978).

like the *Southern Quarterly Review*. Urban life itself offered modes of discourse. In Charleston, there was the Conversation Club, which met every few weeks for papers to be read and madeira to be consumed. In smaller towns were similar if less imposing literary, historical, and debating societies. Colleges, agricultural societies, religious meetings, political occasions generated their own thought and printed expression. Nothing was more common than to have a speech printed. Few things were more usual than this editorial preface to an 1856 *De Bow's Review* essay: "An intelligent gentleman at the South sends us the following article, which we insert without change. In his letter, he says: 'I herewith send an article written by an intelligent gentlemen, for you to publish all, a part or none, as to you may seem proper. The views which it expresses were first presented to me in a conversation, and I was so impressed with their truthfulness, in the main . . . that I suggested to him to write them out, and submit them for publication.'"[3]

This was casual, not in itself inimical to thought but ill-designed to produce professional men of letters. Such a loose structure created, most of all, criticism expressed in periodical literature. George Tucker of Virginia thought the periodical the typical expression of the American mind of his day.[4] It was certainly that of the South. Even then some thought this a mistake. William Grayson observed in 1863, "It is reversing the natural order of production to begin a Country's literature with a Quarterly Review. We should begin with books to be reviewed."[5] But anyone who has read the journals of the nineteenth century, whether issued from Edinburgh, Boston, or Charleston, will know that their definition of criticism was generous. Those sermons, orations, and addresses were reprinted. Essays, independent of any book to be reviewed, were used. Articles purportedly a review were often, perhaps usually, not so. Who now remembers what book prompted Macaulay to write on Chatham? It is doubtful that Macaulay himself cared overmuch. "Look at the Reviews which now form so striking a feature in our general Literature," George Frederick Holmes, then of South Carolina, noted in 1845 in just such a review. "They are no longer expressions of opin-

---

3. "The Union and Its Compromises," *De Bow's Review* 21 (August 1856): 177.
4. George Tucker, "Discourse on American Literature," *Southern Literary Messenger* 4 (February 1838): 85.
5. William J. Grayson, "Autobiography," ed. Samuel Gaillard Stoney, *South Carolina Historical and Genealogical Magazine* 49 (April 1948): 98.

ion upon the merits of new books, but independent essays upon all subjects under the sun."[6]

As has been observed often enough, such journals did not always prosper. William Gilmore Simms buried as many of them as he did children. It has been usual to put this down to the indifference of the reading public, though as often it was the result of feckless editing. Simms liked to blame his readers. His readers as often blamed him, and with equal justice. Such instability was not, however, confined to the South, the impressive and subsidized solidity of the *North American Review* aside. From 1828 to the Civil War the region always had one major review. In the late 1840s and early 1850s, it had three doing tolerably well, despite the endemic and too often cited laments of ambitious and necessarily harassed editors: the *Southern Literary Messenger*, which lasted for thirty years; the *Southern Quarterly Review*, which carried on for fifteen; and *De Bow's Review*, which went on for twenty. The first and the last of these were only stopped by the Civil War itself. On top of these were innumerable more specialized journals, like the *Southern Presbyterian Review* and the *Southern Agriculturalist*.

Into such periodicals the intellectual energies of the region were liberally poured. In them, that energy has been frozen and lost to an indifferent posterity. And the fault has lain partly with journals that observed the convention of an author's anonymity. Not only do *we* not know the identity of many contributors, Southerners themselves were often ignorant. This usage was not peculiar to the South. It was sanctioned by Francis Jeffrey and the elder Stephen Elliott alike. Nor was the secrecy perfect. Occasionally a name was attached to an article, sometimes by mistake or stealth. Initials might offer a delicate hint. Neither was secrecy always intended to be perfect. Periodicals were often products of, and spoke to, small local elites, and few doubted that readers might guess authorship and offer proper congratulations. It is doubtful that anonymity betokened a contempt for writing, let alone ideas, and that to be known as an author made one ineligible for polite society.[7] If that were so,

---

6. [George Frederick Holmes], "The Present Condition of Letters," *Southern Literary Messenger* 11 (March 1845): 174.

7. An anecdote frequently used to illustrate the supposed social inferiority of authorship concerns Lord Morpeth. When visiting Charleston, the Englishman is said to have asked the whereabouts of Simms. His interlocutors confessed ignorance and intimated that Simms was not considered such a great man in Charleston. "Simms not a great man!" replied the visitor, "then for God's sake who is your great man?" Now this story is, for one thing, undocumented. Trent tells it in his life of Simms, but without annotation. There are good reasons for doubting

a remarkable number of the most prominent Southerners were pariahs. Poe was not received for reasons quite other than his association with the *Messenger* and inkwells: being unable to hold even a small drink has always diminished a man's social circle, if drunkenness precipitates roaring abuse of one's host. To write was respectable. *Only* to write was less so. To advertise was vulgar, and the prefix of one's name to an essay was a form of self-aggrandizement. In a society whose authors did not usually depend upon payments for words, it was not only vulgar. It was superfluous.

The consequences of anonymity, however, have been immense, not alone for precipitating our own ignorance. The South lacked a robust book-publishing trade (not to be confused with a printing industry; every Southern town had its printer), and the conjunction of this with the convention of anonymity meant that the transition from essay to book was not often made. There were few publishers who clamored to turn the casual author into the creator of a folio volume. The great merry circle that is modern authorship—the book, the review of the book, the book of the reviews, and so on, round and round, all eased by the public knowledge of and demand for an author freely acknowledged and promoted—this circle was seldom closed in the Old South. Books as such form a smaller part of its intellectual culture than elsewhere. This, it is true, impoverished its critical mind. Its discourse was fragmented. Thought did take place and was expressed. But the barriers between author and reader, author and other authors, periodical and book trade inhibited synthesis and reconsideration.

It was a point that George Frederick Holmes well understood. "As long as it was necessary," he wrote in 1853 of the loosely comparable British situation,

> to purchase and peruse the expensive and extensive series of the Edinburgh or the London Quarterly, in order to possess and become familiar with the modern master-pieces of English criticism and speculation;—as long as we were compelled, even then, without special initiation, to remain ignorant or doubtful of the authorship of the articles most admirable for their grace, in-

---

Morpeth's partiality for Simms. His tastes were more Augustan. Even if the story is true, it scarcely proves its supposed point. That passing strangers should be unaware of Simms's location does not demonstrate the low social standing of the litterateur. And one might consider that, in denying Simms the title of greatness, our anonymous Charlestonians merely anticipated the verdict of modern criticism. See Louis D. Rubin, Jr., *The Writer in the South: Studies in a Literary Community* (Athens, Ga., 1972), p. 13; William Peterfield Trent, *William Gilmore Simms* (Boston, 1892), p. 129; lectures on Alexander Pope and on America in *The Vice-Regal Speeches and Addresses, Lectures and Poems of the late Earl of Carlisle, K.G.*, ed. J. J. Gaskin (Dublin and London, 1865), esp. pp. 406–7.

genuity or depth;—it would have been unreasonable to anticipate, except in rare instances, that the ablest of them should continue to possess any general interest, or should exercise any durable influence on literature and scholarship. The practice of republication . . . affords a great convenience to the anxious student, and revives, with a fresher interest and under more favorable auspices, the pleasure and profit which might have previously attended the cursory perusal of any striking articles. Instead of turning to them as the grateful companions of an idle hour, we may now make them the intimate associates of more sedate studies, and we may consort with the ablest productions of recent times, with an assured confidence in their excellence, and without undergoing the tedium of winnowing the sound grain from the endless amount of chaff with which it had originally been mingled.[8]

This was an observation that prefaced Holmes's own oblivion, for there was no collected edition of Holmes essays.

New England periodicals, of course, observed the same tradition of anonymity. But that region was smaller and more integrated than the South, and it had a lively publishing trade. The South, by comparison, had at least three foci of thought and periodical distribution, radiating from Richmond, Charleston, and New Orleans. The half-secret names would not carry such distances. Even so distinguished a name as Hugh Swinton Legaré, immediately spotted in South Carolina by the literate cognoscenti, could be referred to by the *Messenger* as "little known" in Virginia.[9] But most crucially, New England won the Civil War and the postbellum generation thought it proper to memorialize the ideological authors of that famous victory. Perry Miller has observed, "Scholars diligently hunt out the earliest scrawls of Emerson, Hawthorne, Thoreau; the slightest stirrings of intelligence in New England became part of the national record, for here, the assumption runs, began the problem of the mind in America. The reason is, of course, that New England, by its peculiar coherence, not only presents to the country a body of literature which even those who resent the hegemony have to salute, but that New England scholars have taken care of their own."[10]

If one examines the chronological pattern of reputations objectified in the great multivolume sets of Emerson and Lowell issued by the Riverside Press, if one peruses the biographies by sibling

---

8. [George Frederick Holmes], "Sir William Hamilton's Discussions," *Southern Quarterly Review*, n.s. 8 (October 1853): 289–90.

9. *Southern Literary Messenger* 12 (April 1846): 254.

10. Perry Miller, *The Raven and the Whale: The War of Words and Wits in the Era of Poe and Melville* (New York, 1956), p. 84.

Nortons and Cabots that fixed irrevocably in the American mind the weight and importance of the antebellum New England tradition, one finds books dated in the late nineteenth century.[11] Turn from the bibliopoles of Park Street to the heirs of Legaré in Charleston, turn to a Paul Hamilton Hayne, who had as high a regard for Legaré as Octavius Brooks Frothingham harbored for Emerson, and it is pathetically clear why the postwar Southern generation had neither means nor motive to commemorate the intellectual achievements of their forebears.[12] Look later and the New South is writing essays praising James Russell Lowell and damning Charleston for the curse of slavery. Poverty is a catafalque for fame.

Hayne, fond as he was of the dying fall and romantic about the South Carolina of his youth, could see in 1870 how it might happen. "The great names of the South are dying out. For want of an adequate record, men, whose genius the whole country honored in their lifetime, are beginning to sink into obscurity. With the decay of the present generation, the passing away of all contemporary evidences, all familiar memoranda, of their ability, services and *personel*, we must lose forever those means whereby fresh and vivid portraitures of character are secured, and be forced to content ourselves with such meagre, and imperfect, if not distorted, likenesses, as the hand of the future biographer can draw, with the hesitating aid of Tradition, and the dry details of official documents." This was sentimental, as always with Hayne, but prescient. He wrote this in preface to a biographical sketch of Legaré, based upon the two volumes of Legaré's *Writings* published in Charleston in the mid-1840s. He judged them as botched by their editor, as indeed they were: execrable in arrangement, binding, annotation, incomplete. "We never take the disjointed volumes in hand," he wrote, "without involuntarily regarding them as a species of sepulchre in which the bright genius of Legaré lies buried!"[13] He tried to interest others in a new edition, but failed. And Legaré, ironically enough, was one of the luckier Southern intellectuals. Most never achieved a col-

---

11. The popular Riverside edition of Emerson was published between 1883 and 1893; that of Lowell in 1891; that of Longfellow in 1895; that of Oliver Wendell Holmes in 1896. This is not to say that these were not noticed before the Civil War. But their earlier reputations were more problematical.
12. Paul Hamilton Hayne, *Lives of Robert Young Hayne and Hugh Swinton Legaré* (Charleston, 1878), now obscure; Octavius Brooks Frothingham, *Transcendentalism in New England: A History* (New York, 1878), now reprinted.
13. Hayne, "Hugh Swinton Legaré," *Southern Review* 7 (January 1870): 122, 156–57.

lected edition, however mangled. Twenty years later William Trent ratified the dust on Legaré's *Writings*. "I have to confess that I laid down the two thick volumes of his works with a sigh of relief and regret. Of relief, because I had discharged the duty I owed to one of the few classic writers of my section; of regret, because I could not but acknowledge that here was another instance of the fact that great industry and great learning cannot of themselves make a man a great writer."[14]

Apart from the arid filiopietism of compendia like the *Library of Southern Literature*, the neglect continued until the 1920s and the recovery of the Southern mind itself. H. L. Mencken, it is true, offered his usual swingeing dissent. Prefacing his bastinado of the New South with kind words for its superseded predecessor, he observed that the Old South was "a civilization of manifold excellences—perhaps the best that the Western Hemisphere has ever seen—undoubtedly the best that These States have ever seen. Down to the middle of the last century, and even beyond, the main hatchery of ideas on this side of the water was across the Potomac bridges. . . . The Ur-Confederate had leisure. He liked to toy with ideas. He was hospitable and tolerant. He had the vague thing we call culture."[15] Mencken said this, and may even have believed it. But he was aware that few others would grant his premise, and was glad of it.

In fact the years of the "Southern Renaissance" saw a considerable reevaluation of the antebellum mind. The first to lift the dust were the literary critics. Vernon Parrington's *The Romantic Revolution in America* (1927) was surprisingly thorough. The Jeffersonian considered John Taylor, John Marshall, William Wirt, Beverley Tucker, William Alexander Caruthers, John Pendleton Kennedy, Poe, Calhoun, Alexander Stephens, Francis Lieber, William Grayson, William Crafts, Legaré, and Simms. Parrington was interested in the relationships among economics, politics, and literature. This eclecticism and standpoint were not to prove characteristic of the new indigenous school of literary critics.[16] They have taken—for we

---

14. Trent, *Simms*, pp. 51–52.
15. H. L. Mencken, "The Sahara of the Bozart," in *Prejudices: Second Series* (New York, 1920), p. 137. It is worth pointing out that the *Library of Southern Literature* still has value as a starting point for inquiry into lesser or unjustly obscure writers.
16. Vernon L. Parrington, *The Romantic Revolution in America, 1800–1860* (New York, 1927), pp. 3–125. Some of my remarks on Southern literary critics were used in Michael O'Brien,

are still living in the midst of that school—as their patron saint, not Thomas Jefferson, but Allen Tate. Lewis P. Simpson a few years ago opened a gathering of Southern literary critics with the remark that there is "a particular version of the Southern literary reaction that has prevailed widely among us—although not by any means with doctrinaire uniformity. If this version can be attributed to a single person, we may say that it is probably Allen Tate, whose brilliant critical work is so central to the field of Southern literary studies that we cannot imagine it without him."[17]

Tate's achievement and influence lay in reversing the implicit question of Parrington. The Jeffersonian had asked, what literature has helped to foster a humane society? The New Critic insisted, what society has helped to create a great literature?[18] Reversing the polarities established a new theory about the role of Southern social history in creating favorable or unfavorable contexts for "creative writing." The Old South took its place in a general theory of Southern literature, which has two dimensions.[19] The literary side of the equation between literature and society has, it is said, an ascending theme. The literature of the Old South is deemed inferior, that between the Civil War and the First World War is a shade better but flawed, that of the 1920s and 1930s is an admired "Renaissance" and—here the consensus weakens—that since the Second World War is less impressive. This faltering crescendo is related to a descending theme of social history. The Old South is viewed as a coherent community of values, religion, face-to-face personal relationships, a premodern *Gemeinschaft* culture. The Civil War is said to have strengthened the community of values by the shared experiences of defeat and poverty. But the war permitted the industrial transfor-

---

"The Last Theologians: Recent Southern Literary Criticism," *Michigan Quarterly Review* 17 (Summer 1978): 404–13.

17. Louis D. Rubin, Jr., and C. Hugh Holman, eds., *Southern Literary Study: Problems and Possibilities* (Chapel Hill, 1975), p. 48.

18. See especially Allen Tate, "The Profession of Letters in the South" (1935) and "A Southern Mode of the Imagination" (1960), reprinted in *Essays of Four Decades* (New York, 1970), pp. 517–34, 577–92. Considering the undocumented brevity of Tate's remarks, his influence has been extraordinary.

19. This is distilled from: Rubin, *The Writer in the South* and *William Elliott Shoots a Bear: Essays on the Southern Literary Imagination* (Baton Rouge, 1975); C. Hugh Holman, *The Roots of Southern Writing: Essays on the Literature of the American South* (Athens, Ga., 1972); Lewis P. Simpson, *The Man of Letters in New England and the South: Essays on the Literary Vocation in America* (Baton Rouge, 1973) and *The Dispossessed Garden: Pastoral and History in Southern Literature* (Athens, Ga., 1975); Walter Sullivan, *A Requiem for the Renascence: The State of Fiction in the Modern South* (Athens, Ga., 1976).

mation of the New South which undermined this coherence, shattered the values, and left the Southerner perilously subject to an urbanized mass society, left him with recourse only to an atomistic existentialism or that resistance to fragmentation that is conservative modernism. At the moment at which these two themes crossed, the literary music was most harmonious: that moment was the "Renaissance."

A conundrum was basic to Tate's viewpoint. Both a coherent and a shattered society produce indifferent literature, flawed by excessive complacency or random skepticism. Great literature happens in the delicate moment of transition. Louis Rubin has adapted this doctrine with his customary energy and applied it to the Old South. In *William Elliott Shoots a Bear*, he has set the hunting sketches of Elliott—antebellum South Carolinian, sea island planter, politician, and author—beside Faulkner's "The Bear," so that the unflattering comparison might stand as a metaphor for early impoverishment and later riches in Southern literature. Why is Elliott a bad writer? Rubin asks. Because he was laboring under the neocolonial delusion that significant materials for literature did not happen in the South, but elsewhere, usually in Europe and a long time ago. Thus Elliott penned an uninspired play about political intrigue in Renaissance Genoa, but failed to see the latent opportunity for writing about his own backyard. Mostly the social grip of slavery on the Southern imagination was crippling. Elliott "could not ground his writing in what he knew, the life of a planter and sportsman in the Low Country of South Carolina, because the result would have been a searching scrutiny of a social structure all too flawed in its design and grounded upon an attitude toward a certain segment of the population that involved grave injustice and inhumanity. . . . this would have been . . . . the inevitable direction in which imaginative fiction would have led him, and no doubt certain others as well—others like him, men of education, refinement, talent, possessed of a deep involvement in the life of their time and place. Thus it was that antebellum southern literature remained an affair of surfaces." This theory of alienation—unkind, it must be said, to Jane Austen's domestic comedy of manners, Shakespeare's Italian plays, and, not least, to that intelligent author, William Elliott—has been endorsed by Hugh Holman, a closer student of the Old South: "We would probably all agree that a great writer always transcends his region and is more than a voice of his region, and probably that a great writer is always in some way or other in an antagonistic posture toward the world around him. . . .one of the things that happened to the antebellum southern writers, the men of talent . . . was that they were at home and had at least ostensibly accepted, or thought that they had accepted, the terms of life in the region."[20]

Lewis P. Simpson has argued similarly but with more sophistication. The Old South, he says, chose to defy history by forging the image of an integrated pastoral society, a dream world no less messianic for being conservative. Thereby it lost contact with the mainstream of Western literature. "The South's lack of distinguished literary accomplishment in the nineteenth century . . . can be attributed to its being cut off from the literary sensibility of the larger world, the culture of alienation. . . . The antebellum Southern writer . . . was cut off from what affected the general stream of literary culture because of the involvement of the Southern man of letters in the politics of slavery." All this is an elaboration of Tate's central claim, that antebellum Southern literature was bad because it was "hagridden with politics."[21]

Such critical insights belong, of course, to a particular school of literary criticism. The discussion of the historical nature of Southern literature has been oddly engrossed by an ahistorical aesthetic doctrine. The recent South has had its T. S. Eliot in Tate, but no Edmund Wilson to compete.[22] It has few Marxist critics, next to no structuralists. It has had the New Criticism, dealing incongruously with history. This has led to confusion. Cleanth Brooks has protested that, as his studies of William Faulkner demonstrate, he is not uninterested in history. But he lacks, and wishes to lack, an essential element of the historical vision: the past must be allowed to define its own terms.[23] The Southern version of the New Criticism has worked within history, but not for it. It has given the literary critic a shopping list of the ingredients for a great literature, and he has wandered up and down the face of Southern history to find the market that best fills his requirements. His recipe contains:

---

20. Rubin, *William Elliott*, p. 27; Rubin and Holman, *Southern Literary Study*, pp. 112–13.
21. Simpson, *Dispossessed Garden*, pp. 37–38; Tate, *Essays*, p. 523.
22. Fleetingly, of course, Wilson himself contributed in *Patriotic Gore: Studies in the Literature of the Civil War* (New York, 1962), but Southern literary criticism has been a social circle as much as an intellectual specialty. To the former, Wilson was external.
23. Cleanth Brooks, *William Faulkner: The Yoknapatawpha Country* (New Haven, 1963); Lewis P. Simpson, ed., *The Possibilities of Order: Cleanth Brooks and His Work* (Baton Rouge, 1976).

alienation, but not the capacity for habitual skepticism; a sympathy for religious values and an "organic" society; a hierarchy of literary forms, with short poetry at the apex, the novel further down, and social analysis and polemic at the bottom; a nicely developed sense of irony and "tension"; a vision of literature that is not "relativist, arbitrary, materialistic, but absolute, unswerving, spiritual"; priorities that place the "imaginative artist" above the "limited view of the scientific historian."[24]

The historian may be chagrined at being relegated to the dungeons of literature, if not only for himself, then at least for Gibbon. But what matters here is that such ahistoricism goes hard upon periods with differing preconceptions about the life of the mind. It happens that the Old South is such a period. Now it is true that the roots of the modernist theory of alienation lie partly in the antebellum years. Poe was part of the chain that led from Coleridge to Eliot, and from Eliot to Tate. Simms had some sense that his novels, or his romances, were superior to his political orations.[25] But, on the whole, the Old South saw differently. The attempt of the New Criticism to narrow the definition of literature to a mysterious thing called "imaginative literature"—chiefly the poem and the novel—would have made little sense to a John Pendleton Kennedy, who did not think he had ceased to practice literature when he moved from *Swallow Barn*, a novel, to *Quodlibet*, a political satire, and on to his biography of William Wirt. Charles Gayarré would have been haughtily amused to learn that his *History of Louisiana* would be disregarded as nonliterary. Few citizens of Charleston and Richmond would have thought a political imagination fatal to literary accomplishment. Antebellum intellectual culture moved with no sense of disjuncture between genres that modern criticism has sundered.

Given such perspectives, Southern literary criticism has been most zealous in resurrecting "imaginative literature." Poe was the first and still the most important beneficiary of this. But the researches of literary critics have given us many Simms novels, George Tucker's *The Valley of the Shenandoah*, Beverley Tucker's *The Partisan Leader*, and so forth. But their textual endeavors have been aimed

---

24. Rubin, *William Elliott*, pp. 256–57; Holman, *Roots of Southern Writing*, p. 176. The exception is Jay B. Hubbell, whose *The South in American Literature, 1607-1900* (Durham, 1954) is marked by a breadth of research and eclecticism of standpoint that are invaluable to the historian.

25. Edd Winfield Parks, *William Gilmore Simms as Literary Critic* (Athens, Ga., 1961).

at answering and illustrating their literary theory, and so the agenda they proffer has been limited. Thus we are not given for perusal in modern editions Simms's history or political thought, George Tucker's *Essays on Various Subjects of Taste, Morals and National Policy*, Beverley Tucker's lectures on legal theory. We are offered Legaré's essay on Byron, but not his reflections on D'Aguesseau or Demosthenes.[26] Most of the agenda of the intellectual historian has been absent: theology, philosophy, political theory, social criticism, history, classical scholarship, rhetoric. This is not an accusation, but a fact. There is no reason why the modern literary critic should have done these things, given his sense of what is literature. But it does mean his archaeology of Southern literature has taken us only a short distance into the resurrection of the Southern mind.

The second major development in promoting study of the mind of the Old South has lain with the political and social historians. Three intertwined subjects have fascinated recent historiography: race, politics, and sectionalism. We know far more and subtly about the social organism of the plantation, the nature of slave culture, the character and motives of proslavery and antislavery movements, the complex relationship between local and national politics. In the midst of this, some intellectual history has been written. Where the literary critic has fled at the very mention of politics and slavery, the eyes of the historian have lit up. Political polemic and racist ideology have become central considerations. Eugene Genovese has written on George Fitzhugh, George Fredrickson on the racist anthropology of Josiah Nott.[27] Yet this has been as partial a shopping list. Historians have wished to explain the great facts of slavery and the Civil War and they have culled the mind of the Old South for these purposes. Some believe that Southerners thought seriously *only* about these subjects. Slavery and politics are supposed to be

---

26. See, for example, John Ward Ostrom, ed., *The Letters of Edgar Allan Poe* (Cambridge, Mass., 1948); the University of South Carolina Press is publishing a centennial edition of Simms's novels, and the John Harvard Library of Harvard University Press has reprinted the same author's *Views and Reviews in American History, Literature and Fiction*, with a preface by Holman; the University of North Carolina Press has had a series of "Southern Literary Classics," with novels by Caruthers, Wirt, Beverley and George Tucker, and Caroline Lee Hentz; the Gregg Press, in its "Americans in Fiction" reprints has four novels by John Esten Cooke, four by Simms, and two by Caruthers. Richard Beale Davis et al., eds., *Southern Writing, 1585–1920* (New York, 1970), pp. 326–30 has a snippet of Legaré's Byron.

27. Eugene D. Genovese, *The World the Slaveholders Made: Two Essays in Interpretation* (New York, 1969), pp. 115–244; George M. Fredrickson, *The Black Image in the White Mind: The Debate on the Afro-American Character and Destiny, 1817–1914* (New York, 1971), pp. 78–82.

sufficiently inclusive of the antebellum Southern mind. Others, less extreme, concede the existence of more but insist upon its unimportance.[28]

Hanging between the literary critic and the political historian has been the work of William R. Taylor, whose *Cavalier and Yankee* remains the most thorough attempt to understand thought in the Old South. His achievement and limitation was to ask the historian's question of the literary critic's agenda of texts. How can we understand the coming of war and the growth of intersectional mythologies by looking at the novels and poetry of Simms, Grayson, and Caruthers? It was an important question, making a vital conjunction, yielding many insights, and rightly celebrated. But Taylor was an exponent of the American Studies methodology of Henry Nash Smith, a school never very happy with intellectual history. It disliked formal philosophy, because it was absorbed in the quest for an American national character, a will-o'-the-wisp thought to flee at the mention of epistemology or ontology. It disliked manuscript research and preferred the literary critic's contemplation of the text. It was not adverse to second-rate literature as a guide to the popular mind and was, indeed, incorrigibly democratic in its ideological commitment. Abstruseness suggested elitism and that was to be avoided.[29]

As for the explicators of abstruseness, the American intellectual historians, their record has been a sorry one. In the historiography of the colonial and revolutionary generations, this is less true. Southern names of the seventeenth and eighteenth centuries are there mingled freely with considerations of a wide variety of intellectual problems. The emphasis rests still most heavily upon New England, but not cripplingly so.[30] But the first half of the nineteenth

---

28. For example, David Donald, "The Proslavery Argument Reconsidered," *Journal of Southern History* 37 (February 1971): 3–18.

29. William R. Taylor, *Cavalier and Yankee: The Old South and American National Character* (New York, 1961).

30. The South is given its due in, for example, Henry F. May, *The Enlightenment in America* (New York, 1976); Donald H. Meyer, *The Democratic Enlightenment* (New York, 1976); H. Trevor Colbourn, *The Lamp of Experience: Whig History and the Intellectual Origins of the American Revolution*. The most persuasive, if erroneous, proponent of the America-is-New-England-writ-large school is Sacvan Bercovitch, in *The Puritan Origins of the American Self* (New Haven, 1975). The attempted riposte is Richard Beale Davis, *Intellectual Life in the Colonial South, 1585–1763* (Knoxville, 1978), which, though successful as archaeological bibliography, is less so as historical criticism.

century is a different matter. The South is singled out for separate and brief treatment, the clichés of the literary critics and political historians are indifferently stated, the matter is hastily dropped for more interesting matters: the survival of the Puritan mind, the philosophy of Transcendentalism, the emergence of professionalism, the cultural relationship between America and Europe.[31] Does the Old South have a relevance for any of these and more? Apparently not. There is a recent book, a manifesto of the younger generation, entitled *New Directions in American Intellectual History*. The directions are many, everywhere but below the Potomac. Not a word about the Old South is breathed. (Not a word about the New South either, but that is a different complaint.)[32] And so it is with most new work in American intellectual history; the student of the Southern mind proceeds with hardened skepticism to their indices, looks for "South," looks for the names of Southern intellectuals, finds little or nothing, is absurdly pleased to find the merest reference, however botched. He mutters defiantly, I can summon spirits from the vasty deep, and the American intellectual historian seems sardonically to reply with Hotspur, so can any man. But will they come when you do call for them? It is a fair question. It would be wrong to rail too severely at the less than thorough contributions of literary critics, political and social historians, or American intellectual historians to the study of the antebellum Southern mind. "The South," as I have argued elsewhere, has long functioned as an excluding system of discourse.[33] It is little wonder that other scholarly modes of discourse should have dealt inadequately with it. If Southern historians themselves have not summoned the spirits and produced convincing evidence of an interesting intellectual culture in the Old South, no one else can be expected to do it for them.

This is where we stand. The picture is gloomy. It is only justice to add, however, that in very recent years a few books have trickled

---

31. An older example is Merle Curti, *The Growth of American Thought* (New York, 1943); a fairly standard textbook, Gerald N. Grob and Robert N. Beck, *American Ideas* (New York, 1963), considers thirty-three intellectuals from the "national" period, of which seven are Southerners: Jefferson, Monroe, Taney, Peter Cartwright, Calhoun, Fitzhugh, and Simms.
32. John Higham and Paul K. Conkin, eds., *New Directions in American Intellectual History* (Baltimore, 1979).
33. Michael O'Brien, *The Idea of the American South, 1920–1941* (Baltimore, 1979), pp. 213–27.

forth to hint at the emergence of a Southern intellectual history. It is not a self-conscious trickle. There are no bands of malcontents that gather at historical conventions and declaim the virtues of their subject, foundations are not besieged to finance conferences in agreeable spots, newsletters are not issued to eager Young Turks steeped in the lesser writings of Albert Taylor Bledsoe. A quarter of a century ago, Clement Eaton declared, with that Turnerian turn of phrase so beloved of the American historian, that the "new frontier in Southern historiography . . . is destined to advance into the area of intellectual history."[34] Only a very few wagons have set out.

Some of the most recent prairie schooners, however, have been of hearteningly sound construction. We have now good biographical studies of Beverley Tucker, George Tucker, and George Frederick Holmes, as well as an intriguing collective study of an improbable "Sacred Circle," James Henry Hammond's speeches have been reprinted and Edmund Ruffin's diary published. Aspects of Southern theology have been analyzed. Somewhat earlier, George Fitzhugh's life was studied by Harvey Wish and Clement Eaton tried to fulfill his own prophecy.[35] Such books, and more articles, have been helpful. Yet somehow this research has not cohered in and influenced the American historical imagination. Some of it is too recent to make a prediction of miscarriage altogether convincing. Yet the precedents are not encouraging. Why is this?

I suspect the central reason, waving aside the vexing matter of the South's place in American intellectual life even now, is that the Southern intellectual historian—like any such historian—has a twofold responsibility, part of which is being neglected. He has a duty to narrative synthesis, he must write intellectual biography and analysis, he must trace with all proper deference to social history the changing force of ideas. He must, as Quentin Skinner has force-

34. Clement Eaton, "Recent Trends in the Writing of Southern History," *Louisiana Historical Quarterly* 38 (April 1955): 41. I find since writing this, that I have been involved in arranging a conference in a most agreeable spot, Charleston; reality outruns the ironist, as usual.

35. Brugger, *Beverley Tucker*; Robin Colin McLean, *George Tucker: Moral Philosopher and Man of Letters* (Chapel Hill, 1961); Neal C. Gillespie, *The Collapse of Orthodoxy: The Intellectual Ordeal of George Frederick Holmes* (Charlottesville, 1972); Faust, *A Sacred Circle*; Clyde N. Wilson, ed., *Selections from the Letters and Speeches of the Hon. James H. Hammond of South Carolina* (Spartanburg, 1978); William K. Scarborough, ed., *The Diary of Edmund Ruffin* (Baton Rouge, 1972, 1976); Holifield, *The Gentlemen Theologians*; Harvey Wish, *George Fitzhugh, Propagandist of the Old South* (Baton Rouge, 1943); Clement Eaton, *The Mind of the Old South* (rev. ed., Baton Rouge, 1967). A useful recent article is Robert J. Brugger, "The Mind of the Old South: New Views," *Virginia Quarterly Review* 56 (Spring 1980): 277–95.

Introduction                    17

fully restated, reassemble the context.[36] But he must make available the text itself. For the Old South, this has not been done. It is as though we were obliged to study the French Enlightenment by biographies of Voltaire and Montesquieu and could not read *Candide* and *De l'esprit des lois*, save by expeditions to a Rare Books Room. Southern literary critics have long understood this, and that is one reason their version of the antebellum mind is so dominant.

For to study the Old South is rapidly to learn a central fact. One can read *about* a George Frederick Holmes, but not Holmes himself without elaborate effort. One can, it is true, go to the bibliography in Neal Gillespie's biography, jot down the essays that Holmes published anonymously and prolifically, proceed to the appropriate volume of the *Southern Quarterly Review* or *Methodist Quarterly Review*, if your library has it, and read Holmes. The hardiest student might choose to risk the hazards and inconveniences of interlibrary loan. He may care to peer into the gloom of a microfilm machine. And he might not. It is easier to read Emerson, and that is what he does. Life is short and scholarship is long to waste upon an intellectual culture that all agree is scarcely worth a nod.

What is true for Holmes is true for most of the names that one might plausibly assemble as a Who's Who of the antebellum Southern mind: Beverley and George Tucker, David and Louisa McCord, James Warley Miles, Hugh Swinton Legaré, Stephen Elliott, Thomas Dew, Thomas Cooper, Henry Nott, Robert Henry, James Henley Thornwell, Hugh Blair Grigsby, Frederick Porcher, William Grayson, and many others, known and obscure. They are inaccessible. The orthodoxy argues that these men are obscure because they deserve to be. I am not sure this is true. The orthodoxy's case is weakened, after all, because it shows little evidence of having read these people.

The problem of this culture's stature is, of course, a real one. But it is one that needs evasion for the moment. I doubt that the present state of scholarship permits a convincing answer. As these writers cannot be read without surmounting formidable barriers, the dissonance of opinion and rebuttal has never swirled around them to create an answer—or rather answers—to the matter of stature. I could airily pronounce Holmes's essays exceptionally interesting. The reader could not make an informed response. He has not read

---

36. Quentin Skinner, *The Foundations of Modern Political Thought* (Cambridge, 1978).

Holmes. He could, of course, make an uninformed response and well might. But Holmes would remain my critical prisoner. Now this is always somewhat true of the relationship between a historian and a very dead author, but the measure is modified in the case of a Thoreau because one can expect the literate to have read Thoreau independently. If I say absurdities about Walden Pond, an informed skepticism can be expected. But I could pronounce a series of idiocies about Holmes—that he was a closet abolitionist, that he once raped his daughter and this explains his abomination of Herder, that he wrote with purple Bollandist ink lives of the saints—and need only await chastisement from Holmes's biographer, a small audience.

In short, many scholarly tasks remain unaccomplished. Only the *Southern Literary Messenger* has had its contributors systematically identified, a consequence of the rediscovery of Poe.[37] Without such spadework, much Southern history, not only intellectual, is rendered ghostly and faceless. Historians constantly refer, when they utilize original sources, to a fiction called "a Southern commentator" or "a writer in the *Southern Quarterly Review*."[38] This is disabling to our understanding. The source is made to stand alone, untouched by the specifics of authorship, place, or circumstance. Is the "commentator" a Virginian or a Louisianan, a Methodist or a Roman Catholic, a Whig or a Democrat, an enthusiast for Lamartine or Dugald Stewart? The quotation sits upon the page, indifferently representative of all Southerners, when in all logic it speaks for only one, if we but knew who he or she was. Surely we are past the point when one Southerner is believed to be much like another.

How much more intriguing would have been the quotation in George Fredrickson's discussion of Southern attitudes to race, which he attributes to "a writer in *De Bow's Review*"—a quotation that curdlingly reads: "the brutish propensities of the negro now unchecked

---

37. David K. Jackson, ed., *The Contributors and Contributions to the Southern Literary Messenger (1834–1864)* (Charlottesville, 1936); Guy A. Cardwell, "Charleston Periodicals, 1795–1860" (Ph.D. diss., University of North Carolina, 1936), and Frank Ryan, Jr., "'The Southern Quarterly Review,' 1842–1857" (Ph.D. diss., University of North Carolina, 1956), offer suggestions for the *Southern Review*, *Russell's Magazine*, and the *Southern Quarterly Review*, but not with thoroughness. We badly need a reference volume comparable to the *Wellesley Index of Victorian Periodicals*.

38. For example, Jan C. Dawson, "The Puritan and the Cavalier: The South's Perception of Contrasting Traditions," *Journal of Southern History* 44 (November 1978): 597–614.

[following any possible emancipation] there remains no road for their full exercise . . . but in the slaughter of his white master, and through the slaughter, he strides (unless he himself be exterminated) to the full exercise of his native barbarity and savageness"—if Fredrickson had known that the initials cited in his footnotes stand for Louisa McCord, the daughter of Langdon Cheves. Would not such a feminine outburst usefully have counterbalanced the gentler remarks on slavery by McCord's friend Mary Chesnut, whose views reside so conveniently in paperback?[39] What nonsense is made of Rollin Osterweis's agreeable metaphor for the influence of European Romanticism upon South Caroline nationalism, the assertion that David Flavel Jamison was both a student of Herder and president of the 1860 secession convention, when one knows that Jamison did not write the 1844 essay.[40] Even the student of these matters is easily misled. I find, looking into the matter, that when I cited earlier an observation in the *Southern Literary Messenger* upon the obscurity of Legaré in Virginia, I was quoting William Gilmore Simms: a South Carolinian upon a South Carolinian, and not a Virginian upon a South Carolinian as I inferred from the provenance of the periodical in Richmond.[41]

This is not the place to attempt a full discussion of the Southern mind and its appearance, once scholarly tasks are accomplished: authors identified, collected and usable editions provided, biographies and critical studies written. It is the burden of my argument that we do not know. But I am persuaded a portrait of the southern intellect will look very different, not least because Southern social history has been recently rewritten, and that alone incapacitates half the logic of the traditional historiography. What Allen Tate believed about the Old South is believed by very few historians now. At least five props of the conventional wisdom have badly slipped and they are worth a cursory notice.

The first is the proposition that the isolation of plantation life discouraged opportunities for intellectuality. This idea has faltered,

39. Fredrickson, *Black Image in the White Mind*, p. 54; Mary Boykin Chesnut, *A Diary from Dixie*, ed. Ben Ames Williams (Boston, 1949).
40. Rollin G. Osterweis, *Romanticism and Nationalism in the Old South* (New Haven, 1949), pp. 151–52; Gillespie, *Collapse of Orthodoxy*, p. 251, correctly attributes "Herder's Philosophy of History," *Southern Quarterly Review* 5 (April 1844): 265–311, to Holmes.
41. *The Letters of William Gilmore Simms*, ed. Mary C. Simms Oliphant et al. (Columbia, 1953), 2:124.

not so much because the plantation has been proved especially hospitable to spreading thought, but because the planter himself did not occupy a central place in the region's intellectual elite. Very few writers were planters. Most were ministers, lawyers, college teachers, city or small-town dwellers. This is not to say they were unconnected with the planter class, just as the modern university intellectual is mated to the mechanisms of corporate capitalism. But most Southern intellectuals had as little to do with planting cotton as the *New York Times* book reviewer has with the sweatshops of Wall Street. Their friends might have been obliged to be planters, their relatives equally so, but the young professionals of the Southern mind were urban. Recent economic studies have shown how swift and pervasive was the pace of urbanization in the antebellum South.[42] Outside of the northeastern United States and England, the South was the most urbanized culture in Western society, and did not much repine at the fact. Of the fourteen authors in this anthology, only one, Charles Gayarré, was a planter, and even he controlled his plantation from the distance of New Orleans or Paris. Louisa McCord was a planter's wife, but lived more than half the year in the college town of Columbia, South Carolina. Frederick Porcher had been a planter, but disliked the life and gave it up to teach at the College of Charleston. And this sample was not deliberately biased. In many cases, essays were chosen before the identity of authors was known or their social backgrounds scrutinized.

The second doubtful assertion is the obsession of the Southern mind with slavery. There is little question that slavery was a central concern of Southerners. No amount of revisionism could disturb that assumption. But that does not mean a debilitating obsession. If one surveys, for example, the first *Southern Review*'s contents, one finds that only about 10 percent of its essays were concerned with either slavery or, indeed, any kind of politics, despite its span coinciding with the heat of the Nullification controversy in South Carolina. For the *Southern Quarterly Review*, deeper into the years of sectional controversy, the proportion was about 20 percent. In years of particular stress, under an editor like Simms of markedly political instinct, the share would rise. In 1851, it went as high as 35 percent as the

---

42. David R. Goldfield, "Pursuing the American Urban Dream: Cities in the Old South," in Blaine A. Brownell and David R. Goldfield, *The City in Southern History: The Growth of Urban Civilization in the South* (Port Washington, 1977), pp. 52–91. But see especially J. Mills Thornton III, *Politics and Power in a Slave Society: Alabama, 1800–1860* (Baton Rouge, 1978).

arguments for separate secession were thrashed out. It is in such years, of course, that most political historians have looked into such periodicals, precisely to explain the crisis. The *Southern Literary Messenger*, cultivating belles lettres but starting in the mid-1830s, fell somewhere between the *Southern Review* and the *Southern Quarterly Review*. Its leading piece for its first several issues was a history of Tripoli. *De Bow's Review*, on the other hand, was peculiarly dedicated to the study of economic and political matters and hence of slavery, and dealt only perfunctorily with philosophical and literary matters. So its proportion was the highest of all. The popularity of *De Bow's* as a source for historians has perhaps helped to foster the legend of obsession.[43]

The third proposition, that the South was debilitated by the enthusiasms of an anti-intellectual fundamentalist evangelicalism, is a half-truth. There is no doubt that the deism of a Jefferson or the materialist atheism of a Thomas Cooper grew less common. But a recent study has pointed to a large urban influence upon Southern theology, an influence characterized by a search for a rational theology and not by emotional panache.[44] And it may be a logical error to imagine that, because the terms of the debate had shifted—from disputes between deism and belief to arguments within orthodoxy—any less weighty intellectual endeavor went on. It may be just that historians have found the debates less dramatic and accessible. That most learned of Presbyterian elders, James Henley Thornwell, ranged far and wide to find philosophical errors whose repudiation might strengthen the Westminster Confession of Faith. In the process he kept many extremely well informed about the unorthodox.

The fourth element in the old case, that the South's consensus on the propriety of slavery undermined freedom of thought, seems the most vulnerable to objection. Many did, of course, suffer from dissent on this matter of racial ideology. But it is only a sentimentalism about the seamlessness of freedom and culture, a belief so characteristic of the American passion, that imagines all thought must cease because in one matter consensus, latterly demonstrated

---

43. Figures like this are necessarily crude. I have erred on the side of generosity, however, and they are more likely to be too high than too low. Politics and slavery are scarcely identical, even in the South. And I have included tangential articles, like a travel sketch of Cuba that barely mentions slavery.

44. Holifield, *The Gentlemen Theologians*, esp. pp. 5–49.

pernicious, was strong. Southerners could still think about Coleridge or Vico or whether statues should be naked or clothed, without bearing too closely upon the matter of slavery. Racism itself, of course, elicited discourse. But there is little evidence that Southerners argued less with each other on most things because they agreed with one another on a single thing, however important. Periodicals were clamorous with dispute, mostly of Southerner with Southerner.

The last proposition, that the South was out of touch with innovations in thought, is the most important and most mistaken. The misunderstanding is at least as old as William Trent. He wrote in 1892 of Charleston, "Most of the elegant gentlemen forming those circles were still living, in imagination at least, in the time of Horace. If they had come down the centuries at all, they had certainly stopped at another Augustan age,—that of Pope and Addison. Not a few private libraries in the South will be found, upon examination, practically to have stopped there."[45] The misconception is at least as recent as William R. Taylor, who has observed: "During the first half century of national experience. . . . The South gradually lost touch with Europe at the very time that intellectual leaders in the North, and especially in New England, were establishing new cultural contacts abroad." Taylor contrasts the unintellectual Grand Tour by William C. Preston with the cultural pilgrimage of George Ticknor. He examines the catalog of Legaré's library published in 1843 and finds only six "roughly contemporary writers"—Coleridge, Channing, Goethe, Schiller, Thomas Moore, and Herder.[46] Such evidence, I fear, is unpersuasive even in these particular cases, and is more so in the general instance of the antebellum Southern mind.

The contrast between Preston and Ticknor is a pleasant conceit that proves little. It merely demonstrates that, if you compare Preston and Ticknor, the intellectual advantage would seem to lie with Ticknor. Of the South and New England, the abstractions lying behind the image, it adduces but one partial piece of evidence. Even on the score of Preston, it is probably unsound. William Campbell Preston was a man of no little learning, who liked to appear the casual Hotspur. His *Reminiscences*, upon which Taylor bases his case, are both incomplete and not intended as an intellectual autobiogra-

---

45. Trent, *Simms*, p. 45.
46. Taylor, *Cavalier and Yankee*, pp. 37, 38–45, 56–57.

phy.⁴⁷ If one looks into Preston's correspondence, one finds something else. One finds, for one thing, an 1824 letter to George Ticknor that thanks the Bostonian for passing along a recent edition of the *North American Review*, which contained a letter of Preston's upon the tariff, which praises the *North American* as a valuable influence upon public opinion. And this is not surprising. George Ticknor, William Preston, and Hugh Swinton Legaré had, after all, been friends together in Edinburgh in 1819.⁴⁸ Nor is there anything intrinsically unintellectual about a Grand Tour. Gibbon, at least, would have been surprised to hear of it. It was possible, after all, to learn something outside of a German university. It was sometimes difficult for Americans to learn anything inside one.⁴⁹

As for Legaré's library, the evidence is quite otherwise. There are, in fact, two catalogs of the library. The first of 1843 was used by Taylor, the second of 1848 was not. The second is itself sufficiently damaging to Taylor's case. It would, indeed, be easier to list "roughly contemporary writers" who are not represented. Even to cite the most obvious names in the catalog would be taxing the reader's patience. These, at least, are worth mentioning: Jomini, De Tocqueville, Henri Saint-Simon, Thierry, Michelet, De Maistre, Thiers, Guizot, Lamartine, Balzac, Beranger, Dupin, Villers, Villemain among French writers; August von Schlegel, Tieck, Heeren, Klopstock, Kant, Schiller, Niebuhr, Becker, Grimm among the Germans; Paley, Hallam, Dugald Stewart, Allan Cunningham, Bulwer, Mackintosh, Bentham, Nassau Senior among the British; Manzoni among the Italians; Webster, Jefferson, Hamilton, Washington, Henry Wheaton, Thomas Cooper, Thomas Grimké, Jasper Adams among the Americans; sets of the British Poor Law Reports and the American Congressional Debates and State Papers among official documents. Yet even Taylor's use of the 1843 catalog is curious. One can find even there the following: Bentham, Nassau Senior, Grimm, von Savigny, Tieck, Heeren, Creuzer, Kant, Schiller, Niebuhr, Wheaton,

---

47. Minnie Clare Yarborough, ed., *The Reminiscences of William C. Preston* (Chapel Hill, 1933); they break off, for instance, before Preston began his studies in Edinburgh.

48. Preston to Ticknor, 8 May 1824, Preston Papers, South Caroliniana Library, University of South Carolina, Columbia; *Life, Letters and Journals of George Ticknor*, ed. George S. Hillard (Boston, 1876), 1:278. I strongly suspect that, if we expand the study of the Southern mind away from matters of sectional passion, we shall find many such intersectional friendships and alliances: cf. John Hope Franklin, *A Southern Odyssey: Travelers in the Antebellum North* (Baton Rouge, 1976).

49. Carl Diehl, *Americans and German Scholarship, 1770–1870* (New Haven, 1978), pp. 148–49.

Dupin, Villers, Eichhorn, Schlegel, Klopstock, Webster, Jefferson, Hamilton, Cooper. Moreover, while it is true that the library contained seventeenth- and eighteenth-century editions of the classics in abundance, it also harbored many of the best recent editions from Germany, France, and England.[50] And no one should underestimate the role that philology played in the Romantic movement. These were very modernized classics.

I dwell on this, not to malign an intelligent book, but simply to indicate that closer scrutiny may yield a different picture. The reader will be able to judge for himself in some of the following essays. One can, of course, find Southerners who continued to prefer Pope to Byron, Addison to Disraeli. That is not the point. In general, the Southern intellectual was as likely to be *au courant* as his Northern contemporary. The South was slumbering in no Augustan twilight. We have, it seems, gravely distorted the balance between North and South on this score: as Carl Diehl has recently suggested, it is easy to exaggerate the impact of German thought on New England; it has certainly been easy to underestimate its force in the South.[51]

The desire to identify with New England the modernization of nineteenth-century thought, and to deny the same title to the South, has doubtless proceeded from honest and worthy motives. It has seemed hard to call a slave society progressive. But recent historiography has been moving to an appreciation of the Old South as far from premodern, precisely because our sense of the flexibility of industrial modernity has increased as the phenomenon has spread far beyond its original homes in Manchester or Lowell. In Japan industry has fastened upon older forms of paternalism. In India it has not proved inimical to the caste system. In Korea it has not led to significant democratization. We must entertain the real possibility that the South's peculiar institution did not doom the region to anachronism, that the Old South was a different and evolving ver-

---

50. *Catalogue of the Library of the Hon. Hugh S. Legaré* (Washington, 1843); *Catalogue of the Rare and Valuable Private Library of the Late Hon. H. S. Legaré* (Washington, 1848). Both can be found in the Legaré Papers, South Caroliniana Library, Box 2, Folder 62.

51. Diehl, *Americans and German Scholarship*, pp. 145–53. Diehl's book is a good example of intelligent intellectual history that is flawed by an indifference to the Southern dimension, despite his complaints of having to use yet again the dog-eared manuscripts of Bancroft and a paucity of contemporary American sources. He does not seem to know of Jesse Burton Harrison's German diary, now in Charlottesville, or of Legaré's published German journals. Nor is he aware of the, admittedly scrappy, John T. Krumpelmann, *Southern Scholars in Goethe's Germany* (Chapel Hill, 1965), and so misses the Southern appreciation of German scholarship so important to Basil Gildersleeve.

sion of what an American modernity might have come to look like.[52] I suspect a history of antebellum Southern intellectual life will betray a similar image when seriously undertaken: it may possibly show a modernity more marked in the South's intellectual elite than in even its social structure, contemporary and potential. Liberalism and conservatism were the twin children of the years after 1776 and 1789. In the century of Mazzini and Bismarck, Michelet and Fichte, Emerson and Beverley Tucker, there was nothing old-fashioned in the South's movement to cultural and political nationalism. It was all too modern.

---

52. I have tried to discuss the problem of modernization in the South at greater though insufficient length in Michael O'Brien, "The Nineteenth-Century American South," *The Historical Journal* 24 (September 1981): 751–63.

# Editorial Note

This book is an attempt to resurrect a few neglected passages in the intellectual history of the Old South. Two basic strategies were considered in its planning. The first was to offer a volume like Perry Miller's *The Puritans: A Sourcebook of Their Writings*, a comprehensive survey of the antebellum Southern mind, exemplified in brief excerpts from many authors and embodying a vision of the meaning of the culture. I have rejected that strategy, for several reasons. Firstly, it is idle to emulate Miller's erudition, and, secondly, certain aspects of Southern thought, notably its "literature" and the proslavery argument, have received attention elsewhere, so it would be supererogatory to duplicate efforts well launched. Drew Gilpin Faust has usefully provided a new anthology of proslavery writing, *The Ideology of Slavery: Proslavery Thought in the Antebellum South, 1830–1860* (Baton Rouge, 1981). But, most important, I am persuaded that Miller's premise, that a culture like New England or the South has a coherent "mind" to which individual minds are tributary, no longer makes sense. This atomism dictated the second strategy: to publish a small number of sustained essays, closely annotated to help the reader appreciate the texture of each piece. Random plundering of texts has only inhibited our understanding. Everyone has spoken, it seems, but the antebellum Southerner. He deserves an uninterrupted moment in the court of historical opinion, to persuade or not.

My first instinct was to take certain broad categories of intellectual endeavor—history, social criticism, classical scholarship, and so forth—and offer examples of each. But this proved a straitjacket of little utility. History wandered into memoir, social criticism into philosophy, theology into economics. It was put to me that nineteenth-century categories, such as belles lettres or political economy, might be more useful. But these were divisions as unclear then as now, and mostly existed as unstable pedagogical devices. So I have placed the essays in simple chronological order.

My second instinct was to roam in subject matter as widely as possible. Why not some geology? A little anthropology? Botany? But the reader expects some coherence, rightly so, even if cultures live more randomly than narrative thread cares to allow. So the anthology concentrates upon the reception and understanding of new ideas, since I take it that the open or closed quality of Southern thought is a, if not the, leading issue. As the reader will have surmised from my introduction, I think these essays demonstrate a marked fluidity and variety in Southern thought. He will find, for example, German thought praised and damned, Coleridge relied upon and execrated, an American national literature condemned and espoused, professionalism in literature urged and doubted, Paley approved and called a fool. Very few insights of nineteenth-century thought did not find Southern representatives, and they were often contradictory and the occasion for dispute within the region.

The reader will find the seaboard South, particularly South Carolina and Virginia, heavily represented. This is partly an accident: the issues upon which I have chosen to concentrate were most discussed in the older and eastern South. It is partly intended: I am inclined to think the quality of discourse in a Charleston was higher than that in a Nashville. But this has led to a further unintended distortion, the absence of Jacksonian political thought, more vigorous in the western South and outside the scholarly periodicals. It is my hope, it is worth emphasizing, that this anthology will be taken for what it is, a random sampling probably too conformable to the editor's own tastes and a stimulus to the samplings of others, not a strictly accountable exemplification and portrait of Southern thought.

All but two of these fourteen pieces have been undisturbed by editors since their first publication: the exceptions are Harrison's "English Civilization," which appeared obscurely in a private publication in 1910, and Gayarré's chapter on John Law, for which there is a modern reprint. I hope the annotations make the duplication of Gayarré excusable. I have corrected only the most obvious of misprints. If I have any suspicion that a misspelling or otherwise indicates a misunderstanding of the original author, I have left it to the mercies of the reader. I have done my best to track down quotations and allusions, though the vagueness of the nineteenth century's habits of citation has sometimes made this impossible and has usually made it difficult. If the reader finds the editor silent of identification, he may rest assured that the silence is pained and not slothful. Naturally I have not annotated the obvious, although I am conscious one man's commonplace can be another's exoticism. I have cited poetry simply by line, unless it would prove difficult to locate, when I have been fuller in reference. I have tended to use early editions, if only one could have been used by an author, later if the citation of an earlier would spuriously indicate exactness. I have offered translations from German, Greek, and Latin (except for obvious tags). Anything in the footnotes that is within square brackets is from the original text. I have used these abbreviations for certain periodicals.

RM—Russell's Magazine

SCGHM—South Carolina Genealogical and Historical Magazine (later the South Carolina Historical Magazine)

SLM—Southern Literary Messenger

SQR—Southern Quarterly Review

SR—Southern Review

VMHB—Virginia Magazine of History and Biography

M. O'B.
April 1982
Fayetteville, Arkansas

# 1.

*James Hervey Smith*

"Sismondi's Political Economy"[1]

It was not planned, but it is fitting to begin with an essay of doubtful authorship. One of the sources for identifying anonymous contributors to the first *Southern Review* is a letter, now in the Charleston Library Society, written in 1869 by Peter J. Shand to a Mr. Whitefoord. Shand had lately seen a set of the *Review* with names written against articles, upon the apparent authority of Bishop Stephen Elliott. Elliott had helped to run the periodical, and his father, the senior Stephen Elliott, had been its major instigator and a generous contributor. The Shand letter attributes this essay upon the economic thought of Jean Charles Leonard Simonde de Sismondi to a "James S. Smith." We have no other clue. Now no such person existed in literate South Carolinian circles in the late 1820s. There was, however, James Hervey Smith whose personal history had a quirk that may explain the slip. In 1837 Smith was to change his name to James Smith Rhett, at the same time his more notable younger brother became Robert Barnwell Rhett.[2] It is not implausible that even a bishop, remembering in later years, might

---

1. [James Hervey Smith], "Sismondi's Political Economy," *SR* 4 (November 1829): 261–85, a review of J-C-L Simonde de Sismondi, *Nouveaux principes d'économie politique, ou de la richesse dans ses rapports avec la population* (2d ed., Paris, 1827).
2. Peter J. Shand to Whitefoord, 26 July 1869, Charleston Library Society; Guy A. Cardwell, "Charleston Periodicals, 1795–1860" (Ph.D. diss., University of North Carolina, 1936), p. 390, suggests this may be by Stephen Elliott. I doubt this, because Elliott's role as editor meant he was often ascribed to articles wrongly, other guides to Elliott's writings do not mention this piece, and the unusualness of a contribution from Smith betokens a special knowledge in the Shand letter (in addition, there is a marked copy of the *Southern Review*, formerly belonging to a Drayton Grimke-Drayton and now in the Special Collections of the University of Arkansas Library in Fayetteville, which ascribes this essay to James H. Smith); *SCHGM* 30 (October 1929): 257 reprints the petition by which the name was changed: it was done largely at the behest of James and Albert Smith, with Robert assenting, to honor a forebear whose name was threatened with extinction: see Laura A. White, *Robert Barnwell Rhett: Father of Secession* (New York, 1931), p. 34.

befuddle the transition from James H. Smith to James S. Rhett and write down "James S. Smith." Others have done it.[3]

The Smiths were a Beaufort family, closely allied to the Elliotts.[4] James Hervey Smith was born in 1797, the son of James Smith, a lawyer admitted to the Middle Temple in 1781.[5] The younger Smith married in 1818 and died in 1855. We know little of his profession, though his family connection suggests planting. Of his politics, more is known. He was an energetic Unionist during the Nullification crisis, an orator and alone among Unionists elected to the touchy commission of militia officer during the crisis of the loyalty oath in 1834.[6] Then in dissent from his brothers, Robert and Albert, he was later to move into alliance with them in their tentative pact with John C. Calhoun. He served in the state legislature, but was defeated for Congress in 1842. Later he assisted his brother Robert in a futile attempt to elect Calhoun to the presidency.[7]

His writings were few. Apart from an 1832 Unionist oration, there are four items of note. The South Caroliniana Library has a bound manuscript volume of his juvenile poems. It is full of pieces upon the romantic and cheerful themes of death (of mothers and murdered infants), funerals, graves, the faery world, the fiftieth anniversary of American independence, the melancholy passing of comets in the heavens.[8] Its tone bears out Frederick Porcher's memory of Smith's diligent attendance at the Charleston Conversation Club: a man "very amiable under a frowning exterior."[9] The Shand letter further credits Smith with an essay in the *Southern Review* upon J. L. Alibert's *Physiologie des passions, ou nouvelle doctrine des sentimens moraux*, a piece that betrays the same interest in the mechanisms of perception and action, understanding and morality, that was later to bring him to a laborious study of Kant.[10] But his 1830

---

3. For example, Theodore D. Jervey, *Robert Y. Hayne and His Times* (New York, 1909), p. 462.

4. Beverly R. Scafidel, ed., "The Letters of William Elliott" (Ph.D. diss., University of South Carolina, 1978), pp. 101, 182, 195, 196, 363.

5. E. Alfred Jones, *American Members of the Inns of Court* (London, 1924), p. 201.

6. *SCHGM* 4 (January 1903): 42; James H. Smith, *Oration Delivered by Appointment Before the Union and States Rights Party, on the 4th of July 1832* (Charleston, 1832); James P. Carson, *Life, Letters and Speeches of James Louis Petigru* (Washington, 1920), pp. 88, 138–39.

7. White, *Rhett*, pp. 32–84; Carson, *Petigru*, p. 213.

8. "Book of Compositions by James Smith Rhett, 1817–1826," South Caroliniana Library, University of South Carolina, Columbia; his youthful name has been carefully excised from the title page and Rhett substituted.

9. "The Memoirs of Frederick Adolphus Porcher," ed. S. G. Stoney, *SCHGM* 47 (October 1946): 223: "James Smith Rhett was rather fond of metaphysical discussions."

10. "Physiologie des Passions," *SR* 6 (August 1830): 116–40; "Memoirs of Porcher," p. 223: "He devoted a year, I believe, to the study of Kant."

thoughts seem defined by the traditional categories of Scottish commonsense philosophy. In 1835 Smith delivered a eulogy upon his kinsman, Thomas Smith Grimké, an affectionate evocation of that shabbily dressed oddity in urbane Charleston, the lawyer who advocated a reformed orthography of the English language and the removal of the classics and pure mathematics from curricula.[11] Lastly, Smith (now Rhett) reviewed in 1850 James Warley Miles's *Philosophic Theology*, in a spirit defensive of the pure milk of Kantianism. Kant, he concluded, "lies at the foundation of most of the modern improvements in metaphysical philosophy; and we have always considered our position strengthened when we could have the authority of this great genius to sustain us."[12]

This essay upon the economic theory of Sismondi is a fair example of the good, but not extraordinary, Southern periodical contribution. It betrays a normal awareness of contemporary politics, both domestic and European. Smith cites a recent item in *Niles Weekly Register* and a speech by Robert Peel in the House of Commons, just as his 1832 oration was to mention remarks by Chateaubriand in the Chamber of Deputies.[13] His awareness of economic theory is respectable without being exhaustive, thoughtful but not original. Its striking feature, a sympathetic consciousness of the human costs of industrialism, was partly drawn from Sismondi himself, whose major dissent from classical economics was to draw attention to the endemic suffering of factory laborers—the proletarians as he was the first to call them—both when they worked and when business cycles denied them the chance.[14] Others in the South like Jacob Cardozo, Thomas Cooper, and Thomas Dew were writing with more trenchancy upon political economy.[15] But Smith here added a critical vision of England, the "lazar house" of a Protean

---

11. Smith, *Eulogium on the Life and Character of Thomas S. Grimké* (Charleston, 1835); George A. Wauchope, ed., *The Writers of South Carolina* (Columbia, S.C., 1910), p. 186.

12. "Philosophic Theology," *SQR* 17 (April 1850): 123–45, and 17 (July 1850): 481–99. Both pieces are signed "J. S. R.," and Simms mentions they are by Rhett. See Simms to George Frederick Holmes, 13 April 1850, in *Letters of William Gilmore Simms*, ed. M. C. Simms Oliphant et al. (Columbia, S.C., 1954), 3:32.

13. Smith, *Oration*, p. 8.

14. Joseph A. Schumpeter, *History of Economic Analysis* (New York, 1954), pp. 493–96; Eric Roll, *A History of Economic Thought* (4th ed., London, 1973), pp. 235–40; Albert Aftalion, *L'Oeuvre économique de Simonde de Sismondi* (Paris, 1899), p. 14.

15. B. F. Kiker and Robert J. Carlson, eds., *South Carolina Economists: Essays on the Evolution of Antebellum Economic Thought* (Columbia, S.C., 1969); Melvin L. Leiman, *Jacob N. Cardozo: Economic Thought in the Antebellum South* (New York, 1966); James C. Hite and Ellen J. Hall, "The Reactionary Evolution of Economic Thought in Antebellum Virginia," *VMHB* 80 (October 1972): 476–88.

manufacturing interest. As a vision, it is balanced between two moments in American thought. It harks back to the eighteenth-century Whig cry against British corruption. It looks forward to the Carlylean component of the proslavery argument, that curious occasion when Karl Marx and George Fitzhugh shared an understanding of the aspirations of Chartism. Smith pays little attention to the matter of slavery, surprisingly, in view of Sismondi's sharp condemnation of the institution in the *Nouveaux principes*, and this omission raises the intriguing possibility that roots of the proslavery argument may lie as much in a discrete consideration of classical economics as in the rationalizations of racist ideology.

ECONOMY, in its general acceptation, may be considered as the art of increasing the amount of human comfort and enjoyment, and diminishing the sum of human suffering and want, by the agency of wealth. Domestic economy is this principle applied to the cares of a family; political economy, the same system directed to national concerns.

The immediate object of Political Economy is the accumulation, the distribution and enjoyment of national wealth or capital. The ultimate use of all wealth is the increase and diffusion of happiness and improvement, and the diminution of the distresses and necessities of man. The ultimate and real object of national wealth, therefore, should be the increase and distribution of national happiness, and the relief of national want and suffering. If this position be true, every rule or principle of the science which does not accord to this standard, must be more or less inaccurate. The political economist can never be right in looking short of the end and consequences of his labours.

As the arrangements of Political Economy must, then, eventually be measured by the benefit the nation derives from them, and the evils which may thereby be relieved, it would follow that the utility of all the productions of human labour, or of the materials which human skill acquires from the vast storehouses of nature, when viewed in relation either to the gratification or relief of human wants, constitutes their real value. Such is the view of this subject which M. Sismondi takes, and in his general principles we agree most cordially with him. But when he comes to the application of these principles, we must, in many cases, widely differ. He appears frequently to lose sight of the real results, the ultimate consequences of his own doctrines—to adopt imperfect measures, and to resort to temporary expedients like the unskilful physician, who, instead of applying his remedies to the source and constitutional cause of a disease, should be satisfied with efforts to relieve each unpleasant symptom which may make its appearance.

Neither morals nor politics are legitimately portions of the science of Political Economy, but inasmuch as the moral and political welfare of a nation are objects of the highest value, no principles in Political Economy should be considered as valid or fundamental which are adverse to what ought to be the great ends of all legislation. "Riches," says M. Sismondi, "we cannot be weary of repeating, are not the final object of society, but only one of the means of obtaining this object." And in another page, "thus, Political Economy is not a mere science of calculation, but a moral science, it leads to its end only when it justly appreciates the sentiments, the wants and the passions of men."[16] There are, however, some unquestionably great names who maintain different opinions, and regard accumulation as the sole object of this science. Adam Smith, perhaps, has too little considered the moral view of this subject in his Inquiries;[17] and the English politicians and political economists (as our author asserts) looking to accumulation of capital alone, have probably greatly impaired the comforts of the people by sacrificing the end to the means; but there is another extreme into which M. Sismondi, and the school of economists to which he belongs constantly run.

M. Sismondi arranges his discussions under six heads, which appear to him "to comprehend the whole science of government in its relation to the physical well-being of its subjects." These are, 1st. On the formation and progress of wealth. 2. On territorial wealth. 3. On commercial wealth. 4. On money. 5. On taxation. 6. On population. Each of these forms the subject of a book. Two of them, territorial wealth and population, have not, our author remarks, been specially considered by Adam Smith.[18]

It is not our intention, in the present article, to give a full analysis of M. Sismondi's work. We shall merely glance at its general features, and availing ourselves of such portions as seem most worthy of notice, discuss a few questions connected with this science, which appear to us to merit some attention, whether regarded as points of speculative curiosity, or as doctrines of national importance.

M. Sismondi begins his work with the principle laid down by Adam Smith, that labour is the sole origin of wealth, but differs from him in the opinion that society should be abandoned to the free exercise of all its individual interests.

> "We profess, (with Adam Smith,) that labour is the sole origin of wealth—that economy is the only means of accumulation—but we add, that

16. Sismondi, *Nouveaux principes*, 1:260–61, 8.
17. Adam Smith, *An Inquiry into the Nature and Causes of the Wealth of Nations* (London, 1776).
18. Sismondi, *Nouveaux principes*, 1:1.

enjoyment is the only end of this accumulation, and that there is no increase of national wealth, except when there is also an increase of national enjoyment.

"Adam Smith considering only riches, and perceiving that all those who possess them take an interest in increasing them, concludes that this increase can never be better promoted, than by abandoning society to the free exercise of every individual interest. He has said to the government, the sum of individual wealth forms the riches of the nation. There is no wealthy man who does not endeavour to become more rich. Let him alone, he will enrich the nation by enriching himself. We have seen that the rich may augment their wealth either by new productions, or by acquiring a greater part of what was formerly the portion of the poor. Now to render this distribution regular and equitable, we invoke almost constantly that interference of the government which Adam Smith rejects." Vol. i. p. 51.

In the first position contained in the foregoing extract, that labour, or as Say[19] has more correctly termed it, industry, is the principal origin of wealth, we readily concur; yet there are many cases in which, perhaps, "appropriation to use," would be a more correct expression. In much the most numerous and important concerns of life, labour or well-directed industry gives to all that man possesses, its real or estimated value; but in many commodities an intrinsic value exists independently of the actual labor employed in their acquisition. It would be an abuse of terms to say that a lump of gold found by accident, or a diamond casually taken from a brook, were the products of labour or industry, yet they may possess a high exchangeable value when once they have been appropriated to individual use. Neither can we consider the deer, or fish, or other game acquired by the sportsman in an hour of idle pastime, as the product of labour or industry. In common parlance, it would be held the very reverse of either, the product of idleness and leisure; objects not sought on account of their value, but for the amusement which attended this pursuit. These, however, are but exceptions to the general rule.

There are other circumstances that enter into many of our calculations of value, which ought to be noticed in forming our estimates, and consequently in framing our theorems. The force of a stream of water or of wind which moves the machinery of a mill, is calculated to produce value, and possesses that inherent power previous to its appropriation to the use of man. True, it requires industry or labour so to employ it, but when thus employed, thus appropriated, the value which results from its use, is unquestionably not the product of that labour or industry alone. The acquired value is the joint production of two agents—the industry of man and the inherent powers of nature. The one his own, and therefore

---

19. Jean Baptiste Say, 1767–1832, the chief proponent of Adam Smith in France, a market theorist best known for developing the concept of the entrepreneur.

capable of being applied exclusively to his own benefit; the other, regulated by general laws beyond his control, and though enlisted occasionally in his service, capable, according to the same laws, of destroying his work and sweeping away his labours in the strife of elemental warfare. The power of the elements can only be productive of value, when, more by the intelligence than by the labour of man, they are appropriated to his use. "All value," (says M. Say, in the introduction to his Treatise on Political Economy, though he does not appear to hold sufficiently to this principle throughout his work,) "is derived from the operation of labour, or rather from the industry of man combined with the operation of those agents which nature and capital furnish."[20] If this be true, neither can industry nor labour be in all cases the proper general term for the origin of wealth, for however much capital may be indebted to industry for its creation and increase, still such agents as nature independently furnishes, never could have so arisen, and yet they are here necessarily treated as items of wealth.

With respect to the second position advanced by M. Sismondi, in the passage we have extracted, "that the government should interpose in regulating the individual production of wealth, because the rich have the power of augmenting their riches not only by a new production, but by reducing the condition of the poor," it is here that the great principle of M. Sismondi, which he maintains throughout his work, begins to be displayed. It seems to be his idea, while adopting the mercantile system as the basis of his speculations, that the interference of the government is perpetually necessary to prevent or repair those inequalities which the system has a constant tendency to produce. The parental care of the government must superintend every movement of the great machine, its protecting and guiding hand be every where present. Man must constantly be guarded against his own errors. We view this as one of those vague imaginations, one of those Utopian dreams, which are always floating in the brain of a certain class of politicians, leading them to believe that they can manage every man's concerns better than he can himself, and can remove, if only free scope be given to their sagacity, all the evils with which human society is afflicted. As was the case in some other celebrated speculations of a similar nature, the latter end of their commonwealth frequently forgets the beginning. The great professed object of these systems, is to increase the wealth in order to increase the power and happiness of a nation, and they commence by placing fetters on the intercourse between individuals and states, by controlling men in those pursuits which practice has rendered familiar and easy, and which experience has proved to be most

---

20. Say, *A Treatise on Political Economy: or, The Production, Distribution and Consumption of Wealth*, trans. C. R. Prinsep (Philadelphia, 1827), p. xl: "all value . . . is derived" should read "all values . . . are derived."

profitable;—they acknowledge that national wealth is the result of individual wealth, and yet force capital and labour from productive into unproductive channels, injuring alike those who were engaged in the former occupation, and those who have been attracted into new pursuits—creating inevitably the most pernicious inequalities of wealth, while they affect to reprobate excessive accumulation. Such are the inconsistencies of the doctrines now so strenuously maintained in the United States, and which M. Sismondi himself, against the most enlightened economists of France, continues to advocate.

The truth is (and we are obliged often, however reluctantly, to repeat truisms) that evil is mingled in every cup which man is permitted to taste, and we can acquire no good without some portions of alloy. Wherever the commercial system, the source of the wealth, the power, the active enterprize of modern times is established, riches and poverty, wretchedness and enjoyment must exist in degrees totally unknown to an agricultural age or nation. The accumulation of wealth is the active, we may say, the vital principle of this system. We must take it with its good and evil, but we will be unwise to accelerate its progress, or hasten to that extreme point, where some convulsion, whose termination no man can foresee, must break up the diseased and vitiated state of society, and probably impose on its members a long course of degradation and suffering.

Accidental circumstances, such as the entailment of estates, the existence of hereditary rights and privileges, may increase and perpetuate these evils, and prevent those partial distributions of wealth, that occasional dispersion of the accumulations of successful enterprize, which, in all countries under the operation of equal laws, must frequently take place. We have no doubt, that in Great Britain, to which M. Sismondi constantly alludes, the existence of these feudal principles tends to aggravate the symptoms of the disease which oppresses the lower classes of her population, and has rendered one-half of them paupers; but the vice is inherent in the system, and can never be eradicated.

That the example of Great Britain, which has bewildered the minds of so many politicians, and to which in all these discussions reference is constantly had, is splendid and imposing, it is impossible to deny. That nation, in spite of many disadvantages, presents at this time the most magnificent spectacle of productive industry that the world has ever witnessed. So wonderful, indeed, is her creative power, that authors, among the rest M. Sismondi, seem to dread that the whole world will prove too small a theatre for its display. Her rulers do not trust to the natural progress of other nations, or rely on the commercial liberality or wants of other people, to afford her competent markets, they colonize the remotest corners of the earth, and all the benefit expected from these colonies by the parent state, is that they will furnish raw materials for her workshops, and an increasing demand for her commodities. Her navigators traverse every ocean, and have explored the most desolate islands and inhospitable shores. She has subjugated an immense empire in the Eastern hemisphere, and holds a large portion of the Western subject to her sway. Every continent has witnessed and felt her power. These mighty efforts have been made for the extension of her commerce, to afford markets for her ever increasing production—and the defects of her political system and her national policy have been redeemed by a character of transcendent energy.

But when, from one point of view, we admire the imposing grandeur of the British empire, we must not forget the almost unceasing wars, the waste of blood and treasure, the drafts upon the income and property, perhaps, the welfare of a not remote posterity, by which this empire has been built up and sustained. The foundations were laid by her maritime superiority—they have been extended by her commercial enterprize, and her manufacturing skill and industry have naturally followed the possession of markets almost without limit, of which she had gained the absolute control, and, as far as she wished, the exclusive monopoly. Those who, seduced by the example of Great Britain, wish to follow and imitate her in the career of her commercial and manufacturing prosperity, must adopt also her foreign policy; must acquire or create colonies in the most remote corners of the globe; must give to their productions a market, to their seamen a home on every shore, and in every clime—must conquer the weak, intimidate the strong; and, standing in the attitude of perpetual defiance, maintain their system in despite of the rivalry of jealous and hostile nations. More than a hundred millions of people depend, or can be made, merely by her legislative enactments, to depend upon her for the supply of their most necessary wants, and the shuttle and the loom, the anvil and the forge, might be kept in activity to a degree scarcely known in any other age or country, without seeking a market beyond the limits of her own dominions. This is the sure basis on which her system rests, and it must flourish until these foundations be undermined—until domestic violence shall unnerve the arms that wield her mighty strength—or foreign power wrest from her grasp the scattered fragments of her colossal empire.

But there is another element in the power of Great Britain, or rather the source of all her power which must not be overlooked. Her insular position has unquestionably given her many advantages, and sheltered her from many a storm that has desolated the adjacent continent; but there are many islands as beautiful and fair, superior in size, naturally more fertile, some, even now more populous, on whom these bounties have been wasted. It is not then alone, her insular form which has secured to her these advantages. Her restrictive systems and schemes of monopoly have been extolled, yet nations almost without number, have adopted and pursued similar measures, and to most of them they have proved *telum imbelle*,[21] an inefficient weapon, the source neither of wealth nor power, of domestic prosperity nor of foreign influence. Spain, with greater natural advantages, with accidental appendages to her empire altogether without parallel, on whose dominions the sun never set, and whose colonies covered perhaps the fairest portion of the globe, sunk under this system, which she most rigidly pursued to the impoverishment of her own citizens, and the degradation of all subjected to her. And how many small states— how often have even great nations, encumbering their members with restraints and regulations without number—reaped, in their anxious pursuit of national wealth, nothing but disappointment. Whence has this difference arisen? Why have circumstances apparently similar, even principles in this respect uniform, produced such dissimilar results? Why is Great Britain alone quoted, when it is wished to hold up to our view the beneficial influence of this system? It is that the real causes of the wealth and power of Great Britain are more deeply seated, and too often escape the superficial gaze of those who look with dazzled eyes at the effects rather than the sources of her apparent prosperity. To her, when compared with the other nations of Europe, we may emphatically apply the praise which Adam Smith justly gave to Europe, when contrasted with the other portions of the globe—"Magna Virum Mater."[22] She has produced the men and the government whose energy has accomplished these marvellous works—the men, whose lofty character, whose intrepid courage, whose perseverance, whose integrity, have opened the path to her political and commercial greatness, and the government, whose liberal and enlightened principles have enabled her citizens to triumph alike over the obstacles which other nations had to encounter, the errors and defects of their own character, and the vices engendered and implanted in her own political system by feudal prejudices and ignorance, the parent of monopolies and its attendant evils, which, in fine, have made her prosper in despite of these evils. The liberal spirit of her institutions has supported her against the deteriorating influence of her anti-social doctrines.

We are aware that in addressing a people who boast the same lineage with the British nation, who inherit the same virtues, and not a few of the same frailties, who boast of a government exempted from many of the anomalies and excrescences of the British constitution, and better adapted, as we hope and trust, to promote the welfare of mankind; we

21. Vergil, *Aeneid*, II, line 544, trans. a harmless javelin.
22. Smith, *Wealth of Nations*, ed. E. Cannan (New York, 1937), p. 556: the phrase is adapted from Vergil, *Georgics*, II, lines 173–74, "salve, magna parens frugum, Saturnia tellus, / magna virum": trans. Hail, land of Saturn, great mother of earth's fruits, great mother of men.

speak to those who have reason to be encouraged by her success, rather than deterred by the failure of others, and who may hope to perform whatever enterprize, talent and energy may aspire to accomplish. Well then, let us raise the veil and see what this mighty people has actually acquired, the results, the blessings which the great statesmen of our country are so anxious to confer on us. Great-Britain, in her political aspect, presents a spectacle of almost unrivalled magnificence; she controls a large portion of the human race. The nations of the earth seem tributary to her skill, or fearful of her power—and, like Babylon of old, she stands as "The Golden City, the glory of kingdoms;" but behind this splendid and gorgeous drapery, what does she disclose?—a lazar house, filled with wretchedness and corruption, a population sunk in poverty and vice—the wealth, and consequently the power of the country concentering daily in fewer hands, and indigence and crime extending rapidly through the land—more than half of her inhabitants, by the avowal of her own statesmen, are now paupers, living by the daily or weekly distributions of alms, and the numbers are rapidly increasing. The seats of the arts on which she prides herself, and for which she is so much envied, are now surrounded by military cantonments, the sabre and the bayonet are found necessary to silence the voice, and repress the outrages of desperate misery.[23] Competition in the work shops has been carried to its extreme point—the animal man has been goaded on by an irresistible necessity to labour for the greatest number of hours, and live on the smallest quantity of food which the physical machine can bear. Every glut in a foreign market, every new competitor that springs up in their own; every variation in the price of the raw material they employ; every change of policy among foreign nations causes a vibration that is felt through each fibre of her system. If the price of raw materials falls, each manufacturer is obliged to reduce the wages of his workmen, because, unless this can be done, he cannot bring the stock of raw materials he may have on hand fairly into competition with those who purchase at the new prices. Each one will feel also, that if he cannot reduce the wages of his labourers, he will be undersold by those who may have effected this change, and who may also have the advantage of cheaper materials. If the price of the raw material should rise, similar difficulties occur, the master manufacturer has to contend against the stock of manufactured goods already in market, against his rivals who may have laid up raw materials at the lower prices, and to guard against the future fluctua-

---

23. [Mr. Peel, within a few weeks, congratulating Parliament on the beneficial effects which the emancipation of the Catholics had produced, mentioned by way of exemplifying the fact, that the government had already been able to withdraw from Ireland, where they had been employed to keep the miserable and discontented peasantry in awe, three regiments to add to the military force in the manufacturing districts.] Speech on Daniel O'Connell's election at Clare, 21 May 1829, in *The Speeches of the Late Right Honourable Sir Robert Peel, Bart., Delivered in the House of Commons* (London, 1853), 2:24–25.

tions of the market. On the other hand, if the price of the manufactured article should rise, the workmen begin to clamour for an increase of wages, while their employers have motives, besides the love of gain, to be cautious in raising wages, which it will be so difficult and hazardous again to reduce—and these vibrations are taking place when the mass of the population is on the verge of starvation, when thousands and hundreds of thousands are obliged to depend on casual bounty and the poor rates, for the lowest means of subsistence, and are compelled to watch these changes with the embittered feelings of want, suffering and degradation. Need we wonder, under these circumstances, that we hear of combinations among the masters, combinations among the workmen, 'turnings out,' mobs, the destruction of looms, machines, and manufactories, and finally, the interference of the military, and the suppression of riots, by the destruction of the miserable offenders. This is no exaggerated picture; the testimony of the most correct and most intelligent writers of Great-Britain, the acknowledgements of the journals under the patronage of the government, will corroborate all our statements. She has sought abroad for wealth and power, successfully we readily admit, but she has forgotten the happiness of her people.

It may well become the labouring classes in our country, who are yet free and intelligent, to consider these circumstances, and before they give an additional impulse to this system, to examine its ultimate results, to determine whether they are willing to be reduced to the condition of the operatives in Great-Britain, and to remember, that beyond a certain point, there can be no pause or redemption. The period will approach rapidly when no small capitalist can enter into competition with a great one. It will no longer be the trial of skill, industry or economy, but the contest of machinery, which no small capital can establish or maintain—and no labourer will find employment who will not work for the lowest wages on which life can possibly be supported. It is well for them to know to what they must submit before they can render this country the workshop of the world; what is the only conditon on which competition, in foreign markets, can be maintained with other nations.

Considerations, equally important, should, at some moments, occupy the attention of the capitalists themselves, who are pressing this subject forward with unremitting zeal, apparently unmindful of every thing but their immediate interests. They have before them the history of the British experiment, the advantages under which it has been supported, its triumphant success, and the consequences that appear, almost inevitably, to follow that success. In the midst of that prosperity which appears to foreign nations so specious and so fair, the capitalists find themselves around the crater of a boiling volcano; while the commerce of the world moves at their pleasure, they are obliged to surround themselves with an armed force to protect their persons and property from the lawless violence of licentious mobs, from the very power they must employ to produce their wealth, and to guard against those deeper convulsions with which they are constantly threatened, and which are the more dangerous, because they proceed from misery, hopeless and irremediable. We have already seen some symptoms of this evil in the United States, while wages are twice or three times as high as in Great-Britain, and provisions more abundant; what will be the condition of our manufacturers when these circumstances shall vary—when the population in our manufacturing towns shall become dense and poor, when every change in the political relations of our government with foreign nations, every war at home or abroad, every fluctuation in commerce, nay, every variation in fashion may throw multitudes out of employment, or to speak more correctly, will suspend the demand for certain articles, and leave it a question to be settled between master and workman, whether the former is to continue a business which has ceased to be productive, and may be ruinous, or the latter will quietly consent to be dismissed and starve. In the collisions that must arise under such discussions, whither will those who are physically weak turn for protection. Will the capitalists expect that all the doctrines and principles of our government shall be changed for their convenience—that standing armies shall be created, in order that a military force may be provided to guard and preserve their workshops and their homes? And yet, unless this is done, where is their security? Will they call for the *posse comitatus*, the militia of the district, to suppress disturbances? alas! the militia of the district will be themselves the rioters, and their officers, to whom you must appeal, the very men, perhaps, who are wielding the axe or hurling the torch, directing and inflaming the passions of an excited populace, and ready, upon the slightest resistance or provocation, to turn against persons that violence which, at first, will be directed against property. These consequences are not the less probably, because, in the infant state of our manufacturing system, no serious incidents have yet occurred—some admonitions have already been given that may furnish food for meditation.

 M. Sismondi is fully aware of these results, and, according to the spirit of his system, proposes immediately to regulate society. He supposes there is a point beyond which the invention of new machinery is an evil, as lessening the demand for human labour, and therefore leaving the poor without employment—and that capital may be so amassed as to defeat its own object. When applying his reasonings to Great-Britain, and looking for an illustration of his doctrines, not in the regions of probability, but even beyond those of possibility, he exclaims, "en verité il ne reste plus qu'à desirer que le roi demeure tout seul dans l'isle, et tournant constamment une manivelle, fasse accomplir par des automates, tout l'ouvrage de l'Angleterre."[24] In many respects there is truth in his suggestions; when a new piece of labour-saving machinery, or a cheaper or more productive method of culture is invented, it will unquestionably happen that a large portion of labourers, previously employed, may be dismissed and left to want and misery. But, in a national point of view, their distress is temporary—that is to say, the younger portion will turn while they have strength and ingenuity left, to other occupations, the elder will die off, and give no further trouble. In the mean time, however, the productive power, and consequently the resources of the country are increased, for when a great portion of that work, which was once performed by human labour, is thrown upon the blind forces of nature, or when, by her aid, more is executed by the same labour, there must be a great improvement in her physical, if not moral condition. It has been supposed by many, that man, thus far relieved from the necessity of labour, must become more independent, more enlightened, and more happy. "The faculty of amassing capital, or, in other words, value (says M. Say) I apprehend to be one cause of the vast superiority of man over the brute creation,"[25] and what it has been asked is the use of capital, if it does not tend to increase human production, supply human wants, and relieve human labour? This, if specious in theory, is not always accurate in practice. We have already remarked that the tendency of the commercial system is to excessive and unequal accumulation, the more the labour of a country is performed by machinery, the more all efforts become the mere competition of wealth—of gigantic powers moved by gigantic means—while puny interlopers are disregarded and swept away. If by some new invention, the labour formerly executed by a hundred persons can be performed by ten, it will by no means follow, that the ninety who are dismissed, even if they have more leisure, will enjoy more happiness. Even the position of the ten who remain, may, by no means, be improved. They may only have to do what can be done by any other ten labourers. The whole benefit may, and probably will, result to the capitalist, who will have the means to set in operation the new machinery—at the fate of the ninety, we have already hinted. However, as in no country yet known, has improvement ever advanced so far as to leave no demand for labour, we have no doubt that all who are not physically disabled will find employment, but their condition will not be improved—and as we consider the time as still far off, when machinery shall entirely supersede the necessity for human labour, and extirpate the human race; when, according to the monitory exclamation of M. Sismondi, the last man, sovereign of course he must be, will be employed in turning the wheel, or rather kindling the fires which must drive the whole machinery,

---

24. Sismondi, *Nouveaux principes*, 2:331: "demeure . . . tournant" should read "demeuré tout seul dans l'île, en tournant."

25. Say, *Political Economy*, p. 61; "in other words" should be "in another word."

the mechanical automatons of a nation, and thus concenter in himself all power and all wealth, we shall not enter into any discussion respecting the measures that ought to be adopted to prevent its occurrence, any more than to guard against the advent of that comet which it is said is, at a very remote period, to impinge against the earth and disturb the calculations and speculations of many of its philosophers. The best and simplest system, the most practicable and the wisest, is for the government to employ itself in protecting the country from foreign power, in preserving among the citizens, equal rights, privileges and advantages, and then leave it to the sagacity of each individual to devote his time, his talents, or his wealth to such pursuits as he shall deem most advantageous, and to his prudence, to guard against the evils, which exist, in some degree, in every stage of society. But this doctrine is despised for its simplicity, and those whose lofty minds are incapable of bending successfully to the details of one man's business are too often the very persons who are most anxious to manage and regulate the capital and labour of every individual in the nation.

"Oh fortunatos, nimium, &c."[26] The schoolboy reads these lines with pleasure, as they recall to his memory the thousand enjoyments that the country furnishes to the unsophisticated mind. The aged politician might repeat them when reviewing the happy condition of nations, whilst passing through the early stages of their political existence—when the warmth and freshness and purity of youth still mark and dignify their conduct. If they have not wealth to make them formidable abroad, they have peace and competence at home. If they cannot disturb the uttermost ends of the earth, they can protect their own altars, and their children want neither raiment nor food. How ill exchanged are these blessings for the extremes which accompany the last stages of a commercial system, where the contrast of unbounded opulence and squalid poverty are every where visible, and constantly increasing. These times will come with the natural increase of population, and its usual concomitant, wealth—these extremes will gradually appear, but it would seem to us folly, if not madness, to accelerate their approach. It is like hurrying over, if it were possible, the joyous and vigorous years of youth and manhood to arrive at age and decrepitude, because, at that time, great wealth and higher honours are in expectancy, and may possibly await us.

We have been led further than we intended into this discussion, but we will make some additional observations before we leave it. Of all the attempts which have been made from time to time to build up manufactures by force, none have been so mischievous, and, at the same time, so ridiculous as the one lately made in our own country. In its fundamental

---

26. Vergil, *Georgics*, II, line 458: the full text is "O fortunatos nimium, sua si bona norint, / agricolas!"; trans. O happy husbandmen! Too happy, should they come to know their blessings.

doctrines it is old enough, nay in its dotage; it is only in some of its modifications that it may claim to be original. It endeavours to combine opposing principles, to reconcile contradictions; to make manufactures cheap by raising the price of raw materials and of labour—for it was among the lures it held out to labourers, that employment, under this system, would be more abundant and wages higher—but it was a great object to buy, in its infancy, golden opinions from all men. The leaders of the project were not at all deceived in the bearing of the measure, but they hoped if the yoke could once be fairly fixed on the country, that it might easily afterwards be arranged and adjusted to suit the interest it was intended to subserve. Hence, in order to lower the price of woolen goods, and make, by this means, the system popular throughout the country, a high duty was laid on imported wool, and the price necessarily enhanced. But how else could the wool-growers be enlisted, and bribed to throw their weight into the scale. It was supposed that at a future, and not far distant day, it would not be difficult to prove that this part of the scheme was incorrect, and inconsistent with the true faith of protection, and that the combined power of the manufacturers would be able, easily, to remove this obstruction as one of their own creation, and one, therefore, that ought to be modified at their discretion. While pressing this measure forward, they were willing that the nominal duty on the importation of cotton should continue unaltered; they would even, if it had not been too obvious a farce, have proposed duties on the importation of grain to cajole the farmers with the expectation of an improved price on their staples. If this were not done, it was only because the absurdity would have been too glaring, of appearing to protect those articles which we were actually exporting to almost all quarters of the globe. That the manufacturers understood fully the operations of their own act, no one will doubt, neither will any one suppose that they intended to suffer it to continue unchanged. No men understand better than themselves the principles of free trade, and the benefit of being able to purchase all their materials at the lowest possible prices. They already begin to discover their feelings and views on this subject. In Niles' Register, of the 20th June, a letter from "one of the most respectable and worthy gentlemen of New-England" is prefaced on the part of the editor, by declaring that the attempt to encourage the growth of wool was a political machine that has answered its purpose, and is now laughed at. From the letter itself we will quote a few sentences to show how strongly they support the opinions we have here advanced.

> "The manufacturer has been wronged, cheated, ruined.—The only true friends of the manufacturer are those who now seek to repeal the ridiculous tariff of 1828.—Put a duty for revenue alone on cloths, and *remove the duty on wool*—this process will invite the regular importer back to his old employment, *and finish the vain expedient, already too long adhered to, of growing wool in*

*this country.*—The duties on dye stuffs, oil, soap and wool, taken in connexion with the derangement of trade, by making the manufacturer an exporter, amounts to a much higher protection to the foreigner than all the tariff affords to us.—The system which alone can sustain him (the manufacturer) *is one founded on the principle of monopoly.*"[27]

The whole letter coming from the quarter it does, merits attention. We know not how the wool-growers in the north and west will consider it, but to us it appears a clear and accurate exemplification of the natural and necessary tendency of the whole system. Labour, when employed in one way only, is considered as American industry, and all other occupations are to be sacrificed, as far as may be necessary, to this one paramount pursuit. Great Britain, from whom the friends of the Tariff delight so much to draw their examples, and derive their facts, affords us, on this point, a striking illustration. The landholders in that country, in order to equalize in some measure the restrictive system, have obtained on their part, as protection for their corn, not only a high duty on importation, but an absolute prohibition until the price of grain became so high in England, as to manifest a scarcity almost amounting to famine. As in order to protect manufactures, they paid a higher price for many articles which could have been imported advantageously from abroad, it seemed but reasonable that they should sell at higher prices their own productions. This protection, as in other cases, led to an increased employment of capital in this pursuit. Poor lands which, without such aid, could not have been brought into cultivation, have been improved at a heavy expense. The proprietors, or those who have made investments in these inferior soils, consider themselves as having a strong claim on the government under whose encouragement these investments were made for continued protection. Thus it is, that in this system every step seems to plunge you more inextricably in a labyrinth from where there is no easy escape. For while the farmers of Great Britain demand the continuance of those laws under which they have adventured so much money, very different views of the subject are taken by other parties. The kingdom is now in a state of great excitement on account of the corn laws—great efforts are making to repeal them, expressly on account of the manufacturers. This interest is found alike clamorous, whether the government is disposed to take off duties on articles they produce, or impose them on articles which they consume. They understand perfectly, and maintain strenuously, the doctrines of free trade, as far as their own interests are exclusively concerned. They know the advantages of buying at low, and selling at high prices: but it is themselves only who are to enjoy this privilege. As with us this labour alone is

---

27. *Niles Weekly Register* 3d ser. 12 (20 June 1829): 266–67: Smith has added the emphases.

considered as national, (American we would call it) no other as contributing to national independence. Capital and industry in every other occupation is apparently to be disregarded, and as far as they interfere with this great interest to be trampled under foot.

To manufactures we have no hostility—we rejoice to see them springing up wherever they can arise with native strength and inherent vigour. They possess naturally great advantages in our country, from local circumstances, from the cheapness of provisions, the almost unparalleled command of water power, the abundance of wood and coal, and the distance at which we are placed from foreign competitors. With the duties which, even on account of revenue, we are obliged to impose, these advantages in the home market are quite sufficient to raise up and protect all the articles of general use, unless the labour of the country can be much more profitably employed in other pursuits, and if it can, what prudence, what wisdom, what patriotism is there in diverting by force and hot-bed culture, this labour from its natural and more profitable channel. Manufacturers constitute certainly a great interest in any nation, but it is only one out of many; it is not even the most important, and there is no reason either in policy or justice, why it should be built up at the expense of others, to be elevated as of exclusive excellence, to bear a name above all other names, to become the test of patriotism, the watchword of a party, the shrine at which men must worship and sacrifice judgment and inclination, if they wish to obtain honour and power.

It is not easy to estimate the difference which a few years have made on this subject in the United States. Manufactures were then increasing, slowly perhaps but prosperously, in many parts of our country, new workshops were appearing with every change of season, new and permanent fabrics were every year added to our former productions. Improvements in this department kept pace with improvements in all others, not running ahead, but bearing a close relation to the general and gradual increase of wealth throughout the country. They prospered, and all men rejoiced in their prosperity. But in an evil hour, the capitalists not satisfied with the domestic market which was so fairly opened to them, required a monopoly at home, making all other interests tributary to their idle and mercenary speculations, as a means of enabling them to contend with other nations in foreign markets. Politicians seized upon this excited spirit as a means to promote their personal views. The peace of the country has been shaken. It is now no longer a question of Political Economy, but a contest of higher principles; and hostility and sectional feelings have been created, that may act injuriously not only on this interest, but on the Union itself, for a longer period than the superficial will readily imagine.

Until within a short period, the great kingdoms of Europe were composed of provinces who had distinct laws, privileges and customs. These provinces viewed each other with distrust and jealousy, surrounded themselves with guards and customhouses, prohibited the free ingress of commodities, even from the neighbouring districts of the same nation, lest it might interfere with their own industry, and others might grow rich at their expense. Every fetter of the restrictive system was brightened and burnished, and kept in active employment. Yet strange to tell, they did not get rich under this system, for as all acted on the same principle, there was no means by which each could exchange its superfluous productions; they did not get independent, for each was frequently in want of the most common necessaries of life, and had no wealth with which they could purchase. All were poor and ignorant alike, and filled with those prejudices and foolish opinions that belong to ignorance and poverty, clinging with the most obstinate prepossession to the very source and cause of all their privations. When by accident, for war has sometimes broken these chains, or by the progress of liberal opinions, they have been disenthralled from these shackles, they have found, to their utter astonishment, that the improvement of one district did not necessarily produce the ruin of another, that where all were left to the operation of a free and unrestricted competition, all could find some employment and share in the general prosperity.[28] By the early application of these enlightened principles to national as well as to parochial or provincial intercourse, the United States have afforded an example of extended and rapid prosperity, unparalleled by any other nation. This was the real "American System," not begged or borrowed from the superannuated governments of the old world, to which our country ought to have adhered; it should have been our pride and our boast, and would have secured to us an exceedingly great reward.

We can only touch occasionally on the questions discussed in these volumes—many that are important we are obliged to pass over. On one which has divided the great political economists of the present day—Say, Ricardo, Malthus, Sismondi—we shall offer a few observations. The two former of these writers assert that a nation never can produce too much, because production creates demand; the last two deny this, and assert that

28. [It is very amusing, and might be instructive to read the lamentations of some of the purest Scotch patriots in 1706, over the evils which the union with England was to inflict on that country—her wealth was to be drained away—her industry destroyed—she was not only to be fleeced, but flayed alive. The error with all of this class of politicians, springs from a supposition that there is but a certain amount of wealth or labour in the world, and that whenever any country acquires a new or an unusual quantity, it must be gained by winning the portion of some less fortunate land. They appear not to know, or not to remember, that by the stimulus of free competition, industry can be excited to redoubled exertions—that by improvements in the arts, the results of labour can be prodigiously multiplied—and that by the unrestrained power of exchange, all the productions of industry acquire value, and become real and substantial wealth.]

demand should precede and determine production, that when this is not the case, new production is rather the cause of ruin than of wealth. On this point, however, M. Sismondi shall speak for himself:—

> "Economists are at present divided on a fundamental question, on the decision of which depends in some measure, the first principles of their science. All that we can flatter ourselves to perform, is to show the importance of the question, and to exhort those who, perhaps, have too lightly formed their opinions, to meditate anew on this subject.
>
> "This is the question—Mr. Ricardo in England; M. Say on the Continent, maintain that it is sufficient for the economist to occupy himself with the production of riches; for the prosperity of nations depends on a constantly increasing production. They say that production, in creating the means of exchange, creates consumption; that no one need ever fear that riches (productions of value) will encumber the market, whatever may be the quantity that human industry may produce, because the wants and desires of men will be always ready to convert this wealth to use.
>
> "On the other hand, Mr. Malthus in England, has maintained, as I have endeavoured to do on the Continent, that consumption is not the necessary consequence of production; that the wants and the desires of men are, it is true, without limits, but that these wants and these desires can only be satisfied and occasion consumption so far as they are united to the means of exchange. We have affirmed, that when these means of exchange were created, it did not necessarily follow that they would pass into the hands of those who felt these desires and wants, that it even happened frequently that the means of exchange increased in society, whilst the demand and the wages of labour diminished; that then the desires and wants of a portion of the population could not be satisfied, and consumption must necessarily diminish. In short, we pretend that the unequivocal sign of the prosperity of society is not the increasing production of wealth, but the increasing demand for labour, or the increase of wages which rewards it.
>
> "Messrs. Ricardo and Say do not deny that the increasing demand for labour is a symptom of prosperity, but they affirm that it results inevitably from the increase of productions.
>
> "Mr. Malthus and I deny this. We regard these two increments as resulting from independent, and sometimes even opposite causes. In our opinion, when the demand for labour does not precede and determine production, the market becomes overstocked, and then an increased production becomes a cause of ruin, not of enjoyment."[29]

Even where such men differ, it appears to us that their differences may sometimes arise, if not from a mistatement of a question, at least from viewing it under different aspects, and with different prepossessions. Frequently these discussions approach the confines of metaphysics—they become a mere logomachy—the fair field for the display of keen wits and

---

29. Sismondi, *Nouveaux principes*, 2:408–10.

gladiatorial skill. We know not that we can remove any of the difficulties in this question. We will, however, briefly state our own impressions.

Demand arises from human wants, from the anxious desire of obtaining those objects which minister to the necessity, the comforts, or the mere caprices of mankind—it may be latent or active, expressed or understood. The demand when latent, may yet be as real and ardent as when most actively manifested. It may exist in full force—it may be as well understood as if openly expressed. It is, perhaps, because this circumstance has not been duly considered, that the opinion, as an abstract theorem, has been adopted, that supply should precede demand. We will offer one or two illustrations to explain our position.

There has been no period, probably, since the days of Daedalus, in which men have not anxiously desired to possess wings. Many, before the age of the Psalmist, probably wished for the wings of the morning, not, however, that they might fly away and be no more seen, but that they might rove from place to place with facility, and change climate and country at pleasure. Yet no one runs from street to street inquiring for wings, because it is well understood that no such useful appendages to our frame have yet been invented. But in these days of discovery, should some one of those who load our patent offices with specifications, for the most part, of old things made new, only patent a well-formed, powerful, safe and efficient substitute for wings, who can doubt that the demand would be most extensive and active. But it will spring from a pre-existing want, deeply implanted in our nature.

Again, from the first moment that the power of steam was made known, and applied in the most imperfect manner to machinery, no wish was more strongly felt than that its tremendous agency should be employed to overcome the currents of rapid rivers, and impel boats along those streams, where the labour of men and the unsteady action of the wind are of so little avail. It was perfectly immaterial whether the plan of Fitch, or Rumsey, or Fulton succeeded.[30] This was a mere personal consideration. What the world wanted, was an application of this power in some form, or in any form that could be managed with moderate skill, and could drive boats at a rate of not less than four or five miles an hour, against a rapid current. As soon as this was accomplished, the demand became extensive, and is constantly increasing. It cannot, however, be said that in this instance it was produced by the supply; on the contrary, it sprung from the pre-existing wants of society.

In like manner, men in a savage state, but far more in civilized and refined ages, are always feeling the strong desire of acquiring not only

---

30. John Fitch, 1743–1798; James Rumsey, 1743–1792; Robert Fulton, 1765–1815: all pioneers of the steamboat, though only Fulton with commercial success.

those objects which minister to their physical wants, but those which grow out of the refined taste and artificial distinctions of social life. A fondness for decoration in dress, in equipage, in furniture, in houses, are all modifications of this impulse. The particular form or fashion of these objects is immaterial; this is left to accident, to caprice, to the taste of the manufacturer or of his employer. It is, however, in this wide field for the display of ingenuity, in the fabrication of all things necessary for our convenience and luxury, our arts and our sciences, our serious occupations or fantastic amusements, that supply seems to precede and create demand, and in the wonderful contrivances to gratify the vanity, the indolence, the artificial wants of all classes and conditions of men, to tempt them by novelty, or beauty, or some imaginary advantages to purchase the ever varying commodities which industry and skill are constantly offering to their cupidity.[31] It is in this manner that supply appears to increase indefinitely, and almost without limits, national wealth. For those nations who are most skilful in the arts, and who can command labour at the cheapest rate, draw to themselves the productions of all other countries in exchange for their own. How these productions, this wealth is afterwards distributed, we have already seen. That in this manner supply furnishes the means of exchange as well between nations as individuals, and increases consumption, we do not doubt; yet these means have value only when they conform to the wants and desires of men.

It seems also as if theory were pushed to extremes, when it is supposed that there cannot be an overproduction of any article, at least of any valuable article, "because the wants and desires of men will always be ready to convert all this abundance to use." We fear the experience of the world, even at the present moment, is contradicting this opinion. When we analyze the subject, and take each particular item of which production is composed, no one will doubt of the possibility of over-production. No one will deny, for instance, that more hats could be made than the whole human race could use, or shoes, or ploughs, or swords—or, as we remarked above, any individual article out of the whole mass of national wealth. Surely then it would be illogical to deny of the whole what is true of each part. If we were to make any exception, and even this is questionable, it would be in favour of food, because wages must ultimately depend on the price of food, and life, and to a certain extent, comfort, can be maintained under the greatest accumulation. Thus, if food should be produced to the greatest possible excess, so that the labour employed in its production, becomes almost valueless, yet the price of food would fall in the same proportion, and the modicum the labourer would receive, how-

---

31. Smith seems to be describing what Thorstein Veblen later called "conspicuous consumption."

ever small, would yet procure food, and having this in abundance, the human frame can easily be accustomed to many other privations. But with regard to other articles, the same advantage would not exist. They might be produced to excess, and the wages of the labour employed on them be reduced to nothing, while food, from other circumstances, may be sustained in value or even become scarce and dear—leaving the labourer no means of supporting life.

Our author opposes, and with much ingenuity, the theory of population proposed by Mr. Malthus. He appears to assume the only correct ground on which this theory can be controverted. He undertakes to prove that if the population of the human race increases in a geometrical proportion, the natural increase of vegetables and animals, by which human life is supported, increases in a far more rapid ratio, and that if accidental circumstances obstruct the natural increase of these substances, and limit it within very narrow compass, there is also some inscrutable law of nature acting against the possible increase of man, and defeating also on this point all speculative calculations. We shall, without entering on the question ourselves, present one of the views of M. Sismondi, for the satisfaction and amusement of our readers, for we suspect, after all that has been written on the subject, that it will always be a point of mere speculative inquiry, without ever producing any practical result.

> "Mr. Malthus has established as a principle, that in every country the population is limited by the quantity of subsistence which the country can furnish. This proposition is only true when applied to the globe itself, or to a portion of it which has no possible means of drawing from abroad any portion of its subsistence. He also supposes that the increase of subsistence can only follow an arithmetical progression, as the numbers 1, 2, 3, 4, 5—while population advancing in geometrical progression, will multiply in the ratio as 1, 2, 4, 8, 16, &c. This reasoning which forms the basis of the system of Mr. Malthus, and to which he appeals incessantly through his work, appears to us completely sophistical—and what is more important, this proposition is only true in the abstract, and can never be applied to political economy."[32]

M. Sismondi then goes on to state, that Mr. Malthus puts in opposition, without any regard to circumstances, the *possible increase of the human race*, to the *positive and actual increase of vegetables and animals* in a confined place, and under the most unfavourable circumstances. But when considered in the abstract, the multiplication of vegetables advances in a geometrical progression infinitely more rapid than that of birds or domestic animals, and these in their turn, multiply far more rapidly than men. It is scarcely possible to number the seeds of some plants—but speaking of those which contribute immediately to the support of man, and taking

32. Sismondi, *Nouveaux principes*, 2:269.

even a moderate estimate, it may be said that a grain of wheat will produce twenty grains the first year, four hundred the second, and eight thousand the third. The multiplication of the animals that feed on these vegetables is naturally slower, yet sheep double their number in four years, quadruple in eight, &c. In doubling every four years, in the twenty-fourth year, before, according to Mr. Malthus, the human race would have doubled once, sheep would have multiplied at the rate of sixty-four for one.

A famine caused by the inclemency of the seasons, by accidental occurrences, is not the obstacle to population of which Mr. Malthus speaks. He supposes an impossibility of production, not the loss of what may have been produced. The destruction of harvests, caused by rain or drought, is only a casual misfortune; it may be compensated by an increased abundance in the ensuing season, and can only be considered a counterpoise to the devastations which war or pestilence may occasionally make in the human family.

M. Sismondi is certainly happy in the illustrations he employs to prove that there are some latent and moral causes which act on the production of the human species, and that the mere want or abundance of food, is not the only principle which ought to be taken into consideration, when discussing this doctrine. The nobility, he remarks, are every where in possession of sufficient subsistence. They ought then, according to Mr. Malthus, to multiply until their descendants cover the land, or shall be reduced to the last degree of poverty. But precisely the contrary happens. In every country in the world, ancient families decrease after a certain number of generations, and the body of the nobility is constantly recruited from the commoners. The descendants of those who lived in the time of Henry IV. are not so numerous as their ancestors were.

> "The origin of the Montmorency's is traced back at least as far as the epoch of Hugo Capet, and no one will doubt that from that time all those who had the right of bearing this name, have carefully preserved it. The Montmorencys have never *wanted* bread, their multiplication, according to the system of Mr. Malthus, can never have been stopped through the *want* of subsistence. Their number ought then to have doubled every twenty-five years. At this rate, supposing that the first had lived in the year one thousand, in the year 1600 his descendants ought to have amounted to the number of 16,777,216. France, at that period, did not contain so many inhabitants—their multiplication continuing at the same rate, the whole world, at the present day, would contain none but Montmorency's."[33]

This calculation has an air of pleasantry, but it seems to be a legitimate inference from Mr. Malthus' theory. The obstacles which human vices

---

33. Ibid., 2:274–75. Here, as elsewhere from Sismondi, Smith offers his own translation.

and passions oppose to the increase of population,—obstacles always sufficient to check its progress, and altogether independent of the means of subsistence, will constantly anticipate the evils Mr. Malthus apprehends, for we here perceive that it checks, before all others, those ranks of society which are most elevated and the most sheltered from want.

We are aware while we have been presenting M. Sismondi's observations on this question, that he has not exactly met the strong position of his adversaries. Their theory is that from the naturally slow increase of capital, from the carelessness, the profusion, the general profligacy of the rich, from the many political causes that counteract the accumulation of wealth, capital, which must be the support of population, can only increase by slow degrees, by at most an arithmetical progression, while the natural tendency of population is to multiply in the rapid ratio of the geometrical series. It has always appeared to us, however, that one element which ought to enter into the calculation, has been overlooked. In most countries, not more than one-fifth, or one-sixth; in fertile countries, not more than one-tenth of the population are found to be agriculturalists, to be employed in raising food for the maintenance of the rest. Now, as labour is the source of all capital, is capital itself, it seems to us to have been forgotten that in the very increase of population there is necessarily a proportionate increase of capital, a multiplication of the very power wanted to produce subsistence for the increasing multitudes. As long as there is land unoccupied, or unskilfully or wastefully employed, a small portion of the new progeny may produce food for the rest. When the earth shall be covered with harvests, and no room be left for industry and skill, it will be time then seriously to inquire into the measures which ought to be pursued, with the surplus of the still increasing consumers.

One passage, relative to the United States, we will extract from M. Sismondi. It is unpleasant to notice in the pages of such a writer, opinions we consider as so unfounded, or, at least, so very much exaggerated. Even if derived from the Fearons and other names of equal notoriety, from men who come here purposely to "spy out the weakness of the land," and exaggerate its defects, we regret to find them obtaining currency through the instrumentality of one who holds so high a rank in literature, and evidently bears to our country no ill will.[34] He attributes the character he ascribes to us, to the natural effect of our rapid increase in wealth and population.

> "But the most remarkable consequence of this rapid increase of population and wealth in America, is the influence that this universal and foolish contest for riches has had on the moral character of its inhabitants. There is no American who does not expect for himself a progress, and a rapid progress

34. Henry Bradshaw Fearon, *Sketches of America* (London, 1818).

to fortune. The pursuit of gain has become the first consideration of life, and among the most free people on earth, liberty itself has lost its price, compared to profit—a spirit of calculation descends even to children—it subjects to constant barter all territorial property—it extinguishes the progress of the mind, all taste for the arts, for letters, and for sciences. It corrupts even the agents of a free government, who manifest a dishonourable avidity for offices, and it impresses on the American character a stain which it will not be easy to efface." Vol. i. p. 458.

If M. Sismondi will select such writers as Mr. Fearon, who on this occasion appears to have been his oracle, as guides, he must expect on all and every occasion to be led astray. In all commercial countries, perhaps, in countries not commercial, there exists an ardent desire for wealth. The love of office also is said to pervade more people than one. It is not impossible that in our commercial cities, as in others, the spirit of adventurous speculation is occasionally so much excited, as to lead strangers, who, ignorant of the general tenor of our occupations, should take the exception for the rule, to form sometimes very erroneous conclusions. But from this stain, to any unusual or dangerous extent, we have no hesitation in saying our country is free. Yet the great mass of our population is sound and uncorrupt, and if any crisis should arise, requiring the manifestation of pure and disinterested patriotism, we have no doubt the feelings of those days when our countrymen perilled all that they possessed in defence and vindication of abstract rights, on a question of principle, not for mercenary claims, would instantly be revived, and that the bright days of our Revolution would not be sullied by any unworthy contrast.

M. Sismondi has much merit as a writer. His style is lucid and nervous, his illustrations clear and candid, and his works constantly discover fine moral traits in the man. As a political economist, however, we think him inferior to M. Say; yet we are glad occasionally to see the science considered not merely as a mathematical question, but one into which moral considerations must and ought to enter.

## 2.

## Jesse Burton Harrison

## "English Civilization"[1]

Few Southern intellectuals began with more promise than Jesse Burton Harrison of Virginia.[2] As a young man he was a habitué at Monticello in the years of Jefferson's retirement. James Madison was his patron. George Ticknor taught him the new enthusiasm for German letters at Harvard. Henry Clay was his cousin and adviser. Macaulay corresponded with him over their common enthusiasm for the antislavery movement, and the two latterly met in London. In Paris he conversed with Lafayette and Talleyrand, the Jekyll and Hyde of the French Revolution, and with Benjamin Constant. In Bonn he met August von Schlegel and in Weimar Goethe himself, wrapped in a brown overcoat and coping with an uneasy French accent. In Dresden and Paris he heard the expatriate James Fenimore Cooper ridiculing the author of *Faust* as a "coddled celebrity," whose reputation would not long survive. In Rome he observed, with the fascination of a Protestant of Quaker forebears, the rituals at the death of Pius VIII and the installation of his successor, Gregory XVI: the solemn immurement in the Sistine Chapel, the white smoke and coronation, the fireworks at San Angelo.

His early prospects were less dazzling. He was born in 1805 at Lynchburg. His father, Samuel Jordan Harrison, was a prosperous merchant, chiefly in tobacco. From Jefferson the elder Harrison had purchased land, and they became friends when the president, each spring and autumn, would escape the throng of visitors at Monticello to rusticate in the octagonal house of his Poplar Forest estate.

---

1. Jesse Burton Harrison, "English Civilization," *SR* 8 (February 1832): 462–91, a review of Sir James Mackintosh, *History of the Revolution in England in 1688* (Philadelphia, 1830).

2. The best account of Harrison is still the obscure *Aris Sonis Focisque: Being a Memoir of an American Family, the Harrisons of Skimino* (privately printed, 1910), pp. 84–143. Also useful are John T. Krumpelmann, *Southern Scholars in Goethe's Germany* (Chapel Hill, 1965), pp. 46–76, and Clement Eaton, *The Mind of the Old South* (rev. ed., Baton Rouge, 1967), pp. 3–22, which concentrates on Harrison's antislavery beliefs.

Jesse Harrison first attended Hampden-Sydney College before going on to Harvard and a law degree in 1825. For four years he practiced meagerly in Lynchburg. His prospects were delicately balanced. Young lawyers were not at a premium in the declining fortunes of the state.[3] But Jefferson, Madison, and Ticknor had been working for his advancement. He had started to deliver discourses before literary societies by which his talent might be evidenced.[4] He had tried his hand at politics, albeit unsuccessfully in backing Clay against Jackson in 1828. He had begun to write for the *African Repository and Colonial Journal* in tentative support of antislavery, not yet any obvious disadvantage.[5] Occasionally his mind wandered westward, in emulation of Clay, but he fancied that he might, from a professor's chair at the University of Virginia, still influence matters. Indeed, it would have been difficult for him to repress a certain proprietary feeling for Jefferson's university, since Harrison's father had helped to build the campus. But the university in 1828 preferred to elect a young Cantabrigian, George Long, and this sent Harrison on his travels, armed with a battery of introductions from Virginia, Boston, and the secretary of state, Martin Van Buren.

His journeys took him to London, Paris, Venice, and Rome, but the core of his travel was an academic year at Göttingen, where he acquired German. In Virginia he had learned a characteristically Jeffersonian mistrust and respect for English culture. The experience of Europe turned him decisively against England as a model for American society. German erudition impressed him, though it discouraged his taste for a scholarly career. It would be years, he felt, before such learning could be emulated in the United States, and he might better about other affairs. But, upon his return, he distilled his thoughts in this essay. "I have a thousand and one reasons for not liking England, which I will spare you," he wrote to a German friend in 1831, "only hinting that I am preparing an essay to be *a grand attack on the whole English civilization* in which I shall tear up all things like a very giant of Solfarata."[6] Though he seems to

---

3. Cf. Robert J. Brugger, *Beverley Tucker: Heart Over Head in the Old South* (Baltimore, 1978), pp. 20–44.

4. Harrison, *A Discourse on the Prospects of Letters and Taste in Virginia* (Cambridge, Mass., 1828), delivered at Hampden-Sydney in September 1827, reprinted in *Aris Sonis Focisque*, pp. 271–99.

5. Harrison, "The Colonization Society Vindicated to Virginia," *African Repository and Colonial Journal* 3 (September 1827): 193–208.

6. Harrison to Dr. Froriep of Weimar, 1 September 1831, quoted in *Aris Sonis Focisque*, p. 122.

have thought of the *North American Review*, the essay was published in the expiring issue of the *Southern Review*. This was doubtless at the behest of Hugh Swinton Legaré, who had encouraged Harrison's German venture, even though Legaré was skeptical of Harrison's viewpoint: "The things I object to are your opinions of transcendental metaphysics and prejudice. I am no believer in the one and rather reluctant to believe in the utility . . . of the other. . . . Perhaps in ten years more, or even five you will qualify your confidence in human reason. For the rest I think it very desirable that the mind of the country should be set free from the bondage of English . . . censure."[7]

The essay is very much a summary of Harrison's personal experience. He writes of Goethe, Böttiger, Lady Morgan, and the swarm of English tourists in Rome and had seen them. He cites Madame de Staël, and anyone who had met in succession Talleyrand, Constant, and Schlegel, all her lovers, must have felt no little interest in her writings. It is also an article balanced between his waning commitment to academic scholarship and a decision to abandon Virginia for a new career in New Orleans, where he was admitted to the bar a month before this essay was published. For it is about both abstract ideas and politics, and assumes their interpenetration. The poverty of English empiricism is adduced to explain the moral bankruptcy of English foreign policy. Harrison clearly felt that ideas and action were in tandem. In Louisiana he lectured at Jefferson College, helped to found the Louisiana Historical Society, and edited the *Louisiana Law Reports*. But he also edited a Whig newspaper, the *Louisiana Advertiser*, and worked his way toward a Senate seat. In the event, however, he was denied the ten years of reflection that Legaré had promised him. In January 1841, he caught the yellow fever and died in New Orleans.

THE SUBJECT, of which the present article is to treat, is an august nation. In the statistics of the world, no people count larger items of power than

---

7. Legaré to Harrison, 12 March 1832, Jesse B. Harrison Papers, Library of Congress, Washington, D.C.

England; none rivals her wealth, and in the perfection to which she has brought the arts of life she is the wonder and the benefactress of all. There are other titles, more venerable far, to exalt her in all eyes: these were nobly indicated by Wordsworth in 1802, when he mourned for the tardy arising within her of a spirit commensurate with the great part of liberatress of the world, which he predicted she was to play. He fondly complained that

>                    altar, sword and pen,
> Fireside, the heroic wealth of hall and bower,
> Have forfeited their ancient English dower
> Of inward happiness.[8]

If each single word of this complaint be well meditated, it opens all the characteristic glories of his country. To America, however, this power, thus august and venerable in herself, may stand in a peculiar relation. All men know the intimate intellectual affiliation which has hitherto connected America with her. For ourselves, we have too often felt within us the impulse of doubts touching this interesting relation, to suppose its consideration wholly indifferent to others. We intend to examine it, therefore, in a two-fold view. First, we shall endeavour to put a philosophic estimate on some of those opinions and sentiments, which are the main elements of the English civilization. By the civilization of a nation, we desire here to express the sum of those results which constitute the character, intellectual and moral, public and domestic of that nation. Suppose a Linnaeus of the intellect wished to impersonate all the characteristics distinctive of the European man, from the Asiatic, the African, the American: he would, in the eclectic process of getting materials, find some traits peculiar to single nations of Europe, some so much more strongly pronounced in one than in the rest, as almost to deserve to be called peculiar, and others common to them all as Europeans. Having finished his work he would exult that he had embodied the noblest specimen of all intellectual and moral physiology. He would be at no loss to mark to which nation belongs the glory of any one of his endowments, nor which endowment it is that contributes most to make him the lord of creation. We beg to divine, in our humble way, what he would have borrowed from the *homo sapiens Britannus*, and how far he would consider that the European man, (who has confessedly traced nature "up to the sharp peak of her sublimest elevation," ) owes his supremacy to his British blood. We subjoin, however, that if it be true as Justinian in the first preface to the Pandects, §5th, says: "artes cum etsi vilissimae sint, omnes tamen infinitae sunt,"[9] more true it is, that to take

---

8. William Wordsworth, "London, 1802," lines 3–6.
9. *Corpus Juris Civilis: The Civil Law*, ed. S. P. Scott (New York, 1973), 2:187; trans. the branches of learning have, all of them, no end, however worthless any may be.

the height and depth of a nation's entire reason, is indeed, an infinite work. We, therefore, shall only adventure to throw out some hints on a small number of points in our topic. Secondly, we shall endeavour to weigh the influence which the civilization of England is having on us, for good or ill.

I. The philosophical mind of Hegel has divided the past history of civilization into four Missions, the Oriental, the Greek, the Roman, and the Teutonic.[10] But we think it too vague to embrace all modern civilization under the name Teutonic: there are distinct lines enough in that of Europe at present to admit of a partition, and we avail ourselves of the hint to ask what seems to have been the mission of England in the great toil? In pondering on this inquiry there figures itself to the respectful imagination, something like a solemn vision of the Peers of the Fairy Queen, issuing forth on great and definite vocations, to reclaim a world in barbarism to the cause of truth, honour and justice. There are certain domestic sentiments, which we might almost admit are emphatically English, which the world could as ill spare as any the richest jewels of modern life: these hardly require enumeration. The free inquiring spirit, in matters of religious faith, also might be set down as theirs emphatically, had not Protestant Germany equalled it. Then again, beyond all doubt, there is much about Shakespear's psychology and manner that is essentially English— we should be glad to have time and sagacity enough to develop this and add it to our summary. In no other great light of her literature might it be very profitable to search for the nationalisms. Bacon might have been D'Aguesseau, or Newton Kepler, or Gibbon Bayle, with only the alteration of more or less talent and learning.[11] But we will not detain the reader by an inadequate sketch of these general titles. We love to admit that in the matter of civil liberty, she was blessed with the destiny of maintaining in practice, more or less perfect, many of the principal rights of man. The

---

10. In 1832, Hegel's lectures on the philosophy of history were unpublished, even in Germany, and Hegel himself was but a few months dead. There were no American publications that might have guided Harrison. The earliest American references to Hegel are in Francis Lieber's *Encyclopedia Americana*, which mentions the philosopher twice. Under "Hegel" in vol. 6 (published in 1831), Lieber gives bare biographical details. Under "Philosophy" in vol. 10 (published in 1832), he observes that Hegel "has sought to establish a strict idealism, on Schelling's principles, by considering the absolute as the understanding conceiving itself, and makes three divisions in his philosophy—logic, the philosophy of nature, and the philosophy of mind." So Harrison's is probably the first American reference to Hegel's philosophy of history. Cf. Loyd D. Easton, *Hegel's First American Followers* (Athens, Ohio, 1966), and Henry A. Pochmann, *German Culture in America: Philosophical and Literary Influences, 1600-1900* (Madison, 1957), which have not noticed this. Since Harrison was in Berlin during the summer of 1830, one surmises he either attended Hegel's lectures or, more likely, heard them discussed.

11. Henri François d'Aguesseau, 1668-1751, chancellor of France at various times between 1717 and 1750, and a judicial reformer; Pierre Bayle, 1647-1706, the French Protestant rationalist philosopher, whose *Dictionnaire, historique et critique* (1697) inspired the Encyclopedists.

representation of the Commons, the voting the supplies, freedom of the press from previous censorship, the unlawfulness of arbitrary imprisonment, the trial of accused persons and of differences about *meum* and *tuum* conducted *viva voce*, not before Praetorian Judges merely, but *selecti judices* of the vicinage; of these great rights was she the depositary, and with more or less vestal purity did she preserve them. What, though the civilians always had held that "domus tutissimum cuique refugium atque receptaculum sit"? (1. 18 ff. *de in jus. voc.*)[12]—England only had truly made every man's house his castle. What, though Ulpian could write, and Tribonian sanction under Justinian, the formal declaration that all men are by nature free, and by nature equal?[13] Yet no where but in England was there equality before the law, and true impartiality in the courts. What, though it is written in letters of gold in the German publicists that "the right of voting taxes is as old on the German soil, as the polity of the States itself," nay, that in the old Electorate of Hanover, not to mention the liberal States bordering on France, this right anciently existed in the Provincial Estates, and was still in practice in the Austrian Tyrol up to 1815? Yet still, England, it was, of all the monarchies, who alone kept the right inviolate, that she might serve as a safe model to so many kingdoms whose charters secure that right to their subjects since the General Peace.[14] What though the glory of the rule in Somerset's case is not peculiar to her, but has always been law in France as Dupin declares—or though Madame de Staël pronounces that in France, and not in France only, but in Naples and Spain, what is modern is not privilege—for this is ancient—but it is prerogative that is *parvenu*?[15] Yet to England again, must the liberal monarchies of the present day pay a large homage for her pattern.

The greatest civil glory of England was, when she was alone among nations, in the practice of any thing called liberal; when the great theorists of human rights in other countries, who made all Europe ring from side to side with their dogmas, whether the fearless Voltaire or the wiser Montesquieu, could find but one model and that England. At that era was England the idol of all the paladins of liberty—she had a shrine in every

---

12. *Corpus Juris Civilis*, ed. Scott, 2:275, trans. each citizen's home should be his asylum and inviolable retreat; originally from Gaius, *On the Law of the Twelve Tables*, Book I, it is later attributed to Coke.

13. Domitius Ulpian, d. 228, the Roman jurist from whose writings much of the *Corpus Juris Civilis* derived, the latter being compiled by Tribonian, d. 545?, at the instructions of Justinian.

14. In other words, the Congress of Vienna.

15. In 1772 Lord Mansfield ruled in the case of James Somerset, a slave escaped from a West Indian planter visiting England, that the fugitive had become free upon touching English soil; Charles Dupin, *Forces productives et commerciales de France* (Paris, 1827), 1:xxxix; Madame de Staël, *Considérations sur les principaux evénements de la révolution Françoise* (London, 1818), 1:1–15.

student's tower, a little chapel on the side of the remotest roads for the wayfaring devotee. But, though it may seem invidious, yet it must be said, the moment that nations began to imitate her, she effectually forbade their idolizing her. In fact, English freedom is, at the core, essentially selfish and exclusive, and free England has been fated never to be the champion of struggling freedom in any other country. When Sheridan pictured to the House of Lords that sublime prosopopoeia of Great Britain stretching her arm across the ocean to vindicate the rights of helpless India, the nation adored his rhetoric, but the cause of justice was as fairly in mortmain before Parliament as if it had been in Chancery.[16] While the weary years of the trial were elapsing, what did magnanimous England, who is so scrupulously just in the Common Pleas and King's Bench, communicate to India from her stores of distributive justice? Let Mr. Hastings answer, who like Verres survived the vote of impeachment nearly thirty years in affluence, but happier than Verres, found no Antony come to do tardy justice to his pillaged province.[17] It is a question, how much of the hostility of the British people to the French Revolution is to be traced to this selfish, exclusive quality—to the fact that British liberalism has a wholly different basis from all other, that she builds on precedent not right, on history not theory, on the custom of England not the dicta of the new-created "College of the Rights of Man." However this may be, her opposition to France, until the treaty of Amiens, was far more consistent, more *raisonnée*, than that even of the Sovereigns at Pilnitz.[18] Her system was the truest foe in Europe to the revolutionary principle—truer than that of Austria—just as Arminianism may be said to have its mortal foe not in Paganism or Mahommedanism but in the system of Calvin. From 1803 till 1814 no Frenchman durst pretend that the cause of France was the cause of liberalism, although it was, in part, the cause of national independence, for England distinctly refused ever to recognize the ruler elected by France for herself; but neither can it be asserted that England was fighting the battle of the world's rights. This self-complacent notion is airier than any vanity that floats in Limbo. She was, in truth, fighting for self-preserva-

---

16. Richard Brinsley Sheridan, 1751–1816, moving the impeachment of Warren Hastings on 7 February 1787: "Would not the omnipotence of Britain be demonstrated to the wonder of nations, by stretching its mighty arm across the deep, and by saving by its *fiat* distant millions from destruction?" *Speeches of the late Right Honourable Richard Brinsley Sheridan*, ed. A Constitutional Friend (London, 1816), 1:296.

17. Caius Verres, circa 120–43 B.C., who was prosecuted by Cicero for his allegedly corrupt and rapacious governorship of Sicily (73–71 B.C.); he fled to Massilia (Marseilles) and was later proscribed by Antony.

18. The Treaty of Amiens (1802) between Britain and the powers of France, Spain, and the Batavian Republic lasted barely a year; in August 1791 the Emperor Leopold II of Austria and King Frederick William II of Prussia met at Pilnitz (near Dresden) and vowed to restore Louis XVI to the French throne, though with the crippling proviso that all other European powers should help.

tion, for the destruction of France, and for the unfettering of her commerce from the Continental system.—She ought, too, to be content with her gains. She has acquired command of the mouths of the Elbe, the Weser and the Ems, with Heligoland; has added to the mastery of the Straits of the Mediterranean the control of the Nile with Malta, of the Adriatic with the Ionian isles; has nothing to desire in the passage to India now that she owns the cape of Mauritius, and can wish for nothing in the gulf of Mexico—except Cuba. But the war at an end, let us attend the Liberatress of the World to Vienna. And first comes Genoa; she falls at the feet of England, pleads that a British General had liberated her, and had proclaimed the restoration of the liberties once so jealously maintained within her walls. Sardinia interposes, and England meekly disavows the right of Lord Bentinck to have made such proclamation, and confesses that reasons of high policy have led her to consent to the incorporation of that republic into the kingdom of Sardinia.[19] Behold! poor Genoa departs and is led *sub hastâ*.[20] Next comes the case of the King of Saxony, once co-Elector of the Empire with the head of the House of Hanover. Here Prussia stands up, and exhibits the deed of Lord Castlereagh, signed and sealed before the opening of the Congress, agreeing for England that the whole kingdom of Saxony shall be absorbed by Prussia. Of all outrages on the Law of Nations suffered at that Congress, this would have been the most atrocious. The moral sense of Europe thrilled with the horror of it. Who so well as England, the only power who had preserved her independence from the pollution of a foreign footstep, who so well as England, whose gold, and that alone, had fed and armed the contingents of all the Allies, thus making her the *primum mobile* of the entire campaigns of 1813 and 1814, and therefore entitled to dictate submission at least to what was just—who so well as she, could have covered Saxony with her patronship—Champion of the Independence of States? But she was bound by solemn parchment; had convenanted with the hot haste of shame, before suspicion of their purpose had called out the scorn of the world. It is curious to know who it was that did stand up for Saxony against Prussia, England and Russia. For various reasons, Austria was not inactive on the side of humanity, but there was another voice: it was that of France, conquered France, proceeding from the mouth of Talleyrand. This man (a true Frenchman, we sincerely believe, to whom the Duke of Wellington and Lord Holland[21] do nothing more than justice,) had, by his extraordinary

---

19. Lord William Cavendish Bentinck, 1774–1839, had, after leading a successful expedition to Genoa, issued two proclamations that anticipated the doctrines of Italian independence.

20. Literally, beneath the spear. Originally it was stuck in the ground as a symbol of booty and magisterial authority. Cf. Livy, 23, 38. 7: "comitibus eorum sub hasta venditis."

21. Henry Fox, 3d Baron Holland, 1773–1840, whose London home of Holland House was the social center of Whig politics. Since Wellington was a Tory, Harrison is suggesting some ideological breadth of English political opinion upon the merits of Talleyrand.

English Civilization 63

genius, speedily succeeded in rendering the influence of France as great as if she had been an Ally through the war, and not now the thrall and victim of them all. It was he who admonished them that the war they had all been waging was based, first, on the right of ancient rulers, second, on the maxim, that mere conquest gives no just right of dominion. The indignation of Europe, and the tenacity of the imprisoned King of Saxony, finally induced the British Cabinet to recede from its ground, and Prussia, finding herself unsupported except by Russia, submitted, just as Napoleon was landing from Elba, to accept the larger half of the Saxon territory with the smaller half of the population. So much for the Liberatress! In the summer that preceded the Congress, she had played a *rôle* no less conspicuous and not more to be proud of between Sweden and Norway. Heaven knows what feelings England has when she hears the name of Denmark! But it is a stale topic—that affair of 1807; Denmark had forgotten it we hope.[22] But to signalize her tyrannous might once more in the Baltic, the Liberatress most honourably fulfils a stipulation made with Bernadotte to guarantee him Norway as an appendage to Sweden, in consideration of his consenting to the retention of Finland by Russia.[23] Denmark had been terrified into submission to this spoliation. In vain Norway avouches history to prove hers an independent crown, elects a Prince of the royal line of Holstein for her King,[24] and utterly refuses to be subject to her natural enemy, Sweden. Bernadotte marches in by land, and an English fleet in the exercise of a gentle force, blockades the coast to intercept the annual supply of corn which nature compels Norway to import: this mild admonition soon brings her to reason.[25] Need we behold her on another field, the Peninsula? If there were any country where gratitude was chiefly due to England, it was Spain. While the King was detained a captive and an ignoble trifler at Valençay and the Trianon, England, by her men and money, together with the Junta, went on to achieve what was perhaps the most difficult of all the enterprises against Bonaparte.[26] Wellington swept over the Pyrenees and the Junta held sway over a land not burdened by one single Frenchman. They call to the King with romantic loyalty, he comes among them under promise to accept the Constitution they had framed. That it was the duty of England to see that this noble people received some compensation, in chartered privileges, for their

22. In July 1807 George Canning, to prevent the Danish fleet from falling into French hands, sent unheralded forty-six warships and thirty-one thousand men to Denmark. When Britain's ultimatum was refused, Copenhagen was bombarded for five days before it capitulated. In the nineteenth century, Copenhagen was to become a synonym for the preemptive strike.
23. Jean Baptiste Jules Bernadotte, 1763–1844, early a marshal of France, from 1810 crown prince of Sweden as Charles John, from 1818 Charles XIV of Sweden and Norway.
24. Prince Christian Frederick of Denmark.
25. This occurred in 1814.
26. Ferdinand VII, 1784–1833, displaced by Joseph Bonaparte in 1808 and kept prisoner in France until 1814.

heroism and loyalty, none can deny. She must therefore have been gratified by the King's acceptance of the Constitution, even if she did not wholly approve of the Constitution. It was perhaps quite as good as that brought by Lord Ponsonby from Brazil for Portugal.[27] The King retracts his promises; did England remonstrate in her own right, and demand at least the bestowal of a modified charter? True, when Riego afterwards re-established the Constitution, England was neither aiding nor consenting to the invasion by the French, but a protest is all the world knows her to have used to save Spain.[28] Nor is it enough for her to plead the absence of right to interfere in the internal concerns of other nations: whence then comes the assumption by Five Powers of the Right to hold General Congresses to regulate the highest interests of foreign sovereignties? Whence the share that England herself had in dictating to Russia and Holland that they should grant Constitutions to Poland and Belgium? Consistency and honour alike require that she should not have permitted this interference against liberty.

Admit that she never soiled herself by becoming a member of the Holy Alliance, though it is possible that the main reason was that alleged by Lord Castlereagh at the time, viz: that the instrument was signed by the emperor and kings in their own names, not by their ministers, whereas the King of England can constitutionally do no official act, except it be accompanied by the counter signature of some responsible minister. It is, however, not the accession to the Holy Alliance which need make criminal all its signers. The President of the United States[29] was invited to sign it: he replied that our permanent policy would not permit us to entangle ourselves in European leagues; but, this apart, that there was little in the Act of Alliance that was not already the practice of America. The act itself, the work of Alexander's own pen at Paris, is called by the continental writers *the consecration of politics by religion*, and merely amounts to an engagement of each sovereign who signs, to observe the precepts of Christianity in his relations with other powers and towards his own subjects. It was in the act of the congress of Aix-la-Chapelle, (a congress of the Five Powers rather than of the Holy Allies, who are not fewer than eleven perhaps of fourteen kings) and subsequently at Troppau, Laybach and Verona, that the odious claim of interference to uphold the two principles of morality and legitimacy whenever subverted, was first proclaimed. Now, though true it is, that even Castlereagh protested, through the English

---

27. John Ponsonby, circa 1770–1833, envoy-extraordinary of the British government to Brazil in 1828.

28. Rafael del Riego y Nuñez, 1785–1823, leader of the liberal forces against the restored Ferdinand VII and president of the Cortes: he fought the French who intervened on Ferdinand's behalf and was executed for treason.

29. James Monroe.

Ambassador at Troppau, against the recognition of the right of any one of the Five Powers to invade Naples, and though Mr. Canning not only did the same subsequently with regard to Spain, but also most effectually plucked England from the pollution of longer fraternization with the legitimates, yet with protest it began and with protest it ended. The four other Powers did their will.

A word of two points wherein she assumes to have deserved well of general humanity about this time. She was busy in procuring the consent of the nations, at the first and second treaties of Paris, to the abolition of the slave trade: had this been purely disinterested, we do not know that it would set England *rectus in curia* on that subject.[30] The eagerness with which she bargained to make herself the worst agent in its history, by the *pacto del assiento* in the treaty of Utrecht,[31] whereby she was assured the monopoly of the right to supply the Spanish American Provinces with slaves for thirty years, (about four thousand annually) and the tenacity with which, when war had suspended its exercise, she claimed its liberal execution to the end, will not be easily compensated. Again, Lord Exmouth's treaty with Algiers in 1816, stipulates that "in the event of future wars with any European power," all Christian prisoners should be subject to ransom or exchange during the war, according to the custom of Europe, and to unconditional liberation at the end. Mr. Kent says, there would be no praise too high for this treaty, as for that of which Montesquieu said *il stipuloit pour le genre humain*, "if a great Christian power on this side of the Atlantic, whose presence and whose trade is constantly seen and felt in the Mediterranean, had not seemed to have been entirely forgotten."— (*Comm*. I. 177.)[32] There is something mysterious, in fact, in the unconcern manifested before that time in England about letting these same barbaresques go loose out of the Mediterranean to pillage the American trade. And by the way, her declaration at Ghent that she regarded as a *sine qua non*, our covenant not to purchase any more lands of the Indians, shews that she thinks the interests of general humanity by no means required the farther spread of civilization in America, and that the Mistress of the Ocean, unlike the heathen gods, does not love to see men congregate in cities, except they be under British subjection. But something more conclusive than all this, is the following: there is one department where her liberality and regard for general humanity, may be put to the test with

---

30. Trans. correct in court.
31. Which ended the War of the Spanish Succession in 1713.
32. James Kent, *Commentaries on American Law* (2d ed., New York, 1832), 1:189–90. Montesquieu was speaking of the treaty made by Gelon, king of Syracuse, with the Carthaginians: he insisted that they abolish the custom of sacrificing their children. Kent does not quote the French, so Harrison has reference to the original, "il exigeoit une condition qui n'étoit utile qu'à eux ou plutôt il stipuloit pour le genre humain": Montesquieu, *De l'esprit des loix*, ed. J. B. de la Gressaye (Paris, 1955), 2:24.

peculiar propriety. We mean her administration of international maritime law. This is that part of the great field of sovereign justice, which, it would seem, should differ the least of all codes from the pure maxims *aequi et boni*.³³ Ask how a nation interprets this law, and answer for yourself her claim to be thought philanthropical. Now, if the truth be told, of all tyrannies existing in theory or practice, the maritime law of Great-Britain is the most unmitigated. And all Europe is galled by it. The common prayer of the whole continent is that America (their only hope in this) may speedily attain to a naval strength sufficient to rebuke and check her, and to compel her to renounce her odious doctrines, as do she will, most assuredly one day.

After the events connected with the general pacification in 1814, it were to be imagined that not one foreign admirer would exist to impute to England the chief patronage of liberalism. Madame de Staël was the last of that list of which Montesquieu is the first, and De Lolme the middle name.³⁴ That illustrious lady in her last years, could only say for England that the House of Commons was the tribune of Europe, where the public reason and rights of the Continent were asserted;³⁵ but the voices that she loved to hear were only those of the opposition members, and a liberal opposition alas! makes no epochs in history. Still that this lofty assumption continues to dwell in the English mind, none can forget since the ever memorable speech of Mr. Canning, on the motion for sending troops to Portugal.³⁶ England has scarcely ever shone in a more imposing light than in that speech. The England he that day bodied forth was in truth a Titan, and he lent her words suited to the "large utterance of the early gods."³⁷ It were unfair to note how so noble a speech led to an issue merely the smallest and most imperceptible of all the foreign expeditions on record; for, who knows the end of it? Quite as invidious would it be in any one to carp at his attributing to himself the introduction of the South American States into the circle of nations, calling them in to redress the balance of Europe, though neither was England the earliest among the first-rate powers of the earth to recognize them, nor will they serve in any degree to redress the equilibrium of Europe. A better purpose they will serve England, and that is as a market for those manufactures which the policy of self-preservation among the continental powers has excluded from their own ports. We are so bold as to say, that Mr. Monroe's warning to the Holy

---

33. Plautus, *Curculio*, I, ii, line 65, has "aequi bonique": trans. fair and good.
34. Jean Louis De Lolme, 1740–1806, Swiss jurist and constitutional writer noted for his *Constitution d'Angleterre* (1771).
35. Madame de Staël does not seem to use this precise phrase, but it is the burden of much of her *Considérations sur . . . la révolution Françoise*.
36. George Canning, Speech on 15 June 1808, in *Parliamentary Debates* 11 (London, 1812), pp. 889–91.
37. John Keats, "Hyperion," I, line 51.

Alliance, that we should regard any interference by its members to reduce the colonies under Spanish subjection as an act unfriendly to us, did more for the freedom of those colonies, and for the patronage of liberty, than has been done by England in her whole history, since the day when Queen Elizabeth sent troops to aid the Protestants in the Low Countries. The voice of the earth-born democracy, was indeed, on that occasion, worthy of the reverend listening of Lucretius, of Hooker or of Jones.[38] But we pass by these two circumstances to come to the prediction which the minister hazarded of a general war, and that a war of opinions, at hand. Mr. Canning was a great statesman, but then again he was an Englishman and an insular, as Berkely calls them.[39] He thought he foresaw, if such a war came on, a perilous part assigned to England, for, she would naturally be the Champion of Liberty, avouched by all aspirants, the refuge of the discontented, looked to, prayed to by all liberals, among whom he knew there were many turbulent spirits. This would, indeed, be a responsible part— the Æolus of politics, and would demand immense discretion. To-day we smile at his prescience. He did not dream of the French Revolution, though there were politicians not endowed with second sight who had little doubt, after the fall of Villele, that the throne of the restored Bourbons would not last much longer.[40] In fact, such a war as Mr. Canning described was only to be apprehended from the bosom of France. But suppose France to have remained as in 1823, and a general war of opinion, of the people demanding constitutions in Prussia, Austria, Italy, and the Peninsula, all at once—England is precisely that power in the world which could least play the part of patron-saint and protectress of the votaries of the free opinion. We do but suppose a case which had virtually occurred between 1817 and 1823; and which of the nations was absolutely insignificant, counting for nothing, in that memorable period, except England alone? Austria and legitimatized France quell Naples, Sardinia and Spain, while Prussia and Russia stand ready to back them; the Demagogues of Germany are crushed by Prussia, while England remains the imperturbably neutral, a spectatress of it all. No! no! millions in armament and subsidies to overthrow the Continental System she would freely give again, if needed; but she is of too good a taste for enthusiasm, too fastidious for

---

38. Richard Hooker, 1554?–1600, the theologian and author of *Of the Laws of Ecclesiastical Polity*. "Jones" is more mysterious (possibly Sir William Jones, 1746–1794, the Oriental scholar?), and the relationship between Lucretius and Hooker is far from clear.

39. George Berkeley, "Siris," no. 109, in *The Works of George Berkeley, Bishop of Cloyne* (London, 1953), 5:67–68: "It is much to be lamented that our insulars, who act and think so much for themselves, should yet, from grossness of air and diet, grow stupid or dote sooner than other people, who by virtue of elastic air, water-drinking, and light food, preserve their faculties to extreme old age."

40. Jean Baptiste Séraphin Joseph, comte de Villèle, 1773–1854, French prime minister from 1822 to 1828, who was reluctantly dismissed by Charles X after election reverses.

knight errantry, too aristocratic to patronise levellers, too concrete to give countenance to theory, and too reverend of authority and history ever to uphold subjects against their ancient rulers. This prediction was therefore only the noblest incense that was ever offered to English vanity. It is manifest that there is but one power in Europe gifted by nature with endowments for that sublime part on the scene of history: that power of course is France. Whenever France is mute, kept mute by rulers whose cautious prudence chooses for a while to thwart her ruling passion, then has the struggling freedom of other countries no advocate indeed. That such is the vocation of France in future history, who doubts? Such did she begin to know herself splendidly even under the Martignac ministry.[41] England has another vocation. She would prove the conservative principle in Europe to prevent all change, except that conducted by the extremity of caution. Even Austria will not equal her in this. The problem of the amelioration of human nature, as of the immortal strife between liberty and fate in the Greek tragedies, is to reconcile the perpetual antagonism of the desirable with the actual. France and America will stand for the desirable, but England in consistency only for the actual. This, though not the most amicable of titles, is yet, we submit, very respectable.

But to proceed to another division of our topic. We confess that we put a lower estimate on English civilization, because of the undeniable absence of a love of the ideal which runs through it all. It seems a received canon wherever the English language prevails, that the nature before our eyes, its interpretation, its imitation, its adaptation, is the highest object of intellectual action. We venture to hold this to be far from true. There is an ideal arising out of all the exhibitions of this very nature, which is a just object of that action, and plainly its highest object. Above and beyond nature (but out of materials which nature furnishes) exists the empire of pure philosophy and the just domain of what is strictly called imagination. There is a beauty higher and truer than nature in the physical world; it was in the mind of Claude; for, as Forsyth felt, even when viewing the enrapturing prospect "at evening from the top of Fesoli," and in Vallombrosa, nature but rarely gives more than the elements of superb landscapes which the abstracting artist combines into perfect beauty.[42] In no department of any one of the fine arts, we dare to say, is copying implicitly even from nature the highest reach of the art. The quarry of Raphael is a nature sublimated far above reality, yet in no respect false to the nature it leaves below it. Let no one here imagine that thus to claim a resort higher

41. Jean Baptiste Sylvère Gay, vicomte de Martignac, 1778–1832, replaced Villèle as premier, only in turn to be dismissed by the king for making concessions to the liberals.
42. Claude Lorrain, 1600–1682, the French painter; Joseph Forsyth, *Remarks on Antiquities, Arts and Letters, During an Excursion in Italy in the Years 1802 and 1803* (4th ed., London, 1835), pp. 76, 79–84.

## English Civilization

than nature herself, is to abandon all standard and discard all rules. The contrary holds literally. All just rules are oracles of the ideal: the abstracted principles found true in general experience. Let us illustrate this position. A youthful reader of the Fourth Canto of Childe Harold, would imagine Byron to have most genuine sense of the beauty of the Venus of the Tribune; he is captivated first by the sincere enthusiasm of the poet, and still more by the unaffected scorn expressed for all the *base mechanic rules* of criticism in sculpture.[43] Now, it may be an uncourtly opinion, but every one who travels in Italy, will be apt to utter it for some reason or other: the noble bard was wholly devoid of taste in the arts. For ourselves we will presume to conclude it from this very scorn expressed for rules. It proceeded in him from an undiscriminating sentiment of admiration which is far from being the highest homage due to the marble art, or from an inaptitude to view in detail the beauty which enchanted him in the *ensemble*. The term mechanical is a singular misnomer. Would Byron but have read da Vinci or Mengs,[44] or could he but have listened to Göethe, he would have known that those who feel most intensely, and most unerringly on the subject of the imaginative Sisters, Painting and Sculpture, treat most reverentially the great rules which are the common sentiments of the wise, the refined and definite observers of all countries and ages. Let any common person of that army of English who annually overrun the Tribune, the Vatican and the Studio, bearing under their arm Madame Starke's Guide-book, and in their memory distinct recollection of Tooke's Pantheon, analyze the emotions he experiences on observing any particular piece.[45] If he have obtained a distinct idea of the subject of the painting or statue, in legend or history, and finds it well set forth, he is apt to feel satisfied: this is the pleasure of Eustace.[46] He may go farther than that. If he possess much sensibility, he studies the passion of the work with interest, and if of an exclusive turn, he is apt to feel an imaginary elevation above common mortals whom nature has not privileged with similar nerves: this is the pleasure of Byron. The discipline of the heart through the sensibility thus experienced in galleries, is, it must be confessed, no ignoble effect of the fine arts. The inflation of soul experienced, if from a sound and healthy

---

43. Byron, *Childe Harold's Pilgrimage*, canto IV, stanzas 44–53, on the statue of the Venus de Medici, which stands in the Tribune of the Uffizi Gallery in Florence.

44. Anton Raphael Mengs, 1728–1779, German historical and portrait painter of neoclassical persuasion, author of the *Considerations on Beauty and Taste in Painting* (1762).

45. Mariana Starke, *Travels in Europe, For the Use of Travellers on the Continent* (8th ed., Paris, 1833), pp. 111–249; Andrew Tooke, *The Pantheon, Representing the Fabulous Histories of the Heathen Gods and Most Illustrious Heroes* (London, 1698), an adaptation of Antoine Pomey's *Pantheon*, first published in Latin in 1653, was widely used as a mythological handbook for schoolchildren.

46. John Chetwode Eustace, *A Tour Through Italy* (London, 1813–1819); this may also be a pun upon Eustace of Blois, King Stephen's son, who choked upon a dish of eels, a satiation more comprehensive.

source, becomes the enthusiasm of virtue; this is often permanently ennobling to the character. The operation of the fine arts is in that case parallel to the effect which invariably follows the reading of a page of Seneca: and we are yet to see the justice of the disparagement cast on stoicism by the christian doctors, who have at least unnecessarily striven to render christianity the antagonist principle to it. Methodism is its only necessary opposite.

But to return to our observer. Beyond this effect of the arts he cannot commonly go. Higher than this, perhaps he would assert, no one can go, for he had himself enjoyed the poetry of art. It is, however, possible to go higher, in painting often, in sculpture always. Let us convince him of it. We need not for this purpose call in to our aid a professor from that half-divine southern region, where to be born is to have the true susceptibility for the arts, but a simple traveller from an ungenial northern sky. Our Englishman has not failed to observe that host of uncouth youths and men only less numerous than the English themselves, who too are lookers on. The little cloth-caps, long locks of fair hair, bare necks and dress which would fright St. James'-street from her propriety, indicate the youths to be German *Burschen* just undergoing the process of reassimilation to a world of Philisters, down to which they are degraded by issuing from their university.[47] Let him listen to a traveller of this nation; among the yearly swarm of them, old and young, he may be sure to find at least, one who can dissert scarcely less brilliantly than Winkelman or Böttiger.[48] If he be capable of receiving the ideas of such a person, he soon feels it to have been no airy assertion of the great critics, that the pure dominion of the fine arts is *ideal*. Painting is of the two arts of which we are speaking, the more concrete, but sculpture is undoubtedly only ideal. As far as the historic purport or the *morale* of sculpture reaches, sculpture is an imitative art. But it is not all imitative; at a certain point imitation of nature ends— a statue dare not resemble life. The proper glory of sculpture is its abstractive essence, like the colourless material it works on: now, this is within the resort exclusively of the intellect, we do not mean of the understanding, but of the pure imagination. Every traveller who has been so favoured as to hear such a person descant, has noticed with delight how new beauties before unsuspected, start before his eyes, how fitnesses and harmonies are developed, and as a perception of the ideal enters his mind, he sees the field of the art expand, and the reach of his mind lengthen

---

47. *Burschen* are German undergraduates; *Philister* is a term of opprobrium applied by gown to town in German universities and is the root of Matthew Arnold's later popularization of the phrase *philistine*.

48. Johann Joachim Winckelmann, 1717–1768, archaeologist and historian of ancient art, the chief proponent of neoclassicism in eighteenth-century Germany; Karl August Böttiger, 1760–1835, archaeologist and then inspector of the Museum of Antiquities at Dresden.

almost as if one hitherto limited to the touch in making acquaintance with external objects, had vision suddenly superadded to it. We are above the miserable affectation of originality in the above positions: they are common-places in all languages and infinitely better said by Englishmen themselves, by Smith and Reynolds if you will, than by us.[49] But they are not the less needful to have been touched on in our estimate of English civilization. What we note is, that in other national tastes these doctrines have taken root—in the English, not in the least degree. Now it is amazing how far below, not merely the Italians, but the Germans, and not less the Swedes and Danes, are the English (we include the Americans) in this the true susceptibility for the arts which they carry to their travels. America may stand fairly excused, but England cannot, except she consent to throw the blame on ungentle nature; and this is, we dare say, the literal truth. We have known many who conscious that they were lifted far above the illiterate and the obtuse, by learning enough to enable them to delight in the study of antiques, as an illustration of ancient literature, and by an acute sensibility for the passion demanded by the subject, had yet the mortification to perceive and the candor to admit, that nature had denied them the *entrée* to the sanctuary itself. That judicious instruction may do much to remedy this, is perhaps, truly alleged; but who would not sigh for the happy nature of the ancient Greeks, the people to whom the ideal was a native inheritance! And what do our English bring back with them from their travels? We would by no means deny the prevalence of an infinite deal of cant about styles—what else? Why, the same gold, which inspired the thought of transporting one of the marble palaces from the Grand Canal of Venice to London, has purchased a number of Canovas and Thorwaldsens for England, greater than exists in any country, save Italy and Denmark.[50] Besides this, it is just to add, that, among the younger school of sculptors at Rome, the English Gibson, Wiatt and Gott, are among the most distinguished.[51] But what is sculpture to-day in England, but the carving of busts and profiles? What do the shelves of Chantrey's study display but mere likenesses of his contemporaries, almost exclusively busts?[52] Few candid Englishmen, perhaps none, but Chantrey himself, would contradict us if we asserted that he dare not attempt a group, much less an ideal group, because he knows his incompetency. He himself would

---

49. Probably John Raphael Smith, 1752–1812, portrait and miniature painter, but also a mezzoprint engraver, often after portraits by Reynolds.
50. Antonio Canova, 1757–1822, the Italian, and Albert Bertel Thorwaldsen, 1770–1844, the Dane, were the leading neoclassical sculptors of their day.
51. John Gibson, 1790–1866, studied under Canova and Thorwaldsen; Richard James Wyatt, 1795–1850, worked with Canova and lived in Rome from 1821; Joseph Gott, 1786–1860, went to Rome permanently in 1824.
52. Sir Francis Legatt Chantrey, 1781–1841, an English sculptor noted for busts and memorial statues.

contradict us, point to his only group (the Babes of Litchfield) and allege that there is no encouragement in England for the high ranges of the art. Both are true. The amiable Allan Cunningham who does the honours of Chantrey's study, is known to have said when speaking of a young sculptor, who was one of the exhibitors at Somerset-House last year, that he was sorry he showed a turn for the ideal, for, he could not expect to make his bread in that path in England: just as one would discourage a clerk in a house of business from meddling with poetry.[53]

This unsusceptibility of the English is neither unfairly charged, nor is it an isolated trait. It is of the very essence of her entire civilization; which civilization, we believe too, to be of the most perfect consistency with itself in all its parts. What is the ultimate reach of English music? The regulated perfection of harmony is unknown to it. Scotch music, which only lifts its modest head with pretension to melody and the popular charm of association, pleases from its concentrated nationality. But if any amateur should tell us, that he has discerned harmony or melody in living English music, we can only say, that we wonder what Mozart would have thought of such a phenomenon of taste as he is?

Another chief ground of this lower estimate of English civilization is, that a large class of the essential English opinions, of the present day, have their foundation, not in reason, but in prejudice. The evil here complained of is not that such opinions are therefore false, but that there exists a disposition to prefer prejudice as a foundation of vital opinions. To allude to this idea, of course calls the thoughts of every reader to the renowned defence of prejudice, by ὁ πάνυ Burkius.[54] If there be any passage more characteristic of the great master of political philosophy than all others, it is that passage. In so many words he professes to love a truth the more for the covering of prejudice which envelopes it—its long reception makes it lovely, and incurious custom consecrates it.[55] There is an humble class in the world belonging to this school who seem to mortgage their whole understandings, with all their right of acquiring knowledge, for the consideration of a quantum of old sayings, and are all their lives wondering over the inexhaustible truth of their farthing maxims. We have too genuine a regard for Burke to count him among these. Can any sentiment, however, be more baleful to the cause of truth than this of Burke? There is something more respectable than universal belief, it is Truth; an arbiter far more imperial than Prejudice, it is Reason; a mistress of human life wiser than common sense, it is Good Sense. Is it for a moment doubtful

---

53. Allan Cunningham, 1784–1842, Scottish author and sometime poet, noted for his *Lives of the Most Eminent British Painters, Sculptors and Architects* (London, 1829–1833).
54. Trans. the excellent.
55. "Reflections on the Revolution in France," in *The Words of the Right Honourable Edmund Burke*, ed. F. W. Raffety (Oxford, 1907), 4: 95–97.

what are the limits within which prejudice has an authority sanctioned by philosophy? That it "may safely be trusted to guard the outworks while Reason slumbers in the citadel,"[56] but that Reason, awake, can rarely condescend to take Prejudice into her cabinet council, when she is sending out "her posters by sea and by land" to discover Truth.[57] Often admitted, Prejudice corrupts, perverts, lethargizes, and straightway begins to erect herself into the Mayor of the Palace, the viceroy over the king. There is a tender age when all men are incompetent to investigate the foundations of the maxims necessary to guide them, and there is a large class of men of every age who are incompetent, or must be excused from this investigation. But what shall Philosophy say to the sage, whose business is with another circle of men, with thinking men, who yet pretends to recommend as their safest interpreter of Truth, not that High Priest who alone of all her ministers has ever entered her recesses or will ever see her unveiled visage, but a slave whose station is in the vestibule? Indeed, Reason can never with safety take Prejudice even as an ally, as a mercenary recruit, except for special cases of necessity. It is all one, in the view of Philosophy, when you do confide in Prejudice, whether she be merely Unreason or Anti-Reason; doubtless you may find your account, on some occasions when you have no light to guide you, in surrendering to her blind guidance; but beware how you conceive a preference for her. Never was a truer *tormentum Mezentii* than you inflict on living Truth, by fastening it to decayed Prejudice.[58] These may seem exaggerated generalizations, but to us they appear hardly adequate. English writers all acknowledge that the estimation which the pure search of Truth possesses in England, is very reduced: whether it was formerly very high we shall examine hereafter. What we have said is so far true at the present day, that it only needs a little specification to strike every one. What Prejudice is to Reason, compromise to right, the same is prescription to a legal title. True, among all reasonable men compromise and prescription must be bowed to—they are effectual bars of the rights and titles from which they derogate. But mark the turn of mind which, by preferring to rest in prescription and agreement in things which are their permitted domain, soon comes, and naturally too, to revere the authority of time and precedent more than of justice, in matters wholly without their domain. There needs no illustration of this, but the course of Whig argument for the last forty years in asser-

   56. John Donne, letter to Sir Henry Wotton, 4 October 1622, in *Letters to Severall Persons of Honour* (London, 1651), p. 134, has, "All our moralities are but our outworks, our Christianity is our Citadel."
   57. *Macbeth* I. iii. lines 33–35: "The weyward sisters, hand in hand, / Posters of the sea and land, / Thus do go, about, about."
   58. In other words, the torture of Mezentius, a mythical Etruscan king who caused living men to be bound face to face with corpses and left to die of putrefaction and starvation: Vergil, *Aeneid*, VIII, lines 481–88.

tion of the freedom of the realm. They rarely do more than trace the genealogy of freedom anxiously up to the days of their Anglo-Saxon ancestors, or to the middle times of the bold Barons.[59] It is sufficiently ridiculous in them to limit their titles to those semi-barbarous times, where concessions will be found in no wise adequate to the large demands of an age of perfected civilization. But then were they not justly rebuked by M'Intosh for their manner of claiming more by descent than by original right?[60] It was, indeed, somewhat a degradation of their client to make even a principal prop of her cause to consist in early precedent. If freemen are anxious to vindicate their fathers from the imputation of having lived without freedom, we applaud them; but as the lapse of time cannot deprive in such vital points, it is also a weak argument when favourable. If in geometry there be no prescription or foreclosure available against outstanding truth, so equally can there be no foreclosure in high matters of primary politics. That there is another class of asserters of the freedom of the realm, termed Radicals, we do not forget: but we fear philosophy would be as little disposed to own them for her votaries, as would fashion at Willis' rooms.

What is it which characterizes British metaphysical philosophy? There are illustrious names, none can deny, on its rolls; but neither English nor Scotch books, nor the writings of their French allies or opponents which alone the English consult for information or illustration besides their own, compose the whole school of true philosophy. The philosophy of true British growth and consonant with her whole civilization, the philosophy of Locke, *clarum nomen*, and of Reid and Beattie[61] (we see no propriety in adding the epithet *clarum* or *venerabile* to these last) is that which "inaugurates Common Sense on the throne of Philosophy,"[62] restricts her own domain to the observation of the actions of the mind, regards all ontology (or the science of the nature of being) as an irreclaimable chaos, the

---

59. ["Eis erben rich Gesetz' und Rechte
Wie eine ew'ge Krankheit fort;
\*       \*       \*       \*       \*
Weh dir. dass du ein Enkel bist!
Vom Rechte, das mit, uns geboren ist,
Von dem ist, leider! nie die Frage."—FAUST.

*Translation.*—Laws and Right do but inherit themselves onward, like an eternal disease; wo to thee, that thou art born a grand-child! of the Right that is connate with us, of that alas! not once the question is.] "Faust: Ein Fragment," in *Gendenkaugabe Der Werke, Briefe und Gesprache* (Zurich, 1950), 5: 82. The infelicity of this translation by Harrison must jar when, *infra*, he criticizes Leveson Gower.

60. *Vindiciae Gallicae*, in *The Miscellaneous Works of the Right Honourable Sir James Mackintosh* (London, 1846), 3: 115–21.

61. Thomas Reid, 1710–1796, and James Beattie, 1735–1803, both Scottish common sense philosophers.

62. Samuel Taylor Coleridge, *Biographia Literaria* (London, 1817), 1: 266.

fruitless exploration of which nature has forbidden to the wise by a Limbo of vanities interposed to warn, authorizes faith in no dogma which cannot be subjected either to experiment or observation for the purposes of induction, and encourages the pursuit only of such inquiries as lead to practical, sensible results. The host of useful and valuable truths within these limits with which she has endowed the world is not more characteristic of her system than the indication of that indefinite host of supposed truths which she calls indemonstrable, or those topics which she stigmatizes as without the limits of rational inquiry. We may state these in the words of Professor Jardine: "the general attributes of being, existence, essence, unity, bonity, truth, relations, modes of possibility, impossibility, necessity, contingency and other similar abstract conceptions of pure intellect,"[63] with the vast topics which must be treated and settled in order to attain self-knowledge. Is not the day come yet, when it may be uttered in the English language, that such a philosophy, so limited as the system we describe, though a legitimate portion of the science of spiritual truth, yet is not all of it, nay, is not by any means the highest part of it? We know that the absurdities of schoolmen of the middle ages, and the memorable lines of satirists have made the very name of *entity* ridiculous to English ears. Yet surely we forget that if theory was ridiculous in the schools, experiment was no less so in the laboratory, for experiment and observation were resorted to for the discovery of truth, before as well as after Bacon. Would any one twit us with Butler's wit against logical method, might we not retort, from Aristophanes, on physical philosophers?[64] No choicer wit than that in 'the Clouds' on the experimenters in natural science, who, for aught we see, were Baconians, only not grave enough in their selection of subjects. Nay, may we not say that the most laughable errors of metaphysicians can be paralleled by the conclusions to which the Great Chancellor himself sometimes came by diligent induction? The sovereign efficacy of the inductive method, and its sway over all subsequent philosophy in Europe, are fixed ideas chiefly in the brain of the Scotch and French. Dr. Brewster has admirably treated this matter in his life of Sir Isaac, shown how greatly the claim of the method of induction to be the clue to all modern discovery must be qualified, and reminded us that neither Locke, nor Boyle, nor Newton have once mentioned Bacon in their works—nay, that Newton, so far from being the disciple of Bacon, was really the follower of Galileo and Kepler.[65] And all the learning of Lord

---

63. George Jardine, *Outlines of Philosophical Education* (2d ed. enlarged, Glasgow, 1825), p. 23.
64. Samuel Butler, especially in *Hudibras* (London, 1663–1678).
65. Sir David Brewster, *Memoirs of the Life, Writings and Discoveries of Sir Isaac Newton* (Edinburgh, 1855), 2: 400–406.

Napier in the transactions of the Edinburgh Philosophic Society will do little to disturb these positions.[66] The name of Bacon is inappreciable: but this credit he would not have claimed for himself. But to continue:—the question now is, whether there may not be inquiries made in ontology today, (under the illumination of modern wisdom) as far juster than those of Aquinas, as the induction of Davy is than that of Sir Kenelm Digby?[67] It is in vain to strive to banish the mind from the investigation of the class of topics mentioned by Jardine. Whoever is at all gifted with the true philosophical imagination finds delight in them; feels that they are the native dominion of pure philosophy; that to deny himself their meditation is to curtail the dignity of man; that nature designed to lavish on our species a large birthright, and pronounced him her noblest child who goes farthest to enjoy it all. He knows that nature has given us a soul, and "Reason is her being, discursive and intuitive."[68] That noblest child is the philosopher, and philosophy in its most exalted department would be his occupation, "the science of ultimate truths—*scientia scientiarum*."[69]

Let us not be imposed on by those who would imprison the mind within the visible diurnal sphere. Let us not soil the dignity of this first of sciences by forbidding her to appear in the world, except under the person of popular philosophy which a wise man has pronounced, "the counterfeit and mortal enemy of all true and manly metaphysical research."[70] Let us allot to such as will be content with it, the limited range of empiricism; (the whole philosophy of experiment and observation—a large range but only too limited,) but then this school must consent to admit that it is "neither possible nor necessary for all men nor many, to be philosophers" in the highest sense. Should the empirical school, however, refuse to recognize the other sect, they do but convict themselves of what Bacon called "an arrogant pusillanimity."[71] The precept that descended from heaven was the whole *nosce teipsum*, not so much of it only as the eye and the immediate consciousness could teach.[72] And there are not wanting a few men in England who have learned that all modern researches after ulti-

66. MacVey Napier, "Remarks on the Scope and Influence of the Philosophical Writings of Lord Bacon," privately printed in Edinburgh, 1818, and previously published in the *Transactions of the Royal Society of Edinburgh*. Napier succeeded Jeffrey as editor of the *Edinburgh Review*.

67. Sir Kenelm Digby, 1603–1665, royalist, author, man of affairs, and latterly scientist, notorious for his "powder of sympathy," which was supposed to heal wounds without direct application.

68. John Milton, *Paradise Lost*, V, line 488, quoted in Coleridge, *Biographia Literaria*, 1: 160, 285.

69. Coleridge, *Biographia Literaria*, 1: 239–40, slightly misquoted.

70. Ibid., 1:281.

71. Ibid., 1:135, quotes Bacon on "the arrogance of pusillanimity." Cf. *The New Organon*, in *The Works of Francis Bacon*, ed. James Spedding et al. (London, 1870), 4:296.

72. Trans. know thyself. This motto was inscribed, in Greek rather than Latin, on Apollo's temple at Delphi. Cf. Juvenal, 11, 27.

English Civilization 77

mate truth have not proved either ridiculous or fruitless. The day is coming when auditors may be solicited even in England, for the discoveries of those Germans, who, learned in all systems, have presumed to think that they too may boast trophies, and of conquests in higher fields. Let the English, at least, from what they know of Göethe, of Schiller, of Schlegel, Heeren and Niebuhr,[73] (and how much they have added to the world's stores of good sense) have the modesty to suspect that what their compatriots, the philosophers have written, is not wholly nonsensical. Nay, let them be a little solicitous, lest in their scorn for German metaphysics, of which they are wholly ignorant, they deserve the retort of Schlegel on the Scotch: that Scotch philosophy is a paltry, mechanical art, rather than a science.[74]

In the first place, what can be said of those whose standard in metaphysics is the oracle of common sense, or the general consent of the world? Surely their philosophy is not that being whom Socrates brought down from heaven to dwell among men, but is a genuine *filia terrae*. How just is the remark of Coleridge, that "it is the two fold function of philosophy to reconcile reason with common sense, and to elevate common sense into reason." He adds in another place, "would you assert the Newtonian system, such a pseudo-philosopher might vanquish you by an appeal to common sense, whether the sun did not move and the earth stand still."[75] Secondly, does any one object that the empirical philosophy does in reality contain whatever can be designated by the name of knowledge? We answer that the results of pure philosophy are not of necessity less certain, because theirs is the certainty of reason. True, the wisest may make false moves in it, but this does not declare truth in it to be wholly unattainable. Indeed, if one certain truth has been discovered in it, that is sufficient to encourage progress in this the highest vocation of the mind. So might the portrait painters have objected to attempts to picture the ideal, and thus might they be shamed by a single successful work of Raphael.

The contempt for pure philosophy has naturally fallen heavy on logic, and the poor syllogism is held up to supreme scorn. That, before Bacon, it was not used for the discovery of new facts, some have candidly admitted; that induction was often resorted to by Aristotle for that object is also well known. It ought then to be owned, that the syllogism claimed to be an available instrument only as the *analytic test of reasoning*. Logicians say,

73. Arnold Hermann Ludwig Heeren, 1760–1842, German philologist and historian; Barthold Georg Niebuhr, 1776–1831, German historian of ancient Rome.
74. Harrison is paraphrasing: see Friedrich von Schlegel, *Lectures on the History of Literature, Ancient and Modern* (Philadelphia, 1858), pp. 335–37.
75. Coleridge, *Biographia Literaria*, 1:266, 135; the latter is misquoted and should read: "By the very same argument the supporters of the Ptolemaic system might have rebuffed the Newtonian, and pointing to the sky with a self-complacent grin have appealed to *common sense*, whether the sun did not move and the earth stand still."

that the theory of their syllogism is, that whatever can be affirmed of a class, may be affirmed of every individual in that class. Here English Common Law interposes—and this is the brightest feather in her cap—she declares that then the conclusion was wrapped up in the premises, and if so, it is but farcical to prove to a man by regular steps what he admits *totidem verbis* at first.[76] To this profound objection logicians reply, that true it is, syllogisms cannot discover new facts in physics, though they may new relations in metaphysics; but they submit that, as far as all reasoning reaches, the sole process known to men is to evolve particular truth out of some general postulated truth. The logicians farther submit, that specification and definition are main instruments in all ratiocination, and that whether we reason with three propositions, or with two, or without regularity, all we ever do by ratiocination is to educe disputed truth out of admitted dogmas in which it lay unperceived. We will not hazard ourselves in this abstruse question, though we suspect the longest train of reflection will end in the confirmation of this last assertion of the logicians.

We reassert then that if the philosophy of a nation be the highest index of her civilization, the *Homo Sapiens Britannus* is not altogether the most exalted being possible. His is but the safe mediocrity of nature. And even in that branch of metaphysics wherein she allows her talents full scope, the science of the moral and intellectual function of the mind, she must suffer it to be said that she will not bear a very favourable comparison with the Germans.

Sir William Drummond, as we perceived, says, that the free and philosophic spirit of England was once the admiration of Europe.[77] For freedom in religious inquiry (which we suspect was his drift) certainly England has ever been eminent; and that the unbelieving side has been more ably maintained than that of the true faith, is as sure, as that in the war for and against materialism the English materialists, exceed in ability their English opponents. The conclave of English orthodoxy is *tant qu'il soit peu* unsatisfactory in its reasoning and elliptical in its learning. What has the Bench of Bishops, with all the Presidents of Colleges and Divinity Professors cumulatively, done to purge the blood of the English language of the poison of Gibbon which circulates through every vein of it?

Before we take our leave of this branch, however, we are not afraid of being laughed at for offering to grapple more closely with this popular idol, this Cleon, Common Sense. For a definition we prefer to go to Tully. Ernesti (*clavis ad voc: sensus*) says that as used by Tully, "sensus communis continetur notionibus insitis, et naturali facultate intelligendi, judicandi, ratiocinandi, recti et boni cognoscendi;" it has also the secondary meaning

---

76. Cicero, *Academicae Quaestiones*, 2, 13, 40; trans. in just as many words.
77. William Drummond, *Academical Questions* (London, 1805), 1:xiv.

of sensibility.[78] Let us then proceed to distinguish it as a *ratio cognoscendi* into first merely intellectual, second merely ethical, third merely prudential. That the common moral sense is worthy of all homage, we admit; it is conclusive. Furthermore, we admit that the prudential common sense "*natum rebus agendis*"[79] is an invaluable guide in life. The pity is that "*le sens commun n'est pas si commun.*" We have all due respect for those persons who are such bright concretions of this substantial quality, and only wish they did not think it their duty to scorn all poets, theorizers and other ingenious gentlemen who are lovers of curious and ornamental knowledge, as unproductive drones. Men whose talent is for affairs only, will do well oftener to inform their tenement of clay with a like spirit: they should have the grace to suspect that the assumed superiority of practical shrewdness over speculative wisdom, will never daunt speculation, but that only true theory can dispel false, and only much learning cure the errors of half learned speculators. But when we come to that first branch of Common Sense, wherein it presumes to judge of the true and the false, we unhesitatingly assert that, save where it is perfectly identical with simple consciousness, it is no judge in the courts of Philosophy. A judge in the market and adequate to the market, she is. But where Reason designs to vindicate any province of the true and false as sufficiently enlarged to be worthy of her jurisdiction, the other must give way.

Finally, if the mistress of English opinion be Common Sense, and their dominant aim be practical utility, we must turn them over to Mr. Cooper, to astonish them with the undoubted superiority of the Common Sense of America over their own.[80] But we intercede with the ingenious novelist to term the American quality not Common Sense, but rather *true good sense*. That the English Common Sense is not identical with shrewdness in affairs, or *finesse* of mind, we may perceive by this, that the world agrees, from Commines' assertion down, that England never did produce one eminent diplomatic negociator.[81] Even us the English upbraided, with having taken advantage of their weakness in this particular.

A word or two on some points of her literature. Her own critics have taken it to them to complain of the neglect of pure mathematics and science in general, at the very instant when her practical ingenuity is the miracle of the age. It is honorable to English candour that Professor De

---

78. Johann August Ernesti, *Clavis Ciceroniana Sive Indices Rerum et Verborum Philologico-Critici*, in *M. Tullii Ciceronis Opera* (London, 1830), 16: cccix; trans. Common sense consists in ingrained ideas and in a natural faculty of perceiving, judging, reasoning, and coming to know what is right and good.

79. Trans. born for the conduct of affairs; cf. Juvenal, 14, 72, "utilis rebus agendis."

80. James Fenimore Cooper, 1789–1851, the novelist, whom Harrison had befriended in Europe.

81. *Historical Memoirs of Philip de Comines, Containing the Transactions of Lewis XI and of Charles VIII of France* (London, 1817), esp. pp. 316–21.

Morgan, in his translation of Bourdon's Algebra (we believe) stops at a certain elementary stage and avows, that if any one wished to explore beyond that point he must study the French language.[82] The contemporary classical criticism of England is not often quoted with honour in Continental auditories, though the Germans who are the most learned are the most liberal, insomuch that Thiersch confesses Bentley to have been the first of critics.[83] Little that is enlarged on classical criticism is published in England except what comes out of the German; and that their German translations are not the ripest possible, we may guess from the fact that poor America has been pillaged (from him that hath not, &c.) of the credit of her only two valuable translations, Buttman and Heeren, (Pol. Ancient Greece,) printed in England as British translations, with a modest slur at the want of acquaintance with German manifested by Mr. Everett and Mr. Bancroft[84]—a want which was not suspected in them in Germany.[85] The actual monopoly which the Germans enjoy of the glory of recent criticism in the provinces of ancient history, poetry epic and tragic, ancient philosophy and the genuine original mythic theology, is the loftiest of intellectual trophies, saving only the kindred spoils in the science of celestial mechanics, and such permanent conquest as it has been vouchsafed to mind to make, thus far, in the highest metaphysics. Every body now knows that by the perfect classical learning and taste of the Germans has the true merit of Shakspeare been first reached; that Lessing, Göethe, Schlegel, Tieck and Coleridge (for why not count him among the Germans, *plus Allemand que les Allemands*) have raised the English Poet to an eminence which no one of the editors in the Variorum Shakspeare had dared claim for him.[86] There is even now a more Shakesperian taste in a German audience, when one of Schlegel's translations is played, than at Drury-Lane, as one will perceive by comparing Cibber's miserable patchwork of Rich-

---

82. Louis Pierre Marie Bourdon, *The Elements of Algebra*, trans. Augustus de Morgan (London, 1828).

83. Either Bernhardy or Friedrich Thiersch, both German Homeric scholars, speaking of Richard Bentley, 1662–1742, English classical scholar, indefatigable controversialist, and Master of Trinity College, Cambridge.

84. Phillip Karl Buttmann, *Greek Grammar*, trans. Edward Everett (Boston, 1822), the English edition was published in London in 1824; Arnold Heeren, *Reflections on the Politics of Ancient Greece*, trans. George Bancroft (Boston, 1824); republished in Oxford in 1829.

85. [Germans have several times called the writer's attention to a comical misapprehension of Lord Leveson Gower in his translation of Faust. When Wagner, in a scene with Faust, exposes the deceptions of the demons, he says, "when they lie, they prattle like *angels*," not Englishmen, Lord Leveson; not *Angli*, but *Angeli*. We do not know that this is corrected in any recent editions.] Harrison has reference to the story of Pope Gregory I, who, when shown some slaves in the Roman market, was told they were Angles and observed, "Non Angli, sed angeli." See *Faust: A Drama, by Goethe. And Schiller's Song of the Bell*, trans. Lord Francis Leveson Gower (London, 1823).

86. Gotthold Ephraim Lessing, 1729–1781; August Wilhelm von Schlegel, 1767–1845; Ludwig Tieck, 1773–1853: all helped to introduce the German public to Shakespeare through translations.

ard III, with Schlegel's version which opens with the first line of the true Richard, and proceeds faithfully to the end.[87] A similar critical acumen has rescued Don Juan from the degradation of resemblance to a Faublas, and placed him on a parallel with a Faust.[88]

Another legitimate topic is the actual degree of refinement in England. Observing travellers inform us that the aristocratic sentiment has even advanced with gigantic strides in English society in the last fifty years, while in France it is virtually extinct. That it pervades the Whigs as thoroughly as the Tories, thus rendering that which was the most odious feature of Toryism an essential quality of the name Englishman. That it exhibits itself in its upward aspect servile, and in its downward supercilious and repulsive. Never saw the world such private fortunes, nor so many of them, never such perfection in the common arts of life, never greater luxury and certainly never so artificial a state of society. The leading alteration which manners have suffered in the present century, undoubtedly, is the appearance for the first time of a systematized coldness or apathy, which, beginning in the upper ranks, is spreading every where. Not to admire is all the art they know: were Horace, who was we take it the first of this school, to come among them now, he would be tartly reprimanded we fear for the positive buoyancy of his character. Enthusiasm is the single horror of these people. We wish we had a few specimens of the negative, passionless, unpretending style in our community, which is composed, in two great parts, of men perpetually intent on popular admiration, of over polite, bustling, enthusiastic people. But the stoicism of Grosvenor Square, in becoming national, will not fail to serve as an extinguisher of much vivacity of mind and heart, and may go far to reduce our *Inglese* to a very dull, selfish person. What apology for dullness, and cloak for inferiority of soul, was ever invented equal to this? Of necessity, this new style is accompanied by the introduction of a perfect system of exclusive *castes*. It is quite true that the reign of the Exquisites is ended, and that of the Exclusives begun: the Dandies are voted to have been too violent pretenders, and a recherché simplicity is voted in. In the exclusive system the rival claims of blood and wealth have been nicely adjusted, and now people may associate without losing dignity, i.e. with their own set. To be sure the system makes one Englishman singularly afraid of another, or singularly rude to him, whom he meets without knowing him, at the same time that they both would agree to shower honour on a foreigner to whom they may attribute any sphere they please. We sadly suspect, however, that this artificial arrangement is a miserable servitude,

---

87. Colley Cibber, *The Tragical History of King Richard III* (London, 1700).
88. [See the last chapter of Coleridge's Bio. Litera.] In fact, the penultimate chapter. The reader will have observed that, unacknowledging, Harrison relies considerably upon Coleridge.

that tortures like the rack many a luckless monster with a sympathetic, social, communicative turn. The Englishman is still the best horseman and the gentlest sportsman in Europe—he claims to be the best dressed man: perhaps he is. Though he must be admitted to have the poorest national *cuisine* extant, yet he has the sagacity to hire foreign science, and avenges the unwillingness of *Minerve Gourmande* by unlimited cant. Though he never comes to speak French well, yet he manages to talk more French in his English than Old Burton would have cited of all his languages, in the same length of time.[89] There is something, by the way, singular enough in the perversion which these foreign scraps suffer by transplanting into English use. It is to be well seen by reading a French translation of some book, say Lady Morgan's 'Boudoir,' where the only difficulty for the clever translator is to comprehend her French quotations.[90] The difference between the English *piazza* and the Italian, is but one of many instances of the tendency of words to departure from their original meaning when adopted into English conversation, and may induce the suspicion of what whole sentences may lose by misquotation from mouth to mouth. After all, in point of whatever goes to make up manhood, we fear that the present apathetic, exclusive English, though they have passed the Catholic Bill, and may pass the Reform Bill, yet are hardly worth the men of Merton and Runnymede.

II. We come now to our second head. We are not of those who think it calamitous to America to have inherited the English language and literature. Still less of those who imagine that America has a vocation to make a new era in the mind. And least of all are we of those who believe that this new epoch is to be made by the abandonment of the literature of the ancient democracies, and the dedication of ourselves to what some call useful knowledge. This cant in an American mouth is the veriest unreason and the most pernicious charlatanism that can be conceived. Much rather, if America is destined to make a new era, should it be in the reception and faithful use of the peculiar riches of all nations and of all ages. Our situation is like that of the Colombians, whose equatorial position enables them to behold all the stars of both hemispheres: our visible heaven, figuratively speaking, is the entire concave, and every star is either beneficent or harmless to us. The model of a republic for America is given by Pericles in the funeral oration in Thucydides: it must be a republic that can incorporate refinement, taste and luxury into its system of equality as available agents, or there must be provision made for them as for friction in a machine. Nature and an age too late—an age of commerce and wealth, of civility, of perpetual international intercourse and of contagious example

---

89. Robert Burton, 1577–1640, author of *The Anatomy of Melancholy* (1621).
90. Lady Sydney Morgan, *The Book of the Boudoir* (London, 1829).

on every side—both alike forbid as impossible either the revival of the *farouche* republicanism of Sparta, or the reduction to practice of the pastoral conceits of Raynal.[91] But though America must submit to conform herself to the condition of the world, and may expect no more than a due share of credit for such accession to the general treasury, as the old modes of learning, experiment and meditation will enable her to collect, yet we have a distinct complaint to make. It is that those who furnish us our instruction feed our minds with hardly any knowledge but what comes through English hands. Now, it would not be too hazardous to assert that English literature (if exclusively taken) is not just the most salutary for republican study. But we will not press this. It is enough that her literature does not embrace all the wisdom, nor all the higher wisdom of the human species; golden temptations lead us into other literatures, to correct and supply for our own use the inherent errors and defects of this. Neither shall we ever be satisfied that the knowledge of foreign literatures, or information of foreign history should come to us exclusively or chiefly through the hands of England. Our country is already possessed of those who are competent, if they will, to furnish us proper information on the novelties of letters and science with which France, Italy and Germany are daily adorning the world. What would be the contempt we should deserve for remaining liable to such imposition as that of the sentiments of the Scotch Reviewer of the life of Göethe?[92] As to intelligence of foreign events, the English annalists and newspapers, of all others give the least accurate or complete accounts. Mr. Jefferson formerly was earnest that the Gazette of Leyden, a republican sheet, should be adopted by us as the chronicler of continental news for America. Circumstances are even more urgent now, than hitherto, for renouncing the English medium. The Prussian State-Gazette, and the Austrian Observer give best the authentic expression of the opinions of German cabinets, while the Universal Gazette of Augsburg, not an official organ of any party, though not immaculate, may yet be called the best repertory of news from Turkey, from Eastern, Middle and Western Europe that the world has ever seen. That these sheets should never reach America is lamentable enough: but what is unpardonable is, that so little use is made by our editors of the French papers. If we want the German papers for information on the passing history of Germany, Russia and the North, we want the French not merely for

91. Abbé Guillaume Thomas François Raynal, 1713–1796, philosophe and author of the *Histoire philosophique et politique des établissemens et du commerce des Européens dans les deux Indes* (1770), who believed, amongst other things, that the human species had a natural tendency to degenerate in the New World.
92. Either [William Empson], "Schiller and Goethe," *Edinburgh Review* 53 (March 1831): 82–104, or [Francis Palgrave], "Goethe's Life of Himself (Part I)," *Edinburgh Review* 26 (June 1816): 304–37, probably the former. "Scotch Reviewer" is a reference to Byron's satire, "English Bards and Scotch Reviewers."

their own news, but for doctrine as to all. But from English papers, and from them alone, are we told every thing. What English journalists and historians tell better than others is only English history and news. Let one but study the disquisitions on Continental politics in the Courier, or Morning Chronicle, and in the *Journal des Debats*, or the *Constitutionel*—even take the Tory *John Bull* and the Carlist *Gazette de France*, or any other contemporary remarks, and the superior fairness as well as sagacity of the French journals, is prominently conspicuous. Why cannot the American editors in the seaports spare time enough, or rather get learning enough to supply us with the detailed views of foreign affairs taken by the French?—not merely the debates of the Chambers, but also the essays of the journalists who are the virtual masters of French opinion. Take the English lucubrations on Germany, and submit them to any German statist: they are merely fit for his mirth. From no book in the English language is any just idea of the system of Germany (which is the balance point of that of Europe) to be obtained. Lord Brougham is doubtless one of the best informed of his countrymen on foreign affairs, but even he does not rightly apprehend the relations in which the crown of Hanover stands to that of England: we say this in modesty, yet how avoid saying it, when he declared in the House of Commons two years ago, that "it seemed the Salique Law prevailed" as to the descent of the throne of Hanover. If we inquire either of Montesquieu or of the Archbishop of Canterbury, in the first act of Henry V. what the Salique Law is as to the crown of France, we learn that females are excluded wholly and forever, from the succession. But when all the male agnates are extinct in the line of Hanover, the females begin to succeed. Lord Brougham is a feudist and should know what a fief male and female under this limitation would be called.[93] To her journalists we apprehend Germany is still a Hyrcinian forest tenanted (besides the wild boar, which are capital hunting,) by serfs with a harsh guttural dialect, and a few Lords in *Chateaux*; (how many the German sovereigns are is only known at the foreign office, where credentials for the ambassadors are made out) the amusement of English journals is to shake the fetters of these serfs in the faces of their masters, and demand of them the promised constitutions, though we are not aware that the poor kings have ever yet been allowed a day in court.

To what is it to be attributed that of all European affairs only English politics are well understood in America? Who is to blame that the history

---

93. Henry Brougham, Speech in the House of Commons, 30 June 1830; in justice to Brougham, he did say that "the Salique Law prevails in Hanover," and not "seems to prevail." Moreover, he said nothing as to the situation upon the extinction of the male line, since the House of Hanover had still heirs of that sex. His next words were, "The Princess of Kent [Victoria] cannot succeed to the throne of that kingdom; the Duke of Cumberland must." *Hansard's Parliamentary Debates* (2d Series, London, 1830), p. 792. See also Montesquieu, *De L'Esprit des loix*, pp. 52–66.

of France from the restoration up to the accession of the Polignac ministry, a period as full of instruction for all constitutional governments as the entire period from 1688 until 1832, in the English annals, is scarcely better known in America than the contemporary events in Turkey? We suspect our insulars must bare the blame of keeping us in uncertainty and ignorance. The general mind of America faithful to the hand that feeds it, takes delight in studying English concerns: we will specify a case, where curtailing itself to the acquisition of small things, it would suffice for learning the whole system of Europe. How many Americans know Debrett well, who could by no means count how many independent States there are in Europe? Suppose for Debrett were substituted the genealogical almanac of Gotha; they would thus exchange petty information, no ways concerning them, for knowledge which is history.[94] And thus it must obviously continue; for, if none but English knowledge is put in our reach, the most ingenious student will only become more English than his duller fellows. Let no one sneer at us, trying to subtract the American mind from its only natural and mother-jurisdiction. We aver, before heaven, that we believe the instinct of liberty in America will one day be endangered by the uninterrupted influence of contemporary English literature and manners. Undermine a few principles, and efface this instinct the most vital of all, and our Republic could not sustain itself forever by its own weight. The sentiment of Aristocracy, with which her literature is at present more pregnant than it ever was before—and scarcely more in Scott than in Moore[95]—once fairly introduced, in the train of fastidiousness and exclusiveness, would do the work of our destruction more effectually than sermons preached by a Sacheverel in every village in America for a century.[96] But we should wrong ourselves if we said there was proximate danger of this: enough, that it is a possibility. We dare not go free of all care, knowing the deposit we bear.

The spirit which has animated us, in what we have written, is not of hostility to England, for we profess to fulfil scrupulously the maxim of public jurists, "nations at war are the only enemies, all others, friends." We have only spoken to our countrymen for the interests of democracy. We could by no means permit ourselves to offer wanton reproach to England. What we desired to inculcate was that the dignity of human nature might be alike elevated by searching beyond the English limit, that justice to ourselves demands that we should sometimes follow another guide be-

---

94. *Debrett* gave, and gives, information upon the English nobility and royalty, while the *Almanac de Gotha* gave annual information upon the royalty, governments, and diplomatic corps of Europe.

95. Thomas Moore, 1779–1852, the Irish poet and biographer of Byron.

96. Henry Sachaverel, 1647?–1724, attacked in 1709 the Whig government's policy of religious toleration in two sermons. He was tried, convicted, but only sentenced to a three-year suspension from preaching, which made him a popular hero.

sides the English Sibyl, who neither knows any thing, nor is the fittest to conduct a democracy. Beyond this, we add: the closest bond of union which need bind us to England, is, perhaps, the treaty of commerce between us. Treaties of peace prescribe mutual comity, but do not enjoin companionship. In spite of the humane philosophy of Mr. Irving we cannot think England the most natural bosom companion of America, or that we owe her more, in duty and affection, than is nominated in our bond.[97] Nor, for the reason that we are the two freest people on earth, descended of a common stock, do we feel the touch of nature draw us to her embrace: for, perhaps, our respective liberties are not much akin to each other, and we are candidly of opinion that the two nations of European origin which are the most unlike, are Great-Britain and the United States. Produce your voucher! Captain Basil Hall.[98] Then again, except the occasional blandishments of the Edinburgh Review and Blackwood's Magazine, we are half afraid the English are not more desirous of being the object of our romantic affection, than we, for our simple selves, are of seeing America proffer it. In candour, Captain Hall's book is one of sterling honesty—the genuine avowal of British sentiment with regard to America. It is what every thorough Englishman (and the sailors are the most thorough) must think of us, if they reason and feel logically. But it has done good for America among the aristocrats; for which of them will not blush to see how paltry the sum total of British detraction from our character is, and own with a smile that he never knew the claim of aristocracy to be so brainless a mask, as it is shewn to be by its favourite apologist. Let the English continue to think that Americans are nothing but the men of Liverpool, Birmingham and Glasgow transplanted into a new world: it is our fault if we either are, or long remain second-rate English. The deposit of democratic liberty is little safe in our hands, if we be.

We have thus far not paid any attention to the excellent book, at the head of this paper. Sir James knows that he has a sure place in the heart of America: but it is something more than this book which we expect from him. We are longing for a suitable history of England from the revolution of 1688 up to this day, and we respectfully complain that he is slow to fulfil the world's hope. He will be eagerly read in America, when he comes forth with that work. So far from neglecting the reading of English history, we even doubt if it is not a great deal too much studied in the United States.

It is, no doubt, of the first consequence to a practical lawyer, that he should study well the civil history of England—but as for those speculators who with us usurp the high office of directing our judgments on political subjects, verily one is sometimes provoked to wish that they had

---

97. Washington Irving, 1783–1859, the American novelist and Anglophile.
98. Captain Basil Hall, 1788–1844, British traveler and sailor, author of the irascible *Travels in North America* (1829).

## English Civilization

never heard of that history at all. In the trackless desert, it is necessary sometimes to turn our eyes from the sands around us to the stars above us, but we are lost if we keep them there too long; in the untrodden wilderness it may be well to look to the way behind us, but it is better to ponder well the path before. Politics, is indeed, something better than a set of cunning rules often suspended by a miscounting selfishness, and ever flexible to every emerging circumstance: it is an art founded upon general, and, we believe, certain principles; but it is an art purely practical in its very nature, and it being once perceived that it should be the object of a statesman to provide real securities for the liberty and property of those whom he presumes to govern, it ought never to be forgotten that in choosing efficient means to effect this object, "he must ever have an eye to the place where, and to the men amongst whom he is."

"In the monarchies of Europe different orders and ranks of society are established, large masses of property are accumulated in the hands of single individuals, and standing armies are necessary;" but the condition of these United States is in all these respects wholly different. And yet, let the question be how it is possible in a representative democracy to prevent the majority from abusing the power of laying taxes? Let the question be, whether a man who has two cows has not as good a right to vote as he that owns one horse? Let the question be, whether it is not reasonable that those who act for the people should do as the people tell them? Let the question be what it may, what is the first thing most American politicians are sure to do? They spread their books—they are quite sure that whatever question may arise here, a question *in consimili casu* has already arisen in England; they hunt for an English authority, a case in point, and end with this. They take it all along for granted, that whatever it was prudent and just to do in old England two centuries, or, if you will, two years ago, it is of course prudent and just to do in Virginia or Carolina now. Let no one suppose from all this, that we look upon history as nothing more than, what it certainly is to the common race of readers, the aliment of unthinking curiosity or the amusement of restless indolence. To those who consult it with minds fitted and prepared to learn, it were a silly paradox to deny that it is of all studies that most likely to furnish us with a solid knowledge of those things that concern our conduct. What we wish to say is that it is idle to light the lamp of experience, if we hang that lamp where it can be no guide to our feet; that however well it may be to question the oracle of wisdom, the responses of that oracle can after all be worth nothing to him who cannot interpret, or will not apply them. "History," says Mr. Burke, "is a great improver of the understanding by showing both men and affairs in a great variety of views. From this source much political wisdom can be learned; that is, may be learned as habit not as precept; and as an exercise to strengthen the mind, as furnishing materials to enlarge and enrich it, not as a repertory of cases and precedents for a lawyer; if it were, a thousand times better would it be that a statesman had never learned to read—*vellem nescirent literas.* This method turns their understandings from the objects before them, and from the present exigencies of the world to comparisons with former times, of which after all we can know very little and very imperfectly; and our guides the historians who are to give us their true interpretation are often prejudiced, often ignorant, often fonder of system than of truth. Whereas if a man with reasonable good parts and natural sagacity, and not in the leading-strings of any master, *will look steadily upon the business before him without being diverted by retrospect and comparison,* he may be capable of forming a reasonable good judgment of what is to be done."[99]

---

99. "Remarks on the Policy of the Allies with Respect to France. Begun in October 1793," in *Works of . . . Burke,* 5: 287–88.

# 3.

## Hugh Swinton Legaré

## "German Diaries"[1]

Hugh Swinton Legaré is central to any assessment of the antebellum Southern mind, the quintessential South Carolinian intellectual and man of affairs, whose career was divided between the cultivation of politics and the apprehension of learning. To both he devoted great energy and long hours. From each he derived rewards that brought more honor than understanding. A man who died prematurely in 1843 as the attorney general and acting secretary of state of the dispossessed John Tyler administration, a man whose ambition was to make a translation of the Civil Law theories of Johann Heineccius did not entertain much hope of comprehension by contemporaries or posterity.[2]

He was a Charlestonian, born in 1797 on a plantation on John's Island. His family was mingled Scottish and Huguenot, not splendid but comfortable. But his own fortunes were straitened by his father's early death and complicated by a youthful attack of smallpox induced by innoculation. The latter left him a distorted

---

1. Hugh Swinton Legaré, *Writings*, ed. his sister (Charleston, 1846), 1: 108–39. I have used only the central portion of the diaries, omitting an earlier trip to Antwerp and the second part of his journey after Wittenberg. Portions of the manuscript still survive among the Legaré Papers in the South Caroliniana Library, Columbia. When possible, I have edited from the original text: these passages are enclosed in square brackets. The manuscript shows many differences from the published version. The title, "Journal of the Rhine," was given by Mary Legaré. Since it has no authority from her brother, and is inappropriate for a journey that went far beyond the Rhine valley, I have altered it to "German Diaries." The publishers confessed to a difficulty in transcribing Legaré's hand and warned readers that many errors, especially in names of people and places, may have crept in. They were right to do so, and the published text abounds in mistakes. Mary Legaré did very little bowdlerization of substance, at least intentionally. However, her knowledge of Europe and scholarship was not extensive, so she often made her brother seem to talk nonsense in several languages. She also liberally altered punctuation and put in commas, especially, with manic enthusiasm. I have tried to reproduce Legaré's original text exactly, with two exceptions: he usually wrote "&" for "and," so I have used the latter for the convenience of the reader's eye, and he abbreviated "the" in the old way as "ye," and the modern form seems easier.

2. The standard life of Legaré is Linda Rhea, *Hugh Swinton Legaré: A Charleston Intellectual* (Chapel Hill, 1934), although it is very unsatisfactory.

body, almost dwarfish, strong in the torso but enfeebled in the limbs. When Legaré came, later in life, to review the life of Lord Byron, he wrote of the poet's club foot with a pathos that was personal as well as objective: "He was shy and sensitive to excess, and his mortification about his lameness—a mortification unspeakable in the young, and in Byron's case, approaching to madness—early superinduced upon him that impatience and even horror of ridicule, and those habits of gloomy seclusion and bitter, misanthropic derision and defiance, which grew with his growth and became, at length, so fatally inveterate, as to form a part of his very being."[3] In Legaré's case, mortification led not to Bacchanalian wit but to a sarcastic discipline and the emulation of that Walter Scott whom he used to see, when in Edinburgh in 1818, also limping—not to the bed of Lady Caroline Lamb—but to his work desk in the Parliament House.

Legaré had attended the upcountry school of Moses Waddel, with whom he had small sympathy, before proceeding to the South Carolina College in 1812. He apprenticed himself after graduation to the law practice of Mitchell King, but his immediate ambition was a visit to Europe. For two years, from 1818 to 1820, he lived abroad: Paris, Belgium, Holland, but chiefly Edinburgh where he enrolled in the university. He had planned to attend a German university but an inopportune outbreak of civil unrest among Metternich's wards deflected him to the more traditional Scottish education. There, however, he made a particular friend of the peripatetic Ticknor, then pausing to look over the *Edinburgh Review* set. Upon his return to South Carolina, Legaré was elected to the state legislature before his elevation to the office of attorney general in 1830. Meanwhile he put together a reasonably successful law practice, though his tastes were more scholarly than forensic, even if his ambitions were political. To practice oratory, instead of standing with pebbles on the seashore, he would have a slave row him to the distant parts of Charleston harbor so that his voice could compete with the winds and, losing, be strengthened.[4]

He became the chief support of the *Southern Review* between 1828 and 1832. Some 25 of its 140 contributions can with confidence be ascribed to him, with perhaps another essay of doubtful au-

---

3. Legaré, *Writings*, 2: 373.
4. William C. Preston, *Eulogy on Hugh Swinton Legaré* (Charleston, 1843), pp. 26–27.

thorship. He ranged widely over classical scholarship, social theory, legal thought, and recent belles lettres. Many of these pieces compete for attention, but the diaries he kept on two visits to Germany in 1835 and 1836 have the merit of personal nuance and intellectual insight.

In 1832 Legaré had accepted the position of American chargé d'affaires in Brussels. He had wished to escape the clamors over Nullification, in which he had been a prominent Unionist and from which he knew little could be gained for his advancement. Brussels, freshly asserting its identity as the capital of a new nation, was not the most gorgeous appointment in the miserly American diplomatic service but was one of its most agreeable. His Brussels diaries show Legaré reveling in the round of diplomatic gaiety. These from Germany display a more intellectual determination mingled with his usual fussy but earned vanity.

He went into the maze of German states twice. Briefly in May 1835 he traveled to Bonn, via Cologne, to meet August von Schlegel. A year later, during April and May, he undertook a more ambitious journey: eastward through Düsseldorf, Kassel, and Magdeburg to Berlin and the heart of Frederick William III's Prussia: southward to Leipzig, Dresden, Prague, and Munich: westward back to Brussels via Frankfurt am Main. It was, of course, useful for a diplomat to make such a trip, to meet the Prussian foreign minister and chat to the diplomatic corps elsewhere. And he went to Dresden, no doubt, partly in the spirit of the Grand Tour, to examine its extraordinary collection of art, its Raphaels and Corregios, and to spend a few days with his friend, Ticknor.[5] But his main purposes were to meet representatives of the German culture he had long respected, if not uncritically admired, since his youth; to talk with a Schlegel or an Ancillon, to seek out a Savigny for discourse on the history of the law. The peculiar interest of these diaries lies in their being the prompt observations of, not a young overawed student like Jesse Burton Harrison or the young George Bancroft twenty years earlier, but a man nearing the height of his intellectual powers, already conversant with both the German language and its literary productions, who could meet German culture on its grounds and felt no diffidence in leaving as well as taking.

---

5. *Life, Letters and Journals of George Ticknor*, ed. George S. Hillard (Boston, 1876), 1: 488–89.

I

[Cologne 21 May 1835   I arrived in this venerable old city this evening at ¼ past 7 o'clock, in a sort of hack, of which great use is made in these parts (for I met I know not how many on the road) and which I hired at Aix la Chapelle for four Rix thalers (fr. 15).

My return to Brussells[6] from Antwerp on Sunday evening 10th inst. was extremely opportune. I found a dispatch from the govt. waiting my arrival and demanding my immediate attention. Besides this paper which came to me thro' the Legation at London, there were within the nine days I passed at Brussells, no less than *three* different packets arrived at Hâvre, by wh., after a long interval, I received letters from America, and *lots* of newspapers. I staid much longer at Brussells than was my intention on returning to it, for I purposed proceeding immediately to Aix la Chapelle and the Rhine. But I had public business to occupy me, and it was not until I had written and received several letters to and from Mr. Patterson,[7] and sent two dispatches to the Department, that I felt myself once more at liberty to go, for a few weeks in quest of health. Hélas! I stood in need of continuing *mes courses*. I thought myself quite restored at Antwerp, but in travelling to Brussells, as the weather was particularly bright and genial, I left the inside of my carriage and took my seat upon the coachman's place. It was all very well for some time; but towards evening, I found the wind cold, and descended quite chilled from my exposed elevation. The next day, I felt a slight sour[8] throat; which continuing, I rather inconsiderately took a severe dose, or rather doses, of medicine. What with the remedy and what with the disease, I was very much pulled down in a few days—relapsed into my old dejection and blue devils, and felt that *à tout prix* I must change the air.

By way of having nothing to think of, and getting over the ground as rapidly as I chose, I determined to leave my own carriage at home in Brussells, and to take my place for Liège in the *coupé* of a Diligence. I left town, accordingly, on Tuesday 19th May, at ½-past 7 o'clock, in company with an officer of some sort or other, (judging, at least, from his pantaloons) and an ancient lady, who kept profoundly silent, until we arrived at Liège, when, on the brow of the steep hill that overlooks the town, she

---

6. Legaré consistently used the form "Brussells," rather than Brussels, as in *Writings*.
7. William B. Patterson, the American consul in Antwerp.
8. Not "sore," as in *Writings*.

said to me, with a strong Anglo-Saxon accent, "c'est *un* montagne bien *perpendicular*." I had no idea from her looks that she was English. The officer was a Belgian or German, from his accent—an intelligent man, about 55 or 60, with whom I spoke about the *times* and revolutions. He seemed (like many other people of the better sort in this country) to regard France and Frenchmen with horror. Speaking of their first revolution, he said history told of no such atrocities—and it was easily explained—it was an *impious* revolution—the whole nation continues to this day *profondément corrompue*. Of the Belgian revolution he said the people without leaders, made it; and then some adventurers set themselves up for a moment to be its apparent authors. There was only one thing the Belgians thought worse than a reunion to France—a restoration of the Nassaus.[9] Bonaparte always played his *va-tout* and must sooner or later have lost all. Speaking of Poland, he said its revolution was *sui generis*— Europe would have to suffer yet for that inexpiable partition! This agreeable man left me at St. Trond. I did not arrive at Liège until 8 o'clock, having been a period of 12 hours travelling those 20 leagues. Fatigued to death, my bones all aching, I crawled along after a commissionaire with my portmanteau, to the Hotel de *Pavillon Anglais* and having swallowed two cups of tea as soon as I could make them, went to bed at ½ past 9 o'clock. But hush! what voice sweeter than that of a nightingale, is in broken interrupted notes, beguiling the solitude of some fair creature in the neighbouring chamber. It is, I learn, that of Mad. S———, my neighbour at Brussells; the loveliest woman, to my taste, I have seen this many a day and whose delightful ravishing countenance, struck me and haunted me like a vision of something unearthly, the first time I saw her. Ah! said old Mad. de Baillet LaTour,[10] on hearing me express my raptures, you perceive she is in bad health and *fanée;* but *en* vérité, étant demoiselle, elle était jolie à faire tourner la tête. With such a *lullaby* and a body wearied and worn down, I fell asleep and never woke until 6 o'clock next morning.

Breakfast etc. being over on the 20th. at ½ past 9, I go down to the Diligence office where I had taken my seat and to my inexpressible horror, encounter there the same old Anglo-Saxon dame, whose silence had annoyed me so the day before. I was tempted to ask her, on the spot, if her intention were to extend her peregrinations beyond Aix; for if such were the case, my plans should, without hesitation be altered, so as to avoid a third meeting of the sort. However, I imitated her silence—mounted after her into the coupé, and after receiving our *complement*, a stout German, fresh from London, we were off at 10 for the city of Charlemagne. The

---

9. The House of Orange, hereditary stadtholders of the Netherlands and rulers of Belgium between 1815 and the Belgian revolt of 1830.

10. The wife of Louis Antoine Baillet de La Tour, 1753–1836, formerly an Austrian general but then resident in Brussels.

weather was delightful, tho' on getting out to walk up the high ascent opposite to Liège, I found the sun rather too warm, and was glad to raise my umbrella. The journey was not long—a double delay for examination of passports on the frontier, especially on the Prussian side included, we arrived at Aix la Chapelle before 5 o'clock. We all went to the *Hotel de Ville* immediately and got back our passports, which are examined here with extreme strictness. I then proceeded to the Hotel de l'Aigle Noire, and after ordering dinner for 6 o'clock, went out to see about getting on the next day and cast a glance *en passant* over the town, which I find wonderfully changed since auld lang syne (1819) especially in the neighbourhood of the great fountain and the new Theatre. Taste the water and don't find it by any means so nauseous as I expected. Sir Charles Wale[11] told me last year, having heard it was good for the gout, he intended to drink it, but, after the first attempt, he had posed himself with the question whether it were not better to bear the gout than to take such a diabolical medicine. I was prepared for a potion which could have increased the torments of Dives—but really think that considering its "sulfurous and damned" character, it is *very* far from disagreeable. The Hotel de l'Aigle Noire is kept by a Frenchwoman, and on y est très bien et surtout à très bon[12] compte. For a very good dinner, with a bottle of Seltzer water—bed and breakfast with mutton chops they charged only 6 fr. 50.

I rose early the next morning and visited the great fountain near the theatre where I drank a glass of the medicinal liquid and then walked up to the Cathedral, which I found very much as I remembered of it of old. As I hate descriptions, and have never read Vitmoin's, I shall say nothing of the circular dome, beneath which lies, on the floor of the church, a simple slab bearing the inscription—*Carolo Magno*. After looking round me for a few moments, and especially listening to a mass sung by children who step in here (says my guide) on their way to school I returned to the Spring, and was about to descend by the first staircase I came to, on my left, not observing that people went down the other way and came up this. But if I was unobserving, I was not unobserved. A little blue-eyed urchin about three feet high and nine or ten years old, begirt with a Lilliputian sabre and dressed in a Prussian uniform, was posted there to warn off the unwary visitors that should be about to violate a rule of police, in a country where as one sees at the first glance, every thing is rule and the police is every thing. This tom thumb flies upon me—shrieking out in German, as he fastens his little claws in my frock-coat, you can't go down this way—go the other. I could not help smiling with complacency at this display of diminutive vehemence—and was immediately accosted by an agent of the

11. Sir Charles Wale, 1763–1845, a British general; not "Wales," as in *Writings*. Hereafter "as in *Writings*" will be implicit in my emendations.
12. Not "bien."

police, of riper years, who apologized for the intemperate zeal of his little comrade, and showed me the way I ought to go. After drinking another glass of the running sulfur, I repaired to the Black Eagle and eat my breakfast.

At ½ past 8, I got into the vehicle I had *not* hired the day before. The one I chose was a very nice calèche drawn by two very respectable quadrupeds. This on the contrary was an ugly, shabby little machine, driven not by the man himself, but a servant or agent or partner of his (contrary to his *express* promise) and tied to the tails of two beasts, whose great experience in the journey between Aix la Chapelle[13] and Cöln was but too visibly impressed upon their whole exterior. Yet they did much more than they promised. The distance is 9 German miles (about 45 English). I was at the Cour Royale at Cologne at ¼ past 7, having stopped repeatedly *en route* to refresh the cattle, and once to refresh myself—having dined at Bergheim[14] at 3-4 o'clock, where I had the honor to sit down with a party from Aix to Cöln, consisting of a tavern keeper and his wife and companions of that *ilk*. The woman had very pretty round eyes looking like many I had seen before, and addressed me several times in French, hardened by her strong German accent. One of the *compliments* she made me was to request, in case I repassed by Aix, to bear in mind that they kept *ma foi*! I forget what house there—but a wonderfully pleasant one it was, by their accounts of it. Among other curiosities, they have to show there many crutches left behind, abandoned to the first comer's fate, by ungrateful cripples restored by the healing sulfur.

May 23. Bonn    Arrived at ¼ past 7, at the old Hotel de la Cour Impériale, I found it, like the Black Eagle, all topsy-turvy—undergoing repairs, painting etc. for the approaching "campaign on the Rhine," when England opens her golden sluices to enrich all Europe with the droppings of her *economy* in travelling—(for that is, nowadays the most general motive, and for *them*, it *is* economy to be any where out of the sphere of ruinous London vanity and ostentation. Two years ago Lord Francis Levison Gower, now Lord F. Egerton, was—as Prince Auguste d'Arenberg who was intimate with Lady Charlotte Greville, his mother in law, told me, travelling on the continent like a King, because having *only* 10,000£ a year, he could not afford to live in London!)[15] Notwithstanding the *prematurity* of my tour, I found the apartment next to the one into which I was shown, occupied by

---

13. The text has "Aachen" written in pencil above "Aix," in Legaré's hand.
14. Not "Bergham."
15. Francis Leveson Gower, 1800–1857, 1st Earl of Ellesmere, a liberal Tory and secretary of war in 1830, noted *supra* for his German translations; Auguste Marie Raymond d'Aremberg, 1753–1833, comte de la Mark; Lady Charlotte Greville, née Bentinck, 1775–1862, daughter of the 3d duke of Portland and mother of the diarist Charles Greville.

an English family. Mine was a rather gaudily furnished room, with high ceilings and better fitted for a salon than a bed room. But vain pomp etc. I hate ye, when my bones are broken and the exhausted body, absolute master through its very weakness of its etherial companion, clamors for repose. I called for tea which was served in a silver pot etc. and really was very good. I made it too strong tho' and hence, in part, perhaps the dismal sequel. At ½ past 10, I went to bed: the first thing I look to in a bed, is the pillows and bolster,—in short, the treatment which the head is to undergo during the sleep that one has a right to count on. It was all wrong—the only pillow with a case was too soft and sank down to nothing under the heavy occiput. I called for another: it was a stout one, and with that (there were then *three* and a bolster) I was mounted up too high, and should either fall from it in my restlessness, or have my neck broken by the perpendicular posture. Another defect, for a sore body, was the impenetrable hardness of the upper mattress. However[16] I threw myself *à corps perdu* upon these difficulties, and hardships, and expected my fatigue to carry me thro' them all without a moment's sleeplessness. It was not so. At ½ past 12 I wake, heated, uneasy, with a feeling such as I suppose precedes apoplexy—except that, having lived very low for the last four days and taken so much exercise, it seemed impossible. But I had left Brussells, before I was rid of my sour throat and the accompanying irritation of the blood, which had been greatly increased by the fatigues of the journey and a obstinate costiveness; and hence, my present uncomfortable situation had produced the effect I experienced. I immediately rose—swallowed a dose of calcined magnesia (which I always carry about me) and took a piece of rhubarb root into my mouth. After lying awake and tossing about for nearly two hours I fell asleep again and woke at ½ past 5. The medicine having operated,[17] I found myself better and at 9 o'clock, went out to secure my place in the Diligence for Bonn, and to see once more the Cathedral and the Jesuit's church.

I had a little hobbling fellow about 58 years old, for a guide to these objects. He spoke some French and I some German and thus contrived to be not quite unintelligible to one another.

At the *Diligence* office, I was once more struck with the omnipresence and obtrusiveness of the police in these countries. As it is the first time, for sixteen years, that I have ever been in the territory of an absolute Prince,[18] such things make a great impression on me. The government has

---

16. *Writings* omits here, "I threw myself *à corps perdu* upon these difficulties, and hardships, and. . . ."

17. Not "taken effect."

18. Not "prince." Mary Legaré consistently lowercased the European titles that Legaré usually capitalized. This may be a case of deliberate alteration, if she thought his habit betrayed insufficient republican scruple.

the exclusive *exploitation* of all travelling by *post*: whether in your own or a public carriage (scnell[19] wagen). You are not allowed to take a place in the latter without presenting yourself in person, with your *passport en règle*. If all be right, they take your money and give you a paper, setting forth all the rules and regulations of this mode of travelling, as that each traveller is allowed to take with him *gratis* 30 lbs of baggage, all *excédants*[20] to go by another wagon or diligence etc. On this paper you set down, with the utmost precision, your *effects*, which are to be sent to the *bureau* an *hour* before the coach is to leave: and you are to keep it by you, ready to be produced, as it may be required, at any stage of your future progress etc. etc. The *schnell* machine takes three hours to go from Cologne to Bonn, *15* miles.

The Cathedral—magnificent beyond description so far as it goes—was never finished; but they are now at work upon it, inside and outside, for that purpose. The gothic[21] carving and painted glass of the quire and adjacent parts are richer than anything of the kind I remember. The glass especially, I think, excells the so much and so deservedly vaunted present of Charles V in St. Gudule at Brussells. As I was only refreshing my recollections, I did not ask to be allowed to renew my acquaintance with the famous *three Kings*, or Wise Men of the East, whose real bodies are *unquestionably* deposited in a shrine behind the high altar of this Cathedral and may be seen at any time for *eight* livres tournois; neither did I penetrate into the *Sacristy* replete with curious relics. They were celebrating mass and I listened with profound pleasure to the deep-toned organ—the Christian instrument. The pillars in the nave of the Cathedral are said to be 108 in number and are of a prodigious circumference—much greater than those of the Church at Antwerp. On the whole, however, I was less impressed with the richness and magnificence of this church, than with the vastness, the height and the naked simplicity of that of Antwerp, which I had so recently seen as to have all the impression it made upon me still fresh on my mind. The latter appears to me, judging only by the eye much longer and more spacious—but then the Cathedral at Cologne being in the act of undergoing repairs or, rather, of being completed, was in some degree encumbered with the usual apparatus.

The Jesuit's church is a gaudy affair, like others belonging to the same order which I have seen elsewhere.

Bonn 25th May.    I left Cologne at 2 o'clock in the schnell post and arrived here at 5. Lodgings at the *Stern* or Star. Small room, but neatly

---

19. Not schnell, which is correct; Legaré gets it right elsewhere.
20. Not "excédant."
21. Not "Gothic."

furnished and a good bed, with clean new sheets. As I was to spend several days here, this latter was a matter of infinite importance. I ordered a simple dinner to be served and it was very bad.

The next morning (23d) I wrote a note to M. and Mad. Arconati Visconti[22] announcing my arrival, and at the same time sent to M. Schlegel a letter of introducion I had received from M. Arrivabene,[23] to serve in case the Arconatis were not here. I receive by the return of my commissionaire, an invitation from the latter to dine with them *en famille* at 3, and am informed by M. Schlegel that he will receive me at any time before 1. At ½ past 11 go out to make him a visit. On the way, I meet the Arconatis who are just going, they say, to call on some countrypeople of mine at the hotel where I lodge—Mr. and Mrs. Sidney Brooks. After the usual compliments pass on, and am admitted at M. Schlegels. Shown into the apartments on the ground floor, I see among other things, the *bust* of the master in marble—a very flattering one, as I found afterwards, tho M.S. is rather handsome, in spite of a blink in one of his eyes. His old woman servant presently comes down again and asks me to walk up. After a moment's expectation, an elderly looking gentleman but still active and fresh enough of his age, comes in, quite in deshabille, without cravat and in slippers. I soon saw the whole man, and led on from topic to topic, in order to get as much out of him as possible. Speaking of Pozzo di Borgo, he said he met him once at Vienna in *1808*, when he (S.) was travelling with Mad. de Staël.[24] The gaieties of that dissipated city were at their height. How is it possible, says Pozzo, that people should enjoy themselves so carelessly, while their country is trampled upon as it is. In their joyous *insouciance* they asked Madame de Staël if she thought the peace would last till *after* the hunting and shooting season: and here a loud laugh (quite a frequent accompaniment of M. S's conversation). Then we talk of the University of Bonn—of the perfect religious toleration that exists in Prussia, where young men of the Catholic and protestant communions study together etc.—English politics etc. I get up to take my leave until we should meet again at dinner at the Arconatis, but, as I am doing so, here said he is something you must see. There is a likeness of Mad. de Staël (under it hung a miniature image of Schlegel himself) taken after her death, but

22. Not "Viconti"; Giuseppe Arconati Visconti, 1797–1873, born in Milan but in exile from the Austrians; he lived usually near Brussels, but traveled extensively and counted among his friends many of the leading liberal intellectuals of Europe and the United States; he married Costanza Trotti Bentivoglio in 1818.

23. Giovanni Arrivabene, 1787–1873, a fellow emigré of Visconti, though from Mantua; he translated some of the writings of James Mill into Italian and Nassau Senior into French. His best known book was the *Considérations sur les principaux moyens d'améliorer le sort des classes ouvrières* (Brussels, 1832).

24. Carlo Andrea Pozzo di Borgo, 1764–1842, a Corsican who later served in the Russian diplomatic service, after 1814 as Russian ambassador to Paris and then London; he was an inveterate opponent of Napoleon.

exceedingly resembling her. Corinne[25] is not *so very* ugly in this picture, and has especially very pretty, tho' rather shrewish eyes.

On returning to my lodgings, I see Mr. Brooks' card and shortly after he asks if I can receive him. On my consenting to do so, he comes in and I recognize in him an old acquaintance,—a brother in law of Mr. Edward Everett. He hands me two letters—one of them from my friend Bronson, the other from Mr. A. Everett.[26] As I was about to make my toilette for dinner, our interview was a short one.

At M. Arconati's, find them and a sister of *her's* lately arrived from Milan,—a girl of about 19 years, I suppose, but not pretty, tho' mild and gentle. She has long white eye lashes. Another person present was a M. Bergé, who says he saw me at dinner at Sir. Robt. Adair's when I first went to Brussels.[27] After waiting some time for M. Schlegel, his carriage drives in and he soon makes his appearance, "neat, trimly dressed, fresh as a bridegroom."[28] The *savant* seemed to be very completely sunk in the *petit-maitre*. At dinner, the conversation was very various and agreeable. We talked of foreign countries, with which M. Schlegel is very familiarly acquainted—of *races* of men, negro, *quarteron* etc. The latter he said always retained the African features, *flat nose* etc. I told him it was not so chez *nous* where some of them have the caucasian[29] face in its perfection and are very handsome. A subject we talked a good deal about was the criminal code and trial by Jury. He is evidently full of a reform in the former, which he regretted his friend, Sir James McIntosh had not lived to accomplish.[30] I ventured to say that I knew no problem more puzzling and less likely to be soon satisfactorily solved, than what was the best way of disposing of a *felon*—that is a determined criminal—and that the question would probably have to be answered differently according to circumstances. *Unanimity* in the jury, which he attacked, I stoutly defended, affirming that without requiring that there would be a very insufficient examination of cases by those occasional, undisciplined judges, and I was not sure whether the institution would be worth fighting for without it. Nay, but, said he, even with a majority of only 7 to 5, *we* are very much attached to the system. A case was mentioned in which a man having been convicted, on very doubtful evidence, of a murder committed seven years

---

25. From her semi-autobiographical novel, *Corinne* (1807).

26. Edward Everett, 1794–1865, of Massachusetts, then in the House of Representatives; Oliver Bronson, b. 1799, was a Connecticut friend of Legaré; Alexander Hill Everett, 1790–1847, brother of Edward, and then editor of the *North American Review*. *Writings* has added the initial, "H."

27. Sir Robert Adair, 1763–1855, British Minister to Belgium, a Whig and for many years a political ally and friend of Charles James Fox.

28. *Henry IV, Part I*, I. iii. 33–34.

29. Not "Caucasian."

30. Mackintosh, whose *History* Harrison reviewed *supra*, was a friend to Madame de Staël, Benjamin Constant, and Schlegel himself.

before, the King of Prussia, of his absolute power, set aside the sentence, and had the case rejudged in Silesia, where the accused was acquitted. H. M. in his zeal to do good, violated the forms. Speak also of M. Tocqueville's recent book on the democracy of the U.S.[31] Tell them I have not read it and so get off without giving a general opinion on the subject. Add that from some observations on it in the *Débats*, he seems to have seen things in a truer light than foreigners usually do—e.g. he dates our republicanism, not as people on this side the Atlantic absurdly imagine, from the Revolution, but from the very foundation of the colonies which I explain, adding at the same time, that nothing could be more widely different than such a revolution, and one (like that of '89, for instance) where every thing had to be pulled down and set up again. Witness the So. American abortions.

After dinner, we retire to the salon to take coffee, which I actually did! vae mihi! Mr. S's. *libellus* on the Hippolytus of Euripides and the Phaedra of Racine being mentioned, I say that I had read such a *diatribe* over and considered it as incontrovertibly just and an admirable specimen of comparative criticism.[32] He reads some lines from Pradon, of which the purport was that Hippolytus, at Paris, must be *gallant* to please, and not *sauvage* and intractable to Venus, as he was—in short, that Hippolytus must cease to be Hippolytus.[33] The conversation turns on other kindred topics— Spanish theatre, license of Satire etc. Schlegel mentions no bad joke of Philip IV (I think) who used to recite verses with Calderon, who had a wonderful facility at improvisation.[34] They were doing an *auto*, in which Philip was *God*, and the poet, Adam. The latter had the parole and kept it an unconscionably long time, until the creator becoming impatient interrupts him by saying—"Yes, I am your creator—and I repent me already of having made such a garrulous fellow"—*un Adam tan hablador*.

Presently M. S's. carriage drives in and I am told the arrangement of the evening is that the Arconati's shall go in their carriage and take the Brooks' out to drive. M. S. who proposes to me to join him in a similar promenade, gives Mad. Arconati *rendezvous* at the Botanical Garden. We take leave and get up into a very nice *calèche* drawn by two fine horses, and driven by a coachman in livery, with a footman to suit. I ask M. Schlegel how it happens that his account of the genius of Sophocles being supposed just—as I for one certainly think it, for in reading it *after*, as well as before the original text, I have *felt* it to be so, even to the encomium he

---

31. Alexis de Tocqueville, *De la démocratie en Amérique* (Paris, 1835).

32. August von Schlegel, *Comparaison entre la Phedre de Racine et celle d'Euripide* (Paris, 1807): "libellus" can mean either a pamphlet or a lampoon.

33. Nicholas Pradon, *Phedre et Hippolyte: Tragédie*, in *Les Oeuvres de Mr. Pradon* (Paris, 1744), 1: 202-92, originally published in 1677.

34. Philip IV of Spain, 1605-1665; Pedro Calderón de la Barca, 1600-1681, the Spanish dramatist.

bestows on the Attic grace and sweetness of the Oedipus Coloneus—so many ancient critics seem to prefer Euripides—the τραγικώτατός as he is called—and that not only in reference to *tenderness*, but generally.³⁵ He asks me whom I cite. I tell him Aristotle's Poetics³⁶ and a passage or two in Plato's Dialogues, which, altho' I could not refer to more particularly, I had noted in my *study* book, because] they struck me very forcibly. The mineralogical cabinet is in a fine *ci-devant maison de plaisance* of the ex-Archbishop Elector. We went through all its apartments. In one of them we meet with the Arconatis, and I make the acquaintance of my nice little country-woman, Mrs. Brooks, who looks very English (being very blond, with soft, silky hair, and rather inclined to be fatter than most American women) and speaks the vernacular without any nasal twang at all,—a rare thing for one of my dear country-women. She tells me she has heard so much of me from all her friends, especially Julia Livingston that was, that she can hardly consider me as a stranger.³⁷ I am charmed to see her, and do my best to let her perceive that I am. Find her speaking French extremely well. She is of a Boston family and a niece of Bishop Dehon's.³⁸ Our walk about the garden was very agreeable, and, as we were about to leave it, we mounted a flight of steps which lead one up to one of the principal doors of the palace, from the landing-place of which there is a fine view of the Septmonts in the distance. Thence the conversation turns on the picturesque and the beautiful. M. Schlegel says it is absurd to compare scenes in different countries,—that every country has its own beauties,—the most sterile and ill-favored is not without them; witness Holland which has produced such masters in landscape painting. I answer that, *à force de regarder beaucoup*, they had at last seen, or imagined they saw something, I see, said he, that you are an *incrédule*. After a good deal of conversation, we return to the carriages. He asks me to go home with him and drink tea,—an invitation which I cheerfully accept. On our way, I ask after Hugo and Savigny.³⁹ They do not seem to stand very well in his estimation. Repeats what somebody said, that the civil law was like scenery in twilight,—you may make what you please of it. Savigny, he adds, is of what they call the *historical* school. I tell him, as I interpret the expression, I am half inclined to be of that school myself; and ask him what

35. The Greek is misspelled in *Writings*, chiefly because the text is blotted; the reference is to Aristotle, *Poetics*, xiii.10 (1453a): "Euripides . . . is the most tragic of the poets."
36. Not "Portius."
37. The daughter of Edward Livingston, 1764–1836, of Louisiana, then minister to France; when secretary of state, he had helped to secure Legaré the Belgian legation.
38. Thomas DeHon, 1776–1817, a Bostonian who was later rector of St. Michael's Church in Charleston (1809–1812) and bishop of South Carolina (1812–1817).
39. Gustav von Hugo, 1764–1844, a German jurist who taught at Göttingen for many years, author chiefly of *Lehrbuch eines Zivilistischen Kursus* (1792–1821) and *Zivilistisches Magazin* (1790–1837); Friedrich Karl von Savigny, 1779–1861, the legal historian and first rector of the University of Berlin.

meaning he attaches to the term. He explains it as being a sort of *legislative necessity*, by which every age, *nescio quo fato*,[40] makes the laws that suit it. I then say, all I mean is that the *traditions of a country* must be respected in its constitutional innovations; otherwise one of two things ensues,—either your constitution is dead-born, as in Belgium now, or every thing is turned into chaos as by the *Constituent Assembly*, and refer again to our own history. On the subject of the *Constituante*, he thinks justice is not done it; that, with all its errors and the evils they did or did not lead to, the general result is good; that to get what we have, we must have demanded what they did, etc., etc. The privileged classes never would have yielded to any reform less unsparing.

Arrived at his house, I am shown up (this time) into his study, where the first thing I see is another *bust* of himself, backed by a half-length portrait. Amour propre, it seems, is no *iconoclast*, or rather the contrary. I ask after Niebuhr, whose singularly fine head we had seen at the country palace. Gives me clearly to perceive that he was no friends with the great historian, whose department (that, I mean, of Roman history) M. S. now actually fills, and some of whose opinions he disputes. *Apropos* of his scepticism, I tell him that was obvious enough; but what made him remarkable was not disputing, but the *interpreting* the scanty and hardly intelligible remains of those early annals. He says Niebuhr was altogether impatient of contradiction, and has no doubt but that his end was hastened by the revolutionary events of 1830, which preyed inconceivably upon his mind; although he was here, (he adds,) so as to express it, *en volontaire*, and might have gone away when he pleased, not as I, nailed to the spot by my house, etc. The conversation turns afterwards on Oriental literature, to which (Sanscrit, especially) M. Schlegel is now particularly devoted. Presents me with a letter of his to Sir J. McIntosh on that subject, which he sends me the next day with a note.

I left him at half-past 9, and, on returning to the "Star", call on Mr. Brooks to arrange about the morrow, when we are engaged to visit the Drachenfels with the Arconatis. I had stipulated for permission to go first to *mass*, (it being *Sunday*,) which I never miss in travelling in any Catholic country where there is a cathedral. The Brooks' agree to go with me, and accordingly we repair thither at 9 o'clock, but, after some delay and difficulty (owing to the great crowd) in getting in, find the ceremony begins with a *sermon*, and that in German. After waiting in vain for the fine music we expected, force our way out, and, at about 11, set out with the Arconatis to the object of our morning's visit. Our party filled two open carriages. We passed by the Godesberg, and reached the Rhine (which was very full and muddy, with a strong current, and which we crossed in one

---

40. Trans. I do not know by what destiny.

of their flat-bottomed sail boats) about five miles from the town. Donkeys were waiting on the opposite bank, ready caparisoned [here enter M. Arconati, and afterwards M. de Schlegel, to take leave of me, as I go tomorrow, May 28]: the *male* part of our company all prefer walking up the mountain, but Mad. Arconati and Mrs. Brooks mount two of these long-eared dwarfs. Mrs. B's. goes along very well, but Mad. Arconati's little beast can't be thumped or pulled into any sort of usefulness, so that she is fain to dismount and trudge along with the rest of us; *du reste,* the ascent is not very steep, and we are soon standing on the esplanade formed a little below the ruined castle, and adorned with a monument to the *heroes* who fell in 1814. The view on all sides is delicious; unfortunately for the picturesque, though well for our bodily comfort, there was no sunshine, though the weather was soft and genial. After enjoying this vast and beautiful prospect for a long time, we repair to the sort of eating house built here for the accommodation of visiters, and find a collation prepared for us by the kind attention of our friends, the A's. I had a tremendous appetite, as we all had, though it was only 2 o'clock; and, to make it better, (or, as it turned out, *worse,*) there was a *champagne* foaming and dancing in its crystal bounds, and a bottle of the very finest Johannisberger, which Mr. Brooks had himself bought at McHernich's altar, and brought with him, as if to be offered up in libations on this magnificent altar to the genius of the Rhein gau.[41] After our repast, made agreeable by so many various attractions, not to mention a delightful conversation, we descend once more to the esplanade and feast our eyes upon the beauties of the scenery, now somewhat varied by certain accidents of light, struggling through the haze in the distance. After re-crossing the river, and getting into our caleche with Mesd. Brooks and Arconati, I find, to my great annoyance, that a sore-throat I had brought with me from Brussells, and thought almost cured, had been so much irritated by the mountain air and mounting exercise, not to mention as many as *four* glasses of unmixed wine (merum,)[42] a horrible debauch for me, that I am obliged to send for a doctor on returning to my hotel.

This physician, recommended by Madame Arconati, was M. Nassé, a man of fifty or sixty, a professor of the University. He recommended an *antiphlogistic* treatment; i.e., abstinence and a *tisane,*—told me I was very wrong to take calomel, as I was evidently inclined to *congestions* in the upper regions. He was, I found, a most agreeable person, and I derived so much pleasure from his conversation in the four visits he paid me in three days, that I most cheerfully paid him a fee of five rix thalers in taking leave of him. I had discussed with him all the various systems of

41. Trans. region.
42. "Merum" means unmixed; I suspect Legaré simply wrote "*merum* wine" and his sister amended the text.

medicine. He seemed to like none. When he heard I was an American, he said, "On dit beaucoup de mal de vous." In truth they do, and no better proof of it than that there is no spot so sequestered in Europe, but a clearsighted and quick-eared American finds it out in a couple of days.

As he forbad my going out, this malady, which has detained me up to this present writing, (28th May, 9 o'clock, P. M.,) four days longer than I meant to stay, has also sadly curtailed the pleasures and advantages of my *séjour*: in the first place, I had to renounce a tea-party at M. Schlegel's, though he has repeatedly called on me since.

In the few hours, during which I have felt safe in going out, I have been to the well-furnished *librairie* of M. Weber, publisher of the Byzantine Histories of Niebuhr, (continued by Becker and the other philologists of the Berlin University,) where, besides taking a note of many precious works, I buy Schlegel's Dramatic Literature in German, and a translation into modern German of the Nibelungenlied.[43]

II

Nordhausen, Thursday 22d April 1836.    I left Brussells on Monday evening, 18th April, at ½ past 9 o'clock and travelled incessantly until I arrived at Aix la Chapelle, the next day, at about 4, where I dined. It was not until nearly 7 that I set off again towards Juliers—my resting place for the night. Very good apartment and bed. 23d, at ½ past 6 am off again for Dusseldorf (6¾ German miles) thence to Elberfeldt where I dine. This flourishing manufacturing place filled me with astonishment. I have seen nothing like it in Europe. It has all the freshness and life of an American town in one of the new states. It is built upon the banks of a stream, which sets its mills in motion, and it completely fills up the narrow but beautiful valley for miles together with factories and dwelling-houses—all remarkable for neatness and cleanliness and many for a degree of elegance and grandeur rarely to be met with in great capitals. It is rather a collection of manufacturing towns, than one city and alltogether they contain some 60,000 inhabitants. I do not remember ever to have had a more agreeable drive than this from the time I crossed the Rhine on a *pont volante* at Dusseldorf, until I had passed Elberfeldt some three or four German miles— making in all a distance of about thirty English miles,—but from the last mentioned station to the town (Nordhausen) in which I am writing this,

---

43. *Corpus Scriptorum Historiae Byzantiae*, eds. B. G. Niebuhr, I. Bekker, L. Schopen, G. Dindorf (50 vols., Bonn, 1828–1897); August von Schlegel, *Uber Dramatische Kuns und Literatur* (Heidelberg, 1817); Carl Conrad Friedrich Wilhelm Lachmann, *Der Niebelungen* (Berlin, 1826). These last two are listed in *Catalogue of the Library of the Hon. Hugh S. Legaré* (Washington, D.C., 1843), pp. 13, 15.

that is to say for 150 English miles together, it has been all barrenness and desolation. The road—a most excellent one macadamized—runs the whole way between very high hills approaching very near to each other—so that there is very little prospect. On such an elevation, the spring has as yet made hardly any progress, and so the trees are bare and the heath brown. The towns and villages, with a single exception, are the most miserable, dirty, ragged collection of huts that can be conceived—houses built of wood frames filled up with clay and most of them decaying and dilapidated—in short every thing looks poverty stricken and primitive. This is more strictly true of *Hesse*, which one traverses thro' its pretty capital, Cassel, which is really a charming little town, and where I was almost tempted, in spite of my haste to be at Berlin, to spend a day. As it was I lounged away a pleasant evening in looking down from its fine squares and walks upon the beautiful garden on the hill side and the smiling green valley into which it runs out to a great distance. The public edifices without being particularly fine, are still very respectable in size and appearance and the upper part of the town is laid out with great regularity. There is a statue in the square of the palace of the Grand Duke Frederick II with the date 1783. Was that the man who sold his troops to George III, to reduce us to subjection? And if yea, was it for that his country erected this statue?[44] The peasants have rather a remarkable costume—the men (who seem generally fine—at least so far as I can judge from what I saw in a *residence* amongst them of at least 24 hours from first to last) wear boots or gaiters up to the knees—the women, comb their hair all back from the forehead and gather it in a knot on the top of the head, where it is covered by a black patch, not unlike the calotte of a priest. I must not forget to mention a rather curious incident. In the morning before I set off, I strolled out to cast another glance over the town and suburbs. I remarked very many people walking with great speed down the town, to what I at first supposed was a market-place. I go round a square, and reenter the same street, where I see still as many people all hastening the same way. It now strikes me that this can be no every day matter like a market, nor, indeed, any sort of *business* whatever. There is something extraordinary occurring—I rather think it is an *execution*. I thought, however, no more of the matter, until the head waiter coming in to receive the amount of my bill tells me they are cutting off the head of an assassin that had murdered three people—and that I shall pass very near the spot. I did so, but met the crowd (an immense one for so small a place) all returning, and saw the scaffold, but nothing on it, but some two or three men in cocked hats—who were probably the Jack Ketch and his suite. It seems

44. It was, though the Grand Duke hired out troops to anyone willing to pay, so Legaré's conjecture is doubtful.

they cut off heads here and with a *sword*, in the old fashioned way. I should have been glad to see the *apparatus*, but did not like to discover my curiosity to so many people.

*Magdeburg* 23d April.  I arrived but a couple of hours ago in this famous old town, of which as it was 9 o'clock when I got here, I have as yet seen nothing. Lodging, Stadt London, kept by an Alsacian.
   To go on with my journal where I left off. I was not determined when I left Cassel how far I should travel before I stopped again. Find the posting cheaper, but progress less than in the Prussian dominions heretofore. After going some twenty miles, I arrive at the bank of a rapid stream, where a book is handed me to write my name. Infer (for I can't comprehend the German of the man that offers it) that I am already at the end of the Grand Duke's territory—and on consulting my map find that the stream above mentioned is the *Weser* and the border. Weather charming. At 8 the moon shines beautifully out and the remainder of my drive to Nordhausen a true party of pleasure. Moonlight and motion always make me meditative and romantic. Think what an adventure it will be to pass through the Hartz at this witching time. But *then*, Stolberg, where the ridge of mountains begins (it is about 16 English miles across) is more than two posts beyond Nordhausen; and the moon is only in the beginning of its second quarter and so her smiles upon her benighted wooer not to be expected to continue even so long as a woman's empire usually lasts and a mountainous journey always a long one: Witness a similar attempt and the repentance it occasioned me, on the Saluda mountain in 1830.[45] Besides a morning drive at this season, *must* be so fresh and delicious in these regions, and if one muses less, one sees more by sunlight. I decide, for once, to sacrifice imagination to sense and the senses and determine to "turn in" at Nordhausen. Tell the Postillion I mean to stop at the Post,—wh. d'Arnin[46] describes in the Itinerary he gave me by way of *euphemism*[47] as an *auberge médiocre*. The sight of the town, by moonlight, enough to make night hideous—all the houses built after the fashion described above—a frame of wood, filled up with clay or bricks—so as to leave every rib and rafter exposed to view,—giving to these deformed masses—especially at this hour—the appearance of stuffed skeletons. I verily do not believe the least change has been made in this—nor indeed any other particular in this whole country from Elberfeldt to Stolberg, since the 30 Years War. I had no conception there was in any part of Western Europe, such a miserably lodged peasantry. Many of their huts strongly recalled those of our slaves in the Southern States—But this by the bye.

---

45. In North Carolina, near Asheville.
46. Heinrich Friedrich von Arnim, 1791-1859, Prussian minister in Brussels.
47. Not "euphemisme."

Arrived at mine host of the "Römische Kaiser" I ask for an apartment and am shown up two pair of stairs to a close, unventilated room, wherein are two beds, both together narrower than the one I left at the Hotel de Bellevue. I hate being at too close quarters even with myself, and having found the inconvenience of being stinted in space the night before, the sight of these *couchettes* d'enfer—*not en fer*, like *Gen. Evain's*—makes me nervous.[48] Yielding to the first impression I rush out of the room and down the stair case, protesting to mine host, who speaks a little French, that I can't think of lying down on such a couch and ask if he has nothing better. Nothing—all beds that he has ever heard of made just in the same fashion. I get into my carriage—bawl out in broken German to the Postillion to put his horses to again and take me to the *Post*. "Here *is* the Post," says he. Very well let me have horses and be off. I am better here. They are about complying, when I get down and ask to be shown some other rooms. At length I make choice of one in which the bed is just as narrow, and the ceilings much lower, but which has a window open and is of course well aired. Here I establish myself for better for worse. The bed is made. Another shock for my nerves. There is only one sheet on which one lies down—the place of the upper one, as well as of blankets and counterpane—being supplied by a sort of sack, covered with a linen case like a bolster-case. This puzzles my servant exceedingly—he is no conjuror, it is true. After writing the first part of these notes, I enter with as much resignation as was to be expected upon this new trial, and what with extreme fatigue and what with the idea of rising the earlier to begin my mountain excursion, if I slept little, I make out to pass the night well enough. Rise at five.

The drive from Nordhausen to Stolberg, in this morning air, as delightful as possible. The sides of the mountains are covered with wood—the road is for the most part in a valley and as you approach the latter place, along an impetuous, brawling stream.[49] I should suppose this excursion in the summer as charming as possible to a man of woods and streams, as I am. There are some evergreens—something like stunted cedar—that give great freshness to the scene even now.

The Chateau of the Count of Stolberg hangs in the air abruptly over the miserable village of that name. I get out of my carriage—walk through the village and clamber up the sides of the mountain on which the Chateau does *not* stand, but from which you command a fine view of this part of the Hartz.

Soon after getting again into my carriage and making the best of my way out of the filthy and ill paved streets (the latter to an incredible de-

---

48. Louis Auguste Frederique Evain, 1775–1852, Belgian minister of war.
49. There is an illegible insertion here, in pencil and Legaré's hand.

gree) (by the bye, here is the house in which the famous anabaptist peasant leader Munster[50] was born)—who that sees what their condition *is* now, can wonder that they found it intolerable *then*?) I begin to ascend— and for sixteen miles, am crossing the *ridge*: at first on a magnificent macadamized road, but after getting into *Anhalt*, on a wretched, unpaved crossroad precisely such as I am accustomed to in some of the wildest parts of the Southern country—as narrow as the bed I slept in and as hard too—tho' in bad weather, I suppose, from the terrible ruts that are shaking me to pieces, just the reverse and indeed I do not know how it can be practicable at all. It is a facsimile of that wh. leads from the turnpike to Guesbeck, near Brussells. I tremble at the thought of what it must have been a fortnight since.

The Hartz mountain, as far the present turnpike goes, is completely wooded and the Blue ridge in North Carolina all over again, bating, however, most of its beauties.

I arrive at a post *station*—where I am allowed to wait composedly for half an hour.[51] I was saved from desperation by a rather singular occurrence. There was a posse of boys of various ages and sizes from 17 and 18 downwards, singing psalms (I suppose) in the street. They would stop before one house and raise a stave: then another, at last near my carriage. They sang all the parts of a chorus and very well indeed. I love music— next to women[52]—of all things in this world—and sacred music especially—then in *this* solitude—this mountainous region of pure air and pure morals etc. etc. Religion and music—the worship of God and the worship of nature. In spite of this agreeable *distraction*, however, do not forget I am travelling and so greatly annoyed by the non appearance of the postillion and his gear. The Prussian who brought me hither having pocketed his *Drink geld*, has coolly walked off, and I see no living soul at all interested in my fate—become impatient—make my servant rap at the door— nobody comes—again—again. A girl shows herself and divining my wants, throws a cloak about her (the morning air was shrewd) and runs to a considerable distance. At last appear, in the offing, the Anhalt postillion and his ragged concern. The whole thing dismally poverty striken. Such fare as one gets in an old country house of a decayed gentleman's family. Man very stout and stupid—beasts very spare but not less dull than the man for all that. When we come to mount the first long hill side, I feel the greatest commiseration—especially when the postillion lays hold of the smaller and more willing beast, as if to drag him along. *Descend*, en revanche, very well and at the foot of one of the mountains see a black obelisk. What can an obelisk in these forgotten solitudes mean? Get down

50. Thomas Münzer, 1489–1525.
51. Again, there is some illegible pencil marking here.
52. Not "woman," a possible instance of bowdlerization by Mary Legaré.

and approaching find it is to the "Father of his country"—of course some Duke of Anhalt; every country, like every man, has a father at least. This poor little nation in the wilderness, like any other has its heroes. See, at length after a drive of at least 10 miles, at the top of a high mountain, a vast prospect open before me and descending, descry gradually all the varied beauties of a rich champaign country, covered with green crops just sprung up—and in the distance a towered city—and towering over it, an *abbaye*. See at once it was the seat of an Abbaye Princière, and that, as in so many other cases the land was consecrated to religion because it was fertile, or was fertile because it was consecrated to religion—according to Catholic and heretical versions.

Find myself still doomed to the rack of this infernal cross road—on which I travel till I come within two German miles of Magdeburg, where I arrive as above.

*24d[53] April Potsdam*   I rose this morning at 6. At 7 was on my way, with a Valet de Place, who spoke only German, to see the citadel and the cathedral. The former is famous for having been Trenk's prison and afterwards Lafayette's etc.[54] By paying a trifle, I am let in by the Keeper of it. Am much disappointed in the horrors of the place—indeed, except a rather short allowance of day light, none but such as exist in every prison, *ipso facto*. It is a small guard room, not under the earth, as I had imagined, but on the ground floor; nor yet damp and dripping with water oozing thro' it from the bed of the stream above (this was my strange conceit, God[55] knows why) but dry and comfortable enough. The walls are adorned with rude drawings, Trenk's dismal past time—all in keeping. An *owl*, a death's head and cross bones, a coffin, the date 1761 etc. scratched or rather cut upon the stone floor and what surprized me most was a head of the great Fred[k] himself excellent well done—near by it that of Napoleon had been drawn (by Lafayette *dit-on*, but that can't be true) but the face has been defaced and it is only by the air that one recognizes it. The view up the Elbe towards Dresden, from the walls of the citadel, under the soft morning sky of an April day was charming.

The Cathedral is now used as a Lutheran church. I went half an hour only before their morning service (it is Sunday) began and so was very

---

53. Legaré had written "23d," then changed the "3" to a "4."
54. Franz von der Trenck, 1711–1749, the Austrian commander of a Croatian regiment, was court-martialed by Maria Theresa for his atrocities: he was chiefly confined in the Spielberg Fortress, near Brno, after 1747. Lafayette was imprisoned by the Prussians in Magdeburg during 1793. Later he was moved to Neisse and then, in the custody of the Austrians, to Olmutz. This time in Lafayette's life may have had particular resonance for Legaré, since a young South Carolinian, Col. Francis Kinloch Huger, was involved in an abortive rescue attempt at Olmutz, and ended up imprisoned himself for the pains.
55. Not "heaven."

much hurried. Walked round its long cloisters before the beadle came. The portal is very fine and as of all the Iconoclasts the Lutherans were the most tolerant, some saints are still standing in their niches about the steeples—of which there are two (a rare thing comme l'on sait) but not of the highest. The interior of the church is exceedingly pretty, though not on such a scale as Antwerp or Cologne. It owes as much to Lutheranism as the outside and more. The choir stands as it was—with its fine altar piece of a single block of Carrara marble and its curiously carved *Statues de chanoine*; images, and pictures etc. I did not know until today that wax lights were used—that is, I had forgotten it—in the Protestant service. There were two burning upon the altar. Otho the Great plays a prominent part in this church. Here is his *tomb*, and that of his Anglo Saxon wife Editha.[56] Then there they are, the happy couple, in an old stone chapel, which I suppose was taken out of some still more ancient church (This dates from the beginning of the 13th cent.) as it stands and brought into this. Their majesties, cut in stone cut but a sorry figure there—Punch and Judy.

A really curious thing in this church is part of the armor of Tilly,[57] who in the 30 Years War destroyed and otherwise (if it is not a bull to add this) most villainously entreated Magdeburg—all for its own good as I have no doubt. It seems he left nothing standing but the cathedral: had he not swept them all away, Magdeburg would have resembled in its structures, to this day, the miserable towns with the stuffed skeletons, Quedlinburg[58] included, thro' which I have just passed. Here are his helmet, his general's staff (two of them, one with a lock and barrel) his boots (buskin, with heels 3 or 4 inches high) and his gloves of steel. I put my hand into one of these ponderous gauntlets and thought of *Wallensteins Lager*.[59]

Speaking of Schiller, reminds me of Göthe, and Faust, and Faust of the Brockenberg. I ought to have recorded that as I came rushing down the last of the mountains which break sheer off at the plain of Quedlinburg, looking to the left, I saw a peak higher than the rest, all covered with snow. I have not seen such a sight since I looked on Ben Lomond in April 1819! horrid reminiscence! This peak was precisely the Brocken—the seat of Faust's witches.

The journey from Magdeburg to Potsdam is 16 mortal German miles. You pass thro' a perfectly flat country—as flat as the low country of Carolina—and resembling it unfortunately in more respects than one. It

---

56. Otto the Great, 912–973, Holy Roman Emperor.
57. Johannes Tserklaes, count of Tilly, 1559–1632, Bavarian commander of the army of the Catholic League.
58. Not "Quidlieburg"; it was, incidentally, the birthplace of Klopstock.
59. Friedrich von Schiller, *Wallensteins Lager* (Frankfurt and Leipzig, 1798).

abounds in ponds—called in Europe, I suppose, lakes—so that it occurred to me that in stead of *March*, one should read *Marsh* of Brandenburg. The highway is excellent for use, but detestable for ornament. Besides these barren flats, it traverses for miles a wood of young, (that is, in appearance) pines—and all the way except in this forest, especially from Brandenburg to Potsdam there, you are in an avenue *à perte de vue* of Lombardy poplars. The Elbe it is, I suppose, that swamps this whole district—for one crosses continually streams of considerable width that are rushing with great impetuosity. But that wd. prove the reverse of my position and shew that the Elbe drained the country, by receiving these torrents in its wide expanse. It is a noble river and would be so in America. At Magdeburg, which is 48 Germ. miles by water from Hamburg it is said to be 30 feet deep and tho divided into two branches, each is a mighty flood. But it is dry in summer, dit-on: so is the *Congaree*, almost.

In the course of this long drive from Elberfeldt hither, I am struck with several things. 1st. every man I meet bows with profound, even deferential respect to me, that is, to the man in a post chaise with a servant behind him. In *France*, the *piétons*, who are all philosophers curse you. 2d. I had no idea one could see so much poor land, such miserable towns and villages, a population so vilely lodged yet so primitive and happy,—in short such evidences of things being just as they were a couple of centuries ago, in spite of the schoolmasters and steam engines abroad—in the very heart of Europe. No *Cockerel*[60] has been here yet—and à propos of Cockerel, what a contrast between the Ardennes as it now stands—I mean the road from Liège to Spa—and the Ardennes of the Wild Boar, or the Harz of today. Only let a steam-engine make the tour I have just finished and you'll see. 3d. Every thing is regulated in Prussia. The government has its hand in every thing—and all goes with a mechanical exactness (tho' a little slowly withal) that strikes one who has never lived under an absolute monarch.[61] At every stage or relai you pay in advance for your horses and turnpike—all but the Postillion—and a printed bill receipted is given you. Every time the Postillion approaches a tollgate, he winds his horn (a part of his uniform) and winds it twice, and always in precisely the same manner—the same monotonous note from one end of the kingdom to the other. When you give him his *drink geld* he thanks you, and quietly pockets it without asking for more. At Magdeburg I saw *affiché* behind the door of my appartment a tariff for my host (a Frenchman from Alsace) restraining him to so much for each dish of tea, each slice of bread and butter for which did not prevent his contriving to make me pay seven francs for a

---

60. John Cockerill, 1790–1840, English iron founder of Liège, who helped to build Belgian and other railways.

61. Not "government."

bed and two things he called bougies, which had already served and will no doubt serve again (their own master, j'entend) the useful little things. This *maximum* arrangement, however, I rather think was merciful. In short, one feels that one lives, moves, and has one's being here in the perpetual nurture and admonition of the Government.

To an American, accustomed to precisely the reverse of all this—that is, to every man's doing just as he pleases in all that he has to do, as if he had no account to give, not even to him that pays him, yet generally doing every thing perfectly well and with such results in the long run as there is no record of in the history of human affairs—this go-cart, leading string system appears very strange, and it is for Prussia to shew (if it can be shown) that its effects, on the whole, are really *not* disadvantageous to society. Certainly Elberfeldt seems a *commencement de preuve* to that effect. Meanwhile, it must be owned, that if everything is governed, everything is, for order and happiness merely, *well* governed. The honorable fact that this is a highly enlightened and *moral* government impresses itself upon the traveller as soon as he has had time to look around him and observe the most superficial phenomena.

*April 25.* I am not ready to go out this morning until ½ past 7 and then I find the *valet de place* who was to have conducted me to *Sans Souci, out.* After waiting some time, stroll forth. Am lodged at the Einsiedler near the Palace, where the King happens to be at this moment and is to remain until Wednesday. Everything military—troop of lancers composed of men in the flower of youth—beardless and generally fair, particularly attract my attention. Fine new church—stone—surmounted with a cross. Lounge toward the water—to the bridge—then return thro the parade of the palace, where the Valet de Place overtakes me. I am and have been since I found I had lost an half hour and had my projects frustrated, very *bilious.* Tell him it is too late and I should go to Berlin immediately after break fast—inwardly resolved to do no such thing. Take my tea and coolly go forth with the said *laquais* to see the famous little château: it is distant about a mile from the town. Begin with the picture gallery wh. contains about 200 pictures. More Vandykes than I ever saw altogether. A likeness of some Prince of Orange, in the shape of a little Cupid *skating*—a veritable little *Love*, never was any thing more delightfully beautiful. Several portraits by the same great master—one à cheval—another (admirable) of the sculptor Fiamingo.[62] Many Rubens' some in his daubing style—especially a *Susannah* (like Charlotte in the Werther of the Variete's at Paris) and the Elders—never saw such an uncouth monster as the woman: but *en revanche*, some very fine, tho' none to be compared with those at Ant-

---

62. Denys Calvaert, 1540–1619, a Flemish sculptor known as Dionisio Fiammingo.

werp: among these I remark particularly an *Adoration of the Magi* and a picture of Rubens himself, surrounded by all his wives and his friends—very pretty. The finest picture in the collection is a sleeping Venus by Titian. Homer says of something that it is "softer than sleep"—if you want to *feel* what that means, look at this picture. It is very queer but true that this melting repose reminded me of Taglioni's dancing.⁶³ From this picture gallery (which I forgot to say is about 230 feet long and very fine with gilt cornices etc.) I went to the little chateau of *Sans Souci*. The building it seems was divided between the Royal Host who lived in the right wing and his literary friends who occupied the left. A desk is pointed out at wh. Voltaire used to write. In the King's apartment there is no bed. It seems he died in an armed chair. My valet swore to me the clock points now to the very hour at wh. he died—for it went down as the breath left his body. Always some marvel for the vulgar. His library was an object of particular curiosity to me. It contains, so far as I could discover after a pretty close examination, nothing but French books—that is, books *in* French—for all the classics Polybius, Suetonius, Virgil etc. were translated, as were Macchiavelli (two copies), Don Quixotte, etc. Most of them are historical works—treatises of the art of war, diplomatic correspondence. A book in quarto was lying open upon the table. The running title (as the printers call it) was *Épitres Familières*. It was very dirty at the page I saw and had the appearance of having been much thumbed. It is said to be just as it was left. There is a MS. correction of a verse by Voltaire, in a fine, legible hand. The King had written (and printed) "Chiche de mots mais—" Voltaire substituted "de mots avare". This was what he called *blanchir le linge* of the great Frederick. The view from the front of the château is very beautiful. I had not time to go to the "New Palace" and I am tired of palaces and was fatigued with my walk and so returned to the *Einsiedler* where in half an hour I get into my post chaise and am off for Berlin.

On my way (before I got out of the town) I passed an open carriage in which I thought I recognised Lord Wm. Russell, whom I had seen once at Court at Brussells, with a lady by his side.⁶⁴ Soon after I meet the Crown Prince—and after a few minutes interval—Prince Frederick, followed by the princess in an open carriage and four.⁶⁵

The road continues wholly uninteresting and the country barren. I

---

63. Maria Taglioni, 1804–1884, the foremost Romantic ballerina, was best known for her creation of the Sylph in *La Sylphide* at Paris; the phrase *softer than sleep* occurs, not in Homer, but in Theocritus, *Idylls*, XV, line 25.

64. Lord George William Russell, 1790–1846, British minister to Prussia and brother of Lord John Russell.

65. Frederick William IV, 1795–1863, who succeeded in 1840; "Prince Frederick" is Prince William Frederick Louis, 1797–1888, later William I of Prussia and Emperor of Germany; his wife was Augusta, 1811–1890, the daughter of Charles Frederick of Saxe-Weimar.

arrived here (*Berlin*) at about 3 o'clock and took lodgings at the *Ville de Rome*. Immediately after go to the Table d'Hôte and dine. After dinner walk out to take a general view of the town. See the greater part of the objects mentioned by Reichard, in the course of a two hours' promenade.[66] No opera tonight—so fain to come in and amuse myself with writing this log-book. My *virtu* having been awakened by the gallery of *Sans Souci*, I take out of my Port-Folio my sweet little friend Emma S's[67] *souvenir*, a copy of the *Cena* of Leonardo da Vinci, and gloat for some time upon its beauties.[68]

The street in which I lodge is the great thoroughfare of the city in its most fashionable quarter, and is bisected by a public walk bordered with trees whence, probably, its name, *unter den Linden*.

I have read in my carriage the second vol. of Balzac's *Livre Mystique* which altho it shews the author to be undoubtedly a man of talent does not please.[69] It is a wild story intended to illustrate Swedenborg's nonsense.[70] Also Mad. d'Abrantès *Mémoires sur la Revolution*—a childish, confused, tho cleverish and interesting piece of tittle tattle.[71] The style is colloquial and sometimes not quite *de bonne compaignie*. She repeats the same stories over and over again—rambles from her subject perpetually, and at the end of the second volume, is only at the beginning of her task. Avis au lecteur Madame d'Angoulême[72] is (and deservedly) her heroine—Bonaparte, her hero—*peut-être*. The book, tho purporting to blame the anti-liberal conduct of the Restoration and that unsparingly, seems to be written with an eye to a possible re-restoration, and if it is to be relied on, it is hard to imagine a dirtier gang of ribbalds in high places than those who surrounded the Emperor of the French. She treats Talleyrand with unmeasured and most merited contempt—in *words* at least—Fouché also—but it is hard to say whom she excepts from the charge of treachery—unless it be the Duke de Bassano.[73] If she is to be relied on Bonaparte had completely lost his head when he returned from Elba and still more completely all the prestige of his fortune and name. To think of his dawdling in Paris to put on embroidered shoes or slippers and a coronation robe at the Champ de Mai instead of rushing forward to the frontiers! Would Caesar have done so? He

---

66. Heinrich A. O. Reichard, *Guide des voyagers en Allemagne* . . . (Weimar, 1817).
67. Emma Seymour, the young daughter of a Brussels neighbor.
68. Legaré had first written "Michael Angelo" but then substituted Da Vinci; *cena* is used in the Vulgate for the upper room of the Last Supper.
69. Honoré de Balzac, *Le Livre Mystique* (Paris, 1835).
70. Emanuel Swedenborg, 1688–1772, the Swedish mystic philosopher.
71. Laure Junot, duchesse d'Abrantès, *Memoires de Mme. la duchesse d'Abrantès* (Paris, 1831–1835).
72. Marie Therese Charlotte, duchesse d'Angoulême, 1778–1851, the daughter of Louis XVI.
73. Joseph Fouché, 1759(or 1763)–1820, Napoleon's minister of police; Hugues-Bernard Maret, duc de Bassano, 1763–1839, Napoleon's secretary.

wanted to be sure that he was still a monarch—the Bourgeois Gentilhomme[74] and his robe de chambre. Ney's conduct, according to her acct. was madness or total want of moral sense.[75] She is in love with Metternich. I should judge her to be *spirituelle*, but very foolish. There is a pathetic story of a woman taken in adultery and shut up for mad, really well told. Another book I never read before and of wh. I have read a great deal is Johnson's "Lives of the Poets".[76] Dr. J. is a horribly bad writer. His artificial periods and his pomposity of phrase to express the baldest common place is insupportable to me. Yet his criticism, in every thing that does not soar above a certain height is usually very sensible. For the sublime or the pathetic he had neither soul nor ear to comprehend them. Nothing can be more unworthy of the mighty theme, than his way of treating Milton— except his superficial notes on Shakespear. From his praise of Pope's Homer as *translation*, his significant insinuation that the best scholars have more pleasure in reading the "blind old man" so perverted, (the translation is a good *English* poem, *but*—) than in his own matchless verse, and his absurd remarks on "Samson Agonistes" and Greek tragedy, I shrewdly suspect the Doctor was *no* Greek scholar at all. Nay, I am sure of it. Latin, I dare say he knew to a certain extent—prosody especially—but for deep learning, he had none. His talent is colloquial—ingenious argument, quick turns of thought, ready, pointed, witty repartee, clothed frequently in metaphor wh. looked like reasoning and does often bear a great abundance of maxims and of moralities, uttered with oracular solemnity, even when rather trivial—and withal a taste for elegance, tho' false and a lively but not a sublime fancy—these qualities aided by very considerable, and various literature and by an invincible confidence in himself and a most dogmatical superciliousness in regard to other people account for his prodigious celebrity in that day of *talkers* and *clubs* and will secure to him a certain (greatly curtailed, no doubt) reputation with posterity. But he is in his true element when he speaks of Dryden—Milton was above his pitch. He had not as much heart as head, and not as much soul as heart—and is *never* either very original or very profound.

*Tuesday April 26.* I passed the whole day until the dining hour here (3 o'clock) in the Museum: which was erected so lately at 1826. The ground floor is appropriated to the statuary. The picture gallery if I may use the expression is arranged on a new principle [Tieck[77] made the catalogue of the statues. I don't know whether he was consulted as to the disposition

---

74. Not "bourgeois gentilhomme," which diminishes the allusion to Molière's play.
75. Michel Ney, 1769–1815, Marshal of France.
76. Samuel Johnson, *The Lives of the English Poets; and a Criticism of Their Works* (Dublin, 1779).
77. Not "Teick": Christian Ludwig Tieck, 1776–1851, professor of the Academy of Arts in Berlin and director of the picture gallery: he was also a sculptor.

of the pictures]. They are divided into a great number of different compartments, intended to illustrate the diversity of schools and the progress of the art—Venetian, Flemish etc. In this point of view the gallery is extremely interesting to an amateur, and the collection very precious, as it is very extensive.

Dine by way of curiosity again at a *table d'hôte*. Only "mine host" and two guests—very respectable persons, one saluted the other (an aged person, with good manners) as *M. le Président*. Scanty and ordinary dinner—served from another room by a dish at a time.

After dinner Sir G. Hamilton sends me word he will call at 6.[78] Accordingly does so. Gives me a horrid account of old Sir Robert A's conduct as British ambassador. Servile court to *Carlistes*, studious avoidance of all liberals. Kept out of the way of our old friend Count Joseph de Baillet, Belgian envoy, who I know counted very much on Sir Robert's countenance in a strange place. Regrets Brussells, wh. he thinks, as I do, the pleasantest residence after Paris. Berlin dull. One reception a year and only one at Court—after that, all over. Fortunately he (Sir G.) was in time for that.

Takes me to the King Street *Theatre*—where he sets me down. They give the Barber of Seville and a *Cantatrice* from Vienna plays Rosina. Detestable exhibition—which sends me home in the course of an hour. N.B. The spectacle begins here at 6 and ends at 9. Dine at 2 and *sic de similibus*.

Took up Balzac's "Pere Goriot" this afternoon and found it so interesting, that I laid it down with regret and hasten to resume it: read till 11.[79]

*Wednesday April 27*. Before I am out of my bed-room, some one knocks at the door. I open it and see a little *laquais* in livery who asks me if I be "Herr Legaré" and on receiving the right answer proceeds to invite me, in the name of M. Ancillon[80] (to whom I had a letter from my friend d'Arnin, Prussian minister at Brussells) to dine with him to-day at *3*. The *hour*, as well as the *form* of the invitation (verbal and without *carte de visite*) rather surprise me; but heard from Hamilton yesterday that the old minister (he is past 70) is rather an *original* and so, after asking the boy if he is sure of the hour and the occasion, I accept.

On coming out receive an invitation from Count Jos. de Baillet to dine on Sunday or Monday, as may best suit my convenience, he being engaged every day till then. My arrangements compel me to be off before Sunday and so I have to decline. I express to M. de Baillet the very sincere regret with which this necessity inspires me and the strongest wish to see him in person. Sends me word he will call at ½ past 11.

78. Sir George Baillie Hamilton, 1799–1850, British secretary in Brussels.
79. Honoré de Balzac, *Le père Goriot* (Paris, 1835).
80. Johann Peter Friedrich Ancillon, 1767–1837, a philosopher and Prussian minister of foreign affairs.

*Berlin 27 April.* Presently after Hamilton writes me a note informing me that Lord William Russell to whom I was to have made a visit to-day, will be too much occupied with business (his courier goes) but requests I will dine with him *to-morrow en famille*, that he may have a better opportunity of making my acquaintance. I suspect a mistake of *to-morrow* for *to-day*.

This is a great religious *fête*, of some sort or other and I am curious to attend divine service in the Cathedral of this city but fear my arrangements will not permit it.

Before I go out M. de Baillet comes in. Expresses his regret that I cannot dine with him. It is his intention he says to return to Brussells at all events in the month of June. Wanted to go to Vienna in May, but requested by his Court to remain here. Supposes it is on acct. of the Duke of Orleans'[81] visit, which he thinks (as it *is*) quite an event: says the King of P.[82] has acted towards him (M. de B.) like a *parfait honnête homme*—having told him at his reception, that, of course, the Belgian revolution gave him great *pain*, but that it was now a *fait accompli* in which he had bound himself to acquiesce and would do so in good faith—adding that he would go further and say that if the whole controversy had not been already settled the fault was not the Belgian govt's—but the King of Holland's. I told him I was to dine at M. Ancillons: said he was glad to hear it, and had no doubt the old minister would wish to have my opinion on the state of affairs in Belgium: advertised me, therefore—after remarking that the whole policy of this government was cautious, and even timid, and directed to the preservation of the *status quo* to all events,—that they suspect the Belgian people of a propensity to France, which you *know*, says he, does not exist; should be glad if I would contribute to rectify this error. Tell him I shall not fail to do so if occasion serve especially as it were only telling a truth. Says the K. is determined to receive the French princes with all possible distinction—but that his sons—especially the Prince Royal—will do their part very much *à contre coeur*. Recommends to me by all means to visit Charlottensberg and not to miss seeing the Mausoleum of the Queen[83] and the statue of Her Majesty by a sculptor who had been her *valet* and whose talents for drawing etc. being accidentally revealed to her, she had him sent to Rome to study his art, where he became one of the greatest masters in it. *There* he executed this monumental statue of his Royal patroness after her death—a first rate likeness—which after many adventures (it

---

81. Ferdinand Philippe Louis Charles Henri, duc d'Orleans, 1810–1842, the son of Louis Phillippe, was on a visit to Berlin and Vienna in search of a wife: he found Princess Hélène of Mecklenberg.

82. Frederick William III, 1770–1840.

83. Sophie Charlotte, 1668–1705, wife to Frederik I of Prussia, sister of George I of England and friend to Leibnitz.

was captured by a barbary corsair and redeemed) at length arrived at its destination.

Hamilton by a note informs me the error I suspected in his invitation did in fact exist and that both he and Lord Wm. being engaged tomorrow, we must adjourn over our expected *symposium* for the present.

Go out to see the churches—the *Cathedral* first. Pretty church in Modern (and Protestant) style. Vaulted roof—pillars—the altar adorned by three pictures, a crucifix and two wax lights. Learn that the preservation of these ornaments was a part of the arrangement by wh. the govt. reconciled the differences of the Lutherans and the "reformed" and so that they exist in all the churches. Ascend the Belfry (not very high) whence under a perfectly clear sky, a fine view over the town. The great bell is 400 y. old and when rung, is made to discourse its music by rather a clumsy contrivance—one man above swings it, while another by its side catches the clapper as it comes with his hands and forces it into contact with the brass above, then lets it fall upon upon [sic] the lower side.

This church contains the monuments of the Margrave of Brandenburg who secularized his dominions at the Reformation, and of three of the Kings of Prussia—not the Great Frederick's who is buried at Potsdam. The royal pew is here in a gallery.

Went thence to the Old Church of St. Nicholas just before the service began. I could see thro' a glazed window from the corridor what existed or was passing within the church. Very antique affair built of brick. Service began at 2 with a hymn, sung principally by a choir in a gallery, with accompaniment of organ. After waiting a quarter of an hour, obliged to retire to dress for M. Ancillon's dinner at *3*. First put on boots according to our fashion at Brussells; but fearing lest there might be ladies and a different rule here and being an entire stranger—think it safer to go in shoes. Do so and repent, no womankind and everybody in boots. Arrived am trotted through several apartments *au premier* (including the dining room) to the *salon* of "His Excellency". Surprised at first sight of a stout, hale looking man whom I should have judged to be about 58 or 60, had I not been informed how much was to be added to that *chiffre*. Rises as I enter, receives me very politely and with an apology for having taken the liberty to invite me so unceremoniously, but that the multiplicity of his engagements made it necessary he should seize the first opportunity etc. etc. I tell him I am very fortunate in seeing him in a way that will enable me to see more of him etc. etc. There was a baron somebody, secretary of legation at Copenhagen, who was just about to return to his post—a professor Michelet of this University[84]—a young French painter from Metz (very clever and agreeable youth) a Mr.———the host and myself. I see

---

84. Karl Ludwig Michelet, 1801–1859, a disciple of Hegel.

Arnin has given him a very particular account of me: knows I am from the South, that I have read Schiller, study history laboriously and am an amateur of Greek literature. Talk of Belgium, in which I say almost all I have to say on that subject in a few words. M.A. remarks on the singularity of the fact of Belgium's coming out of the 20 years of French contact and domination, quite uncontaminated in religion. I tell him it was what had struck me most forcibly at first—that with all foreigners, I had been led to regard the Belgians as an inferior sort of French while, on the contrary, there was hardly any resemblance between them, even in Hainault and Brabant, and none at all in the Flemish country; and of a French party, some noisy individuals about Mons etc. constituted the whole. The K. of Holland had lost his throne by not seeing this palpable truth: he was haunted by the *idea* of a *réunion* (as it is called) with France, and in trying to counteract that imaginary tendency, wounded and revolted all the national sensibilities of this people, so singularly wedded to their usages and traditions—that they have made two revolutions, not to change, but to preserve them.

At dinner—a little tea table scarcely large enough to allow elbow room to the six guests. Service and furniture very simple and ordinary, a maitre-d'hotel and two other serving men. Nothing on the table but a plate of oranges, two of sugar plums of various sort and one other—about a centre piece—it was I really forget what. Very frugal dinner served from a side board. I began with the *Bouillie* (which was the second dish, the first I did not recognize and so, with my horror of all strangeness, did not touch) next asparagus—next a suprême de volaille, or volaille of some other sort aux champignon, followed by *fish*. Then *Hare*—with a cake and a jelly and there I think was the whole dinner. Good enough for me, however—who in eating as in other things, *video meliora proboque—deteriora sequor*.[85] Conversation of arts, music, literature; find M. Ancillon *very* agreeable, clever, enlightened and *well read*—with great douceur and kindness of manner, and an ardent *love* of talk—for I know my *own* by instinct. Speaks of Roman metaphysics as studiously and systematically unintelligible: contrasts it with the French style—repeating the "what is not clear, is not French"—hence the language of diplomacy—*beaucoup parler sans rien dire*—or saying much without appearing to make a mystery of it, say I etc. etc. But in solemn treaty perfectly precise.[86] Talk of history. I remark that to write or even to appreciate history, perfectly, one must have lived in the world and even been engaged in public affairs. M.A. assents, but the literary men, cry out against what so trenches upon the privileges of their caste. This leads to a long discussion of Herodotus, Sallust, Tacitus

---

85. Ovid, *Metamorphoses*, VII, lines 20–21; trans. I see and approve the better course; I follow the worse. The speaker is Medea.

86. "But . . . *precise,*" omitted in *Writings.*

and Jul. Caesar, and the Lord knows what. M.A. takes occasion to say to me, "M. d'Arnin tells me you cultivate Greek literature[87] a good deal". I answer, rather confused, as I always am, I know not why, when allusion is made to my studies of *that kind*—that I am a mere amateur and amuse myself in that way, in my leisure moments. Whereupon some one says he did not know people took an interest in Greek in America. I tell him, as much as anywhere else, except, perhaps, in Germany. But "England" says another. I am left to think, say I from all that I know of English scholarship that it is rather superficial. But see how they quote *Latin* in Parliament. Horace and Juvenal, I reply—some of the Augustan authors and their school books—and that too merely for rhetorical purposes—"to draw a moral or to point a tale"—nothing more. I have seen an excellent scholar bred in England, to whom Tacitus was Greek. Then a discussion of Tacitus' Latinity. I assert that every one accustomed only to the Latinity of the purest[88] aera, would be embarrassed at the first reading of the Historian and cite the "spatium exemplorum"[89] of the life of Agricola—a use of *exempla* that occurs else where in his works and no where in those of Cicero or any writer of the Augustan aera. Another discussion thereupon— "None speak English with purity in America." All things considered, with surprising purity, tho some provincialisms, many archaisms, and an almost universal tendency to a nasal twang—which I attribute in a good degree to the puritan habits of our ancestors and the *cant* of all sectarians—a thing remarked not only in our English fathers at home, but among Catholics in[90] devout orders, cloisters etc. Conversation turns on M. de Savigny, who, I regret to learn is not in Berlin, it being a vacation. M. Ancillon says] excellent as his works are, his lectures are still better; delivered with a charming ease, grace and clearness, and giving you the idea of a man who is quite above the subject he treats of, and makes a pastime of it. I tell him it is just the impression made on me by his famous History of the Roman Law in the Middle Ages.[91] Speak of his general doctrine, and that of the historical school, in opposition to *Abbé Sieyès'* constitution on mathematical or astronomical principles.[92] Profess myself of that school *hautement*. Say the merit of Tocqueville's book consists in his being the only foreigner, except Heeren,[93] who has seen that *republicanism*

---

87. "literature" omitted in *Writings*.
88. Not "Juvenal," an obvious nonsense as Juvenal was a contemporary of Tacitus.
89. Not "spatium exemplum": Tacitus, *Agricola*, 8.2; trans. room for setting glorious precedents; Legaré is correct that this usage occurs nowhere in Cicero.
90. "catholics in" omitted in *Writings*.
91. Savigny, *Geschichte der Römischen Rechts in Mittelalter* (Heidelberg, 1834): all six volumes are listed in the 1843 catalog of Legaré's library (p. 13).
92. Emmanuel Joseph Sieyès, 1748–1836, French revolutionary and constitutional theorist, author of *Qu'est ce que le Tiers État?* (1789).
93. Arnold H. L. Heeren, 1760–1842, the German historian.

is the primordial law and condition of American society, and that our revolution was merely external and confined to the question of sovereignty, and, chiefly, executive power; in short, that *tout ce qui est republique* has always been so,—brought with them by our founders,—and only what is *federal* is new. Much more said of this. Mention Elberfeldt, and tell him the impression it had made on me, that it resembled a flourishing American town. "I hear it looks like an English town." "More American," say I: "for after all, in English towns there are always some unwashed holes and corners, and filthy retreats of wretchedness, or rotting relics of the past,—whereas, with us, all is hope and vigor." "One might know you to be an American by this admiration of what is *new*," said one of my neighbors; "whereas many persons here admire a thing the more for an antique and ruinous air." "In its *place*, I reply, "a ruin is a fine thing,—on the Drachenfels, for instance,—mais il y en a tout partout en Europe; and it is as a rarity that I admire a creation like Elberfeldt, which has more *avenir* than *past* in it, and reminds you that, after all, the human race have not seen their *best* days,—as Cicero said of Catiline's gang,—*vixere*."[94] The minister seizes the idea and heartily assents, parrying the ill-aimed blows of my not very quick-sighted adversary. Apropos of ruins, speak of the chateau of Heidelberg, to which I object that it is only of yesterday; and a ruin, like *nobility*, ought to be enveloped in the *nuit des temps*. An *artificial* ruin is as bad as what I have heard called, in America, "a *made* gentleman." Speak of the prejudice against African blood in the United States. At 5 take leave. M. Ancillon regrets my stay is so short, and apologises again for having invited me so unceremoniously. Mr. Wheaton spoken of with great respect, and said by the secretary of legation to have been very much regretted there,—his wife, too,—is she a distinguished woman, says M.A. "Qui. . . . .c'est une *bonne* femme." That is too true, thinks I.[95]

It is worth recording that, on my mentioning what Lord Brougham had said in my presence, viz: that Talleyrand, Roederer and Cambacères,[96] all agreed Sieyès was the *veritable homme du siècle*,—M.A. cried

94. When Cicero reported to the Romans the execution of the Catilinarian conspirators, it was his shortest speech: *vixere* or *vixerunt*, "They have lived." See Plutarch, *Cicero*, 22.2

95. Henry Wheaton, 1785-1848, then American chargé d'affaires in Berlin (which makes this reference puzzling); he had been reporter to the U.S. Supreme Court. A letter by Lord William Russell casts some light on the matter of Mrs. Wheaton: "I found the wisest of my colleagues to be Wheaton the Yankee. He has established his family at Paris & goes to visit them without ever asking leave. He lives here in a small lodging, keeps no carriage, never gives a glass of water to a soul, & dines with everybody. Everybody likes him, respects him & speaks well of him. He pockets his *quattrini* & laughs at the world. This fine man then I shall take as my model & grow rich & wise myself": Russell to Lady William Russell [Berlin, 1839], quoted in Georgina Blakiston, *Lord William Russell and His Wife, 1815-1846* (London, 1972), p. 420.

96. Legaré probably met Brougham in Edinburgh in 1818 or 1819, or possibly in London in the early 1830s; Jean Jacques Regis de Cambacérès, 1753-1824, consul with Sieyès under Napoleon; Pierre Louis Roederer, 1754-1835, French senator.

out against it; and, speaking of his famous pamphlet, *Qu'est ce que le Tiers?* he and the professor assert that somebody (I forget whom) suggested to him the manner of putting the question. What has the Tiers been? nothing. What is it like? what ought it and is it to be? *every thing.* Which is the sum and substance of the whole work.

This dinner and conversation make me very much regret the necessity of leaving Berlin so soon. I leave M. Ancillon with a profound respect for his abilities, and a great prepossession in favor of his person and society, although he is, perhaps, somewhat ambitious in conversation. After dinner to Charlottensberg, about a league from the fine Brandenburg gate. You pass through a wood like the Bois de Boulogne, before you arrive at the palace and its garden, and which is traversed by the Spree. There is a château (not very magnificent)—a hot-house of great length, filled with exotics. Then there are groves now resounding with voices of nightingales on every bough; and that sweet stream flowing quietly through these tranquil recesses; and the mausoleum of the queen—but, to my eternal mortification, I find that I am debarred from all access to the interior, for want of some precautionary arrangement which I wist not of, and so have not made. The loss is irreparable,—yet the depth of the enjoyment which I find in my hour's ramble in these shades, under such a delicious evening sky, reconciles me to the disappointment, and I return to my hotel at 8 in peace. *C'est tout dire.* There are many people, it being a *fête* day, and remark that one sees, in all places of public resort, individuals obviously of the lowest order,—that is, of the shabbiest appearance. At the picture-gallery, the other day, I saw a fellow so dirty and ragged, that I am sure a French sentinel would have driven him away with scorn from the gates of the Tuilleries, the very day after the revolution of 1830.

Leipsic, 29th April, 8 o'clock, P.M.    I arrived here just now, and, after applying unsuccessfully for lodgings at two hotels, (the town is swarming for the fair,) I establish myself for the night at a rather shabby, dirty-looking place, called the Stadt-Wien.

I passed yesterday at Berlin, which I left after 10 in the evening, [in a very unedifying manner. Indeed I did nothing that I can remember but lounge for an hour in the picture gallery and pay and receive some visits. I called on Hamilton at his lodgings, which are very comfortably and prettily fitted up—he is *dans ses meubles* and was not a little proud of having the opportunity of showing them to one who will report on them at Brussells.

After dinner Lord Wm. Russell calls: find him quiet, unaffected and gentlemanlike—very English and so a little stiff and angular. Tells me M. Ancillon has the name of being rather insincere in his relations with the *corps diplomatique,* tho' he is sure the imputation is not just—the frequent vacillations and retractations that have occasioned it, being caused by the absence of firmness, or consistency, or something else in the Prussian govt., whatever that is and wherever it may reside—a thing, it seems, not easy to decide. The King is getting old and loves repose, and so is not unwilling to be freed as much as possible from the troubles of business— tho' his great memory he is very firm—and positive. After about a half hour's conversation his lordship retires with regrets etc.

Count de Baillet succeeds him and stays with me until I am getting ready to set out.

The night is perfectly bright with moonlight and fair weather—but it is excessively cold—my servant says *freezing*.

At ½ past 8 I arrive at *Wittenberg*, and alight at the *London* tavern, near the church in which are the graves and pictures of Luther and Melancthon.[97] After shaving and drinking tea, I go out upon the to me most interesting excursion of the sort I ever made accompanied by, beyond all comparison, the most singular cicerone that ever conducted me. He was an excessively small man—much shorter than myself—with a woebegone countenance, such I thought as beseemeth a sexton carries in advance of the rest of the body at an angle of 45 from the back, while, by some means natural or artificial, but quite incomprehensible to me, he took the longest and made the most rapid strides imaginable. He spoke to me at first in German, but finding that he seemed to be quite *au fait* in reading the Latin inscriptions on the tombs of the reformers, I asked him in that language if he spoke it. He answered me immediately in the affirmative and went off full gallop in a style worthy of Melancthon himself and which quite surprised me—to such a degree, indeed, that I took the liberty of asking him who he was, τίς πόθεν εἶ etc.[98] He told me he was a *man of letters*, it being found necessary that the *aedituus* of those interesting edifices should be so. He was charmed to find how perfectly intelligible my pronunciation was to him—which he said was very often not the case. To increase his surprise, I told him I was an American legationem apud Belgarum regem nunc obiens—but his fluency was much greater than mine, from frequent practice, and what is still more remarkable he spoke generally with the greatest purity, and with a certain swelling, rhetorical pomp of style, like the prefaces and dedications of the 16th and 17th cent. When I complimented him, he declined the honor with such phrases of studied humility, and such acknowledgments of the *singularis tua humanitas vir amplissime, et doctissime*, etc.[99] However, like other Germans, he slights quantity. e.g.

97. Philip Melanchthon, 1497–1560, born Schwarzed, the Lutheran religious leader; it will be observed that Legaré consistently misspelled the name.
98. Trans. Who are you and from what place? A Homeric greeting, although Legaré puts it into Attic; cf. *Odyssey*, I, line 170.
99. Trans. Your extraordinary courtesy, most eminent and learned sir. The comma should come after "humanitas."

*occurret*—with the *second* short. But for Luther himself (of whom my learned beadle is a prodigious enthusiast) you see his likeness at all ages here—up to the very article of death. The ardent apostle! the invincible champion! the audacious iconoclast! the sage and serious reformer of morals and opinion! you see it all in his robust form, his capacious head, his square broad visage, with firm-set under jaw in that deep, grave countenance—and fixed look—etc. The inscription on his tomb stone in the church (a little oblong slab in the pavement, covered with a sort of trap door) merely records the day of his birth and that of his death. Melancthon's the same. After my curiosity had been satisfied here we proceeded to the monastic building in which the famous Doctor lived and lectured. There is a table at which he sat—an old, worm-eaten wooden slab bearing its experience upon its face—then the professor's pulpit from which he delivered his productions. Likenesses of the two princes of Saxony, Fredk. and *John*[100] accompany those of Luther and Melancthon, both here and at the church. They are remarkable for the same expression of deep, solemn earnestness, befitting men that had a conviction and a conviction to fight for. I told my little mystagogue that standing in that room I felt that I was *in templo quodammodo orbis terrarum libertatis*[101]—at the wh. he was not a little pleased. In the first room are the letters *Petr.* in chalk (I think) an autograph of Peter the Great—another mighty founder. To preserve it, it has been covered with glass. Here is a book in which pilgrims inscribe their names. I added to it mine. The first name in the first volume is that of the present King of Prussia written with his own hand. That reminds me that Wittenberg is no longer Saxon and that the ashes of Luther lie in what may be called foreign ground. To be sure the King of Saxony is a Catholic and perhaps it is fit that the chief of Protestant Germany should have the guardianship of its most precious and sacred shines. Potsdam—Frederick—Voltaire—Wittenberg, the unfortunate Elector, Luther—What a contrast.]

---

100. Frederick III, 1463–1525, and John, 1467–1532.
101. Trans. In the temple, so to speak, of the world's liberty.

# 4.

## Thomas Roderick Dew

## "Republicanism and Literature"[1]

Thomas Dew stood crucially at the transition between the Enlightenment of Jefferson and the modernized conservatism of Beverley Tucker. Perhaps because his nuances were thus eclectic, he became the most influential social philosopher, certainly of Virginia, possibly of the South. And he did it from an academic position. Though deeply interested in politics and influence, he declined the gift of office, preferring the propagation of thought and believing in the utility of theory.[2] He wrote in 1829 that "theory and practice can never be adverse to one another: that sound theory is indispensably necessary to successful practice. . . . when men arise in deliberative bodies, and thank their God they are no *political economists, no theorists*, they in a short time shew by their unwarrantable generalizations, how much they stand in need of that sound theory against which their philippics are directed."[3] Dew was the ideologist of Virginia, as Calhoun was to South Carolina, and could only have agreed when the senator spoke in 1838 in praise of those "powers of analysis and generalization, those higher faculties of the mind (called metaphysical by those who do not possess them) which decompose and resolve into their elements the complex masses of ideas that exist in the world of mind . . . and without which those deep and hidden causes which are in constant action, and producing such mighty changes in the condition of society, would operate unseen and undetected."[4]

1. Thomas Roderick Dew, "On the Influence of the Federative Republican System of Government upon Literature and the Development of Character," *SLM* 2 (December 1836): 261–82.
2. Stephen Mansfield, "Thomas Roderick Dew at William and Mary," *VMHB* 75 (October 1967): 434.
3. Dew, *Lectures on the Restrictive System* (Richmond, 1829), p. 194.
4. "Speech on the Independent Treasury Bill, in reply to Mr. Clay, delivered in the Senate, March 10th, 1838," in *The Works of John C. Calhoun*, ed. Richard K. Crallé (New York, 1853), 3: 274.

Dew was the second of the six sons and four daughters of Thomas Dew, planter in and founder of Dewsville, Virginia.[5] He was born in 1802. All his life he was to be associated with the College of William and Mary: as graduate in 1820, as professor of Civil Law in 1827 and as president in 1836. He was particularly rooted in Williamsburg and in Virginia, though he did travel twice to Europe: for two years after his graduation, and to Paris in 1846 upon his marriage trip, when he was taken ill with consumption and died. It was once thought that he spent time at a German university. But this seems doubtful. He could not speak or read the language. He did, it was true, have an interest in German thought, in Friedrich von Schlegel, Niebuhr, and Heeren, but the absorption was scanty compared to his awareness of American, English, and French thought.[6] His 1829 *Lectures on the Restrictive System*, an adept Ricardian defence of free-trade doctrine, show him using: of the Americans, Jefferson, Thomas Cooper, John McVickar (Ricardo's chief American disciple), Daniel Raymond, and George McDuffie; of the British, Adam Smith, James Mill, Ricardo, James McCulloch (the main Scottish propagator of both Ricardo and Smith), Malthus, Robert Owen, Dugald Stewart, Thomas Brown, Burke, Hume, Southey, and Alison; of the French, Quesnay, Say, Diderot, and Constant; of the Swiss, Sismondi. This was typical of Dew, the eclectic mixer of eighteenth- and nineteenth-century thought, the mediator. It was not so evident in his most famous production, the "Review of the Debate in the Virginia Legislature, 1831–32," which directed and ratified the drift in Virginian thought from vague antislavery to powerful proslavery sentiment. Later, as simply "Dew on Slavery," it found even wider celebrity as one of the essays in *The Proslavery Argument*.[7] But it is an eclecticism clear in this essay upon the relationship between republicanism and literature, intended as an oration before the Virginia Historical and Philosophical Society in 1836, though never delivered.

Many of the themes of the piece are very eighteenth century and Virginian. Its emphasis upon the radical Whig tradition of republicanism, its invocations of Locke, Hampden, and Sidney, its derogations of Hobbes and Filmer would not have been out of place in the discourse of Jefferson. James Madison would have smiled to read,

---

5. H. B. Gresham, "Dewsville and Providence," *VMHB* 46 (April 1938): 112–15.
6. Mansfield, "Dew," pp. 429–30, 437.
7. *The Proslavery Argument* (Philadelphia, 1853), pp. 287–490.

if he had lived a few more months, Dew's plundering of the essays of David Hume. The anti-monarchical tone, the deprecation of medievalism and scholasticism are themes that the Enlightenment in England transmitted to a receptive Virginia, and lived to see confirmed in the ideology of the American Revolution. Most of all, Dew thinks here with traces of the eighteenth century's faith in mechanism, the belief that one can design a political structure that will induce liberty, morality, and lucid thought.

But Dew was also a nineteenth-century man, one of its molders in the South. Un-Jeffersonian is the insistence that slavery and republicanism are natural allies in the maintenance of social and individual liberty. "Let us cherish this institution which has been built up by no sin of ours—let us cleave to it as the ark of our safety. Expediency, morality and religion alike, alike demand its continuance; and perhaps I would not hazard too much in the prediction, that the day will come when the whole confederacy will regard it as the sheet anchor of our country's liberty." But most nineteenth century is Dew's worrying of the problem of national literatures. He had read Madame de Staël, Sismondi, Schlegel, and Chateaubriand and absorbed their sense of the historical organism called a nation. How that could be mated with the federal system, both national and yet not, tending to consolidation and yet resisting, was Dew's major problem. His resolution, that literature could and should flourish in the cracks of federalism, in the South or in the individual states, was an answer with great influence and no little ingenuity.

MR. President and Gentlemen of the Society,

I have consented to appear before you this evening with feelings of the deepest solicitude—a solicitude which has been increased by my knowledge of the ability and eloquence of the gentleman who was first chosen by you to perform this task, and by the fact that this is the first time that circumstances have permitted my attendance on your sessions, though early admitted by the kindness of your body to the honor of membership.

The subject upon which I propose to address you is one which I hope will not be considered as inappropriate to the occasion. I shall endeavor to present to your view some of the most important effects which the Federative Republican System of government is calculated to produce on the progress of literature and on the development of individual and national character.

When we cast a glance at the nations of the earth and contemplate their character, and that of the individuals who compose them, we are amazed at the almost endless variety which such a prospect presents to our view. We perceive the most marked differences, not only between the savage and civilized nations, but between the civilized themselves—not only between different races of different physical organizations, but between the same races—not only between nations situated at immense distances from each other, but among those enjoying the same climate, and inhabiting the same region. How marked the difference, for example, between the nations of India and those of Europe—how different the citizen who merely vegetates under the still silent crushing despotisms of the East, from that restless, bustling, energetic being who lives under the limited monarchies and republics of the West! And again, what great differences do we find among the latter themselves! What differences do we observe between the French and the English, the Germans and the Spaniards, the Swiss and the Italians! How often does the whole moral nature of man seem to change, by crossing a range of mountains, passing a frontier stream, or even an imaginary line! "The Languedocians and Gascons," says Hume, "are the gayest people in France; but whenever you pass the Pyrenees you are among Spaniards." "Athens and Thebes were but a short day's journey from each other; though the Athenians were as remarkable for ingenuity, politeness and gaiety, as the Thebans for dulness, rusticity, and a phlegmatic temper."[8]

There is no subject more worthy the attention of the philosopher and the historian, than a consideration of the causes which thus influence the moral destiny, and determine the character of nations and individuals. Among the generating causes of national differences, none exert so powerful, so irresistible an influence as Religion and Government; and of these two potent engines in the formation of character, it may be affirmed, that if the former be sometimes, under the operation of peculiar circumstances, more powerful and overwhelming, directing for a season the spirit of the age and overcoming every resistance to its progress, the latter is much more constant and universal in its action, and mainly contributes to the formation of that permanent national character which lasts through ages.

Of all the governments which have ever been established, it may per-

---

8. "Of National Characters," in *The Philosophical Works of David Hume* (Edinburgh, 1826), 3:232, 231–32. It is interesting that there is, in this same essay (p. 236), a passage upon the inferiority of blacks.

haps be affirmed, that ours, if the most complicate in structure, is certainly the most beautiful in theory, correcting by the principle of representation, and a proper system of responsibility, the wild extravagances and the capricious levities of the unbalanced democracies of antiquity. Ours is surely the system, which, if administered in the pure spirit of that patriotism and freedom which erected it, holds out to the philanthropists and the friends of liberty throughout the world, the fairest promise of a successful solution of the great problem of free government. Ours is indeed the great experiment of the eighteenth century—to it the eyes of all, friends and foes, are now directed, and upon its result depends perhaps the cause of liberty throughout the civilized world. In the meantime it well behooves us all to hope for the best, and never to despair of the republic. Let me then proceed to inquire into some of the most marked effects which our peculiar system of government is likely to produce, in the progress of time, upon literature and the development of character.

Some have maintained the opinion that the monarchical form of government is better calculated to foster and encourage every species of literature than the republican, and consequently that the institutions of the United States would prove unfavorable to the growth and progress of literature. This opinion seems to be based upon the supposition that a king and aristocracy are necessary for the support and patronage of a literary class. I will briefly explain my views on this point, and then proceed to the consideration of that peculiar influence which our state or federative system of government will, in all probability, exert over the character and literature of our inhabitants. It is this latter view which I wish mainly to present this evening—it is this view which has been neglected or misunderstood in almost all the speculations which I have seen upon the character and influence of our institutions.

In the first place, it has been affirmed that republics are too economical—too niggardly in their expenditures, to afford that salutary and efficient patronage necessary to the growth of literature. To this I would answer, first, that this argument takes for granted that the literature of a nation advances or recedes in proportion to the pecuniary wages which it earns. Now, although I do not say with Dr. Goldsmith, that the man who draws his pen to take a purse, no more deserves to have it, than the man who draws his pistol for the same purpose,[9] yet I may safely assert, that of the motives which operate on the literary man—the love of fame, the desire to be useful, and the love of money—the former, in the great majority of cases, exerts an infinitely more powerful influence than the latter. And if I shall be able to show, as I hope to do in the sequel, that the

---

9. "An Enquiry into the Present State of Polite Learning," in *Collected Works of Oliver Goldsmith*, ed. A. Friedman (Oxford, 1966), 1:310.

republican form of government is the one which is best calculated to stimulate these great passions of our nature and throw into action all the energies of man, then must we acknowledge its superiority, even in a literary point of view.

But even supposing that the progress of literature depends directly upon the amount of pecuniary patronage which it can command, it by no means follows that it will flourish most under a monarchical government. For granting that this kind of government may have the ability to patronise, it is by no means certain that it will always possess the will to do so. Augustus and his Maecenas may lavish to day the imperial treasures upon literature, but Tiberius and Sejanus may starve and proscribe it to-morrow. That which depends upon the will of one man must ever be unsteady and uncertain. It is much easier to predict the conduct of a multitude—of a whole nation—than of one individual. The support then which monarchs can be expected to yield to learning, must necessarily be extremely capricious and fluctuating. It is not however by sudden starts and violent impulses, that a sound, solid, wholesome literature can be created. Ages must conspire to the formation of such a literature. Constantine the Great, seated on the throne of the Eastern Empire, with all the resources of the Roman world at his command, could not awaken the slumbering genius of a degenerate race, nor revive the decaying arts of the ancient empire. The literature of his reign, with all the patronage he could bestow upon it, did but too nearly resemble those gorgeous piles, which his pride and vanity caused to be erected in his *own* imperial city, composed of the ruins of so many of the splendid monuments of antiquity.

Not only, however, is the support a capricious and uncertain one which a monarchy is calculated to yield to literature, but there are only certain departments of learning, and those by no means the most important, which such a government can ever be expected cordially to foster. Monarchs may patronise the fine arts and light literature—they may encourage the mathematical and physical sciences, but they can rarely feel a deep interest in the promotion of correct and orthodox moral, political and theological knowledge, which is, at the same time, much the most important and most difficult department of literature. The great law of self-preservation prompts us to war on every thing which threatens our interest and happiness. Moral and political philosophy has too often aimed its logic at the throne, and questioned the title of the monarch, ever to be a favorite with rulers. Hence, while even the absolute despot may encourage the arts, light literature and the physical and mathematical sciences, he dares not unbind the fetters of the mind in the region of politics, morals and religion. He can but tremble at that bold spirit of inquiry which may be aroused on those subjects—which dares to advance to the throne itself and loosen even the foundations on which it is erected. Napoleon Bonaparte, in the plentitude of his power, could give the utmost encouragement to all those departments of learning, whose principles could not be arrayed against despotism. In these departments he delighted to behold the genius and talent of the country. In the provinces and in the capital he called to the physical and mathematical chairs of his colleges, his universities and his polytechnic schools, some of the most splendid lecturers of the age; but selfishness forbade him to tolerate a free and manly spirit of inquiry in morals and politics, and he whose armies had deluged Europe with blood, whose name was a terror and whose word was a law unto nations, could not feel secure upon his throne while such men as Cousin[10] were illustrating the nineteenth century by the splendor of their professorial eloquence, before the youth of France, or such writers as De Stael were making their animated appeals to the nation, in behalf of liberty of thought, and freedom of action. It is impossible, without full freedom of thought, and a single eye to truth and usefulness, that the scientific investigator, no matter how great his genius may be, can unravel the difficulties of moral and political philosophy. The very patronage of the throne enthrals his intellect, and his fears or his avarice tempt him to desert the cause of truth and humanity.

> "Thus trammell'd, thus condemn'd to flattery's trebles,
> He toils through all, still trembling to be wrong:
> For fear some noble thoughts like heavenly rebels
> Should rise up in high treason to his brain,
> He sings as the Athenean spoke, with pebbles
> In's mouth, lest truth should stammer through his strain."[11]

If we look even to those epochs under monarchical governments, which have been designated by the high sounding title of the golden ages of literature, we shall observe a full exemplification of the remarks which I have made on this subject. Let us take the Augustan age itself. Under the patronage of the first of the Roman Emperors we find, it is true, the arts and light literature rising to a pitch which perhaps they had not reached under the republic. After the death of Brutus the world of letters experienced a revolution almost as great as that of the political world. The literature of the Augustan age is distinguished by that tone and spirit which mark the downfall of liberty, and the consequent thraldom of the mind. The bold and manly voice of eloquence was hushed. The high and lofty spirit of the republic was tamed down to a sickly and disgusting servility. The age of poetry came when that of eloquence and philosophy was past; and Virgil and Horace and Propertius, flattered, courted and enriched by an artful prince and an elegant courtier, could consent to sing the syco-

---

10. Victor Cousin, 1792–1867, the French eclectic philosopher.
11. Byron, "The Prophecy of Dante," canto III, lines 92–97.

phantic praises of the monarch who had signed the proscriptions of the triumvirate, and rivetted a despotism on his country.

But the men who most adorned the various departments of learning during the long reign of Augustus, were born in the last days of the republic. They saw what the glory of the commonwealth had been—they beheld with their own eyes the greatness of their country, and they had inhaled in their youth the breath of freedom. No Roman writer, for example, excels the Lyric Bard in true feeling and sympathy for heroic greatness. We ever behold through the medium of his writings—even the gayest—a deep rooted sorrow locked up in his bosom, for the subversion of the liberties of the commonwealth. "On every occasion we can see the inspiring flame of patriotism and freedom breaking through that mist of levity in which his poetry is involved." "He constrained his inclinations," says Schlegel, "and endeavored to write like a royalist, but in spite of himself he is still manifestly a republican and a Roman."[12]

"In the last years of Augustus," says the same writer, "the younger generation who were born, or at least grew up to manhood, after the commencement of the monarchy, were altogether different. We can already perceive the symptoms of declining taste—in Ovid particularly, who is overrun with an unhealthy superfluity of fancy, and a sentimental effeminacy of expression."[13] Even History itself, in which the Romans so far excelled, yielded to the corrupting influence of the Caesars. Tacitus concluded the long series of splendid and vigorous writers, and he grew up and was educated under the comparatively happy reigns of Vespasian and Titus, and wrote under the mild government of Nerva. Unnatural pomp and extravagance of expression seem, strange as it may appear, to be the necessary results of social and political degradation. And it is curious indeed to behold among the writers under the first Caesars, the extraordinary compounds which genius can produce, when impelled on the one hand by the all-powerful and stimulating love of liberty, and vivid glimpses of the real dignity of human nature, while checked and subdued on the other by the fear of arbitrary power. Take Lucan for an example. "In him we find the most outrageously republican feelings making their chosen abode in the breast of a wealthy and luxurious courtier of Nero. It excites surprise and even disgust, to observe how he stoops to flatter that disgusting tyrant, in expressions the meanness of which amounts to a crime, and then in the next page, exalts Cato above the Gods themselves, and speaks

---

12. Friedrich von Schlegel, *Lectures on the History of Literature, Ancient and Modern* (Edinburgh, 1818), 1:144. [Horace fought under Brutus and Cassius, on the side of the Republic, at the battle of Philippi, and he was after the battle saved from the wreck of the republican army, and treated with great respect and kindness by Augustus and his minister Maecenas.]

13. Ibid., 1:151: "In the last years of Augustus" should precede "we can already perceive . . ."

of all the enemies of the first Caesar with an admiration that approaches to idolatry."[14]

Let us now look for an exemplification of the same great truths, to the reign of Louis the fourteenth, a reign which has been celebrated as the zenith of warlike and literary splendor—and here I borrow the language of Macintosh. "Talent seemed robbed of the conscious elevation, of the erect and manly port, which is its noblest associate and its surest indication. The mild purity of Fenelon, the lofty spirit of Bossuet, the masculine mind of Boileau, the sublime fervor of Corneille, were confounded by the contagion of ignominious and indiscriminate servility."[15] Purity, propriety and beauty of style, were indeed carried during this reign to a high pitch of perfection. The literature of this period was "the highest attainment of the imagination." An aristocratic society, such as that which adorned the court of Louis XIV, is particularly favorable to the delicacy and polish of style, the fascinations of wit and gaiety, and to all the decorations of an elegant imagination. No one has ever surpassed Racine, Fenelon, and Bossuet, in purity of style and elegance of language.

The literature of this age, however, as well asserted by Madame de Stael, was not a "philosophic power." "Sometimes indeed, authors were seen, like Achilles, to take up warlike weapons in the midst of frivolous employments, but, in general, books at that time did not treat upon subjects of *real* importance. Literary men retired to a distance from the active interests of life. An analysis of the principles of government, an examination into religious opinions, a just appreciation of men in power, every thing in short that could lead to any applicable result, was strictly forbidden them."[16] Hence, however perfect the compositions of this age in mere style and ornament, we find them sadly deficient in profundity of reflection and utility of purpose. The human mind during this period had not yet reached its proper elevation, because it was enthralled by arbitrary power. The succeeding, was one of more grandeur of thought, and consequently of a more bold, daring, and profound philosophy. In vain would we look over the annals of the age of Louix XIV, to find a parallel to Voltaire, Montesquieu, Rousseau and Raynal. And what, let me ask, had so soon produced this mighty difference in the philosophy of France? It surely could not be the patronage of that base, profligate, licentious libertine, who during the period of his unfortunate regency, loosened the very foundation of human virtue, polluted the morals of his country, and weakened or destroyed those dearest of ties which bind together in harmony, in happiness and in love,

---

14. Ibid.: "disgusting tyrant" should read "detestable tyrant."
15. *Vindiciae Gallicae*, in *The Miscellaneous Works of the Right Honourable Sir James Mackintosh* (London, 1846), 3:11.
16. Madame de Staël, *The Influence of Literature on Society* (Hartford, 1854), p. 64: "frivolous employments" should read "frivolous ornaments."

the whole social fabric. It could not surely be the patronage of a monarch who had been reared and educated in such a school as this. No! it was the new spirit which animated the age—the spirit of liberty—the spirit of free inquiry—the spirit of utility. It was this spirit which quickened and aroused the stagnant genius of the nation, and filled the soul with the *"aliquid immensum infinitumque,"*[17] which had in the days of antiquity inspired the eloquence of a Tully and the sublime vehemence of Demosthenes. It was this new spirit, and not the puny patronage of a monarch, that called forth those intellectual giants of their age, Voltaire, Montesquieu and Rousseau, who have traced out three different periods in the progress of reflection—and if I may borrow the language of De Stael, like the Gods of Olympus, have gone over the ground in three steps.[18] It was this new spirit in fine, which in spite of the influence of the monarch and his nobility, sapped the foundation of the throne and hastened on the awful crisis of revolution in that devoted country.

Thus do we see that it is only the lighter kinds of literature, and the physical and mathematical sciences, which the patronage of a monarch can be expected to foster. In those nobler and more useful branches of knowledge—moral, mental, religious, and political,—the patronage of the throne clips the wings of philosophy and arrests the growth of science and the progress of truth.[19]

So far from this particular species of literature flourishing most under the bounty and patronage of a monarch, we find, in almost every monarchy, the party arrayed against the government, at the same time the most talented and the most philosophical party. The remark is susceptible of still greater generalization. I may, perhaps, with truth assert that in every age and in every nation, the men who have arrayed themselves against the usurpations of government, whether monarchical or republican—the men who have arrayed themselves on the side of liberty, who have led on the forlorn hope against the aggressions of despotism, have been the men who against the patronage of power and wealth, have reared up those systems of philosophy that time cannot destroy—they are the men who have performed those noble achievements which most illustrate their country, and weave for it the chaplet of its glory—these are the men whose eloquence has shaken senates and animated nations. These are the men, who, whatever may be their destiny whilst they live, will ever be remem-

17. Trans. something immense and enormous: cf. Cicero, *In Verrem*, II, 3, 64.149.
18. De Staël, *Influence of Literature*, p. 66.
19. [In the great Austrian university established at Vienna, the Professor of Statistics is strictly forbidden to present to the view of his class any other statistics than those of Austria, lest this country should suffer by comparison with others. How limited must be the range of intellect on political subjects under such fatal restrictions as this, imposed by the narrow jealousy of arbitrary power!]

bered and honored by a grateful posterity. Where now are those writings which contend for *jure divino* rights and patriarchal power?—past and gone! The Filmers are forgotten, the Hobbes are despised—while the writings of Locke will live forever, and the memory of Sidney and Russell and Hampden will be cherished through all ages. What were the Grenvilles and the Norths in more recent times, when compared with Chatham, Burke, Fox and Sheridan, in England, or with the Washingtons, Franklins, Henrys, Jeffersons and Adamses of our own revolutionary crisis.[20] And thus would a review of the history of the world bear me out in the assertion, that in almost every age and country since the annals of history have become authentic, the opposition literature, in moral, political and religious philosophy has been purer, deeper, more vivifying and useful, than the sickly literature which has grown up under the shadow of the throne, though encouraged and stimulated by the smiles of power, and sustained and fostered by the lavish expenditure of exhaustless treasures.

The only additional remark which I shall make upon the general question of the relative influences exerted upon the progress of literature and the development of character, by the monarchical and republican forms of governments is, that in the former the aspirants to office and honors look upwards to the throne and the nobility, in the latter they look downwards to the people. This simple difference between the two governments is calculated to produce the most extensive and material consequences. In the first place, the kind of talent requisite for success under the two governments, is very different. Even Mr. Hume himself acknowledges, that, to be successful with the people, it is generally necessary for a man to make himself *useful* by his industry, capacity, or knowledge; to be prosperous under a monarchy, it is requisite to render himself *agreeable* by his wit, complaisance, or civility. "A strong genius succeeds best in republics: a refined taste in monarchies. And consequently the sciences are the more natural growth of the one, and the polite arts of the other."[21] We are told, that in France under the old monarchy, men did not expect to reach the elevated offices of government either by hard labor, close study, or real efficiency of character. A *bon mot*, some peculiar gracefulness, was frequently the occasion of the most rapid promotions; and these frequent ex-

---

20. Familiar except perhaps Sir Robert Filmer, d. 1653, the English royalist theorist whose writings Locke repudiated in the *Two Treatises on Government*; Algernon Sidney, 1622–1683, the Whig martyr whose *Discourses Concerning Government* (1698)were so influential in the American colonies; Lord William Russell, 1639–1683, was executed along with Sidney for a supposed participation in the Rye House Plot; George Grenville, 1712–1770, was responsible for the Stamp Act; and Lord North, 1732–1792, as prime minister (1770–1782) prosecuted the American War; Chatham, Burke, Fox, and Sheridan all had in common an opposition to British policy in North America.

21. "Of the Rise and Progress of the Arts and Sciences," in Hume, *Works*, 3:140.

amples, we are told, inspired a sort of careless philosophy, a confidence in fortune, and a contempt for studious exertions, which could only end in a sacrifice of utility to mere pleasure and elegance.

The fate of individuals under those circumstances is determined, not by their intrinsic worth or real talents, but by their capacity to please the monarch and his court. Poor Racine, we are told by St. Cimon, was banished forever from the royal sunshine in which he had so long basked, because in a moment of that absence of mind for which he was remarkable, he made an unlucky observation upon the writings of Scarron in presence of the king and Madame de Maintenon, which could never be forgotten or forgiven.[22] We all know that the Raleighs, Leicesters, Essexes, &c. under the energetic reign of Elizabeth, were much more indebted to their personal accomplishments and devoted and adulatory gallantries, for their rapid promotions, than to any real services which they had rendered, or extraordinary talents which they had displayed. And in the time of Queen Anne, it has been said that the scale was turned in favor of passive obedience and nonresistance, by the Duchess of Marlborough's gloves; and the ill humor of the Duchess caused the recall of Marlborough, which alone could have saved the kingdom of France from almost certain conquest at that eventful crisis.

Another consequence which almost necessarily follows from the difference just pointed out between the monarchical and republican forms of government, is, that the stimulus furnished by the former, both to thought and action, is much less universal in its operation that that furnished by the latter. In the republican form of government, the sovereignty of the people is the mainspring—the moving power of the whole political engine. This sovereignty pervades the whole nation, like the very atmosphere we breath—it reaches to the farthest, and binds the most distant together. In a well administered and well balanced republic, it matters not where our lot may be cast, whether in the north or the south, at the centre or on the confines, the action of the political machine is still made to reach us—to stimulate our energies and waken up our ambition. The people under this system become more enlightened and more energetic, because the exercise of sovereignty leads to reflection, and creates a demand for knowledge. Aspirants to office must study to become useful, intelligent and efficient, for by these attributes they will be the better enabled to win that popularity which may ensure the suffrages of those around them, so necessary to their attainment of political elevation—and thus does the republican system operate on all, and call into action the latent talent and energy of the country, no matter where they may exist.

In the monarchy, on the contrary, the moving spring of the whole ma-

---

22. *Historical Memoirs of the Duc de Saint-Simon*, ed. Lucy Norton (London, 1972), 1:124.

chinery lies at the centre—the virtual sovereignty of the nation reposes in the capital. The want of political rights and powers sinks the dignity of the people, stagnates the public mind, and torpifies all the energies of man. In such a body politic you may have action and life, and even greatness at the centre, whilst you have the torpor and lethargy of death itself at the extremities. The man who is born at a distance from the capital has no chance for elevation there. If he aspires to political distinction he must make a pilgrimage to the seat of government. He must travel up to court, where alone he can bask in the beams of the royal sunshine. How partial is the operation of such a system as this! How many noble intellects may pass undiscovered and undeveloped under its sway! How many noble achievements may be lost, for want of a proper opportunity to display them! And all this may happen while the monarch and his court are disposed to foster literature, to encourage talent, and to stimulate into action all the energies of the nation.[23]

But how debasing does this form of government become, when the monarch, either from policy or inclination, shuns the talent and virtue of the country, addresses himself to the lowest, the most vulgar and most selfish passions of man, and draws around him into the high places of the government men taken from the lowest and most despised functions of life. "Kings," says Burke, "are naturally lovers of low company; they are so elevated above all the rest of mankind that they must look upon all their subjects as on a level."[24] They are apt, unless they be wise men, to hate the talent and virtue of the country, and attach themselves to those vile instruments who will consent to flatter their caprices, pander to their low and grovelling pleasures, and offer up to them the disgusting incense of sycophantic fawning adulation. Every man of talent and virtue is an obstacle in the path of such a monarch as this—he holds up to his view a most hateful mirror. When such monarchs as these are on the throne, the government exercises the most withering influence on the intellect and virtue of the country. Science is dishonored and persecuted because she is virtuous, because she will consent to flatter neither the monarch on his throne nor his sycophantic courtier—she will consent to mingle in no degrading strife, nor does she bring up any reserve to the dishonest minister, either to swell his triumph or to break his fall. When men of rank thus sacrifice all ideas of dignity to an ambition without a useful and noble object, and

---

23. [Hence we see at once the error committed by the great author of the Decline and Fall of the Roman Empire, in the assertion, that the absolute monarchy would be the most desirable form of government in the world, if such men as Nerva, Trajan, and the Antonines could always be upon the throne.] Cf. Edward Gibbon, *The History of the Decline and Fall of the Roman Empire*, ed. J. B. Bury (London, 1896), 1:78.

24. "Speech, 11 February 1780, on the Economical Reform of the Civil and Other Establishments," in *The Works of the Right Honourable Edmund Burke*, ed. F. W. Raffety (Oxford, 1906), 2:363.

work with low instruments and for low ends, the whole composition becomes low and base. Whilst Tiberius surrenders himself into the keeping of so vile a being as Sejanus—whilst Nero is fiddling and dancing, and Commodus in the arena with the gladiators—all that is noble and great in the empire must retire into the shade and seek for safety in solitude and obscurity.

When Louis XI dismissed from the court those faithful nobles and distinguished citizens, who had stood by his father and saved the monarch and his throne in the hour of adversity, and filled their places with men taken from the lowest and meanest condition of life, with no other merit than that possessed by the eunuch guard of the Medio-Persian monarch, of adhering to the king, because despised by all the world besides, he conquered, for the time at least, the virtue, the chivalry, the real greatness of France. Well, then, may we say, in the emphatic language of England's most philosophic statesman, "Woe to the country which would madly and impiously reject the service of the talents and virtues, civil, military or religious, that are given to grace and to serve it; and would condemn to obscurity every thing formed to diffuse lustre and glory around a state. Woe to that country too, that considers a low education, a mean contracted view of things, a sordid, mercenary occupation, as a preferable title to command."[25]

But it may be asked, may not some of the effects which I have just described as flowing from monarchy, be produced under the republican form of government? To this I answer that almost all of them may be expected to be the result of one homogeneous republic, stretching over a great extent of territory, including a numerous population and a great diversity of interest; but, as such a government as this has been wisely provided against in our country at least, by a system of confederated republics, I will now proceed to the main object of my discourse this evening—to point out the peculiar influence which our federative system of government is calculated to produce upon literature and character.

And in the first place, supposing our system to continue as perfect in practice as it undoubtedly is in theory, a mere statistical exposé of its future condition in regard to numbers and wealth at no very distant period, is of itself sufficient to present to our view prospects of the most cheering and animating character. We have a territory extending over three millions of square miles, composed of soils of every variety and every degree of fertility, stretching almost from the tropics to the poles in one direction, and from the Atlantic to the Pacific in the other. We have spread sparsely over a portion of this immense territorial expanse, a population of fifteen millions, principally descended from that nation in Europe, which is at the

---

25. This is not Burke.

same time the most wealthy, the most powerful, the most enterprising, the most free, the most civilized, and perhaps the most moral, purely religious and intellectual nation, among all the great powers of Europe. This population, which has, so far, shown itself worthy of the immortal stock of ancestors from which it is descended, is rapidly advancing in numbers and in wealth. Our censuses have hitherto shown a duplication of our population, in periods of less time than twenty-five years. We will assume, however, this period in our calculation, and we shall find this elastic spring of population, (if we can only bind down the movements of the governments of our system within their prescribed orbits,) of itself, like the magic wand of the enchanter, or the marvellous lamp of Aladdin, capable of achieving all which may confer glory and power and distinction on nations. In a period of seventy-five years, which is but a short time in a nation's history, we shall have a population of one hundred and twenty millions of souls, and yet not so dense as the population of many of the states of Europe. We shall then have an empire, formed by mere internal development, as populous as that of Rome and much more wealthy, speaking all the same language, and living under the same or similar institutions.

Let us then for a moment contemplate the inspiring influence which the mere grandeur of such a theatre is calculated to produce on literature and character. Whether the author write for wealth or for fame, or for usefulness, he will have the most unbounded field open to his exertions. The law which secures the property in his productions throughout such as immense empire, will ensure the most unlimited pecuniary patronage to all that is valuable and great, a patronage beyond what kings and princes can furnish. And the most powerful stimulus will be applied to every noble and generous principle of his nature, by the simple reflection that complete success in his literary efforts will introduce him to the knowledge of millions, all of whom may be edified by his instruction, or made more happy by the enjoyment of that literary repast which he may spread before them.

Do we not read of the mighty influence produced upon mind and body in ancient Greece, by the assemblages at the Olympic games? It was the hope of winning the prizes before these assemblages which called forth energy and awakened genius. It was under the thrilling applauses of these bodies that Herodotus recited his prose, and Pindar his poetry. And what, let me ask, was the great idea which animated every Roman writer? It was the idea of *Rome* herself—of Rome so wonderful in her ancient manners and laws—so great even in her errors and crimes. It was this idea which was breathed from the lips of her orators and embalmed in her literature—it is this idea which stamps the character of independent dignity and grandeur on the page of her philosophy, her history and her poetry.

But what were the multitudes that could be assembled together in Elis, or the heterogeneous half civilized polyglot people of the Roman Empire, bound together by the strong arm of power and overawed by the presence of the legions, in comparison with the millions that will ere long spring up within the limits of our wide spread territory,—speaking the same language,—formed under similar institutions,—and impelled by the same inspiring spirit of independence?

Another advantage which it is proper to present, as growing out of that condition of our people, which a mere statistical exposé will exhibit, is the security furnished by the magnitude and resources of our country, and by the immense distance of all bodies politic of great power and ambition, from our borders, against foreign invasion, or foreign interference in domestic concerns. I shall not here dwell upon the consequent exemption of our country from those mighty engines of despotism, overgrown navies and armies, and the deleterious influence which these essentially anti-literary establishments exercise over the genius and energy of man. I shall merely briefly advert to some of the effects which this security of individuals and states against foreign aggression is calculated to produce on individual enterprise and state exertion.

Since the governments of the world have become more regular and stable, and the great expense of war has made even victory and conquest ruinous to nations, rulers are beginning to look to the development of the internal resources of their countries, more than to foreign conquest and national spoliations. The great system of internal improvement in all its branches, is without doubt one of the most powerfully efficient means which can be devised to hurry forward the accumulation of wealth, and speed on the progress of civilization. The canal and the rail road, the steam boat and the steam car, the water power and steam power, constitute in fact the great and characteristic powers of the nineteenth century—they are the mighty civilizers of the age in which we live. They bind together in harmony and concord the discordant interests of nations, and like the vascular system of the human frame, they produce a wholesome circulation, and a vivifying and stimulating action throughout the whole body politic.

These great improvements in our own country, with but few exceptions, and those well defined, ought to be executed solely by states and individuals. But neither states nor individuals would execute those necessary works, without security from interruption and invasion, and consequent security in the enjoyment of the profits which they might yield. What wealthy individual in our own state, for example, would erect a costly bridge across one of our rivers, or embark his capital in the construction of a canal or rail road, if foe or friend might blow up his bridge during the next year, or a war might interrupt trade, and perhaps a treaty of peace might cede the canal or rail way to a different state?

Of all the nations in Europe, England is the one which has been most exempt from foreign invasion, and we find in that country that individual enterprise has achieved more in the cause of internal improvement than in any other nation in Europe; and the prosperity and real greatness of England are no doubt due in a great measure to the energy and enterprise of her citizens. In the continental nations we find this constant liability to invasion every where paralyzing the enterprise of both individuals and states. One of the most skilful engineers of France tells us that in passing through some of the frontier provinces of that country, he every where beheld the most mournful evidences of the want of both national and individual enterprise, in miserable roads, in decayed or fallen bridges, in the absence of canals and turnpikes, of manufactures, commerce, and even of agriculture itself, in many almost deserted regions. Paris, the second city in Europe in point of numbers and wealth, and the capital of the nation hitherto most powerful on the continent, has not yet in this age of ardor and enterprise, constructed either a canal or rail road to the ocean, or even to any intermediate point. If our federative system contained within its borders a city thus wealthy and populous, and so well situated, can there be a doubt that it would long ere this have sent its rail roads and canals not only to the ocean, but in all probability to the Rhine and the Danube, to the Rhone, the Garonne, and the Mediterranean.

This spirit of improvement, under the hitherto benign protection of our government, is already abroad in the land. New York and Pennsylvania have already executed works which rival in splendor and grandeur the boasted monuments of Egypt, Rome or China, and far excell them in usefulness and profit. The states of the south and west too are moving on in the same noble career. And our own Virginia, the *Old Dominion*, has at last awakened from her inglorious repose, and is pushing forward with vigor her great central improvement, destined soon to pass the Blue Ridge and Alleghany ranges of mountains, and thus to realize the fable of antiquity, which represented the sea-gods as driving their herds to pasture on the mountains.

"Omne cum Proteus pecus egit altos
        Visere montes."[26]

One certain effect of our great systems of improvement must be the rearing up of large towns throughout our country. I know full well that great cities are cursed with great vices. The worst specimens of the human character, squalid poverty, gorgeous, thoughtless luxury, misery and anxiety, are all to be found in them. But we find, at the same time, the noblest and most virtuous specimens of our race on the same busy, bustling theatre. Mind is here brought into collision with mind—intellect whets up intellect—the energy of one stimulates the energy of another—and thus

26. Horace, *Carmina*, I, 2, line 7: trans. When Proteus [the Sea God] drove forth all his livestock to see the high mountains.

we find all the great improvements originate here. It is the cities which constitute the great moving power of society; the country population is much more tardy in its action, and thus becomes the regulator to the machinery. It is the cities which have hurried forward the great revolutions of modern times, "whether for weal or woe." It is the cities which have made the great improvements and inventions in mechanics and the arts. It is the great cities which have pushed every department of literature to the highest pitch of perfection. It is the great cities alone which can build up and sustain hospitals, asylums, dispensaries—which can gather together large and splendid libraries, form literary and philosophical associations, assemble together bands of literati, who stimulate and encourage each other. In fine, it is the large cities alone which can rear up and sustain a mere literary class. When there shall arise in this country, as there surely will, some eight or ten cities of the first magnitude, we shall then find the opprobrium which now attaches to us, of having no national literature, wiped away; and there are no doubt some branches of science which we are destined to carry to a pitch of perfection which can be reached no where else. Where, for example, can the great moral, political, and economical sciences be studied so successfully as here? And this leads me at once to the consideration of the operation of the state or federative system of government, which I regard as the most beautiful feature in our political system, and that which is calculated to produce the most beneficial influence both on the progress of science, and on the development of character.

It has been observed, under all great governments acting over wide spread empires, that both the arts and literature quickly come to a stand, and most generally begin to decline afterwards. In fact, Mr. Hume makes the bold assertion in his Essays, "that when the arts and sciences come to perfection in any state, from that moment they naturally or rather necessarily decline, and seldom or never revive in that nation where they formerly flourished."[27] His remark is certainly much more applicable to large monarchical governments than to such a system as ours. In large countries, with great national governments, there will be quickly formed in literature as perfect a despotism as exists in politics. Some few great geniuses will arise, explore certain departments of literature, earn an imperishable reputation, die, and bequeath to posterity in their writings a model ever after to be imitated, and for that very reason never to be excelled. And thus it is that certain standard authors establish their dominion in the world of letters, and impose a binding law on their successors, who, it has been well said, do nothing more than transpose the incidents, new-name the characters, and paraphrase the sentiments of their great prototypes.

27. "Of the Rise and Progress of the Arts and Sciences," in Hume, *Works*, 3:152.

It is known that under the Roman emperors, even as late as the time of Justinian, Virgil was called *the poet*, by way of distinction, throughout the western empire, while Homer received the same appellation in the eastern empire. These two poets were of undisputed authority to all their successors in epic poetry.

We are told that in the vast empire of China, speaking but one language, governed by one law, and consequently moulded into one dull homogeneous character, this literary despotism is still more marked. When the authority of a great teacher, like that of Confucius, is once established, the doctrine of passive obedience to such authority is just as certainly enforced upon succeeding literati as the same doctrine towards the monarch is enforced on the subject.[28] Now all this has a tendency to cramp genius, and paralyze literary effort.

The developing genius of the modern world was arrested in the career of invention at least, and the imagination was tamed down by the servile imitation of the ancients immediately after the revival of letters. And perhaps one of the greatest benefits conferred on learning by the reformation, consisted of the new impulse that was suddenly communicated to the human mind—an impulse that at once broke asunder the bonds which the literature of the ancient world had rivetted—set free the mind after directing it into a new career of inquiry and investigation, unshackled even by the Latin language, which had so long robbed the vernacular tongues of Europe of the honors justly due to them from the literati of the age.[29]

But not only do great writers in large nations establish their authority over their successors, and thus set bounds to the progress of literature, but they repress the genius of the country by discouraging those first intellectual efforts of young aspirants for fame, which appear insignificant by comparison with established models. Now in literature, as well as in the accumulation of wealth, the proverb is strictly true, that it is the first step which is the most difficult, "*c'est le premier pas qui coute.*" The timid and the modest, (and real genius is always modest,) are frequently deterred from appearing in a particular department of literature, because of the great distance at which their first efforts must fall in the rear of the

---

28. Cf. ibid., 3:136.

29. [I would not by any means be understood as advancing the opinion that the language and literature of the ancients have been always an impediment to the progress of modern literature. On the contrary, at the revival of letters, the moderns were an almost immeasureable distance in the rear of the ancients. Ancient literature then became a power, by which the moderns were at once elevated to the literary level of antiquity; but when once we had reached that point, all farther *exclusive* devotion to the learning and the language of antiquity became hurtful to the mind by the trammels which it imposed. The study of the classics will forever be useful and interesting to him who aspires to be a scholar. But it becomes injurious when we make it an exclusive study, and substitute the undefined and loose system or morality—the high sounding and empty philosophy of the ancients, for the purer morals and deeper learning of the moderns.]

standard authors who have preceded them. They are overawed and alarmed at the first step which it is necessary to take, and frequently recoil from the task, sinking back into the quiet obscurity of listlessness and mental inactivity—whereas, if a proper encouragement could have been furnished to their incipient labors, it would have cheered and animated them in their literary career, and finally conducted them to proud and exalted rank in the world of letters.

The splendor, profundity, and irresistible fascination of Shakspeare's plays, have perhaps deterred many a genius in England from writing plays. So Corneille and Racine have no doubt produced similar effects in France. Even the great names which I have mentioned, would have been overawed, if in the commencement of their career, they had been obliged to contend with their own more splendid productions. "If Moliere and Corneille," said Hume, "were to bring upon the stage at present their early productions which were formerly so well received, it would discourage the young poets to see the indifference and disdain of the public. The ignorance of the age alone could have given admission to the *'Prince of Tyre;'* but it is to that we owe *'The Moor.'* Had *'Every Man in his Humor'* been rejected, we had never seen *'Volpone.'*"[30]

Now there is no system of government which has ever been devised by man, better calculated to remove the withering and blighting influence of great names in literature, and at the same time to insure the full possession of all the great benefits which their labors can confer, than the federal system of republics—a system which, at the same time that it binds the states together in peace and harmony, leaves each one in the possession of a government of its own, with its sovereignty and liberty unimpaired. In such a condition as this, there is a wholesome circulation of literature from one state to another, without establishing, however, any thing like a dictatorship in the republic of letters. A salutary rivalry is generated; and a true and genuine patriotism, I must be allowed to assert, will always lead us to foster and stimulate genius, wherever we may perceive symptoms of its development, throughout the limits of that commonwealth to which we are attached. The soldier in the field may love the marshal, and feel an attachment to the grand army which has been so often led to conquest and glory; but I must confess that I admire more that warm, generous, and sympathetic attachment, which his heart feels for that small division and its officer with which he has been connected—for that little platoon in which his own name has been enrolled, and where his own little share of glory has been won.

---

30. "Of the Rise and Progress of the Arts and Sciences," in Hume, *Works,* 3:154: the reference is to works of Shakespeare and Ben Jonson.

The history of antiquity, and the history of the modern world, alike show that small independent contiguous states, speaking the same language, living under similar governments, actuated by similar impulses, and bound together by the ties of cordial sympathy and mutual welfare, are the most favorable for the promotion of literature and science—in fine, for the development of every thing that is great, noble, and useful. On such a theatre, the candidate for literary honor is not overawed by the fame of those who have won trophies in adjoining states. He looks to the commonwealth to which he is attached, for support and applause; and when his name begins to be known abroad, and his fame to spread, his horizon expands with the increasing elevation of his station, until it comprehends the whole system of homogeneous republics. In such a system as this, the literature of each state will be aided and stimulated by that of all the rest—it will draw from all the pure fountains in every quarter of the world, without being manacled and stifled by the absolute authority of any. In such a system as this, there is no *jure divino* right in science—there is no national prejudice fostered in a national literature; respect, and even veneration, will be paid in such a system to all true learning, wherever it may be found; but there will be no worship, no abject submission to literary dictators. And if such a people may fail to form a regular homogeneous national literature, they will perhaps for that very reason be enabled to carry each art and science, in the end, to a higher pitch of perfection than it could reach if trammelled by the binding laws imposed by an organized national literature.

Among the nations of the earth which have made any progress in civilization, we find from the operation of causes which it would be foreign from my object to explain, that Asia most abounds in great and populous empires. And it is precisely in this quarter of the globe that we find a most irresistible despotism in both government and literature. Europe is divided into smaller states, and in them we find more popular governments, and more profound literature. Of all the portions of Europe, Greece was anciently the most divided; but as long as those little states could preserve their freedom, they were by far the most successful cultivators, in the ancient world, of every art and every science. The literature of the little republics of Italy, during the middle ages, illustrates the same great principles; and the rapid progress of the little states of Germany, since the general pacification of Europe in 1815, in literary and philosophical research of every kind, proves likewise the truth of the remarks made above.

Germany was accused by Madame de Stael of having no national literature: but the German state system of government, though by no means equal to ours, bids fair to carry German literature beyond that of any other nation in Europe. Although the literati of these small states are not trammelled either by their own or foreign literature, yet there is no body of learned men in the world who profit more by all that is really good and great in the learning of their neighbors. Without any narrow prejudices, they go with eagerness in search of truth and beauty wherever they are to be found. Every literature in the world has been cultivated by the Germans. We are told that "Shakspeare and Homer occupy the loftiest station in the poetical Olympus, but there is space in it for all true singers out of every age and clime. Ferdusi, and the primeval mythologists of Hindostan, live in brotherly union with the troubadours and ancient story-tellers of the west. The wayward, mystic gloom of Calderon—the lurid fire of Dante—the auroral light of Tasso—the clear, icy glitter of Racine, all are acknowledged and reverenced."[31]

Of all modern literature, the German has the best, as well as the most translations. In 1827, there were three entire versions of Shakspeare, all admitted to be good, besides many that were partial, or considered inferior. How soon, let me ask, would the literature of Germany wane away, if all her little independent states were moulded into one consolidated empire, with a great central government in the capital?

But the most beneficial influence produced upon literature and character under the federative system of government, springs from the operation of the state governments themselves. We have seen that the monarchical government, in a large state, fails to stimulate learning and elicit great activity of character, because its influence does not pervade the whole body politic—while the centre may be properly acted on, the confines are in a state of inextricable languor. A great consolidated republican government, if such an one could exist, would be little better than a monarchy. The aspirants for the high offices in such a nation, would all look up to the government as the centre for promotion, and not to the people. The talent and ambition of the country would have to make the same weary pilgrimage here as in the monarchies—to travel up to court—to fawn upon and flatter the men whom fortune had thrown into the high palaces of the government. The stimulus which such a government could afford, must necessarily be of the most partial and capricious character. A system of state governments preserves the sovereignty unimpaired in every portion of the country; it carries the beneficial stimulus, which government itself is capable of applying to literature and character, to every division of the people. Under such governments as these, if properly regulated, and not overawed or corrupted by central power—it matters very little where a man's destiny may place him, whether he may be born on the borders of the Lakes, on the banks of the Mississippi, or even in future times on the

---

31. Mention of the Persian poet, Firdusi, is characteristic of Friedrich von Schlegel, but these are not his remarks.

distant shores of the Pacific—the sovereignty is with him—the action of the state and federal governments reaches him in his distant home as effectually as if he had been born in the federal metropolis, or on the banks of the Potomac, or the waters of the Chesapeake.

Under such a system as this, there is no one part more favored than the rest; but all are subjected to similar governments, and operated on by similar stimulants. In all other countries the term province is a term of reproach. Neibuhr tells us that in France the best book published in Marseilles or Bordeaux is hardly mentioned.[32] *C'est publie dans la province* is enough to consign the book at once to oblivion—so complete is the literary dictatorship of Paris over all France. In such a system as ours, we have no provinces; if the governments shall only move in their prescribed orbits, all will be principals, all will be heads—each member of the confederacy will stand on the same summit level with every other. While this condition of things exists, the institutions of one state will not be disparaged or overshadowed by those of another—not even by those of the central department. A great and flourishing university for example, established in one state, will but encourage the establishment of another in an adjoining state. The literary efforts of one will not damp or impede those of another, but will stimulate it to enter on the same career.

Where, in all Europe for example, can be found so large a number of good universities for the same amount of population as in the states of Germany. The number, it is said, has reached thirty-six—nineteen Protestant, and seventeen Catholic; and nearly all of them, particularly the Protestant, are in a flourishing condition. Even as early as 1826 there were twenty-two universities in Germany, not one of which numbered less than two hundred students. And Villers[33] tells us that there is more real knowledge in one single university, as that of Gottingen, Halle, or Jena, than in all the eight universities of San Jago de Compostella, Alcala, Orihuela, &c. of the consolidated monarchy of Spain.[34]

---

32. Bartold Georg Niebuhr, *Lectures on Ancient History*, ed. L. Schmitz (Philadelphia, 1852), 2: 31–32.

33. Charles F. D. de Villers, *Essay on the Spirit and Influence of the Reformation by Luther*, trans. B. Lambert (London, 1807), pp. 217–18.

34. [The literature of Spain has never revived since the consolidation of her government under Charles and Philip. It flourished most, strange as it may appear, when the Spanish peninsula was divided among several independent governments, and when the spirit of independence and individuality was excited to the highest pitch by that spirit of honor, love of adventure, and of individual notoriety, infused into the nations of Europe by the Institution of Chivalry. "The literature of Spain," says Sismondi, (Literature of South Europe) "has, strictly speaking, only one period, that of Chivalry. Its sole riches consist in its ancient honor and frankness of character. The poem of the Cid first presented itself to us among the Spanish works, as the Cid himself among the heroes of Spain: and after him, we find nothing in any degree equalling either the noble simplicity of his real character, or the charm of the brilliant fictions of which he is the subject. Nothing that has since appeared can justly demand our

If we look to that period of greatest glory in the history of modern Italy, when her little states with all their bustle and faction were still free—still unawed by the great powers of Europe, we shall behold in her universities a beautiful exemplification of the truth of the same principles. Almost every independent state had its university or its college; and no matter how limited its territory, or small its population, the spirit of the state system—the spirit of liberty itself, breathed into these institutions the breath of life, and made them the nurseries of genius and independence, of science and literature.

How soon was the whole character of Holland changed by the benign operation of the federative system, after she had thrown off the odious yoke of the Spanish monarchy! Soon did the spirit of freedom give rise to five universities in this small but interesting country. "When the city of Leyden, in common with all the lower countries, had fought through the bloodiest and perhaps the noblest struggle for liberty on record, the great and good William of Orange offered her immunities from taxes, that she might recover from her bitter sufferings, and be rewarded for the important services which she had rendered to the sacred cause. Leyden however declined the offer, and asked for nothing but the privilege of erecting a university within her walls, as the best reward for more than human endurance and perseverance." This simple fact, says the writer from whom I have obtained this anecdote, is a precious gem to the student of history; for if the protection of the arts and sciences reflects great honor upon a monarch, though it be for vanity's sake, the fostering care with which communities or republics watch over the cultivation of knowledge, and the other ennobling pursuits of man, sheds a still greater lustre upon themselves.

In our own country, it is true that we have not yet passed into the gristle and bone of literary manhood. But we have already established more colleges and universities than exist perhaps in any other country on the face of the globe. We have already about seventy-six in operation, and some of them even now, whether we consider the munificence of their endowments, or the learning which they can boast of, would do credit to any age or country. If the time shall ever come when our state governments shall be broken down, and the power shall be concentrated in one great

---

unqualified admiration. In the midst of the most brilliant efforts of Spanish genius, our taste has been continually wounded by extravagance and affectation, or our reason has been offended by an eccentricity often bordering on folly." Spain then furnishes a most convincing illustration of the melancholy influence of great consolidated governments on mind and literature. The poem of the Cid, so highly eulogized by Sismondi, is supposed to have been written about the middle of the twelfth century.] The first two sentences of this quotation are in J. C. L. Simonde de Sismondi, *Historical View of the Literature of the South of Europe*, trans. T. Roscoe (London, 1823), 4:245; the rest is in ibid., 4: 243–44.

national system, then will the era of state universities be past, and a few bloated, corrupt, *jure divino* establishments will be reared in their stead, more interested in the support of absolute power, and the suppression of truth, than in the cause of liberty and freedom of investigation.[35]

But it is said by some that the state system tinges all literature with a political hue—that under this system politics becomes the great, the engrossing study of the mind—that the lighter kinds of literature and the fine arts will be neglected—that the mathematical and physical sciences will be uncultivated—in fine, that the literature of such a people will be purely utilitarian. This objection is perhaps, founded principally upon too exclusive a view of the past literary history of our own country. Up to this time there has, if I may use the phraseology of political economy, been a greater demand for political knowledge in this country than for any other species of literature. The new political condition into which we entered at the revolution—the formation of our state and federal governments—the jarring and grating almost necessarily incident to new political machinery just started into action—severely tested too as ours has been, and is still, by the inharmonious and too often selfish action of heterogeneous interests on each other—the formation of new states, and the rapid development of new interests and unforeseen powers, together with the great sparseness of our population, have all contributed to turn the public mind of this country principally to the field of politics and morals—and surely we have arrived at an eminency on these subjects not surpassed in any other country.

One of the most distinguished writers on the continent of Europe, even before the close of the eighteenth century, says most justly, "the American literature, indeed, is not yet formed, but when their magistrates are called upon to address themselves on any subject to the public opinion, they are eminently gifted with the power of touching all the affections of the heart, by expressing simple truths and pure sentiments; and to do this, is already to be acquainted with the most useful secret of elegant style."[36] The Declaration of American Independence, the Constitution of the United States, the speeches delivered on it in the conventions of the states, particularly in Virginia—the collection of essays known by the name

---

35. [Perhaps in our country we have multiplied colleges to too great an extent, and consequently have lessened their usefulness by too great a division of the funds destined for their support. The spirit of sectarianism co-operating with the system of state governments, has produced this result. The college and university ought, to some extent, to partake of the nature of a monopoly. There should be some concentration of funds, or you will fail to obtain adequate talents for your professorships. In our country particularly, professors should be paid high, or they cannot be induced to relinquish the more brilliant prospects which the learned professions hold out for them. But the evil of too great a number of colleges and universities, is one which will correct itself in the course of time, by the ultimate failure of those not properly endowed.]

36. De Staël, *Influence of Literature*, p. 68.

of The Federalist—the resolutions on the Alien and Sedition Laws, and the report thereon in the Virginia Legislature of '98 and '99—with the messages of our Presidents, documents from the Cabinets, speeches of our congressmen,[37] and political expositions of our distinguished statesmen,

37. [There is no species of talent which republican institutions are better calculated to foster and perfect than that of public speaking. Wherever the sovereignty resides with the people, this talent becomes an engine of real power, and one of the surest means of political advancement to the individual who possesses it. Mr. Dunlop remarks, in his Roman Literature, that Cicero's treatise *De Claris Oratoribus*, makes mention of scarcely one single orator of any distinction in the Roman Republic, who did not rise to the highest dignities of the state. We may certainly expect then, in the progress of time, if our institutions shall endure, that the great art of oratory will be carried to perhaps greater perfection here than in any other country. Our federal system is particularly favorable to the encouragement of this art. Had we but one great legislature in this country, very few could ever be expected to figure in it, and those would be the more elderly and sober. Under these circumstances, the more ardent eloquence of the youthful aspirant might fail to be developed, in consequence of the want of a proper stimulus. The state governments now supply that stimulus in full force, and furnish the first preparatory theatres for oratorical display. When in addition to all this, we take into consideration the training which our public men receive during the canvasses, at the elections, in public meetings, and even at the festive board, we must acknowledge that our system is admirably calculated for the development of the talent for public speaking. Perhaps I would not go beyond the truth in making the assertion, that we have now in this country more and better trained public speakers than are to be found in any other. Judging from our own legislature and congress, I would say, without hesitation, that our public men are generally the most efficient speakers in the world, in comparison with their general ability and the learning which they profess. In the latter, unfortunately, they are too often very deficient.

It is very true that our style of speaking is too diffusive. Our orators too often seem to be speaking against time, and to be utterly incapable of condensation. It has been observed, that it would take three or four of the great speeches of Demosthenes, to equal in length a speech which a second rate member of Congress would deliver *de Lana Caprina*. I am well aware that the style is frequently the result of confused ideas, and an indistinct conception of the subject under discussion. But it arises in part from the nature of our republican institutions. Most of the speeches delivered in Congress are really intended for the constituency of those who deliver them, and not to produce an effect in Washington. They are consequently of an elementary character, long and labored too, to suit the pleasure and the capacity of the people. From this cause, combined with others, it has happened that the division of labor in our deliberative bodies has never been so complete as in the British Parliament. When particular subjects are brought up in that body, particular men are immediately looked to for information, and for the discussion of them. Men who are not supposed to be qualified on them, are coughed down when they interrupt the body with their crude remarks. But in our own country, particular subjects have not been thus appropriated to particular individuals; and when a matter of importance is brought up for discussion, all are anxious to speak on it, and it is not to be wondered at that the clouded intellect of some of the speakers, together with the great courtesy of the body, should sometimes lead on to long-winded and tiresome effusions.

No body in ancient times displayed so much patience and courtesy towards its speakers as the Senate of Rome, and we are told that the speeches delivered before the Roman Senate were much longer than those delivered before the *Comitia*. There is no body in modern times which displays more impatience than the French Chambers, and accordingly you find generally that the speeches delivered before them are very short. But whatever may be the cause of this tendency to prolixity in many of our speakers, we may console ourselves with the reflection that it is not the fault of all—that there are some now in the United States who can compare with any in the world—that the eloquence of our country is decidedly advancing,

Republicanism and Literature 151

form altogether a mass of political learning not to be surpassed in any other country. We are not to wonder then that a German writer of much celebrity, and a defender too of the Holy Alliance, in full view of the nascent literature of our country, should have proclaimed the 4th of July, '76, as the commencement of a new era in the history of the world;[38] nor that that eloquent royalist of France, the Vicompte de Chateaubriand, should assert that the representative republic, which has been first reduced to practice in the United States, is the most splendid discovery of modern times.[39]

May we not then judging even from the past, form the most brilliant conceptions of the future? When our wide spread territory shall be filled up with a denser population—when larger cities shall be erected within our borders, the necessary nurseries of a literary class—when physical and mental labor shall be more subdivided, then will the intellectual level of our country begin to rise; the increasing competition in every department of industry will call for greater labor, greater energy, and more learning on the part of the successful candidates for distinction. And then may we expect that every branch of literature will be cultivated, and every art be practiced by the matured and invigorated genius of the country.

But although in the progress of time we may expect that literature in all its forms and varieties will be successfully cultivated here, yet we must still acknowledge that the character of our political system will give a most decided bias towards moral and political science. Under a system of republics like ours, where the sovereignty resides *de jure* and *de facto* in the people, the business of politics is the business of every man. Men in power, in every age and country, are disposed to grasp at more than has been confided to them; they have always developed wolfish propensities. To guard against these dangerous propensities in a republic, it is necessary that the people in whom the sovereignty resides, should always be on the watchtower; they should never be caught slumbering at their posts; they should take the alarm not only against the palpable and open usurpations of power, but against those gradual, secret, imperceptible changes, which silently dig away the very foundations of our constitution, and create no alarm until they are ready to shake down the whole fabric of our liberties. Under these circumstances, it is the business of every man—it is more, it is the duty of every man—to think, to reflect, to instruct himself, that he may

---

and will no doubt shed a much brighter lustre over our future history, if we can only preserve our federal system in all its original purity and perfection.] John Dunlop, *History of Roman Literature* (London, 1824), 2:183; *de lana caprina* is a proverb meaning to dispute about trifles (literally, about carding goats wool); cf. Horace, *Epodes*, I, 18, line 15.

38. Arnold H. L. Heeren, *A Manual of the History of the Political System of Europe and Its Colonies* (Oxford, 1834), 2:93, quotes Vergil's "novus saeclorum nascitur ordo" about the Declaration of Independence. See *Eclogues* 4, line 5.

39. Chateaubriand, *Travels in America*, trans. R. Switzer (Lexington, 1969), p. 15.

be prepared to perform that part at least which must necessarily devolve on each freeman in the great political drama of our country. He must recollect that the great experiment of a free government depends upon the intelligence and the virtue of the people. It is this knowledge and this virtue which constitute at once their power and their safety. It is in the reliance on this power, resulting from the intelligence and virtue of the people alone, that the honest patriot may well exclaim in the glowing language of Sheridan on a different subject, "I will give to the minister a venal house of peers—I will give him a corrupt and servile house of commons—I will give him the full swing of the patronage of his office—I will give him all the power that place can confer, to overawe resistance and purchase up submission; and yet armed, with this mighty power of the people, I will shake down from its height corruption, and bury it beneath the ruins of the abuse it was meant to shelter."[40]

Surely then it can be no disadvantage to a country to direct the virtue and talents of its citizens principally to that science whose principles, when well understood and practiced on, will secure the liberty and happiness of the people, but when mistaken by ignorance, or perverted by corruption, will subvert the one, and dissipate the other. Look to the past history of the world, from the days of the Patriarchs to the days of our Presidents, and we are at a loss, after the review, to determine whether the world has been injured more by the unwise and unskilful efforts of statesmen and philanthropists to benefit, or by the nefarious attempts of wicked men and tyrants to injure it. We shall find from this review, that where a Hampden, a Sidney, and a Russell have been crushed by the tyrannous exercise of power, and been wept over by posterity after they had fallen, thousands have been reduced to misery, or sent untimely out of the world, unpitied and unmourned, by the stupid legislation of ignorant statesmen. Of such bodies of functionaries, we may well exclaim, in the language of England's bard,

"How much more happy were good Aesop's frogs
Than we?—for ours are animated logs,
With ponderous malice swaying to and fro,
And crushing nations with a stupid blow."[41]

The statistics of the densely populated countries of Europe and Asia inform us, that there are large masses of population in those countries constantly vacillating, if I may use the expression, between life and death; a feather may decide the preponderance of the scales, in favor of one or the other. In view of such a pregnant fact as this, how awfully responsible becomes the duty of the legislator! Suppose, whilst he is endeavoring to

40. I can find no trace of this in Sheridan's speeches.
41. Byron, "The Age of Bronze," stanza VIII, lines 29–32.

organize the labor and capital of the country, he should unfortunately tamper with the sources of production, and, if I may use the beautiful simile of Fenelon, like him who endeavors to enlarge the native springs of the rock, should suddenly find that his labors had but served to dry them up,[42]— what calamities would not such legislative blunders at once inflict upon that lowest and most destitute class, which is already holding on upon life, with so frail a tenure! How many would be hastened prematurely out of existence! And these are the melancholy every-day consequences, too often misunderstood or unnoticed, of ignorant legislation. How vastly different is the benign influence of that wise legislator, whose laws, in the language of Bacon, "are deep, not vulgar; not made on the spur of a particular occasion for the present, but out of Providence for the future, to make the estate of the people still more and more happy!"[43]

But not only should political science be a prominent study in every republic, in consequence of its immense importance and universal application, but it demands the most assiduous cultivation, because of the intrinsic difficulties which belong to it. There is no science in which we are more likely to ascribe effects to wrong causes than in politics—there is none which demands a more constant exercise of reason and observation, and in which first impressions are so likely to be false. The moral and political sciences, particularly the latter, are much more difficult than the physical and mathematical. There is scarcely any intellect, no matter how common, which may not by severe study and close application, be brought at last to master mere physical and mathematical science. Eminence here is rather a proof of labor than of genius.[44]

But in matters of morals and politics how many must turn their attention to them, and how few become eminent! Suppose that the exalted talents which have been turned into a political career in this country, had been employed with the same assiduity in physics or mathematics—to what

---

42. Fénelon, *Adventures of Telemachus*, trans. Hawkesworth (New York, 1854), p. 196: quoted also in Dugald Stewart, *Dissertation: Exhibiting the Progress of Metaphysical, Ethical, and Political Philosophy*, ed. Sir William Hamilton (Edinburgh, 1854), p. 168.

43. "History of King Henry VII," in the *Works of Francis Bacon*, ed. B. Montagu (Philadelphia, 1887), 1:335, a passage in which Bacon suggests that Henry VII was, after Edward I, England's "best lawgiver."

44. [A very able reviewer in Blackwood, of Allison's History of the French Revolution, says of Napoleon, in attempting to disprove his precocious greatness, "even his faculty for mathematics, which has been frequently adduced as one of the most sufficient proofs of his future fame as a soldier, fails; perhaps no faculty of the human mind is less successful in promoting these enlarged views, or that rapid and vigorous comprehension of the necessities of the moment, which form the essentials of the great and master soldier. The mathematician is generally the last man equal to the sudden difficulties of situation or even to the ordinary problem of human life. Skill in the science of equations might draw up a clear system of tactics on paper. But it must be a mental operation, not merely of a more active, but of a totally different kind, which constructed the recovery of the battle at Marengo, or led the march to Ulm."] [George Croly], "Alison's *History*," *Blackwood's Magazine* 38 (August 1835): 173.

perfection might they not have attained in those sciences? If the genius and study which have been expended upon one great subject in political economy, the Banks for example, could have been directed with equal ardor to mathematics and physics, with what complete success would they have been crowned? And yet this whole subject of Banking is far, very far from being thoroughly comprehended by the most expanded intellects of the age. Thus do we find the moral and political departments of literature the most useful,[45] and at the same time much the most difficult to cultivate with success. They require too a concurrence of every other species of knowledge to their perfection, and hence the literature of that country may always be expected to be most perfect and most useful, in which these branches are made the centre, the great nucleus around which the others are formed.[46]

45. [Dr. Johnson in his Life of Milton has given us his opinion on these subjects, and as it is perfectly coincident with my own, I cannot forebear to add it in a note. "The truth is," says the Doctor, "that the knowledge of external nature and the sciences which that knowledge requires or includes, are not the great nor frequent business of the human mind. Whether we provide for action or conversation—whether we wish to be useful or pleasing, the first requisite is the religious and moral knowledge of right and wrong; the next is an acquaintance with the history of mankind, and with those examples which may be said to embody truths, and prove by events the reasonableness of opinions. Prudence and justice are virtues and excellences of all times and of all places. We are perpetually moralists, but we are geometricians only by chance. Our intercourse with intellectual nature is necessary; our speculations upon matter are voluntary, and at leisure. Physical learning is of such rare emergence, that one may know another half his life, without being able to estimate his skill in hydrostatics or astronomy; but his moral and prudential character immediately appears. Those authors, therefore, are to be read at schools that supply most axioms of prudence, most principles of moral truth, and most materials for conversation."] Samuel Johnson, *The Lives of the English Poets* (London, 1828), p. 28.

46. [Although our political institutions have the effect of directing the matured minds of the country into the field of politics and morals, yet we are not to suppose, on that account, that the mathematical and physical sciences will be neglected here. In almost all our colleges, particular attention is paid to these latter branches. In fact, so far as I have been enabled to examine into the condition of our colleges and universities, I would say the moral and political sciences are almost always too much neglected. It is easy generally to fill the mathematical and physical departments with able professors, because those who are well qualified to fill those departments, can find no other employments so lucrative and honorable. But those who would make eminent moral and political lecturers, would be generally well qualified, with but little additional study, to enter into the learned professions, or into the still more enticing field of politics, with the most unlimited prospects before them. Hence, whilst in many of our colleges the physical and mathematical chairs are most ably filled, you find the moral and political professors but second rate men. Now talent and real comprehension of mind are particularly required on the subjects of morals and politics. In the mathematics and physics, the merest dunce, if he teaches at all, must teach correctly. He may not give the most concise, or the most beautiful, or the most recent demonstration; but if he gives any demonstration at all, his reasoning is irrefutable, and his conclusions undeniably true. How vastly different are our speculations in politics and morals! What fatal principles may ignorance or dishonesty inculcate here! In our colleges, then the fixed sciences do now, and are likely in future to receive most attention; and consequently, we need not fear that they will be neglected. On the contrary, the danger seems to be, that they may be studied too exclusively.

Again, the wide extent of our country, the variety of our soils, our immense mineralogical resources, our mountains and rivers, our diversified geological phenomena, our canals,

But again, the state system of government, in all its details, awakens the genius and elicits the energies of the citizens, by the high inducement to exertion held out to all,—from the stimulating hope of influencing the destinies of others, and becoming useful to mankind and an ornament to our country. Under the benign operation of the federative system, the hope of rising to some distinction in the commonwealth, is breathed into us all. From the highest to the lowest, we stand ready and anxious to step forth into the service of our country. This universal desire to be useful—this constant hope of rising to distinction—this longing after immortality, arouses the spirit of emulation, excites all the powers of reflection, calls forth all the energies of mind and body, and makes man a greater, nobler, and more efficient being, than when he moves on sluggishly in the dull routine of life, through the unvarying, noiseless calm of despotism. All the rewards, all the distinctions of arbitrary power, can never inspire that energy which arises from the patriotic hope of being useful, and weaving our name with the history of our country.

Philosophy is the most frivolous and shallow of employments in a country where it dares not penetrate into the institutions which surround it. When reflection durst not attempt to amend or soften the lot of mankind, it becomes unmanly and puerile. Look to the literature of those deluded beings, who immured within the walls of their monasteries, separated themselves from the great society of their country, and vainly imagined that they were doing service to their God, by running counter to those great laws which he has impressed upon his creatures, and by violating those principles which he has breathed into us all. What a melancholy picture is presented to our view—what waste of time, of intellect, and of labor, on subjects which true philosophy is almost ashamed to name! What endless discussions, what pointless wit, what inconsequential conclusions—in fine, what empty, useless nonsense, do we find in that absurd philosophy reared up in seclusion, and entirely unconnected with man and the institutions by which he is governed![47]

our rail roads, our immense improvements of all descriptions, open a wide and unlimited range for the research and practical skill of the physical and mathematical student, which will always stimulate the talent of the country sufficiently in this direction. Our past history too, confirms my remarks; and the great names in mathematics and physics, and the great and useful inventions in the arts, which have already shed a halo of glory around our infant institutions, point us to that brilliant prospect in the vista of the future, when our mathematical and natural philosophers, if not the very first, will certainly rank among the greatest of the world.]

47. [As a specimen, let us take the work of the celebrated St. Thomas Aquinas, with the lofty title of Summa Totius Theologicae, 1250 pages folio. In this work there are 168 articles on Love, 358 on Angels, 200 on the Soul, 85 on Demons, 151 on Intellect, 134 on Law, 3 on the Catamenia, 237 on Sins, and 17 on Virginity. He treats of Angels, says D'Israeli, their substances, orders, offices, natures, habits, &c. as if he himself had been an old experienced Angel. When men are thus cut off from the active pursuits of life, it is curious to contemplate the very trifling character of their discussions and labors. D'Israeli tells us that

Nothing so much animates and cheers the literary man in his intellectual labors, as the hope of being able to promote the happiness of the human race. Hence the custom among the ancients of blending together military, legislative, and philosophic pursuits, contributed greatly to the progress of mental activity and improvement. When thought may be the forerunner of action—when a happy reflection may be instantaneously transformed into a beneficent institution, then do the contemplations and reflections of a man of genius ennoble and exalt philosophy. He no longer experiences that embarrassing timidity, that crushing shame, which genius, condemned to mere speculation, must ever feel in the presence of even an inferior being, when that being is invested with a power which may influence the destiny of those around him—which may enable him to render the smallest service to his country, or even to wipe away one tear from affliction's cheek.

I am not now dealing in vague conjecture; the history of the past will bear me out in the assertions which I have made. In casting a glance over the nations of antiquity, our attention is arrested by none so forcibly as by the little Democracies of Greece. I will not occupy the attention of this society by the details of that history which is graven upon the memory of us all. I will not stop here to relate the warlike achievements of that extraordinary system of governments which, covering an extent of territory not greater than that of our own state, even with division among themselves, was yet enabled to meet, with their small but devoted bands, the countless hosts of Persia, led on by their proud and vain-glorious monarch, and to roll back in disgrace and defeat, the mighty tide upon the East. Nor will I recount the trophies which they won in philosophy, or describe their beautiful and sublime productions in the arts, which they at once created and perfected. Nor will I detain you with an account of that matchless eloquence displayed in their popular assemblies, which the historian tells us drew together eager, gazing, listening crowds from all Greece, as if about to behold the most splendid spectacle which the imagination of man

---

the following question was a favorite topic for discussion, and thousands of the acutest logicians through more than one century, never resolved it. "When a hog is carried to market with a rope tied about its neck, which is held at the other end by a man, whether is the *hog* carried to market by the *rope* or the *man*?" The same writer too, tells us of a monk who was sedulously employed through a long life, in discovering more than 30,000 new questions concerning the Virgin Mary, with appropriate answers. And it was the same useless industry which induced the monks often to employ their time in writing very *minutely*, until they brought this worthless art to such perfection, as to write down the whole Iliad on parchment that might be enclosed in a nutshell. In the Imperial Library of Vienna, there is still preserved an extraordinary specimen of chirography by a Jew, who had no doubt imbibed the *in*utilitarian spirit of the monks. On a single page, eight inches long by six and a half broad, are written without abbreviations and very legible to the naked eye, the Pentateuch and book of Ruth in German; Ecclesiasticus in Hebrew; the Canticles in Latin; Esther in Syriac; and Deuteronomy in French.] Isaac D'Israeli, *Curiosities of Literature* (London, 1858), 1:63, 65, 369.

Republicanism and Literature 157

could conceive, or even the universe could present. The history of Greece is too well known to us all to require these details. A people with such historians as Herodotus, Thucydides, and Xenophon, acquires a strange pre-eminence—a wonderful notoriety among the nations of the earth. The extraordinary power of this cluster of little states, the superiority of their literature, the resistless energy of the minds and bodies of their citizens, whether for weal or woe—in short, their real greatness, are acknowledged by all.

What then, we may well be permitted to ask, could have generated so much greatness of mind, so much energy and loftiness of character in this apparently secluded corner of Europe, scarcely visible on the world's map? It was not the superiority of her climate and soil. Spain—worn out and degenerate Spain, enjoys the genial climate of the Athenian, and possesses a soil more fertile. It was not the superior protection which her governments afforded to persons and property, which generated this wonderful character. Property was almost as unsafe amid the turbulent factions of Greece, as under the despotisms of the East; and the stroke of tyranny was as often inflicted upon patriots and statesmen, by the ungrateful hand of a capricious and unbalanced democracy, as by the great monarchs of Persia, or by the barbarian kings of Scythia. No!—it was the system of independent state governments, which, badly organized as they were, without a proper system of representation and responsibility, and often shaken by faction and torn to pieces by discord, nevertheless extended their inspiring, animating influence over all, and drew forth from the shade of retirement or solitude the talent and energy of the people, wherever they existed. It was this system of state government which so completely identified each citizen of Greece with that little body politic with which his destiny was connected—which breathed into his soul that ardent patriotism which can sacrifice self upon the altar of our country's happiness, and which could make even an Alcibiades, or a Themistocles, whilst laboring under the bitter curse of their country, stop short in their vindictive career, amid their mediations of mischief and vengeance, and cast many a longing, lingering, pitying look back upon the distresses of that ungrateful city that had driven them forth from its walls.

The great moral which may be drawn from the history of Greece, is one which the patriot in no age or clime should ever forget. In looking over this little system of states, we find uniformly that each displayed genius, energy, and patriotism, while really free and independent; but the moment one was overawed and conquered by its neighbor, it lost its greatness, its patriotism—even its virtue. And when, at last, a great state arose in the north of Greece, and placed a monarch upon its throne, who substituted the obedient spirit of the mercenary soldier and crouching courtier, for the independent genius of liberty and patriotism—who overawed Greece by his armies, and silenced the Council of Amphictyon by his presence—then was it found that the days of Grecian greatness had been numbered, and that the glory of these republics was destroyed forever; then was it seen that the Spartan lost his patriotism, and the Athenian that energy of mind almost creative, which could lead armies and navies to battle and to victory, adorn and enrich the stores of philosophy and literature, agitate the public assemblies from the *Bema*, or make the marble and the canvass breathe. The battle of Cheronea overthrew at the same time the state governments, the liberties, the prosperity, and, worst of all, the virtue and the towering intellect of Greece.

With the destruction of the governments of her independent states, Greece lost the great animating principle of her system. Forming but an insignificant subject province of the great Macedonian kingdom, and afterwards of the still greater empire of Rome, her sons preserved for a time the books and the mere learning of their renowned ancestors; but the spirit, the energy, the principle of thought and reflection,—the mind,—were all gone. "For more than ten centuries, (says an eloquent historian) the Greeks of Byzantium possessed models of every kind, yet they did not suggest to them one original idea; they did not give birth to a copy worthy of coming after these masterpieces. Thirty millions of Greeks, the surviving depositaries of ancient wisdom, made not a single step, during twelve centuries, in any one of the social sciences. There was not a citizen of free Athens who was not better skilled in the science of politics than the most erudite scholar of Byzantium; their morality was far inferior to that of Socrates—their philosophy to that of Plato and Aristotle, upon whom they were continually commenting. They made not a single discovery in any one of the physical sciences, unless we except the lucky accident which produced the Greek fire. They loaded the ancient poets with annotations, but they are incapable of treading in their footsteps; not a comedy or a tragedy was written at the foot of the ruins of the theatres of Greece; no epic poem was produced by the worshippers of Homer; not an ode by those of Pindar. Their highest literary efforts do not go beyond a few epigrams collected in the Greek Anthology, and a few romances. Such is the unworthy use which the depositaries of every treasure of human wit and genius make of their wealth, during an uninterrupted course of transmission for more than a thousand years."[48] And such will always be the destiny of states as soon as they are moulded into one consolidated empire, with a controlling despotism at the centre.

But while the states of Greece were thus sinking into insignificance, under the crushing weight of one great consolidated government,—in an-

---

48. This passage is almost a parody of certain passages in Gibbon, although the references to morality and the enthusiasm for Greece suggest a nineteenth-century author.

other part of Europe, almost as small and secluded as Greece, little confederacies or associations of independent states were rapidly developing a literature and a character equal to those of the ancient Greek, and affording perhaps a still more striking and beautiful illustration of the truth of the principles for which I have contended this night. It was Italy that first restored intellectual light to Europe, after the long and gloomy night of ignorance and barbarism, which the Goth, the Vandal and the Hun had shed over the western half of the Roman world. It was Italy which recalled youth to the study of laws and philosophy—created the taste for poetry and the fine arts—revived the science and literature of antiquity, and gave prosperity to commerce, manufactures and agriculture. And what was it, let me ask, which made this small peninsula the cradle of commerce, of the arts, sciences and literature—in one word, of the civilization of modern Europe? It was because the whole of this beautiful and interesting country was dotted over with little republics or democracies, which, like those of Greece, applied their stimulating power to every portion of the soil of Italy. These little states, it is true, were factious, turbulent and revolutionary, but they awakened the genius and stimulated the energies of the whole people.

The exertions of this people were truly wonderful. No nation in any age of the world has ever raised up in its cities, and even in its villages, so many magnificent temples,—which even now attract the stranger from every country and clime to the classic soil of Italy. We find throughout this land, whether on the extensive plains of Lombardy, or on the fertile hills of Tuscany and Romagna, or on the now deserted *campagna* of the Patrimony of St. Peter, towns of the most splendid character, reared during the palmy days of modern Italy; and in those cities we find long lines of once stately palaces now tumbling into ruins. Their gates, their columns, their architraves, says the eloquent historian of Italy,[49] remain, but the wood is worm-eaten and decayed, the crystal glasses have been broken, the lead has been taken from the roofs, and the stranger from one end to the other of this *monumental* land, asks in mournful sadness in each town through which he passes,—Where now is the population which could have required so many habitations? Where is the commerce which could have filled so many magazines? Where are those opulent citizens who could have lived in so many palaces? Where now are those numerous crowds that bowed in reverential awe and devotion before the altars of Christ, of the Virgin and the Saints? Where now are the grandeur and magnificence of the living, which should have replaced that grandeur and magnificence of the dead, of which their monuments so eloquently tell? All are gone. While other

---

49. J. C. L. Simonde de Sismondi, *Histoire des républiques Italiennes du moyen âge* (Paris, 1826), 16:354ff.: these passages do not occur in the abridged English translation of 1832.

nations have been growing in importance and multiplying the materials of their history as they approach the age in which we live, how different has been the mournful destiny of Italy! The present has well been called the epoch of death in that lovely land. When we observe, says the historian, the whole of Italy, whether we examine the physiognomy of the soil, or the works of man, or man himself, we always regard ourselves as being in the land of the dead; every where we are struck by the feebleness and degeneracy of the race that now is, compared with that which has been. The sun of Italy now sheds as warm and vivifying rays over the land as before—the earth remains as fertile—the Appenines present to our view the same varient smiling aspect—the fields are as abundantly watered by the genial showers of heaven, and all the lower animals of nature preserve here their pristine beauty and habits. Man too, at birth, seems in this delightful climate, to be endowed still with the same quick creative imagination, with the same susceptibility of deep, passionate feeling—with the same wonderful aptitude of mind—and yet man alone has changed here! In contrast with his fathers—

> "As the slime,
> The dull green ooze of the receding deep,
> Is with the dashing of the spring-tide foam,
> That drives the sailor shipless to his home."[50]

It is the change in government—the fatal change in the political destiny of the Italian, which has wrought this melancholy change in his whole nature. When this beautiful land was covered with leagues of independent states, inspired with the genius of liberty and political independence,—the stimulating influence of the government was felt every where—it animated and aroused all—it communicated the spirit of activity and enterprise, the love of home and the ardent love of country to all the citizens alike—from the proud lord of Venice, whose stately palace was lashed by the wave of the Adriatic, to the poor peasant whose thatched and humble cottage lay in some secluded solitary hollow of the Alps or the Appenines. Under this system of government there was no favored spot upon which the treasures of the nation were expended; there was no Thebes, no Babylon, no imperial Rome built up, adorned and beautiful by the degradation and utter prostration of all the rest. We might almost say of Italy what has been affirmed of Omnipotence itself—its centre was every where, its circumference no where. Every little independent state, no matter how limited its area or small its population, had its men, its thriving cities, its noble monuments. The little Florentine democracy with but eighty thousand souls, had more great men within its limits than any of the great

---

50. Byron, "Ode on Venice," lines 8–11.

kingdoms of Europe; and all were animated with the spirit of patriotism, of industry,[51] of learning.

No wonder then that the citizens of Italy should have prospered amid their domestic broils, their factions, their revolutions—even amid the sanguinary conflicts of the Guelph and the Ghibeline. If the energy and elasticity of the mind be not destroyed by the pressure of despotism, it is curious to contemplate the wonderfully recuperative powers of man, and to behold the appalling difficulties which he can surmount, undismayed and unscathed. You may prostrate him to day, but the energy and vitality that is within him will raise him up on the morrow.[52] Of all sorts of destruction, of every kind of death, that is the worst, because the most productive of melancholy consequences, which reaches the mind itself. That system of government which slays the mind, is the system which, at the same time reaches the sanctuary of the heart, overthrows the purity of morals and forges the fetters for the slave. And such a government as this have the Spaniard the Frenchman and the German rivetted but too fatally upon Italy. The day that saw those modern Goths and Vandals pouring their mercenary hordes over the Alps to rob and plunder, was a black day for Italy, and well might the friend of that lovely land have then exclaimed in the language of the poet,

> "Oh! Rome, the spoiler or the spoil of France,
> From Brennus to the Bourbon, never, never
> Shall foreign standard to thy walls advance,
> But Tiber shall become a mournful river."[53]

The independence of the little states of Italy is now gone, and with it all the real greatness of that country. The power that now sways the Ital-

---

51. ["The habit of industry," says Sismondi, "was the distinctive characteristic of the Italians even to the middle of the 15th century. The first rank at Florence, Venice, and Genoa, was occupied by merchants; and the families who possessed the offices of the state, of the church or the army, did not for that reason give up their businesses. Philip Strozzi, brother-in-law of Leo X, the father of Mareschal Strozzi, and the grandfather of Capua, the friend of several sovereigns, and the first citizen of Italy, remained even to the end of his life chief of a banking house. He had seven sons, but in spite of his immense fortune, he suffered none of them to be brought up in idleness."] Sismondi, *Histoire des républiques Italiennes*, 16:223.

52. [Whilst Italy was free, there was no country which could repair its losses with so much despatch; the town that was sacked and burnt to-day, would be built up and stored with wealth on the morrow, and the losses of one excited the sympathies and support of all those engaged in the same cause. When the Emperor Frederic carried fire and sword through the Milanese territory, and left the treasury of that state completely exhausted, we are told that the rich citizens soon replenished it from their private purses, contenting themselves in the mean time with coarse bread, and cloaks of black stuff. And at the command of their counsuls they left Milan to join their fellow citizens in rebuilding *with their own hands* the walls and houses of Tortona, Rosata, Tricate, Galiate, and other towns, which had suffered in the contest for the common cause.]

53. Byron, "The Prophecy of Dante," canto II, lines 97–100.

ian, emanates from a nation situated afar off on the banks of the Danube. And we can wonder while the Austrian soldier stands sentinel in the Italian cities, that their citizens should

"Creep,
Crouching and crab-like, through their sapping streets."[54]

But enough of a spectacle so sad as this![55]

Did the limits which I have prescribed to myself in this address allow it, I could easily adduce the history of the Swiss Cantons, the Netherlands and Holland, the Hanseatic League, the little states formerly around the Baltic, and even the Germanic Confederation, as confirmation strong of the truth of the positions which I have taken in favor of the federative system. Indeed I might go farther than this, and show that the feudal aristocracy of the middle ages, horrible as was its oppression, calamitous as were its petty wars, and feuds, and dissensions, intolerable as was that anarchical confusion which it generated in Europe towards the close of the tenth century, was nevertheless the instrument which kept alive the mind of man in the great nations of Christendom, by splitting up the powers of government among the Baronial Lords, and thereby preventing that fatal tendency to centralism and consolidation, which would inevitably have shrouded the mind of Europe in inextricable darkness. Far be from me that vain presumption which would dare to scan the mysterious plans of Providence; but I have always thought that the regeneration of the mind of Europe required that the barbarian should come from the North and the East—that an Alaric, a Genseric and an Attila, should pour out the vials of their wrath upon the Roman's head—that the monstrous, corrupt

---

54. Byron, "Ode on Venice," lines 12–13.
55. [Small states, if truly independent, are very favorable to the production of great characters, and even great virtues. "The regeneration of liberty in Italy," says Sismondi, "was signalized still more, if it were possible, by the development of the moral, than by that of the intellectual character of the Italians. The sympathy existing among fellow-citizens, from the habit of living for each other, and by each other—of connecting every thing with the good of all, produced in those republics virtues which despotic states cannot even imagine." But the moment the independence of the small states is destroyed by the overshadowing and overawing influence of larger ones, then does the system work the most disastrous consequences upon the political, moral, and literary character of the citizens. A little state overawed by a large one, instantly has recourse to cunning, intrigue, and duplicity, to accomplish its ends. Caesar Borgia in Italy, says Mr. Hume, had recourse to more villainy, hypocrisy, and meanness, to get possession of a few miles of territory, than was practised by Julius Caesar, Zenghis, or Tamerlane for the conquest of a large portion of the world. Hence we are not to wonder that Italy should become the most infamous of all schools, in the production of subtile, intriguing, hypocritical politicians, and that the literature should soon become as corrupt as the political morals of the country. The Marini, the Achillini in Poetry, and the Bernini in the arts, had a reputation similar to that of Concini, Mazarini, Catherine, and Mary di Medici in politics.] Sismondi, *History of the Italian Republics* (Philadelphia, 1832), p. 167; I can find no such reference to Borgia in Hume, and I assume Dew has misremembered a passage from elsewhere.

and gigantic fabric of his power might be broken to pieces by barbarian hordes, who had not the genius and political skill requisite to establish another great military despotism on its ruins.

After this review I turn with pleasure again to our own system of government. We have seen how stimulating were the little republics of Greece and of Italy, to the genius of those countries. But their systems were not made for peaceable endurance—they were too disunited, too turbulent, too prone to civil wars; hence they either fell a prey to some ambitious state in their own system, or invited by their reckless internal dissensions the foreigner into their land, who broke down their institutions, overthrew their liberty, and imposed upon their submissive necks the galling yoke of military despotism. But those venerated fathers of our republics, who framed the federal constitution, came forward to their task in full view of the history of the republics of the ancient and modern world, with that almost holy spirit of freedom and patriotism which gave them that undaunted courage and unremitting perseverance that enabled them to wade through the blood and turmoil of the revolution. They completed their task, and the wisdom and virtue of our confederacy did sanction their work, and long may that work endure if administered in that spirit of purity and virtue which inspired those who framed it.

Our states are much larger than the little democracies of ancient Greece or of modern Italy—the new and improved principle of representation, combined with the modern improvements in the whole machinery of government, have rendered the republican form much better suited to large states than formerly. Some of our states may perhaps be too large, and others too small. But our ancestors very wisely avoided that geometrical policy, which would have divided our country into equal squares, like France in the dark days of her revolution. "No man ever was attached," says Burke, "by a sense of pride, partiality, or real affection, to a description of square measurement. He never will glory in belonging to the chequer No. 71, or to any other badge ticket. We begin our public affections in our families. No cold relation is a zealous citizen. We pass on to our neighborhoods and our habitual provincial connection;"[56] and these ties and habits were respected by our forefathers. No sovereign state, no matter how small, was disfranchised—the giant and the dwarf had their rights and liberties alike respected and secured in this new system, and all were bound together by a wise and beneficent plan of government, based upon the mutual interests and sympathies of all the members of the confederacy—a plan which was wisely framed to give lasting peace to our country, and to demonstrate the inapplicability to our portion of the western hemisphere at least, of the gloomy philosophy of the European statesman, that the natural condition

---

56. "Reflections on the Revolution in France," in *Works of . . . Burke*, 4:218.

of man is war. Thus organized, our system was calculated to apply the beneficial stimulus of government to every portion of our soil and every division of our population, and at the same time in the midst of profound peace and freedom of intercourse, both social and commercial, among the states, to secure that enlarged and extended theatre for action, which may stimulate and reward the exalted genius and talent of the country, and crown the pyramid of our greatness.

But I must turn from this view of my subject, which has ever been so delightful to my mind, to the contemplation always gloomy, of the dangerous evils which may beset us in our progress onwards. It is too true that there can be nothing pure in this world; good and evil are always intertwined. It has well been said that the wave which wafts to our shore the genial seed that may spring up and gladden our land with luxuriant vegetation, may unfold the deadly crocodile.

One of the most fatal evils with which the republican system of government is liable to be assailed, is the diffusion of a spirit of agrarianism among the indigent classes of society. This spirit is now abroad in the world— it is fearfully developing itself in the insurrectionary heavings and tumults of continental Europe, which, however ineffectual now, do nevertheless mark the great internal conflagration—"the march of that mighty burning, which however intangible by human vigilance, is yet hollowing the ground under every community of the civilized world." England's most eloquent and learned divine, tells us but too truly that "there now sits an unnatural scowl on the aspect of the population, a resolved sturdiness in their attitude and gait; and whether we look to the profane recklessness of their habits, or to the deep and settled hatred which rankles in their hearts, we cannot but read in these moral characteristics of this land, the omens of some great and impending overthrow."

In our own more happy country, the almost unlimited extension of suffrage in the most populous states, the frequent appeals made to the indigent and the destitute by demagogues for the purpose of inflaming their passions, and of exciting that most blighting and deadly hostility of all, the hostility of the poor against the rich—the tumults and riots at the elections in our great cities—the lawless mobs of the north which have already set the civil authority at defiance, and have pulled down and destroyed the property of the citizen—all are but premonitory symptoms of the approaching calamity—they are but the rumbling sound which precedes the mighty shock of the terrible earthquake. If these things happen now, what may we not expect hereafter? At present the great territorial resources of our country offer the most stimulating reward to labor and enterprise. The laborer of to-day looks forward, and hopes, yes, knows, that by his industry he is to be the capitalist of to-morrow. He feels a prospective interest in the defence of property. The little German farmer with a hundred acres of poor land in the Key Stone State, clad in the coarsest raiment, contented with the simplest food, and saving from his hard earnings the small sum of one hundred dollars a year, would not wish the property of the country to be thrown in jeopardy—he would shudder at the idea of a general scramble, lest he might lose that little patrimony around which the very affections of his heart have been twined.

But the time must come when the powerfully elastic spring of our rapidly increasing numbers shall fill up our wide spread territory with a dense population—when the great safety valve of the west will be closed against us—when millions shall be crowded into our manufactories and commercial cities—then will come the great and fearful pressure upon the engine—then will the line of demarkation stand most palpably drawn between the rich and the poor, the capitalist and the laborer—then will thousands, yea, millions arise, whose hard lot it may be to labor from morn till eve through a long life, without the cheering hope of passing from that toilsome condition in which the first years of their manhood found them, or even of accumulating in advance that small fund which may release the old and infirm from labor and toil, and mitigate the sorrows of declining years. Many there will be even, who may go to and fro and be able to say in the melancholy language of Holy Writ, "the foxes have holes, and the birds of the air their nest, but the son of man has not where to lay his head."[57] When these things shall come—when the millions, who are always under the pressure of poverty, and sometimes on the verge of starvation, shall form your numerical majority, (as is the case now in the old countries of the world) and universal suffrage shall throw the political power into their hands, can you expect that they will regard as sacred the tenure by which you hold your property? I almost fear the frailties and weakness of human nature too much, to anticipate confidently such justice. When hunger is in the land, we can scarely expect, by any species of legerdemain, to turn the eyes and thoughts of the sufferers from the flesh pots of Egypt. The old Roman populace demanded a regular distribution of corn from the public granaries; the Grecian populace received bribes, fined and imprisoned their wealthy men, or made them build galleys, equip soldiers, give public feasts, and furnish the victims for the sacrifices at their own expense.[58] The mode of action in modern times may be changed, but the

---

57. Matthew 8:20.

58. [When an individual was tried before an Athenian tribunal, his wealth was generally a serious disadvantage to his cause, and there was nothing which the defence labored harder to establish than the poverty of the accused. "I know," says the orator Lisias, in his defence of Nicophemus, "how difficult it will be effectually to refute the report of the great riches of Nicophemus. The present scarcity of money in the city, and the wants of the treasury which the forfeiture has been calculated upon to supply, will operate against me." In the celebrated dialogue of Xenophon, called the Banquet, he makes a rich man who has suddenly become poor, congratulate himself upon his poverty; "inasmuch," he says, "as cheerfulness and confi-

result will be the same if the spirit of agrarianism shall once get abroad in our land. France has already furnished us with the great moral. First comes disorganization and legislative plunder, then the struggle of factions and civil war, and lastly a military despotism, into whose arms all will be driven by the intolerable evils of anarchy and rapine. I fondly hope that the future may bring along with it a sovereign remedy for these evils, but what that remedy may be, it is past perhaps the sagacity of man now to determine. We can only say in the language of Kepler upon a far different subject,— "Haec et cetera hujusmodi latent in pandectis aevi sequentis, non antea discenda, quam librum hunc deus arbiter seculorum recluserit mortalibus."[59]

In the mean time I may boldly assert that the frame work of our southern society is better calculated to ward off the evils of this agrarian spirit, which is so destructive to morals, to mind and to liberty, than any other mentioned in the annals of history. Domestic slavery, such as ours, is the only institution which I know of, that can secure that spirit of equality among freemen, so necessary to the true and genuine feeling of republicanism, without propelling the body politic at the same time into the dangerous vices of agrarianism, and legislative intermeddling between the laborer and the capitalist. The occupations which we follow, necessarily and unavoidably create distinctions in society. It is said that all occupations are honorable. This is certainly true, if you mean that no honest employment is disgraceful. But to say that all confer equal honor, if well followed even, is not true. Such an assertion militates alike against the whole nature of man and the voice of reason. But whatever may be the vain deductions of mere theorists upon this subject, one thing is certain—Reason informed me of its truth long before experience had shown it to me in actual life—The hirelings who perform all the menial offices of life, will not and cannot be treated as equals by their employers. And those who stand

---

dence are preferable to constant apprehension, freedom to slavery, being waited upon, to waiting upon others. When I was a rich man in this city, I was under the necessity of courting the sycophants, knowing it was in their power to do me mischief which I could little return. Nevertheless, I was continually receiving orders from the people, to undertake some expenses for the commonwealth, and I was not allowed to go any where out of Attica. But now I have lost all my foreign property, and nothing accrues from my Attic estate, and all my goods are sold, I sleep any where fearless; I am considered as faithful to the government; I am never threatened with prosecutions, but I have it in my power to make others fear; as a freeman I may stay in the country or go out of it as I please; the rich rise from their seats for me as I approach, and make way for me as I walk; I am now like a tyrant, whereas I was before an absolute slave; and whereas before I paid tribute to the people, now a tribute from the people maintains me." This picture, though perhaps overwrought, marks still but too conclusively the agrarian spirit in Greece.] Lysias, *On the Property of Aristophanes*, 11; Xenophon, *Banquet*, 4:29–32.

59. Trans. These and other things of this kind lie hidden in the encyclopedia of the next generation, not to be understood before God, the arbiter of the ages, opens this book to men: in the conclusion of Kepler's *Epitome of Copernican Astronomy*, which Dew probably derived from Dugald Stewart, *Dissertation*, p. 37, where this passage is quoted.

ready to execute all our commands, no matter what they may be, for mere pecuniary reward, cannot feel themselves equal to us in reality, however much their reason may be bewildered by the voice of sophistry.

Now, let us see what is likely to be the effect of universal suffrage in a state where there are no slaves. Either the dependent classes, the laborers and menial servants, will be driven forward by the dictation of their employers and the bribery of the man of property, thus giving the government a proclivity towards an aristocracy of wealth;[60] or they become discontented with their condition, and ask why these differences among beings pronounced equal—they look with eyes of cupidity upon the fortunes of the rich. The demagogue perceives their ominous sullenness, and marks the hatred which is rankling in their hearts—then the parties of the rich and the poor are formed—then come the legislative plunder and the dark train of evils consequent on the spirit of equality, which is in fact, in such a community, the spirit of agrarianism.

But in our slaveholding country the case is far different. Our laboring classes and menials are all slaves of a different color from their masters—the source of greatest distinction among the freemen is taken away; and the spirit of equality, the true spirit of genuine republicanism may exist here,—without leading on to corruption on the one side or agrarianism on the other.[61] Political power is thus taken from the hands of those who might abuse it, and placed in the hands of those who are most interested in its judicious exercise. Our law most wisely ordains that the slaves "shall not be sought for in public council, nor sit high in the congregation: they shall not sit high on the judges' seats nor understand the sentence of judgment;

---

60. [Men whose impulses are all communicated by the expectation of small pecuniary rewards, quickly acquire that suppleness of conscience, which renders them peculiarly liable to bribery. Take, for example, the waiter in a hotel—it is the hope of little gains that moves him in any direction which you may dictate, and which makes him a ready tool for the execution of any project whatever. His motto is, *I take the money and my employer the responsibility*. Bring this man to the polls, and offer him money for his vote, and the probability is that he would not refuse that which the whole education and training of his life would impel him to receive.]

61. [I will take leave here to introduce a short extract from my Essay on Slavery, in corroboration of the assertions which I have made. "The citizens of the north will not shake hands familiarly with his servant, and converse, and laugh, and dine with him, no matter how honest and respectable he may be. But go to the south, and you will find that no white man feels such inferiority of rank as to be unworthy of association with those around him. Color alone is here the badge of distinction, the true mark of aristocracy; and all who are white are equal, in spite of the variety of occupation. The same thing is observed in the West Indies. 'Of the character common to the white resident of the West Indies,' says B. Edwards, 'it appears to me that the leading feature is an independent spirit, and a display of *conscious equality* throughout all ranks and conditions. The poorest White person seems to consider himself nearly on a level with the condition of the richest; and emboldened by this idea, he approaches his employer with extended hand, and a freedom which, in the countries of Europe, is seldom displayed by men in the lower orders of life towards their superiors.'"] *The Proslavery Argument*, pp. 461–62; Bryan Edwards, *The History, Civil and Commercial, of the British Colonies in the West Indies* (3rd ed., London, 1801), 2:7–8: Dew has added an emphasis, tinkered with the phrasing, though not the sense, and lower-cased the word *white*.

they cannot declare justice and judgment; and they shall not be found where parables are spoken. How can he get wisdom that holdeth the plough, that glorieth in the goad, that driveth oxen and is occupied in their labors, and whose talk is of bullocks?"[62] Lycurgus, more than two thousand years ago, in his celebrated system of laws, was so well aware of the aristocratic feeling generated by diversity of occupation, that he decreed in order that a perfect spirit of equality might reign among the Spartans, that slaves alone should practice the most laborious arts, or fill the menial stations.[63] And in this particular he showed perhaps as much sagacity as in any other law of the whole system. We want no legislation in the south to secure this effect—it flows spontaneously from our social system.

But whilst the political effects of our social system are so peculiarly beneficial, the moral effects are no less striking and advantageous. I have no hesitation in affirming that the relation between capitalist and laborer in the south is kinder, and more productive of genuine attachment, than exists between the same classes any where else on the face of the globe. The slave is happy and contented with his lot, unless indeed the very demons of Pandemonium shall be suffered to come among us and destroy his happiness by their calumnious falsehoods and hypocritical promises. He compares himself with his own race and his own color alone, and he sees that all are alike—he does not covet the wealth of the rich man, nor envy that happiness which liberty imparts to the patriot, but he identifies all his interests with those of his master—free from care—free from that constant feeling of insecurity which continually haunts the poor man of other countries, he moves on in the round of his existence, cheerful, contented and grateful.[64] We have no Manchester and Smithfield riots here—no breaking of machinery—no scowl of discontent or sullenness hovering over the brow—no midnight murders for the money which we have in our houses—no melancholy forebodings of that agrarian spirit which calls up the very demon of wrath to apply the torch to the political edifice. The statistics of the slaveholding population prove that it is the most quiet and secure population in the world—there are fewer great crimes and murders among them than in any other form in which society can exist. I defy the world too, to produce a parallel to the rapid improvement of the slave on our continent since the period of his landing from the shores of his forefathers. And when the philanthropist tells us to plant our colonies on the coast of that benighted region, that the tide of civilization may be rolled

62. Ecclesiasticus [the Apocrypha] 38:33, 24.
63. Plutarch, *Lycurgus*, 24, 28.
64. [Any one who has ever seen the negro at hard labor by the side of a white man, or who has noticed him while performing menial services along with his white associate, has marked no doubt the striking difference. The negro is all gaiety and cheerfulness—his occupation seems to ennoble him. His companion, on the contrary, whom the world calls a freeman, but really treats as a slave, is seen sullen and discontented, and feels himself degraded for the very reason that he is called a freeman.]

back on Africa, the very enthusiasm of his language marks the inappreciable improvement which slavery has here wrought upon the character of the negro. On the other hand the master is attached to his slaves by every tie of interest and sympathy, generated by a connection that sometimes lasts for life. He does not work them to-day for sixteen hours, reducing them to mere bread and water, and capriciously discharge them to-morrow from his employment, and turn them adrift without money or resource, upon a cold and inhospitable world. When their labor will not support themselves, the master is bound to consume his capital for their sustenance. There are evils, no doubt, incidental to this relation—but where is the relation of life exempt from them?[65]

65. [Whatever philanthropists may say upon the subject, I believe the history of the world will bear me out in the assertion that slavery is certainly the most efficient and perhaps the only means by which the contact of the civilized man with the barbarian can contribute to the advantage and civilization of the latter. The relation of master and slave is the only means which has ever yet been devised by the wisdom of man, capable of bringing the element of civilization into close union with that of barbarism, without either dragging down the civilized man to a level with the barbarian, or corrupting and then exterminating the latter in the attempt to elevate him. Every one who is acquainted with the condition of society in our southern country, will bear witness to the truth of the assertion, that whilst slavery by producing the closest and most constant intercourse between the whites and blacks, elevates the character, purifies the morals, and speeds on the civilization of the latter, it has not the slightest tendency to introduce their barbarism or their vices among the former. It is for this very reason, while virtue and knowledge may travel downwards, and vice and barbarism cannot move upwards, that the institution of such slavery as ours becomes the greatest security for virtue, and the most certain preservative of morals. It is this inestimable feature in this most slandered institution, which keeps the upper stratum of the social fabric in the healthiest and soundest state, which makes the character of the slaveholder so lofty, generous, chivalrous, and sternly incorruptible wherever we find him. It is this same feature too which contributes most to elevate and adorn the character of the mistress of slaves—which enshrines her heart in the very purity and constancy of the affections, and makes her the ornament and immaculate blessing of that delightful domestic sanctuary, which is never to be polluted by the vile and wicked arts of the base designing corruptor of the female heart.

What then, in the presence of these facts, must we think of the slanderous tongues that would dare asperse the character of southern females—that would endeavor to blacken that almost spotless purity of heart, which I hope will forever remain the proud characteristic of southern women? Ignorance does not excuse such calumniators. The men who can attack, without having taken even the trouble to ascertain the facts, that class whose virtue constitutes their greatest ornament, and whom the usages and customs of the world have driven from the active bustling arena of life into the shade of retirement, there to be loved, honored, and protected by all who are noble and generous, show to the world the real hollowness of their hearts and the reckless impurity of their intentions. But when they cannot even plead such ignorance, their past lives should not be suffered to shield them from the imputation of crime, and the mantle of that pure and beautiful religion, preached by the meek Saviour of mankind, was never designed to cover the canting hypocrisy of the insidious calumnious slanderer. It is Sterne who says that the man who is capable of doing *one dirty trick* can do another—he thus at once unmasks his real character, and stands forth confessed in all his naked deformity before the world. And we may perhaps but too truly assert, that those whose minds are incapable of comprehending the purity, whilst they maliciously asperse the innocence of female character, are the beings who are most apt at last to be displayed as the true Tartuffes of the world.] Tartuffe is the hypocrite of Molière's play of that name; Dew was particularly interested in the social problem of women; cf. Dew, "Dissertation on the Characteristic Differences Between the Sexes," *SLM* 1 (May, July, August 1835): 495–512, 621–32, 672–91.

I would say then, let us cherish this institution which has been built up by no sin of ours—let us cleave to it as the ark of our safety. Expediency, morality and religion, alike demand its continuance; and perhaps I would not hazard too much in the prediction, that the day will come when the whole confederacy will regard it as the sheet anchor of our country's liberty.

I will now conclude my long address, by a brief notice of two results which may happen to our system of government, either of which would be fatal to the system—dismemberment on the one side, or consolidation on the other. Separate governments, or confederacies, would of course have rivalries and jealousies and wars. Our militia would be found inadequate to our defence; standing armies and navies would be established: and all history has shown that these will trample upon the civil authority. War with their concomitant establishments, navies and armies, entail the heaviest expense of nations.[66] These expenditures require taxation; and heavy taxation in an extensive range of country, whether levied on imports or on native productions, would be sure to lead on to partial and vicious legislation, to the intolerable oppression of one part for the benefit of another. And all the guards and checks which constitutional charters would impose on government, could not prevent the rapid concentration of power into the hands of the executive, in most of our independent states, amid wars, armies, navies, taxation, expenditures and increasing patronage of the governments. We should, I fear, exhibit the picture of Europe to the world, with governments perhaps less balanced[67] and more sanguinary in their wars. It is more than probable, then, that if ever disunion shall come, as has been said by a distinguished statesman,—we shall close the book of

---

66. [It may perhaps be affirmed with truth, that there is scarcely a nation in Europe, with a population equal to the United States, whose army does not cost more than the whole expenses of our federal government. The military statistics of Europe are truly formidable. Great Britain keeps at home an army of 100,000 men, and 250,000 in India. France has a standing army of 280,000; Austria 271,000; Prussia 162,000; and Russia 800,000. The United States have 6,000, with a population of a little more than the half of Austria, and greater than that of Prussia. Even the kingdom of Sardinia, with a population of a little more than one-fourth of ours, has an army more than seven times as great: and Spain, with a population not so great as ours, has an army fifteen times as great. Comment is unnecessary.]

67. [If a nation must have monarchy, I have no hesitation in saying that it should not be isolated. It should be "buttressed by establishments." If we must have Kings, it would be better that the Lords and Commons should follow. Kings, Lords, and Commons are perhaps the nearest approach which the monarchical form of government can make towards liberty. When there is no intermediate power between the king and the people, every dispute between the parties, for want of a conciliatory compromise, brings the nation at once to blows; and the immediate issue is necessarily either a despotism established, or a dynasty overthrown. The chances against a perfect balance are infinite. But in our country we can never have a regular nobility. Antiquity is absolutely necessary to such an establishment. Bonaparte tried the experiment of a suddenly created nobility, and it entirely failed; although his nobles were much more talented and efficient than the ancient noblesse. Bonaparte's nobles besides were the most unprincipled, and the most remorselessly rapacious of modern Europe; and this perhaps is the almost necessary character of an upstart nobility.]

the republics, and open that of the kings, not in name perhaps—but in reality.

This would certainly be the result of the non-slave-holding states, where the agrarian spirit, co-operating with executive usurpation, would inevitably overthrow the balance of the government, and lead on eventually to military despotism. But such is my confidence in the influence of slavery on the slaveholder—so certain am I, judging from all fair reasoning on the subject, and from the past history of the world, that the spirit of liberty and of equality, glows with the most unqualified intensity in the bosoms of the masters of slaves, that I believe the slaveholding states, with all the horrors of disunion against them, would nevertheless, under the impulse of this spirit, so ineradicable among *them*, be enabled to preserve their liberties, and arrest their governments in their dangerous proclivity towards monarchy. It is true, circumstances might often even here concentrate too much power in the executive department; but the owners of slaves, with a spirit like that of the Barons at Runnimede, would embrace the first opportunity to take back the power that had slipt from their hands; and the absence of any thing like a formidable agrarian party, would deprive the executive of that infallible resource to which, under other circumstances, it might resort, to obtain the power necessary to break through the trammels of constitutions, and finally to entrench itself safely behind military power. Where has a greater love for liberty been shown, or a more noble struggle made for its preservation than in Poland? And in our own country, it is a matter of history, that in no portion of it has the spirit of freedom so fervently developed itself as in the Southern States, nor has any portion been found more constantly and effectually battling against power. Two administrations have been overthrown since the constitution went into operation, and it has been Southern talent, and Southern energy, which have accomplished it. Whenever the South shall present a solid unbroken phalanx against usurpation, I hazard little in the prediction, that it will generally accomplish its ends.

But disunion, with all its attendant evils, would not so completely prostrate the mind, and relax all the energies of man, as the other more dangerous result which may happen—I mean consolidation! A number of independent governments, no matter how bad, no matter how despotic, must to some extent at least, exert a stimulating influence, each over a portion of its own territory. The greater the number of governments therefore, the greater the number of stimulants, as long as each one remains independent. And the probability is, that a sort of political equilibrium would be formed very soon on our continent, which would, as in Europe, preserve the territorial integrity of the smaller states, and prevent the larger from a dangerous accumulation of power.[68]

68. [It is curious to look now to the condition of Europe, and compare it with the same quarter of the world three hundred years ago, and to see how small the change in the division

But if ever our state institutions shall be overthrown, and the concentration of all the powers into one great central government shall mould this system of republics into one grand consolidated empire, then will the last and greatest evil which can befal our country have arrived. The wide extent of our territory, and the numbers of our population, which under a system of confederated republics, would awaken the genius and patriotism of the country, and call forth an almost resistless energy and enterprise in our citizens, would then be a blighting curse—the bane of our land. All eyes would be turned to that great and fearful engine at the centre, whose oppressive action would paralyze all the parts, whilst it would bind them together in indissoluble union—in the numbness and torpor of death itself.

Could it be possible for our government, after such consolidation, to retain its democratic form, then would it become the most corrupt, the most demoralizing, the most intolerably oppressive government which the annals of history could furnish. That diversity of climate, of soil, of character, and of interest—that great difference of condition springing from the existence or non-existence of slavery, all of which, under a mild, federative system, would increase the general happiness and add to the blessings of union, by interlocking, in the harmony of free trade, all the interests of the parts, would then lead on to vicious combinations in our national legislature, for the purpose of robbing one portion of the union for the benefit of another—then would be formed our fixed and sectional majorities, who by their unprincipled and irresponsible legislation, would prostrate the rights and suck out the very substance from the minority. The history of past ages informs us that physical force has hitherto been the great engine which has distributed the wealth and overthrown the liberties of nations. But the system would be changed here. Governmental action and legislative jugglery would accomplish more effectually what the sword has done elsewhere. And to the oppressed there would be but one

---

of countries after all the wars, bloodshed, and expense which have been inflicted on it. And some of the greatest gainers too have been the small states. The Duke of Savoy, for example, now takes honorable rank among the second rate monarchs, under the more imposing title of King of Sardinia, and with a territory more than doubled in extent. The Marquis of Brandenburg now hails as King of Prussia, and takes his station among the great powers in Europe with a greatly augmented dominion. It is the system of the political equilibrium in Europe which has bridled the great nations, and prevented them swallowing up the smaller. "Consider," says Sir James Macintosh, in one of his ablest speeches, "the Republic of Geneva—think of her defenceless position, in the very jaws of France; but think also of her undisturbed security, of her profound quiet, of the brilliant success with which she has applied herself to industry and literature, while Louis XIV was pouring his myriads into Italy before her gates. Call to mind that happy period, when we scarcely dreamed more of the subjugation of the feeblest republic of Europe, than of the conquest of her mightiest empire—and say whether any spectacle can be imagined more beautiful to the moral eye, or which affords a more striking proof of progress in the noblest principles of true civilization."] "A Speech in Defence of Jean Peltier," in *Works of . . . Mackintosh*, 3:248: Dew has badly knocked this quotation about, without materially altering the sense.

right left—the right that belongs to the worm when trodden on—the right of turning upon the oppressor and shaking off his iron grasp, if possible. This is the most valuable of all rights to the European citizen—because there the few, the units, are the oppressors, and the millions are the oppressed; and when tyranny has passed beyond the point of endurance, and the people are at last roused to a sense of the injustice and wrongs which they are suffering, they rise in their might and pull down the pillars of the political edifice.

But in our own country, if the state governments shall ever be broken down, and state marks obliterated, what will the right of resistance be worth to us? When the oppression comes from the greedy many, and is exerted over the proscribed few, is it not worse than mockery to tell them they may resist in the last resort—that the minority, enfeebled and impoverished by legislative plunder, without army, navy, or treasury, disorganized, unsteady, and vacillating in its plans, may rise against the many who possess the advantages of physical force, wealth, organization, together with the whole power of an energetic government, which can break the ranks of the minority, and sow the seeds of dissension among them, by the corrupting influence of its mighty patronage, or attack and conquer by its force those who shall first have the temerity to take the field against its oppression? Resistance is worth but little, when the strong man, armed and resolute, has pushed me, feeble and unarmed, to the wall.[69]

But let not the many console themselves with the vain belief that democracy would long survive the consolidation of our government—that very power which they would endeavor so sedulously to concentrate in the hands of one great central government, would be quickly made to recoil upon their own heads. The executive department, which would be built up and established by the dominant majority, the better to accomplish its own selfish purposes, would quickly become omnipotent; and when once safely entrenched in the impregnable bulwarks of its power, like Athens enclosed in the walls of Themistocles, it would bid defiance to all assaults, and all

---

69. [The principle of the *absolute majority* claimed by a great central government, would make the republican form of government more intolerable than any other, for the following reasons: 1st. The parties may be permanent, and consequently the oppression may be permanent also. 2d. An individual with power to oppress may or may not do it. Even Nero or Caligula may refrain from exactions—but a multitude being *always* governed by the selfish principle, will be *sure* to oppress if they have the power; the operation of the selfish principle on *one* man is a matter of chance,—on the *multitude*, it is a certainty. 3d. In such a government, the influence of the public opinion of the oppressed produces the *least possible* influence on the oppressors, first, because the majorities and minorities being almost always sectional, the opinions of the latter are not likely to be known to the former; and secondly, if they were known they would produce little effect, because the former have on their side the majority of public opinion, and therefore would generally disregard that of the minority. 4th. The rapacity of such a government would be increased, from the necessity of procuring a large *dividend* for so great a number of *divisors*.]

would then be ground down to the same ignominious common level. The Executive, in such a system, would be all—the People, nothing! We should then be reduced to the condition of the silent crushing despotisms of Asia— with every principle of improvement gone, and the whole elasticity of mind destroyed. Soon would we, then, hug the chains which bound us; and bend the knee in degrading servility before him who had rivetted them on us. Soon would we be ready to use the idolatrous language of the Roman bard,

> "Erit ille mihi semper Deus: illius aram
> Saepe tener nostris ab ovilibus imbuet agnus."[70]

A great empire speedily assimilates every thing to its own genius. No long season is requisite to generate the spirit of submission. The monarch that first mounts the throne is often the most worshipped. The first emperor of Rome had not descended to his grave before the servility of his subjects had become so disgusting as to call forth censure from even the monarch himself.[71]

These great despotisms too, when once established, are likely long to endure. Great empires have an extraordinary vitality—a wonderful tenacity of existence; they but too closely resemble that fabled serpent whose parts when forced asunder were quickly drawn together again and united into a living body. There has always been something painfully revolting to my mind in the contemplation of the history of great empires. From our boyhood we contract a horror of eastern despotisms, with their great monarchs, their satraps and tyrants; and who that has read the *luminous* page of Gibbon and contemplated the imperial despot with his

> Praetors, pro-consuls to their provinces
> Hasting, or on return, in robes of state,
> Lictors and rods the ensigns of their power,
> Legions and cohorts, turms of horse and wings,[72]

but sickens at the bare contemplation of such despotic machinery. And whilst we peruse the eloquent recital of these internal throes and convulsions, which to-day would seem to break the empire into fragments and scatter them to the very winds of heaven,—but would cease on the morrow, by the elevation to the throne of perhaps some barbarian military chieftain from the banks of the Rhine or the Danube, binding again to-

---

70. Vergil, *Eclogues*, I, lines 7–8: trans. a god he shall ever be to me; often shall a tender lamb from our folds stain his altar. Dew has capitalized *deus*.

71. [Augustus, at the expiration of his third term in the imperial office, was accosted by the people at the public entertainment with the title of "Lord," or "Master," which so much disgusted him, that he published a serious edict on the following day, forbidding such a title, and saying, "*My name is Caesar, and not Master.*"] Suetonius, *Twelve Caesars, Augustus*: 53.

72. Milton, *Paradise Regained*, IV, lines 63–66.

gether in the rude embrace of military power the conquered parts of the empire,—we cannot but weep over the fearful immortality with which such a nation seems almost to be endowed. It reminds us but too strongly of that persecuted being, gifted with a cursed immortality, whom the fables of antiquity reported to have been bound down upon the mountain, with a vulture forever lacerating his liver, which grew as fast as it was destroyed. When contemplating the horrors of such a government, we almost hail with pleasure the advent of the Goth and the Vandal, whose barbarian power alone could break it into fragments. The death of such an empire is always hard—painfully, fearfully hard! Unless its destruction is prepared from without, there are no elements within that can achieve it. The gravity of the parts too towards the centre, is so wonderfully great, that disunion can never be effected.

It is mournful to behold how the rights of man, and of nations, may be destroyed by the mere magnitude of empire. Humanity now weeps when wronged and injured Poland shows symptoms of a revolt,—we know that the blood of the patriotic Pole will be shed in vain, and that the Russian and the Cossack soldier will soon come to place the galling yoke again upon his neck; and yet if Poland were united to a nation no larger than herself—Poland would have rights, and what is better still, Poland would have the power to defend them. And when she should send her petitions to the throne and demand redress, the Autocrat would dare not answer her deputies by pointing them to his Marshal, and telling them that *he* had his orders and would execute them.

Let us then forever guard against the dangerous evil of consolidation. Let us foster and cherish and love our State institutions as the palladium of our liberties and the nursery of our real greatness. Let the motto inscribed upon the banner of each patriot, in regard to his state, be that which was placed upon the urn that enclosed the heart of the philosopher of Ferney,[73] "*Mon coeur est ici, mon esprit est partout;*" and sure we may be, that this elementary training of the affections will not destroy a proper love for the whole, but is absolutely necessary, to keep the State and Federal governments moving, in those distinct orbits which have been prescribed to them by the wisdom of our ancestors.

But, whatever may be the course of other states,—I hope our own Virginia,—so rich in soil, but so much richer in her noble sons who have grown up on that soil and illustrated her history, will ever cherish with becoming affection her own institutions—for certain she may be, when a great consolidated central government shall have fixed its embrace on the Union—the sun of her glory will have set forever—certain she may be, that in the awful silence of central despotism, no such statesmen as Wash-

---

73. Voltaire.

ington, Jefferson or Madison, will ever again arise upon her soil—no such men as Wythe, Pendleton and Roane, will grace her benches—nor will the thrilling eloquence of the Henrys, the Masons and the Randolphs, be ever again heard within her borders.[74] The power that then reposes at the centre, may, after the example of the most wily and politic of Roman emperors, suffer the mere state forms to remain, but the spirit, the energetic life, the independence that once animated them, will all be gone. They will then obey an impulse that comes from without; and like the consuls, the senate, and the tribunes of imperial Rome, they will but speak the will and execute the commands of the Caesar upon the throne. Then indeed may the passing stranger, when he beholds this capital, once the proud theatre for the exhibition of the conflicts of mind and talents, exclaim—Poor Virginia! how art thou fallen!

But I sincerely hope, that the patriotism and the intelligence of the people of this country, will be sufficient to keep our state and federal governments moving on harmoniously in their legitimate spheres,—avoiding at the same time dismemberment on the one side, or the more dangerous tendency of consolidation on the other. All, however, depends on the virtue, the intelligence, and the vigilance of the People. Power to be restrained must always be watched with Argus eyes—the people must always be on the alert—they must never slacken their vigilance. If they have succeeded to-day in stripping the usurper of his assumed powers—let them not remit their exertions on the morrow, but let them remember that power after "these gentle prunings" does sometimes vegetate but the more luxuriantly. If we shall wisely avoid the evils with which we are beset in our onward progress, then I would boldly assert, that never since the foundation of the world has the eye of the philanthropist rested on a country which has furnished so grand, so magnificent a theatre for the creation and the display of arts, science and literature, and for the production of all those virtues and high intellectual energies, which so ennoble and adorn the human being and render him the true image of his Maker, as our own most beautiful system of Confederated Republics will then present.

Mr. President, I have done. The great importance and interest of the topic I have so unworthily discussed, must be my apology for having detained you so long.

---

74. George Wythe, 1726–1806, jurist, signer of the Declaration of Independence, reviser of Virginia law; Edmund Pendleton, 1721–1803, jurist and Continental congressman; John Roane, 1766–1838, congressman and member of the Virginia Constitutional Convention of 1788.

# 5.

## George Frederick Holmes

### "Schlegel's Philosophy of History"[1]

George Frederick Holmes belongs in an anthology of Southern intellectuals, more because there is nowhere else to put him than because he was an unmitigated Southerner.[2] He was born, in fact, in British Guiana in 1820 and lived between the ages of two and seventeen in the North of England, where he latterly attended the University of Durham. He came, uncertain of purpose, in 1837 to the United States via Canada, partly to make his fortune, a task for which he was always singularly ill-equipped. He lived for a while in Virginia, went for a few months to Macon in Georgia, moved on to Decatur, thought about Russia or Missouri, settled briefly on a legal career in Orangeburg but failed at it, taught at a college in Richmond until he was elected to a chair at William and Mary in 1847, resigned two years later, was reinstated but decided to accept the presidency of the new University of Mississippi at Oxford, was a catastrophic failure at that, went to live in rural isolation in western Virginia upon his wife's meager establishment, until his election to a professorship at the University of Virginia in 1857 ended his peregrinations. He died in 1897. Along the way, he acquired some friends, more correspondents, and some sense of identity with the South. But it is little wonder that he stares out from his photographs, owlish and startled, or that his writings were a search for intellectual order.

As an earner of bread, he was incompetent. As an author, he had critical talents. No one wrote more and few better for Southern

---

1. George Frederick Holmes, "Schlegel's Philosophy of History," *SQR* 3 (April 1843): 263–317.
2. The best source for Holmes's life and thought is Neal C. Gillespie, *The Collapse of Orthodoxy: The Intellectual Ordeal of George Frederick Holmes* (Charlottesville, 1972).

periodicals. His output was prodigious, which is one reason posterity has been ill-disposed to appraise him. His bibliography for the antebellum years contains some 114 items, most of them far from brief, many on subjects extremely diverse: scientific theory and Indians, medieval Greek and Russian literature, Disraeli and Californian gold, spiritualism and Gibbon, demographics and the Reformation.[3] He wrote, one is tempted to say, almost obsessively. He certainly read that way. It was true he usually needed the money, even though the periodical essay was not a sensible way to fashion a fortune. But money was as much an excuse as a reason. Publication was the tip of an iceberg of letter books, memoranda, and notes.

Among such an outpouring, the editor's task of selection is more than usually absurd. This piece upon the historical philosophy of Friedrich von Schlegel is one of his earliest pieces, written when he was fleetingly a lawyer in South Carolina, still just twenty-three, and patronized by that other notable Southern Francophile, David Flavel Jamison.[4] But Holmes, apart from a few youthful effusions of fiction in the *Southern Literary Messenger*, struck the stride of his forte very quickly and maintained it almost invariantly until the Civil War interceded and destroyed his natural medium, the Southern periodical. And many of his characteristic themes are stated here: his suspicion and pondering of German thought; his enthusiasm for French letters, which was later to make him the first American disciple of, and correspondent with, Auguste Comte;[5] his worrying over the problem of Christianity and the grounds for a rational theodicy; his desire to find a grand pattern in the course of human history; his apparent devotion to the traditions of English empiricism, which often masked his instinct for theory, even from himself; his conviction that the nineteenth century was poised upon an intellectual revolution. His sense of the balance between these themes was to fluctuate. In the early 1840s he was most sanguine that "intellect is claiming her throne, and though we live in the day of battle, we cannot doubt the issue of the contest."[6] He was still diffident about

---

3. Ibid., pp. 250–57.

4. See especially David F. Jamison, *The Life and Times of Bertrand du Guesclin, A History of the Fourteenth Century* (Charleston, 1864), translated as *Bertrand Guesclin et son époque* (Paris, 1866); "The French Revolution," *SQR* 5 (April 1844): 1–102; "Lamartine's Histoire des Girondins," *SQR* 16 (October 1849): 53–76.

5. Richard L. Hawkins, *Auguste Comte and the United States, 1816–1953* (Cambridge, Mass., 1936) and *Positivism in the United States, 1853–1861* (Cambridge, Mass., 1938).

6. "Whewell on the Inductive Sciences," *SQR* 2 (July 1842): 195, quoted in Gillespie, *Collapse of Orthodoxy*, p. 41.

the claims of orthodox Christianity. Later his faith in mind and doubt of religion were to lessen, but even in 1843 the Bible was never far from his thoughts.

The intellectual hero of this essay is Jules Michelet. As Holmes himself was at pains to indicate, Michelet was still barely known in the United States and largely untranslated. Through Michelet, Holmes grasped less surely at the writings of the forerunner of historicism, Giambattista Vico. With both, and using Schlegel as a whipping boy, Holmes tried to grapple with a characteristic problem for Southern intellectuals. What is the nature of the divisions in human culture? Upon what do they rest? Climate, race, religion, the chance or ordered managements of historical development? Was human progress linear or cyclical or—as Vico argued, Michelet seemed to misconstrue, and Holmes reasserted under the impression that he was correcting Vico—spiral? If cultures were imbedded in history, and the two changed together, how should the historian devise periodizations to comprehend the evolution? To all these questions, Holmes worried out preliminary answers. In later years, more impressed with traditional Christianity, he was to reflect that he had been too ruthlessly secular in 1843, had written too much in the spirit of a Thomas Cooper and of Michelet himself, the scourge of medieval Christianity's historical reputation. "In this article," Holmes was to write in a private notebook, "I have not done justice to Schlegel, and have overpraised Michelet. Were it now to be written over again both the censure and the praise would be very much modified. I have most unpardonably neglected to take any notice of the Catholic view of history which Schlegel develops throughout his work."[7] The later reader might be more disposed to forgive.

TO STUDY history as merely the narrative of a series of disconnected events, which have in their day been attended with national weal or national wo;—to regard it as simply a record of battles gained and battles lost,—of heroic actions crowned with eternal glory, or of individuals consigned to merited

---

7. Ibid., p. 103.

obloquy and contempt;—or worse, to peruse it as a barren chronicle of kings, and princes, and rulers, who have lived, and reigned, and passed away, leaving behind them such scanty cause for remembrance, that they only serve to indicate periods in the march of time:—this is to view history as a strange diorama, wherein a few figures here and there stand out, connected together by little more than a common canvass and sequence in respect of time. If we suffer ourselves to entertain such considerations of history, we are certainly obnoxious to the charge, which Sir William Davenant brings against historians, that they "worship a dead thing."[8] We are not to examine into the "*acta*" and "*gesta*" of earlier times, as if it were the sole requisite of history to collect the "*disjecta membra*"—the torn and mutilated remnants of the past,—into a heap, and to string together upon the wires of chronological succession, the blanched and mouldering bones, so as to defy all recognition of them as organic parts of a once existent body. Such a mode of prosecuting the study, (though frequently adopted,) loads the memory at the expense of the judgment, and interests the feelings for the moment, without repaying us with any of those instructive lessons, which render history the most profound of all philosophies. Pursued in this spirit, it may possibly afford to the mind relaxation and amusement; but is scarcely entitled to that high degree of consideration, which has been usually conceded to it. Indeed, we lose the greater and the more important part of its value, if we content ourselves with studying it as the mirror of human nature in the abstract, as some have done; or referring to it solely for the maxims of present political wisdoms, or the secrets of possible political change. But it becomes the noblest study which can employ the mind of the sage, when we regard it as the chart of the moral, social and intellectual advancement of mankind,—showing how one nation and one era have paved the way for the superior intelligence of the next; or have fired the train which produced its ruin;—how one race of men has impregnated and civilized all succeeding ages, while another has infused new fire and vigor into the smouldering embers of a declining world; and revealing at the same time the mysteries of the downfall of nations, and the successive cycles which have arisen upon the ruins of their precursors. In this manner, the long progression of human events is linked together in one connected scheme; each phenomenon of the world's civilization and advancement appears holding that station, which the nature of the world's career required; and the mighty scroll of history becomes the page, on which is written in mystic, but intelligible characters, the nature, the di-

---

8. Sir William D'Avenant, preface to *Gondibert*, ed. D. F. Gladish (Oxford, 1971), p. 10: "But by this I would imply, that Truth narrative, and past, is the Idoll of Historians (who worship a dead thing) and truth operative, and by effects continually alive, is the Mistresse of Poets, who hath not her existence in matter, but in reason." It is quoted in Samuel Taylor Coleridge, *Biographia Literaria* (London, 1817), 2:141.

rection and the causes of the onward march of humanity, during the centuries of its existence. To study history in this way, is to study it philosophically; and history expounded in such a manner as to exhibit the results of this mode of investigation, is what we understand by—THE PHILOSOPHY OF HISTORY.

This branch of human knowledge, is undoubtedly of very late origin. There are, indeed, not a few passages in the Treatise De Augmentis Scientiarum, which might lead to the impression, that the main features of the science had been contemplated by the remarkable author of that work, and had been alluded to by him among the literary desiderata of his day. But such is the wonderful pregnancy of Lord Bacon's masterly style, that his language frequently appears to carry in its womb the embryos of sciences subsequently discovered, in cases where we could scarcely conjecture a possible anticipation of them. And if we once admit the propriety of the dogma, laid down by St. Augustine in reference to the interpretation of Scripture, that every expression is intended to convey by implication, whatever, by constructions the most forced, we may be able to deduce from it,[9] we sweep away at one blow all the land-marks of scientific discovery, and deny to the real and meritorious inventor the credit due to his successful exertions, that we may heap up honor on the head of some antecedent speculator, whose loose phraseology may be made to disgorge, *ad libitum*, whole sciences of which the writer knew nothing. In this way, Newton might be despoiled of his laurels that they might wither on the brow of Hooke;[10] and the first blind wanderer, that lost his way and stumbled over the ground, might receive all the praise which might afterwards be merited by the laborious planter of the vineyard. Far be it from us to apply to Lord Bacon any part of these observations, which may seem in

---

9. [I quote this remark of St. Augustine from memory, but think it occurs in his Confessions. A serious reply to such a dogma, is almost as ridiculous as the proposition itself. The most suitable answer is the following extract from the great Iconoclast of the follies of the intellect. "Croiez vous en vostre foy qu'oncques Homere, escrivent l'Iliade at Odyssée, pensast es allegories lesquelles de luy ont calfreté Plutarche, Heraclides Ponticq, Eustatie, Phornute, et ce que d'iceulx Politian a desrobé? Si le croiez, vous n'aprochez ne de pieds ne de mains à mon opinion, qui decrete icelles aussi peu avoir esté songéez d'Homere que d'Ovide en ses *Metamorphoses* les sacremens de l'Evangile, lesquelz un Frere Lubin, vray croquelardon, s'est efforcé demonstrer, si d'adventure il rencontroit gens aussi folz que luy, et (come dict le proverbe) couvercle digne du chaudron."—Rabelais. Vie du Grand Gargantua, liv. I, Prologe de l'Autheur.] I have corrected this text, not from any wish to disguise any possible incompetence on Holmes's part, but because it is so egregiously botched that I can only imagine the printer was astounded at old French, or at Holmes's handwriting, or both. See *The Confessions of Saint Augustine*, trans. E. B. Pusey (New York, 1951), pp. 334-35: "So when one says, 'Moses meant as I do;' and another, 'Nay, but as I do,' I suppose that I speak more reverently, 'Why not rather as both, if both be true?' And if there be a third, or a fourth, yea if any other seeth any other truth in those words, why may not he be believed to have seen all these, through whom the One God hath tempered the Holy Scriptures to the senses of many, who should see therein things true but divers?"

10. Robert Hooke, 1635-1703, the English physicist.

the slightest degree to detract from his learning and genius, for in both he was pre-eminent; but if we acknowledge that he anticipated the authors of the last century in inventing the Philosophy of History, we have reasons, almost equally strong, for carrying many ages further back its earliest anticipation, and finding its glimmering dawn in the writings of the sage of Samosata.[11] There will be found, however, among us, none sufficiently adventurous to maintain this thesis, unless a second Dutens[12] should arise, or the grave restore to the world the *Arch-Archaeist* himself.[13]

Bossuet's celebrated Discourse on Universal History,[14] was the first pioneer in the new route, but it is not without justice that Giambattista Vico has been termed *the Father of the Philosophy of History*.[15] His great work, the Scienza Nuova, first appeared at Naples towards the close of 1725, and again under an enlarged form in 1730.[16] This is the corner-stone of the new temple. Yet, the work lay almost wholly neglected and forgotten for more than a century, after the first burst of astonishment had subsided, which its novelty excited. It was neither appreciated nor understood by his own contemporaries, for it was far in advance of the age in which he lived, and the name of Vico had nearly sunk into oblivion, when the Scienza Nuova was re-produced, a little more than ten years ago, by M. Michelet, of the College Royal de France, under the form of an abridged translation, accompanied with a luminous Introduction, on the System and Life of Vico. Between the dates, however, of its first publication and its subsequent resuscitation, several valuable works had appeared, either directly and professedly written upon the Philosophy of History, or bearing incidentally upon it, from the mode in which separate branches of historical investigation were treated. Of the latter class, the most celebrated are Montesquieu, sur l'Esprit des Lois, les Oeuvres de Turgot; Voltaire, Essai sur L'Esprit et les Moeurs des Nations; and V. Cousin, Histoire de la Philosophie:[17]—of the former, the most worthy of note are Herder's Outlines

11. Lucian, circa 125–80 B.C., the Greek satirist and historian, who was born at Samosata in Syria.

12. Louis Dutens, 1730–1812, a French writer who worked in the British diplomatic service, author of *Recherches sur l'origine des découvertes attribuées aux modernes* (1766); it may be significant that Samuel Taylor Coleridge, *The Friend*, ed. B. E. Rooke (Princeton, 1969), 1:484, 462, mentions Hooke and Dutens on not unadjacent pages.

13. "Archaeist" means an antiquary; the *Oxford English Dictionary* gives its first usage as 1851, by Elizabeth Barrett Browning. It is not clear to whom Holmes has reference, unless it is St. Augustine.

14. Jacques Benigne Bossuet, *Discours sur l'histoire universelle* (Paris, 1681).

15. [S.Q.R.—No. IV] "Oeuvres de Vico," *SQR* 4 (October 1842): 404–15; the author is as yet unidentified.

16. [Vie de Vico, ecrite par lui-meme—trad. Michelet.] *Principes de la philosophie de l'histoire, traduit de la Scienza Nuova de J.B. Vico, et précédes d'un discours sur le système et la vie de l'auteur*, ed. Jules Michelet (Paris, 1827).

17. Montesquieu, *De l'esprit des loix* (Geneva, 1748); Voltaire, "Essai sur les moeurs et l'esprit des nations," *Mercure de France* (1745–1746, 1750–1751); Victor Cousin, *Cours de philosophie* (Paris, 1828–1829) and *Cours d'histoire de la philosophie moral au dix-huitième siècle* (Paris,

Schlegel's Philosophy 183

of a Philosophy of the History of Man, which appeared at Weimar in 1784, being only an enlarged edition of a similar work, published by the same author ten years before Schlegel's Philosophy of History, delivered in a series of Lectures at Vienna in 1828; and several of the works of Guizot, Cousin, Michelet, etc.[18]

Within the last few years, this subject has been daily attracting more and more attention abroad. New treatises connected with it have been given to the world, principally by the French school; and these, together with the work whose title we have prefixed to our present article, have added a new impulse to the study, and furnished us with many aids, of more or less value, to the successful prosecution of it. But all these new discoveries have been made by laborers in France and Germany, and it is to them that our thanks are due. Occasional notices of their works, with, however, but small apprehension or appreciation of their import, may indeed be found, like gleams of unexpected—*starlight*, in the Reviews of England and America. These are of very different degrees of excellence, but any thing like a comprehensive understanding of the connected scheme, which the science of history would build up, appears to have been wholly foreign from their habits of thought. One Irish scholar, indeed, if not better informed than the rest, at any rate with all the rashness of his country, did venture, in 1840, under the high sanction of the Primate of Ireland, to publish an original treatise on this subject, which cannot pretend to be on a par with the philosophy of the times of Montesquieu, notwithstanding the vast variety of new materials within his reach, and has, therefore, proved its author to be at least a hundred years behind the present stage of the science in France. "W. Cooke Taylor, LL. D., M. R. A. S., of Trinity College, Dublin," is the writer to whom we allude; and from this merited censure, neither the marked array of honorable appendages to his name, nor the scrutinizing eye and over-shadowing wing of the arch-episcopal logician of Dublin, can shield him, for we have meted out his portion to him according to his deserts. His work, professing to be "The Natural History of Society, in the Barbarous and Civilized States," though so misnamed, has been welcomed by many with a degree of approbation, to which it was not in the least entitled.[19] This was not to be wondered at, when the great majority of readers were so lamentably ignorant of every thing relating to the task which he had undertaken, and so totally unconscious even of the nature and amount of their own ignorance. Dr. Taylor has,

---

1839–1842); Herder, *Auch eine Philosophie der Geschichte* (Riga, 1774) and *Ideen zur Philosophie der Geschichte der Menschheit* (Leipzig, 1784), the latter translated as *Outlines of a Philosophy of the History of Man* by T. Churchill (London, 1800).

18. [We are under the impression that Michelet's Translation of Vico appeared either in 1827 or 1828, but do not know whether it did or did not precede Schlegel's lectures.] Both were 1827.

19. William Cooke Taylor, *The Natural History of Society, in the Barbarous and Civilized State* (New York, 1841).

however, the merit of having opened the eyes of English and Americans to the existence of this department of historical investigation; and if he has done little to introduce them to the treasures collected abroad, he has, at any rate, called attention to the subject; and each individual is at liberty to inquire for himself. Moreover, his book, notwithstanding all its imperfections and deficiencies, may serve to throw a flickering light thro' the Cimmerian gloom, even though it be wholly unfit to be taken for a guiding star.

If there were not so much more to be surprised at in the work of Dr. Taylor, we might express some astonishment that he did not avail himself of the opportunity afforded him of introducing to the particular attention of English scholars, the remarkable productions of the recent historical school of France. We are convinced that a thorough familiarity with them, would contribute much towards elevating the views generally prevalent in regard to the functions of history, both in England and in the United States. Not that we are so blindly enamoured of the writings of Guizot, Cousin, Michelet, and their respective followers, as to imagine them to be without fault or flaw; they are far enough removed from any such perfection,— they do not pretend to exhaust the subjects they handle, and frequently present us with crude and incomplete speculations, instead of mature reflections. Yet there is no room for doubt that, in historical science, the Parisian school of the present day is far, very far in advance of any other people, and we would do well to have constant recurrence to their writings, in preference to any other sources of information, with which the most of us content ourselves.

Instead of this reference to Guizot, Michelet, &c., Herder and Schlegel have been accepted as the parents of what little speculation this subject has elicited in England and the United States. Both of these authors were reprinted in New-York in the year 1841, by the respectable house of D. Appleton & Co., which may be taken as some evidence of our assertion. For a long time previously, however, Herder had ceased to attract much attention beyond the closet of the studious, and had been left to moulder in most of our libraries unopened, and often unknown. The name of the distinguished author might have been sufficient to keep the interest in his work alive, had not the English and American nations, and, perhaps, from their position, necessarily, opposed to the genius of history; in consequence of which the Science, or Philosophy of History, has been held by many among them to be quite as mysterious, and nearly as unprofitable, as the Cabbala and the Talmud. Herder and Schlegel have been almost the only writers on the subject translated into the English tongue. Herder was for a long time scarcely remembered, and accordingly Schlegel has become the principal fountain to quench the thirst of the curious, and has thereby been received with a much more cordial greeting than was his due.

Schlegel's Philosophy of History is open to very many objections; his

History of Literature, though exceedingly valuable, was not immaculate,[20] but the work under review has no title to any share of the praise which the other might deserve. It has neither the feelings nor the profundity, which the learning and reputation of the author, and the nature of the subject, might have naturally led us to expect. Its views are vague, fantastical and unsatisfactory,—there is a constant straining towards some invisible end,—a continual groping amid fogs, and clouds, and darkness, for something which the writer supposes to be latent there, but which remains wholly untangible to him. He starts some wild dream about Providence and man, and, pursuing the shadow which he has evoked, gives utterance to the thick-thronging fancies with much more of the air of a rhapsodist than a philosopher. The facts, however, on which the details of the work have been built, were well selected and respectably arranged,— it is in the comprehension of the philosophic import of his materials that Schlegel failed. In consequence of this merit, he has undoubtedly contributed somewhat to advance the department of knowledge to which it was devoted, though we may have some hesitation in admitting, that it was not behind the age in which it was produced, like Dr. Taylor's, commemorated above. Some of its faults were necessarily entailed upon it, by the adoption of the form of Lectures, for the Philosophy of History is not a matter that can be safely treated in a popular strain, as it pre-supposes a tolerable familiarity, in the readers or the audience, with all the main points of historical knowledge. What a German audience may be, we would hardly presume to say; we might admit that Schlegel's lecture-room, at Vienna, contained more varied information, and more extensive learning, than could be brought together in any lecture room in London, Edinburgh or Dublin,—in Boston, Philadelphia or Charleston; and, yet, we might still with reason infer, that lecturing even before them was not the best mode of doing justice to a subject so novel, and requiring such varied and copious elucidation. For this reason, we regret exceedingly that Guizot's works on kindred subjects should have been promulgated under the form of Lectures, for much must necessarily be sacrificed to the demands of the moment.[21] These views may be correct, or they may not be so: we would very willingly refer the numerous deficiencies which strike us in Schlegel's Philosophy of History, to extraneous causes, for we feel some degree of reluctance, if not of absolute timidity, in charging home these faults upon an author of such merited and established reputation as Frederick Von Schlegel, and referring them to the *"culpa ingeni"*[22] of a writer whom we ourselves so highly esteem. Moreover, such extravagant praise has been lav-

---

20. Cf. Holmes, "History of Literature," *SQR* 2 (October 1842): 472–517.
21. Francois Guizot, *General History of Civilization in Europe from the Fall of the Roman Empire to the French Revolution* (New York, 1838).
22. Trans., literally, the blame of the creative intellect, in other words, the defect of his virtue.

ished upon this book, that it cannot be surprising if we feel some honest hesitation in withholding the usual amount of commendation, more especially as the encomiasts have themselves been men of learning, ability and eminence. We cannot, however, suffer ourselves to be drawn in with our eyes open into the crowd of astonished gazers,—wherever our frailty will permit, we will not "follow the multitude to do evil,"[23]—we cannot join in the full cry of Schlegel's admirers, without being first assured of the propriety of their warmth. The applause with which the work has been received, both in this country and in England, is easily accounted for, by recalling to mind the fact, that in neither place has any degree of attention been devoted to the subject, and that the little which may be known about it, has been derived, almost exclusively, from the very work which they so immoderately laud, and from Dr. Taylor's "Natural History of Society," which we have spoken of above with as much generosity of commendation as our sense of common honesty would allow. As these two authors have been the principal sources to which the majority have had access, we do not wonder at the amount of indiscreet praise bestowed upon them, for there was an utter ignorance of all that had been achieved elsewhere. Accordingly, we feel a double obligation resting upon ourselves to expose errors, so far as our own limited ability and information may permit, and by so doing to open the eyes of others to the true merits of the case. To show the lazy indifference which has hitherto prevailed on this most important subject,—the Philosophy of History,—we need only specify the fact, that to many, if not to most readers, Vico is unknown, or, if known at all, known only by name, and that his works remain to this day untranslated; that Guizot's second series of Lectures, by far the most profound and erudite of the two, is still sealed up in the French language; that only scraps of the writings of Victor Cousin and his school have been rendered into the vernacular; and that no one has as yet presented us with an English version of the magnificent productions of Michelet.

Under these circumstances it need not be matter of surprise, if learning without reflection reap the rewards due to profound philosophy alone; and if astonished mortals hail in unthinking rapture the first traveller, as a god, who announces to them the wonders of the newly discovered regions. But it is not to be expected that those, whom circumstances, perhaps accident, have introduced to a fuller cognizance of them, should fall down and worship the same idol with themselves, merely because "the sound of cornet, flute, harp, sackbut, psaltery, dulcimer, and all kinds of music," may have burst forth in Dura to do it honor.[24] But it may be, on the contrary, reasonably expected that they should seek to wean the multitude from the objects of their unreflecting adoration; that they should

23. Exodus 23:2.
24. Daniel 3:15, 1. Dura was a plain near Babylon where Nebuchadnezzar set up a golden image.

## Schlegel's Philosophy

endeavor to show them more of the same countries, so that their praise may hereafter be leavened with discretion; and that they should exhort them to examine for themselves, and to become themselves the discoverers of even more precious treasures, in the same imperfectly explored regions. Such is the effect, which we trust our scanty article may be able to produce.

Before commencing our examination of the present work of Schlegel, it will be proper to establish with precision what is the aim of the Philosophy of History, and the plan to be adopted in all our investigations of the subject. And if our views on this, as on other points, should chance to be novel and strange, we hope that our readers will not reject or assent to them at first sight, but will deem them worthy of deliberate examination, as we do not offer them hasty and undigested speculations, but have formed our conclusions after close scrutiny and long and mature reflection. They are not the idle thoughts of an idle hour, but the studied meditations of years, and we would not wish them to be either received as mere novelties, or rejected as unworthy of impartial and attentive consideration.

We have already, at the close of our opening paragraph, given a concise definition of what seemed to us the import of the term; but, as so laconic an explanation may be unintelligible or insufficient, it may be well in this place to enlarge somewhat upon it, and to compare our own views with those of other writings, so as to determine, with as much accuracy as practicable, the limits within which it should be comprehended.

To commence with the author more immediately under consideration, Schlegel unfolds the objects of the science thus:

> "To point out historically, in reference to the whole human race, and in the outward conduct and experience of life, the progress of the restoration in man of the lost image of God, in the various periods of the world, constitutes the object of the Philosophy of History." Pref. vol. I. p. 77.

This is certainly very German, though not equally intelligible; such light, however, as it is capable of receiving, is thrown upon it by a subsequent passage in the body of the work:

> "But, since man hath been the prey of discord, two different wills have contended within him for the mastery—a divine and a natural will. Even his freedom is no longer that happy freedom of celestial peace—the freedom of one who hath conquered and triumphed—but a freedom as we now see it—the freedom of undetermined choice—of arduous, still undecided struggle. To return to the divine will, or the one conformable to God—to restore harmony between the natural and divine will, and to convert and transform more and more the lower, earthly, and natural will into the higher and divine one, is the great task of mankind in general, as of each individual in particular. And this return—this restoration—all the endeavors after such—the progress or retrogression in this path, constitute an essential part of universal history, so

far as this embraces the moral developement and intellectual march of humanity." Vol. I. p. 117.

Interpreting these paragraphs in the most favorable spirit, and extracting from them a little more sense than, perhaps, they can be legitimately said to contain, we are led to infer, that, according to Schlegel's idea, it should be the aim of humanity, both collectively and individually, to attain again that original type and excellence imprinted upon Adam, in the beginning; and that such is its tendency, that the advancement of the world in civilization is veritably a retrogression towards the primeval condition of man—that the only criterion of a nation's progress in all the elements of national superiority and perfection, is the purity and sincerity of its religious faith and practice—and that the history of the changing phases of morals and religion among the several generations of the earth, constitutes the Philosophy of History. When we speak of the religious phases of humanity, as contemplated by Schlegel, we do not mean to confine the significance of these words to the religious service of the temple and the church, but consider them in their application to religion as it is blended with the habits of action, and the modes of thought of every day life.

We regard this view of the Philosophy of History as erroneous and imperfect, because it proceeds upon the supposition that the nature of man remained unaltered by the change of the circumstances in which he was placed, after his fall; and that when he was subjected to a host of influences wholly diverse from those operating upon him in his original condition, his feelings, his desires, his necessities, his duties, and the relations of life, springing from all these, were left unaffected by the difference in his moral destinies and his physical wants. Because it indirectly assumes the dangerous and unchristian fallacy, that the workings of God's Providence in the world are clearly cognizable by human intelligences, and that men are so far authorized and able to look into very heart of hearts of their fellow mortals, and of nations, as to pronounce an impartial, just and righteous judgment upon the relative degrees of humanity of all their thoughts and actions. Because it argues according to the old, but rather childish presumption, that we may reason about masses of men and aggregate bodies in exactly the same way that we would about individuals separately, and may apply, without modification, to the former, the same rules that we might with propriety have recourse to in forming our judgment of the latter. Because, as a necessary corollary from this, it merges the historical character of nations in the private characters and the moral conduct of the members composing it. And, lastly, because it assumes that the purity of national and individual morals and religion, is a satisfactory and conclusive evidence of advancement and civilization, thus reasoning against all that the experience of the world inculcates, confounding the historical characteristics of all ages and generations, and overthrowing what must always be the fundamental idea of every Philosophy of History—the progressive development of humanity. If we are to adopt Schlegel's test as the criterion of civilization in different periods, we ought to turn away from the refinement of modern times, and go back with Homer "μετ' ἀμύμονας Αἰθιοπῆας," or to the tents.

ἀγαυῶν Ἱππημολγῶν
γλακτοφάγων, Ἀβίων τε, δικαιοτάτων ἀνθρώπων[25]

And place these, by right of moral superiority, on the scale of civilization, far, infinitely far, above the Athenians under Pericles, the Romans under Augustus, and the French under the Grand Monarque. Such is the view taken by Schlegel of the objects proposed by the Philosophy of History, and such are the grounds on which we venture to dissent from him, and to protest against the abundant praise which has been so lavishly poured out upon him. And now let us to the speculations of more profound thinkers, and first to the greatest of all, the Neopolitan Vico.

The phrase, Philosophy of History, is not employed by Vico, but the name which he has adopted—Scienza Nuova, or the New Science—is intended to convey precisely the same idea; and, perhaps, as has been remarked by a contemporary Reviewer, is the more appropriate designation of the two. What was comprehended by Vico under his system, may be best sought from the commentary of his French translator:

"The grand truth of the Scienza Nuova is this, *humanity*[26] *is its own creation, operating on and for itself. God acts upon it, but through its intervention.*" Michelet's Pref. Hist. Rep. Rom.[27]

---

25. Homer, *Iliad*, I, 423, trans. to the blameless Ethiopians; *Iliad*, XIII, 5–6, trans. of the noble Hippemolgi, who drink mare's milk, and of the Abii, the most just of men.

26. [As this word *humanity* will necessarily play a very prominent part in our future remarks, and as we employ it here and elsewhere in a signification somewhat novel to the English language—and equally so to the French, beyond the limits of the French Historical School, if we may judge from the Dictionaries of the Academy and of Laudais—it may not be out of place to attempt, in a note, an explanation of its peculiar significance. Michelet makes use of the word and all its kindred forms; *humanité, humaniser, s'humaniser, humanisation*, the latter of which alone has been naturalized in the English: see Mickle, Disc. on the Lusiad, quoted in Richardson's Eng. Dict. tit. Human. By *humanity* then we understand human nature, not as an abstract and independent thing, but as existing in all its varied relations to the world in which it is placed, thus comprising the aggregate of all human faculties, viewed as combining to educe the specific changes of the world's career. *The progress of humanity* will, therefore, be the development of all the resources of human nature, the mutations of human society, and every thing which conspires to the perfectionating of mankind. After this explanation the other cognate terms will be easily intelligible.] Napoleon Landais, *Grammaire générale ou resumé de toutes les grammaires françaises* (2d ed., Paris, 1839); *Dictionnaire de l'Académie française* (6th ed., Paris, 1835); *A New Dictionary of the English Language*, ed. Charles Richardson (London, 1836), 1:1024, quotes from William J. Mickle's translation of Luis de Camoëns, *The Lusiad* (Oxford, 1776): "A voyage esteemed too great for man to dare: the eastern world happily, and for ever indissolubly joined and given to the western, the grand Portugese empire in the east founded; the *humanization* of mankind, and universal commerce the consequence."

27. Michelet, *Histoire romaine: Première partie: République* (2d ed., Paris), 1:6.

And this is enlarged upon and explained in the same writer's Introductory Essay on the System and Life of Vico:

> "The miracle in the constitution of humanity is, that in each of its revolutions, it finds in the corruption and decay of its former condition the elements of that renovation which will preserve it. Truly therein is a wisdom above that of man.
>
> "This overruling wisdom does not constrain us by positive laws, but it employs for our governance, instruments which we freely adopt. Here, then, let us repeat the fundamental principles of this *New Science; men have themselves made this social world such as it is*; but this world has not the less, on that account, sprung from a Divine Intelligence, often contrary, and invariably superior in its aims, to the private ends which men have proposed unto themselves. These ends, dictated by limited views, are for that Intelligence only, the means of attaining far grander and more distant aims. Thus, men might individually have desired only animal gratification, yet from this has arisen the sanctity of the marriage contract, and the institution of the family. The heads of the family seek to abuse the power they possess over their servants, and the city is founded: the ruling class of nobles endeavor to oppress the plebeians, and is itself subjected to the sovereignty of the law, which constitutes the liberty of the people: a free people attempts to shake off the yoke of the law, and sinks itself under the authority of a despot: the despot hopes to strengthen his throne by corrupting and degrading his subjects, he only paves the way for their subjugation by a more valiant race: and, at length, when nations aim at their own destruction, their elements are dispersed and scattered abroad—and the phoenix of society springs regenerated from the ashes of its parent." Michelet's Disc. sur la Syst. and la Vie de Vico.[28]

According to the understanding of Vico, then, the progress of society is the gradual and outward development, under continually recurring and improving forms, of all the powers and resources of humanity. The passions and the necessities of the human race form the main-spring of this development; but these act, though for the most part unconsciously to the individual, yet in direct and immediate subordination and subserviency to the higher purposes of Providence in the world. As the seeds of the advancement of mankind are to be found in the breasts of individuals, so the whole series of history—the records of the successive transactions of man—can furnish us only with a picture, more or less distorted and *anamorphosed*, of the outward workings of the inward feelings; that is to say, all that is most valuable in history, is the representation of the embodiment of these in the form of institutions. Human institutions are the most trustworthy witnesses of the condition of humanity at any epoch; thus, by way of illustration, the habit observed in modern nations of sending resident ambassadors to foreign courts, is, in itself, the most convincing evidence

---

28. Michelet, *Vico*, pp. xliv–xlv.

that the day has passed by when *stranger* was regarded as identical with *enemy*,[29] as is the case in the early history of all nations. And of this we have a very recent example in the case of China, which, at the same time that she opens her ports to foreign commerce, is to receive within her dominions a resident British ambassador, and herself to send one to the Court of St. James. Human institutions, indeed, are, as it were, the most vital feelings of the period arrested in the moment of their highest action and most perfect development, and chrystallized there to be the foundation for all future improvement, and a perpetual testimony of the past, the truth of which may be irrefragable. Wars, and dissensions, and civil discords, and seditions, and broils, and party struggles, are only phenomena of *the works of humanity unto itself*, they are merely sparks that fly off in the rapid rotation of the heated metal, giving evidence of some obstruction to the quiet working of the machine, or of some collision between its parts. Under this system the Philosophy or Science of History will be the exposition of the recorded transactions of the nations of the earth, according to the properties and necessities of human nature; the deduction of the one from the other, and the connection of the two together, as cause and effect, in such a manner as to show the character of the revolutions in society, the gradual advancement of humanity, and the mode in which men have themselves been made, in their struggles for private gratification or private interest, the immediate though unwitting instruments of God's will, in effectuating higher purposes for the civilization of the world, than any they contemplated themselves.

To limit, however, the above statements in some measure, and to complete our analysis of what Vico understands by the Science of History, we must not omit all notice of his celebrated doctrine of the *"corso"* and *"ricorso"* of humanity. By these terms he intended to signify that, as the progress of society is born of the increasing wants of man, which when most fully gratified, pave the way for the decline of States, by giving place to luxury and indolence, and as this is a general law with regard to nations, so the peoples of the earth, in their rise and in their decline, all pass through a career analogous to that with their predecessors. "Corso" and "ricorso," advancement and decline is the destiny of one nation, and all follow in the same path.

"Kingdoms are shrunk to provinces, and chains
Clank over sceptred cities: nations melt
From power's high pinnacle, when they have felt

29. [Every one will remember the words of Cicero,—"*Hostis* enim apud majores is dicebatur, quem nunc peregrinum dicimus." Cic. De Off. lib. I. c. xii. §. 37] Trans. For among our ancestors that man was called an enemy whom we now call a stranger; Holmes has omitted "nostros" after "maiores," and it should be "dicimus," certainly a misprint.

The sunshine for a while, and downward go
Like lanwine loosen'd from the mountain's belt."[30]

There is one fate measured out for all, *"omnium Versatur urnâ serius ocyus sors exitura;"*[31] through a like narrow stadium have the destinies of all nations been driven. But the "corso" and "ricorso" are not confined to states. Vico would further declare, that it is equally true of systems and institutions; thus, for example, religion emerges in faith, changes to superstition and credulity, and after passing through its varied phases ends in scepticism, after which it is either purified and re-modelled, or it is supplanted.

These views of Vico are certainly more purely and genuinely philosophical than those of Schlegel, already considered; yet, to these we have our objections. Though profound and strictly true, so far as they go, they are incomplete, and therefore unsatisfactory. They exclude entirely from the calculation all those accidental causes which produce the characteristic differences between ages, races and nations, and stamp their peculiar type upon each. There is no estimation made under this system of the influences of climate, local situation, and the habits of life which spring from the two combined. We have exactly the same measures and the same tests for all periods; the changes produced by anterior civilization are not regarded as legitimate elements of the calculation. Various races may become amalgamated together, yet no attention is paid either to the peculiarities of the original races, or the results of the combination. A new migration may transform the hunters of the forest, or the rovers of the sea, into keepers of sheep, or tillers of the ground, and these again into inhabitants of cities, merchants and manufacturers. Yet, not withstanding the change in national character which invariably follows a change in national habits, all races, all periods, all conditions of life are to be subjected to the same unvarying scale. We are further dissatisfied with the views of Vico, because they do not sufficiently account, nor make any provision in the calculation, for that constant tendency towards change, which is manifested in the career of each individual, and may be read with equal distinctness in every page of the history of nations. The doctrines of *"corso"* and *"ricorso,"* the constant recurrence of the same successive order of changes, will not explain the marked difference which is impressed upon each new revolution of the same cycle. The orbit in which the alternations of a system move, may be unchangable in its character, but it widens at each return, and a different spirit travels over the concentric circles at each rep-

---

30. Byron, *Childe Harold's Pilgrimage*, Canto IV, stanza 12, lines 3–7; "lanwine" should be "lauwine," an avalanche.
31. Horace, *Carmina*, II, 3, lines 5–6; trans. The lot of every one of us is tossing about in the urn, destined sooner or later to jump out.

etition. Like the gyrations of a spiral, widening from the top, there is similarity not sameness, resemblance yet accompanied with difference; the coils run not again into themselves, but are continued into each other. The *"corso"* and *"ricorso"* will explain the obvious analogy of the orbits; they will not explain their diversity, nor the mutations of the impelling influence. We object also to these views, because, while they do reduce the science to the pure metaphysics of history, agreeably to the desire of their author, they gather together only the dry bones and dead elements, without giving to them the fulness, the freshness, or the varied energy of life. All is not inanimate and clay-cold matter in the world; but in the actual genesis of the mutations of society, in their progressive flow, even in the regular periodicity of their returns, there are every where manifest that conscious effort and that diversity of action, which may usually be traced in all the developments of organized beings. In the history of humanity the blood is warm in the veins, the pulses beat under the skin, the breath of existence is at work in the body,

"Spiritus intus alit, totamque infusa per artus
Mens agitat molem, et magno se corpore miscet."[32]

Such is the case in nature; but when we enter the dissecting room of the Neapolitan philosopher, we look around for the living creature, and discover only an unmeaning skeleton. It should not suffice, however, for the Philosophy of History to enable us only to bring together in their proper order the sibylline leaves, on which the oracles of the world's mysterious progress are written; it is not enough that we should be taught by it to build up a lifeless counterfeit of life; it is not enough to point out the bones and the sinews, and to say here was a muscle and there an artery, here ran the wonderful complexities of the venous system, there the infinite ramifications of the nerves. Something more than this should be effected; the fallen limbs should be raised and reinvigorated, the breath of life should be breathed into the torpid frame, the warm blood should be made to course through the body—the whole figure should be raised from the tomb and reanimated, the skeleton of bones and sinews should be clothed again with its natural vesture of flesh, the motions and actions of life should be recalled, and form, and figure, and coloring, and truth, given again to the whole being. Vico's metaphysics of history will not enable us to do this.

Not satisfied with the views taken of the Philosophy of History either by Schlegel or Vico, and, as a necessary consequence, not satisfied with those modes of treating the subject which have flowed from them, we turn to discover whether any other system, diverse from these two, has been

---

32. Vergil, *Aeneid*, VI, lines 726–27: trans. A spirit within nourishes, and mind, poured through the separate parts, sets in motion the whole mass and mingles with its great frame.

projected and acted upon. There still remains one other to be considered, that which has given character to the works of Montesquieu, Herder, and, perhaps, we ought to add, some of those of Michelet; though, in most of his writings, the latter author is identified with the system of Vico. This third mode of considering history refers the career of humanity almost exclusively to the plastic influences of external and *accidental* causes. (We employ the word *accidental* in the strict Aristotelian signification, to denote all that modifies the *subject* ὑποκείμενον, without forming an *essential* part of it.)[33] Of these influences the most important are climate, proximity to the sea or to navigable rivers, and all that may be included under local situation, the face of the country, the character of its soil, the nature of its productions, its intercourse with other nations by neighborhood or by commerce, and the whole concatenation of circumstances which alter or modify the habits and operations of men, individually or in society. As the spirit of a system, this appears under very different forms, and in very unequal proportions in the works of the three great authors, to whom we have alluded above, but in all it may be taken as the main characteristic.

After what has been said of the other two modes of regarding the Philosophy of History, the defects of the present system will be at once apparent. It does not account for the gradual change in the manners, feelings and institution of nations, nor for their progress and decline. It looks upon man almost in the light of a creature purely passive, moulded by a plastic force working on him from without, from which he receives his habits, his dispositions, and, in a great measure, his desires, yet makes neither resistance nor effort after independence. It wholly overlooks the truth, which a scrutinizing examination of history will teach, that the potency of the influence of external causes is not equally strong in all the stages of human progress and civilization, but is inversely proportioned to the advancement of the latter, being most manifestly and powerfully operative as we recede into barbarism, and daily diminishing in the subse-

33. [For the benefit of those who make a study of the logic of the school, and with very much the same feeling that led to the composition of the works of Harris, of Salisbury, we give the definition of the phrase *accidental* from Porphyry. "Συμβεβηκὸς δέ ἐστιν ὃ γίνεται καὶ ἀπογίνεται χωρὶς τῆς τοῦ ὑποκειμένου φθοϱᾶς—ὁϱίζονται δὲ αὐτὸ καὶ οὕτω συμβεβηκός ἐστιν ὃ ἐνδέχεται τῳ αὐτῳ ὑπάϱχειν καὶ μὴ ὑπάϱχειν ἢ ὃ οὔτε γένος ἐστιν οὔτε διαφοϱὰ οὔτε εἶθος οὔτε ἴδιον, ἀεὶ δέ ἐστιν ἐν ὑποκειμένῳ ὑφιστάμενον. Porph. Isagog, in Categ. Aristot. c. 5.] The word in the text means "the essential matter"; Holmes presumably means James Harris, 1709–1780, the eccentric grammarian, and John of Salisbury, circa 1110–1180, the scholastic philosopher; the quotation is from Porphyry, "Introduction to the Categories of Aristotle," see *Commentaria in Aristotelem Graeca* (Berlin, 1887), IV, p. 12, lines 25–26, 30–32 (Holmes has put a dash, instead of an ellipsis); trans. The accidental is that which exists and ceases to exist apart from the corruption of the essential matter. . . . They define it also in this way: the accidental is that which may happen or not happen to someone, or that which is neither kind nor differentia nor species nor particular thing, but is always predicated upon the essential matter. Porphyry, 233–circa 301, was one of the chief exponents of Neoplatonism.

quent stages of humanity, being checked, modified, and sometimes nearly obliterated by the controlling action of other causes. Hence any mode of explaining the phenomena of human development by these external influences, as the key note of the system, must of necessity be imperfect, for they are merely accessary to other causes, and are declining in energy at each remove. If we adopt them exclusively, or even principally, as the talismanic charm to explain in all ages the phases through which humanity may be passing, we will soon bewilder ourselves in a labyrinth of fallacies, and the further we sail down the stream of time, the more deeply and desperately false will they be found. We object further to this system of Montesquieu, because it cannot admit the direct government of God in this world, nor the intervention of His power in moulding events and shaping consequences; and without this the page of history becomes either a blank or wholly unintelligible; and further, because it does not allow to man himself any conscious or purely voluntary instrumentality in working out his own destiny.

In justice to Michelet, we ought, before proceeding, to take some further notice of his writings, and to be somewhat more explicit in characterizing them. This it may be difficult to do satisfactorily, because it appears to us that the author in a great measure modifies his opinions in different works. There is only one of them indeed which we could confidently refer to as fully justifying our classification of him along with Montesquieu and Herder. The "Introduction to Universal History" is the work to which we allude.[34] We believe it was the first published of all, and it is certainly the most boldly and genuinely original. With the exception of the abridgment and translation of Vico, it is the only one of Michelet's productions which is devoted professedly to an exposition of the Philosophy of History. After the publication of the translation of Vico, the ideas of the latter author became so completely transferred in the mind of Michelet, that we think his just admiration of the great Neapolitan has exercised rather an unfavorable influence over himself, by limiting the range of his own views within the precincts prescribed to himself by his Italian predecessor. As it is, however, Michelet has in some degree combined the systems of Vico and Montesquieu, and comes more nearly up to our ideas of perfection in this department than any other writer whom it has been our fortune to consult. In all the requisites of a great writer on history, Michelet stands almost without a rival. Gibbon and Niebuhr are the only authors who can compete with him in a majority of his qualifications, and in some even these must yield to him. His learning in all necessary branches is very extensive and singularly accurate; his judgment remarkably sound, cool and impartial; his perception of the importance of the several facts and

---

34. Michelet, *Introduction à l'histoire universelle* (Paris, 1834).

events in history keen and discriminating, and his imagination of that high and rare creative order, which can without effort call up the dead from the graves, and revivify the past with a single touch of the enchanter's rod. His range of vision seems bounded only by the wide, and, to ordinary eyes, limitless horizon of his subject; his philosophical discernment penetrating, profound and convincing; his sincerity and earnestness of purpose almost without parallel. Add to this the perfectly unique beauty, the magnificence, the melancholy grandeur of his style;—the words burthened with unwonted majesty, the pregnant sentences sounding like the oracles of the world's destinies, mysteriously sent forth from lips touched by the hands of seraphim with live coals from the altar. Such is the guiding star we would look to, though even him we may not always or entirely follow.

To proceed with our subject. Of the three systems which we have examined, none appears to be altogether satisfactory. The first in order of time is that of Vico, which makes man the central point of the system from which all reasoning about the progress of human improvement ought to radiate. The second is that of Montesquieu, written before the publication of the *Scienza Nuova*, as we learn from a note in the biography of him by Valckenaër,[35] though not given to the world until many years afterwards. This regards material, external nature as the true point of vision. It has been, perhaps, most fully and judiciously elaborated by Cabanis, in his celebrated work, "*Rapports du Physique et du Moral*," though we have not alluded to him above, as his writings have no immediate connection with history.[36] The third is the system of Schlegel, which considering Providence as the immediate fountain of all the changes in the world, looks upon the Philosophy of History as merely the unravelling, from the web of recorded events, of so much as may be supposed to make clear the successive manifestations of the Divine will, the fulfilment of the Divine purposes, and the effort of mankind to return, with God's aidance, to that original condition, in which he lived in the closest and most perfect harmony with his Creator. These three systems may be appropriately shadowed forth under three separate vocables, representing the central ideas of each respectively—HUMANITY—NATURE—PROVIDENCE.

After refusing our assent to any of these systems, sustained as they all are by names to which we look up with reverence and admiration, it becomes us to point out what we deem to be the cause that all have failed. The reason we take to be this: they have each taken separate and single elements, whereas all of them are invariably found to be combined together in action, though not always in equal proportions, and which ought therefore always to be combined together in our speculations. In most

---

35. Montesquieu, *Oeuvres complètes* (Paris, 1835), has a "Notice sur la vie de Montesquieu par M.C.A. Walckemaer."

36. Pierre Jean Georges Cabanis, *Rapports du physique et du moral de l'homme* (Paris, 1802).

cases, we are diametrically opposed to anything approximating to eclecticism. We think that those who expect to avoid the difficulties presented by clashing theories by uniting them, are much more apt to extract from the combination the aggregate of evil, than the tithe of the good which may be existent in any of them separately. In the present instance we do not recommend eclecticism—the harmonizing of opposite views by selection and exclusion, but the aggregation of three things which separately are parts, but conjointly form a perfect whole. For the character of a nation does not depend upon climate and local situation alone, but is derived, perhaps even more, from the peculiarities of the race whence it drew its origin, and the state of civilization attained at the time it was subjected to those influences. The advancement of mankind may be well explained by a reference to the passions, the necessities, and the properties of man, but not without referring much to the action of external causes, and much also to the direct supervention of the Divinity. Again, Religion may with the utmost propriety be taken as a clue to guide us through the labyrinthine obscurities of history, but we must view it with very different eyes from Schlegel's, and must not disconnect it from all other efficient influences. It is necessary, therefore, if we would read the enigma of the world's development, that we should consider as operating together in all the mutations of the earth and the fortunes of its inhabitants, the agency of man, the plastic force of circumstances, and the controling supervision of God.

The Philosophy of History thus becomes the exposition of the progress of humanity; the connection together of different eras and systems by the laws of natural and necessary antecedence and succession; the detection of the causes which effectuate change, and those which engender the characteristics of nations and periods; the explication of the mode and extent of their influence; and the recognition of the phenomena arising from the peculiarities of specific races, and from their intermixture. These are the points which the Science of History should invariably keep in view, not separately and distinctly, but in their combined and harmonious action.

Having thus pointed out the imperfections in the modes of treating the subject, hitherto proposed, and having opened the path to a much more comprehensive Philosophy of History, than any that has hitherto been attempted, we would turn to the more particular consideration of the work of Schlegel, which we have taken up as a text for our remarks. It may indeed seem rather late to examine into details when we have expended nearly half our article in apparently introductory remarks, but the ground which we have been travelling over is not merely preliminary—it has a more extensive bearing upon Schlegel's Treatise than may be manifest from our hurried notice of it. And as our main object on the present occasion is the elucidation of the Science of History, our secondary purpose the confutation of Schlegel, whatever tends to illustrate the former is naturally more important in our eyes than the bare prosecution of our intentions with regard to the latter. During the remainder of our article, the work of Schlegel will occupy prominently our attention, although the scope of our labors will not be altered.

The first lesson which Schlegel would inculcate, is that which must be the foundation-stone of all Science of History—the curse passed upon Adam. "Cursed is the ground for thy sake, in sorrow shalt thou eat of it all the days of thy life.—In the sweat of thy face shalt thou eat bread, till thou return unto the ground."[37] It is by virtue of this curse that the human race is condemned to unending labor; and it is from the absolute necessity of labor that civilization becomes possible, and that man is made, in the hands of God, the instrument in working out his own destinies.

> "This first divine law of nature," says Schlegel, "by virtue of which labor and struggle became from the beginning the destiny of man, has retained its full force through all succeeding ages, and is applicable alike to every class, and every nation, to each individual as well as to mankind in general, to the most important as to the most insignificant relations of society." Vol. I. pp. 116–17.

The constant change and progress of humanity is to be attributed to this, as the mainspring of all its action, united with that vague but ardent struggling after an unknown and unattainable *je ne sais quoi*—that *élan après quelque chose d'inconnu*, to alter slightly an expression of Chateaubriand. This solves, as far as mortal man may solve it, the first enigma in the history of the world—its restless activity—and it will be noted, that herein, as in all the grand movements of mankind, the hand of God, the energy of man, and the resistance of external nature, all conspire to produce the result.

The second lesson that we are to learn, is taught us by "the fratricide and curse of Cain"—which Schlegel denominates "the first historical fact." Of this event and the doctrine inculcated by it, he says,

> "The origin of discord in man, and the transmission of that mischief to all ages and all generations, is indeed the first historical fact; but on account of its universality, it forms at the same time a psychological phenomenon; and while in this first section of sacred history, every thing points and refers to the mysteries of religion, the fratricide of Cain, on the other hand, and the flight of that restless criminal to Eastern Asia, are the first events and circumstances which properly belong to the province of history. In this account we see, first the foundation of the most ancient city, by which undoubtedly we must understand a great, or at least an old and celebrated city of Eastern Asia; and, secondly, the origin of various hereditary classes, trades and arts; especially of those connected with the first knowledge and use of metals, and

---

37. [Gen. c. iii. vv. 17–19.]

which doubtless hold the first place in the history of human arts and discoveries." Vol. I. p. 123.

Abandoning altogether these speculations about the locality, population and character of *Caïnopolis*, as the city itself appears to be very much of the nature of a *Spanish castle* or city *in nubibus*, we are willing to limit ourselves to the consideration of the legend of Cain as a *psychological phenomenon* alone. The murder of Abel—the first fruits of that apple of discord

"Whose mortal taste
Brought death into the world, and all our woe,"[38]

when considered as a psychological phenomenon, points out to us the early dissension of races, and the inherent opposition of different employments. The story of Cain is the history of two races, originally from the same stock, but daily diverging further and further from each other; the patriarchal children of Seth earning indeed the bread of life with the sweat of the brow, but apparently content with supplying the absolute and immediate necessities of nature; the progeny of Cain, on the other hand, for whom the ground had been a second time cursed, not limiting their labors to their actual wants, but haunted, as it were, by an irresistible though unwelcome impulse to labor, which might lull, in the pursuit of vague ulterior aims, the *unvoiced, unvoiceable* agony of the soul. "When thou tillest the ground it shall not yield thee her strength.—A fugitive and a vagabond shalt thou be in the earth."[39] When the Lord cursed Cain, He cursed the ground a second time for him and his progeny. Yet from this curse flowed a greater blessing—it was this that rendered civilization possible. Had the earth freely yielded her increase without any further exertion on the part of man than the trifling labors of the pastoral life, the whole face of humanity would have represented stagnation alone. But the ground was not idly or vindictively cursed by God, it was cursed for man's sake,[40] that it might thenceforward be, by virtue of this very curse, the main instrument in effectuating the progressive amelioration of the human race. Fugitives and vagabonds in the earth and before God might Cain and his offspring be; the ground might be for them a second time accursed; and the punishment might seem to Cain greater than he could bear. The brand might be seared upon his brow, and himself driven from the neighborhood of Eden, but it was under the influence of the sentence of condemnation which the Lord had passed upon him that he journied to the East, built a city, and in his children instituted the arts, trades and manufactures, which in long after

---

38. Milton, *Paradise Lost*, I, lines 2–3.
39. Genesis 4:12, 14, somewhat misquoted.
40. ["And the Lord said in his heart, I will not again curse the ground any more *for man's sake.*" Gen. viii, v. 21.]

ages were thence to flow back and illuminate the West. In the Cainites commenced and was first illustrated the natural opposition between the artificial life of the *city*[41] and the nomad life of pastoral men. Thus they became the first link in the progress of human society. Cain then is the type of humanity as capable of progressive civilization, and not Abel or Seth. It may seem singular, nay, even paradoxical, that the race on which a double curse rested, should be the one chosen to carry forward the destinies of mankind. A careful study, however, of the tale of Cain, accompanied with mature reflection of the truths which the Science of History teaches, will, we think, bring others to the same conclusion with ourselves, unnatural as, at first blush, it may appear. Let those who may be disposed to reject without examination, remember, that the Lord said unto Cain, "Therefore whosoever slayeth Cain vengeance shall be taken on *him* sevenfold."[42]—Wherefore?—We profess our total ignorance, and until we can answer this question, we may yield assent to the doctrines above, though utterly unable to solve the mystery. If it be true, what becomes of Schlegel's hallucination that religion or morality are evidences of civilization, or are even parallel to it?

We have purposely considered "the fratricide and curse of Cain" as a *psychological phenomenon* rather than as an historical fact, in order that our conclusions might be of general application, and throw light upon the whole history of mankind. Our inferences are much wider than those which Schlegel has ventured to draw from the same source, and in many respects different from them. He sees in the consecrated legend little more than the opposition and discord existing between the early races of the earth, the *antagonism* of impiety and religion, and the commencement of moral degeneracy.

The pregnant and melancholy story of Cain is nearly all that the records of the antediluvian world have handed down to us of importance in an historical point of view; and much that it conveys is an anticipation of truths, which are not fully illustrated till after the deluge. The flood swept away not only the former dwellers on the earth, but obliterated also the landmarks of that elder civilization, which had preceded it, and imposed on mortals the task of weaving anew the web of their own destinies. It might not be necessary to commence the whole work *ab ovo*, but men had to be drawn again into society by various affinities, many of them diverse from those that had prevailed before, and all of them operating under different circumstances. All that was saved of the created things of the antediluvian world, flowed thro' the narrow limits of the ark; through the same narrow channel was conveyed all that was transmitted to postdilu-

---

41. [We employ the word *city*, in the strict philosophical import attached to it by the writers on the subject, to denote the association of men together, so as to form society, and all the institutions and peculiarities arising from that association.]
42. Genesis 4:15.

vian times of the anterior civilization. With the olive leaf that the dove bore back to Noah, while as yet she "found no rest for the sole of her foot,"⁴³ with the stablishment of the bow of the Lord in the clouds to be a covenant with the earth, commenced a new cycle,

"Magnus ab integro saeclorum nascitur ordo."

We cannot add with the poet,

"Jam redit et Virgo, redeunt Saturnia regna."⁴⁴

The subsidence of the waters of the flood was followed by the promise of the Lord, "neither will I again smite any more every thing living, as I have done. While the earth remaineth, seed-time and harvest, and cold and heat, and summer and winter, and day and night, shall not cease."⁴⁵ And thus the cycle which then commenced is not only new but also continuous, and all that preceded it belongs not historically to the consideration of the advances of humanity.

This statement was necessary to account for our unwillingness to notice the supposed *historical* import of any facts preceding the deluge, and also for the mode in which we shall feel ourselves called upon to dismiss the "vexed question" of the origin of society. Whatever historically precedes the present cycle, and is not historically connected with it, is beyond its range, and ought not, except for other purposes, to be introduced into the Philosophy of History.

The original institution of society, and the change from barbarism to civilization, or *vice versa*, has often before afforded a very wide field for fanciful imaginations, under the name of inquiry. The first problem Vico solves, as Alexander untied the Gordian knot—he cuts it with a single blow. "Nothing remains long out of its natural state; man, therefore, is naturally sociable, for he continues to exist in society."⁴⁶ In this view Cicero had preceded him—"The first cause of the formation of society is less the weakness of men individually, than a sort of aggregation among mankind in obedience to nature; for man is not constituted an isolated or solitary being * * * *."⁴⁷ We leave this question where we find it, for specula-

43. Genesis 8:9.
44. Vergil, *Eclogues*, 4, lines 5–6; trans. The great order of ages is born anew; now even the maiden [Astraea, the goddess of justice] returns; the reign of Saturn returns.
45. Genesis 8:21–22.
46. *Oeuvres choisies de Vico*, ed. Michelet (Paris, 1835), p. xviii, has: "Nulle chose ne reste longtemps hors de son état naturel; l'homme est sociable, puisqu'il reste en société."
47. [Ejus autem caussa coeundi est non tam imbecillitas, quam naturalis quaedam hominum quasi congregatio; non est enim singulare nec solivagum genus hoc, sed ita generatum, ut ne in omnium quidem rerum affluent— . . . *cetera desunt*. Cic. De Rep. lib. I, c. XXV. Most of Cicero's philosophic opinions were little more than translations from the Greek; this may be derived from Aristotle:—"ἐκ τούτων οὖν φανερὸν ὅτι τῶν φύσει ἡ πόλις ἐστί, καὶ ὅτι [ὁ] ἄνθρωπος φύσει πολιτικὸν ζῷον, καὶ ὁ ἄπολις διὰ φύσιν καὶ οὐ διὰ τύχην ἤτοι φαῦλός ἐστιν

tion is wholly useless in cases where the inferences drawn cannot by any possibility be confirmed, and even if the historical origin could be discovered, it would be altogether unprofitable, as it would give us no insight into its nature which we could not much more easily obtain from a study of society, as an institution already formed. It would be infinitely worse than an idle waste of time to speculate on subjects, on which our speculations could throw no light even if successful.

Much more attention than requisite has also been devoted to the solution of the difficulty, whether barbarism or civilization was the primary state of man. Most philosophers have proceeded on the supposition that the former was: Schlegel impugns this position, and gives his voice in favor of civilization. His words are

> "That this (the savage state) was the really original condition of mankind is by no means proved, and is arbitrarily assumed, nay, on the contrary, the savage state must be looked upon as a state of degeneracy and degradation—consequently not as the first, but as the second phenomenon in human history—as something which, as it has resulted from this second step in man's progress, must be regarded as of later origin." Vol. I. p. 115.

And again,

> "Thus in his origin and by nature, man is no savage." Vol. I. p. 121.

This view Dr. Taylor also adopts in his "Natural History of Society,"

> "It follows then," says he, "that the capacity of becoming civilized belongs to the whole human race—that civilization is natural to man—that bar-

---

ἢ κρείττων ἢ ἄνθρωπος, ὥσπερ καὶ ὁ ὑφ᾽ Ὁμήρου λοιδορηθεὶς ἀφρήτωρ, ἀθέμιστος, ἀνέστιος." I Pol. II.

The above quotation from Cicero is a fragment of his Republic, recovered in 1822, by Cardinal Maio, from a palimpsest of St. Augustine, found in the Vatican. Nobbe has edited "affluentia" in the close of the quotation. Recte. The whole sentence may be completed thus,

"Ut ne in omnium quidem rerum affluentia sine socio possit esse contentum, sed semper quaerit quibus aliquid ex abundantia sua impertiat.

Our Latin may be far from Ciceronian; indeed, it is long enough since it was our good fortune to look into any "Elegantiae Linguae Latinae." The probable correctness of our completion of the sentiment may be confirmed from Cic. De Amicit. c. XXIII. and Senec. Ep. IV, §§. 3-4. If our memory does not play us false, there is a kindred passage in the First Book De Officiis.

This is a long note on so small a matter; the classical scholar will pardon it from the goodness of our motive in writing it; the unclassical reader will perhaps have the complaisance to overlook it.] The Latin in the text translates the Cicero as far as "genus hoc"; Holmes's completion of the text translates, "but is created in such a way that not even in an abundance of everything is he able to be content without a comrade, but he always seeks those with whom to share something of his own store"; Aristotle, Politics, book I, 9 (1253a), trans. From these things therefore it is clear that the city state is part of the natural order and that man is by nature a political animal and that he who by nature and not by fortune is without a city is either subhuman, or superhuman or a man like that reviled by Homer, "without family, without law, without home" (Iliad, IX, line 63); Elegantiae Linguae Latinae is a treatise by Lorenzo Valla, 1407-1457; Mai actually found the palimpsest in a Ligurian monastery.

barism is not 'a state of nature,' and that there is no *prima facie* evidence for assuming it to be the original condition of man." Taylor's Nat. Hist. Soc. vol. I. p. 30.

We would notice a signal *non sequitur* here, in the deduction of these inferences from the arguments which are supposed to sustain them, had we either time to spare or space to devote to the consideration of a point so trivial in comparison with the much grosser blunders with which the Doctor's volumes are filled. We would only remark in passing, that his Grace of Dublin can hardly have supervised this author's logic. Accepting, however, the proposition above as the independent assertion of Dr. Taylor's own opinion, let us consider the point immediately in dispute.

Those who advocate either of the extremes of this question, appear to us equally in error. We cannot possibly affirm that either barbarism or civilization was the original condition of mankind. Not the former, because the starting point of historical inquiry is changed by the deluge, and it may be conclusively shown that Noah brought with him out of the ark the arts and civilization of the antediluvian world, such as they were. Not the latter, because civilization is a gradual and *forced* growth, and exists only under those circumstances which compel its development. A certain degree of civilization might exist in the world directly after the flood; it might exist as long as men had but one language, and lived together in one society, but when the dispersion at Babel scattered them abroad, and gave to them diverse habits and modes of life, the savage state would be rapidly superinduced on the dwellers of the forest, while the builders of cities would lay the foundation of a new civilization. The early *postdiluvian* civilization could be termed so only by comparison with actual barbarism, not with modern times; indeed these terms are of necessity always relative. We might add that any thing like civilization, according to modern notions, would be an unnatural state, and therefore incapable of long continuance. Moreover, after the flood many new elements were introduced to cause immediate change and rapid degeneracy. Many mistaken notions upon this subject might be prevented by considering that civilization is not a state which can at any moment, and under any circumstances, be forced upon peoples from without, but that it is the spontaneous but necessary production of certain antecedent causes, and the development from within of mankind in certain definite positions.

We have been more particular in alluding to this difficulty, than we should otherwise have been, from the fact that other writers, as well as Dr. Taylor, and of far higher mark than he is, have endeavored on this to build up the thesis that all the races of the world are equally capable of civilization. And this they do in utter defiance of history, which unanswerably disproves the fallacy. The Zingalee or Gypsies, the North American Indians, the negroes of St. Domingo, have shown themselves wholly incapable of civilization. They have all been subjected to the test, they have all signally displayed their incapacity for it. In reply to this it may be said that the Zingalee and the North American Indians have never been so situated that the influences of civilization bore upon them with sufficient power to counteract the force of their wild habits. True; but this is begging the question, for it would be necessary to prove that under any circumstances their savage nature could yield to the spirit of civilization. There are some races which will suffer themselves to be exterminated before they will submit to a settled and civilized life. Where are the aborigines of the West India Islands, whom Las Casas[48] labored to preserve? Obliterated—entombed. Where are the thousand tribes of the North American Indians that ranged over this wide continent from the ragged shores and storm-beat isles of New-Brunswick to the waters of the Pacific ocean, from the mighty St. Lawrence on the North, to the Gulf of Mexico on the South? They have melted away before the steps of civilization, like snow before the morning sun, until only a scanty remnant is preserved for a short breathing while under the shadows of the Rocky Mountains.[49] They cannot co-exist with civilization; they wither away and die whenever brought into contact with it.

"An over free intercourse with the whites," says a writer, infinitely better informed on the subject than Dr. Taylor can be, "is fraught with so many evils to the unsophisticated Indian, that he must be secured against it, or his destruction is inevitable. To this cause may be attributed the extinction of some of the most powerful tribes of this continent; and we see whole tribes now, in the receipt of large annuities from the government, and enjoying advantages which an equal number of whites hardly any where possess, gradually declining in numbers, and daily becoming more licentious, though not less barbarous and miserable, under the same destructive influence. Here is the greatest evil they are subjected to. The remedy is, perhaps, easier to hope for than expect."[50]

It cannot be expected, it cannot be even reasonably hoped for. No race has ever been civilized without commixtion with some more civilized race.

48. Bartolome de Las Casas, 1474–1566, the Spanish missionary and historian who urged the abolition of Indian slavery.
49. [The whole number west of the Mississippi, or on their way thither, appears to be only 168,682, from the latest and most authentic returns. With such a scanty remnant, well may we exclaim by anticipation, "Troja fuit, fuit Ilion." Mr. Crawford, the Commissioner of Indian Affairs, appears more sanguine than we can be, of the possible civilization of the Indians. He admits, however, the destruction which flows from the proximity of the white race. A diligent perusal of the interesting and deeply affecting Report of Mr. Crawford, and the accompanying documents, (State Papers, 1842) will establish the truth of our position above, against such theorists as Schlegel, Dr. Taylor, &c.]
50. [D. P. Bushnell to Gov. J. D. Doty, Sept. 30, 1842.—Papers accompanying the President's Message, 1842, p. 406.]

If the Indians die of the proximity of the whites, what possibility can there be of their civilization, what ground for such a thesis as that of Dr. Taylor?

Driven from this foot-hold the advocates of the universal capacity for civilization may say, respecting the negroes of St. Domingo, that we cannot fairly judge of the Haytians, for they are yet in their infancy as a nation. It is not the first time that we have had occasion to remark, that this application of the peculiarities of individual existence, as an argument to extenuate the condition of nations, affords the weakest but most fallacious of all modes of reasoning. There might be some sense in talking of the infancy of nations in this manner in those ancient times when they sprung up singly and successively, by the sole action of their own elements upon themselves, after their first impregnation from abroad. But it is an absolute absurdity to speak thus in reference to an age when a nation is at once and continually subjected to the influences of the most perfect civilization for the time, in all other parts of the world. The sole reply to such an argument, as we suppose to be brought forward, is this; if the Haytians had been susceptible of civilization they would have given conclusive proofs of progression before this day.

Connected with these questions about the original condition of mankind, and the universal capacity for civilization, and introduced sometimes as cause and sometimes as corollary, is the proposition of the unity of the human species. Retaining our own opinions on this point, which we think very doubtful, we might admit, for the sake of argument, the truth of the doctrine, and yet deny the influence which it is intended to support, that all races are capable of civilization. We have denied it above, and we have adduced what seemed to us sufficiently strong evidence against it;—the question has a very important bearing on the Science of History, inasmuch as it seriously affects the determination of the mode in which the progressive civilization of the world is generated. We are ourselves convinced that the stream of the world's development had its fountain-head in India, that thence flowed the spirit which has fecundated in their just succession all the historical nations, not indeed in all cases deduced immediately from the original spring, but brought down in different channels, which frequently unite again in one bed; and that no nation can take an active part in forwarding the civilization of humanity, unless impregnated directly or indirectly from that source. If this be so, different races must have different peculiarities and different destinies; and the possible unity of nations originally can give no promise of any future adunation. The fallacy, which would infer a similarity of capacities from identity of origin, springs from overlooking altogether in the calculation the changes which took place in humanity in consequence of the circumstances at and subsequent to the deluge, and from forgetting the indelible diversities which were then stamped upon different races. Dr. Taylor endeavors to prepare the way for his thesis, and to bolster it up by the assertion,

> "The American and Negro types disappear by intermixture with the Caucasian. A similar wearing away of the negro type may be observed among the descendants of black servants who have married. We have had an opportunity of observing the continuous process through three generations, and can aver that not a trace of the negro peculiarities could be found in the great grandchild of the African." Vol. I. p. 29.

That is to say, that when there is one-eighth of negro blood in the veins, the seven-eighths of Caucasian blood will be predominant and obliterate it. We have had better opportunities of noticing the consequences of the commixture of the races than Dr. Taylor, and should be far from adopting his assertion as a correct general law. Nevertheless, it is the proportion which in South-Carolina entitles a free colored person to the privileges of a white, provided that *status* have already been conceded to him by the society in which he resides.[51] Yet this will not sustain the Doctor's inference, any more than it would prove the possibility of a wolf's being made a good fox-hound, or a fox a good yard-dog, to say that the wolf and the fox will both unite with the dog, and that in process of time the *lupine* and *vulpine* peculiarities are obliterated. To sustain his point, it must be shown that the negro can be resolved into the Caucasion type, under any variety of circumstances, by the admixture of the negro races among themselves. By mixture with the Caucasian the negro race does not become white, but the scanty portion of negro blood is invisible in the excess of the Caucasian—it becomes the rain-drop in the salt sea.

The conclusions that we draw from all the preceding observations, to aid us in forming a Science of History are these: firstly, that the progress of humanity is governed like all the other operations of the created world, by certain fixed and definite laws: secondly, that the agents in the production of civilization are Providence, man, and material, external nature: thirdly, that the necessity of labor is the cause of human progress and development: fourthly, that there is an essential antagonism of different races and occupations: fifthly, that some races seem set apart for carrying on the work of civilization, while others appear incapable of it: sixthly, that the admission of a common origin for all the varieties of mankind is no argument in favor of any supposed return to this hypothetic identity: and, lastly, that the character of civilization bears a direct relation to the circumstances of each age and people, and is not possible in all nations and

---

51. [State vs. Davis, and State vs. Hanna—2d Bailey, 558. State vs. Cantey—2d Hill, 614.] Henry Bailey, *Reports of Cases Argued and Determined in the Court of Appeals of South Carolina* (Charleston, 1833), 2: 558–60; William Randolph Hill, *Reports of Cases . . . South Carolina* (Columbia, 1834–1841), 2:614–17.

at all times. These are fundamental principles, without which the phenomena of the world's history become either unintelligible or anomalous.

Our readers may fancy that these are trivial and unimportant matters, that we have been dwelling on with so much diligence and care, but they form the very basis of the Philosophy of History. And having thus cleared the way before us, we will plunge, without hesitancy, into an examination of the method adopted by Schlegel for the unfolding of his subject. And when we come to this part of our inquiry, we have even more cause to censure his work severely, than we had when exposing the unsoundness of particular propositions. His plan we give at length, and in his own words:

> "Now that we have seen mankind divided and split into a plurality of nations, our next task, in the period which follows, is to discover the most remarkable and most civilized nations, and to observe what peculiar form the *word*, whether innate in man or communicated to him—the word which may be considered as the essence of all the high prerogatives and characteristic qualities of man; to observe, we say, what peculiar form the word assumed among each of those nations, in their language and writing, in their religious traditions, their historical sagas, their poetry, art, and science. In the account of ancient nations, we shall adopt the ethnographical mode of treating history; and it will be only in modern and more recent times that this method will gradually give place to the synchronical; and the reasons of this change will be suggested by the very nature of the subject. It is only at a later period that political history becomes the main object of attention, and almost the leading principle in the progressive march, and even the partial retrogressions of mankind." Vol. I. p. 138.

And further,

> "Corresponding to the divine image implanted in the breast of individual man—the main subject of all history—the *word* of divine truth originally communicated to man, and which the sacred traditions of all nations attest in so many and such various ways,—forms the leading clue of historical investigation and judgment, during the first stages of the progress of society. But in the second stage of social development, which must be fixed in that full noonday period of refinement, when victorious power shines forth so conspicuously in the ascendancy obtained by nations, to whom universal pre-eminence was accorded—the right notion of this power, or the question how far it were just and godly, or pernicious in its application—whether it were inimical to God, or at least of a mixed nature—must constitute the true standard of historical investigation. In the third or last stage, however, of this progress, which occurs in the modern period of the world, the pure truths of Christianity, as they influence science and life itself, can alone furnish the right clue of historical inquiry, and can alone afford any indication as to the ulterior advances of society in future ages. Thus then the *Word*, the *Power*, and *Light* from this three-fold divine principle, or the moral classification of historical philoso-

phy—a classification which is founded on historical experience and historical reality." Vol. I. p. 272.

In reading these passages, as frequently indeed in other parts of Schlegel's work, we were forcibly reminded of Byron's remarks upon his style:

"He is like Hazlitt in English, who *talks pimples*—a red and white corruption rising up, (in little imitation of mountains upon maps,) but containing nothing, and discharging nothing except their own humors.
"I dislike him the worse because he always seems upon the verge of meaning; and, lo, he goes down like sunset, or melts like a rainbow, leaving a rather rich confusion,—to which, however, the above comparisons do too much honor." Moore's Life of Byron, c. xlii. p. 484. Murray's 8vo. Ed. London: 1838.

Let us interpret these passages, however, as if they really signified so much as a charitable imagination may suspect them to imply; and as such let us examine them. In the former of the quotations, Schlegel seems disposed to invert the process, which the scientific inquirer into the spirit of history ought to pursue. He says, it is his object to discover the peculiar form which the *word*, (the intellect we suppose he means, if the phrase, as employed by him, has in reality any meaning,) assumes in the language, writing, religion, poetry, art, and science of the nations. The object of the Philosophy of History should be, on the contrary, to learn from these, which are at best only its outward manifestations, the hidden intellectual spirit by which they were generated. Schlegel's system could not by possibility produce any thing more than a connected and harmonized *resumé* of general histories of particular developments of human thought and feeling. The Philosophy of History should seek its foundations much deeper than this, and should regard these as merely the outward trappings through the instrumentality of which to detect the *vis formativa*, the causative energy latent within.

Schlegel treats the earlier period of history ethnographically, the later synchronically, he does not attempt to assign any philosophical grounds for so doing, but dismisses the announcement of his plan with the dexterous statement, that "the reasons of this change will be suggested by the very nature of the subject." True: they are so suggested, but they do not lie so tangibly upon the surface, as to justify the author in omitting all mention of them in this way. He had no cause to presume that they would be obvious to every reader, nor that "the nature of the subject" would suggest the same reasons to all. They are to be drawn from the very depths of the science, and cannot be detected without long and minute attention to the whole scope of history: and we trust that there will not be many to whom "the nature of the subject" will suggest the same weak and insufficient grounds, that seem, from the whole tenor of his work, to have contented

Schlegel. He has looked merely upon the face of history, instead of sounding the depths of its waters; he has been willing to follow mechanically the stream of the world's progress in its outward developments, instead of endeavoring through a study of these to arrive at the history of its inward spirit. The only reasons, which "the nature of the subject" suggested to him for the sudden and abrupt change, appear to have been the ethnographical advancement of civilization in antiquity, and its synchronical march in modern times. There is little philosophy in thus blindly following appearances; it might all have been learnt, without Schlegel's assistance, from the bare inspection of the most meagre manual of history ever thumbed by a school-boy.

We do, indeed, admit most readily the perfect propriety of the distinctions observed by Schlegel in treating the Philosophy of History in the two eras of the world, but we cannot remain satisfied with any reason that we can discover from his work. To content our own minds we are obliged to seek after something more convincing. And to us the following reason appears to be sufficient. With the ancients each stage of civilization was perfected by distinct and successive nations, for the diversity in the spirit of each epoch was of that nature, that the elements of any precedent states of civilization could not by internal modifications alone bring forth any succeeding state, but required the aid of some new and very different elements from without to produce an effective fermentation. We find in the intellectual character of Greece and Rome peculiarities, which could never have been solved from the spirit of the Oriental nations, operating upon itself. In modern times on the other hand, all the civilized and *civilizing* nations form one connected whole, and advance synchronically, though not *co-equally* in civilization. The different nations influence each other as the separate parts of a complex machine, and by their reciprocal action producing the development of one common system. It would be as absurd to separate the Caucasian or Indo-Germanic nations of the present day in the same manner that we do India, Egypt, Greece and Rome, as it would be to treat the several Grecian States as essentially distinct in ancient times, and wholly independent of each other for their character and the spirit of their institutions. The European peoples, and those which have sprung from them as colonies, are more closely allied to each other, and more instantaneously affected by mutual action, than even Athens, Sparta, Corinth and Thebes were wont to be of old. And if the variety of events in the particular history of the several modern nations be so great, and the events themselves so important, as to demand a separate history for each, yet the Philosophy of History, which looks or should look at the core and not at the surface, must treat them as one whole when it recognizes the unity of civilization prevailing among them. Thus, that unity, which antiquity presents in the succession of races, and the delivery of the torch from one hand to the other, in the analogous, but changing, career of advancement, undergoes a mutation in modern times, and becomes a unity of spirit in contemporaneous civilization, and a synchronical development of it. And for this reason we assent to the propriety of Schlegel's distinction, and not on the strength of his affirmation, that "the nature of the subject" suggested the change.

As Schlegel has not attempted to give any philosophical reason for the difference of his mode of treating the Science of History in the two eras of the world, so he seems to think it wholly unnecessary to explain the cause why politics should assume such a prominent place in the modern period. To do Schlegel justice, unflattering though it be, he did not even suspect the necessity of any explanation—he noticed the fact, and deemed it wholly arbitrary and independent of intelligible cause. The doctrine that the movements of the social, the moral, and the intellectual world is governed by laws as fixed and definite as those that dictate the motions of the spheres, never presented itself to him, and, if it had, would not have been properly appreciated by him, to judge from other parts of his work. History teaches us that the political development of modern times is the most striking feature of its civilization, and this has been enough to satisfy Schlegel; the Philosophy of History should not be content to borrow the observation, but should endeavor to analyze the cause. It arises, as will be more clearly seen hereafter from the fact, that whereas in antiquity the worship of deified matter, the religion of nature, if we may so term it, was the centre around which every thing revolved, the individual man is now the pivot on which the whole scheme of civilization turns. This may seem a novel view, but we think it will be fully sustained by our subsequent investigations. In ancient times the fulcrum of the lever was thus placed out of humanity, hence political changes were only of secondary importance; in the modern era, the fulcrum is at its core, and politics, or the civil subjection of the individual, becomes the principal fact in his existence. Combine with this the fact that the progress of civilization is the gradual disenthralment of the human mind from all the chains that fetter it, and is identical with the progress of human liberty, and we arrive at the full explanation of the phenomenon. For as government, either in chief or in its numerous minor ramifications, is necessarily the most important enigma to be solved by those who have or affect to have individual liberty, the prominence of politics in recent ages depends on the fact that man is now individually and consciously the centre of the system of humanity, and is by unceasing efforts daily increasing his personal freedom.

These topics are difficult of explanation, for they do not suggest themselves as readily to the mind as Schlegel would have us suppose. They bring us to perhaps the most arduous point of all—the determination of the distinctive historical eras for the purposes of historical inquiry. Schlegel, in the second of our quotations from him, divides the philosophical history of the world into three separate parts, the epoch of the *Word*, the epoch of *Power*, and the epoch of *Light*, but he does not favor us with any necessary or even natural connection between them. To those who are not besotted admirers of every thing issuing from the German school, it will not appear presumptuous in us to declare, that this division is as ridiculous and unphilosophical as it is fanciful and obscure. And we are by no means disposed to mitigate the severity of our remark, when we read afterwards such an unblushing confession as the following:

> "And hence the Philosophy of History is not a theory standing apart and separated from history—but its results must be drawn out of the multitude of historical facts—from the faithful records of ages, and must spring up, as it were, of themselves, from bare observation. And here an unprejudiced mind will discern the motive, and also the justification of the course we have pursued, for in the Philosophy of History, we have not to do with any system—any series of abstract notions, positions and conclusions, as in the construction of a mere theory—but with the general principles only of historical investigation and historical judgment." Vol. II. p. 195.

There cannot be very much room for philosophy, where "the results spring up, as it were, of themselves from bare observation:" nor is the Philosophy of History of so simple a nature that it can be built up with "the general principles only of historical investigation and historical judgment." Something more is requisite; a systematic form is absolutely demanded, although Schlegel declares, "we have nothing to do with any system." Nay, more, all our learned author's asseverations to the contrary notwithstanding, we cannot hope to make any better progress in the Science of History than himself, without "abstract notions, positions and conclusions;" nay, even without a theory, so as to render the result of our labors something more than a superficial glance over universal history. Our theory need not be a fanciful assumption of baseless principles as the origin of our speculations; we need not dream over the progressive development of the *Word*, and the epochs of the *Word*, the *Power*, and the *Light*: of any such imagination we have more horror than Schlegel himself. But the Philosophy of History certainly demands an harmonious and consistent system for its support, derived by strict induction from a careful scrutiny of all the elements of human history. The outcry against theories, which some authors have raised, is an empty and vain declamation, where the theory is not a preconceived hypothesis, but a rational induction from observed facts. We are not so indifferent to the Philosophy of History ourselves, as to be frightened by such unmeaning babblement of the tongue as this, and to leave it as Schlegel has done, a series of loose, unconnected, superficial and unphilosophical observations. It is essential to philosophy that it should be systematic; and we do not wish to see the Philosophy of

History divorced from every thing like philosophy by a purblind rejection of all system.

To return, however, from this apparent digression to Schlegel's division of the Philosophical History of mankind. If we throw aside altogether the mystical and utterly worthless supposition which he would assume for the fundamental principle of this division, and substitute for his three epochs the periods of time to which they correspond, we are still constrained again to declare the distinction to be false, frivolous and unphilosophical. It entirely breaks up that natural division which history imperatively demands; it throws together in most unfathomable confusion, eras and nations essentially opposed; and in place of a Pharos to direct our course, it builds up an airy superstructure on a flimsy and purely arbitrary basis, which is either wholly inefficient, or efficient only to mislead. Divide, if you please, the history of the world into three periods, and it will be very evident from a study of the progress of civilization, that the first period must extend from the earliest ages of which we have authentic traditions, down to the first efforts of Roman power after universal dominion, the epoch at which Greece could no longer boast of an independent or even healthy existence. Within this space will be included the whole scheme of ancient advancement, and all the various phases which a sensuous religion, the adoration of the deified powers of nature, passed through. The second period will comprise the centuries during which all the elements of the preceding civilization were absorbed and amalgamated in the Roman State, then gradually destroyed by internal corruption and decay, and lastly supplanted by the germs of a new era, which burst forth into active and vital movement about the year 1300. We do not intend to bring this period down to what is usually considered the termination of the middle ages, which is generally placed one hundred, and sometimes nearly two hundred years later; but we think the jubilee proclaimed by Pope Boniface VIII. may be well taken as the commencement of a new era.[52] This second period formed the route through which humanity had to pass, in its transition from the civilization of antiquity to that of these later ages, and was necessary to level the road for the latter. The third epoch, which is now in progress, developes a new scheme of which Christianity is at once the soul and the type, and runs in an orbit directly parallel to the first era of the world. And as the Roman dominion was requisite to absorb, engulph, and then efface all the elements of anterior civilization, in order to make straight the way for a brighter and more perfect successor, so a peculiar race was by the foreknowledge of God set apart from the earliest times in order to furnish the electric spark which should give form, and character, and life to the subsequent civilization. This spark is Christianity; the Hebrews are

52. In 1300 Boniface VIII proclaimed the first Holy Year.

the peculiar people who were destined to impart this new leaven to the world. That singular and remarkable people, chosen from the beginning of the Lord, appear on the stage of the world's history in connection with the advance of civilization, only during that one moment of time, in which they present to the whole human race, Jew and Gentile, in ignominy and on the cross, Him whose Gospel has breathed a second and a higher existence into humanity. It is well worthy of remark, that though the records of the Hebrews run further back than those of any other people, the previous annals of that people display only a constant preparation for this single event; and that their whole subsequent career is of no importance whatever to the world, except as illustrating, attesting, and confirming the truth of the Messiah's mission.

Of all the writers on this and kindred subjects, whom we have had an opportunity of perusing, none appears to have been conscious of the full and true historical import of the Hebrew nation;[53] nor of the exceedingly narrow limits of time, within which its immediate agency in the advancement of civilization was confined. This, too, is the only instance in which the carrying forward of the torch of the world's advance, has proved a curse to the bearers; again we are reminded of the fate and the destinies of Cain, though the judgment has fallen most heavily here. A single hour, and the fifteen centuries of previous struggle are forgotten in the fruit they have produced; that single hour is followed by a new light over the rest of the earth, but by heart-burning, and anguish, and degradation, and almost despair to themselves. The God crucified upon the cross on Calvary, the Roman soldiers with their centurion, agents in the deed, the myriads clustering round and jeering Him they knew not, until the veil of night at broad day miraculously fell upon the land, and the last expiring words of the Saviour divorced the world that had passed from the world that was come, and the Jews from all the nations—this one scene within Jerusalem and about her walls, overpowering in its stupendous awe, in the one moment of time when the existence of the Jews connected itself with the fortunes of the world. The darkness which was over all the land from the

---

53. [The manner in which the career of the Gentiles operated upon that of the Jews, and assisted in working out the destinies of that remarkable people, themselves all the while isolated among the nations, has been ably and eloquently set forth by C. G. Memminger, Esq., in an Oration, delivered before the Euphradian and Clariosophic Societies of the South Carolina College, in December, 1842. He therein shows, also, the absolute necessity of recognizing the overruling hand of Providence in the history of the world, and points out how "the Father hath put in his own power the times and the seasons." The nature of his subject led him to regard the history of the Jews from a point of view, differing from that we have taken, and this difference enables us without inconsistency to subscribe most cordially and admiringly to the greater part of his doctrines.] Christopher Gustavus Memminger, 1803–1888, was born in Germany, lived in South Carolina, and was later secretary of the treasury to the Confederacy: see Memminger, *Oration on the Bible, As a Key to the Events of Sacred and Profane History* (Charleston, 1843).

sixth to the ninth hour, passed away and left a brighter and more glorious sunshine to other nations, but from Jerusalem and her children that curtain has never been withdrawn. Mysterious, indeed, has been the fate of the Jewish people, yet not without meaning. With conscious pride they carried for long centuries the destinies of the world in their hands, unconsciously they scattered the seed upon the ground, and they have not shared the harvest.

Perhaps, from the remark that all writers hitherto have failed to appreciate the true import of the Jewish history, we should except Michelet, by far the boldest and most original among them, on the strength of the following passage:

> "It was sufficient for the Holy City to preserve within its tabernacle the priceless deposit of that unity, which the world would ask of her on its knees, when it had commenced its work in the west by Greece and by Rome." Int. Hist. Univ.[54]

This may seem a slight and uncertain passage to sustain the supposition that the views of Michelet on this subject are the same with our own, but we are unwilling to make the slightest pretensions to originality in the present article, when any semblance of similar opinions can be even suspected of being shadowed forth in the writings of others. Moreover, Michelet does certainly appreciate rightly the historical peculiarity of the isolated existence of the Jews, and he is so infinitely in advance of Herder, Schlegel, and Taylor, whom for once we must mention in the same category, that he is well entitled to our passing notice.

Though we have thus explained what should be the distinction of periods if a division into three is chosen, we are far from considering this partition of times as the most satisfactory or philosophical. The third period, which is the transition state between the other two, is evidently compounded of the conclusion of the first and the commencement of the second. True, the vanishing shades of the one and the brightening hues of the other are so intermingled and confused, as to be inseparable by any ordinary analysis. But this must not deter us, while we would investigate the career of the world, from determining with philosophic accuracy the periods into which the history of humanity has resolved itself. When treating historically of the advancement of civilization, we may adopt this division into three epochs, on account of the greater facility of explication which it promises us; but in determining the actual fact of existence we must not suffer ourselves to be led away from the true path by such considerations. The most philosophical of all divisions appears to us to be into two periods, which are definitely separated from each other by that single moment of

---

54. Michelet, *Introduction à l'histoire universelle*, p. 19.

time in which the Jewish people appears as the *Protagonist* on the theatre of the world. All that followed that hour was directly preparatory for the new system, and as such may be legitimately termed its commencement. The orbits of these two periods are analogous, and so far as the latter has extended, have been parallel. The history of the Jews is as isolated from that of the world, as the Jews themselves ever have been from the nations; it is to be studied only to throw light upon that one moment which connects the two schemes of civilization.

We have said that the later period of the world's history in which we are now living is a direct parallelism to the former. But this parallelism is not to be sought in any fancied similarity of facts and events, but in the analogy which the progress of the human mind in one period bears in its nature to the same in the other. The history of antiquity teaches us that in each successive stage of ancient civilization, man liberated himself more and more from an absolute subserviency to the powers of the natural world—to a material *fatalism*, if we be allowed to borrow a very expressive phrase from Michelet. Speaking with reference to the advancement of humanity, that author remarks:

> "With the world began a war which can end only with the world; that of humanity against nature, of mind against matter, of liberty against *fatalism*. History is nothing else than the recital of this interminable struggle."—"If the present treatise attains its aim, history will appear as the eternal protestation (or rather protestantization—to coin a word much wanted,) and the progressive triumph of liberty." Introd. Hist. Univ. ad init.[55]

The progress of humanity is the gradual victory obtained by man over all opposing influences, the regaining of as much freedom of action as his nature will allow. It is the triumph of the self-conscious and self-relying intellect over all counteracting forces; it is the continual *protestantism* of liberty—the assertion by action of the supremacy of man over the influences by which he is surrounded—the progressive disenthralment of the human mind from its subjection to any power but that which it intelligently establishes or recognizes itself.

In antiquity the contest was carried on almost entirely against the material world; what it has been in modern times will be seen hereafter. To illustrate the opposition between the human race and nature, and to show how the advance of humanity depends upon the emancipation of the former from the restraint of the latter, and is, indeed, often identical with it, we will refer to a few facts. Seas and oceans had been interposed so as to separate the different parts of the earth from each other, but men "sought out many inventions," and trusting to their rafts, their canoes, their boats,

55. Ibid., p. 9.

their ships, they floated proudly over the waves, and laughed at the obstacle,

> Ne quicquam Deus abscidit
> Prudens oceano dissociabili
> Terras, si tamen impiae
> Non tangenda rates transsiliunt vada.[56]

It is because the human race is *"audax omnia perpeti"*[57] that civilization becomes practicable; a tame submission to the tyranny of nature would render stagnant all the present currents of social and intellectual advance. This very obvious truth has been dimly perceived and feebly appreciated.

> "Without this freedom of choice innate in man or imparted to him,—this faculty of determining between the divine impulse and the suggestions of the spirit of evil, there would be no history, and without a faith in such a principle, there could be no Philosophy of History. If free-will were a mere psychological illusion; if consequently men were incapable of sentiment or deliberate action; if all in life were pre-determined by necessity, and subject like nature to a blind, immutable destiny; in that case, what we call history, or the description of mankind, would merely constitute a branch of natural science." Vol. II. pp. 192–3.

This passage, divested of its *Germanism* and *Schlegelism*, and rendered into intelligible language, would seem to involve something of the idea that we would insist on, that the development of humanity is owing solely to the constant struggle against external influences. From this it follows, as we find to be the case in history, that the advancement of the human race, and the progress of civilization become more rapid and determinate in proportion as the yoke of material nature, of *fatalism*, is more effectually shaken off. It should be remarked, too, that if another obstacle appears after a former has been overcome, the confidence inspired by the first victory is a sure prestige of success in subsequent attempts; and in time the difficulties that have been surmounted become the most available and effective instruments of success in achieving further advances. Thus the ocean at one period seemed insuperable; it is now, and has long been the high-way of civilization. A barren soil refused a spontaneous harvest, agriculture and commerce arose, both important aids in furthering the development of humanity, both protesting against tyranny of matter, and asserting the gradual subjection of the soil, the sun, the rains, the winds, the waves, to the purposes of man.

56. Horace, *Carmina*, I, 3, lines 21–24; trans. In vain did the provident god divide the lands by the estranging sea, if nevertheless impious ships should leap across depths which ought not to be touched. "Ne quicquam" should be "Nequiquam."
57. Ibid., line 25; trans. bold to endure everything.

Such is the nature of the emancipation of man from foreign influences; as far as intellectual and physical independence was concerned the progressive liberation from the powers of material nature was nearly complete in antiquity. Yet the continued belief in omens, in portents, in auguries showed that man was not entirely freed from his fetters. If however, the emancipation of humanity was so far perfected in antiquity, in what is the modern period parallel to it? Is it in outward form? Far from it—as the experience of every day will prove. Has it traversed—is it now traversing the same beaten track of continual protestation against the powers of nature? If it were doing only this, the periods would be identical, not parallel. The protestation of humanity against nature has, indeed, been continued in these later ages, as the downfall of astrology will prove, but this has occupied a subordinate place in modern times, instead of giving character to the advances of civilization as was the case in antiquity. In what then does the supposed parallelism consist? In this—that both periods equally protest against the tyranny of external influences, and that the progress of that protestation has assumed similar phases in similar succession. The scheme of the ancient epoch was the disenthralment of man from a blind subjection to nature: the scheme of modern times is the assertion of the independence of the individual man against the aggregate masses. The civilization of antiquity emancipated humanity from the thraldom of matter; modern civilization is liberating each individual man from the tyranny of his fellows. Let us recall to mind that the faith of the ancient world was a sensuous adoration of material nature, and it will be seen that, as a necessary corollary from the diversity of the two schemes, the protestantism of antiquity was essentially religious and mythological; that of modern times essentially political. It is this difference which affords the philosophical reason for that prominence of politics in the third period of the world's history, which Schlegel perceives, and we have been laboring to explain. Yet our assertion may seem strange and untenable to many, who will cite the Reformation of Luther as conclusive proof that modern civilization proceeds by a religious, rather than a political *Protestantization*. Let it be remembered, however, that Luther's Reformation consisted of two elements totally distinct from each other; the protestation against the tyranny of human authority over the mind—and the promulgation of his own peculiar tenets on the subject of religion. Of these, which was it that gave character to the Reformation, and made it the most important event in modern history? Certainly not the latter, for many of his opinions were objectionable, and have as such been discarded by all the sects that have sprung from the excitement of that day. The mode in which Luther promulged his opinions was also wholly repugnant to the spirit of his own protestation. And were Zuinglius, and Melancthon, and Munzer, and Carlostadt, and Socinius, and Calvin less deeply, if less intelligently, than Luther imbued with the spirit of Protestantism?[58] Many of them possessed it in excess; but they all maintained their own religious dogmas to be the guide of faith, with an obstinate inconsistency truly characteristic of human nature. If they all, being equally Protestants, differed from each other in theological views they espoused, the genius of protestantism could certainly not be involved in these. It is that in which they all agreed, that must be taken as the index of the predominant and motive spirit. And this principle of union which made them all equally Protestants, was the resolute opposition to the supremacy and infallibility of human authority. It is this common feeling which forms the characteristic of Protestantism. Luther began the great work while a priest of the Roman Catholic Church; had that hierarchy not opposed the requisitions of the times, (for Luther was merely the embodiment and expression of a general want,) the Reformation might have been completed without ever being carried out of the bosom of that body, and without any important religious schism. It was the tyranny of the Church that was battled against, rather than any particular dogmas of faith. Religion merely chanced to be the common ground on which individual freedom and a tyrannical authority assumed to be infallible, met in contention. If we would know what the Reformation really was in its essence, we must look at the fruits which it produced in every department of knowledge in which the intellect and the heart of man develope themselves—Revolt every where, and in all cases against those authorities whose assumed power possessed only the right of prescription. In letters, in science, in politics, in religion, the same opposition to tyranny over the mind manifested itself. In religion we perceive a diversity of sects all warring furiously against this tyranny over opinion, while with pertinacious but natural inconsistency each endeavored to impose its own dogmas upon others. The same spirit, which dictated the Reformation of Luther, produced the opposition to him of Carlostadt and Munzer. Luther would reform, the others would *radicalize*. The war of the anabaptists, the immediate offspring of the Reformation, is sufficient to display its tendency. On this point we will quote a few remarks from our favorite author and invaluable guide—Michelet.

> "The Reformation itself seemed to turn against the Reformer. His old friend Carlostadt ran in the same path in which Luther was content to walk. No longer was the dispute only about religious authority; the civil authority itself was about to become the point in dispute. Behind Carlostadt was seen Munzer; behind the sacramentists and Iconoclasts appeared in the distance a revolt of peasants, a *Jacquerie*, a servile war, more reasoning, more levelling, but not less bloody than those of antiquity." Mémoirs de Luther, liv. II. c. ii.
> "This polemic violence of Luther against Carlostadt, was more and more

58. Melanchthon was the Latinized name of Philip Schwarzed: both mean "black earth."

embittered every day, by the frightful symptoms of general revolution which threatened Germany. The doctrines of that bold theologian answered to the wishes and the secret thoughts with which the masses of the people were preoccupied in Suavia, in Thuringia, in Alsatia, in the whole western part of the Empire. The lower classes, the peasants, who had been slumbering so long under the weight of feudal oppression, heard philosophers and princes speaking of liberty, and applied to their own condition what was never meant for them. The demand of the poor peasants of Suavia, in its barbaric naïvete will remain as a monument of courageous moderation. By little and little the eternal hatred of the poor against the rich awoke, less blind, however, than in the *Jacquerie*, but already looking for a systematic form, which it was to attain only in the English *Levellers*. It absorbed into itself all the germs of religious democracy, which had been believed to have been stifled in the Middle Ages. Lollardists, Beghards, a host of obscure visionaries re-appeared. At a later period their rallying cry became the necessity of a second baptism. In the beginning the aim was a dreadful war against established order, war against property, as a robbery of the poor; war against learning, as a violation of the equality of nature, and a tempting of God, who reveals all things to his saints;— books and pictures were held the inventions of the devil." Mémoirs de Luther, liv. II. c. iii.

If we required further evidence to establish our position, we would point to the Civil Wars of France, and the whole conduct and career of the Puritans in England. The tendency of the Reformation was strictly political, (in the widest sense of that word,) indeed, no change in religion, sufficient to characterize it as a religious revolution, was either proposed or contemplated. A few doctrines, which had been interpolated among the fundamental principles of Christianity, might be disavowed, but it was ecclesiastical and secular tyranny, as exercised by the Church, that was the target for every shaft. Let it not be objected to our doctrine of the political nature of modern *protestantism*, that as religion was the first index of the change, so it should be assumed as characteristic of the change. Nothing can be further from the truth than the supposition that the first ripple on the surface of the waters is a sufficient indication of the nature of the commotion beneath. And, indeed, the changes in the religious feeling of antiquity appear among the Greeks most clearly in literature and art, among the Romans in law, thus disproving the validity of any such objection.

We have dwelt at some length upon this point, but it was necessary to place it in its proper light, that our views of the scheme of human advance might be rendered intelligible. The result then of this part of our inquiry is, that the civilization of the world may be best divided into two historical periods, but if the preference is given to a division into three, the epochs should respectively be, first, the emancipation from his subjection to nature, which epoch bears a religious type: second, from A. C. 280 to A. D. 1300, furnishing the link of connection between the ancient and modern worlds, and containing the absorption and destruction of the elements of antiquity, and the development of the germs of a new order of things: and, third, the modern civilization, having a decidedly political character, yet running parallel to the first period of the world's history. Such is the grand division which we would make before attempting a Philosophy of History: though, as we have said before for accurate analysis, we would prefer the portion of the second epoch between the other two.

We have now pointed out the defectivenesses of Schlegel's views on the aim of the Science of History, and have stated our objections to the erroneous plan adopted by him as the groundwork for the explication of his opinions. Our remarks have been necessarily confined to what may be termed the metaphysics of the science, for our intention was not to illustrate its parts, but to determine its form. Hence we have spoken of the advancement of civilization and the development of intellect as both identical with the progress of humanity, whereas in strictness they are only component parts of it. They are both, however, equally due to the same general laws, and as our eye was fixed upon these, the soul and moving principle of the whole, a comprehensive and generalized view of the scheme of the world's advance, might very properly overlook the minor differences which characterize and distinguish them.

And here we might with great propriety bring our long article to a close, but to smooth the way for any future investigations in the same field, we will detain our readers for a short while longer, and occupy the few pages still at our command with a rapid and cursory examination of the principal influences which affect and modify the advancement of humanity, and form the character of nations. We will also consider the different developments of human intellect in which we ought to search for the materials of the Science of History. This part of our inquiry will be easy and our labor light, as the subject is more within the sphere of our ordinary cogitations. It is not, however, to be regarded as unimportant, because our investigation may be less painful and laborious than the task which we have just accomplished. We have not touched in this article the lesser details of the Philosophy of History, but if such had been our intention, the inquiry which we are now about to enter upon, would have formed a necessary preliminary to our undertaking.

Montesquieu, in his Spirit of Laws, when speaking of the various influences which contribute to produce the specific differences of national character, mentions "climate, religion, laws, government, traditions of the past, manners and habits."[59] These, as M. Villemain truly remarks, operate with different degrees of force in the different periods of a nation's

59. [Liv. xix. c. iv.]

history;[60] and Montesquieu is perfectly correct in asserting, in the same chapter from which we quote the above, that men in the savage state are governed almost entirely by nature and climate. We do not, however, adopt without scrutiny the influences enumerated by Montesquieu, for there are some which he has omitted, and others which he mentions that are not strictly admissible. Of those which he has specified, only two, as it is very evident, are not themselves the productions of other human forces—Climate and Religion. Even religion is, perhaps, as much influenced by the intellectual character of each age arising from other causes, and is as violently reacted upon by them as it acts thereon. But as religion never springs up spontaneously in the heart of the people, but is brought to them from without, it may very properly be taken, under certain limitations, as one of the original influences in forwarding the development of humanity. Montesquieu's list may be a very correct though scanty catalogue of the forces which form the character of the several periods in the existence of a particular nation, but is altogether insufficient and unsound when the whole history of mankind is before us for our examination. Of those which may be supposed to act upon intellect at large the principal will be climate, local circumstances and situation, the character of the component races of a nation, temperament, and the antecedent state of civilization among those peoples from whom it derives its own. Of these, perhaps the most important of all are the previous condition of humanity, and the character of races. In all ages of the world these are nearly equally operative, whereas the others are all liable to be more or less modified by the progress of society. Thus the Anglo-Saxon race, in many parts of the world, retains much of its energy and activity where the long settled aborigines become enervated and yield without resistance to the enfeebling influences of a hot climate. And universally a nation is less susceptible of the peculiarities of climate as it advances in civilization; this might be inferred from what we have said in a previous part of this article, and is amply confirmed by the experience of history.

The importance of a diligent attention to the characteristics of particular races, has never, it appears to us, been sufficiently insisted on. Yet if we would not have all our conclusions drawn from a scientific study of history rendered inconsistent with each other, or inapplicable to the facts, we must always admit the character of each race as one of the principal elements in all our calculations regarding the nations descended from it. The characteristics of particular races remain ineradicable, they undergo slight changes and modifications, according to the admixture of foreign

---

60. Abel François Villemain, *Cours de littérature française: tableau du dix-huitième siècle* (Paris, 1838), 2: 62–66.

blood, but the original type remains. Thus we may detect many of the strongest peculiarities of the Anglo-Saxon race in the Germans while inhabiting their wild woods, as described in Tacitus, and those peculiarities are not supplanted at the present day. The character of the French nation may be traced in some of its most distinctive features in Caesar, Cicero, Tacitus, and other classic authors, and the portrait drawn of the Armoricans, by a writer in the early part of the middle ages, might be applied, with slight alteration, to the French people now:

"Gens inter geminos notissima clauditur amnes,
Armoricana prius veteri cognomine dicta,
Torva, ferox, ventosa, prorux, incanta, rebellis,
Inconstans, disparque sibi novitatis amore,
Prodiga verborum, sed non et prodiga facti."[61]

The importance of a due consideration of the character of races may be seen in the matter of colonization alone; the Anglo-Saxon colonies have been always successful, the French have as invariably failed. This point may be slight in comparison with many others; as for instance, what nation subsequent to the Greeks has aided in the civilization and advancement of humanity, which does not refer to them as the fountain whence their own refinement flowed? Tyre was, in many respects, the rival of Greece, Carthage of Rome: what memorials of its existence has the Phoenician race left to posterity? A few coins and inscriptions—a few glosses and proper names—two or three passages in the Paenulus of Plautus,[62] and one record of its conflict with those nations of the world in whose hands the advancement of civilization was placed. And this is all: the Punic wars, the record of the successive defeats of the Phoenician power in its attempts at supremacy—this is all that the Philosophy of History, when it takes a general view, notices of the Phoenician race.

Of the other influences, which we have mentioned as affecting the character of civilization in different ages, it will be wholly unnecessary for us now to speak at large. Their operation must be obvious to any one; their extent, mode of action, and limitation, if touched upon at all, would require much more space than we are able to devote to them. It is sufficient for the present to have indicated them. Let it be understood, however, that

---

61. [Errichus Monachus, cited by Gibbon.] Edward Gibbon, *The History of the Decline and Fall of the Roman Empire*, ed. J. B. Bury (New York, 1907), 5:281, n. 180 (Erricus Monachus was the author of a life of Saint German); "prorux" should be "procax," and "incanta" should be "incauta." Trans. A very famous tribe is contained between twin rivers, once called Armorican (its ancient name): savage, cruel, fickle, insolent, heedless, insurgent, inconstant, unlike itself by its craving for novelty, lavish with its words but not with its deeds.

62. [Anthon's Class. Dict. Tit. Phoenice.] *A Classical Dictionary*, ed. Charles Anthon (rev. ed., New York, 1849), p. 1052.

in enumerating these influences as giving character to the mutations of the civilization of the world, we consider them as all acting together, and combining by their opposition or agreement to produce the particular results, although their degree of power may vary with circumstances and times. The laws to which the world of God is subjected may be simple themselves, but always act in combination with each other, and thus produce a complicated system for us to unravel in our investigations of their effects. We cannot arrive at any satisfactory conclusions if we take them separately, but must always examine into the character and results of their combined action. And in no department of philosophic inquiry is this more necessary, or more arduous than in the Science of History. We must, however, submit to the necessity and overcome the difficulty, if we would achieve any profitable aim.

The only remaining point of inquiry is to determine in what way we ought to trace the current and character of the development of humanity. By a careful scrutiny and examination of all those arts and sciences, practical and theoretical, by which the mind and the feeling of mankind declare, and in which they unfold themselves. All the departments of human knowledge, arts, literature, science, religion and philosophy—all are but diverse developments and outward manifestations of the same indwelling spirit, which fructifies, and, by its plastic force, moulds them all into harmony with itself and with each other. These are the works of the intellect and not the intellect itself—they are the visible effects whence we judge of the invisible cause, for every tree is known by its fruit.—The same energy has given birth to them all, the same family likeness is stamped upon them all—they are all blossoms budding upon the same stem. But it is the hidden energy which produces them, and its changes, which we seek, and this we are to discover by noting the changes in the savour and appearance of its fruits. The expressed and recorded feelings of nations, which may be considered as furnishing us with their intellectual character, are not, however, all that we are to mark; the greater part of the feelings of their heart they have never been able to shape into words, though they may live in actions. Those of which they are fully conscious find vent in language, while manners, customs, institutions, &c. frequently embody a hidden feeling unconsciously to the possessors. Thus, by a little attention, we are easily rendered conscious of our mental operations, and can describe them, but the silent processes of the physical system cannot be brought to our knowledge by any degree of attention, nor expressed in language, though they may produce changes as great as any caused by the former. Hence our calculations respecting the progress of humanity would be futile and imperfect, if we were to omit all attention to those unconscious processes in the bosom of nations, which have never found utterance for themselves in words, but which may be often traced in actions or in monuments. Are not the manners and customs of people as significant of some hidden truth as the record of their battles? Do not the myriads employed in the building of the pyramids point as conclusively to the existence of a despotism in Egypt, as the pages of any historian could do? Do we require any further evidence of the superstition of the middle ages, of the vague, indeterminate longing for some unknown good, of the authority of the Church, than the cathedrals of Salisbury and Durham, of Strasburg and Milan? The actions of men as races and as nations must, therefore, be sought out and explained; and no shred of information in regard to their habits of life, and the character of their deeds, can be so scanty and worthless, as not to merit attention.

If then a light can be thrown upon the progress of humanity by all these things, even by the most minute, the Science of History will absorb into itself all possible information on all subjects. It may do so; but that extent and accuracy of knowledge will not be requisite in delineating the broad outlines, which might be demanded in filling up the picture, and finishing the details. So much would, indeed, be necessary to be known, weighed and appreciated, before the task of writing a Philosophy of History, in such a manner as to leave nothing to be desiderated, could be completed, that we fully concur with Herder, "that a philosophy of the history of man cannot yet be written," but doubt whether it will probably before "the end of this miliad."[63] Yet a cool and impartial judgment may collect from a study of the main features of the different elements we have specified above, enough to furnish the outlines of the whole scheme, though it must be left to future times to complete the undertaking. We look forward with hope, but with fear, to the day when this shall be accomplished. In the mean time we shall not be without our own reward, if we suceed in bringing the subject into more general notice, and thus increasing the chances of accomplishment and facilitating its performance. Our feeble aid may contribute little to the work, but we will not be ashamed of the office of herald in a good cause.

Of these various developements of human feeling and intellect, which form the progress of humanity, there are some which may be more serviceably employed than others as our guides. They are all serviceable, all important, but for the purposes of a general investigation the inductions we would seek cannot be obtained with equal facility from all. Those, however, which best merit our attention are religious, literary, and political change, in the same order that we have mentioned them. Literature is the running commentary upon all ages, the universal exponent of the thoughts, feelings, views, desires and intentions of all periods at which it may exist, and it has existed more or less in all times which have aided in the progress

---

63. [Herder, Pref. Phil. Hist. Man. p. x. Ed. 1800. 4to.]

of humanity since the Greeks seized the torch of civilization. Religion is the inward consciousness, and outward declaration of the highest and most vital belief; and politics is the mirror in which we discern the struggle of men to adapt circumstances to themselves. The three are all indicative of the same spirit, acting in different ways upon diverse materials and for diverse aims. They throw mutual light upon each other by their specific differences, and illustrate the action of the one common energy by their generic identity. If literature be multiform and Proteus-like in its infinite diversities, still it is always deeply imbued with the dominant feelings of the epoch. The progress of the French Revolution may be traced with greater ease and distinctness in the works from Voltaire and Jean Jacques Rousseau downwards, than in the protocols and diplomatic missives of government. A glance at the literature of any age, and a comparison of it with its previous condition, will always enable us to trace most of the changes of nations. It is, however, too uncertain, too fluctuating, too liable to assume an outer vesture, concealing its real character, derived from the idiosyncrasies of each author, to be adopted as our sole, or even as our principal dependence in following the stream of historical advancement. For this and other reasons, we must seek some additional aid, less liable to be affected by individual peculiarities, to guide us through the mazes of the labyrinth. And what we seek we find both in religion and politics, which derive their character from the feelings of large masses of men. Of the two, religion is the most prominent, for when it does not stand alone, it identifies itself with politics, and always expresses the most vital feeling of the day, exhibiting it in action. For belief, hope, faith, call it what you will, (though metaphysically distinct, they are nearly synonymous when applied to our future prospects,) is necessarily the pivot of all human action working towards its own advancement, as its opposite unbelief is the soul and incarnate spirit of destruction. Now both of these, belief and unbelief, find their highest and most complete development in religion, which is the faith of man in his moral duties and moral destinies. This then is the most important of all the guides we can take, as it is always in action, and, being common to whole nations, or to large bodies of men, exists more free of the impress of individual peculiarities. If in contravention of this remark, Pope Gregory VII., Luther, and Knox be cited, as men who have left the impress of their own character upon papacy, Lutheranism, and Scotch presbyterianism respectively, we reply that, so far as the essence of these creeds was concerned, their opinions and views were only the legitimate exposition of the age and country to which they belonged: and that all that was immediately derived from their genius was the form and vesture. Many of us have yet to learn that a great revolution is not the work of one man, but of a change in the feelings of whole nations: that a great man himself is but the creation of the times, catching the spirit of the coming change before others are aware of its approach, and communicating the spark to the materials already prepared for ignition. We might as well refer the impression on the coin to the die alone, without attributing anything to the mind and art of man and the experience of ages, which have formed the letter, as to say that the temporal sovereignty of the successor of St. Peter was due only to the genius of Pope Gregory VII., or the production of the protestantism to the Augustan friar of Wirtemberg alone, when Europe had already been *protestantizing* so long. Those who would hazard such a supposition have read the history of nations to very little purpose.

The third guide we have mentioned is politics, and by this we mean to include all the institutions of a country established for its own internal regulation, and the maintenance of its welfare, as well as what is usually comprehended in the term. And though we place this last of the three we have specified, its importance must not be overlooked, for one of the strongest evidences of national prosperity, is the excellence of its government, and easy operation. We have placed it after religion and literature, because it was always rife in vain speculations and useless experiments. Before it is possible to trace the advance of a nation in its political history, it is necessary to winnow the whole, and then you may often find only one grain of wheat to two bushels of chaff. But that one grain, will amply repay all previous labors, its existence is fixed and certain, it is a landmark to all future time, and it is nearly impossible for an impartial mind to mistake its significance. These three then—religion, literature and politics, may be taken as our best aid in tracing the stream of human advance, but, though we rely principally upon these, the others must not be overlooked, nor must any one be regarded independent.

We will now conclude these long labors, which their novelty may render unwelcome to many readers, with a notice of the grand lessons which the Philosophy of History inculcates. And first we learn from it, that the progress of the world has not been brought about by loose, blind, and disconnected efforts, but that its advance has been in one connected chain, each link of which has been formed in obedience to certain fixed laws, so that the future has been invariably the legitimate offspring of the past. That the civilization of man has been truly *"the work of humanity unto itself,"* acting in subjection to certain influences, and impelled to exertion by the consequences of the curse upon the ground "for his sake." That the march of the world has been continually forward, and that even in those ages where the pall of night seemed to darken over the nations, the retrogression was itself the necessary condition of a further advance. That it has also been one unbroken system, carried on under all changes of time, place, and circumstances, from the first day, when the ground was cursed for man's sake, to the present hour. And, though the course of this article has not let us insist upon it, we may add that the Philosophy of History forces upon our minds the continual superintendence of Providence, as marshalling events, so as at the proper time to be submitted to the proper influences. Three things are essential to the existence and progress of humanity, the partial opposition of nature, the active and conscious energy of man, and the controlling hand of God, without which the whole scheme becomes unintelligible. And as God did constitute the laws of nature in the beginning with a just view and foreknowledge of all their possible effects; as he did stamp upon humanity the impress and character which it bears, so as to adapt it to the career which it was to run and the influences to which it was to be exposed;—let our closing words be—ΤΩ ΘΕΩ ΔΟΞΑ.[64]

---

64. Trans. Glory be to God.

# 6.

## Henry Augustine Washington

### "The Social System of Virginia"[1]

Henry Augustine Washington, who was born in Westmoreland County, Virginia, in 1820 and died young in Washington in 1858, was deeply imbedded in the kinship network that was Virginian intellectual and political society.[2] He was a Washington, itself a comprehensive legacy; he married a daughter of Beverley Tucker; he edited the first systematic edition of Jefferson's papers;[3] he assumed Thomas Dew's chair of History, Political Economy and International Law at the College of William and Mary and prepared Dew's history lectures for press in 1853.[4] But the striking fact of Washington's intellectual career was his attempt to fashion a skeptical appreciation of his Virginian inheritance.

Washington was persuaded that the nineteenth century was formulating a newly detached and scientific historical understanding. "Never before," he observed in 1852, "has such immense erudition, enlightened skepticism and patient, laborious and comprehensive learning been brought to bear on this [history] or any other subject. The result has been almost startling. Stale common-places

---

1. Henry Augustine Washington, "The Social System of Virginia," *SLM* 14 (February 1848): 65–81.
2. Right Rev. John Johns, *Memoir of Henry Augustine Washington* (Baltimore, 1859), is the only printed source for Washington's life. Johns spends about half of this slim pamphlet upon establishing that Washington had, under the influence of Cynthia Tucker, abandoned religious skepticism for orthodoxy. See also Carol H. Sturzenberger, ed., "The Diaries of Henry A. Washington, 1842–1845" (Master's thesis, College of William and Mary, 1979).
3. Henry A. Washington, ed., *The Writings of Thomas Jefferson* (9 vols., Washington, D.C., 1853–1854); Jefferson's modern editor observes, "Though Washington's edition . . . was a noteworthy accomplishment in its day and added greatly to the public knowledge of Jefferson in the mid-nineteenth century, it was characterized by the sort of editorial liberties with the text which reflected the inexact scholarly standards of that day," *The Papers of Thomas Jefferson*, ed. Julian P. Boyd (Princeton, 1950), 1:xviii.
4. Thomas Dew, *A Digest of the Laws, Customs, Manners and Institutions of the Ancient and Modern Nations* (New York, 1853).

have been refuted, consecrated errors exposed—established dogmas shaken—ancient rubbish removed—a full broad light thrown upon things which have been hitherto enveloped in impenetrable myth and fable."[5] The heroes of this historicist revolution were Guizot, Niebuhr and Macaulay; and in America there was Bancroft. One feels Washington aspired to be for Virginian history what Niebuhr was for ancient Rome, an aspiration truncated by ill health and an accident with an air gun that propelled a bullet through Washington's skull. It was to be a revolution of documents carefully preserved and located, but also of theory and sociological analysis; committed to a mild reformism in the spirit of a modernized Whiggism; secular, save in that vague commitment to Carlyle's natural supernaturalism which spoke of the usefully indistinct forces of Providence.

This discourse upon "The Social System of Virginia" was Washington's first attempt to apply his revolution to Virginian history. It is a young man's piece, too long, overargued, circling around the act of dissociation. But to argue that the Virginian contribution to American political history and theory derived from special social conditions, and that the inheritance was a very mixed blessing, was a bold move. Parts of his analysis were traditional, notably his invocation of the Cavalier myth and his emphasis upon the English and specifically Anglo-Saxon origins of Virginian society. His mild antislavery tone is reminiscent of Jefferson, although a memoir of Washington notes that he undertook the editing of Jefferson's papers with distaste and emerged "with diminished admiration for the political character and aversion for the moral views" of the former president.[6] Washington, at the time he was writing this, was living on a farm in King George County, and his ambivalence toward the moral and intellectual benefits of country life must have had more personal significance.

Later, in a discourse upon the Virginia Constitution of 1776 given to the Virginia Historical Society in 1852, he was to develop a more sophisticated analysis. Both pieces betray a fascination with the problem of aristocracy's function in the history of political liberty and social equality. In 1852 Washington offered a drastically revised version of traditional Virginian Whig theory. In 1848 he had dwelled

---

5. Washington, "The Virginia Constitution of 1776," *SLM* 18 (November 1852): 664.
6. Johns, *Washington*, p. 13.

upon the indigenous social influences upon the emergence of American liberty. Later he turned more to the burden of European political experience. Earlier Whig theory had held, just as later Herbert Baxter Adams was to insist in the Germanic seminars at Johns Hopkins, that liberty had been initiated in the German woods and been defined within the Anglo-Saxon tradition under the exigencies of the Norman yoke. This, Washington insisted, was in error. American liberty was feudal in origin, certainly, but on the distaff side. Its roots were Norman and aristocratic. Magna Carta was not an assertion of popular rights, but a pact between king and barons. Its importance was to create the principle of resistance to absolutism, a definition of legal independence to which it was later possible to admit other ranks of society. English history was precisely that process of assimilation and levelling up. Indeed Washington thought he saw a general historical law in this: that "society always begins in inequality and tends towards equality, and that, in its earliest stages, all rights, privileges and franchises—even liberty itself—are the possession of an exclusive cast, from which they descend in successive stages, with the progress of society, to the great body of the nation." This was scarcely Jacksonian, nor even Jeffersonian, since Washington specifically dissented from natural rights theory. He even went so far as to praise that bête noire of Whiggery, Hobbes, as "a man of genius and erudition—a great, bold, original thinker—the first philosopher of his age and country" and to speak slightingly of "Algernon Sidney and other writers of less note." This repudiation of orthodox Whig historical theory released Washington to the organicist historicism of a Herder. Without natural right, man was left with time and place. One could not therefore dispraise a culture that chose other ways. "Despotism then at Rome was as legitimate as democracy now at Washington. . . . we cannot judge governments in the abstract."[7] Washington might have paused at these words, to listen for a cacophony of Virginians revolving in their graves.

---

7. Washington, "The Virginia Constitution," pp. 663, 671, 669–70.

IT has long been a matter of surprise and regret, that the people of Virginia have manifested so little interest in regard to the early history of their State. The amount of ignorance which prevails in the commonwealth upon this subject is absolutely astonishing. It is by no means confined to the illiterate. Our educated men—men of intelligence and general information—are equally amenable to the charge. Young gentlemen, who have been to college, and who are reasonably well-read in general history, are yet, (with some few honorable exceptions,) profoundly ignorant of the State whose soil they tread and whose air they breathe. They have been carefully instructed in the annals of Greece and Rome—every phase of French and English history is familiar to them—they know by heart the whole line of Plantagenets, Tudors, Stuarts, Guelphs and Capets, and yet can tell you nothing of that race of men from whose loins they have sprung, and if they have heard, by accident, that such men as Smith and Bacon[8] have lived and died, this is the extent of their information in respect to these colonial heroes.

This neglect of their early history by the Virginians is altogether unpardonable. Even were the subject uninviting, its dignity and importance would entitle it to their consideration. But nothing could be further from the truth. No such reproach as this attaches to our colonial history. Upon the contrary, we venture to affirm that the annals of no people whatever, ancient or modern, more abound in interesting incident. The mere fact that the early annals of Virginia present to us two distinct states of civilization and two distinct races of men placed in direct juxtaposition to each other, and that, too, under the most novel circumstances, must invest them with an interest which attaches to the history of few countries. They present to us barbarism and civilization—the red man of the American forest and the cultivated European, thrown face to face upon the shores of the Western world, there to wage a war of extermination—the one in defence of his country and his home—the other to make conquests, settle colonies and amass wealth. The history of such a struggle, and of a society compounded of such strange elements, and in which men occupied such novel relations to each other, could not, in the nature of things, be otherwise than entertaining and instructive. And we accordingly find that new phases of human life—novel and striking developments of the individual man—romantic adventure, bold achievement, and thrilling incident, meet us at every step of colonial progress. The simple story of Smith and Pocahontas, if there was nothing else, would redeem the annals of any people from the reproach of dulness.

But it is the importance, rather than the romance of our colonial his-

---

8. John Smith, circa 1580–1631, the colonial adventurer; Nathaniel Bacon, 1647–1676, the leader of Bacon's Rebellion.

tory, which claims for it the attention of every educated man—particularly of every educated Virginian. It was upon the banks of our favorite river, not many miles from the present capital of the State, that the Anglo-Saxon race first took root in the soil of the Western world. We do not hesitate to pronounce this one of the most memorable epochs in modern history. In our judgment, the landing of Smith at Jamestown, followed, as it was, by the subsequent occupation of the country by men of Anglo-Saxon origin, has exercised, and is destined to exercise, in its remote consequences, a greater influence over the destinies of the human race than any event which has occurred since the Reformation. It would not be difficult to make good this proposition, but it would lead us too far from our present purpose. We believe, however, that it will be generally conceded, and, if so, how recreant has Virginia heretofore been to her early history.

It is gratifying, however, to find that there has been some improvement in this matter. A disposition has recently manifested itself in several quarters to wipe away this reproach from the Ancient Dominion, and rescue, as far as is now practicable, her early annals from oblivion. The Virginia Historical Society has been recently reorganized under new auspices, and with flattering prospects of success.[9] This Society, if it can once be established on a permanent basis, will no doubt prove a useful institution. It deserves the patronage of the State, and we should be pleased to see an appropriation made for it during the present winter by the Legislature, if such appropriation be fairly within the scope of its legitimate powers. Virginia, even yet, abounds in rich historical fragments, which must soon be lost, unless they be collected and arranged with some regard to order and system. New York, Massachusetts, and, we believe, several of the other States, have similar societies, which are in a prosperous condition. Their collections are already large and interesting, and have been found valuable in illustrating the colonial history of the country. There is no good reason why the Virginia Historical Society should not also prosper, and we feel confident that, with equal industry and enterprise, it will meet with equal success. We believe that the loose material yet floating about in the commonwealth is quite as valuable as that either of New York or Massachusetts, and if diligently collected and arranged, will be found no inconsiderable contribution to our historical literature. Let our people then, for once, at least, lay aside their repugnance to combined action—let them come to the aid of this public and patriotic enterprise—let them send in their interesting historical manuscripts and other documents to the Society, where they will be preserved; let them do this and the Virginia Historical Society will be placed upon an enduring basis, and its labors will redound to the honor of the State.

9. First organized in 1833, the Virginia Historical Society was revivified at a meeting in Richmond in December 1847.

Valuable contributions to Virginia history have also been made from other quarters. Within the last year or two, we have been favored with a volume from R. R. Howison, Esq., upon the colonial history of Virginia, and a history by Charles Campbell, Esq., covering very much the same ground.[10]

We have only had it in our power to read the first two or three chapters of Mr. Campbell's history. With the part which we have read, however, we are much pleased. Indeed, we shall be greatly disappointed if Mr. Campbell's book does not prove to be the most valuable history of Virginia which has yet been given to the public. We have the pleasure of a personal acquaintance with that gentleman, and know that the best energies of his life have, up to this time, been devoted to its preparation. It has been with him, for many years, a labor of love—every faculty of mind and body has been enlisted in the undertaking; and, in the collection of material, he has been indefatigable. We are persuaded that there is no man in Virginia so intimately acquainted with her colonial history as Mr. Campbell, and we believe that his industry has led to the discovery of matter which has never before been published and which will enable him to present some portion of Virginia annals in a new point of view.

We have read Mr. Howison's volume, and can, with pleasure, bear testimony to its merits in many respects. It is a clear and interesting narrative of the most prominent facts connected with the colony of Virginia from its first settlement in 1607 to the peace of Paris in 1763. And, so far as our limited information enables us to judge, it is a correct narrative. We know of no book which we would sooner place in the hands of one who desired to make himself acquainted with the general outline of Virginia history in the shortest possible time and with the least possible trouble. Matter which is elsewhere spread over a large surface and dispersed in books, some of which are out of print and others not readily accessible to all, is here compressed into a single volume of moderate size, arranged in chronological order and the whole woven into a narrative, conducted with no inconsiderable skill. As a mere record of important public events—the settlement of Jamestown—the early adventures of the colonists—their bloody battles with the savages—their "moving accidents by flood and field"[11]—the laws which were at various times enacted—the revolutions through which the colonial government passed, and the relations which subsisted at different times between the colony and the mother country—as a record, we say, of these and such like external matters, Mr. Howison's book leaves us not much to be desired. But at this point we must stop.

10. Robert Reid Howison, *A History of Virginia from Its Discovery and Settlement by Europeans to the Present* (Philadelphia, 1846–1848); Charles Campbell, *Introduction to the History of the Colony and Ancient Dominion of Virginia* (Richmond, 1847).

11. *Othello*, I. iii. line 135.

Having pointed out what we believe to be merits of Mr. Howison's history, the laws of independent criticism demand that we should next point out what we conceive to be its defects. And, in the first place, the style in which his book is written is open to many objections. It is upon a key altogether too high for historical writing. Mr. H. will, by no means, consent to tell us what he has to say in plain English. But whatever he is narrating, however trivial and unimportant it may be, must be set down in the swelling periods of Johnson or Gibbon, and the consequence is, that Mr. H. is frequently eloquent upon occasions when it would have been much better to have been merely natural. This is, however, in our eyes, a very venial offence; for style, after all, is not the body, but the mere outward vestment, and we care not much for the setting, if the diamond itself be genuine. In our judgment, a bold, manly utterance of the honest convictions of one's own intellect, is the best style in which a man can write, and, dismissing this whole matter of style, we proceed immediately to what we esteem to be the great defect of Mr. H's history: and in order that we may be distinctly understood, it will be necessary to premise a word or two in respect to the revolution which has taken place in historical literature within the last half century.

He who has observed, with any degree of attention, the progress of modern civilization, must have noted the rise of a new spirit which presides over the investigation of truth in all the departments of human life. It is a spirit of strict reserve, rigid analysis and cautious deduction—a spirit which observes facts carefully, and admits generalization slowly. This spirit has, for sometime, prevailed in the conduct of those sciences which employ themselves in the material world, Natural philosophy, chemistry, geology and astronomy. It explains their progress and has been the source of their glory. And it is a spirit which is now extending itself to all those sciences which have for their object, the investigation of *facts* and the ascertainment of *truth*, as it exists in the world around us. But where the object is not so much the investigation of facts and the establishment of pre-existing truth, as the improvement of the social relations, there a very different tendency prevails. In political economy, government and the administration of public affairs, for instance, we no longer observe that servile subjection to *facts*, as they were called, which was once manifested. These general ideas, reason, principles—what are called *theories*, are introducing themselves and causing themselves to be respected. The movement of which we speak is, therefore, a double movement. Facts are intruding themselves into the intellectual order, and ideas are intruding themselves into the social order. The outer world is governed more according to reason and the intellectual world more according to reality. Thus, in our times, are fact and theory brought together and made to move in company. This is the last and greatest intellectual achievement of the age— the glory of modern civilization. It was not so a hundred years ago. Then, in the intellectual order—in abstract science and philosophy—little respect was paid to reality, and the imagination of men, refusing to be controlled by facts as they existed in the world around them, ran into the wildest excesses of theory and hypothesis. On the other hand, in the social order, general ideas found no place at all, and he who attempted to assert for them any influence in political economy or the administration of public affairs, was forthwith branded as a visionary and a dreamer. The provinces of facts and general ideas were then entirely distinct and independent— each was supreme in its own dominion and would tolerate no intrusion by the other. The consequence was, as has just been stated, that speculation ran into the wildest excesses and the intellectual world was filled with fantasies and chimeras; while the social world remained a dead chaotic mass. The progress of modern civilization has, at last, corrected this state of things. We can find fact and theory every where moving in company, acting and reacting upon each other—modifying each other—fact controlling the excesses of theory, and theory expounding and interpreting fact. Guizot, in his History of Civilization, (whence we have borrowed it,) has developed so fully and forcibly the idea which we have been endeavoring to express, that we will take the liberty of quoting the passage.

He says:

> "We are now compelled to consider—science and reality—theory and practice—right and fact—and make them move side by side. Down to the present time these two powers have lived apart. The World has been accustomed to see theory and practice following two different routes, unknown to each other, or at least never meeting. When doctrines, when general ideas, have wished to intermeddle in affairs, to influence the world, it has only been able to effect this under the appearance and by the aid of *fanaticism*. Up to the present time the government of human societies, the direction of their affairs, has been divided by two sorts of influences; on the one side theorists, men who would rule all according to abstract notions—Enthusiasts; on the other, men ignorant of all rational principle—Experimentalists, whose only guide is expediency. This state of things is now over. The world will no longer agitate for the sake of some abstract principle, some fanciful theory, some Utopian government, which can only exist in the imagination of an enthusiast; nor will it put up with practical abuses and oppressions, however formed by prescription and expediency, when they are opposed to just principles and the legitimate end of government. To ensure respect, to obtain confidence, governing powers must now unite theory and practice; they must know and acknowledge the influence of both. They must regard as well principles as facts; must respect both truth and necessity—must shun, on the one hand, the blind pride of the fanatic theorist, and, on the other, the no less blind pride of the libertine practician."[12]

---

12. François Guizot, *General History of Civilization in Europe from the Fall of the Roman Empire to the French Revolution* (3d ed., New York, 1856), 1:83; Washington has emphasised *fanaticism* and capitalized *Enthusiasts* and *Experimentalists*.

This scientific method of investigating truth is extending itself in every direction. It has, as we have seen, taken possession of science and philosophy, it prevails in political economy, government and the administration of public affairs generally, and is now reaching into the domain of history. Indeed, the revolution which it has wrought in historical literature, within the last half century, is unprecedented. The historian of the nineteenth century is no longer, a mere *Gazetteer*, and his history a dry record of battles, treaties and public acts of government. He feels that he has a higher province than that of merely collecting public facts and setting them down in chronological order. Besides these outward and material facts, open to the inspection of all, there are other moral and hidden facts, which, although we cannot attach to them precise name or date, it yet concerns us quite as much to know as those battles, treaties and public acts of government, of which we have spoken. To bring those hidden facts to light, to evolve those general principles which lie buried under the chaos of innumerable isolated facts—to elucidate those great moral problems which connect themselves with the social progress of every people—this is the mission of modern history. And it is this recent alliance between *philosophy* and *history* which precisely measures and characterises that revolution in historical literature, which it is our purpose to note. The results of that revolution have been immense. It has, indeed, changed the whole course of history, and given a new direction to the labors of the historian. Heretofore, history has been occupied almost exclusively about courts, camps and battle-fields, forgetting that it is not in courts or camps, nor yet on battle-fields that the life of a people is spent, or their true history discovered; but far away from scenes like these, in the field, the work-shop, and the factory—on the highway and in the retired valleys of the world, causes which few eyes see and which are chronicled in no records, are silently, but steadily and irresistibly moulding the destinies of the human race. To detect these latent causes, and record them for the instruction of the present and future generations, is the province of history, and, hereafter, he who does this will alone be esteemed an historian; while he who writes to us about courts and camps and battle-fields—who collects and sets down in chronological order, under their appropriate heads, so as to be of easy reference, the *remarkable events* of the past, such as the birth of princes, the death of kings, the dates of battles, the change of dynasties, political revolutions, general laws, and public acts of government, may be regarded as a more or less instructive Gazetteer; but nothing more. Mankind, if they could only be induced to think so, have a much deeper interest in those arts, sciences, discoveries and inventions, by which the comforts of human life have been extended and civilization advanced, than in those wars, revolutions and public acts of government by which the world has been so often scourged and whole nations devastated.

With much force and beauty does Carlyle ask—

"Which was the greater innovator, which was the more important personage in man's history, he who first led armies over the Alps, and gained the victories of Cannae and Thrasymene; or the nameless boor who first hammered out for himself an iron spade? When the oak tree is felled, the whole forest echoes with it; but a hundred acorns are planted silently by some unnoticed breeze. Battles and war-tumults, which for the time din every ear, and with joy or terror intoxicate every heart, pass away like tavern brawls; and, except some few Marathons and Mogartens, are remembered by accident, not by desert. Laws themselves, political constitutions, are not our life, but only the *house wherein our life is led*: nay, they are but the bare walls of the house; all whose essential furniture, the inventions, and traditions and daily habits that regulate and support our existence, are the works, not of Dracos and Hampdens, but of Phoenician mariners, of Italian masons, and Saxon metallurgists, of philosophers, alchemists, prophets and all the long train of artists and artisans; who, from the first, have been jointly teaching us how to think and how to act, how to rule our spiritual and our physical nature."[13]

It is these "Phoenician mariners, Italian masons, and Saxon metallurgists, philosophers, alchemists, prophets, and all the long train of artists and artisans; who, from the first, have been teaching us how to think and how to act," who have been the real benefactors of mankind. It is this hitherto neglected and despised class, who only appear on the pages of history, when they are gathered together on some battle-field to be slaughtered for the glory of their masters, who have given to the world those arts and sciences which have redeemed the world from barbarism, and preserved civilization as a trust for their children and future generations. Honor and glory are attached to their names; but we know nothing of them; for history, which should have recorded their praises, was in the service of those who lived by their toil, and rewarded them with oppression. Their very names lie buried in the dark untenanted places of the past, while every school-boy knows by heart the genealogy of a whole line of barbarian kings. Truly has the world been slow to recognize its benefactors! These men have a history—it is the history of art, science, discovery, invention, philosophy, and literature—in a word, the history of civilization itself. Though long neglected, it is yet destined to be written. The honor of doing so has been reserved for our times. We have histories in abundance of kings, rulers and statesmen. We are now, at last, to have a history of the PEOPLE.

We return from this long digression. Our object has been to point out the revolution which has taken place in historical literature within the last half century. We have done so, though in the most crude and imperfect

13. "On History," in *The Works of Thomas Carlyle* (New York, 1904), 27:86–87; the emphasis is Washington's.

manner, and found that revolution to consist essentially in an alliance, which has never before existed, between philosophy and history, and in the new direction which has been thereby given to the labors of the historian. We are now prepared to state in a very few words what we regard as the great defect of Mr. Howison's book. It is not written in the spirit of modern history. There is none of that blending of philosophy and history which, as we have seen, constitutes the characteristic feature of modern historical literature. The volume before us is, as we have stated, a clear, consecutive narrative of the prominent public events connected with the colonization of Virginia, and it pretends to nothing more. It nowhere attempts a solution of those many interesting social problems which are indissolubly interwoven with our early progress, nor does it seek to evolve those important general principles which lie buried under the rubbish of colonial civilization. We regret this very much; for those problems and general principles lie directly across the path of the Virginia historian, and if, instead of evading them, Mr. H. had taken them boldly in hand and treated them with success, as he might have done, he would have entitled himself to the gratitude of the people of Virginia, and have secured for his book a position in the historical literature of the country, which, we fear, it is not now destined to attain. For all must admit that the Social System of Virginia is, in many respects, a peculiar system—unlike most of the social systems by which it is surrounded—a sort of anomaly in our times. It has no parallel except in the other slave-holding states of the union, and, when closely inspected, looks very much like the remnant of an older civilization—a fragment of the feudal system floating about here on the bosom of the nineteenth century. As we have just stated, many novel and interesting problems necessarily connect themselves with such a system—problems the solution of which will, we believe, throw much light upon our past history and future career as an independent people. If Virginia has always been poor—if she has accomplished but little for the improvement of man's social and material well-being—if she has fallen behind her sister states in the accumulation of wealth; if, upon the other hand, she has done much for the melioration of man's moral and intellectual nature, if she has been eminently fruitful in great men and general principles, if she has given to the nation those warriors whose valor has led its armies to victory, those statesmen whose wisdom has guided its councils in peace, and those principles of civil and religious liberty upon which our institutions are founded—if all this be true, an explanation of it and of every other problem connected with the past history or present condition of the commonwealth, will be found in the peculiar elements which prevailed in her social organization during the colonial period. We repeat, therefore, that it is a source of regret to us that Mr. H. has not entered somewhat into this interesting subject. It would, in our judgment, have greatly increased the value of his history. Bancroft is the only writer who has undertaken any thing like an analysis of the Social System of Virginia, and the consequence is that, although he has performed his task but imperfectly, and has fallen into some errors of fact, yet, every thing considered, he has given us the best History of Virginia which we have yet come across. He does not tell us as much as some others, but he tells us more that we want to know.

We have one other objection to allege against Mr. H.'s book. He tells us nothing about the *people* of Virginia: gives us no new insight into their character, habits, and mode of life. He has written a history of the *Government* of Virginia, and not much more. The King, Parliament, London Company, Governor, Council, and House of Burgesses are his dramatis personae. The PEOPLE rarely appear upon the stage. This is a great omission. We have heard much of those old-time Virginians, and have long desired, above all things, to make their acquaintance. It is certain that they were, in many respects, a remarkable race of men. They are illustrious in colonial annals, and were, beyond question, the master spirits of the age in which they lived. We sometimes imagine that we can see them standing in the twilight of those early times, a head taller than their cotemporaries. These men were our fathers, and what we, their lineal descendants, desire is to know something of them—to be placed face to face with them—to visit them at their homes in the country and set with them around their fire-sides and at the social board. We desire to see what manner of men they really were—what they did, thought and felt, and how they spent their daily being. A race from whose loins have sprung a line of warriors and statesmen—such men as Washington, Henry, Marshall, Jefferson, Madison, and a hundred others—all names,

"Worthy on fame's eternal bead-roll to be filed,"[14]

deserves to be studied and remembered. We do not think that Mr. H. has paid attention enough to this branch of his subject. He might well have devoted a whole chapter to the *people* of Virginia, and it would have been the most interesting chapter in his book.

We have now, in the discharge of that duty which is due to the public, and in the spirit of independent criticism, pointed out the defects of Mr. H.'s History of Virginia as they have appeared to us. Of its merits we have already spoken, and they are such as are not likely to be overlooked. They are of a character which will commend the book to the public, and cause it to be generally read. And while we think that Mr. H. leaves much yet to be accomplished, we cannot withhold from him the credit of having made a valuable contribution to our historical literature. Although his book does

---

14. Edmund Spenser, "The Faerie Queene," book 4, canto II, stanza 32: "Dan Chaucer, well of English undefyled / On fames eternall beadroll worthie to be fyled."

not go all the way, yet it is certainly a step in advance, and will do much to clear the way for those who may come after him. And we here dismiss Mr. H.'s history, with the remark already made that it is, so far as we are able to judge, a correct and interesting narrative of the important public events connected with the colonization of Virginia, and, as such, we take pleasure in recommending it to all who desire to acquaint themselves with the general outline of colonial history with the least possible expenditure of time and trouble.

We have said that there were many interesting questions connected with the Social System of Virginia. We propose, briefly, to call public attention to one or two of these questions. We can only do so in a very imperfect manner; for although the views, which we are about to express, have been long entertained; yet, for the want of time for arrangement, they must necessarily assume a crude and undigested form, and we send them to press, rather with the view of calling attention to an interesting subject, than with any expectation of illustrating it. He, indeed, who shall present the public with a thorough analysis of the Social System of Virginia will have performed a useful task, and made an invaluable contribution to the State. It is unnecessary to say that the crude matter which follows has no such pretension.

When the confusion, which necessarily attended the conquest and occupation of the country by the English colonists, had, in some degree, subsided, and the Social System of Virginia began to develop its true features, the first thing which attracts attention is the division of society into two distinct classes—*Masters and Slaves*. Under the latter denomination, we include *indented servants*. We do so, because there was really little or no difference, in social position, between the slave and the indented servant. They both stood in the same relation to their master, and the indented servant was, to all intents and purposes, a slave, during the period of his servitude. And the only important difference in the condition of these two classes of men was in the *duration* of their servitude—the slave, in almost every instance, being doomed to servitude for life; while the indented servant was only bound for the time mentioned in his indenture. But, during the period of servitude, their social position was, in all important particulars, the same. Mr. Jefferson, speaking of the early population of Virginia, says:

> "Indented servants formed a considerable supply. These were poor Europeans, who went to America to settle themselves. If they could pay their passage, it was well. If not, they must find means of paying it. They were at liberty, therefore, to make an agreement with any person they chose, to serve him such a length of time as they agreed on, upon condition that he would repay, to the master of the vessel, the expenses of their passage. If, being foreigners, unable to speak the language, they did not know how to make a

bargain for themselves, the Captain of the vessel contracted for them, with such persons as he could. This contract was by deed indented, which occasioned them to be called *indented servants.*" 1 *Jeff. Works*, p. 406.[15]

But Bancroft has described, with more minuteness, the social condition of this class of the early colonial population of Virginia, and we make a short extract from his history—

"Conditional servitude, under indentures or covenants, had from the first existed in Virginia. The servant stood to his master in the relation of a debtor, bound to discharge the costs of imigration by the entire employment of his powers for the benefit of his creditor. Oppression early ensued: men who had been transported to Virginia at an expense of eight or ten pounds, were sometimes sold for forty or fifty, or even three score pounds. The supply of white servants became a regular business; and a class of men, nicknamed spirits, used to delude young persons, servants and idlers, into embarking into America, as to a land of spontaneous plenty. White servants came to be a usual article of traffic. They were sold in England to be transported, and, in Virginia, were resold to the highest bidder; like negroes, they were to be purchased on shipboard, as men buy horses at a fair. In 1672, the average price in the colonies, whose five years of service were due, was about ten pounds; while a negro was worth twenty or twenty-five pounds."—*Bancroft's Hist. U. S.*, *vol. 1, p.* 175.

Again:

"The condition of apprenticed servants in Virginia differed from that of slaves chiefly in the *duration of their bondage.*"—*Ibid*, *p*. 176.

We thus see that the relation subsisting in Virginia between master and indented servant was, during the period of servitude, the same with that subsisting between master and slave, and that the only material difference in the condition of the two classes was in the *duration* of their bondage—the slave, in almost every case, being bound to servitude for life, and the indented servant for the time specified in his deed of indenture. We have, therefore, for the sake of brevity and perspicuity, classed them together, and we now return to the proposition with which we started—viz: that from an early period in colonial history, the population of Virginia was divided into two distinct classes—*Masters and Slaves*. With the relation subsisting between these two classes, all are familiar, and it is only necessary to remark, in passing, that it was a relation of perfect control on the one side, and of complete subjection on the other. The master was the absolute lord of the slave. And this *relation*, so far as we have been able to discover, was nearly universal. Almost every man who was not himself either a slave or indented servant, was the owner of slaves or

---

15. *Memoir, Correspondence and Miscellanies from the Papers of Thomas Jefferson*, ed. Thomas Jefferson Randolph (Charlottesville, 1829), 1:406; the emphasis is Washington's.

indented servants—some of many, others of few—each man according to his means; for, at that time, property in Virginia almost always assumed the form of land and slaves. And, between the lord of thousands and the proprietor of a single slave, there was every variety of gradation, as there is in the apportionment of property in other communities. Almost every man, we repeat, then, who was not himself a slave or indented servant, was the owner of slaves or indented servants. Such a thing as *free labor*, or an *independent body of laborers*, was not known at that time in Virginia. If a man was compelled to rely exclusively upon his own labors to support him, he labored in subjection to another—if, upon the other hand, he had capital to invest, however inconsiderable it might be, he invested it in land and slaves, or indented servants. This was the form which labor and capital almost universally assumed at that time in the colony—the laborer was a slave and the capitalist was his master, and thus the relation of master and slave became almost universal. At all events, if this relation was not so nearly universal as we believe it to have been, it was certainly so general as to prevail over all other relations and constitute a controlling element in the social system of the colony.

The relation, thus established between these two classes, was confirmed by the fact, that almost every slave owner was, at the same time, a landed proprietor, and the laborer, therefore, became a *serf of the soil*. Most of the colonists of Virginia were men of Anglo-Saxon descent, and love for the soil is said to be an Anglo-Saxon passion. On the shores of the Chesapeake and its tributaries, this passion had ample room for indulgence. Land was cheap and large tracts could be procured at low prices. Not only so, but, for the purpose of encouraging immigration, the government of the colony had provided, at a very early period, that each planter should receive fifty acres of land for every person whom he should transport into the plantations. Thus the Virginia planter, by the same operation, increased the number of his serfs and enlarged his territorial possessions. The result was, as we learn from authentic documents, that there existed in the colony, from a very early period, a body of wealthy landed proprietors, who cultivated large tracts of country with African slaves, or European serfs. Along the banks of James river, York river and its tributaries, the Rappahannock, Potomac and other water courses of the country, there resided, in almost baronial state, the *Gentry* of Virginia—as they were styled in the language of those times—a class of men holding vast landed possessions, rivalling in extent and fertility the estates of many of the English nobility, and controlling, with absolute despotism, a body of serfs, which a feudal lord of the middle ages might have envied.

And here the question naturally suggests itself—who were these lords of the soil and masters of slaves, whom we find, in those early times, standing on the summit of society, and controlling the social and political destinies of the colony? Our records furnish satisfactory information upon this point. A considerable portion, in point of numbers, and a much larger portion in point of wealth, education and influence, were Cavaliers, and younger branches of noble English houses. As was to be expected, they brought with them, into the colony, the feelings, habits and principles in which they had been educated at home. Nothing had occurred to wean them from the mother country. The colonists of Virginia, were not, like the Puritans of New England, fugitives from persecution. They embarked, upon the contrary, under the auspices of the crown and the nobility—their emigration was voluntary, undertaken, for the most part, to repair their broken fortunes, and, not unfrequently, with intentions of ultimately returning to the land of their nativity. It is not wonderful, therefore, that the affections of the first colonists should have clung, as we know they did, for a long time, to England, and that, in the wild forests of Virginia, they should have pined for their homes across the ocean. They could not divest themselves of the idea that they were sojourners here, and were ever looking forward to the time when, their pilgrimage being over, they would return to their country and their friends. The consequence was that society in Virginia was, as far as circumstances would admit, a *continuation* of English society. From the beginning, a decided preference for England and her institutions manifested itself every where, and there was a disposition among all classes to conform the infant colony to the model of the mother country. So strong was this partiality for old England, and so loyal were the colonists to her ancient institutions, that they never manifested the slightest sympathy with Cromwell in his effort to erect a commonwealth on the ruins of monarchy. The Virginians were always true to the Stuarts, and, through all the vicissitudes of that ill-starred house, they never, for a moment, abandoned its fortunes. They did, it is true, submit, for about eight years, to the dominion of Cromwell; but it was through necessity, and, immediately upon the restoration of Charles II., the fact was proclaimed in Virginia, which heartily responded to the passionate joy manifested by England on that memorable occasion. Berkeley, who then governed the colony by virtue of powers delegated by the *people*, now, by common consent, issued writs for a new Assembly in the name of the *King*, and the royalists carried the elections every where.[16] The first Assembly which convened after the restoration was composed of royalists and cavaliers—men loyal to the house of Stuart and devoted to England and her ancient institutions. And this Assembly was the type of those which succeeded it for many years.

We thus discover, in the very infancy of the colony, the elements of a *Landed Aristocracy*. There existed, from the first, a class of men, descended from the nobility of England—embued with the tastes, feelings and prin-

---

16. Sir William Berkeley, 1606–1677, governor of Virginia, 1642–1652 and 1660–1677.

ciples of their order, and confirmed in power by their superior culture, the extent of their possessions, and the character of the laboring classes. These men naturally aspired to the government of the colony, and we accordingly find that all the important offices were filled from their ranks. They were made Councillors, returned as members of the Assembly, commissioned as officers in the militia, and appointed by the Governor to be justices of the peace. In this latter capacity, their powers were large and anomalous, as are to this day the powers of justices of the peace. Men, in no manner, delegated by the people, but commissioned by governors, who were themselves, in turn, commissioned by the Crown, were authorized, contrary to the first rudiments of American liberty, to fix the amount of the county levies, which are generally much larger than the State tax, to apportion those levies, and control their collection and disbursements. We thus find power of every sort—legislative, executive, judicial and military, uniting in the hands of a class of men who, as descendants of the ancient nobility of England, had been educated in aristocratic habits and feelings, and who, as proprietors of large estates, masters of indented servants, and lords of slaves, controlled the social destinies of the colony. And the influence thus acquired by this order was confirmed and augmented by the lamentable state of education among the great mass of the people. Indeed, there seems to have been no provision whatever for general education at that time—common schools were unknown—and each man had to instruct his children at home as best he could. The consequence was, of course, that, as a general rule, they grew up in absolute ignorance. Not only was this so, but it seems to have been the good pleasure of the government, that it should continue so. This certainly was the case during the administration of Berkeley, which lasted for about thirty-six years. We quote from Bancroft's history:

> "The system of common schools was unknown. 'Every man,' said Sir William Berkeley, in 1671, 'instructs his children according to his ability;' a method which left the children of the ignorant to hopeless ignorance. The instinct of aristocracy dreaded the general diffusion of intelligence, and even the enfranchising influence of the preaching of the ministers. 'The ministers,' continued Sir William, in the spirit of the aristocracy of the Tudors, 'should pray oftener and preach less. *But I thank God, there are no free schools, nor printing*; and I hope we shall not have these hundred years; for learning has brought disobedience, and heresy, and sects into the world, and printing has divulged them, and libels against the best governments. *God keep us from both.*"—Vol. 2, p. 192.

With this disposition upon the part of the government, and that lamentable ignorance among the masses, of which all the co-temporaneous writers speak, it is easy to see that the administration of affairs must necessarily have fallen into the hands of those wealthy proprietors, who had brought with them into the colony the culture which belonged to the English gentry of that day, or into the hands of their children, who had been sent to England to be educated—as was the fashion of those times.

In this connection, we should not omit to mention the laws of *Primogeniture* and *Entails*, as they exerted great influence in building up the aristocracy of Virginia, and confirming its power. It can scarcely be necessary to say that these laws were brought into the colony by the first settlers as a part of the laws of the mother country, and that, down to the period of the Revolution, their policy was much favored. Indeed, the principle of entails was carried much further in the colony than it had ever been carried in England. In the first place, nothing but *land*, or something issuing out of, or appurtenant to, land, could be entailed in England. But, by an Act of Assembly passed in 1727, *slaves*, as well as land, could be entailed in the colony. There was another most important distinction between the law of entails in Virginia and in England. In England, fines and recoveries, as they were called, were always a part of the law of Entails. This was a provision which put it in the power of the tenant in tail, at any moment, to defeat the estate tail, and vest in himself an absolute fee simple, over which he had complete dominion, to alien, devise, or transmit by descent to his heirs general, as he saw fit. And when the law of entails was received into the colony, fines and recoveries, as a part of that law, were, as a matter of course, received with it. But, as early as October, 1705, it was enacted by the Assembly, that "fines and recoveries, and *every other act for the purpose of avoiding and defeating estates tail*," except by act of the General Assembly, "shall be utterly null and void." And, although this restraint was so far removed in 1734, as to allow the entail of lands not exceeding £200 in value to be defeated on certain conditions, yet all entails of estates *over* £200 sterling in value were indestructible. And, if our memory serves us aright, this continued to be the law until 1776, when all entails were abolished. By this course of legislation, restraints upon the alienation of property in the colony became more burthensome than in the mother country, and it was in the power of the owner to bind up his property in a particular line of transmission for an almost indefinite period. All this, of course, favored the growth of wealthy families, and tended to confirm and perpetuate their power.

From these elements, and others which it is not necessary to enumerate at this time, sprung the *Landed Aristocracy* of Virginia, which, for more than a century, controlled her destinies—in many respects, a remarkable race of men, illustrious first in the annals of the colony, and afterwards in the history of the commonwealth and the councils of the nation.

We have now pointed out, in an imperfect manner, what we understand to have been the character of the population of Virginia during the colonial period, as also the relations subsisting between the two great classes into which that population was divided. Let us next ascertain, if we can, how the people of Virginia lived in those times—what manner of life they led. And here the first thing which attracts our attention is *preponderance of country life over town life*. We find that the people of Virginia were, from the first settlement of the colony, an agricultural people. They lived isolated upon their farms, at long distances apart, rarely congregating together in towns or cities, as did the Puritans of New England. We learn from the best authority that, as late as 1660—fifty-three years from the foundation of the colony—"*Virginia possessed no considerable town.*" And Bancroft, writing of the year 1674, says—

> "There was scarcely such a thing as a cluster of three dwellings. Jamestown was but a place of a statehouse, one church, and eighteen houses, occupied by about a dozen families. *Till very recently the legislature had assembled in the hall of an alehouse.* Virginia had neither towns or lawyers." Vol. 2, p. 212.

And again describing the manner in which the Virginians of that period lived, he says—

> "The generation now in existence was chiefly the fruit of the soil; they were the children of the woods, nurtured in the freedom of the wilderness, and dwelling in lonely cottages, scattered along the streams. No newspaper entered their houses; no printing-press furnished them a book. They had no recreations but such as nature provides in her wilds; no education but such as parents in the desert could give to their offspring. The paths were bridleways rather than roads; and the highway surveyors aimed at nothing more than to keep them clear of logs and fallen trees. We doubt if there existed what we should call a bridge in the whole dominion, though it was intended to build some. Visits were made in boats, and on horseback through the forests; and the Virginian, travelling with his *pouch of tobacco for currency*, swam the rivers, where there was neither ferry nor ford." Vol. 2, p. 212.

Let us, for a moment, visit one of these Virginia farmers in his forest home—let us see the course of life he leads there, and the society by which he is surrounded. Having selected a suitable location, generally on an eminence and "in sight of a lovely river," he builds his mansion. Here he locates himself and family. In addition to his wife, children and other relatives, he has around him a few menials—sometimes indented servants, but generally slaves. These constitute his household. At a distance from the mansion-house, in some retired corner of his estate, we find huddled together, in log huts, the serfs who cultivate his lands. The number of these will, of course, vary in each case according to the wealth of the proprietor and the extent of his possessions. Here, in the depths of the forest, with no society but that of his family, surrounded by slaves and indented servants, the Virginia farmer spent his life, seldom leaving home except to visit the horse-race, the county court, and sometimes, perhaps, the parish church. *Isolated country life was a controlling element in colonial society.*

We have now described what we conceive to have been the three most prominent features in the Social System of Virginia during her colonial existence, and which still continue such, though in a mitigated form. *First*, the general prevalence of the relation of *master and slave*. *Second*, the existence of a *Landed Aristocracy*, who gave tone to society and controlled, for a long period, the destinies of the colony. *Third*, isolated country life.

And now a deeply interesting problem presents itself. What was to have been expected of a social system thus constituted? What progress was such a system likely to make in civilization? What would be its probable fate among the other systems by which it was surrounded? No more interesting problem could possibly be presented to the consideration of the present generation of Virginians. For we believe that a truthful solution of it will throw a flood of light upon our past progress and future destiny as an independent people. If, as has been already stated, Virginia has hitherto done little for the melioration of man's social condition—if she has made but inconsiderable progress in material greatness, and, notwithstanding her rich soil, her genial climate, and vast natural resources, has always been, and is to this day, poor, *very poor*; if, upon the other hand, she has been always fertile in general ideas, if she has abounded in great men and striking developments of character and passion—if all this be true, as we believe it is, it may, in our judgment, be traced directly to those elements which, as we have seen, preponderated in her social system during her colonial existence. Let us then return to this system, and, by an examination of those elements, ascertain, if we can, what progress it was likely to make in civilization.

A word or two, by way of explanation, before we attempt a solution of this problem. In order to ascertain what progress the social system of Virginia was likely to make in civilization, it is necessary that we should first get some distinct idea of what the thing we call *civilization* is. And the first idea comprised in it, as it seems to us, is that of improvement in *civil life*—of melioration in man's outward condition and social relations. When applied to a community, it awakens at once the notion of general prosperity, social progress, and increase in the means of subsistence, comfort, and material well-being. This much is certainly implied in the term civilization; but is this all? Our nature at once rejects the definition as too narrow—it tells us that man was formed for a higher destiny than this—that the full development of his nature involves something more than progress in material well-being and social melioration. To feed and clothe the body, and keep the social relations well adjusted are very excellent things; but man has a soul as well as a body—he has a spiritual nature as well as a carnal nature, endowed with moral and intellectual faculties, the cultivation, of which is quite as essential to his development and civilization, as eating, drinking, dressing, house-building and keeping the social machine well adjusted. And when we come to look closely into the matter, it will be found, we think, that civilization consists essentially of two elements—the improvement, first, of the *individual*, and then of *society*. Neither of these elements alone is sufficient—neither the development of man's social condition, nor of his inward and personal nature, taken separately, constitutes civilization. Its progress pre-supposes their union and combined movement. In proof of this, let us imagine, for a moment, a society abandoned to the absolute dominion of either one of these elements, and trace, if we can, the probable destiny of such a society. In this manner, it will appear, we think, that our definition is correct, and that civilization presents itself under the double aspect which we have described.

First, let us imagine a society where the moral and intellectual elements prevail. We will suppose that this society has made eminent progress in the development of the individual man—that his moral and intellectual nature have been highly cultivated, and that general ideas and striking manifestations of character abound. Looking at the individual man, one would say that this people possess the elements of a fine civilization. But when we come to look at their *social* condition we find that it has not kept pace with their moral and intellectual progress—the individual is greater than society. Among this people there are few common ideas, but little public feeling, and such a thing as a general interest is scarcely known. Individualism reigns almost supreme. The principle of association, if it exists at all, exists in its weakest form, and men's powers and faculties are exhausted in isolated effort. There is force enough to carry society forwards, but society does not move, because that force is dissipated over a large surface, and there are no means of collecting it and directing it to a common purpose.

It is obvious that such a social system cannot advance. There is much effort but no progress. Generation after generation sweeps by and leaves no trace of its existence. This society contains *one* of the elements of civilization, but the other is absent, and, until it arrives, immobility, if not dissolution, is its necessary condition. The development of man's inward and personal nature, without a corresponding progress in his social condition, can do little for the cause of civilization. It prepares the way, and that is all.

Let us now reverse the hypothesis. Let us suppose the case of a people whose outward condition is easy and agreeable. They have made vast progress, we will suppose, in material well-being—all their physical wants are supplied, and their social relations happily adjusted. They are well fed, well clothed, well housed and well governed—in a word, their whole physical existence is comfortably regulated—they eat, drink, and are merry. But the moral culture of this people has been neglected—their intellectual energies are in a state of torpor and inertness—their whole inward and spiritual nature has remained barren and unimproved. They resemble a well-kept flock of sheep more than any thing else. Society has made prodigious progress, wealth has rapidly accumulated, material comforts have multiplied—the social relations have been perfected; but in the midst of this general movement, man himself has remained stationary—his moral and mental faculties have withered and decayed. It is manifest that this civilization is unsound, precarious and illegitimate—that it has no just foundation to stand upon, and that, however imposing it may be for the time, it is destined to be short-lived. Such is the aspect generally presented by those countries whose civilization, after a long and prosperous career, has at last exhausted itself, and, its vital elements having deserted it, is verging to speedy dissolution.

We repeat, then, that civilization consists essentially of two elements—that it manifests itself under two forms—the improvement of the exterior and general condition of man, and that of his inward and personal nature—in a word, the improvement both of society and humanity. We do not pretend that these two elements always move *abreast*. The reverse is much more frequently the case. We sometimes find one in advance, sometimes the other. Sometimes man's moral and intellectual nature progresses faster than his outward and social condition; at others, society, taking a start, far outstrips man's moral and intellectual development. But these two elements, however they may separate for a time, must ultimately come together and advance shoulder to shoulder. For, so soon as one progresses any great distance without the other and their union has long been interrupted, a painful hiatus is produced—a general conviction of unfitness, illegitimacy and incompleteness takes possession of the minds of men. They feel that the relation of things, and the harmony of society, have been disturbed. If any important social improvement, any great progress in material well-being, manifests itself among a people, unaccompanied by a corresponding mental movement, such improvement and progress seem to us strange, unaccountable and almost unjust. One desires immediately to know how it has been produced—upon what foundation it rests—to what principle it attaches itself. Not only so, but men feel that an obligation rests upon them to correct this state of things—to conform their inner nature to this new improvement which has manifested itself in the outer world, and thus restore the relations which should subsist between man's mental progress and social condition. So, on the other hand, if any great moral and intellectual movement makes its appearance in the world, unaccompanied by a social progress, we find this same uneasiness, restlessness and discontent. Men feel the necessity immediately of carrying this new improvement, which they have experienced in their inward nature, into their outward, social condition, to conform the external world which they inhabit to this new truth which they have conceived, nor can they rest satisfied until this has been accomplished—so closely are man's social and intellectual development bound together and so essential are both to his civilization.

We thus perceive that civilization consists essentially of two elements—the development of man and the improvement of society—that these two elements are strictly connected and act reciprocally on each other, that man's moral and intellectual nature may be instructed by his social condition and his social condition elevated by his moral and mental progress, that these two elements, though they may separate for a time and impress their peculiar character upon the age or country over which they preside, must, by the laws of their own movement, ultimately come together and advance in company. We also believe that it is upon this union that the hopes of civilization rest, which, though it is often delayed for long intervals, is not, for that reason, any the less certain. An eloquent modern author says,

> "The movements of Providence are not restricted to narrow bounds: it is not anxious to deduce today the consequences of the premises which it laid down yesterday. It may defer this for ages, till the fulness of time shall come. Its logic will not be the less conclusive for reasoning slowly. Providence moves through time, as the gods of Homer through space—it makes a step and ages have rolled away! How long a time, how many circumstances intervened before the regeneration of the moral powers of man by christianity exercised its great, its legitimate influence upon his social condition? Yet who can doubt or mistake its power?"

Having now got some distinct idea of what the thing called civilization is, let us return to the problem which we have in hand, viz: what progress was the Social System of Virginia likely to make in civilization, what its probable success as compared with the other social systems by which it was surrounded. And, if the definition which we have given of civilization be correct, in order to solve this problem, it will be proper that we should put to that system the two-fold question—what was it likely to do for or against the development of *man* for or against the development of *society*. And we remark in the threshold that no one at all acquainted with the Social System of Virginia during the colonial period, can fail to discover immediately the preponderance of those elements which favoured the development of *man* at the expense of *society*. We have seen that, from the first settlement of the colony, *isolated country life* constituted a prominent feature in Virginia. There were no towns or cities, and the inhabitants of the colony lived in the woods, scattered in dwellings along the streams and watercourses of the country, at long distances apart. Many of them, much the most considerable for power and influence, were large landed proprietors and the masters of slaves. There they collected around them a little society, of which they were themselves the center, and over which they presided with absolute sway. That these men should come to be regarded as of great importance, not only by themselves but by all around them, was naturally to be expected. Observe for a moment, if you please, the social position of the Virginia farmer. He was the head of a family, a landed proprietor, the master of indented servants and the lord of slaves. Above him no superior, near him no equal, beyond the influences of general society, with no rule of conduct but his own good-will and pleasure, he lived in his forest home like a feudal baron in his lonely castle. He was everywhere supreme in the sphere in which he moved and which he rarely left. That a feeling of consequence and superiority, together with a sentiment of personal independence and individual liberty should have sprung up in the bosom of this society was unavoidable. And what the Virginians of that day meant by liberty was quite a different thing from the modern acceptation of that term, and what their cotemporaries, the Puritans of New England, meant by it. The liberty for which the men of New England labored so zealously was civil, political, or religious liberty—the liberty of the *citizen*; but the liberty to which the Virginians were so passionately attached was personal liberty—the liberty of the *individual*. And while our northern neighbors were devoting every faculty to the improvement of their social relations and condition as citizens, our ancestors in Virginia could, with difficulty, be induced to submit to the restraints of society at all. They loved their free forest life, and cared infinitely more for their liberty as men than their franchises as citizens. They could not understand why they should abridge their natural rights for the improvement of their social relations, when they felt society to be a burden, and only desired to be relieved of its trammels. They asked nothing from it, and were willing to concede nothing to it—they felt able to protect themselves, and did not lean upon the arm of government for safety. Aversion to much government has been, from the settlement of the colony, and is, at this day, a Virginia instinct. Listen to Bancroft.

> "Shall the Virginians be described in a word? They were Anglo-Saxons in the woods again, with the inherited culture and intelligence of the seventeenth century. The major part of the House of Burgesses now consisted of Virginians that never saw a town. The Anglo-Saxon mind, in its serenest nationality, neither distorted by fanaticism, nor subdued by superstition, nor wounded by persecution, nor excited by new ideas, but fondly cherishing the active instinct of personal freedom, secure possession and legislative power, such as belonged to it before the reformation, had made its dwelling place in the empire of Powhatan." Vol. 2, p. 454.

This isolated country life, together with that love of liberty and personal independence which it fostered, has, beyond doubt, been one of the controlling elements of our civilization. It meets us at every point of our progress—has moulded our institutions and lays at the foundation of our political creeds.

No one can fail to see that a social system thus constituted was admirably adapted to the progress of the individual man, to the development of his sentiments, affections and ideas. His secluded life favored meditation; and that independence, that love of liberty, that conscious superiority and habit of command, which we have just described, gave power to his nature and elevation to his views. And we accordingly find that, when the Virginia farmer left his native forests, it was to be translated to some higher sphere of action, either the cabinet, the legislative hall, the rostrum, or the field of battle. For the counting-house or the factory, he never manifested any taste or talent. In addition to this, society did not then present the chess-board uniformity of modern times. The people of Virginia had not yet submitted themselves to that Procrustean operation by which all the inequalities of nature are corrected, and mankind reduced to one stature. In the depths of the forest they recognized no common social standard to which they were obliged to conform, nor had they been subjected to that modern system of grading, by which it is sought to equalize every thing, to "make all mountains and valleys exactly of the same level, plane down universal creation into a Westphalian flat, and metamorphose the irregular grandeur of nature's Alps into a methodical circumvallation of Dutch dikes;" but society, like one of nature's own landscapes, was broken into hill and dale, mountain and valley, where the royal oak and the stinted pine grew side by side, and man walked abroad in his native majesty. The air he breathed was free, the soil he trod was his own—relieved from all conventionality, his sentiments, passions and ideas had ample space for expansion, and his nature full room for growth and development. All this was eminently favorable to individual progress; nor has the civilization of Virginia been false to its constituent elements. If, as we have seen, those elements preponderated which favored the development of the individual man, we find that they have produced their legitimate results, that the fact has corresponded with our expectations. It is impossible to deny that the civilization of Virginia has exercised a vast and salutary influence upon individual progress—upon the development of man's sentiments, passions and ideas. At every page of her annals we meet with a crowd of noble sentiments, elevated ideas, and striking manifestations of character and passion, evidently generated in the bosom of that country life, so peculiar to her people. No where has man risen to greater moral and intellectual grandeur—warriors, statesmen, orators and civilians seem to be the natural products of her soil. The men who have ruled in the cabinet, who have guided the legislative councils of the country, and led her armies to victory, have most of them come from the woods of Virginia. The greatest statesman, the greatest warrior and the greatest orator that

America has yet produced, have each been Virginia products. Washington, Henry and Jefferson are the true types of her civilization—she claims them as peculiarly her own. In the bosom of that country life which we have described, far away from towns and crowded cities, in the solitude of the forest, were their great virtues cultivated and their natures developed. These men, and others almost as great, have been the contributions which Virginia has made to the nation. Indeed, no impartial man can read the history of the country without discovering the vast influence which Virginia ideas and Virginia men have exerted over its destiny in peace and war. Truly has the great statesman of South Carolina said, that "Virginia, like the mother of the Gracchi, when asked for her jewels, points to her sons."[17]

But Virginia has not only abounded in great men,—she has been equally fruitful in general ideas: her soil has been the hot-bed of political creeds. Those great principles of civil, political, and religious liberty, upon which all our institutions rest, grew naturally in the bosom of that society which we have described. And no one can fail to see that those principles are eminently characteristic of our civilization—that they are just what might have been expected from its constitutive elements. Their object is to "preserve, as far as possible, the independence of individual action and pursuit; and they reject all limitations upon this independence, which are not essential to the great ends of social organization. They regard all those powers which man wields in his aggregate or corporate capacity as so many limitations upon his individual rights, and they yield those which are indispensable to the institution of society as so many concessions which necessity has extorted from liberty." These are the principles which lie at the foundation of the political creed of Virginia, and upon which her own constitution and the constitutions of almost all the States of the Union are based. We conscientiously believe that those early Virginians—those "Anglo-Saxons in the woods," understood the nature of government better and did more to solve that great social problem by which individual liberty shall be reconciled with social order, than any race of men that have ever lived.

We must now reverse the picture—from the bright side we must turn to the dark side of our civilization; for, like the civilization of most other countries, it is Janus-faced. We have seen the ascendancy of those elements which favored individual progress; but unfortunately those very elements, which were thus favorable to individual progress, were hostile

---

17. Robert Y. Hayne, "Speech on Mr. Foot's Resolution, Thursday, January 21, 1830," has, "Look at the 'Old Dominion,' great and magnanimous Virginia, 'whose jewels are her sons'"; Hayne is adapting the famous remark of Cornelia about her sons, the Gracchi, first reported in Valerius Maximus, *Facta et Dicta Memorabilia*, 4:4, preface.

to social improvement. That isolated country-life—that love of liberty and personal independence which were so propitious for the development of character and passion, were every where opposed to general order and the establishment of society. The very notion of society implies the existence of a certain number of ideas and sentiments common to a majority of the members. Not only must there be a common stock of ideas and sentiments, but there must be a disposition to rally around those ideas and sentiments and a willingness to make sacrifices for their advancement. Where individualism reigns absolute and each man insists upon all his natural rights, it is manifest that there can be no society. This was too much the case in Virginia. Not only was the stock of common ideas small; but there was no disposition to rally to their support—the principle of association, if it existed at all, existed in its weakest form. The Social System of Virginia was at that time, substantially a federative system—it was composed, as we have seen, of a number of little societies scattered through the country, each with a distinct organization, and it proceeded upon the principle of leaving in each of these little societies all the power which could abide there, and carrying to the great central society only so much as was absolutely necessary to the ends of social order. It is manifest that the success of such a system presupposes a very advanced state of civilization—a strong conviction of the necessity of society, and a general disposition and willingness upon the part of individuals to submit to social restraints; for it possesses in a less degree than any other system, the means of coercion. The general society was, in point of fact, the creature of the little local societies of which it is composed, holding its power by no other tenure than their sufferance, and stood to them in very much the same relation that the Federal Government does to the States of the Union. It is manifest that such a system, however beautiful it may be in theory, and salutary, sometimes, in practice, was not adapted to a society composed of such elements as was the colonial society of Virginia. It was altogether incapable of maintaining its ascendancy and establishing general order among a people to whose tastes and habits the restraints of government and the conventional arrangements of society were so repugnant; who valued their natural rights more than their civil franchises, and cared for nothing half so much as personal liberty, and we accordingly find that these little local societies resisted all encroachments by the general society of which they were a part, and maintained their independence and individual importance with the same resolution and pertinacity that a modern nullifier resists all encroachments by the General Government upon the reserved rights of the States. We doubt whether any society, laying claims to civilization, has ever existed, in ancient or modern times, where there was so little government, and the citizen enjoyed so large a liberty, as in this early colonial society.

## Social System of Virginia

We have now shown, by an examination of its elements, that the early civilization of Virginia did not favor *social improvement*. A further analysis will also show, if we mistake not, that it was equally unfavorable to the production of *wealth and progress in material greatness*. And we are now prepared, we think, to answer the question which has been so repeatedly asked—*Why has Virginia, with her great natural resources, always remained so poor?* In the beginning of this article, we remarked that the population of Virginia, from a very early period, was divided into two great classes. *Masters and Slaves*. The Slaves were the producers and the Masters the consumers. The relation, as we know, subsisting between these two classes, was that of an absolute control on the one side, and perfect submission on the other. The slave was the *property* of his master, as much so as his ox, his ass, or any thing else that was his—he and his latest posterity were bondmen, and, like any other chattel, the slave might be sold, made the subject of devise or bequest, and, in the case of intestacy, passed with the rest of the intestate's estate either to the heir at law or the distributee—according as slaves were declared to be realty or personalty for the time being. There is no relation, so far as we know, which has ever been established between man and man, either in ancient or modern times—not even that of lord and serf—which theoretically implies such absolute despotism on the one side, and servile subjection on the other, as that of *master* and *slave*. And this was the relation which prevailed almost universally in Virginia between the two great classes into which the population of every country is divided—*producers* and *consumers*—the producers were slaves, and the consumers were their masters. As we have already said, such a thing as free labor, or an independent body of laborers, had, at that time, no place in the social system of the colony. It is not difficult to estimate the influence which this fact was likely to exert over material progress. History is full of admonition upon this point. The great truth stands recorded on every page, in letters of living light, that, so soon as one part of the population of a country reduces the other to subjection, and the system of *castes* succeeds to that of *classes*, that moment all further progress is at an end, and society becomes stationary, if it does not retrograde. Take the history of any people—it matters not what—and you will find that the conquest of one class by another, and their reduction into subjection, has been invariably followed by torpor or decay; while the periods of greatest progress have always been periods of greatest emulation and struggle. So certain is it that rivalry, competition and effort are every where the conditions of progress and improvement. You see this clearly illustrated in Asiatic civilization. No one can fail to observe the simplicity and unity of that civilization. It seems to be the development of a single principle, which has excluded every other principle, and taken possession of society. It is sometimes the theocratic principle, as in India; sometimes the democratic principle, as in the republic of Phoenicia; sometimes the despotic principle, as in Turkey and Persia; in other quarters, other organizations have obtained. But the aspect of Eastern civilization is every where the same—the domination of an exclusive power, which admits no rival, proscribes every other power, and takes into its own hands the absolute control of government and society. The consequence of which is that monotony, torpor, decay, every where characterise that civilization. It seems as if society, having exhausted its vital energies, was about to lie down and die. How different from this has been the civilization of Europe. Diversity, complexity, emulation and struggle are every where met with in its history. For the last thousand years, it has had scarcely a moment's rest. Its whole career has been stormy and adventurous. All the social elements—all classes and conditions—every gradation of wealth and influence—political creeds and religious creeds—powers temporal and powers spiritual—every conceivable form of organization—the theocratic principle, the monarchical principle; all these diversified elements have been thrown together in incessant rivalry, each struggling for victory and none able to secure it. This, beyond doubt, has been the productive, and, at the same time, the conservative element in European civilization. It has been at the same time, the source both of its strength and of its glory. If that civilization is superior to all others which have preceded it—if it has done more for the melioration of man's personal and social condition—if, after the lapse of fourteen centuries, it still retains all the vigor of youth, and manifests no symptoms of exhaustion—it is because of that emulation and rivalry, which we have noticed. Society has never, for any considerable time, fallen under the dominion of any single principle; no one class has ever been able to conquer all the others and reduce them to subjection; but all have advanced together, and developed themselves side by side, amidst undying jealousies and rivalries. And it is this emulation between contending principles and classes—this desire to conquer without the ability to do so—this effort for victory unaccompanied by success—which chiefly distinguishes European from Asiatic civilization, and gives to the former its vast superiority. It is obvious that a society, thus agitated by conflicting elements, can never fall into repose and inertness. It may, perchance, be overwhelmed in the storms of revolution, but can never sink into torpor and gradual decay.

Thus history teaches us that emulation and rivalry, which liberty encourages, is every where the condition of progress, while that lethargy and inertness, which follows upon the subjection of one class by another, leads to a stagnation, if not a dissolution, of society. And the voice of history is, in this matter, as in most others, but the echo of reason. The masses of mankind are not *amateurs* in labor. To induce them to labor, *motives* must be addressed to them, and, as a general rule, the amount of exertion which they will make will be in exact proportion to the weight of the motives to which they are subjected. This principle will scarcely be denied. Let us, then, apply it first to the case where the producing classes of a country are free and independent, and next, to the case where they are in bondage and subjection; or, to come at once to the case in point, let us apply the principle to the *systems of free labor and slave labor*, and see what result it gives us. It informs us that that system of labor is best, and will prove most productive, which supplies to the laborer the strongest *motive* to exertion. Now, the strongest motive which can be addressed to the laboring masses is, beyond doubt, the *hope of reward*—the reasonable prospect of improving their material well-being. All experience demonstrates that, with the vast majority of the human race, this motive takes precedence of all others; indeed, there is none which can enter into competition with it. The *fear of punishment* is, it is true, in many instances, a powerful motive to effort; but no one at all acquainted with human nature, and the springs of human conduct, will venture to compare it, for a moment, with the hope of reward. Taking it, then, as true, that the hope of reward is the most powerful motive which can be addressed to the laboring masses of mankind, it follows necessarily that the system, which adopts this motive and establishes the most intimate connection between labor and the rewards of labor, must be the most productive. Now, free labor presents, in its strongest possible form, the hope of reward as a motive to exertion; while slave labor rejects it altogether, and substitutes in its stead, the far inferior motive of the fear of punishment. And it has always appeared to us, that the superiority of free labor over slave labor, in point of productiveness, is just precisely that superiority which the hope of reward has over the fear of punishment, as a motive to human exertion. Where labor is free, the laborer is rewarded in exact proportion to the amount of exertion which he uses. What he sows he reaps; if he sows much, he reaps much; if he sows little, he reaps little; if he sows nothing, he reaps nothing. While, therefore, the prospect of comfort and abundance invites the laborer to industry, the apprehension of destitution and want deters him from idleness. He is placed, therefore, in a position which, of all others, is best calculated to elicit exertion. Rewards surround him on one side, and penalties on the other. Industry is the highway to comfort and happiness, and idleness the certain road to want and misery. But how is it with the slave? *What motive to exertion has he?* Does his condition in life depend upon the exertion which he shall use? By no means. His condition is determined by causes over which he has no manner of control, and it is not in his power, by any conduct of his, to affect it materially, either for good or for evil. He can neither improve it by industry nor impair it by idleness. The great and universal motive to honest industry, that of bettering one's lot, is lost upon him. The great law of human progress is not for him. As he is born, so must he die. "Why, then, should I toil and sweat?" the slave may well ask himself. "I am not to eat the bread which my own hands have sown. If I plant, another gets the increase. It is a matter, therefore, of indifference to me whether I work or am idle. The most industrious slave, and the veriest drone in the hive, upon a common footing—they share pretty much alike their master's bounty—they are fed alike, clothed alike, and housed alike. Seeing, therefore, that whether I work or am idle, my condition is the same, I have a direct and positive interest to be idle." Is it not obvious that a system, which thus takes from labor its legitimate rewards and relieves idleness from its proper penalties, is fatal to exertion, and, consequently, to production. It is true that the fear of punishment is substituted for the hope of reward as a motive to exertion; but, as we have already stated, it will be readily admitted by all acquainted with the motives of human conduct, that the substitute is a very imperfect one.

It can scarcely be necessary for the writer of this article to remark, in this connection, that he has no sort of sympathy with that false philanthropy which, both in this country and Europe, has expended so much indiscriminate sympathy upon the condition of the African slave in the Southern States. We have never been able to discover why that portion of the laboring mass should be made the *peculiar* objects of sympathy. It is true that the slave is doomed to labor, and, at the same time, realize but a small proportion of the products of his labor. But this, as every reflecting mind must see, is the condition of the laboring masses every where. One portion of the community always has and always will live upon the labor of the other portion. In every age and country *capital* has held labor in subjection, and always must hold it in subjection and no where has the laborer received, or is he ever destined to receive, more than a very small proportion of the products of his own labor. And we are firmly persuaded, after a somewhat careful examination of the subject, that the distribution of the products of labor between the laborer and the capitalist is no where more favorable to the laborer than in the Southern States of the union. For it can be demonstrated from immutable general principles, and it is confirmed by experience, that bare subsistence, together with the means of perpetuating the race, is all that simple labor has ever received or can ever expect to receive. And, if so, it seems to us that the slave has reason to rejoice, rather than repine, over his lot. He is well fed, well clothed, well housed, and secure in the enjoyment of all the necessaries and many of the comforts of life. And this, as we have recently had much melancholy reason for knowing, is more than can be affirmed of the laboring masses of Europe. It is in the name of the *master*, therefore, and not of the *slave*, that we assail the institution of slavery. It is political economy and not humanity which raises its voice against it.

We have now pointed out, in a very imperfect manner, the preponderance, from a very early period, of those elements in the social system of the colony which favored the development of man's moral and intellectual nature, but were hostile to the melioration of his material and social condition. And the fact, as we all know, corresponds, in every particular, with what might have been expected from this state of things. We are prepared, did space permit, and could we believe that it would be acceptable to the public, to carry this analysis of the Social System of Virginia yet further, and show that, whatever there may be characteristic in her present condition or past history—whatever she may, at any time, have done for the development of man, or whatever she may have failed to do for the improvement of society, is fairly attributable to those elements which, as we have seen, have always controlled her civilization. But this article has already extended to an unreasonable length, and we must bring it to an end. We cannot, however, dismiss this subject without calling attention, in a very few words, to one other feature in the Social System of Virginia, an explanation of which will be readily found in the preponderance of those elements which we have already described. We allude to *Domestic Manners*. This, from the first settlement of the country, has been a remarkable characteristic of the civilization of the colony, and, afterwards, of the commonwealth. No where have domestic manners ever been more prevalent—no where have they ever arrived at greater perfection. This was the necessary result of that isolated country life, of which we have so frequently spoken. Placed beyond the reach of general society, the only refuge of the Virginia farmer was in the bosom of his family. Here he found his wife and children, and but few besides—they alone were his companions—they alone divided his sorrows, and shared his joys. Whatever concerned him, deeply interested them, and the members of this little circle became gradually united to each other by the strongest ties that can bind human beings together. And we accordingly find that the ties of family and kindred, the associations which connect themselves with *home*, and make it a shrine in after years, and "all the charities of father, son and brother," acquired a force in Virginia that is seldom seen elsewhere. The preponderance of domestic life in the colony, and, since, in the commonwealth, is not, therefore, to be wondered at. It was, as we have just stated, the necessary consequences of that retired country life which the people then led, and still lead, to a great extent. By the force of his position, the affections of the Virginia planter were oblige to center in his *Home*. Here his life was spent, here were his only friends and companions, here all his visions of happiness in this life clustered. Feelings which, under other circumstances, would have been weakened by diffusion, were here strengthened by concentration, and, almost, by exclusiveness. And here we remark, in passing, upon the *social position of woman in Virginia*. No where is woman held in higher respect. And this is attributable to the prevalence of those domestic manners which we have just been describing. Here her importance and value became manifest. Woman, at one time man's drudge, and, at another, his toy in the bosom of that isolated country life which the people of Virginia have always led, became at once his friend, companion and guide. And, as is always the case, this improvement in her social position, has been accompanied by a corresponding improvement in her moral and intellectual faculties. As her influence and importance have increased, her mind has been expanded, and her virtues illustrated. And it will, accordingly, be found that if woman has always commanded cordial and unfeigned respect and admiration in Virginia, this has been but a just tribute to her many virtues. No where, in our judgment, has the female character ever attained to greater excellence—no where has woman ever been more chaste, more lovely, more self-devoting. A Virginia mother, in the circle of her family, with her children around her, is the noblest specimen of her sex.

A word in conclusion. We have now pointed out, though in a very imperfect manner, what, in our judgment, constitutes the strength and weakness of the Social System of Virginia. We have seen that its strength consists in the preponderance of those elements which favor individual development, and its weakness in the subjection of those elements which favor social progress. But, if we be right in another proposition of ours, this latter evil will, in time, cure itself. For we have argued that the two great elements of civilization—individual development and social melioration—however they may separate for a time, must, by the laws of their own movement, ultimately come together, and advance *abreast*. And, in the meantime, until these two movements shall become parallel, there is, as we think, nothing discouraging in the present condition of the commonwealth. She is, at least, in possession of one, and that the most valuable of the great elements of civilization. And, indeed, grave doubts have been entertained by wise and reflecting men whether, after all, the prodigious progress, which modern society is making towards perfection in social organization, is the *summum bonum* which it has all along been supposed to be. It is argued that order and harmony in the social arrangements are very beautiful things, and, in no wise, to be neglected; but, upon the other hand, it is said that the tendency of the present system is to destroy all *individuality*, to make men mere conventional machines and respectable drudges. And thus, while you erect a grand and imposing social edifice, with all its parts adjusted in perfect harmony and order, you sap the foundation upon which it rests. Society progresses for awhile with wonderful rapidity, but the individual man deteriorates. It is not difficult to predict the ultimate fate of such a community. And in respect to progress in material wealth, it is argued that, while it is certainly a very good thing that men should be well-fed, well-clothed, well-housed, and that their external condition, in every respect, should be comfortable and happy, yet that society has now passed that point, and the tendency of the present order of things is to engross men exclusively in the miserable work of accumulation, and to chain down their minds to low and perishable interests, to the neglect of higher and more enduring interests and the cultivation of those spiritual and intellectual faculties which distinguish man from the brute, and connect him, in the gradation of being, with higher intelligencies. They say that Mammon is the "Great God" of the age, and that it has none other God but him. We must not be understood as approving these views—upon the contrary we, for the most part, reject them. But yet we have thought proper to state them for the encouragement of those who are inclined to regret and despair over the present aspect of civilization in Virginia. For ourselves we need consolation from no such source. We find it in the Social System of the State itself. We believe that that system, while it has its imperfections, is full of hope and promise, and destined to future greatness. And we found this opinion upon that preponderance, which we have so often pointed out, of those elements which favor the development of the individual man. While the constituent members of a community remain sound and healthy—their moral and intellectual natures improved and cultivated—however imperfect its social organization may be, it possesses the materials for a fine society; for, after all, it is the noble people that make the noble government, rather than the converse. Institutions are much; but they are not all. And it is a truth which should never be forgotten, that those memorable revolutions in religion, morals and government, as well as those important inventions and discoveries in art and science, which have added so largely to the stock of human comfort and happiness, have resulted, not from social or political mechanism and organization, but from isolated and individual energy and devotion. They have, each and all of them, been either the legacies which some silent thinker has bequeathed to his country and his age from the retirement of his closet, or the achievements of some bold reformer, who, overflowing with love for his race and burning with indignation at their wrongs, has fired the human soul with new hope and new daring, and changed the course of history. And now, perhaps, when we least expect it, some such thinker or reformer may be in our midst. In the bosom of that isolated country life, which still constitutes a distinguishing feature in Virginia society, there may linger, obscure and unknown, and only awaiting a fit occasion to develop his priceless worth, some Jefferson, who shall expound to his country and the world the great principles of civil and religious liberty, and teach mankind how individual liberty may best be reconciled with social order—some Henry, whose burning words shall again stir up men's souls, and whose voice, as of old, shall sound to arms in the hour of peril—or some Washington, upon whose broad shoulders his country may again repose in the day of need, and feel that his constant soul and outstretched arm are a better safeguard than fleets and armies. "The glory of an age is often hidden from itself."

# 7.

## James Warley Miles

### "The Possibility and Nature of Theology"[1]

James Warley Miles is one of the exceptions to the rule of Charleston thought, an aberration common enough to make the historian doubt the existence of a rule. For much of a gloomy life, Miles moved with consummate unease between Episcopalian ministries and academic posts.[2] Born in Orangeburg in 1818, he took the not unusual course of the Willington Academy and the South Carolina College, though his prompt expulsion from the latter for planning a duel with another student betrayed an uncharacteristic élan. A few years later he went to the General Theological Seminary in New York, where he acquired some taste for the medievalism of the Oxford Movement. Later his interests grew more cerebral and less sensual, freed from "the mists of a new-fangled Theology from a distant Island."[3] But he did catch the Seminary's missionary evangelicalism, sufficient to serve in rural South Carolina parishes, and for four years from 1843 in Mesopotamia and Constantinople. There his interest in languages, which had already extended to French and German, stretched to Arabic, Persian, Aramaic, Armenian, Sanskrit, and Turkish. An enthusiastic admirer put the tally of Miles's languages at thirty or forty, which is doubtful. But it is probable that Miles was one of the most accomplished linguists in the United

---

1. James Warley Miles, *Philosophic Theology: or, Ultimate Ground of All Religious Belief Based on Reason* (Charleston, 1849), pp. 47–72.
2. The best discussion of Miles is Ralph E. Luker, "God, Man and the World of James Warley Miles, Charleston's Transcendentalist," *Historical Magazine of the Protestant Episcopal Church* 39 (June 1970): 101–36; see also E. Brooks Holifield, *The Gentlemen Theologians: American Theology in Southern Culture, 1795–1860* (Durham, 1978), pp. 66–71, and George Walton Williams, *The Reverend James Warley Miles* (Charleston, 1954), a pamphlet with an incomplete bibliography.
3. Miles, *Farewell Sermon* (Charleston, 1843), p. 11.

263

States, one of only a handful whose range went beyond the European tongues and that tool of the theologian, Hebrew.[4]

The Near Eastern mission, like many such ventures, fell victim to poverty, illness and dissension. Miles's health undoubtedly suffered. Back in South Carolina, he drifted into temporary ministries, until he ended up, also *ad interim*, at St. Michael's Church in Charleston. In 1850 he was elected to a chair of the History of Intellectual Philosophy and Greek Literature at the College of Charleston. But the need to instruct the diffident young irked him as much, if not more, than the exigencies of the weekly sermon. In 1854 he resigned on the grounds of ill health and, after auctioning off his precious library, he fled to Paris and there moped for two years. A passing friend found him depressed and lonely, and hauled him back to Charleston.[5] He was found a job, flattering to neither ego nor pocket, as librarian of the college by friends careful of his prospects and his books, but conscious that Miles had little capacity for great responsibility. The war forced him to rusticate, but Reconstruction merely repeated the pattern of ill health, interim ministries, and teaching in Charleston. He died in 1875.

In the midst of this melancholy disruption, Miles found time to write, mainly in the form of sermons and orations, usually printed as pamphlets. But he also contributed to the *Southern Quarterly Review* and *Russell's Magazine* in an anonymity that was, for him, a matter of insistent principle. Most importantly, he published in 1849 his *Philosophic Theology*, from which this excerpt is drawn. Miles knew much recent French and German theological research. He was a student particularly of Schliermacher, and, though there is no evidence that he had read Hegel (oddly so, in view of his persuasion), he was deeply influenced by Hegel's German disciples. From France he drew upon the eclectic philosophy of Victor Cousin, and from England upon Coleridge. Not surprisingly, since they in turn were influenced by Schliermacher, Broad Church Anglicans like Thomas Arnold and Richard Whately were also prominent in Miles's aware-

---

4. *Catalogue of the Library of the Reverend James Warley Miles* (Charlottesville, 1955) lists about 1,600 volumes, of which 154 are in or about Oriental languages; see Miles, "The Turkish Language," *SQR* 13 (January 1848): 54–78; "On the Philosophy of Language," *SQR* n.s. 4 (October 1851): 390–433; *The Student of Philology* (Charleston, 1852).

5. Robert Newton Gourdin to William Porcher Miles, 17 October 1856, in W. P. Miles Papers, Southern Historical Collection, University of North Carolina, Chapel Hill; Miles had also traveled to Holland and Berlin, where he preached an Independence Day sermon at the home of the American Minister. See Luker, "Miles," p. 116.

ness of theology. *Philosophic Theology*, almost alone of Southern books, was noticed in its turn in Europe. Fredrika Bremer, the Swedish traveler and novelist, praised it in her *Homes of the New World*. With more discrimination, one of the chief German disciples of Schliermacher, Johann Neander, took comfort in the spread of his beliefs to such remoteness as Charleston and encouraged a German translation of Miles's book, which duly appeared in Leipzig in 1850.[6]

This chapter was written with uncluttered simplicity, with little explicit reference to others, and it would be easy to miss the force of its heterodoxy. Miles's point was simple. Man's awareness of a God begins in human consciousness. The offense against orthodoxy lay in Miles's denial of other sources. Miracle, divine intervention, the Scriptures themselves were not the beginning. The Bible, he was to write in 1864, "I regard as a historical book—that is, whose origins, contents, growth, development, arose and can be traced and accounted for, by the laws of criticism and historical development and also of psychology." This standpoint lifted God out of active participation in human affairs, left him immanent in human consciousness, so immanent that man, charged with awareness, could in turn discern the movement of Providence by his power of intellectual insight. Such beliefs left Miles open to the charges of pantheism and presumption.[7] James Smith Rhett clucked that Miles was insufficiently Kantian, but most theologians criticized from the right flank.[8] Miles was unimpressed. "I would rather be called an infidel in the noble company of Neander and Arnold," he wrote, "than be lauded for the narrow-minded *orthodoxy* (?) of Thornwell." Elsewhere he told Mrs. Thomas John Young, the wife of a fellow minister with whom he kept up a strange and intense correspondence, "Oh! my Dear Friend, I am so weary of the emptiness and ignorance of the religious teachers of the day! Men who *know nothing* of what criticism has achieved—, who do *not wish* to keep pace with the learning and science of the world. . . . Fichte . . . was actually persecuted by the clergy of his day, because his religion was too earnest

---

6. Fredrika Bremer, *The Homes of the New World: Impressions of America* (New York, 1854), 1:378–79; the Neander review originally appeared in *Deutsche Zeitschrift für Christliche Wissenschaft und Christliche Leben*, but is reprinted in *SQR* 2 (September 1850): 259–60.

7. Holifield, *Gentlemen Theologians*, p. 69, notes, however, that Miles, though radical in the United States, was on the right flank of the new European theology, since he insisted that God was incarnate not only in man but also in the historical figure of Christ.

8. [James Smith Rhett], "Philosophic Theology," *SQR* 17 (April 1850): 123–45 and (July 1850): 481–99.

and real for their cold formalism."⁹ Gentle as it reads, this was an embattled essay.

FROM the most general point of view, THEOLOGY presents itself as *that department of knowledge which embraces what is supposed to be known respecting the nature and character of God, and the relations of man towards Him.*

The first and most obvious fact with regard to the subject, is the immense *discrepancy* between the various systems of Theology, as the Hindoo, the Mohammedan, the Christian, etc.; but upon a closer inspection, we find ourselves compelled to limit our investigations for truth in this department of knowledge, to *Christian* Theology, both because it is the prevailing system among the most cultivated and enlightened portions of mankind, as well as because all other systems have become virtually effete for the intellectual and learned, to such a degree, as renders it morally certain that they can never supersede Christian Theology; that whatever truth they may contain will be found embraced in this latter; and that if the religious element in cultivated humanity finds not satisfaction in this system, it can not in any other which is known. Even if it be supposed that that element can find its adequate satisfaction in a Philosophical Theology, which shall not be distinctively christian, it certainly will not be denied that it is unnecessary to examine any other system than the christian, to arrive at such a result; since if this fails, some Philosophical Theology must be at once adopted, without seeking the desired satisfaction in any of the known systems, mohammedan or pagan. At all events, whatever conclusions be arrived at, there are certain general principles and questions relating to *Theology itself*, which must be antecedently discussed, if we would proceed in a scientific manner.

The first query which naturally occurs, is—*whence does Theology arise?* Without entering into the history of religion, we can certainly deduce from the very existence of such a history, the fact of a religious element in man. Amidst the various subjective phenomena which are identified with the peculiar development of particular religions, there is one universal element pervading the whole, and belonging essentially to the religious nature of man. This is *the sense of finiteness, imperfection, dependence, which seeks to attach itself to the infinite, the perfect, the supernatural and divine.*

---

9. Miles to David J. McCord, 24 April 1851, quoted in Luker, "Miles," p. 123; Miles to Mrs. T. J. Young, circa 1858–1859, quoted in Luker, "Miles," p. 124.

Something beyond itself the soul must have to stay upon, and to satisfy its religious instincts. It must seek some solution of the mysteries of being, creation, death, and futurity; and when it is too debased to rise to the conception of a God, of destiny, of an eternal law, or of some sentimental abstraction of ideal beauty, it will cling even to the grossest devilism and magic. This religious element has even appeared in a remarkable degree, where many would least expect to find it; namely, in the great systems of pantheism, where it seeks vent in losing its sense of feebleness in the all-embracing infinite; and even in the philosophic atheism of the acute and sceptical Lucretius, a lurking, instinctive superstition, can not wholly escape the critical eye. It is, doubtless, from this primary religious element that Theology takes its rise.

But although man is impelled by an inner necessity to speculate upon such subjects, and to form theories and systems of Theology, it does not thence necessarily follow (the contrary indeed we clearly see,) that he will hit upon the exact truth, or not mingle inextricably truth with error, or arrive at a positively real Theology. Another query, therefore, immediately springs from the former, namely, whether any thing can be certainly known upon the subject, or *how does a valid Theology become possible?* The only solid principle upon which an answer to this query can be based, is self-evident; it is this, the possibility of conceiving and becoming satisfied of the existence of God. If a conviction of the existence of God can not be attained, all Theology must appear as mere empty speculation. The conception of God, however, can be, and is, attained, although it is only from man's self-consciousness of his own reason, understanding, will, power, moral affections, convictions of right and wrong, and of accountability, that he is able to form any conceptions of the wisdom, power, attributes and moral will or law of Deity. It is upon these conceptions and facts of self-consciousness that a conviction of the real existence of God can alone be founded, and to them every proof of his Being and will must be addressed. It is, then, the first condition of a valid Theology that it does not contravene, but is accordant with, the universal reason and moral instincts or convictions of man. But still, a Theology based *solely* upon these conceptions, while it would embrace the vital conclusions that God must be just and good, and hence that only justice and goodness can please Him, would only amount to a reasonable hypothesis, and could not rise to an absolute character. For this, a revelation from Deity is manifestly necessary. If there is no revelation, it is impossible to affirm absolutely theological truth. *Is a revelation, then, possible?* If God be the absolute, unoriginated, intelligent cause of all existence, not bound by the fatal necessity of all inability to communicate with the intelligent beings whom he has created, a revelation is undoubtedly possible. If he be even supposed moved by some mysterious necessity in the infinite energies of his own nature, to manifest himself by creation, this would oppose no reason against the possibility of revelation, but rather, from the intimate connection with his creatures which such a necessity would involve, it becomes even more probable that that connection would manifest itself at times in the higher degree of revelation; the eternal energies of the all-sustaining Being coming forth in fuller manifestation through the finite intellect, as they put forth themselves at times in the mighty operations of nature. In short, God can not be conceived as the absolutely Supreme intellect, without the possibility of revelation to finite intellects being involved in the conception.

But although God be not bound except by the absolute and eternal fitness of things in relation to his perfect nature and infinite wisdom, yet the finite creature is bound by the conditions of its limited nature, and once constituted under those conditions, without their total change, a revelation is only possible to it in accordance with those conditions. Since, then, the finite intellect, from the very limitation of its faculties, can not comprehend the infinite, a revelation would only be so far possible and intelligible as it could fall within the scope of the conceptions and understanding of the finite intellect. Those conceptions might be elevated and that understanding enlarged by the revelation from Deity, but they would be the same in kind, and if the recipient of a revelation was to communicate its contents intelligibly to others, whose intellect had not been illumined in the same manner, then such communication must fall within the ordinary comprehension of men, or it would be valueless. The subject of a revelation from Deity could doubtless be assured of the fact of a special illumination of his intellect by God; but how could others be satisfied that the ideas which he declared as derived from divine instruction were really from such a source? If they were unintelligible, no judgment could be pronounced upon them; if they were intelligible, by what criteria could they be judged to have proceeded from divine illumination? Prophecy could only verify itself by fulfilment, and could only afford indirect proof as to theological doctrines announced by the Prophet, since it would not necessarily follow that because he had predicted an event which mere human sagacity could not have foreseen, therefore his declarations as to duties and articles of belief were infallible. In the same way miracles would only prove the connection of the worker with a power beyond that of man; but could not prove that the worker was absolutely infallible in his statement of doctrines and duties. It is only through his actually existing faculties that the recipient of a revelation could receive and comprehend the divine communication, or communicate it to others, and unless a miracle was wrought in the minds of men to produce at once conviction,—when a fellow man declared to them that the ideas he communicated had been immediately given to him by God, they would be obliged to judge of the truth of his declaration by conceptions of which they were already in possession. That is, the revelation would approve itself to them by its accordance with the great principles of morality, reason, and the character of Deity, enlarging their ideas on these subjects, reaching their conscience, and taking hold of their religious nature and wants. If God gave an individual knowledge, surpassing, and wholly different from any which the faculties of man can comprehend, it could never be communicated by the recipient to others. A revelation from God, then, intended to be conveyed by the recipient to others, must be communicated to him through his ordinary faculties and comprehension. All which can be acquired through the faculties with which God has constituted man, is to him a revelation, as the knowledge of the objective world, and all which pertains to the subjective domain of intellect. God has bound up man in these conditions, as those by which alone he can acquire or receive any knowledge; and hence any higher revelation touching the will of God and spiritual truth, must be made by enlarging the ideas and conceptions and intellectual perception of the recipient, so that he may be able to communicate comprehensible ideas to others. As the only method by which *we* can *communicate* newly acquired ideas or knowledge, is through language, a revelation must also be communicable in intelligible language, and every recipient of revelation must relate in his own manner the subjective impressions which he has received, unless the conditions of his humanity be violated. A finite intelligence, then, (that is, a man, for we know nothing of the conditions of other intelligences,) can only receive a revelation in the same manner as all information is received,—through existing faculties, (or if he receives it in any other manner, other men can not judge of it, until they possess the same experience,) and thus receiving a revelation, he can only communicate it in the same manner as all men communicate their increased information to their fellow men. And revelation thus necessarily passing into the sphere of language, must be judged as all other communicated information is, by the laws of language and reason. If, then, it can be determined that a professed revelation has really proceeded from enlightenment and information furnished by Deity to the finite agent of the revelation, a basis is obtained for a really valid Theology in the contents of that revelation.

But to obtain such a ground for Theology, it must first be determined *how a revelation can be established.* It must come to those not the subjects of an inspiration, upon the testimony of the deliverers of it; and in case they are removed by some interval of time from the original deliverers, upon the conjoined testimony of those who have recognized it as revelation. In every case, in which those to whom an alleged revelation is delivered, are not themselves inspired, the revelation must depend upon human testimony; and as, from the very nature of the case, this can reach no further than the facts that such declarations were delivered and received as revelation, and that the original deliverers were of trust-worthy character, the whole force of the revelation must depend upon its own intrinsic character. That is, it must be probable as relating to matters of such import to man, and yet so beyond his ordinary means of knowledge, as to warrant the bestowal of information from God; it must contain intelligible truths of so superior a character, as to warrant the belief of their having been communicated by God; and it must approve itself to the conscience and moral wants of man. Revelation must thus be suited to the degree of development man had attained, in order that he might comprehend and judge of it, however it might be always adapted for enlarging his conceptions, and elevating him towards a higher degree of development. To us, then, who are at so great a distance from any original revelation on spiritual truths, and who must take the records alleged to contain such a revelation, upon very complicated testimony, as to their genuineness and authenticity; those records must be utterly valueless, unless they can approve themselves to our reason and religious nature, by their own contents. Whether they were revelation or not to those in past times,—if they do not meet *our* state of development, *our* intellectual, moral, and religious wants, in reference to religion,—they can possess no vitality, no real utility, even if we admit that they were originally revelation. But a revelation to be valid for all time, for man in every period of development, and calculated ever to further his moral and spiritual growth, must contain truths which will ever be applicable to his religious wants, and ever vital for his conscience and moral nature. It is, then, to the intuitive reason and conscience of man, as a moral and religious creature, that the subject-matter of an alleged revelation must appeal, in order to establish itself as divine. For, if that character is only to rest upon human testimony, even should this establish the genuineness and authenticity of the records, man could never appreciate the complicated evidence and critical details upon which it rests; and even if the testimony be admitted, the question might still be asked, how can we know that God really communicated with the original deliverers of those records, and that their contents may not otherwise be accounted for? But as man is created with religious instincts, moral intuitions, and deep wants with regard to theology, which however perverted and darkened, are an original revelation in the depths of his own soul, it is to them all revelation must appeal; and by answering, elevating, satisfying them, that it must establish itself as truly divine.

The question now inevitably arises, *with what must Theology occupy itself*? A valid basis being given it, in a revelation which approves itself to the reason and conscience of man, what is the true function of Theology in relation to that revelation? If it would keep within its appropriate sphere of truth and certainty, it must encroach as little as possible upon the field of dogmatic divinity, where the systems carefully and logically built up by one, are demolished zealously by another; where theories once held as absolute divine truth, which it was sacrilege to doubt or question, are superciliously cast aside, as superannuated, in a succeeding age; where the doctrine, an assent to which is made a condition of salvation by one, is regarded by another as endangering the eternal safety of him who holds it; and where the endless conflicts of diverse systems and theories, may well plunge one into despair of ever obtaining a certain reply to the query— 'what is truth?' In this vexed field, the divine must battle for what he regards the true, or truest, system. Hard and ungracious is his task, but let him bravely battle on; contest must ever further the truth,—time will vindicate the right,—God will protect what is truly his revelation. But it is the privilege of Theology to move in a higher and calmer sphere. If not freed from the necessity of doing battle for the truth, her contests are for no scholastic forms, no logical processes, upon which certainty is ever problematical, and which rest for their validity upon the acceptance of the individual judgment; but hers are the dignified, the vital, the heroic conflicts, in which the very "fortresses of the faith" must be defended. It is for religion itself, and not for the system of this or that man, or body of men, that she stands as champion. The true office of Theology is to vindicate the great religious truths which appeal to the deepest consciousness of man; to awaken him to a realization of the Personal God in whom he lives, who is at once the author and the end of his existence; to elevate his consciousness to a perception of the vital and quickening ideas which God has given to the world, through the experience of Prophets and Apostles; to purify him, by bringing him into contact with eternal verities; to place him in communion, as it were, with all the good and noble and holy of every age and clime; to cheer him on in the fulfilment of his eternal destiny; and to actuate in him the religious life as a redeemed heir of immortality. Holiness is its lofty aim, and faith its immortal strength. It regards revelation, not as material given, whereon men shall exhibit their astounding temerity, in presuming to dogmatize upon the most abstruse and hidden mysteries, but as a moral and religious power for kindling in the soul a holy life, ennobling it with the faith and hopes of redemption, and empowering it by the love of God in Christ, to fight nobly the battle of life, until its immortal aspirations shall be swallowed up in the fruition of eternity.

When we proceed to apply these principles to the criticism of what is currently received as Theology, we find two elements which need to be carefully distinguished, and also a general fact of the highest importance. We find the element of religious sensibility and perception, with which Theology proper has to do, in cultivating the religious life in man; and we find the logical understanding, to which divinity addresses itself, in definite or sharply defined systems and propositions. We also find the general fact, that amidst all diversity and opposition, there is an underlying unity which characterises all as *christian*, in distinction from every other religious development. There are two points from which Theology may indifferently start. Either from the Being of God, and the probability and need of revelation which that grand truth involves, to the actual records of revelation as established and interpreted by the universal consciousness of christianized humanity, or from the phenomena of the christian life up to the revelation and its author in which those phenomena are grounded, and which alone adequately explain them. Having already stated the grounds upon which a valid Theology can rest in the truths and ideas of a revelation commending itself to, and realized in, the deepest consciousness of man, we shall briefly analyze the phenomena of christian life, in order to point out what are its universal, invariable and necessary characteristics, which stand forth as a beacon against enthusiasm, superstition and fanaticism, as well as against frigid formality, scepticism and rationalism.

When we distinguish what is *material* from what is *formal*—what belongs to *religion* from what pertains to *divinity*—what is the substance of truth and reality beneath the guises of form in which it is variously expressed, it is evident that amidst all the difference in christendom, even amidst the jarring of dispute and recrimination, there is something common to all as christian, in which any pretence to christian life or experience must profess to be grounded; and this, as a fact, neither the coldest scepticism nor the haughtiest bigotry can deny. There is a universal principle beneath the various modifications of the christian element itself, upon which it rests, and in which the unity of the christian consciousness is grounded.

When the primary religious element is developed under the influence of christianity, it assumes a phase which distinctly marks it as christian, and distinguishes it from its developments in any other form of religious belief. It can scarcely be disputed as historical fact, that the central idea and ultimate aim of all religion is *reconciliation*. But the root from whence grows all development of the christian religious element, is *reconciliation through a Personal Redeemer*. However this may be supposed to be effected; from the most ardent and enthusiastic view of "conversion," to the coldest and most passive theory of an "opus operatum;" from the most strenuous conviction of "resistless grace," to the most absolute assertion of "human ability;" there is still the unanimous grounding of all views of reconciliation upon the *Personal Christ*, as the author of the new relation of man towards God, Truth and Duty. It is by realizing a personal relation through the spiritual consciousness, towards this Personal Redeemer, that there is realized that confidence in God, wherein filial duty and love are harmonized in the sense of paternal reconciliation with the individual man. And it is the great practical problem of christianity, (the appointed means for the resolution of which we do not here discuss,) to awaken the spiritual consciousness to the realization of that personal relation towards the Re-

## Nature of Theology 273

deemer, and to foster and maintain the religious life of the soul. The most general characteristic, then, of the *christian* feeling of religion, we would state to be, *that sense of confidence in God, wherein filial duty and love are harmonized in the sense of paternal reconciliation through the Personal Redeemer.*

This characteristic, however, manifests itself under a variety of degrees and modifications, as it is more or less purely developed, and as the peculiar relation of sonship towards God, is realized with more or less clearness under the modification of accompanying conceptions. For example, where the conception predominates, of God ruling through a strict and defined monarchical polity, the sense of sonship will be modified by the feeling of the appointed service of the subject. Where the preponderating conception is of the absolute sovereignty of the divine will, in its own mysterious and secret counsels, the feeling of sonship will be modified by the sense of the subjection of all to the mighty decrees of the supreme wisdom and pleasure. Where, again, there predominates the conception of God as boundless love, the feeling of the relation of sonship will be chiefly merged in the grateful sense of the freely reconciled creature. And so, again, the sense of that peculiar relationship will be correspondingly modified, as there predominates the conception of God, viewed through the provided means of reconciliation, as they stand in relation to his own character, or to the wants and nature of the creature himself. So that strict and submissive duty,—or dutiful resignation and submission,—or confiding and trustful affection,—or careful and thankful obedience,—or earnest and grateful acceptance,—will come out most prominently in one or the other case. Not that they may not all be commingled in a certain degree; but that some one, as the case may be, will appear as the most prominent phase, under each predominant conception of God. We also know, as historical fact, that in various developments of the religious element in christianity, there prevail stern views of duty, or narrow conceptions of submission, or loose notions of obedience, or other modifications of the christian feeling of religion; as well, as that there sometimes predominates the subjective condition of the individual, or the objective appointed means of reconciliation, as the most prominent modifying element of systems of divinity. But we can trace through all these modifications, that sense of confidence in God, founded upon the filial relation realized through reconciliation by a Personal Redeemer, which characterizes the religious element of christianity.

Now, we are compelled to ask, *what is the origin of this christian religious element*? For eighteen centuries, the christian life has developed itself in humanity, flowing on in the consciousness of man, through every age, with undying vitality, actuating the same phenomena in every diversity of clime, development, and race, and supplying a boundless and imperishable aliment to the spiritual wants and life of man. We can fix the period when this extraordinary phenomenon began to manifest itself in the human consciousness, and it has ever continued propagating itself through that consciousness down the flow of time, like a mighty wave, gathering strength from its vast and onward swell. Under its impulse and control, a development of humanity has manifested itself, wholly different from any which preceded, and evincing that a new element had been introduced into the world. Civilization, politics, international and national law, social life, and intellectual processes in every department, have been signally influenced, modified, and directed into before unknown channels, by this mighty element. Even the region of speculative philosophy has felt its control; and the very sceptic who rejects christianity, is enabled to speak of God, morals, and duty, with a clearness and definiteness of apprehension, and a lofty nobility of conception, sublimely and infinitely surpassing all to which the highest genius of the world had attained before the introduction of christianity. And all which he can oppose to the origin which christians claim for this element, is the postulate that in the natural, uninterrupted progress of humanity, that clear apprehension, and those noble conceptions of God and duty, would have inevitably developed themselves. But such a position is entirely unphilosophical, in as much as it is at direct variance with the known course of human development. It is impossible to affirm what would inevitably have been the actual development of humanity, had any of the great facts in the chain of its moral and intellectual growth been wanting. Had not the Greeks existed, and received their peculiar development, and stood in the exact place they occupied in the history of mankind, it is doubtless true, that the development of the human race and its history would have been different from what it was; but it is impossible to take a phase of humanity, subsequent to the period assigned to the Greeks as their historical era, and to erect that into a postulate claiming any deference, as to what the development and history of man would inevitably have been, independent of the modifying elements alleged to have flowed from the Greeks. Nor can we any more, in philosophically examining the progress of humanity, strike out so obvious and undeniable a modifying element as christianity. The most we could do, would be to deny that the modern civilized world is indebted to that source for its sublime ideas of a Personal God, clothed with a mercy as resplendent and attractive, as the notions with which the ancients invested their conceptions of the divine, were gross, terrific, or Platonically undefined and shadowy. We may affirm that the lofty conceptions of morality and duty, before which every page of ancient literature must blush; or that the religious life of purity, holiness, charity, faith, and hope, of which, before christianity, the world had known no realization, and the best of the ancients had only faintly and confusedly dreamed, were no offspring from that astonishing element, before whose appearance in the world, those grand and vital ideas had been unknown or profoundly dormant. We must not only, in asserting such a denial, show how those ideas originated and took their place in the growth of humanity, but we must also explain the origin of christianity itself, and account for the coincidence of its appearance with the putting forth of those high conceptions, as well as for their invariable connection ever since with the progress and influence of pure and vital christianity. We know well that attempts to satisfy such demands, have been made with subtlety and ability, but they all involve the manifest sophism and assumption, that christianity itself is a gradual offspring from the development of humanity; while it evidently did not gradually grow into the world, but was at once introduced—a germ full of new ideas, which still in every age are loftier than the age itself, and pour forth exhaustless treasures to the ever increasing expansion of intellect and civilization; an expansion incited and modified by christianity itself, which arose, like a conquering vision of light, upon the mists and gropings of the world, from the midst of the retrograding, sinking civilization, and the rapidly petrifying vitality of the formal religion of degraded Palestine. At a period, when the world had sunk to such a point of demoralization and scepticism, as almost to justify the speculation of Plato, that there are cycles in which the world reaches such a condition of intense moral disharmony, as imperatively to call for the rectifying interposition of Deity, lest the whole frame of society should go to utter wreck, in the wild deluge of corruption; at such a period, when every hope of rational liberty, settled religious consolation and faith, and regenerating morality, seemed to have died out of humanity, in the vast and gloomy triumph of despotism, superstition, infidelity, and luxurious vice, there arose from the very base of society, in a wretched province, such a light, such a mighty, vital, regenerating element, as the world had never witnessed or experienced; and which has shaped, and elevated, and ennobled humanity in every subsequent development, with a deathless and ever growing energy. And now, when every thing indicates that humanity is to be hurried into a mighty battle for its most precious and vital possessions,—for the absolute basis of law and constitutional liberty,—of public morals,—of religious hope,—when the awful contest will rage around the very central life of man—the belief and trust in a Personal God; the vigor with which christianity gathers up her strength for the battle, undaunted, undismayed, is an earnest of her triumph,—is a proof that she is alone adequate to meet the foe,—is a glorious assurance that she is able to save the hopes of the world. She will herself be benefited and purified by the contest. The mists and corruptions, with which the lapse of centuries and the follies of men have obscured her divine lineaments, will be swept away; and she will again beam upon the world, as the uniter and sanctifier of humanity, radiant as she was in the Apostles' days with the glory of God.

But the christian life, which has existed in the world ever since the introduction of christianity, an actual experience, realized and propagated from age to age, in the vital consciousness of man, would exist, and grow, and continue, even if every record of the origin of christianity should perish. This christian consciousness is too wide spread, too manifestly recognizable under every variety of development, too deep-seated and sympathetic, too much inwrought into man's highest civilization and inmost life, to be at all affected by the results of speculative criticism. Even suppose that the records alluded to could be indubitably proved to be rather mythical accretions, than veritable history, this could not touch the actual, existing fact of the power and vitality of christianity, as realized in the religious consciousness of man; but, at most, it could only prove that we knew no authentic *details* respecting the wonderful Being, who so mightily impressed the energy of his own personality upon humanity, that it has modified its entire subsequent development, and lives ever in the hearts, the conscience, the hopes, the belief of men, although no positive history respecting his life has been preserved, but who was so awfully great and majestic and mighty and sacred, that within a half century of his moving among men, and leaving his spiritual image impressed forever upon the world, there grew up around the single central fact of his appearance upon the stage of life, the most wonderful myths which the word has ever beheld. What must have been his character, that the mere memory of his existence and the impression which he left in the hearts of men, could have gathered around them such a splendid halo as the Gospel narratives, weaving all the glories and hopes which humanity had ever lavished upon its Gods and Heroes and Redeemers, into a radiant crown for the most resplendent, consistent and divine impersonation of nobility, inspiration and holiness, which ever won the hearts and attracted the devotion of men! Christ, as the Personal Redeemer, the root of the christian life, is too deeply incarnated in the heart of humanity, too intimately inwoven with the dearest and noblest hopes, the most lofty and mighty motives, the most earnest and sacred life of man, to be torn thence by any historical destruction of the mere records of his life. More wonderful, more divinely mighty must he appear, who has thus introduced the greatest modifying element into the progress and development of the human race, which has ever influenced it, and thus lives in the consciousness of christianized humanity, ever extending his sway, while no reliable record of his life exists; a life whose reality and power are nevertheless immortally stamped in the history and the firmest convictions of mankind. So that we can only adequately account for the existing phenomena of the christian life, by tracing its vitality back to that Christ, whose actual existence, not even the hardy criticism of Strauss[10] attempts to question, (for without that basis, at least,

---

10. David Friedrich Strauss, 1808–1874, the German neo-Hegelian theologian.

the Gospel myths could never have grown up,) and through that Christ, to God himself, who alone could have introduced that new and suddenly appearing, and astonishing element into the development of humanity. Strauss's theory starts from two postulates which he does not condescend to substantiate, taking them as acknowledged science, but a denial of which is fatal to the force of his arguments. One of them is, that there can be nothing miraculous or supernatural; and the other is, that within so brief a period as the time between Christ's flourishing, and the latest date which can be assigned to the oldest existing Gospel, it was possible for such a mythical legend to arise and shape itself, absolutely swallowing up every authentic fact, and yet embodying the most perfect conception of a sublimely harmonious, consistent and faultless character. The admission of a Personal God destroys the former assumption; the latter, which it is attempted to substantiate by a criticism of the internal evidence of it afforded by the contents of the Gospels, is invalidated by the direct external evidence to the substantial historical character of those books, and to the essential integrity of their existing text. Strauss's theory is the highest effort of criticism to destroy historical records. It appears that criticism can go no further, except in the denial of the very possibility of any history whatever; and his own words, upon the contemplation of his labors, are the truest and most eloquent judgment of what he has accomplished; they are the funeral oration, the perpetual epitaph, of such fruitless efforts. "The results" he says "of the inquiry which we have now brought to a close, have apparently annihilated the greatest and most valuable part of that which the christian has been wont to believe concerning his Saviour Jesus, have uprooted all the animating motives which he has gathered from his faith, and withered all his consolations. The boundless store of truth and life which for eighteen centuries has been the aliment of humanity, seems irretrievably dissipated; the most sublime levelled with the dust, God divested of his grace, man of his dignity, and the tie between heaven and earth broken. Piety turns away with horror from so fearful an act of desecration, and strong in the impregnable self-evidence of its faith, pronounces that, let an audacious criticism attempt what it will, all which the scriptures declare and the church believes of Christ will still subsist as eternal truth, nor needs one iota of it to be renounced."[11]

Profound and philosophical insight! It is not in the record of the letter, but in the spiritual sanctuary of the heart, that christianity is enshrined and lives. And if it were possible to destroy the record, the Christian Consciousness would *then*, perhaps, form glorious legends of the mighty Christ, whose power and truth will ever continue to be actuated in the experience

---

11. Strauss, *The Life of Jesus Critically Examined*, trans. George Eliot (Philadelphia, 1972), p. 757.

of man, thus testifying the divinity of the source whence it drew the first impulse of its immortal life.

*What relation, then, does the christian consciousness bear towards the christian records?* It finds in them a corrective and an exhaustless nourishment. A corrective against superstitions and notions unwarranted by the contents of the records, and an ever fresh and vitalizing spring of truth and holiness, for perfecting and elevating the religious life. The christian consciousness arose and took ineradicable root in humanity, before any christian records existed, and these were written evidently for the fostering and elevation of that divine life in the soul of man. Emanating from those in whom that life had been kindled by direct communion with its mighty author and his apostles, those records express the experience afforded their writers by God, with a depth, and vigor, and elevation of spiritual perception, far beyond anything that ordinary christian writings can present, unless indeed the writers be elevated by God to the same keen and vivid and extraordinary perception and realization of spiritual truth. They are the profoundest expression which the world possesses, of the affections, hopes, faith, consolations, charity, convictions of duty, of union with and redemption by God in Christ, with which humanity was ever inspired; and they will thus be ever regarded by the church as a most precious legacy. Basing itself upon the christian consciousness, upon christianity, not as a *science*, but a *divine life*,—Theology must ever strive to give more adequate form and expression to the subjective facts of christian experience, and to expound the deep, vitalizing, religious idea, which is embodied in "every objective expression respecting the relation of man to God."[12] Thus finding christianity actuated in the soul, the conscience, the spiritual experience of man, Theology will feel no nervous apprehension and jealousy at the boldest investigations of science and criticism; she will pronounce no profound conviction of an earnest soul, sincerely and candidly expressed, "dangerous," because it harmonizes not with some phraseology or dogma which depends upon the conviction of the individual judgment; and feeling assured that the christian life having God for its author, neither depends upon logical propositions or critical details, nor can ever die out of humanity, but will flow on sanctifying, ennobling, saving it, until the flood of time shall be lost in eternity; she appeals to us, by every demand of reason, to reverence, and love, and confide in the omnipotent God, whom we can not deny without abandoning and contravening reason itself; and who not only proclaims his existence to our intellect, but speaks in the depths of the conscience, as our Creator, our Judge, and our Father; pro-

---

12. [Bunsen.] Christian Charles Josias Bunsen, *The Constitution of the Church of the Future* (London, 1847), p. 33.

claiming, through his amazing displays of goodness and redemptive mercy in the Gospel, that man's highest nobility, is his creation in the image of God, and his supremest glory, is his being conformed to the likeness of Christ.

# 8.

## Charles E. A. Gayarré

## "The Rise and Fall of John Law"[1]

Charles Étienne Arthur Gayarré of Louisiana came as close to embodying the Cavalier myth as any sane mythologist might wish. Of old and aristocratic Creole stock, both French and Spanish, he was born in 1805, not long after the inauguration of what he himself dubbed the "American domination." He grew up close to New Orleans, on a plantation where the slaves would gather each dawn to kneel for prayers before the master or his deputy. Gayarré first performed the ceremony at the age of eight. Mature, he was very tall, elegant, proud, and presumably lusty, since he sired a bastard at the age of twenty-one.[2] For most of his life a Democrat—although he occasionally received preferment at the hands of Whigs and in the 1850s dallied, unsuccessfully and oddly for a Roman Catholic, with the Know-Nothings—he was elected to the United States Senate when barely past the legal age of thirty in 1836. But ill health, always to be his bane, compelled resignation before he even reached Washington. Thereafter he spent eight years in France, between 1836 and 1844, where he became interested in historical narrative and mingled, it is unreliably said, with De Tocqueville, Balzac, and Lamartine.[3] Back in Louisiana he served at various times in the state legislature and as secretary of state, but politics were an avocation hindered by his Creole origins and indifferent health. Rich in

---

1. Charles E. A. Gayarré, *Louisiana: Its Colonial History and Romance* (New York, 1851), pp. 197–238; this is an untitled chapter, so I have offered one.
2. Edward M. Socola, "Charles E. A. Gayarré, A Biography" (Ph.D. diss., University of Pennsylvania, 1954), pp. 320–23; the evidence for this, though persuasive, is not unimpeachable (but then such things seldom are).
3. Grace King remembers Gayarré speaking of his French sojourn and mentioning these names; see King, *Creole Families of New Orleans* (New York, 1921), p. 279. Gayarré, one must note, was as inclined to romanticize his own life as that of Louisiana.

the antebellum years, richer for a judicious marriage, the Civil War reduced him to poverty, charity, and novel-writing.

It is as a historian that he is remembered. His *History of Louisiana* is still in print and some are still disposed, with no little justice, to call him the Old South's greatest historian.[4] Certainly he undertook more serious manuscript research than any contemporary, save perhaps William Gilmore Simms. In France he personally examined archives, when his mind first turned to the project of a Louisiana history. In Spain in the late 1840s, he employed an agent to copy documents in Madrid, Seville, and Cadiz, as Prescott had done before him and Henry Adams was to do after.[5] And certainly Gayarré had a better grasp of narrative techniques than did most of the dull men who began the writing of Southern state history in the early nineteenth century. George Bancroft, for one, before the Civil War embittered their relations, thought Gayarré eminently reliable as a scholar.[6]

Gayarré's history was cut in a pure romantic mold, gorgeous and dramatic, avowedly indebted to the persuasion of Walter Scott. His biographer claims, with some force, that the earliest writings—the *Essai Historique sur la Louisiane* of 1830–1831 and the *Histoire de la Louisiane* of 1846–1847—were most romantic and unreliable, but that his later revisions, expansions, and additions betrayed a greater devotion to documentary evidence and less for melodrama.[7] Gayarré himself felt so. In 1847 he had given a series of lectures in New Orleans under the title *Romance of the History of Louisiana*. Published, they had brought him censure for wilder fancy. In a second series of lectures, from which this account of the financier John Law is drawn, he insisted that he had got his facts rights, but would get them more right: "I was informed that many had taken for the invention of the brain what was but historical truth set in a gilded

---

4. Clement Eaton, *The Waning of the Old South Civilization* (Athens, Ga., 1968), pp. 53–78.

5. In fact, Gayarré employed the same agent as Prescott. In 1882 Gayarré met Adams at the home of Oliver Wendell Holmes and wrote to George W. Cable: "At Holmes' table I met Henry Adams, one of the sons of Charles Francis Adams. He is writing a book on Burr's conspiracy and Wilkinson's treason. He wondered at my having procured the documents embodied on that subject in my History of Louisiana, and spoke of the difficulties he had personally met, notwithstanding his opportunities of position, in attempting to search the archives of Paris, London, and particularly Madrid. I sympathize with him in consequence of my own experience in the matter"; Gayarré to Cable, 6 August 1882, quoted in Socola, "Gayarré," p. 261.

6. Ibid., pp. 83, 207–9.

7. Ibid., p. 87.

frame, when, to use the expressions of Sir Joshua Reynolds, I had taken but insignificant liberties with facts, to interest my readers, and make my narration more delightful, in imitation of the painter who, though his work is called *history painting*, gives in reality a poetical representation of facts. The reader will easily perceive, that in the present production, I have been more sparing of embellishments, although '*I well noted, with that worthy gentleman, Sir Philip Sidney*,' as Raleigh says in his history of the world, '*that historians do borrow of poets not only much of their ornaments, but somewhat of their substance*.'" It was thus a half-hearted concession, more tactical than strategic, and one the reader doubts when he discovers with a smile that Gayarré proceeded, in his narrative, to change the name of Anthony Crozat's daughter from Marie Anne to Andrea because of, as he candidly and charmingly admitted in a footnote, "some capricious whim."[8]

This text shows how much Gayarré liked the melodramatic flourish. The ghost of the Duc de Sully is made to stalk a terrified Law, the parvenu and alien usurper. Of such interpolations, the reader is given fair warning. More interesting is the silent structuring of facts by which Gayarré heightened the drama of his narrative. Most contemporary historians did this, of course, and this is no censure. History in the early nineteenth century was still fluid in its strategy and identity, not yet settled upon the sepulchral ethic of modern historiography. The best of historians rearranged texts or altered for the purposes of seemliness. Gayarré did it more often and radically than most, one suspects, but then he strove for more gorgeous effect. Here the adjustments to the facts were designed to hasten the pace, to keep the rise and fall of John Law's fortunes swift and linear, to increase the effect of design, duplicity, and wonder in the Scotsman's good and bad fortune. Events actually devious and slow are compressed. Law is made peculiarly the author of his own fate, and men, like the Duc d'Orleans himself, are turned into mere ancillary ciphers. Evidence of sobriety in Law, though abundant, is suppressed and rococo touches of vice are added, so that his standing as an adventurer be unimpugned. Certainly the effect is both entertaining and rhetorically persuasive, which Gayarré intended. And the reader who has examined Gayarré's novels may believe the

---

8. Gayarré, *Louisiana: Its Colonial History and Romance*, pp. xiii–xiv, 194.

Louisianan wrote more engaging fiction as history than history as fiction.⁹

NOTHING could be more insignificant than Louisiana in the estimation of her European rulers, when Crozat's charter became one of those things that are among the past.¹⁰ But by one of those rapid transitions so common in human affairs, she was suddenly destined to exercise a wonderful influence over the powerful kingdom of which she was the weak progeny. In her very name there was soon to be discovered something as dazzling to the imagination, as the richest diamond is to the eye of woman. A subtile conjurer arose, who, waving aloft his magical wand, and using that name, then so obscure, to give more force to his incantations, prepared for France an intoxicating draught which made her reel as in drunkenness, and nearly prostrated her to the ground, despite of her ever-reviving energies. The star of John Law had risen on the horizon of France: and the Company of the Indies, the great Mississippi scheme, of which he was the chief projector, the destinies of France and of Louisiana, the expected results of such commerce as the world had never known before, the reports of hidden treasures concealed in inexhaustible mines of silver and gold, were to be indissolubly united in the annals of history and of folly.

On the 13th of August, 1717, the situation of affairs in the colony of Louisiana having been brought before the Council of State, at Versailles, it was decided by that body, presided over by the Duke of Orleans, Regent of France during the minority of Louis the XVth, that, "for many essential reasons which it would be superfluous to recite, because they were known to every one, it was to the interest of France that the colony of Louisiana should be fostered and preserved."—Such were the terms of that decree, which went on, saying that, "whereas it had been demonstrated, in the case of Crozat, that the colonization of the province of Louisiana was an

---

9. See especially Gayarré, *The School for Politics: A Dramatic Novel* (New York, 1854) and the more accomplished *Fernando de Lemos. Truth and Fiction: A Novel* (New York, 1872).

10. Anthony Crozat had been granted in 1712 a charter to trade exclusively in Louisiana for fifteen years, to work its mines, supply its slaves, and to own in perpetuity all land that he caused to be cultivated, all buildings erected, and all manufactures. In exchange he was to send two shiploads of colonists each year and to bear, after nine years, the administrative costs of the colony. In the meantime he was to be allowed by the crown fifty thousand livres a year. He found the arrangement unworkable.

undertaking beyond the strength of any private individual: and whereas this undertaking would not become the King, on account of the commercial details which were its inseparable concomitant, it was resolved that Louisiana should be intrusted to the administration of a company." From this resolution sprang the creation of the Western Company, or Company of the Indies, whose charter of incorporation was registered by the parliament of Paris, on the 6th of September, 1717.

Thus the monopoly granted to Crozat ceased, merely to be transferred to a Company. The government of one ruler was to be succeeded by an oligarchy, and the worst of all, a commercial oligarchy, an association of cunning stockjobbers, or robbing directors, and of silly dupes in the shape of stockholders. There were not men wanting at the time who foresaw that the creation of the famous Company of the Indies, of which Law was the soul, and which became one of the most popular schemes that ever flourished in France, was destined to impart to the colonization of Louisiana only the short-lived appearance of galvanic vitality, but that, ending soon as all delusions do, it would, in its collapse and bursting, be fatal to the speculators engaged in the experiment, and be productive of the most mischievous results to France. Some of these readers of coming events attempted in vain to warn their fellow-citizens against the evils which they predicted. But the weak voice of individual reprobation was drowned in the loud acclamation of the multitude. When the current of the public mind runs impetuously in one direction, when was it ever checked? It sweeps furiously over such obstacles as wisdom or patriotism may interpose, and it even derives fresh impetus from the very attempt to arrest its course.

Who was John Law, to whom the use of the name of Louisiana was destined to give so much celebrity in the beginning of the 18th century?[11] In the romantic city of Edinburgh, the pride of Scotland, he was born in 1671. A checquered and a singularly varied life his was doomed to be, as checquered and varied as the changeful appearance of those ever-flitting clouds which chase each other through the fields of heaven, now assuming fantastic shapes, now dyed in splendor with the morning or evening rays of the sun, or black with the conception of coming storms. Gay halls and gloomy cells there are in the palace of Holyrood, within sight of which that obscure child was cradled, and of which the projecting battlements so often darkened with their shade his curling locks, as he indulged in the gambols of his age. When in his youth he strolled through that antiquated abode of departed royalty, and there gazed with mixed feelings of admiration and awe at the hoary relics of time, did any prophetic spirit shadow forth to

---

11. I have relied for recent knowledge about Law upon H. Montgomery Hyde, *John Law* (London, 1948), which—though partial to Law and unfootnoted—uses the most reliable scholarship, including French. Apart from Marcel Giraud, *Histoire de la Louisiane française: L'Époque de John Law (1717-1720)* (Paris, 1966), there seems to be nothing better available.

him the gay halls and gloomy cells of his future existence, when he should attain to manhood? The boy had in him the seeds of exalted talent and over-wrought passion—talent and passion!—Those unruly steeds upon which, when seated, man not unfrequently speeds away in a mad career, faster than he chooses, whither he heeds not or cares not, and oftener for his ruin than his good, if he does not check them with the reins of morality or the curb of religion.

John Law, or Jessamy Law, or Beau Law, as his playmates called him, for he was as handsome as a mother's heart could wish him, was the son of a goldsmith or banker. Did this circumstance have any influence on his future career, and did he inherit his passion for the precious metals and for banking operations? He was educated in Edinburgh, and he is said to have been no mean adept in versification, if not in poetry. But he soon intuitively discovered that a scribbler's lot was not very enviable, and following the natural bent of his genius, he became so remarkably proficient in mathematics that he could, with the greatest facility, solve the most difficult problems of that abstruse science. He also devoted his attention to the study of trade and manufactures, and made himself master of the principles of public and private credit. He minutely investigated the theory and practice of taxation, and all matters constituting the arcana of political economy. Such were the deep laid and solid foundations of his future eminence.

But John Law was a votary of pleasure as well as of study, and whenever he emerged from his closet, it was to attend the gambling-table, the racing-ground, and to indulge in convivial and amorous exploits. To some men, excitement of some sort or other is the very breath of life. It is the air which inflates and expands their intellectual lungs. Without it, the flow of their mind would stagnate. Such was John Law. An orphan at the age of fourteen, free from paternal control, and the heir to an ample fortune, he had within his reach all the means of vicious indulgence, and sadly did he avail himself of them to barter away the very altars of his household gods. In 1694,[12] goaded on by the desire of extending his sphere of enjoyments, he paid a visit to London, that great center of attraction, where his wit, his graces, his manly beauty, his numerous attainments, gained him admittance into the best society. There, however, his profusions of every sort, his love for deep play, and his gallantries soon rid him of his patrimonial lands of Lauriston and Randleston. Their broad acres were converted into guineas which melted away in the hands of prodigality, and thus, in early life, through his own folly, John Law stands before us a bankrupt![13]

12. Law went to London in 1691, not 1694.
13. Law was not declared a bankrupt in his London days.

That bankrupt was also an adulterer, and the acknowledged paramour of a Mrs. Lawrence. That intrigue brought him into collision with a Mr. Wilson, whom he killed in a duel. Tried for murder, he was found guilty, sentenced to death, and pardoned by the crown.[14] But an appeal was taken by a brother of the deceased, and the appeal was pending before the King's Bench, when Law, not deeming it prudent to await the result, escaped from his prison, and fled to the continent. Law was then twenty-three years of age. A bankrupt, an adulterer, a murderer, and an exiled outlaw! If to feel is to live, Law had thus gone through an intensity and variety of feelings, which, in the spring of youth, must have made his soul and mind as gray with age, as if over them a century had passed.

To Holland, Law retired for an asylum:—he could not have made a choice more congenial to his tastes, and no place in Europe could afford more facilities to his favorite investigations on trade, finances, public credit, and political economy, than that country, which, of all others, was peculiarly indebted to them for its national importance, and even for its existence. During his residence there, he took care to improve every opportunity to make himself thoroughly acquainted with the constitution and the practical operation of the Bank of Amsterdam.

John Law was not the man, even in a foreign country, to remain long without friends or protectors, and he soon contrived to ingratiate himself with the British Resident in Holland, of whom he became the secretary.[15] But the phlegmatic temperament of the Dutch not presenting him with the materials which he wished for the accomplishment of such schemes as were ripening in his brain, and having received the assurance that he had no longer any thing to fear on account of the death of Wilson, he returned to Edinburgh in 1700, and in the following year he published a pamphlet under this title: "Proposals and Reasons for establishing a Council of Trade."[16] The proverbial prudence of the Scotch received this work with coldness. Not discouraged by this failure, Law showed the remarkable aptitude which he had to possess himself of the favor of all those whom he thought proper to propitiate, and he gained the support of the Duke of Argyle, his sons, the Marquis of Lorn and Lord Archibald Campbell, the Marquis of Tweeddale, and other persons of rank and distinction.

14. Law was not pardoned, but reprieved. There is also some evidence that his escape, suspiciously easy, was abetted by the authorities.
15. The evidence that Law was Matthew Prior's secretary is unclear. Gayarré omits the travels that Law made to Switzerland, Genoa, and Venice.
16. Law went back to Britain in the winter of 1703–1704, not in 1700. Nor did he receive any assurance, other than that implicit in a return to Scotland and not England where he committed the offence; the two countries were still separate kingdoms, and his English conviction carried no force under Scottish law. Law did not publish the "Proposals and Reasons for Establishing a Council of Trade"; these were by William Paterson. Here, however, Gayarré was repeating a common error: the second edition of the "Proposals," printed in Glasgow in 1751, attributed the original anonymous pamphlet to Law.

Under this patronage, he presented to the Scottish parliament, in 1705, a plan for removing the difficulties under which the kingdom had then been suffering from the scarcity of money and from the stoppage of payments by the bank; and in illustration of his views on that subject, he gave publicity to another work, entitled "Money and Trade considered, with a proposal for supplying the nation with money." What could be more tempting! and what a pity that this grand projector did not live in this projecting age of ours! Like other men, he came too soon.

The proposal of Law, says one of his biographers, was that commissioners, to be appointed by an act, under the control of parliament, should be empowered to issue notes, either in the way of loan, at ordinary interest, upon landed security, provided the debt should not exceed half, or at the most, two thirds of the value of the lands, or upon land pledges, redeemable within a certain period, to the full value of the land:—or, lastly, upon sale irredeemably to the amount of the price agreed upon. Paper money thus issued, would, he conceived, be equal in value to gold and silver coin of the same denomination, and might even be preferred to the metals, as not being like them liable to fall in value. But this scheme, though powerfully supported by the court party, and by the influence of such men as the Duke of Argyle and others, was rejected by the parliament on the ground that, "to establish any kind of paper credit, so as to oblige it to pass, was an improper expedient for the nation." Wise Scotchmen! They also apprehended that if Law's plan were adopted, all the estates of the kingdom would thereby be brought to a complete dependence upon the bank, or collaterally upon the government, the bank itself being dependent upon the government. It is remarkable that more than a century after, in 1827 and 1833, Law's plan, or one very similar, was put into operation in Louisiana, under the titles of "The Citizens' Bank" and "The Consolidated Association of the Planters of Louisiana," and that it produced the same disastrous effects that were anticipated by the Scotch in 1705.

It soon became evident to Law that his countrymen and the English were not sufficiently imaginative to allow him to tempt them into his gigantic experiments, and that to better his fortune, it was necessary that he should seek elsewhere for more pliable instruments.[17] Accordingly he returned to the continent, whither let us follow him, as he flits, like an ignis fatuus, from place to place. Now we see him a man of fashion in Brussels, where his constant success at play brought him into unfavorable notoriety. Then he dashes into the vortex of Paris, where it is said that he introduced the game called Faro, and became still more conspicuous than

17. It seems the most compelling reason for Law's departure was the impending Act of Union, which threatened the jurisdiction of English law. A desire for advancement may also have been a motive, of course.

at Brussels by his enormous gains at the gaming-table. His graceful person, the charms of his conversation, his insinuating manners, were rapidly favoring his ascent into the highest regions of society, when D'Argenson, the Lieutenant or Minister of Police, thought proper to cut short his brilliant career, and to order him out of the kingdom, with this pithy observation, "That Scot is *too expert* at the game which he has introduced."[18]

He retired to Geneva, where he gave an extraordinary proof of his power of extracting money from the dryest sources, by gaining large sums at the expense of the sober-minded and close-fisted citizens of that puritanic little commonwealth. In Genoa and in Venice, he gave such evidence of his invariable luck at play, that the magistrates of these two cities deemed it their duty to interfere for the protection of their fellow-citizens, and to banish Law from these over-exhausted theaters of his exploits. At Florence, he became acquainted with the Duke of Vendôme, whom he favored with the loan of a large sum of money. At Neufchatel, he obtained access to the Prince of Conti, to whom, as to the Duke of Vendôme, he imparted his financial schemes. He was thus skillfully securing protection for the introduction of his plans into France, on the first favorable opportunity. For several years Law rambled over Europe, proposing his financial systems everywhere and to every body. During a short residence at Turin, he pressed the subject on the King of Sardinia, Victor Amadeus—but that prudent sovereign answered: "I am not rich enough to afford being ruined. France is the proper field where your speculative genius ought to cast its seeds, and where you will reap rich harvests. I am sure that your schemes will be to the taste of my mercurial neighbors. To them, therefore, I would advise you to repair."[19]

This advice seemed to Law a sensible one, and acting under it, he returned to Paris with the enormous sum of two millions and five hundred thousand francs, which were the result of his success in gaming, and of his speculations in stocks and public funds.[20] Soon after his arrival Louis the XIVth died, which was a circumstance favorable to his pretensions. He had no longer to deal only with the prudent Desmarets, comptroller-general of the finances of the state, whose wisdom had discarded the tempting propositions of that adventurer in 1708. But now, in 1716, when the Duke of Orleans, as Regent of France, found himself at the head of the government, the financial situation of France had become desperate. The public debt was immense: it was a legacy bequeathed by the military glory of Louis the XIVth, and the other pompous vanities of his long reign. The

---

18. It is inference that D'Argenson was responsible for Law's expulsion; the quotation is invented.

19. This quotation is invented and improbable.

20. Law did not go straight from Turin to Paris, but spent a year in the Hague between 1712 and 1713.

Rise and Fall of John Law 289

consequence was that the load of taxation was overwhelming, merely to pay the interest of this debt, without any hope of diminishing the capital. All the sources of industry were dried up: the very winds which wafted the barks of commerce seemed to have died away under the pressure of the time: trade stood still: the manufactures were struck with palsy: the merchant, the trader, the artificer, once flourishing in affluence, were now transformed into clamorous beggars, and those who could yet command some small means, were preparing to emigrate to foreign parts. The lifeblood that animated the kingdom was stagnating in all its arteries: and the danger of an awful crisis became such, that it was actually proposed in the Council of State to expunge the public debt by an act of national bankruptcy. But the Regent has the credit of having rejected the proposition; and a commission was appointed to inquire into the financial situation of the kingdom, and to prepare a remedy for the evil.

It was at that time, when the wisest heads in France were not able to see their way through the embarrassments of the treasury, that John Law came forward with his panacea. It was to liquidate the debt of the state, to increase its revenue, to diminish taxation: and all these prodigies were to be suddenly produced by the easiest process in the world—the creation of a bank, by which fictitious capital, quite as good as any real one, would be produced at will. The Regent, who was incessantly in want of money, and whose ardent imagination was always easily captivated by every daring and extraordinary conception, eagerly jumped at the conclusions presented by Law, or L'as, as he was called by the French.[21] He became even a favorite of that prince, and was admitted into all the licentious privacies of the *Palais Royal*.[22] Soon after, in May, 1716, in spite of the opposition made by all the financiers of the kingdom, Law obtained letters patent, not, it is true, complying with all his magnificent schemes, but establishing on a very limited scale, the bank of which he was the originator, and which was to bear his name, with a capital of six millions of livres, divided into shares of five hundred livres. It was to be a private undertaking, and intended by the government as an experiment.

This institution met with so much success, and became so popular, that in April, 1717, the Council of State assumed the responsibility of ordering that its notes be received as specie by the royal treasury, in all its branches. The influence of Law on the Regent was daily on the increase, and it was he who prevailed on that prince to purchase for the king the celebrated diamond, which, from that circumstance, was called the *Regent*,

---

21. Orleans was far from as eager as Gayarré suggests, and first turned down Law's scheme. Nor was the Regent ignorant of economics; indeed, Law claimed the Regent to be the only other man in France to understand the project.
22. While there is no doubt of the Regent's indefatigable and ingenious profligacy, there is little evidence that Law was involved and much to counter the suggestion.

and which is still the property of republican France, and a part of its public domain.[23] It was a curiosity then thought to be unique of its kind; and the Regent, although strongly tempted, had long hesitated to invest millions in such an unproductive manner, when tbe revenue of the kingdom was far below its expenses. But Law removed his scruples, by persuading him that he had the means not only of remedying the necessities of France, but of making her richer than she had ever been.

Law now began to develop the stupendous projects he had so long meditated. The success of his private bank had gained him so much credit, that the Regent was induced to change its character, and to make it a royal institution. Law's bank was abolished in December, 1718, to give way to the Royal Bank, of which Law was named the director-general. From that fruitful parent trunk, sprung branches which were established at Lyons, Tours, La Rochelle, Orleans, and Amiens.

It will be remembered that, as before stated, the charter of the Mississippi Company had been registered by the parliament of Paris on the 6th of September, 1717. The capital of the company was one hundred millions of livres, to be furnished by stockholders, and to be divided into shares of five hundred livres. Aliens were permitted to become members of the company, and their shares were exempted from the *"droit d'aubaine,"* and from confiscation in case of war. The "droit d'aubaine" is the right which the king had to inherit all the property which an alien left at his death. To entice subscribers, their shares were made payable in a depreciated paper currency, called *"billets* d'état," or state bonds, which, however, in the hands of subscribers, were taken at par or full value, although their depreciation amounted to between sixty and seventy per cent. This was such a tempting bait, that it was greedily gulped down by the public, and the subscription was soon more than filled up.[24] By this operation of taking the depreciated paper currency of the state in payment of subscriptions, the company became the creditor of the state for a sum of one hundred millions of livres, on which interest was to be paid at the rate of four per cent.

The following were the principal articles of the company's charter:—

It had the exclusive privilege of trading with Louisiana during twenty-five years, and also the monopoly of the beaver trade with Canada, it being understood that the king reserved to himself the right of determining the number of skins that the company should be bound to purchase annually from the Canadians, at the price fixed by the government of his Majesty.

The company was authorized to make treaties with the Indians, and

23. This is a half-truth. Law did go to the Regent to suggest buying the diamond, but Orleans turned down the idea. It was Saint-Simon, after discussing the matter with Law, who prevailed upon the Regent. Gayarré certainly knew this, since Saint-Simon's memoirs are the source for this story.

24. The first floating of the shares was slowly subscribed, and they quoted at below par for nearly two years.

to wage war against them in cases of necessity. It had taken care to secure the absolute owernship of all the mines which it could discover and work, and it is needless to say that much reliance was placed on this article of the charter.

The faculty was given to the company of making grants of land, of levying troops, of raising fortifications, of appointing the governors of the colony and the other officers commanding the troops, provided they should, on presentation, be accepted and commissioned by the king. The right of recalling or altering these appointments was also reserved to the company.

To build ships of war and cast cannon, to appoint and remove judges and officers of justice, except those of the Superior Council, was one of the numerous powers granted to this mighty company.

Military officers in Louisiana and all others in the French service were allowed, with the king's license, to enlist in the pay of the company. While in that service, their respective grades in the navies or land forces of the realm were to be retained, and they had the gracious promise of the king that whatever service they might render to the company would be acknowledged as rendered to himself.

By the consular jurisdiction of the city of Paris, all civil suits to which the company might be a party, were to be determined; with a right of appeal, in cases above a certain amount, to the parliament of Paris.

The company was prohibited from employing other than French vessels and crews in trading with Louisiana, and all goods found on the company's vessels were to be presumed its property, unless the contrary was proved.

Frenchmen, removing to Louisiana, were to preserve their national character, and their children, born there, were to be considered as the natural born subjects of the king. The same privilege was granted to the children of all other European settlers in Louisiana, provided they professed the Roman Catholic religion. To encourage emigration, it was stipulated that during the continuance of the company's charter, the inhabitants of Louisiana were to be exempted from the payment of any tax, duty, or imposition whatever.

To promote the building of vessels in Louisiana, where it was reported that the most magnificent timber existed in its boundless forests, a bounty was to be awarded for every vessel there built, on its arrival in France.

In anticipation of wars with the Indians, it was agreed that forty thousand pounds of powder were to be delivered annually to the company, out of the royal magazines, at the rate of the manufacturing cost.

The stockholders were to have a vote for every fifty shares. During the two first years, the affairs of the company were to be conducted by directors appointed by the king, and afterward, by others, elected triennially by the stockholders.

In order to minister to the religious wants of the colonists, the obligation was laid upon the company to build churches and to provide for a sufficient number of clergymen. It was understood that Louisiana was to remain part of the diocess of Quebec, under whose spiritual authority it has always been since it had been settled by the French.

The company obliged itself to transport to Louisiana, before the expiration of its charter, six thousand white persons and three thousand negroes: but it was stipulated that these persons should not be brought from another French colony, without the consent of the governor of that colony.

In consideration of the charges assumed by the company, its goods were to be exempted from the payment of any duty, and the king promised not to grant any letters of dispensation or respite to any debtor of the company. He also gave the company the solemn assurance of his effectual protection against any foreign nation.

If the company, as it is seen, took special care to keep its debtors irredeemably within its reach, it was no less solicitous to withdraw itself, as much as possible, from the grasp of any one of the creditors of its stockholders, and it had a clause inserted in its charter, by which the effects, shares, and profits of the stockholders could not be seized and sold either in the hands of its cashier, its clerks, or agents, except it be in cases of open and declared bankruptcy, or on account of the death of the party.

All the lands, coasts, harbors, and islands in the colony of Louisiana were granted to the company, as they were to Crozat, on condition of its taking the customary oath of faith and homage, as practiced in such cases, and of furnishing to every King of France, on his accession to the throne, a crown of gold, of the weight of thirty marks.

Thus Louisiana was constituted into a sort of commercial fief, and the Mississippi Company rose almost to the dignity of those great feudatory vassals who, in the days of old, had been, alternately, the pride, the support, and the curse of France. It did not spring into existence, it is true, in the shape of a Duke of Burgundy, who, backed by one hundred thousand men, could, if he pleased, set at defiance his liege Lord, and could proudly enter through the battered walls of Paris, with crested helmet on his head, and the trucheon of command in his hand. But it was perhaps a being more powerful and more dangerous—it was a company—an incorporeal conglomeration, an unfathomable, uncontrollable, unaccountable creation—an agent with such divided responsibility that it amounted to nothing, and, as Lord Coke says of corporations—a thing without a soul, to which, nevertheless, a power more efficacious and more fearful than that exercised over armed men was delegated—the power of controlling commerce!

Law was appointed director-general of the Mississippi Company, as he had been of the Royal Bank, and both institutions were merged into one another. That would have been power enough to satisfy a less craving ambition, but Law was not the man to stop short in his career of aggrandizement. Thus, he soon obtained that the farm of tobacco, that is the exclusive privilege of selling this favorite weed, be made over to the company by the government, at an advance of rent exceeding two millions of livres. This was a pretty rich feather in his cap, but it was not enough; and stepping from one acquisition to another, he immediately afterward procured for the company of which he had the absolute control, the grant of the charter and effects of the Senegal Company. It was piling up Pelion upon Ossa, and the world stood aghast with astonishment at the extent of the concessions made by the French government to a foreign adventurer. A Royal Bank, the Tobacco farm, the Mississippi Company, and the Senegal Company, with all their millions, rights, privileges, effects and powers, all combined into a gigantic unity!—and that unity put as an instrument into the hands of another unity in the shape of a man! This was something curious to look at and to study in its operations.

Wise people thought that the climax of folly had been reached; but John Law laughed in his sleeve at their inexperience, or their ignorance of his skill, and before they had breathing time to recover from their surprise, he gave another proof of his wonderful legerdemain, by purloining from the French government a still more extraordinary grant than the preceding ones:—which was the exclusive privilege of trading to the East Indies, China and the South Seas, together with all the possessions and effects of the China and India Companies, now dissolved, upon condition of liquidating all just claims upon them. It was then that the Company of the West, or Mississippi Company, dropped its original name to take up that of the Company of the Indies, with the privilege of creating additional shares to the amount of twenty-five millions, payable in coin.

This, it seems, ought to have been enough to satiate the most inordinate appetite. Not so with John Law. On the 25th of July, 1719, the mint was made over to the already overgrown Company of the Indies, that huge financial Polyphemus, which owed its existence to the great Scotch projector. This other concession was made for a consideration of fifty millions of livres, to be paid to the king within fifteen months. This time, it might have been permitted to believe that the digestive organs of this boa constrictor, of this king of speculators, were more than overgorged with the accumulation of superabundant nutrition, with which they had been so lavishly favored. But John Law asked for something more! Was he shut up in a lunatic asylum for his mad presumption? No!—he obtained what he begged. Will not the dullest mind be stimulated into curiosity, and will not the quick inquiry be: What more could John Law presume to grasp? This:—on the 27th of August, 1719, he obtained for his progeny, the prodigious Company of the Indies, the great farms of the revenues of the kingdom, which the Regent took out of the hands of the farmers general and gave to the company, in consideration of its paying an advance of rent of three millions and a half of livres: and on the 31st of the same month, to cap the climax of all these almost supernatural wonders, Law obtained again for the same company the general receipt or collection of all the other branches of the king's revenues.

Through this curious process of complex annexation and assimilation, John Law had succeeded in erecting the most stupendous financial fabric that has ever been presented to the world. In one company, and through it, in one man, was vested nothing less than the whole privileges, effects and possessions of the foreign trade companies of France, the great farms of the kingdom, the mint, the general receipt of the king's revenues, and the management and property of a royal bank, with an immense capital! Thus, one man, an obscure foreign adventurer, through his creature, the company, had condensed into one lump, which his hands encircled, all the trade, taxes, and revenues of one of the most powerful kingdoms of Europe, and through the Royal Bank, he might, according to his will, increase to any amount the circulating medium of that country! Does not this strictly historical sketch smack of the wild conception of a delirious mind? Is not truth often more incredible than fiction, and in reading these lines, would not misanthropy be tempted to exclaim: "Hail to thee, mischievous sorcerer! Three times hail to thee, John Law!"[25]—while poetical fancy would be permitted to inquire if the Weird Sisters, the foul witches of his native heaths, had not furnished him with the spell, under the influence of which so many millions of his fellow-beings had been touched with insanity.

It is not astonishing that on the showering of so many grants on the company, its shares gradually rose from 500 to 1000, to 5000 and to 10,000 livres, which was more than sixty times the sum they were originally sold for, if the depreciation of the *"billets d'etat,"* or state bonds, with which they were paid, be taken into account. The desire to become stockholder in a company which promised to realize the fable of the hen with golden eggs, was fevered into frenzy. There was a general rush of greedy subscribers, far exceeding the number wanted, and in their struggles to be ranked among the privileged ones whose claims were to be admitted, the greatest interest was exerted, and every stratagem put in practice.

At the same time, the press was teeming with publications on the Mississippi, or the Colony of Louisiana, and France was flooded with pamphlets describing that newly-discovered country, and the advantages which it offered to emigrants. The luxuriant imagination of prolific writers was taxed, to clothe Louisiana with all the perfections they could invent. It was more than the old Eden, so long lost to mankind. There, the pictur-

---

25. Adapted from *Macbeth*, I.iii.48.

esque was happily blended with the fertile, and abundance smiled on rocky mountains as on the alluvial plains of the valleys. The climate was such that all the vegetable productions of the globe existed, or could be introduced with success in that favored land. To scratch the soil, would call forth the spontaneous growth of the richest harvests of every kind. All the fruits ever known, were to be gathered in profusion from the forests, all the year round, and the most luscious peaches, pears, apples, and other like nutritious delicacies, dropping from their parent boughs, were piled up in heaps under cool shades and on the velvet banks of bubbling streams. There, dust and mud were equally excluded, as the ground was lined in all seasons with a thick carpet of flowers, endless in variety, and perfuming the air with their sweet breath. The finest breed of all domestic or useful animals was there to be found in all the primitive vigor and gentleness of their antediluvian perfection. The poor peasant who, during a long life in France, had never dreamed of eating meat, would there feed on nothing less than wild ducks, venison, pheasants, snipes and woodcocks. The birds kept up a never-ceasing concert, which would have shamed the opera singing of Paris. The rivers and lakes were stocked with fish, so abundant that they would suffice to nourish millions of men, and so delicate that no king ever had any such on his table.

The seasons were so slightly marked that the country might be said to be blessed with a perpetual spring. None but gentle winds fluttered over in their gamboling flight through boundless prairies and forests, they produced the effect of Eolian harps, lulling enchanted nature to sleep with heavenly music. The sky was brighter, the sun more gorgeous, the moon more chastely serene and pure, and the nights more lovely than anywhere else. Heaven itself seemed to bend down upon earth in conjugal dalliance, and to environ it with circumambient love. There, it is true, it could not be said to have been positively ascertained that the fountain of eternal youth had been discovered, but it was beyond doubt that there was in the atmosphere a peculiar element which preserved from putrefaction;—and the human body, being impregnated with it, was so little worn out by the action of its organs, that it could keep itself in existence almost indefinitely; and the Indians were known to retain the appearance of youth even after having attained five or six hundred years. Those very Indians had conceived such an attachment for the white men, whom they considered as gods, that they would not allow them to labor, and insisted on performing themselves all the work that might be necessary for the comfort of their pale-faced brethren. It was profanation in their eye not to minister to all the wants of their idolized guests.

More enticing than all that, was the pretended discovery of inexhaustible mines of gold and silver, which, however, it would not be necessary to work by the usual tedious process, because the whole surface of the country was strewed with lumps of gold, and when the waters of the lakes and rivers were filtered, particularly the thick water of the Mississippi, it yielded an invaluable deposit of gold. As to silver, it was so common that it would become of no value, and would have to be used in the shape of square stones, to pave the public roads. The fields were covered with an indigenous plant which was gifted with the most singular property. The dew which gathered within the perfumed cups of its flowers, would, in the course of a single night, be converted into a solid diamond: and the soft texture of the flowers bursting open and dropping down under the weight of its contents, would leave the precious gems ticking on the stem in unrobed splendor, and reflecting back the rays of the morning sun. What is written on California in our days would appear tame when compared to the publications on Louisiana in 1719: and the far-famed and extravagant description of the banks of the Mississippi given at a later period by Chateaubriand, would, at the time I speak of, have been hooted at, as doing injustice to the merits of the new possession France had acquired.

When the extreme gullibility of mankind, as demonstrated by the occurrence of every day, is taken into consideration, what I here relate will not appear exaggerated or incredible. Be it as it may, these descriptions were believed in France, and from the towering palace to the humblest shed in the kingdom, nothing else was talked of but Louisiana and its wonders. The national debt was to be paid instantaneously with the Louisiana gold, France was to purchase or to conquer the rest of the world, and every Frenchman was to be a wealthy lord. There never had been a word invested with such magical charms as the name of Louisiana. It produced delirium in every brain: the Louisiana every one wished to go, as now to California, and some of the most unimproved parts of that colony were actually sold for 30,000 livres the square league, which, considering the difference in value in metallic currency between that time and the present, makes that sum almost equal to twenty thousand dollars, worth of our money in our days!

Who could describe with sufficient graphic fidelity the intense avidity with which the shares of the Company of the Indies were hunted up? All ranks were seized with the same frantic infatuation. To be a stockholder was to be reputed rich, and the poorest beggar, when he exhibited the proof that by some windfall or other, he had become the owner of one single share, rose at once to the importance of a wealthy man, and could command the largest credit. There was a general struggle to raise money, for the purpose of speculating in the stocks of the marvelous company which was to convert every thing it touched into gold. Every kind of property was offered for sale, and made payable in stocks. Castellated domains which had been for centuries the proudly cherished possessions of the same families were bartered away for a mess of financial porridge, and more than one representative of a knightly house doffed off the warm lining that had been bequeathed to him by his ancestors, to dress himself, like a bedlamite, in the worthless rags of unsubstantial paper. Such rapid mutations in real estate the world had never seen before! Lands, palaces, edifices of every sort, were rapidly shifted from hand to hand, like balls in a tennis-court. It was truly a curious sight to behold a whole chivalrous nation turned into a confused multitude of swindling, brawling, clamorous, frantic stock-jobbers. Holy cardinals, archbishops, bishops, with but too many of their clergy, forgetting their sacred character, were seen to launch their barks on the dead sea of perdition to which they were tempted, and eagerly to throw the fisherman's net into those troubled waters of speculation which were lashed into fury by the demon of avarice. Princes of the royal blood became hawkers of stocks: haughty peers of the realm rushed on the Rialto, and Shylock-like, exulted in bartering and trafficking in bonds. Statesmen, magistrates, warriors, assuming the functions of pedlers, were seen wandering about the streets and public places, offering to buy and to sell stocks, shares, or actions. Nothing else was talked of; the former usual topics of conversation stood still. Not only women, but ladies of the highest rank forgot the occupations of their sex, to rush into the vortex of speculation, and but too many among them sold every thing, not excepting their honor, to become stockholders.

The company having promised an annual dividend of 200 livres on every share of 500 livres, which, it must be remembered, had been originally paid for in depreciated *billets d'état*, or state bonds, making the interest to be received on every share still more enormous, the delirium soon culminated to its highest point. Every thing foreign to the great Mississippi scheme was completely forgotten. The people seemed to have but one pursuit, but one object in life: mechanics dropped their tools, tradesmen closed their shops; there was but one profession, one employment, one occupation, for persons of all ranks—that of speculating in stocks: and the most moderate, the few who abstained from joining in the wild-goose chase, were so intensely absorbed by the contemplation of the spectacle which was offered to their bewildered gaze, that they took no concern in any thing else. Quincampoix Street, where the offices of the company were kept, was literally blocked up by the crowd which the fury of speculation and the passion for sudden wealth attracted to that spot, and persons were frequently crushed or stifled to death. "Mississippi!—Who wants any Mississippi?"—was bawled out in every lane and by-lane, and every nook and corner of Paris echoed with the word, "Mississippi!"

Immense fortunes were lost or acquired in a few weeks. By stock-jobbing, obscure individuals were suddenly raised from the sewers of poverty to the gilded rooms of princely splendor. Most amusing anecdotes might be told of persons thus stumbling by chance into affluence; and heart-rending stories might be related of such as, from the possession of every luxury, were precipitated into the depths of absolute destitution; while those who had become spontaneously rich, being made giddy with their unexpected acquisitions, launched into such profusions and follies that their return to poverty was as rapid as their accession to wealth, through which it might be said they had only passed with the velocity of steam locomotion. He who could write in all its details the history of that Mississippi bubble, so fatal in its short-lived duration, would give to the world the most instructive composition, made up of the most amusing, ludicrous, monstrous and horrible elements that were ever jumbled together.

The distribution of property underwent more than one grotesque change. The tenants of the parlor or saloon went up to the garret, and the natives of the garret tumbled down into the saloon. Footmen changed places with their masters, and the outside of carriages happened to become the inside. Law's coachman made such a large fortune that he set up an equipage of his own. Cookmaids and waiting-women appeared at the opera, bedizened in finery like the Queen of Sheba. A baker's son, who used to carry his father's loaves in a basket to his customers, was, by a sudden turn of the wheel of fortune, enabled to purchase plate to the amount of four hundred thousand livres, which he sent to his wife, with the recommendation of having it properly set out for supper, and with the strict injunction of putting in the largest and finest dish his favorite stew of onions and hog's feet. The Marquis d'Oyse, of the family of the Dukes of Villars Brancas, signed a contract of marriage, although he was at the time thirty-three years of age, with the daughter, three years old, of a man named André, who had won millions at the Mississippi lottery. The conditions of the marriage were, that it should take place when the girl should reach her twelfth year, and that, in the mean time, the marquis was to receive three hundred thousand livres every year until the day of the wedding, when several millions would be paid to the husband by the father of the bride. All these meteors, who were thus blazing in their newly-acquired splendor, were called "Mississippians," on account of the source of their fortune.

Let us now turn from the system, to its inventor—to John Law, who, under such circumstances operating in his favor, was adored by the people; and as usual, they were few indeed who refrained from worshiping the idol of the hour, and from burning incense at his shrine. He was a favorite with the Duke of Orleans, Regent of France, of whom he was known to possess the ear; and on his abjuring in the hands of Abbé Tencin, since a cardinal, the Protestant religion, which was the only obstacle to his advancement to the highest offices of the state, he was appointed, on the 5th of January, 1720, comptroller-general of the finances of the kingdom. To so eminent a personage, England sent, of course, a free and absolute pardon for the murder of Wilson; and Edinburgh, proud of having given him birth, tendered him the freedom of the city in a gold box.[26] Poets, tuning their lyres to sing his apotheosis, declared him to be the Magnus Apollo of the age, and the Academy of Sciences elected him one of its honorary members. It is impossible not to pay a tribute of admiration to the talents of that lowborn adventurer, who, in less than four years, by his own unassisted exertions, and even in despite of the most strenuous opposition from formidable adversaries, rose from a suspicious position in private life, to be one of the ministers of one of the most powerful and enlightened nations of the world. The Duke of St. Simon, who knew him well, and who writes of him with partiality in his celebrated memoirs, says, that Law had a strong Scotch accent, but that although there was much English in his French, he was extremely persuasive, and that he had the peculiar tact, by assuming an air of exquisite candor, frankness, straightness, and modest diffidence, to throw off their guard those he wished to seduce. With prodigious powers of insinuation and persuasion he must indeed have been gifted, to have operated all the wonders we have seen!

Law, who had the pretension of enriching every body, did not, as it is very natural to suppose, forget his own pecuniary interest, and had purchased no less than fourteen of the most magnificent estates of France with titles annexed to them, and among which was the Marquisate of Rosny; that domain had been owned, and its splendid castle had been occupied as a favorite residence by the illustrious friend and minister of Henry the IVth, the great Sully, who, before he was created duke of that name, had borne the title of Marquis of Rosny. But Law had attained his highest degree of prosperity, and the wind was already blowing which was to prostrate him to the ground from his towering altitude.

The year 1720, which saw him at the zenith of his prosperity, witnessed also his rapid declension, and his ultimate fall into the abyss of adversity, where he was forever lost. But how dazzling his position was on the 5th day of that year, 1720, when he was appointed comptroller-general of the finances of the kingdom! At that time, he was literally besieged in his splendid palace by a host of applicants and supplicants of every description. His friendship was courted with cringing eagerness by princes, dukes, peers of the realm, marshals and prelates, who reverentially bowed, and bent a supple knee to the upstart, in the mean hope of securing his patronage. Nobles crowded his anti-chambers in democratic conjunction with a motley crew of people of every hue and feather. It was thought to be a lucky accident or a high honor to attract even his passing notice, and ladies

---

26. George I sent no such pardon, although he did, remarkably to a convicted felon, offer the Garter and a dukedom, both of which were declined. Law did not get a pardon until, after his expulsion from France, he went to England in 1721.

of the most exalted rank were not ashamed to ply meretricious smiles to win his favor.

With no very great stretch of the imagination,[27] we may easily conceive the occurrence of such a scene as the following: far from the bustle of the street, and from the crowd which encumbers his apartments of reception, in a retired but richly and tastefully decorated room of his princely residence, John Law is taking his luncheon in the sole company of his son, his daughter, and his pretended wife, who, says the Duke of Saint Simon, was a high-born English lady. Enamored of Law, she had left her family and dignified position in society, to follow him. She was very haughty, and the superciliousness of her manners was such, that it frequently became impertinent. She rarely paid visits except to the chosen few: she received homage as her due, paid none, and exercised in her house a despotic authority. Her well-shaped person looked noble, and she would have been thought handsome, if a horrid stain of the color of red wine had not covered half of her face and one eye. It is well known that Law always treated her with the utmost respect and tenderness.

Sitting in front of her at a table adorned with exquisitely carved gold and silver implements, Law seemed to be enjoying with peculiar relish the quiet atmosphere of his family circle. Now and then his confidential groom of the bed-chamber glided in, and whispered into his ear the arrival of some distinguished personage who had come to swell the retinue that filled his apartments, and anxiously expected his appearance. At each announcement of a high-sounding name, of a duke, a marshal, a great dignitary of the church, a smile of triumph would flit across his face, and he would cast a look of exultation at his wife, whose natural pride appeared to be intensely alive to the enjoyment which was administered to it by her husband. But Law, keeping his self-composure, would answer, with the utmost unconcern, and without hurrying his meal, whenever a new name was brought in to him: "Well! well! let him wait!" On a sudden, the servant entered again, but not with the same measured step, and cried out with a voice which emotion raised far beyond its usual key: "My lord, his highness the Prince of Conti." Law jumped up as if the irresistible action of a spring in his seat had forced him into his erect attitude, his face became flushed, and his limbs trembled. "Ha!" exclaimed he, "a prince of the royal blood under my roof!" But a thought flashed through his brain, he knit his brows, compressed his lips, looked at his wife with an expression of intense pride, and resuming his chair, composedly turned to his servant, and with the same tone of voice with which he had answered every other call, he said: "Let him wait." Here is something to moralize upon, if moralizing was not so flat, stale and unprofitable. A Bourbon, the descendant of a long line of

27. The next few pages are, of course, fantasy and owned as such.

kings, to be kept waiting in the ante-chambers of the son of a Scotch goldsmith! A prince of the royal blood of France to dance attendance on a low adventurer, an exiled outlaw, who had successively and collectively been called the gambler, the swindler, the profligate, the bankrupt, the adulterer, the murderer, the apostate. O the power of gold! Can we not divine the feeling that made Law's blood thrill with excitement! Ours must be one of unmitigated contempt.

Now the scene has shifted, and John Law is rusticating at his castle of Rosny, the once proud seat of Sully, in Normandy. Reclining in a gothic, richly carved chair, with a high back still retaining, chiseled in its oak, the coat-of-arms of Sully, and tapering into a point surmounted by a ducal crown,—in the very chair of state of that haughty feudal baron, and with his feet resting on the lower and more modest chair of the Duchess of Sully, for in those days Sully's wife would not have dared to occupy a seat of equal dignity with that of her lord,—our great financier, John Law, before indulging in his nightly repose, is reckoning up in his mind his acquired wealth, and building up calculations still to increase its already enormous bulk. It is midnight—and the solemn hour of twelve strikes at the big tower's clock! Hist!—a slow, solemn step is heard—it comes from the stair running up the turret which opens into Law's room. What can it be? The light burns blue on his table:—Law's soul is suddenly awed with the consciousness that an unnatural atmosphere is gathering round him. His hair stands erect: a cold chill shoots through his body, and his eyes involuntarily turn to that iron door which the strange visitor is gradually approaching. Oh, wonder! There is no using of the key—no unbarring—and yet the door grates on its rusty hinges—and opens wide. God! can it be true?—can such things be?

It is Sully himself, with his so well-known stern face, and with the same antiquated dress in which he was clad, when in the latter part of his life, being summoned from his retirement to the court of Louis the XIIIth, to give advice on matters of importance, and his unfashionable appearance having provoked a laugh from those butterfly courtiers who surrounded the young king, he frowned them down with an air of inexpressible majesty and contempt, and then, looking at the crowned son of his old friend, Henry the IVth:—"Sire," said he, "whenever the king, your respected father, sent for me, he used to dismiss from his presence all the buffoons, masqueraders and jackanapes of the palace."—It is the same Sully, to whom the king having exhibited a paper which, to the disgrace of royalty, he had signed in a moment of weakness, seized it, tore it to pieces, and on the king having exclaimed: "Are you mad, Sully!" answered, "Would to God that I were the only madman in your kingdom!"—It is he, whose sense of his feudal and personal dignity was such, that he never would descend to his terraced garden, even to indulge in an early morning walk, without having before and behind him a file of halberdiers escorting him in state. A bold man John Law was. But when this apparition met his sight, drops of cold sweat pearled down his forehead, his voice stuck in his throat, and terror fettered him to his seat, as if his limbs had been bound with chains of adamant. Indeed, a stouter heart than his would have been frozen by the gaze which Sully bent upon him, a gaze in which were so vividly expressed intense, indignant surprise at the witnessed profanation, and the scowling threat of condign punishment. Ay, a bolder man than John Law would have sunk to the ground when, with rapid strides, Sully advanced toward him, and lifting up the hunting whip which his hand tightly grasped, exclaimed, "Dog of a stock-jobber! vile Scotch hound, darest thou pollute—" A shriek!—a fearful shriek was heard—and John Law shook off his agonizing dream. Yea—it was only a dream. But some dreams are prophetic.

It must not be supposed that Law had carried on all his projects so far, without encountering incessant opposition. Among his adversaries the parliament of Paris had been the most redoubtable, and that powerful body had been always on the watch to seize a favorable opportunity to crush Law and his system. That opportunity was soon to present itself. Undermined by the intrigues of his other colleagues in the ministry, carried away by the innate imperfections of his system farther than he had intended, terrified at the mighty evolutions of the tremendous engine he had set at work, and could no longer control or stop, the victim of a combination of envy, apprehension, ignorance and avarice, which interfered with his designs, and made him pay too dear for protection or assistance, Law felt that the moment of his fall was approaching, and saw with terror the threatening oscillations of the overgrown fabric he had reared. He tried to conceal his embarrassments by inducing the company to declare that they had such a command of funds as to be able to propose lending any sum on proper security at two per cent. But in vain did they put on this show of confidence in their own resources:—the smiling mask deceived nobody. There were symptoms which too plainly denoted approaching dissolution and death. Among those dark spots was the number of bank notes which had been manufactured, and which, on the 1st of May, 1720, exceeded 2600 millions of livres, while the whole specie in the kingdom amounted only to 1300 millions.

Then happened what has been frequently seen since: the superabundance of paper money produced a scarcity of specie. It became evident to the most obtuse that those bank notes had no representative, and that sooner or later they would be no more than worthless rags. As soon as that discovery was made, every one hastened to convert his shares or bank notes into gold or silver, and to realize the fortune he had acquired. The most keen-sighted, or the most prudent, not only exchanged their notes for specie, but sent it out of France; and it is calculated that in this way the kingdom was drained of 500 millions of livres. To avert the danger with which his system was threatened, Law, in less than eight months, promulgated thirty-three edicts to fix the value of gold and silver, to preserve and to increase the metallic circulation, and to limit the amount of gold and silver which might be converted into plate and jewelry. No payment in specie could be made except for small sums: the standard of coin was kept in the most bewildering state of fluctuation, while the value of bank notes was decreed to be invariable. Rents, taxes, and customs, were made payable in paper only:—and as a climax to these high-handed measures, individuals as well as secular or religious communities were prohibited, under very severe penalties, from having in their possession more than 500 livres in specie. This ordinance established the most intolerable inquisition, and gave rise to the most vexatious researches on the part of the police. The house of no citizen was free from the visits of the agents of power, and every man trembled to see denunciation lurking by his fireside, and to harbor treason by the very altars of his household gods.

The alarm of the public mind became such, that it was thought necessary to equalize the proportion between the bank notes and the coin; and on the 21st of May, 1720, an edict was issued, which, in violation of the pledge of the state, and of the most solemn stipulations, and as a beginning of bankruptcy, reduced the value of the company's bank notes to one half, and cut down the shares from 10,000, and even 20,000, which was their highest ascent, to 5000 livres. The effect of this edict was instantaneous and overwhelming.[28] At once, all confidence was lost in the bank notes:— general consternation prevailed: and no one would have given twenty cents in hard coin for millions in bank paper. There was a rush on the bank for payment, and one will easily form a conception of the fury, despair and distress of the people, when he is informed that on the stopping of payment by the bank, there was paper in circulation amounting to 2,235,085,590 livres. The whole of it was suddenly reduced to zero. In the whole of France there was but one howl of malediction, and guards had to be given to Law, who had become an object of popular abhorrence. Even the life of the Regent himself was put in jeopardy, and it became necessary to station troops in different parts of Paris, where seditious and inflammatory libels had been posted up and circulated, to increase the confusion and tumultuous disorder which reigned everywhere. It was apparent that France had been transformed into a volcano, from which the slightest cause would have produced an eruption.

With regard to Louisiana, there had been also a great revolution in

---

28. The effect upon the company's shares was immediate, but upon the bank's notes, a different matter, the decline was less precipitate.

the public estimate of her merits. She was no longer described as the land of promise, but as a terrestrial representation of Pandemonium. The whole country was nothing else, it was said, but a vile compound of marshes, lagoons, swamps, bayous, fens, bogs, endless prairies, inextricable and gloomy forests, peopled with every monster of the natural and of the mythological world. The Mississippi rolled onward a muddy and thick substance, which hardly deserved the name of water, and which was alive with every insect and every reptile. Enormous trunks, branches and fragments of trees were swept down by the velocity of the current, and in such quantity as almost to bridge over the bed of the river, and they prevented communication from one bank to the other, by crushing every bark or canoe that attempted the passage. At one epoch of the year, the whole country was overflowed by that mighty river, and then, all the natives betook themselves to the tops of trees, where they roosted and lived like monkeys, and jumped from tree to tree in search of food, or they retired to artificial hills of shells, piled up by preceding generations, where they starved, or fed as they could by fishing excursions.

In many of its parts, the country was nothing but a thin coat, one foot thick, of alluvial soil, kept together on the surface of the water by the intermingled teguments of bind-weeds and the roots of other plants, so that if one walked on this crust, he made it, by the pressure of the weight of his body, heave up around him, in imitation of the waves of the sea, and great was the danger of sinking through this weak texture. Temptingly looking fruits and berries invited the taste, it is true, but they were all poisonous. Such portion of the colony as was not the production of the Mississippi, and therefore a mere deposit of mud, was the creation of the sea, and consisted in heaps of sand. Hence it was evident, that the country was neither fit for the purposes of commerce nor for those of agriculture, and could not be destined by the Creator for the habitation of civilized man. The sun was so intensely hot, that at noon it could strike a man dead as if with a pistol shot:—it was called a stroke of the sun. Its fiery breath drew from the bogs, fens, and marshes the most pestilential vapors, engendering disease and death. The climate was so damp, that in less than a week a bar of iron would be coated over with rust and eaten up by its corroding tooth. The four seasons of the year would meet in one single day, and a shivering morning was not unfrequently succeeded by a sultry evening. The ear was, by day and by night, assailed by the howls of wolves, and with the croakings of frogs so big that they swallowed children, and could bellow as loud as bulls. Sleep, sweet sleep, nature's balmy restorer, was disturbed, if not altogether made impossible, by the buz and stings of myriads of mosquitoes, which thickened the atmosphere and incorporated themselves with the very air which the lungs inhaled.

In such a country, the European race of men rapidly degenerated, and in less than three generations was reduced from the best-proportioned size to the dwarfish dimensions of misshapen pigmies. As soon as the emigrant landed, he was seized with disease, and if he recovered, the rosy hue of health had forever fled from his cheeks:—his wrinkled and sallow skin hung loosely on his bones, from which the flesh had almost entirely departed:—his system could never be braced up again: and he dragged on a miserable, sickly existence, which fortunately was not of long duration. In such a climate, old age was entirely unknown, and the statistical average of life did not exceed ten years. There, man lost the energies both of his body and mind, and through the enervating and baleful influence of the atmosphere, soon became stultified into an indolent idiot. Even the brutish creation did not escape the inflictions to which humanity was subject, and experienced the same rapid transformations. Thus, in a short time, horses were reduced to the size of sheep, cattle to that of rabbits, hogs gradually shrunk up so as to be no bigger than rats, and fowls dwindled into the diminished proportions of sparrows. As to the natives, they were cannibals, who possessed all the malignity and magical arts of demons, and waged incessant war against the emigrants, whose flesh they devoured with peculiar relish. This delineation of the features of Louisiana was very different from those of the first portrait, so many copies of which had been industriously circulated through France. It had been Hyperion; now it was a Satyr.

It is easy to conceive the startling effects produced on the minds of a people already in a paroxysm of consternation, by such malicious misrepresentations, which the enemies of Law took care to scatter far and wide. Thus, the tide of emigration which was pouring onward, rolled back, and the prospect of establishing a powerful colony in Lousiana, which, at first, had appeared so feasible, and loomed out to the imagination of the speculator in such vivid colors, and with such fair proportions, was nipped in the bud, and was looked upon as an impossibility. Under the exaggerated and gloomy apprehensions of the moment, no actual tender of money, and no promises of future reward, could have tempted any body to embark for Louisiana. So universal was the terror inspired by the name of the Mississippi, that, as it is a well-known fact, it became even a bugbear of the nursery, and that, for half a century after the explosion of Law's great Mississippi scheme, when French children were unruly and unmanageable, and when all threats had proved ineffectual, the mother would, in the last resort, lift up her finger impressively, and in a whispering tone, as if afraid of speaking too loud of something so horrible, would say with a shudder, and with pale lips to her rebellious progeny: "Hush! or I will send you to the Mississippi!" The child looked imploringly into his mother's face, his passion vanished, his cries and sobs were stifled, and under the soft kisses of maternal affection, coupled with the assurance that he never would be sent to the Misisssippi, he fell into gentle and undisturbed sleep.

However, the Western or Mississippi Company having contracted the obligation to colonize Louisiana, and to transport thither, within a fixed time, a certain number of emigrants, found itself under the necessity, in order to comply with the terms of its contract, to have recourse to the most iniquitous and unlawful means. As it was indispensable that there should be emigration—when it ceased to be voluntary, it was necessary that it should be forced.[29] Thus violence was resorted to, and throughout France agents were dispatched to kidnap all vagrants, beggars, gipsies, or people of the like description, and women of bad repute. Unfortunately, the power given by the government to these agents of the company was abused in the most infamous manner. It became in their hands an engine of peculation, oppression, and corruption. It is incredible what a number of respectable people, of both sexes, were put, through bribery, in the hands of these satellites of an arbitrary government, to gratify private malice and the dark passions or interested views of men in power. A purse of gold slipped into the hand, and a whisper in the ear, went a great way to get rid of obnoxious persons, and many a fearful tale of revenge, of hatred, or of cupidity, might be told of persons who were unsuspectedly seized and carried away to the banks of the Mississippi, before their voices could be heard when crying for justice, or for protection. The dangerous rival, the hated wife, or troublesome husband, the importuning creditor, the prodigal son, or the too long-lived father, the one who happened to be an obstacle to an expected inheritance, or crossed the path of the wealthy or of the powerful, became the victims of their position, and were soon hurried away with the promiscuous herd of thieves, prostitutes, vagabonds, and all sorts of wretches of bad fame who had been swept together, to be transported to Louisiana.

Guarded by a merciless soldiery, they, on their way to sea-ports, filled up the public roads of France like droves of cattle, and as they were hardly furnished with means of subsistence or with clothing by their heartless conductors, who speculated on the food and other supplies with which they were bound to provide their prisoners, they died in large numbers, and their unburied corpses, rotting above ground, struck with terror the inhabitants of the districts through which the woe-begone caravan had passed. At night, they were locked up in barns, when any could be found, and if not, they were forced, the better to prevent escape, to lie down in heaps at the bottom of ditches and holes, and sentinels were put round to watch over them. Hunger and cold pinched the miserable creatures, and their

---

29. The enforcement of emigration had also preceded the debacle of the company.

haggard looks, emaciated bodies, and loud wailings, carried desolation everywhere. Such sights, added to the horrifying descriptions which were given of Louisiana, made its name more terrific to the minds of the people of France than that of the celebrated Bastile and its dark dungeons. Dull indeed must be the imagination of the novelist, who, out of these strictly historical facts, could not extract the most romantic and heart-rending tales!

Law was considered as the author of all these cruelties and misfortunes, and he became still more odious to the people. The parliament of Paris thought that the moment was come at last to pounce upon Law; and to gratify their long-cherished resentment, he was summoned to appear in person before that high tribunal, to answer for his misdeeds and for his violations of the laws of the kingdom. On his refusal or neglect to do so, the parliament ordered him to be arrested, and had determined, on his being brought to the palace where they sat, to close their doors; and in order to prevent the expected interference of the Regent, their intention was to try summarily the hated foreigner, and to hang him in their courtyard. Thus, if the Regent, as it was anticipated, sent troops to batter down the gates of the parliament-house, to save his favorite, they would arrive too late, and would find there nothing but a gallows and a corpse. Aware of this plan, Law left his residence and fled to the Regent's palace, which was the only place where he felt himself secure against the pursuit of his enemies. There he cast himself at the feet of his august protector, and bathed his hands with tears. What a change!

> "This is the state of man: to-day he puts forth
> The tender leaves of hope, to-morrow blossoms,
> And bears his blushing honors thick upon him:
> The third day comes a frost,—a killing frost:
> And—when he thinks, good easy man, full surely
> His greatness is a ripening—nips his root,
> And then he falls."[30]

The Regent gave to Law assurance of his protection and vouched for his life; but this was all he could do. He had to bow to the force of public opinion, and to bend to the storm which menaced even his royal person. It was evident that Law could no longer stay in France. In the mean time, the Regent, irritated at the presumption of the parliament, exiled that body to Pontoise; but public indignation still gathering fresh fuel from that very circumstance, the Duke of Orleans provided Law, who resigned the office of comptroller-general, with the means of escaping out of the kingdom. On the 22d of December, 1720, Law arrived at Brussels, where he

30. *Henry VIII*, III.ii.352–58: the speaker is Cardinal Wolsey.

waited for some time in the vain expectation of being recalled. Far from it, he discovered, to his dismay, that when a man is sliding down the hill of prosperity, his best friends, instead of endeavoring to arrest his fall, will not unfrequently help him down with a kick. Thus, the Great Western or Mississippi Company, to which he had stood sponsor or godfather, lifted up a parricidal hand against him; and under the allegation that his accounts had not been faithfully kept and rendered, had proceeded to seize all his property, and had thereby deprived him of all means of subsistence. He did not lose however the favor of the Regent, who appointed him minister of France at the court of Bavaria, where he resided until the death of that prince.[31] Then he traveled through many parts of Europe, but found everywhere that dame Fortune was tired of smiling upon him.[32] He became but too sensible that he was a discarded lover, and that her favors were bestowed on some other favorite.

In October, 1721, he returned to England, and at first was received with distinction by persons of high rank: he was even presented to George the Ist. It had been shrewdly suspected that he had retained a considerable portion of his enormous wealth, of which it was presumed that he had been prudent enough, in his palmy days, to send not a small fraction out of France. But when it was discovered that he was reduced to beggary, people railed at his supreme want of discretion at not providing better for himself, and they felt indignant at the presumptuous cheat, who had been wheedling himself into their society under the false impression that he was rich. As soon as it was ascertained that he was poor, it followed of course that he was nobody, and no longer to be countenanced or noticed. Out of an innumerable host of friends, the Countess of Suffolk was the only one that remained true to him.[33] Let it stand on record in justice to her and for the honor of woman! This indeed was another of those but too striking instances of the mutability of fortune and of the instability of friendship.

In 1722, John Law turned his back upon England for the last time, and returning to the Continent, retired to Venice, where he lived in obscurity, and where he died on the 21st of March, 1729, in a state of indigence, and in the fifty-eighth year of his age. He had lost his wife and his only son, and there remained with him to solace his last moments but one faithful heart, a sweet Antigone, who closed his eyelids.[34] That was his daughter. She afterward married Lord Wallingford in England. A branch of the

---

31. The Regent made no such appointment nor did Law live in Bavaria until Orleans's death in December 1723, the news of which reached Law in England.

32. Law's fortunes, though declined, were not so bad. He received invitations from both Peter the Great and the King of Denmark to assume the finances of Russia and Denmark; Law declined.

33. Both the Duke of Argyll and Lord Londonderry helped.

34. Law was not indigent. Moreover, his wife survived him by eighteen years and his son by five.

family of Law has preserved to this day in France a very honorable position in society. A brother whom he left in that kingdom when he fled from it, was taken under the special protection of the Duchess of Bourbon. Through her favor, two of his sons found employment, in 1741, in the service of the East India Company, and greatly distinguished themselves. The eldest one, Law de Lauriston, rose to the rank of major-general, and to be governor-general of the French possessions in India. He left several sons; two perished in the unfortunate expedition of La Peyrouse, and one of them lived to be known under the reign of Louis the XVIIIth, as Marquis de Lauriston, a lieutenant-general and a peer of France.[35]

We have followed Law through all the phases of his eventful career, until, crossing with him the Bridge of Sighs, we have left him dying in Venice, "that sea Cybele with her tiara of towers—the revel of the earth—the masque of Italy."[36] A fit tomb for such a man! Now that the last act of this varied drama has been played, let the curtain drop, leaving to the judgment of impartial posterity the memory of John Law of Edinburgh.

---

35. He was a Comte, not a Marquis.
36. Gayarré has altered and compressed lines from Byron, *Childe Harold's Pilgrimage*, canto IV, stanza 2, lines 1–2, which are, "She looks a sea Cybele, fresh from Ocean / Rising with her tiara of proud towers," and stanza 3, line 9, "The Revel of the earth—the Masque of Italy."

# 9.

*Frederick Adolphus Porcher*

## "Modern Art"[1]

Few Southerners were more insistently enchanted by the memory of childhood than Frederick Porcher. He constantly returned, in the midst of a discontented adulthood, to the apparently simpler, rural days of youth. He came from the low country of South Carolina, where he was born in 1809 on his father's plantation in St. John's Berkeley. His family was not rich, but well-connected, established enough to have its eccentricities indulged. His first home was modest enough to pass for poverty in the modern American suburb: "a single two story house, with two rooms on each story; it was afterwards enlarged by the addition of two rooms at the back and they were subsequently built upon, so that in the end it became a two story house, with four rooms on each floor, and was as comfortable internally and as imposing externally as any gentleman's house in the country."[2] To this was annexed a slave quarter for some eighty blacks and a resolutely eighteenth-century library: Hume, Gibbon, Smollett, Robertson, the Junius Letters, Jefferson's *Notes*, Knox's *Elegant Extracts*. He grew up in a society, still dominated by the citizens of the late Revolution, "consisting entirely of planter's families, all of whom occupied the same social position . . . [with] a total absence of affection or pretension." "I looked with confidence upon these men, whose blue cloth coats, knee breeches, high boots with tassels hanging down the front, distinguished them from the people of the parish in a humbler walk of life and the queue which gently flapped the collar of the coat gave them an appearance of respectability in strong contrast with the closely cropped hair of the other people."[3]

1. Frederick Adolphus Porcher, "Modern Art—Powers' Statue of Calhoun," *SQR* n.s. 5 (January 1852): 86–114.
2. See especially, "Historical and Social Sketch of Craven County," *SQR* n.s. 9 (April 1854): 377–428; "The Memoirs of Frederick Adolphus Porcher," ed. S. G. Stoney, *SCHGM* 44 (April 1943): 78.
3. Ibid., pp. 79, 80.

Porcher wrote his memoirs in 1866 and 1867 in despondency, which colored his nostalgia. They begin bleakly, "In the fifty eighth year of my life after severe domestic trials and afflictions, and in great uncertainty whether any persons will take the least interest in the perusal of my manuscript, I commence the Memoirs of my life and perhaps of my times." But the nostalgia had been his before the Civil War wrecked his never-great fortune. He portrayed himself as having drifted unthinking through the young life of a planter's son: hunting, shooting, fishing, drinking, going into the legislature for motives of rank rather than competence. But the portrait is by a man who had abandoned the life and is thus suspect. Even on his own admission, he had been too bookish. William DuBose of Yale and St. John's Parish had abjured the young Porcher "never to read, a planter he would say has no business with books . . . he thought I was in danger of becoming too speculative, and of neglecting my business in the interest of my books."[4] And he had been right.

Porcher was educated at a military academy in Vermont and then at Yale. He returned to become a planter and stayed one until 1848, when nearly forty. But he was, as he knew, inefficient and bored. So he gave it up to become professor of History and Belles Lettres at the College of Charleston. He was to remain there until he died in 1888. Previously he had dabbled in a few French translations for Simms's periodical, the *Magnolia*, when living in Charleston away from the vexations of the rural life.[5] Now he wrote with more seriousness, chiefly for the *Southern Quarterly Review* and *Russell's Magazine*, upon a variety of topics: the school system of South Carolina, women in eighteenth-century France, historical philosophy, ancient political institutions, sectional differences, the social life of a South Carolina county, the nature of paradox, the conflicts of labor and capital, Bancroft's *History*, and Webster's Dictionary. In addition, he did the usual amount of orating, notably to the South Carolina Historical Society, of which he was the first president.[6]

4. Ibid., p. 66; *SCHGM* 45 (April 1944): 82.
5. *SCHGM* 47 (April 1946): 95–96.
6. "Free School System in South Carolina," *SQR* 16 (October 1849): 31–53; "Julia Kavanaugh's *Woman in France, during the Eighteenth Century*," *SQR* n.s. 4 (October 1851): 433–58; "False Views of History," *SQR* n.s. 6 (July 1852): 23–48; "Political Institutions of Sparta and Athens," *SQR* n.s. 8 (October 1853): 451–80; "Southern and Northern Civilization Contrasted," *RM* 1 (May 1857): 97–107; "The Nature and Claims of Paradox," *RM* 1 (September 1857): 481–89; "Conflict of Capital and Labor," *RM* 3 (July 1858): 289–98; "Bancroft's History of the United States," *RM* 3 (September 1858): 521–30; "Webster's Dictionary," *RM* 5 (August 1859): 410–19. This list is not exhaustive.

Porcher's chief virtue was detachment. He was in, but not of, the Charleston literary set, an entity that required little specific allegiance of ideas. He observed and went his own way. Not a thorough scholar at anything, he was intelligent about most things. Of the great about him he was no respecter, of the obscure he could be pithily evocative. His memoirs are scattered with insight and anecdote: of mulattoes received in polite circles, of the odd characters who haunted the Charleston Library Society, of James Henry Hammond reproved for a capitalist, of the political shenanigans of the Nullification crisis. Next to those of William J. Grayson, they are the liveliest of South Carolinian memoirs.

This essay is a sample of Porcher's skepticism. No figure loomed larger in South Carolina than Calhoun, no aesthetic doctrine was more entrenched than neoclassicism, no historical belief was more held than that the South should be identified with the sensual peoples of the Mediterranean. Porcher quietly flouted them all. He knew what he thought about art, and his beliefs were outraged by the neoclassical statue of Calhoun that the City of Charleston commissioned to sit before the City Hall: Calhoun wrapped in a toga. Porcher had traveled in Europe in the 1830s and had seen his share of statuary and painting. And he had traveled extensively along the eastern seaboard of the United States. This essay, though it has reference to books, is more a distillation of Porcher's visual experience and sense of what was fitting for his time and place. It is historicism applied to art. Anyone who rises from Porcher's memoirs, persuaded of the planter as an eighteenth-century survivor, will find here a very Victorian standpoint, one that John Ruskin would not have found uncongenial.

IN remote antiquity, the spirit of hero-worship, alike honourable to the devotee and its object, erected temples to consecrate the memory of those whose names men would not willingly let die. In modern times, the hero usually constructs his own monument; which, either in the glowing page of the historian, or in the impassioned words of the hero himself, has a vitality and an endurance far superior to any material fabric which veneration for departed greatness may raise. Yet, with a sense of gratitude which is honourable to humanity, mankind are not content to let the hero be the sole builder of his monument, and they therefore endeavour, by cenotaphs and sculptured images, to express their sense of his worth and their admiration.

The noblest of these monuments is the statue. By means of it, men desire to transmit to posterity the features of him whom they revere as one of the master spirits of the age. Rejecting all other forms as unsuitable, they select that of humanity itself as the fittest emblem of him who was an honour to his race.

We believe men are, in general, disappointed in the execution of such works. Critical indeed is the situation of the artist who undertakes to give expression to the popular idea of the object of their veneration. It is his duty to convey, as far as sculpture can do so, the thought of the age; to become to all succeeding ages the exponent of the characteristics of the great man of his period; and, at the same time, to preserve the dignity and the sublimity of art. A statue, therefore, is to serve a two-fold purpose. It is a work of art, and therefore a monument of the condition of art at the period when it was designed. It is to be also a means of illustrating the history of the times. In the latter respect, the artist frequently fails. Artists may applaud the execution, but it does not succeed in touching the chord which should vibrate responsive to the emotions which he would excite. The marble generally tells no story to the popular eye. The admiration bestowed on sculpture is too often forced and conventional. We are not slow to appreciate the merits of the master-pieces of antiquity, but we receive with cold approval the productions of the modern artists.

He who will honour these pages with a perusal, will readily discover that the writer has no technical or professional knowledge of art. Our remarks, therefore, can carry no authority. But it may be that our ignorance may aid in giving force to our observations in the inquiry, What is demanded of the artist, and in what spirit should he execute his work? Is he to work for artists alone, who can appreciate his productions as works of art? or is he to labour for the mass of mankind, who expect to be pleased without taking the trouble of devoting profound study to that in which they do not, and can not be expected to, feel more than a passing interest?

We hold it as a fact never to be lost sight of, in the discussion of this question, that, wherever our fortune may have placed us on this continent, the people of the United States are originally and essentially members of a Northern Race. We call ourselves Americans, but we are not the less, on that account, Saxons or Kelts. Without entering into the vexed question of the origin of races, we take the generally undisputed admission, that the races, as they now exist, are characterized by essential differences in their moral and mental constitution—that these differences are so deeply rooted, that education can do little more than modify them in individuals—that whenever the instinct of the race is touched, all conventional trainings disappear, and nature asserts her dominion over the heart of man. The instinct of race arrayed the Doric Greeks against the Ionians, and involved Greece in a civil war, which terminated in the ruin of that country. The hatred of the English to the Irish, and the pertinacity with which the Northern sects resisted the English government, can be accounted for on no other principle. The French and English regard each other as natural enemies. The Celtic population of Flanders, though quick to resist, yielded at length to the persuasions and perseverance of Philip the Second; while the Germans of Holland, acting in the same cause, achieved their independence. In later times, no political contrivance has succeeded in making these two neighbouring people coalesce, though every maxim of sound political philosophy seems to indicate the propriety of such an arrangement. These are not the results of moral causes, but the natural workings of instinct. In religion, too, the doctrines of Luther have obtained the ascendancy in all the countries which acknowledge the Teutonic origin, while Rome still holds the allegiance of the Celtic families of Europe; and neither Rome nor Wittenburg has made any serious impression on the Greek faith of the Sclavonic race.

All races of men are, to a greater or less degree, the votaries of art. Wherever man has been found, he is found also in possession of some specimen of sculpture however rude, and some token of his passion for that mysterious art which imitates the aspects of nature. The wonderful development of art in ancient Greece was such that we are accustomed to hail that country as its birthplace. This is not strictly true. Greece developed art only as the illustrator of the sublime and beautiful.

How large a proportion of the original races, whose exploits made the soils of Greece and Italy classic ground, still remain in those countries, is a question not easy of solution. It may aid us, however, in determining the question, to remember that no wars of extermination have ever been waged against either of them; and that, in spite of the various political revolutions which have been forced upon them from abroad, the languages of both countries continue still to bear unmistakeable traces of their descent from those which flourished when Pericles and Augustus respectively governed them. This fact, in the absence of historic proof to the contrary, affords strong presumption against any radical change of race. What Grecian art was, in the days of its glory, we know; what it might be under the influence of modern refinement, can be but a matter of conjecture. In ancient Greece, art was characterized by chaste beauty. In modern Italy, the principle of beauty exists, but it is voluptuous rather than chaste. The arcana of the great museum of Naples, contains specimens of art in which voluptuousness is carried even to licentiousness. If this tendency has not, in modern times, reached a similarly extreme development, it has probably been checked by the powerful influence of a purer religious principle.

It is not easy to ascertain what may have been the earliest development of the Imaginative Arts among the Northern nations. But, from the time that they began to exercise an influence over the civilization of Europe, we find them in the possession of a high degree of art. The noble temples which form a characteristic feature of the scenery of France and England, those gorgeous monuments of an age which we arrogantly call Dark, are splendid galleries of medieval art. Viewed in this light, they have not, we think, been justly appreciated. The different genius of the North and the South is strikingly exemplified in the art of architecture. The people of the latter selected a commanding highland, and on it erected their monuments; which, as if growing out of the rocks on which they are founded, are characterized by a bold and severe simplicity and beauty. The former, generally, sought in sheltered and sequestered vales, to elevate those fabrics which, even in their ruins, are the shrines at which the traveller in search of the picturesque pays his humble and heartfelt adorations. In the development of Southern architecture, the eye at once takes in the whole; the details offer no excitement to the curiosity of any but the professional eye. Northern architecture, on the contrary, is gorgeous as well as grand. The choir of the unfinished Cathedral of Cologne, fills the mind with admiration, not because it is suggestive of what the whole was designed to be, but because, mutilated and unfinished as it is, it contains enough to provoke wonder and excite the curiosity. Gothic architecture is said to violate the precision and severity of classic taste, but the universality of its diffusion shows that it must have satisfied the taste of those for whom it was designed: and even, now, when every one pretends to have imbibed the spirit of the classic taste, the mind involuntarily turns from the wonders of the Parthenon, and revels in the glorious beauty of the ministers and old abbeys of the North.

If the difference between the architecture of the North and that of the South is great as to their form, it becomes infinite when we consider the ornaments with which they are respectively decorated. In the South, the column is surmounted by the volute, the ovoid, or the acanthus leaf, and the metope or ox head, and the trigliph, are the invariable ornaments of the entablature. On the front of the temple we see a group of figures, severe, simple, grand. Every thing is beautiful, appropriate, chaste, perhaps sublime. In Gothic architecture, we know not what to expect until the temple actually stands before us. It may be, that, as we approach it, our admiration of its beauty and grandeur is suspended by the appearance of a figure starting from one of its salient buttresses, which would terrify us, were it not for a certain air of *bonhommie*, which, in spite of its formidable aspect, deprives it of its hideousness. We find the entrance to be an arched doorway, which we would pronounce entirely too low for the stupendous height of the fabric to which it seems as a portal; but we cannot criticise, for our attention is diverted by the strange figures by which it is decorated and surrounded. There is no classical beauty, no severe simplicity. No one would say that this door deserves to be the portal of Paradise, as Michel Angelo said of the grand portal of the Baptistery of Florence; but we unconsciously ask whether it may not conduct to Pandemonium. Still there is no terror. Wonder is awakened, and curiosity, strongly excited, urges us forward to see the mysteries which lie hidden within. For the interior, the description of the Collegiate Church at Manchester, by Miller, will suffice:

> "In the interior, all is fresh and sharp as when the field of Bosworth was stricken. Daylight streams in through numerous windows, mullioned with slim shafts of stone, curiously intertwisted atop, and plays amid tall slender columns, arches of graceful sweep, and singularly elegant groinings, that shoot out their clusters of stony branches, light and graceful as the expanding boughs of some lime or poplar grove. The air of the place is gay, not solemn, nor are the subjects of its numerous sculptures of a kind calculated to deepen the impression. Not a few of the carvings, which decorate every patch of wall, are of the most ludicrous character. Rows of grotesque heads look down into the nave, from the spandels; some thrust their features to one side of the face, some to the other; some wink hard, as if exceedingly in joke; some troll out their tongues; some give expression to a lugubrious mirth, others to a ludicrous sorrow. In the choir, of course a still holier part of the edifice than the nave, the sculptor seems to have let his imagination altogether run riot. In one compartment there sits, with a birch over his shoulder, an old fox, stern of aspect as Goldsmith's schoolmaster, engaged in teaching two cubs to read; in another, a respectable looking boar, elevated on his hind legs, is playing on the bagpipe, while his hopeful family, four young pigs, are dancing to his music, behind their trough. In yet another, there is a hare, contemplating, with evident satisfaction, a boiling pot, which contains a dog, in a fair way of becoming tender. But in yet another, the priestly designer seems to have lost sight of prudence and decorum altogether. The chief figure in the piece is a monkey, administering extreme unction to a dying man, while a party of other monkeys are plundering the sufferer of his effects and gobbling up his provisions. A Scotch Highlander's faith in the fairies is much less a reality now than it has been; but few Scotch Highlanders would venture to take such liberties with their neighbours, 'the good people,' as the old ecclesiastics of Manchester took with the services of their religion."[7]

---

7. Hugh Miller, *First Impressions of England and Its People* (London, 1847), pp. 40–41; Porcher has altered the punctuation, made a few small slips, and omitted, after the first sentence, "What first impresses as unusual is the blaze of light which fills the place. For the unexpected dim solemnity of an old ecclesiastical edifice, one finds the full glare of a modern assembly room: the daylight. . . ."

Modern Art 317

With the exception of those which decorate the temples, few works of sculpture are to be found in the northern countries of Europe. A remarkable exception, however, is the celebrated Mannikin pipe of Brussels, an old and grotesque monument, which ornaments one of the principal streets of that city, and which is regarded with filial reverence by the people of that capital, as their oldest burgher.

Leaving, for a while, those arts which are purely imitative, we may ascertain the genius of a people by the contemplation of those airy creations which the poets and story-tellers have invented, for the edification and amusement of their countrymen.

Three great poets flourished in England, so nearly contemporary with each other, that the eyes of the eldest were hardly closed in death before those of the youngest were open to the enjoyment of that light, the extinction of which he was destined to bewail in tones of manly, sublime and affecting sorrow. The subject of Spenser's muse was the homefelt mythology of England; that of Milton, the great truths of the religion which every Englishman acknowledges; Shakspeare found a kindred muse in every topic.

Of these three names, doubtless, contemporary reputation gave to the first two whom I have mentioned, a far higher place than to the last. Spenser was a man of great learning, of high classical attainments, and eminently a poet. The same is true of Milton. And we must not infer that Milton's reputation was not great, because of the oft-told story of the wretched price for which he sold the copy-right of his great poem. That is only a proof that literary property was not as valuable then as it has since become. An author then depended on the patronage of an individual, rather than on that of the public. The latin Secretary of the Commonwealth, the great apologist of the English people, must have enjoyed, in his own day, an enviable reputation, in spite of the lowerings of political storms. A better proof that his book was no failure to his publisher, may be found in the fact, that, though published only seven years before the death of its author, he lived long enough to receive the price which, according to the contract, was to be paid on the issuing of the second edition. This fact proves that Milton had precisely the same sort of reputation in his own day that he now enjoys—that his works were read and admired by the learned. I say by the learned, designedly. Milton never was, and never will be, popular. I infer nothing from the fact that the press teems with stereotyped editions of his works. Men buy his works, because they regard it as a sort of religious duty to have them in the house. They look upon them as a sort of commentary on the Bible. But few are found to read the writings, which are yet bought by everybody. Milton and Spenser drew on the classical model, and their works are consigned to the libraries of the learned; Shakspeare drew after the old Teutonic model of·his countrymen, and finds a responsive chord vibrating in the heart of every man of Gothic blood. Examine, for example, two of the most beautiful productions of these noble authors, Comus and the Midsummer's Night Dream. Where only the more dignified pictures of the poets are concerned, one may, perhaps, award the palm of superiority to Milton. But leave the regions of sober truth, and enter into those of the imagination, and how infinitely does the genius of Shakspeare soar above that of Milton! Not because his conceptions are better or more noble, but because they are, if the expression may be allowed, more natural. Milton's fairies are quiet, calm and dignified personages. Those of Shakspeare are full of frolic and fun. The sports of the fairies, their loves, their quarrels and their cross purposes, are felt and enjoyed by readers of every class. The incantations of the spirits, in Comus, are dull to all but those who have drunk at the fount of classical inspiration.

Take another creation of Shakspeare. What classic fancy ever conceived the idea of a Caliban? Pan cannot answer, for he is an object of worship. The satyrs are not beings of the same class. Caliban is a northern devil—a wretched and malicious devil. But he inspires no fear. Like a vile cur, he is used when his services are required, and his master, knowing his temper, keeps him in constant obedience by severity.

A striking characteristic of the English mind is its healthfulness. Even the sins of an Englishman are natural, we might almost say wholesome. In illustration of this remark, let us contrast two productions on the same fable, the one by an old English dramatist, the other by a modern German, of the mystico-classical school. It is an old and popular northern faith, that a man may purchase great temporal enjoyment by selling his soul to the devil. The well known story of Dr. Faustus has exercised the genius of Marlowe and of Goethe. Marlowe adheres closely to the popular belief. Faustus sells his soul, and obtains a devil as his servant. His life becomes a mingled scene of frolic and remorse. He indulges in all sorts of drollery, and amuses himself to the top of his bent. But it is remarkable, that, except so far as the playing of mischievous tricks extends, he appears to be powerless to injure his fellow men; and, when the term of the contract is over, his despair and remorse are such as might reasonably be expected from one who has been trained in the Christian belief. In the German poet, no such truth to nature is to be found. Faustus becomes devilish from his association, and makes a devilish use of his dearly bought power. He exercises it, with fearful effect, on the only interesting character in the drama—indeed, but for the interest excited by the sufferings of Margaret, the work would want readers. But, even Goethe, with all his affectations, is unable to repress entirely the northern spirit. We now find him puzzling a student of theology; now he is amusing himself by fomenting quarrels among a set of roystering students, and, with characteristic drollery, he plays upon the vanity and jealousy of the widow, whose aid is essential to the prosecution of his designs against his victim.

It has been reserved to the present age to furnish a true illustration of Shakspeare. All attempts hitherto made in England were made on the classical model, and failed. The great Northern artist, Retzch, has appropriated Shakspeare to himself; and we venture the prediction that the poet and the artist will descend together to posterity, as the most faithful delineators of the emotions and conceptions of the Northern heart.[8]

We consider it a subject of heartfelt gratitude to every man who speaks the English language, that Shakspeare was the precursor of Milton. Had it been otherwise, had the mighty genius who tuned his harp to justify the ways of God to man, first uttered his divine notes, and caught the favourable ear of England, the impetus given to the classic taste might have been too great for even the genius of Shakspeare to resist. He might have been to Milton what Racine was to Corneille, and England and the North would have lost the noblest exponent of their poetical style. This is no mere hypothesis. The course of French poetry was, like that of the English, picturesque and natural, until the mighty hand of Corneille stamped it with the impress of classicality, and, from that day, French poetry has been grand, sublime and majestic, but incapable of uttering a word which finds a response in the great heart of humanity. Corneille may be the breviary of kings, but Shakspeare deserves to be the vade mecum of mankind.

In the department of painting, with the exception of the schools of Holland and of Flanders, the North is confessedly inferior to the South. The great masters of Italy and Spain are the great masters of Europe, and none venture to contest the palm with them.

We think it not insusceptible of proof, that the superiority of the South is due mainly to the fact, that their artists have, like those of Holland, followed nature. The Dutch are eminently the painters of domestic life. The Southern artists are able to draw upon the legends of Catholic christianity, which, to the people of those countries, are realities. The popular belief sanctions the free exercise of the artist's fancy, and he works without the restraint imposed by the fear of tape and compass criticism. The heathen mythology, too, which doubtless lies at the bottom of the Christian hagiology, is so familiar to the masses, that the artist has no fear of employing a language unintelligible to his compatriots. In these respects, unfortunately, they have been followed by their Northern imitators; and hence Northern art has now taken possession of the heart of the people. Of the prizes offered for competition by the French Academy of arts, for nearly

---

8. Friedrich August Moritz Retzsch, 1779–1857, a German engraver after scenes of Goethe, Schiller, and Shakespeare; see his *Gallery to Shakespeare's Dramatic Works in Outline* (Leipzig, 1847).

thirty consecutive years, nearly all the subjects selected for painters, as well as sculptors, are borrowed from ancient poetry and history. The few exceptions are selected from the sacred Scriptures. Such subjects as these are offered to the sculptor: the visit of Pericles to Anaxagoras; the departure of Gracchus from his house; Cleobis and Biton; the exile of Cleombrotus. And to the painter, the discipline of Manlius Torquatus; the wrath of Achilles; Antigone burying Polynices, etc., etc. Can the public spirit of the Academy discover, in the annals of French history, or in the drama of France, no subjects calculated to exercise the genius of her artists, but they must be transported to an age which cannot call into action the best feelings of our nature? It is not surprising, therefore, that art, in France, has no popular life. The endless display of allegory which characterizes that school, requires an amount of study which places it beyond the reach or the appreciation of the masses. Allegory is cold, not persuasive, and the artist who depends upon it can never hope to kindle a flame in the hearts of his spectators.

We cannot help believing that Sir Joshua Reynolds has hung like an incubus upon the English school of art. Excelling, himself, in the most lucrative branch of his profession, and enjoying a reputation which was unquestionably his due, he inspired the artists of his country with a taste for that which, except in the limited opportunities afforded him as a portrait painter, he never practiced—the ideal and the grand. He possessed, in an eminent degree, the faculty of giving dignity to indifferent features, and if he had not been a most successful portrait painter he might have become a very respectable imitator of the classic style. But, unfortunately, he was only an imitator. Nature appears to have had no charms for him. He either could not, or would not, recognize the claims of Hogarth to the character of an artist, because Hogarth had the genius to appreciate and embody the peculiar taste of his countrymen. But time is silently bringing about the reign of truth, and, whilst Reynolds is fading away from the memories of men, the genius of Hogarth is daily kindling a sentiment, which is destined to give birth to a new and characteristic school of art. West painted under the influence of Reynolds's doctrines, and succeeded him as President of the Royal Academy. Not so successful as a portrait painter, he had more time and opportunity to devote himself to the study of the grand style, and in this he was aided by the royal patronage, which conferred upon him the office of historical painter to the king. Everybody goes to see West's pictures. Who brings away with him a single sentiment which repays him for his visit? Carefully correct in drawing, unexceptionable in colouring, they repose upon the walls, which are afraid to acknowledge that they are encumbered, because, like all great bores, they are intolerable from the weight of their respectability. West undertook great subjects, and was therefore considered a great painter, and the people have not yet recovered from the influence of the prestige of his name.

Notwithstanding, however, the great disadvantage under which the art of painting has laboured, in consequence of the mistaken views, and, we may add, the want of true genius, of those who have confessedly stood at the head of this department, it has taken a tolerably firm hold on the heart of the people, and promises to grow in their good opinion. In landscape painting there is perhaps nothing to be desired, and the worshippers of nature may always be sure of a wholesome draught from the scenes of Claude, of Wilson, of Gainsborough, of Doughty and of Fraser.[9] Nor have the labours of Hogarth remained without their fruit. To them we may ascribe the works of Wilkie and of Landseer, whose success, in their peculiar departments, gives us reason to hope that a high degree of art, purely Northern, may exist, without any infusion of caricature.[10]

But if modern painting has been clogged and trammeled by the influence of the great masters of our times, sculpture has been kept absolutely in leading strings. No sculptor of our times dares hope to become anything but a humble imitator of Phidias or of Chomenes. The amateur walks over the immense collections of Rome and of Naples, and cannot distinguish between the works of Phidias and those of Canova; and Canova and his host of admirers proclaim this as the greatest triumph of which he is capable. Now, this circumstance, alone, shows how wide is the difference between sculpture and every other art. It would be a desirable accomplishment to be able to write Latin in such a manner that scholars might compare one with Cicero; but how infinitely more desirable is the ability to speak English with the eloquence of a Henry or a Chatham. Suppose old Burton had written his Anatomy of Melancholy in Latin, as he apologizes for not having done, would he not have stepped immediately from the printer's press to the tomb of the Capulets? Who, but the scholar, has ever heard of George Buchanan?[11] and where, that the English language is spoken, do we not find the writings of Macaulay? The age preceding the reformation is called *dark*, not because genius and learning existed not, but because they chose to shut themselves behind the veil of antiquity. The language of the people—of their mothers—they despised, as a vulgar tongue. Disdaining the language, they had no sympathy with the predominant thought of their age; they neither cultivated it nor reflected it; they

---

9. Richard Wilson, 1713?–1782, an English landscape painter in the school of Claude; Thomas Doughty, 1793–1856, an American painter of the Hudson River school; Charles Fraser, 1782–1860, the South Carolina miniaturist.

10. Sir David Wilkie, 1785–1841, a Scottish genre painter; Sir Edwin Landseer, 1802–1873, the English animal painter.

11. George Buchanan, 1506–1582, a Scottish humanist, satirist, and theorist upon monarchy.

lived for antiquity, wrote for antiquity, and posterity has rewarded them by condemning them to hold eternal companionship with those whom they had spent their lives in humbly imitating.

The world has room enough for Homer and for Milton. The latter need not shelter himself under the protecting wings of the former. Both have performed the great work allotted to them by Providence. Homer was the Greek poet; Milton that of England. Neither rejected his peculiar age, and posterity has therefore embalmed the memory of both. And as it is with letters, so will it be with sculpture, as well as every other art. He who is sedulously taught to disdain his age, will find himself rejected by his age. He who has no sympathy with his contemporaries—who lives only for antiquity—has a small chance of living with posterity. The sculptor is guilty of this neglect. To appreciate the merits of Canova, one must understand the excellence of Phidias; and, to the uninitiated, Michael Angelo is the contemporary of those great artists whose names have perished, but whose works, redeemed and restored by his hand, flourish, the pride and glory of Italy and of ancient art.

This would be very well if Art had but one phasis of existence. If the great Masters of Greece have fathomed it in all its bearings, and have completed all of the possible conceptions of the Ideal, then would it be wise to select some master-piece of antiquity, make our canons to suit its structure, and condemn inexorably every work which does not correspond with the standard. Similar to this was the rule of literary criticism, which long governed the world of letters. The poet was judged, not according to the laws of nature and the sentiments of humanity, but by a rigid comparison with Homer or Virgil. Instead of testing the merits of Homer by the touchstone of moral truth, they make Homer the test of truth—and such appears to be the condition of sculpture in the present age. Sir Joshua Reynolds, says "I would recommend that an implicit obedience to the rules of Art, as established by the practise of the great masters, should be exacted of the Student—that those models which have passed through the approbation of ages, should be considered by them as perfect and infallible guides; as subjects for their imitation, not their criticism."[12]

It would be difficult to lay down a better rule for the instruction of mere learners in any department of life; follow without question, the precept or model submitted to you. But, when we reflect that this rule is extracted from the discourses which were delivered before the Royal Academy, to young gentlemen whose admission as pupils into that Institution, was itself a proof that they had conquered the elementary difficul-

---

12. "Discourse I, Delivered at the Opening of the Royal Academy, January 2, 1769," in *The Works of Sir Joshua Reynolds*, ed. Edmond Malone (London, 1797), 1:9; Porcher has omitted "chiefly" before "recommend," and "the Student" should be "the young Students."

ties of their art, and were to be considered really promising artists,—the rule must be considered a declaration, that, in the author's opinion, Art had reached its *ne plus ultra*. If this is true, we may ask, whether this consideration is not calculated to repress the ardor of genius, and to deter from the pursuit of this art, any one who feels that he has within himself a talent which he would not willingly let die.

Sir Joshua Reynolds, says:

"It is the sense of nature or truth, which ought more particularly to be cultivated by the professors of Art; and it may be observed, that many wise and learned men, who have accustomed their mind's to admit nothing for truth but what can be proved by mathematical demonstration, have seldom any relish for those arts which address themselves to the fancy; the rectitude and truth of which is known by another kind of proof; and we may add, that the acquisition of this knowledge requires as much circumspection and sagacity, as is necessary to attain those truths which are more capable of demonstration.

"Reason must, ultimately, determine our choice on every occasion; but this reason may still be exerted ineffectually, by applying to taste, principles which, though right as far as they go, yet do not reach the object—no man for instance can deny, that it seems at first view, very reasonable, that a statue which is to carry down to posterity the resemblance of an individual, should be dressed in the fashion of the times, in the dress in which he himself wore. This would, certainly, be true, if the dress were part of the man; but, after a time, the dress is only an amusement for an antiquarian, and if it obstructs the general design of the piece, it is to be disregarded by the artist. Common sense must here give way to a higher sense. In the naked form, and in the disposition of the drapery, the difference between one artist and another is principally seen—but if he is compelled to exhibit the modern dress, the naked form is entirely hid and the drapery disposed by the skill of the tailor. Were a Phidias to obey such absurd commands, he would please no more than an ordinary sculptor, since in the inferior parts of every art, the learned and the ignorant are nearly upon a level. These were, probably, among the reasons that induced the sculptor of that wonderful figure of Lacoon to exhibit him naked, notwithstanding he was surprised in the act of sacrificing to Apollo, and consequently, ought to have been shown in his sacerdotal habits, if these greater reasons had not preponderated. Art is not yet in so high estimation with us as to obtain so great a sacrifice as the ancient's made; especially the Grecians, who suffered themselves to be represented naked, whether they were generals, law-givers, or kings."[13]

Notwithstanding the great name of the President, we must confess our inability to discover the reasons which he declares himself to have

---

13. "Discourse VII, Delivered to the Students of the Royal Academy, on the Distribution of Prizes, December 10, 1776," in *Works*, 1:141–42; the punctuation, here as elsewhere, is altered by Porcher.

given—and in fact, we do not think he has given any reason at all. Sir Joshua Reynolds must have known, as well as any other man of his day, that the grandeur, the dignity, the elevation of the statue, or picture, is derived from something *internal*, and altogether independent of the dress,—something beyond the reach of the stone-cutter or mere copyist, and which can be caught only by one who shares the inspiration of the artist. Of this, every one must be convinced who has ever examined the numerous attempts to multiply works of art. Of the numberless casts of the Medicean Venus, where is one that can be received as a true copy of the original? No where. And yet, if measured by tape and compass, they are in every respect counterparts of the original. It is the soul, the incommunicable touch, perhaps the faintest stroke of the artist's chisel, which finishes the work and sheds over the whole a loveliness which is irresistible and inimitable. And the same is true of all the master-pieces of antiquity. It is not, therefore, the mere manner, style, or fashion, in which the figure is conceived and executed, nor the skill with which the drapery is arranged, that constitutes the finish of a work of art. It is a something which must be felt, not described. The naked figure will naturally be best exhibited by the artist who understands Anatomy, the clothed figure by him who has served an apprenticeship to a tailor or modist—and it is probable that the adjustment of drapery was as diligently studied in ancient times as the art of fitting coats and trowsers is at present. But, without the creative spirit of true genius, the anatomist and the tailor, will both, like the Frankenstein, produce a monster, having nothing of humanity but the figure.[14]

As to the opinions of the President, on the subject of the naked figure, we will only observe that the day for such exhibitions has gone by forever. Modern European civilization revolts at it, and will, we hope, forever continue to do so.

We have never been able to overcome the feelings of disgust with which we once beheld a painting, if we mistake not, by David,[15] of Themistocles, a suppliant before the king of the Molossians. David was an enthusiastic admirer, and a successful imitator of the ancients; and in this, his great picture, the noble Athenian,—he who wrote that remarkable letter to the great king,—is made to stand naked before the petty chieftain whose hospitality he demands. To us, all sense of dignity is lost; there is nothing but abject humiliation, utterly inconsistent with the sympathy due to fallen greatness. To the civilization formed under the influence of Christianity, nakedness is revolting and humiliating—"Naked came I out of my mother's womb, says Job, in his misery, and naked shall I return

---

14. The first American edition of Mary Shelley, *Frankenstein: or, The Modern Prometheus* (London, 1818), was in 1833.
15. Jacques-Louis David, 1748–1825.

thither."[16] This is the extreme aspect of humiliation, and to modern civilization can never be reconciled with the dignity of generals, law-givers, and kings.

The primary object of Art in all its departments, is to excite an emotion of taste. In the departments of architecture, of painting, and of poetry, this emotion has been sought by every variety of mode and every conceivable form of expression. Sculpture alone remains servilely attached to original forms and original rules. It enthrones itself on a dignity so exalted, that ordinary mortals dare not look up to her, and then the artist complains that the heart of the people is dead. Death there is, it is too true, but it is not in the popular heart: that rejects sculpture because *it* is dead. Humanity acknowledges no sympathy with the dead. We instinctively reject the past, and cannot consent to live over again the scenes through which we have acted. The great men of this world are they who live in advance of their age, and impress their mighty spirit upon that which succeeds them. Even the conservative politician feels the influence of the onward tendency of humanity, and his efforts are directed to stay and prevent the too rapid growth of new ideas; never to re-produce those which have gone by. Whether for good or ill, the past lies behind us, and we may seek in vain to find it in the future which lies before us.

But in spite of this great law of nature, which extends to every department of life, practical as well as poetical, men are always to be found, eager to impose limits on our aspirations, and to keep us within the bounds of the actual. We have already alluded to the old canons of criticism, which are based upon the practice of Homer. But long after the absurdity of these canons was acknowledged, men still labored hard to repress the aspirations of genius. No great man has ever flourished in modern times who has not had to encounter the shafts of respectable criticism. But genius makes rules for herself, and rides triumphant over the heads of those who, we will not say, in envy, for that is not necessarily implied, but, in ignorance of the great ends of her mission, impotently strive to clip her wings.

We suppose it will not be denied, that, wherever the English language is spoken, Wordsworth is regarded as a great poet. His is, unquestionably, the merit of founding a new school of poetry; one in which, life in all its various phases is viewed in the light of poetry, and the humblest condition of humanity elevated into a source of the highest poetical aspirations. Possessing unbounded sympathy with nature, Wordsworth wants no hero to kindle his poetic flame. Suffering humanity is to him an inexhaustible theme, and the artless simplicity of infancy is to him as welcome as the profoundest pathos of a struggling Titan.

16. Job 1:21.

And yet Wordsworth had to struggle against the ablest and the most uncompromising criticism. Jeffrey reviews one of his poems with the positive declaration:—

> "This will never do! The case of Mr. Wordsworth, is now manifestly hopeless, and we give him up as altogether incurable, and beyond the power of criticism. We cannot, indeed, altogether omit taking precautions now and then, against the spreading of the malady; but for himself, though we shall watch the progress of his symptoms as a matter of professional curiosity and instruction, we really think it right, not to harass him longer with nauseous remedies—but, rather to throw in cordials and lenitives, and wait in patience for the natural termination of the disorder." And again he says: "An habitual knowledge of the few settled and permanent maxims (*mark the expression*) which form the canons of general taste in all large and polished societies—a certain tact which informs us at once, that many things which we still love and are moved by in secret, must necessarily be despised as childish and derided as absurd in all such societies—though it will not stand in the place of genius, seems necessary to the success of its exertions; and though it will never enable any one to produce the higher beauties of art, can alone secure the talent which does produce them, from errors that must render it useless. If Mr. Wordsworth, instead of confining himself almost entirely to the society of dalesmen and cottagers, and little children, who form the subject of his book, had condescended to mingle a little more with the people that were to read and judge of it—we cannot help thinking that its texture might have been considerably improved. At least, it appears to us, to be absolutely impossible that any one who had lived or mixed familiarly with men of literature and ordinary judgment in poetry, could ever have fallen into such gross faults, or so long mistaken them for beauties. * * We cannot refuse him the justice of believing that he is a sincere convert to his own system, and must ascribe the peculiarities of his composition, not to any transient affectation, or accidental caprice of imagination, but to a settled perversity of taste or understanding."[17]

Such were some of the criticisms made on Wordsworth. His school of poetry was called in derision the Lake School, and in every way did the professors of the classic style of poetry show their contempt for the new aspirant after poetical fame. And what was his fault? The old conventional notions of the grand and the Ideal had been disregarded by the rash innovator, and the truth of nature set up in opposition to artistic and conventional truth. And the issue of the conflict was not doubtful. Words-

---

17. Francis Jeffrey, "The Excursion," *Edinburgh Review* 24 (November 1814): 1, 2, 3–4; after the famous first sentence, Porcher jumps to p. 2, adds (from p. 3) "mark the expression," and omits (after "render it useless"), "Those who have the talent, however, commonly acquire this knowledge with the greatest facility; and . . . ," and (after "judgment in poetry"), "(of course, we exclude the coadjutors and disciples of his own school)."

worth now stands among the giants of the age, and his illustrious critic was compelled in his latter days, to do homage to his genius.

As it is with poetry, so is it with other departments of Art. The grand, the beautiful, the sublime, lie not in the works of departed genius alone—but nature, to the eye of the poet and of the artist, is an inexhaustible store-house of poetic truth.

It appears to us essential to the perfection of any work, that it should have some characteristic features, which shall in some way create a sympathy with its author. God has impressed a character on man, and it is but reasonable to expect to see some traces of that character in the works of man. It is no derogation to the art of painting, but rather an excellence, that all the great productions of this art, may be grouped in schools. We have the school of Spain, of Rome, of Bologna, of Flanders, of Holland—and yet, in all of them, every artist has his own peculiar mark by which he may be recognized. And though no reason can perhaps be shown why this or that feature should distinguish a school, it would yet appear, from the universality of its existence, to have operated upon every member of it, and we recognize it as one of the connecting links which bind the artist with his kind. But the sculptor who blindly follows antiquity strips himself of all personality. The man is lost in the art, and he renounces forever the hope of living in his work. In seeking after the ideal, grand and sublime, he loses his own individuality.

We have said, that a great Artist, like every other great man, will be in advance of his age, and the teacher of that which follows him. But let us not be understood as implying that he should either despise or neglect his own. On the contrary, he who is not eminently teachable, can never pretend, with success, to teach others. The great man stands in advance of his age, but he is also its best monument; just as Shakspeare is the best illustrator of the age of Elizabeth.

And here we would incidentally remark, that to this extent a natural literature is desirable in this country; not one full of affectations and mannerisms, such as would inevitably revolt from any attempt to force it, but one which will unconsciously and spontaneously reflect the American character. Such a literature will be found whenever a decided tone shall be given to our national character—but it must be spontaneous; no effort of individuals to produce such a result can be successful.

But we have, perhaps, devoted more time than may be agreeable to our readers, to the consideration of art in general—we shall, therefore, proceed at once to a practical application of these preliminary remarks.

It is said, that, notwithstanding the meagre appearance of that portion of the Crystal Palace, allotted to American Industry, the citizens of our Republic, in London, always pointed with exultation to *one* American production, which is unrivalled. This is the "Greek Slave," from the chisel of Hiram Powers.[18]

It may, perhaps, be considered significant of the tendency of the English and American mind, that, in an exhibition of the Industrial Arts, calculated to promote the material comforts of nations, statuary should find a place by the side of starch, and take the precedence, merely on account of its alphabetical position, of steam and steam engines; that pictures should be classed in the same page with poudrette; and that poetry has actually claimed a premium for its intrinsic merits, no less than the arts of pickling and printing.

Known to us for some time by reputation, Mr. Powers has, for about 18 months, been familiarly known here, by his heads of Psyche and Persephone; and it is nearly a year since his statue of Mr. Calhoun has adorned our City Hall.[19] These works are alone sufficient to establish Mr. Powers' position as an artist of no ordinary merit. His works are finished with consummate skill. He possesses the art of giving to his marble the softness of flesh, and he happily conceives and expresses the ideas of beauty and of grandeur.

Europeans as well as Americans have expressed their astonishment that the palm of excellence, in a classic art, should be borne away by an Ohio lad; but, indeed, when we consider that it is in the humblest sense of the word an imitative art, it is not surprising; not that it should be matter of surprise that Ohio should bear the palm in a noble art, but that, in an art purely imitative, dexterity of manipulation may as readily be predicated of one portion of the world as of another.

Every clever and promising artist is sent to Italy to study the great models of antiquity. The consequence is, that modern genius has no opportunity of giving expression to its conceptions. When first we saw the

18. Hiram Powers, 1805–1873, carved "The Greek Slave" in Florence, where he lived after 1837. It was exhibited in various American cities during 1847 and in Columbia, South Carolina, in December 1851. His chief patron was Col. John S. Preston, the brother of William Campbell Preston.

19. Powers had executed a bust of Calhoun while in Washington in the winter of 1836–1837, a plaster copy of which is now in the Yale University Art Gallery. The City Council of Charleston commissioned a full statue in the spring of 1845, which Powers based upon his earlier head. It was shipped from Lisbon in 1849, but its carrier, the *Elizabeth*, sank off Fire Island, Massachusetts, on 19 July. The statue went down with, among other things, Margaret Fuller. It, though not she, was salvaged at the behest of the Charleston authorities in late 1850 and arrived in Charleston on 12 November 1850. The arm and portions of the scroll, bearing the words "Truth, Justice and the Constitution," had been damaged but were later replaced. During the Civil War it was moved to Columbia, where it perished in the fire of 1865. There is a photograph of it, in situ before the Charleston City Hall, reproduced in *Art in the Lives of South Carolinians: Nineteenth Century Chapters*, ed. David Moltke-Hansen (Charleston, 1979). Otherwise it can only be viewed in an inferior Parian ware copy in the Gibbes Gallery, Charleston.

Psyche of Mr. Powers, we were struck with an indescribable air of modest assurance and rustic bashfulness, curiously and beautifully blended, and gazed at it with a sort of personal interest, from a spontaneous conviction that, in that creation, the artist had consecrated the features of some rustic beauty who had, in earlier and happy times, made a conquest of his affections. Under this impression we were painfully impressed with the mischievous tendency of conventional training. We could not but ardently desire to witness, in what manner native genius would have idealized the beauty which had touched his heart, and given expressions to the emotions which had been called into existence by the prestige of a hallowed first love.

It is not for those who utterly disclaim any knowledge of art, who pretend to no creative fancy, ever to suggest a hint; but we think it may be safely asserted, that the idea would not, naturally, be developed in the American mind, under the form of a Psyche. An artist is such, not by keeping himself aloof from the sentiments of his age and country, but by sympathizing largely with them. Now, though we cannot imagine in what form an American lover would clothe his conceptions of his young love, we think it may be concluded that it would be in conformity with a type existing in the northern mind, and not after the classical mould. Even to an intelligent mind, not too familiar with the classics, the idea of Psyche is vague and indistinct. One regarding solely her emblem, would consider her the impersonation simply of life, fleeting and evanescent, but warm, passionate, and beautiful. Another would regard her as typical of life purely intellectual. And another might see in her a combination of moral, mental and physical excellence. If such are the various conceptions of men of cultivation, how infinitely crude must be imagined those of the uneducated.

But, whatever may be the conceptions of the poet of the Northern race, we may be sure that they would be characterized by the most scrupulous modesty. To our minds, beauty never appears so perfect as when it leaves much to the imagination. Man, as well as woman, is essentially a clothes-wearing animal. Nudity is revolting, as striking at the basis of that modesty which lies at the source of all beauty; and the most impassioned lover will turn instinctively from the exposure of those charms which custom and propriety cover with a veil.

We know that it is a common observation, that, in art there is no scandal; but it is only the initiated who acknowledge the truth of the maxim. Happy is that work which needs not its protection. Habit and education have implanted in us certain notions, and it is unreasonable to expect us to put off all of our accustomed notions in order to enjoy the emotions of taste, called out by the contemplation of a work of art. When Greenough sent his first works to Boston, for exhibition, two naked figures which he called the Chaunting Cherubs, the popular sense was so shocked, that the figures were a long time furnished with napkins.[20] But Boston is a city of classic taste, and her citizens succeeded, after a while, in shaking off their Anglo-Saxon and puritan prejudices. It is not much more than a dozen years ago, since, in the museum of Philadelphia, separate hours were allotted to men and women, for the purpose of viewing a statue,—we believe of Ariadne,—which was naked. Education was then too strong for classic art. Since that time, it is true, a change has been wrought in the spirit of our people. Foreign travel has stripped us of our prejudices, and we contemplate now, without alarm or disgust, sights which would even in our younger days, have been avoided with horror. Those who are determined to conquer prejudice can do so; it may be at the price of principle; but the masses have no particular ambition to possess a reputation for classic taste, and generally prefer to have their prejudices consulted.

But it may be objected that we would degrade art by making it subservient to the prejudices and the ignorance of the masses. No degradation can result unless it stoops to vulgarity. But vulgarity does not, necessarily, follow a popular character, and art can flourish as a living principle, only in so far as it is popular. The dramatic poet who pleases the fastidious taste of the dress circles, may be a critical scholar and an accomplished writer; but, if he is a *true* poet and artist, he touches chords which vibrate in unison from the pit to the gallery. If this chord is *not* touched, if any part of the audience is incapable of responding to his call, he may be a clever man, but no artist. So too, the sculptor, who is compelled to appeal to men of classical education for support, when condemned by the sentiments of an uneducated mob, may be capable of executing a work which Phidias would condescend to approve, but unfortunately, he dooms himself to live only in the approbation of the contemporaries of Phidias. We live in our own age, and not in any other. Our only hope of living in the future, is to live for our age, and in sympathy with it. All prejudice is not the result of ignorance. A great deal of what is commonly so called, is in truth, the deep moral sense of a reasoning and intelligent community. We question whether the most enthusiastic classicist in America, would be pleased that his wife, his sister, or his daughter, should appear in marble, as either the Psyche or the Persephone, of Powers.

To the great work of the sculptor, the same objection applies. A "Greek Slave" presents no definite idea to the northern mind, in America. An African slave would, perhaps, have left too little to the imagination; a Greek slave, perhaps, has the opposite fault. A naked woman in chains is not a

---

20. Horatio Greenough, 1805–1852, the American sculptor and writer, studied under Thorwaldsen and was a protégé of Washington Allston. *The Chanting Cherubs*, done in Florence in 1830 with the encouragement of James Fenimore Cooper, was exhibited in Boston in the spring of 1831.

very pleasing subject of contemplation, nor do we suppose the actual exhibition, calculated to excite emotions higher than those which belong to art, merely as art. But, if we say any more on this subject, we may only betray our ignorance, having never seen more of it than is represented in the statuettes.

In executing the statue of Mr. Calhoun, for the city of Charleston, Mr. Powers had a peculiarly favorable opportunity of distinguishing himself as an historical sculptor. He is said, too, to have considered his work as a labor of love, so that his own feelings, as well as the exalted character of his subject, combined to inspire him with the idea of moral and intellectual greatness. Perhaps, therefore, it would not be unjust to the artist, to consider it as not merely a noble effort of art, but also a sort of tribute to his own conceptions of human excellence. Here then, if any where, was afforded an opportunity of linking the artist with his subject; of indissolubly connecting the name of Powers with that of Calhoun; of descending to posterity as the poetical illustrator of mighty intellect.

We have neither the wish nor the pretension to criticise this statue as a work of art. On this head, we bow implicitly to the decision of more enlightened critics, who have pronounced it to be worthy of the reputation of the author, and of the dignity of his subject. But we feel that we may say something of it as the statue of Mr. Calhoun. The question is, not whether it satisfies the expectations of professional artists, and of the fortunate few, who have been taught to feel as they prescribe; but whether the friends and admirers of Mr. Calhoun recognize, or are likely to recognize, in this statue, their own, or anything approximating to their own conceptions of the manner in which the object of their unbounded reverence should be made to descend, embodied, to posterity.

With respect to the execution of the statue, however, we must first observe, that, to our uninstructed eye, it appears to have been a beneficent storm which caused the statue to be submerged, so that it could not be recovered without being mutilated. As originally finished, the left arm was raised on high, holding up a scroll, on which are inscribed words indicating the great principles, in behalf of which, Mr. Calhoun was, through life, a conspicuous champion. This position appears to violate that calm repose which seems so necessary to the success of sculpture. To behold the arm continually held in that paralyzing posture, could not but be inexpressibly painful to those who were obliged to see it from day to day. Fortunately, that portion of the statue has been broken off, and it is to be hoped that it will never be restored. When not very closely inspected, the figure now appears to be reposing easily against the neighboring palmetto.

With the exception of the Palmetto stump and the broken scroll, Mr. Powers has laid aside, entirely, the historical features of the work, and, following in the wake of other artists, has chosen rather to be a humble imitator of antiquity, than to strike boldly for a work which would identify his name with his age—his country and his race. Mr. Calhoun is represented after the antique. He is made to appear before the people of Charleston, in a garb, which, when living, Mr. Calhoun would never have allowed himself to wear. The people of Charleston are called upon to admire Mr. Calhoun in a costume, which, if Mr. Calhoun had worn during his life time,—such was the affection borne to his person, they would have veiled their faces rather than witness the humiliating masquerade.

In defence of the ancient costume, it has been urged, that the artist has done enough if he satisfies our conceptions of moral and intellectual dignity—that if he does this, the dress is a mere adjunct; and that, as the ancients have pre-occupied the ground and left us noble models to work by, we do well to adopt them. In the artists' imagination, therefore, Mr. Calhoun stands out as a great man. His greatness is absolute, not relative; and it is becoming to his character, and to our high estimation of his worth, that he should live in art, as a great model of humanity, independent of age, race, or condition.

Now this may be an established canon in art, and may conform strictly to artistic truth—but, it is not true in nature, nor is it admitted by common sense. It may be reasonably doubted, whether any thing under the character of the Deity, is in itself either grand or beautiful. Even moral qualities appear to require concomitant associations and circumstances to aid in their development. Washington, or Calhoun, would have been insignificant in the French Revolution; in that of America, Bonaparte would, probably, have been no more distinguished that Gates, or Arnold. Now, in executing a statue or picture of Washington, or of Bonaparte, the artist should strive to inweave his national character into his conception, and not assign to him a mere conventional greatness. Washington was a great *American*. Would he have been a great Frenchman, a great Roman, a great Grecian? We believe not, and we feel disposed to glory in this belief, because we fancy that greatness, like his, so far superior to anything in the conception of the Gallic, Grecian, or Roman mind, adds a new lustre to the great *Northern* race to which he belonged, and which he honored and adorned.

But here we may urge a serious objection to the blind imitation of antiquity. When books were rare, and art popular, every work of art, whether of architecture or of sculpture was supposed to represent, in some way, the predominant sentiment of the age. The great works of the Grecian and of the Northern artists, were books addressed to the popular eye, and exhibiting, in a manner not now perfectly intelligible to us, the great thought of the times. Hence, our critics perceive the differences of style, in works of antiquity, which they regard as evidences of improvement or decline. It is significant of this truth, that, with the revival of letters, gothic architecture has fallen asleep. If, from time to time, it arouses itself, it is only to reproduce a feeble imitation, or carricature, of an already existing model. The architect has not learned the language of him whose work he attempts to reproduce; so too, with the artist. He follows antiquity without a knowledge of the key by which, alone, the true meaning of his model is to be deciphered. He imitates merely that which is obvious, but has no conception of the *thought* which his model was designed to express. Hence his productions have no vitality. Like the daguerreotype impressions of the face of a corpse, they present an accurate likeness of the features, but they are images of death.

The sculptor, who adheres pertinaciously to antiquity, like the writers who composed in the dead languages, will find his reward in being enrolled among the dead lights of the preceding generations. And the aspirant after artistical fame must feel a cold gloom at his heart, when he calls over the catalogue of sculptors who have toiled in this vocation from the time of Michel Angelo, to the present, and reflects how few are familiar to the ears, even of the intelligent. None but an *habitue* of the galleries of Rome and Florence, can, without the aid of a guide book, enumerate a tythe of the names of those who, in their day, were considered famous. Another generation may forget the name of Canova, and even now, Chantry and Flaxman, are strange names to all but English ears.[21]

> "Sculpture," says Sir Joshua Reynolds, "is formal, regular and austere, disdains all familiar objects as incompatible with its dignity; and is an enemy to every species of affectation."[22]

Unless these words of the President have a technical sense, they must be condemned by the common sense of mankind as false; if they are true, they condemn sculpture! Where is the austerity of Venus, or of Hebe, or of Diana; or of any of those inimitable productions which adorn the tribune of Florence. How, if such had been its early character, could it ever have become popular. The President seems, in every department but his own, to measure the merit of a performance by the extent of its heaviness. Art does not possess austerity so long as it is a living principle; it is only *dead art* which becomes rigid and austere. Mankind have commonly supposed, that art is to minister to the enjoyment of life, by exciting emotions of pleasure in the beholder; but, the critic dooms it to no existence higher than that which may be strictly canonical. Every thing that links it with humanity is to be remorselessly cut away. If the Parian marble, from its softness, bears too close a semblance to flesh, it is to be cleaned; if a ray of light comes into the room, which in the least degree heightens

21. John Flaxman, 1755–1826, an English sculptor and draftsman who worked for Josiah Wedgewood: he was later noted for a memorial sculpture of Reynolds.
22. "Discourse X, Delivered to the Students of the Royal Academy, on the Distribution of Prizes, December 11, 1780," in *Works*, 1:218; Porcher has omitted, after "affectation," "or appearance of academical art."

the effect of the work, the intrusive softness must be banished. The marble is to remain but marble, clear, cold and lifeless; and then, the critic will venture to pronounce it a perfect work of art. Strip it of every attraction, and judges, with hearts as unimpressible as the marble itself, will calmly award it their approbation. But let a spark of life animate the marble, let a single natural emotion be raised in the bosom of the beholder,—let the artist show himself at all conscious of his humanity,—that he has any life but classical life,—which is not life but death,—and he is denounced as aiming at the picturesque—as being grotesque! In the name of common sense, are we to be reasoned out of our very natures by such dogmatists? Is not the grotesque, the very essence of our imaginative life? Have we, in our inmost heart, any sympathy with the cold and formal regularities of classic taste? Our whole history denies it. We have rejected classicality in every department of art but one, and until sculpture rejects it too, her votaries live not for posterity, but for antiquity, and that too, in the humble capacity of imitators.

Sir Joshua Reynolds, says again:

"He who wished not to obstruct the artist, and prevent his exhibiting his abilities to their greatest advantage, will certainly not desire a modern dress. The desire of transmitting to posterity the shape of modern dress, must be acknowledged to be purchased at a prodigious price, even the price of every thing that is valuable in art. Working in stone is a very serious business, and it seems scarce worth while to employ such durable materials in conveying to posterity a fashion, of which, the longest existence scarce exceeds a year * * * Even supposing, no other objection, the familiarity of the modern dress by no means agrees with the dignity and gravity of sculpture."[23]

This opinion is pronounced *ex cathedra*, and, in the true spirit of a Dictator;—no reason is alledged to support it. Habit, doubtless unconsciously, governs our tastes, and it is not unlikely that, when the sister art of painting first ventured to exhibit the costume of the living age, the conservative party in the profession denounced the innovation as grotesque, and too familiar for the dignity of art. If Sir Joshua could paint the costume of his day, without doing violence to the dignity of his art, surely Flaxman or Chantry needed not to hesitate to follow his example. Suppose that, when Mr. Healy's portrait of Mr. Calhoun shall arrive here, we find that, instead of the American Senate, we are presented with a view of the Roman Senate?[24] Would not the popular feeling instantly reject the work, as a miserable parody? Why, then, should sculpture fear to live as well as painting? If the object of sculpture was merely to transmit to posterity the shape of a certain fashion, the objection would be reason-

---

23. Ibid., 1:217; "artist" and "sculpture" should be capitalized.
24. George Peter Alexander Healy, 1813–1894; the portrait proved to be in modern dress.

able, simply as a utilitarian's argument. But when we consider that, to our notions, dress is essentially a part of a man, it becomes invested with dignity. It is true that we regard with some emotions of ridicule the exhibition of a fashion of dress which we remember to have worn a few years since. He who appears in such a dress appears to be either an inferior or an ignorant person—in either case, an awkward one. But no such emotion is experienced when we examine the costume of our fathers. We never view with any emotions but those of respect, the aged gentleman, who declines departing from the costume to which he was accustomed in the prime of his life. We cannot conceive how the sculptor can be said to labour with more liberty, when he is obliged to clothe his subject like an ancient Roman, than when the truth of history requires that he shall be dressed like a Christian. When Houdon was executing the statue of Washington, he consulted that illustrious man on the subject of his dress, and he, acting on the principles of that common sense which so greatly distinguished him, but which Reynolds held in contempt, chose the costume of his day.[25] And Houdon's Washington remains, the statue of the father of his country. Chantray and Canova sent their statues, robed like Roman Senators, the one to Boston, the other to Raleigh, and Greenough sent his half-naked statue to Washington; but the hero of '76, the man of America, the Virginia planter, is to be found only in Richmond.

Who would venture the risk of failure, by attempting to represent Bonaparte as an ancient? In his statues, the cocked hat, the overcoat, and the military boot, have become classical. France would instinctively reject any other form of representing the man of destiny. A great opportunity was afforded to Powers, of striking a blow in defence of modern art. He might have made an historical statue of Calhoun. He appears to have the power of imparting to his work a dignity and majesty which would have triumphed over the difficulties of the novelty of a modern costume. He might have made Mr. Calhoun the type of the great man of the nineteenth century; he has preferred to invest him with conventional greatness. He might have founded a school of art, Northern as well as American; he has neglected his opportunity. He might have made a name for himself, as enduring as we hope that of Calhoun will be; he has condescended to swell the long list of humble imitators of a school which is dead beyond the hope of resuscitation.

25. Jean Antoine Houdon, 1741–1828, the French sculptor; he visited the United States in 1785 and met Washington at Mount Vernon. Cf. Thomas Jefferson to Washington, 14 August 1787, written from Paris on the matter of modern dress for the Houdon statue: "I found it strongly the sentiment of West, Copley, Trumbull, and Brown, in London; after which it would be ridiculous to add that it was my own. I think a modern in an antique dress as just an object of ridicule as a Hercules or Marius with a periwig and a *chapeau bras*," quoted in Bernard Mayo, *Jefferson Himself: The Personal Narrative of a Many-Sided American* (Charlottesville, 1942), pp. 122–23. I am grateful to Gene Waddell, director of the South Carolina Historical Society, for bringing this to my attention.

Who, that has ever seen, does not remember Thom's group of Tam O'Shanter, that wonderful production of an untutored Northern genius?[26] It was hailed with no cold approbation, but took forcible possession of the popular heart. It might have been condemned by the schoolmen, as picturesque and grotesque; but it touched the popular heart. It has been reproduced, in every variety of form. It is to be found, in some shape, in every house, a convincing proof that there is something in Northern art which can captivate the Northern heart. The name of Thom is now as inseparably connected with Burns as that of Retzch is with Shakspeare.

It is true that Mr. Calhoun is not to be conceived in the same spirit in which the artist conceives the figures in that group. But we have referred to it to show that the daring attempt of true genius to shake off conventionalities must be successful. The man of genius will no more imitate Thom than he will Phidias or Michael Angelo. If the character, conduct and services of Mr. Calhoun deserved the meed of a statue, the garb in which he was accustomed daily to appear cannot be otherwise than respectable. The genius and virtue of the man impart a dignity to the circumstances which moulded his life and character. He was great only through them and by them. He was a man who will probably live with posterity, because he lived with and for his contemporaries. His greatness was the reflection of the moral and intellectual excellence with which he was surrounded. In him they were embodied and concentrated. No other sort of greatness is recognized among men, because men cannot depart out of themselves, to appreciate a greatness which has no sympathy with them. And such greatness is to be represented only by adhering to historical truth. The people, who loved and venerated their representative, hailed the arrival of his statue a short time after they had followed his remains to the tomb. They saw the venerated features, in a stone curiously carved. They were told to admire it, as a work of art beyond all price, and they have coldly submitted to the mandate. They are proud to possess the statue of the first statesman of the age, executed by the first sculptor of the age; but their sentiment is the pride of the man who possesses wealth which ministers not to his happiness. They respect it, they please themselves in its possession; *but they do not love it*. The first glance of curiosity satisfied, the statue stands unheeded, in the City Hall, and there it will stand, a monument of the public spirit of the citizens and of their disappointment. We asked for our statesman, and have received a Roman Senator. We asked for the citizen of the nineteenth century, and have received a specimen of the antique. We asked for our Calhoun, the Carolina planter, and have received an elaborately carved stone.

26. James Thom, 1799–1850, a Scot who moved to the United States in 1834; his group, *Tam O'Shanter*, was owned by the Franklin Institute in Philadelphia and exhibited regularly at the Pennsylvania Academy between 1850 and 1870.

# 10.

## *Louisa Susanna McCord*

## "Enfranchisement of Woman"[1]

Southern intellectual culture was chiefly a male affair at its most learned levels. There were exceptions: the main translator of German literature in the Charleston of the 1840s was Mary Elizabeth Lee;[2] less grandly, popular magazines like the *Southern Rose* and the *Southern Lady's Book* teemed with lady writers of sentimental verse and fiction. Louisa McCord was not entirely free of the latter impulse; after all, a volume of verses upon her dreams was published in 1848, though it was done by her husband without her knowledge. And she did, with no such excuse, write a Roman tragedy upon the Gracchi that would do no injustice to "Savanarola" Brown, the possessed playwright of Ladbroke Crescent. Her "Huzza! Huzza! (Exeunt Citizens, with Pomponius)" has less panache than his "To the Piazza! Ha, ha, ha, ha, har! (Seizes ring, and exit. Through open door are heard, as the Curtain falls, sounds of a terrific hubbub in the Piazza)," but she had the disadvantage of seriousness. In general, Louisa McCord did not lack for certainty, seriousness, or vigor.[3]

She was the daughter of Langdon Cheves, a fact that was central to her life in the way that Necker dominated the sentiment of Madame de Staël. Born in Columbia, South Carolina, in 1810, she moved north to Philadelphia in 1819 when her father was appointed president of the United States Bank by James Monroe, a position he held for nearly ten years. Philadelphia, though the first home of American antislavery, taught her no radical doctrines and seems only to have reinforced her adolescent preference for the established institutions of the South. She was a strong daughter to a

---

1. Louisa Susanna McCord, "Enfranchisement of Woman," *SQR* n.s. 5 (April 1852): 332–41.
2. Lee translated extensively for Simms's *Magnolia*.
3. Louisa S. McCord, *My Dreams* (Philadelphia, 1848); *Caius Gracchus: A Tragedy* (New York, 1851); *The Bodley Head Max Beerbohm*, ed. David Cecil (London, 1970), p. 123.

strong father. Tall, not soft of demeanor or tongue, she was unsurprisingly late to marry and then to a widower. David James McCord was, like his wife, a contributor to the periodicals, but also a politician and a lawyer of local distinction. The union was doubtless not unaffected by her rich dowry, from an indulgent father and a few fortunate inheritances. But there is little evidence that so traditional an alliance brought less happiness. They would work, like the Brownings, at their separate desks positioned around the fire at "Langsyne" plantation on the Congaree River. They had three children, to whom she seems to have been particularly devoted. Her husband, however, died in 1855, and she was obliged to face a difficult war and its aftermath, the prostration of her estates, alone.[4]

It was during the brief fifteen years of her marriage that she did most of her writing. No one, I fancy, would rest her claims upon her verse. But her periodical essays were another matter. She wrote critically upon feminist issues, as here. But her major theme was slavery in all its ramifications: the diversity of the races, Mrs. Stowe's despised novel, the nature of labor both black and white, the slave trade, British antislavery movements. In addition, she published a translation of Bastiat's *Sophisms of the Protective Policy* in 1848.[5] She pled the causes of the Southern conservative—the traditional role of the woman, proslavery, class distinction, free trade—with the excited indignation of the reformer.

Unlike the Paris of Madame de Staël, South Carolina offered a woman like Louisa McCord little discretion of action, not even that of the salon. In Paris, she would have gone into the drawing rooms and stood censoriously to contribute her denunciations of *Les Amis des Noirs*. In South Carolina she spent much of her time on the plantation, tending to her slaves with more than ordinary zeal. As it was, she claimed more of a social role than society was usually disposed to grant. Being the daughter of Langdon Cheves and the wife of David McCord helped. Being socially inviolable, she need fear no gossip of her presumption, the rumor that to write on manly subjects betokened an unnaturally manly woman. But still her prose is

---

4. Jessie Melville Fraser, *Louisa C[heves]. McCord* (Columbia, S.C., 1919); Margaret Farrand Thorp, *Female Persuasion: Six Strong-Minded Women* (New Haven, 1949); Louisa McCord Smythe, *For Old Lang Syne* (Charleston, 1900).

5. *Bastiat's Sophisms of the Protective Policy*, trans. Louisa S. McCord (New York, 1848); there is a bibliography of McCord in Evert Duyckinck, ed., *Cyclopedia of American Literature* (New York, 1855), 2:28.

shot through with a restlessness, a violence of sentiment, a hint of frustration with her place, sublimated into a severity of belief and commitment. Much of the interest of this piece upon the merits of female enfranchisement, aside from the polemical adeptness of its chilling racism, lies in observing how Louisa McCord contrived to fend off radical feminism, while still carving out a claim for the intellectual independence of woman. Its two central arguments—that man must predominate through superior physical strength and capacity for violence, and that it is woman's lot to suffer nobly—are familiar enough. But the vividness of her vision is striking. Her descriptions of the hustings, of brawling in the legislature seem exaggerated, until one's mind goes to the scene of Preston Brooks caning Charles Sumner in the Senate chamber, until one reads that David McCord was not above settling an argument with his fists.[6] And her analysis of the essential lot of woman, to suffer and so ennoble herself and those around her, is resonant with her own experience. Thought itself, the product of Louisa McCord's struggle for self, came to seem so echoing with the difficulties of social role that it became identical with pain, however fruitful. "Is not all intellect suffering?" she asks here. Mary Chesnut, a lighter spirit and a friend, would not perhaps have agreed: she had not quite Louisa McCord's capacity for gritting her teeth and plunging ahead and shrank, indeed, from the sanguinary nursing that her neighbor undertook in the Civil War.[7] But the diarist would have understood the motive for the question, and the tension of the answer.

GLANCING lately over a quaint old history of the Albigenses, by Pierre de Vaulx Cernay, we were amused by a remark of the author, that *"dans ce moment, le Seigneur qui semblait s'être endormi tant soit peu, se reveillait au secours de ses serviteurs."*[8] To judge from the movements of certain portions

---

6. Thorp, *Female Persuasion*, pp. 190–91.
7. *Mary Chesnut's Civil War*, ed. C. Vann Woodward (New Haven, 1981), pp. 372, 361: "Mrs. Preston and I whisper. Mrs. McCord scorns whispers."
8. Pierre de Vaulx-Cernay, *Histoire de l'hérésie des Albigeois*, in *Collection des memoires relatif à l'histoire de France*, ed. F. Guizot (Paris, 1824), 14:90: "Dans ce moment" should be "dès ce moment." The copy of this in the Thomas Cooper Library, University of South Carolina, has this passage marked, and was probably used by McCord.

of society just now, one is led to suppose that they agree with the warlike Pierre as to the disposition of *Le Seigneur* to nap, "*tant soit peu,*" now and then; and are, like the savages of certain of the Pacific islands, who, as we have somewhere read, endeavour, with drums, rattles, and other hideous noises, to rouse their sleeping Deity, now attempting, by all manner of singular commotions and bustle extraordinary, to effect a similar end. To this laudable aim, the ladies seem at present disposed to lend a helping hand, and if Providence is not to be roused, evince no little disposition to take the arrangement of affairs into their own hands.

> "C'est dommage, garo, que tu n'es point entré
> Au conseil de celui que prêche ton curé;
> Tout en eut été mieux."[9]

We must try, however, to rectify, since we are too late to have things made to order. So, go it, ladies! On, for "the whole hog!" while your hands are in for it. Let's have no half-way measures, sickly things, "at war 'twixt will and will not."[10]

> Now o'er the enemy's battlements we'll stride,
> And cry our loudest war-cry in his ear,
> Nor pause until each coward drop of blood,
> To tell the story of its fears hath run,
> And whispering to the panic-stricken heart,
> Quick bids it summon forth the cringing knee,
> And own its victor's might.

Universal equality! *Fraternité* extended even to womanhood! And why not? Up for your rights, ladies! What is the worth of a civilization which condemns one half of mankind to Helot submissiveness? Call ye this civilization, with such a stained and blurred blot upon it? "Out, damned spot! Out, I say! One; two; why then 'tis time to do it!"[11] The knell of injustice has sounded! The world is awake! All men (and women too) are born free and equal. Every man shall have his rights, according to his own reading of them. Let A knock down B, and B trip up C. *Vogue la galère!*[12] Reform! Reform! If the world should be turned somewhat topsy-turvy thereby, and chance, in the hustle, to be kicked back to barbarism and the dark ages, or even to something worse, perchance, than man has yet the memory of—

---

9. Livre IX, Fable 4, in *Fables de La Fontaine*, ed. E. P. et F. Dauphin (Paris, 1960), p. 223; "garo" should be capitalized.
10. *Measure for Measure*, II. ii. line 43.
11. *Macbeth*, V. i. lines 34–35.
12. A common French phrase, meaning "Here goes!" It is the heading of chapter 6 of Charles Kingsley, *Yeast* (London, 1851), from which McCord later quotes.

never mind. *Fiat Justicia ruat Coelum.*[13] Capital motto that, by the way. Like the prince's tent of the fairy-tale, it is capable of limitless extension, and all can find shelter under its interpretations. *Justicia,* says the communist beggar—*Justicia* means, whip me down those rich fellows and let me revel in their luxuries. Why should not I too ride in the king's carriages? *Justicia,* says Louis Napoleon, means, that I shall do what I please in this realm of France.[14] Shoot down the beggarly rascal who disputes it. *Justicia,* says Austria, means that Hungary shall not breathe without my permit. *Justicia,* growls the Russian bear, means imperial might. *Justicia,* answers Kossuth, means democratic might.[15] *Justicia,* shouts Cuffee, means that I am a sun-burned white man. *Justicia,* responds Harriet Martineau,[16] means that I may discard decency and my petticoats at my own convenience; and, *Justicia,* echo her Worcester Convention sisters, means extinction to all law, human and divine.[17] God is a bugbear—decency a dream. *Fiat Justicia ruat Coelum.* The beggar shall have his *patés de foie gras*; the negro shall be christened a white man; and woman—surely she, too, shall profit by this general revolution! Stand to your colours, ladies! Take for your flag the whole animal, *in extenso,* from snout to tail, with the motto, *ab actu ad posse valet consecutio*;[18] i.e.—if a man swallows the head, surely he may take in the tail also. Follow close, ladies. The door of privilege is open pretty wide for the admission of Cuffee. Should *he* get in, surely *you* might follow. Woman is awake. "You see her eyes are open." "Ay, but their sense is shut."[19] Forgive us, you true women; you, the noblest of practical philosophers; you, who bear and forbear, humbling yourselves, that others may rise upon your efforts, and yet ceasing those efforts, never; you, who see with love and without envy, husband, brother, or son, too often in the pride of manhood, with slight and sneer contemning his "womankind," and holding her even in his love, as

"Something better than his dog—a little dearer than his horse;"[20]

13. Cf. "Of Passive Obedience," in *The Philosophical Works of David Hume* (Edinburgh, 1826), 3:533: "The maxim, *fiat Justitia, ruat Coelum,* let justice be performed, though the universe be destroyed, is apparently false, and, by sacrificing the end to the means, shows a preposterous idea of the subordination of duties."

14. Louis Napoleon had staged his coup d'état on 2 December 1851.

15. Louis Kossuth, 1802-1894, the Hungarian revolutionary leader who was briefly prime minister in 1849.

16. Harriet Martineau, 1802-1876, the English abolitionist and author of *Society in America* (1837).

17. The Woman's Rights Convention met in Worcester, Massachusetts, in October 1851.

18. Trans. And action necessarily implies the ability to repeat the action; this is medieval, rather than classical, Latin.

19. *Macbeth,* V. i. lines 23-24.

20. Tennyson, "Locksley Hall," line 50; the full quotation is, "As the husband is, the wife is: thou art mated with a clown, / And the grossness of his nature will have weight to weigh thee down. / He will hold thee, when his passion shall have spent its novel force, / Something better than his dog, a little dearer than his horse."

you, who can see this, feel it, and yet strive on; you, whose heart may ache, and yet lovingly labour still, seeking no reward, knowing no reward, save the fulfilment of that high duty, of that great mission of love, which is woman's mission on earth. *Your* eyes are indeed open, nor is their sense shut. A true woman, fulfilling a woman's duties, (and do not let our masculine readers suppose that we would *confine* these to shirt-making, pudding-mixing, and other such household gear, nor yet even to the adornment of her own fair person,) a high-minded, intellectual woman, disdaining not her position, nor, because the world calls it humble, seeking to put aside God's and Nature's law, to *her* pleasure; an earnest woman, striving, as all earnest minds can strive, to do and to work, even as the Almighty laws of Nature teach her that God would have her to do and to work, is, perhaps, the highest personification of Christian self-denial, love and charity, which the world can see. God, who has made every creature to its place, has, perhaps, not given to woman the most enviable position in his creation, but a most clearly defined position he *has* given her. Let her object, then, be to raise herself *in* that position. *Out* of it, there is only failure and degradation. There be those, however, and unfortunately not a few, who look upon these old-fashioned ideas as exploded. God's and Nature's laws have nothing to do with the question. A Harriet Martineau, or a Fanny Wright,[21] would prefer a different position in the picture, and many a weak sister is misled by them.

In every error there is its shadow of truth. Error is but truth turned awry, or looked at through a wrong medium. As the straightest rod will, in appearance, curve when one half of it is placed under water, so God's truths, leaning down to earth, are often distorted to our view. Woman's condition certainly admits of improvement, (but when have the strong forgotten to oppress the weak?) but never can any amelioration result from the guidance of her prophets in this present move. Here, as in all other improvements, the good must be brought about by working with, not against—by seconding, not opposing—Nature's laws. Woman, seeking as a woman, may raise her position,—seeking as a man, we repeat, she but degrades it. Every thing contrary to Nature, is abhorrent to Nature, and the mental aberrations of woman, which we are now discussing, excite at once pity and disgust, like those revolting physical deformities which the eye turns from with involuntary loathing, even while the hand of charity is extended to relieve them. We are no undervaluer of woman; rather we profess ourselves her advocate. Her mission is, to our seeming, even nobler than man's, and she is, in the true fulfilment of that mission, certainly the higher being. Passion governed, suffering conquered, self forgotten,

21. Frances Wright, 1795–1852, a Scot who later lived in the United States. She was a disciple of Robert Owen and latterly an advocate of women's rights, abolition, birth control, and universal education; she had also founded a colony for free blacks in Nashoba, Tennessee.

how often is she called upon, as daughter, wife, sister and mother, to breathe in her half-broken but loving heart, the whispered prayer, that greatest, most beautiful, most self-forgetting of all prayers ever uttered,—"Father, forgive them, they know not what they do." Woman's duty, woman's nature, is to love, to sway by love; to govern by love, to teach by love, to civilize by love! Our reviewer may sneer,—already does sneer,—about "animal functions" and the "maternity argument."[22] We fear not to meet him, or rather her; (for we do not hesitate to pronounce this article to be the production of one of the *third* sex; that, viz. of the Worcester Convention petticoated would-be's;) true woman's love is too beautiful a thing to be blurred by such sneers. It is a love such as man knoweth not, and Worcester Conventionists cannot imagine. Pure and holy, self-devoted and suffering, woman's love is the breath of that God of love, who, loving and pitying, has bid *her* learn to love and to suffer, implanting in her bosom the one single comfort that she is the watching spirit, the guardian angel of those she loves. We say not that all women are thus; we say not that most women are thus. Alas! no; for thus would man's vices be shamed from existence, and the world become perfect. But we do say, that such is the type of woman, such her moral formation, such her perfection, and in so far as she comes not up to this perfection, she falls short of the model type of her nature. Only in aiming at this type, is there any use for her in this world, and only in proportion as she nears it, each according to the talent which God has given her, can she contribute to bring forward the world in that glorious career of progress which Omniscience has marked out for it. Each can labour, each can strive, lovingly and earnestly, in her own sphere. "Life is real! Life is earnest!"[23] Not less for her than for man. She has no right to bury her talent beneath silks or ribands, frippery or flowers; not yet has she the right, because she fancies not her task, to grasp at another's, which is, or which she imagines is, easier. This is baby play. "Life is real! Life is earnest!" Let woman so read it—let woman so learn it—and she has no need to make her influence felt by a stump speech, or a vote at the polls; she has no need for the exercise of her intellect (and woman, we grant, may have a great, a longing, a hungering intellect, equal to man's) to be gratified with a seat in Congress, or a scuffle for the ambiguous honour of the Presidency. Even at her own fire-side, may she find duties enough, cares enough, troubles enough, thought enough, wisdom enough, to fit a martyr for the stake, a philosopher for life, or a saint for heaven. There are, there have been, and there will be, in every age, great hero-souls in woman's form, as well as man's.

22. "Enfranchisement of Woman," *Westminster Review* 55 (July 1851): 153–54; this is not by Harriet Martineau, as McCord guessed, but by John Stuart Mill and his wife-to-be, Harriet Taylor.
23. Longfellow, "A Psalm of Life," line 5.

It imports little whether history notes them. The hero-soul aims at its certain duty, heroically meeting it, whether glory or shame, worship or contumely, follow its accomplishment. Laud and merit is due to such performance. *Fulfil* thy destiny; *oppose* it not. Herein lies thy track. Keep it. Nature's sign-posts are within thee, and it were well for thee to learn to read them. Poor fool! canst thou not spell out thy lesson, that ever thus thou fightest against Nature? Not there! not there! Nothing is done by *that* track. Never; from the creation of the world, never. Hero-souls will not try it. It is the mock-hero, the dissatisifed, the grasping, the selfish, the low-aspiring, who tries *that* track. Turn aside from it, dear friends—there is no heaven-fruit there; only hell-fruit and sorrow.

We regret to believe that this move for woman's (so called) enfranchisement, is hitherto, entirely (at least in its modern rejuvenescence) of American growth. Thank heaven! our modest Southern sisters have held aloof from the defiling pitch, and Worcester Conventions are entirely a Yankee notion. Not a little surprised have we been to see, in so long-established and respectable a periodical as the Westminster Quarterly, a grave defence of such mad pranks as are being enacted by these petticoated despisers of their sex,—these would-be men,—these things that puzzle us to name. They should be women, but, like Macbeth's witches, they come to us in such a questionable shape, that we hesitate so to interpret them. Moral monsters they are; things which Nature disclaims. In ceasing to be women, they yet have failed to make themselves men. Unsexed things they are, we trust, like the poor bat in the fable, who complains, "neither mouse nor bird will play with me," destined to flit their twilight course, alone and unimitated.[24]

Such is the point of view in which we have hitherto looked upon this subject, that we feel as though to attack it seriously, were scarcely less ridiculous than to defend it. But the poison is spreading; and, truly, except that the fashion of the thing is a little newer, it is but a piece with negro emancipation; a subject with which the world has been stunned for many a year, until, at last, it now seems ready, with fanatic zeal, to sacrifice all that it has gained, of good, of beautiful, and of true, at the shrine of this fearful phantom. Madness becomes, sometimes, contagious; and, to judge from the symptoms, society labours, at present, under a high state of brain-fever—delirious, decidedly—raving over one fantastic dream or another. Communism and abolitionism have been dancing their antics through its bewildered brain; and now behold the *chef d'oeuvre* of folly! Mounted on Cuffee's shoulders, in rides the lady! The genius of communism bows them both in, mouthing over Mr. Jefferson's "free and equal" sentence, and banishing the motto, *par nobile fratrum*.[25] Woman! woman! respect thyself and

---

24. Livre II, Fable V, in *Fables de La Fontaine*, p. 52.
25. Horace, *Satires*, II, 3.243; trans. a notable pair of brothers.

man will respect thee. Oh! cast not off thy spear and thy shield, thine Aegis, thine anchor, thy stay! Wrapped, thou art, in a magic cloud. Cast it not off to destroy thine own divinity. Man worships thee and himself; he knows not why. Ignorantly, in thee, he bows to his "Unknown God." The benevolent, the true, the holy, the just; in a word, the God of Love speaks to him through *thee*. Woman, *cherish thy mission*. Fling thyself not from the high pedestal whereon God has placed thee. Cast not from thee thy moral strength—for, lo! what then art thou! Wretchedly crawling to thy shame, thy physical weakness trampled under foot by a brutal master, behold thee, thou proud mother of earth, to what art thou sunk!

We have said that this move is entirely of American growth. Our reviewer tells us, exultingly, that there are indications of the example being followed in England, and that a petition of women, agreed to by a large public meeting at Sheffield, and claiming the elective franchise, was presented to the House of Lords by the Earl of Carlisle.[26] Heaven bless the mark!—surely our poor world is moon-struck! Let us, however, hear some of the reviewer's arguments, though we confess it is with a sickening loathing that we turn them over.

What first do these reformers ask? "Admission in law and in fact, to equality in all rights, political, civil and social, with the male citizens of the community." "Women are entitled to the right of suffrage, and to be considered eligible to office." "Civil and political rights acknowledge no sex, and therefore the word 'male' should be struck from every state constitution." "A co-equal share in the formation and administration of laws,—municipal, state and national,—through legislative assemblies, courts and executive offices." Then follows the memorable quotation from the "memorable document" about all men being created free and equal, the ladies arguing, with some reason, that "men" here, certainly stands for human beings, and thereby prove their right at least equal to Cuffee's. In fact, the reviewer remarks, that such being American principles, "the contradiction between principle and practice cannot be explained away. A like dereliction of the fundamental maxims of their political creed, has been committed by the Americans in the flagrant instance of the negroes; but of this (she charitably remarks) they are learning to recognize the turpitude. After a struggle, which, by many of its incidents, deserves the name of heroic, the abolitionists are now so strong in numbers and influence, that they hold the balance of parties in the United States. It was fitting that the men whose names will remain associated with the extirpation, from the democratic soil of America, of the aristocracy of colour, should be among the originators, for America, and for the rest of the world, of the

---

26. Mill and Taylor, "Enfranchisement," p. 161; George William Frederick Howard, 7th Earl of Carlisle, 1802–1864, was then chancellor of the Duchy of Lancaster; as Lord Morpeth, he had visited the United States, including Charleston, during 1841 and 1842.

first collective protest against the aristocracy of sex; a distinction as accidental as that of colour, and fully as irrelevant to all questions of government."[27]

This is certainly taking a position, and we are glad to see that the advocates of this move class themselves exactly where they should be, cheek by jowl with the abolitionists. We thank them, at least, for saving us the trouble of proving this position. Of the first Worcester Convention, that of 1850, (which is, in fact, the second Woman's Rights Convention, the first having been held somewhere in Ohio,) "the president was a woman, and nearly all the chief speakers women,—numerously reinforced, however, by men, among whom were some of the most distinguished leaders in the *kindred cause* of negro emancipation." One of the resolutions of this meeting declares "that every party which claims to represent the humanity, the civilization, and the progress of the age, is bound to inscribe upon its banners, equality before the law, *without distinction of sex or colour.*"[28] Oh! there are things so horrible that man, in sheer terror, will mock at what he hates, and think to sneer the scoffing fiend away. We laugh at this, but it is frightful;—frightful to think that thousands of women, in these United States, have signed, and thousands more, if these accounts be correct, are willing to sign their names to such a document. Oh! woman, thou the ministering angel of God's earth, to what devil's work art thou degrading thyself!

But, their reasoning in all this? for they have an argument. First, then, as we have just seen, they claim that the distinctions of *sex and colour are accidental and irrelevant to all questions of government*. This is certainly clinching the argument, and that by an assumption which is so extremely illogical, that we are forced to say, if this reforming sisterhood can advance no better ground for their pretensions, it shows them but ill-fitted for the reins of state which they propose taking in hand. The distinction of colour has for many years been a point in discussion, and science has now settled that, so far from being accidental, it is an immutable fact of creation, that the black skin and woolly head are distinctive marks of race, which no age, climate, nor circumstance, has ever been able to efface; and there is no more accident in a negro's not being born a white man, than there is in his not being born a baboon, a mouse, or an elephant. As to the distinction of sex being accidental, this is a remarkable discovery of the present enlightened and progressive age. Sex and colour are severally so essential to the being of a woman and a negro, that it is impossible to imagine the existence of either, without these distinctive marks. We have hitherto understood that the sex of a human being was fixed long before its entrance into

---

27. Mill and Taylor, "Enfranchisement," pp. 149, 150.
28. Ibid., p. 149: the first convention was in Seneca Falls, New York, in 1848, but McCord has transcribed the error from Mill and Taylor.

# Enfranchisement of Woman 347

this world, by rules and causes, which, entirely unknown to man, were equally beyond *his* reach, and that of accident. Such has, we believe, been the received opinion of the learned; but Miss Martineau (who is, we take it, our reviewer) has determined to assume the position of vice regent to Deity, (a power, by the way, which she seems inclined entirely to depose,) and, like *Sganarelle*, in Molière's witty play of the *"Medecin malgré lui,"* she arranges things to suit her own ignorance. Sganarelle having assumed the fact that the heart was on the right side of the human system, has the suggestion made by one of his bewildered admired admirers, that the generally received opinion of science and experience has universally placed it on the left. Oh! answers the ready quack, *"celà était autrefois ainsi: mais nous avons changé tout celà."*[29] If Miss Martineau and her sisterhood should prove powerful enough to depose *Le Bon Dieu*, and perfect their democratic system, by reducing His influence to a *single* vote, we do not doubt that, according to the approved majority system, it will be clearly and indisputably proved that Cuffee is Sir Isaac Newton, and Mrs. Cuffee, Napoleon Buonaparte, and Miss Martineau herself may stand for Cuffee, unless, indeed, she should prefer (as some of her recent works seem to indicate) to have it decided that she is *Le Bon Dieu* himself. She could probably carry the votes, with equal ease either way, and get rid of these little accidental distinctions. We, however, must, at this point of the question, be old-fashioned enough to declare ourselves conservatives. We cannot entirely shake off old prejudices, and still, spite of Dr. Sganarelle and Miss Martineau, are inclined to look for our hearts on the left side of our bodies, and for our God in the glorious works of his creation. We prefer His rule to Miss Martineau's, and believe that He has given the distinctions of race and sex, not accidentally, (with Omniscience there is no accident,) but distinctively, to mark the unchanging order of His creation—certain beings to certain ends.

All the further arguments of our reviewer are based upon the assumption we have been discussing, and with it fall to the ground. If beings are created to different ends, it is impossible to consider in them the point of equality or inequality, except in so far as their differences are of a kind to still allow them to be cast in the same category. As, for instance, the man, as animal, is superior to the beast, whose subordinate intellect makes him, as co-labourer of the soil, or as rival candidate for its benefits, inferior to man. The white man is, for the same reason, superior to the negro. The woman, classed as man, must also be inferior, if only (we waive for the moment the question of intellect) because she is inferior in corporeal strength. A female-man must necessarily be inferior to a male-man, so long as the latter has the power to knock her down. In womanhood is her

---

29. Molière, *Le Médecine Malgré Lui*, 2: vi.

strength and her triumph. Class both as woman, and the man again becomes the inferior, inasmuch as he is incapable of fulfilling her functions. A male woman could as ill assume the place and duties of womanhood, as a female-man could those of manhood. Each is strong in his own nature. They are neither inferior, nor superior, nor equal. They are different. The air has its uses, and the fire has its uses, but these are neither equal nor unequal—they are different.

"A reason (says the reviewer) must be given why any thing should be permitted to one person and interdicted to another."[30] A reason!—a reason why man cannot drink fire and breathe water! A scientific answer about hydrogen and oxygen will not answer the purpose. These are facts, not reasons. Why? Why? Why is anything on God's earth what it is? Can Miss Martineau tell? We cannot. God has made it so, and reason, instinct and experience teach us its uses. Woman, Nature teaches you yours.

"The speakers at the Convention in America, have (says the reviewer) done wisely and right, in refusing to entertain the question of the peculiar aptitudes, either of women or of men, or the limits within which this or that occupation may be supposed to be more adapted to one or the other."[31] In the name of all that is foolish, what shall we consider, if not the aptitude of a person or thing to his or its uses? It is fortunate that Miss Martineau has never descended from her high sphere, to allow herself to be burthened with the cares of a family; for had she, in that capacity, forgotten to consult the aptitudes of things to their uses, she might, in some inauspicious fit of philosophic experiment, have committed the unlucky blunder of packing her children in December ice to warm them, or, perchance, cast the little unfortunates into the fire, by way of cleansing their dirty faces. And what might the philosophical and reforming world have thus lost! The ignorant mob, who persist in judging of the uses of things by their aptitudes, might have committed the egregious mistake of taking this doubty philosopher—this Wilberforce[32] of women—this *petit bon Dieu*—for a murderess, and hung her for the interesting little experiment of burning her brats.

We, of the conservatives, who judge of the uses of things by their aptitudes, can read woman's duties any where better than in an election crowd, scuffling with Cuffee for a vote. Imagine the lovely Miss Caroline, the fascinating Miss Martha, elbowing Sambo for the stump! All being equals, and no respect for persons to be expected, the natural conclusion is, that Miss Caroline or Martha, being indisputably (even the Worcester conventionalists allow that) corporeally weaker than Sambo, would be thrust into the mud. "Hello da! Miss Caroline git two teet knock out, and Miss

30. Mill and Taylor, "Enfranchisement," p. 151.
31. Ibid., p. 152.
32. William Wilberforce, 1759–1833, the leading British antislavery advocate.

# Enfranchisement of Woman 349

Marta hab a black eye and bloody nose!" "Well, wha' faw I stop fa dat? Ebery man must help hisself. I git de stump anyhow, and so, fellow-citizens, Sambo will show how Miss Marta desarve what she git." Or, let us suppose them hoisted through this dirty work. The member is chaired— some fair lady, some Mrs. or Miss Paulina Davis, who, we see, figures as President of the last convention, or one of her vices, Angelina Grimké Weld, or Lucretia Mott[33]—let us imagine the gentle Paulina, Angelina, or Lucretia fairly pitted, in the Senate, against Mr. Foote, for instance, or Mr. Benton, or the valourous Houston,[34] or any other mere patriot, whom luck and electioneering have foisted there. We do not doubt their feminine power, in the war of words—and again we beg to defer a little the question of intellect—but are the ladies ready for a boxing match? Such things happen sometimes; and though it is not impossible that the fair Paulina, Angelina and Lucretia might have the courage to face a pistol, have they the strength to resist a blow? La Fontaine tells us a fable of a wax candle, which, being ambitiously desirous of immortality, and seeing a handful of clay, that, hardened by the fire into a brick, was enabled to resist time and the elements, turned the matter over for a while in its waxen brains, and finally determined to try the experiment in its own person. A fire being conveniently near, and concluding, we presume, like the lady conventionalists, that all arguments on aptitudes and uses was quite *de trop*, in so clear a case of logical induction,

"Pars sa propre et pure folie
Il se lança dedans. Ce fut mal raisonné.
Ce cièrge ne savait grain de philosophie."[35]

The fact, that women have been queens and regents, and filled well these positions, as cited by the reviewer in the cases of Elizabeth, Isabella, Maria Theresa, Catharine of Russia, Blanche, etc.,[36] proves that woman, as a woman and a monarch—with the double difference, that the habits of the civilized world accord to these positions—has had the intellect to fill the position well; but it does not prove, and rather goes to disprove, her power of struggling with the masses. As woman and queen, doubly isolated from those masses, she kept her position, simply because of such isolation—because, supported by the laws and habits of society,

---

33. Paulina Kellogg Wright Davis, 1813-1876, a New Yorker; Angelina Emily Grimké Weld, 1805-1879, a Charlestonian; Lucretia Coffin Mott, 1793-1880, from Massachusetts; all were prominent feminists.
34. Henry Stuart Foote, 1804-1880, then in transition from being Mississippi's senator to being its governor; Thomas Hart Benton, 1782-1858, for many years senator from Missouri, but defeated in 1850; Samuel Houston, 1793-1863, late president of the Republic of Texas, then its senator.
35. Livre IX, Fable 12, in *Fables de la Fontaine*, p. 232.
36. Mill and Taylor, "Enfranchisement," p. 153.

none dared insult or resist her. But, suppose those laws and habits abrogated, what would have become of the virago, Elizabeth, when she gave the lordly Essex a blow on the ear? If ever it should happen to the fair Paulina, Angelina or Lucretia to try, under the new *regime*, a similar experiment on any of their male coadjutors, or opponents, it is rather probable that they may receive, upon the subject of aptitudes and uses, a somewhat striking lesson. Of the combatant ladies, similarly cited, the same remark is to be made. Ladies of the feudal ages, they generally were petty monarchs: that is to say, defending their strongholds. These were always supported and strengthened, rather than impeded by their sex, the *prestige* of sex seconding and doubling the admiration accorded to their remarkable actions. Joan of Arc, (decidedly the most remarkable of heroines, and, strange to say, not cited by the reviewer,) was a wonderful woman; great as a woman; a phenomenon in her way, certainly, but still a woman-phenomenon. Her deeds were unusual for woman, but, nevertheless, done as a woman, and claiming, for their sanction, not the rights and habits of manhood, but divine inspiration. She never levelled herself to man, or, so doing, must have sunk to the rank of the coarse *femmes de la Halle* of the French revolution. Such, too, would of necessity be the case with the man-woman that our conventionists would manufacture. Deprived of all which has hitherto, in separating her from man, wrapped her, as it were, in a veil of deity; naked of all those observances and distinctions which have been, if not always her efficient, still her only shield; turned out upon the waste common of existence, with no distinctive mark but corporeal weakness; she becomes the inevitable victim of brutal strength. The reviewer acknowledges (or rather, remarks, for she does not seem to be conscious that it is an acknowledgment) that to account for the subjection of woman, "no other explanation is needed than physical force."[37] Setting aside, then, for the moment, all other differences, we would be glad to have the lady explain how she would do away with the difficulty arising from this acknowledged physical inferiority? Man is corporeally stronger than woman, and because he, in the unjust use of his strength, has frequently, habitually, (we will allow her the full use of her argument,) even invariably, oppressed and misused woman, how does she propose to correct the abuse? Strangely, by pitting woman against man, in a direct state of antagonism; by throwing them into the arena together, stripped for the strife; by saying to the man, this woman is a man like yourself, your equal and similar, possessing all rights which you possess, and (of course she must allow) possessing none others. In such a strife, what becomes of corporeal weakness? Perhaps we will be told how man conquers the wild beast, and, by knowledge and intellect, holds in sway the mighty elephant and the for-

---

37. Ibid., p. 152.

est's king. True, by *intellect*. He has the superiority of intellect, and he uses it. It is God's and nature's law, that he should use it. Man, generally, uses it to subdue his inferior, the beast. The white man uses it to subdue his inferior, the negro. Both are right, for both are according to God's law. The same argument has been used, to prove the necessity of woman's subjection. This, we think, is taking mistaken ground, and unnecessarily assuming a doubtfully tenable position. Woman's bodily frame is enough to account for her position. The differences of mind between the sexes, we are, ourselves, inclined to regard rather as differences than inequalities. More of this anon, however. Granting, for the moment, exact mental equality, how will the conventionists redeem corporeal deficiencies? They do not pretend that woman is the superior mind, only the equal. Still, then, man—where they are matched against each other—where woman assumes manhood, and measures herself hand to hand with him—has, of necessity, the superiority—a brutal superiority, if you please, but still the superiority—and, in proportion as it is brutal, will the triumph it gives be brutal. Woman throws away her strength, when she *brings herself down* to man's level. She throws away that moral strength, that shadow of divinity, which nature has given her to keep man's ferocity in curb. Grant her to be his equal, and instantly she sinks to his inferior, which, as yet, we maintain she has never been.

Many women—even, we grant, the majority of women—throw themselves away upon follies. So, however, do men; and this, perhaps, as a necessary consequence, for woman is the mother of the man. Woman has allowed herself to be, alternately, made the toy and the slave of man; but this rather through her folly than her nature. Not wholly *her* folly, either. *Her* folly, and *man's* folly, have made the vices and the punishment of both. Woman has certainly not her true place, and this place she as certainly should seek to gain. We have said that every error has its shadow of truth, and, so far, the conventionists are right. But, alas! how wide astray are they groping from their goal! Woman has not her true place, because she—because man—has not yet learned the full extent and importance of her mission. These innovators would seek to restore, by driving her entirely from that mission; as though some unlucky pedestrian, shoved from the security of the side-walk, should, in his consternation, seek to remedy matters, by rushing into the thickest thoroughfare of hoofs and wheels. Woman will reach the greatest height of which she is capable—the greatest, perhaps, of which humanity is capable—not by becoming man, but by becoming, more than ever, woman. By perfecting herself, she perfects mankind; and hers, we have said, is the higher mission, because, from her, must the advance towards perfection begin. The woman must *raise* the man, by helping, not by rivalling, him. Without woman, this world of mankind were a wrangling dog-kennel. Could woman be transformed into man, the same result would follow. She it is who softens; she it is who civilizes;

and, although history acknowledges her not, she it is who, not in the meteoric brilliancy of warrior or monarch, but in the quiet, unwearied and unvarying path of duty, the home of the mother, the wife and the sister, teaching man his destiny, purifies, exalts, and guides him to his duty.

> "Under a nominal recognition of a moral code, common to both [says our reviewer] in practice, self-will and self-assertion form the type of what are designated as manly virtues; while abnegation of self, patience, resignation and submission to power, unless when resistance is demanded by other interests than their own, have been stamped, by general consent, as preeminently the duties and graces required of women. The meaning being merely that power makes itself the centre of moral obligation, and that a man likes to have his own will, but does not like that his domestic companion should have a will different from his."[38]

Now, all this means, if it means anything, that woman, in the present condition of the world, is a self-denying, patient model of Christian love and charity; while man, unable to conquer his harsher passions, still benefits by her virtues. The reviewer, envying him the lordly privilege of getting into a passion, raving and ranting, would advise all womankind to disturb him in his monopoly, and to rave, rant and be selfish along with him. We confess, for ourselves, that where a poor woman, borne away by human weakness, and restive under oppression, catches the raving malady a little, we seldom feel inclined to be harsh in our judgments of her. Nature is frail—we pity her, and confess that her case is a hard one. Even Zantippe, "the famous old scold,"[39] could, no doubt, have shown cause for exasperation; and it is not unlikely that, as philosophers are men, the good dame had no little reason on her side. Still, if she had borne life meekly, although her present great renown in history and spelling-book, spreading the knowledge of her name as far as that of old crooked back Z himself, would never have been attained; even Miss Martineau, we think, must confess that, while less celebrated, Mrs. Zantippe would have been a more perfect and more amiable character; and we, while we feel a deep interest in the sorrows of this far-famed personage, would hardly deem her a desirable model for our daughters. Wrath and power are hideous and fearful; wrath and weakness are hideous and contemptible. We trust that such of our sisters as may have attained the beautiful point of perfection, which our reviewer rather contemptuously refers to, will be sufficiently rewarded by the proud consciousness of duty fulfilled, to induce them to work on, in their righteous course—if not a flashing beacon of light to a benighted world, at least a holy ray of God's own sunlight, to purify and to bless. If ladies fear that these concessions are too great, and the pride

38. Ibid., p. 155.
39. The wife of Socrates.

of sex inclines them to rebel a little, let them remember that they are concessions, not to man, but to God;—not to the husband or the brother—who, if he raves too hard, it is not in human weakness not to feel a little spiteful against—but to nature and mankind. Each,—the lowliest individual woman,—is in bearing and forbearing, in earnest striving and in patient suffering, doing her share towards softening and civilizing this hard world. Such is God's task to her, and she must fulfil it, or pass away either the frivolous plaything of a day, or the scorned abortion of a misplaced and grovelling ambition.

As regards the question of intellect, it is a most difficult one to argue. We are ourselves inclined to believe that the difference of intellect in sexes exists, as we have said, rather in kind than degree. There is much talk of the difference of education and rearing bestowed upon individuals of either sex, and we think too much stress is laid upon it. Education, no doubt, influences the intellect in each individual case; but it is as logically certain, that intellect, in its kind and degree, influences education *en masse*;—that is to say, Thomas, the individual man, may be better suited to woman's duties, than Betty, the individual woman, and *vice versa*. Thomas might make a capital child's nurse, in which Betty succeeds but badly; while Betty might be quite competent to beat Thomas hollow in a stump oration; and yet we have a fair right to argue, that Thomas and Betty are but individual exceptions to a general rule, which general rule is plainly indicated by the universal practice of mankind. The fact that such relative positions of the sexes, and such habits of mind, have existed, more or less modified, in all ages of the world, and under all systems of government, goes far to prove that these are the impulses of instinct and teachings of Nature. It is certainly a little hard upon Mrs. Betty to be forced from occupations for which she feels herself particularly well qualified, and to make way for Mr. Thomas, who, although particularly ill-qualified for them, will be certain to assert his right; but laws cannot be made for exceptional cases, and if Mrs. Betty has good sense, as well as talent, she will let the former curb the latter; she will teach her woman-intellect to curb her man-intellect, and will make herself the stronger woman thereby. The fact that less effort has been made to teach woman certain things, is a strong argument that she has (taking her as a class) less aptitude for being taught those certain things. It is difficult to chain down mind by any habit or any teaching, and if woman's intellect has the same turn as man's, it is most unlikely that so many myriads should have passed away and "made no sign." In the field of literature, how many women have enjoyed all the advantages which men can command, and yet how very few have distinguished themselves; and how far behind are even those few from the great and burning lights of letters! Who ever hopes to see a woman Shakspeare? And yet a greater than Shakspeare may she be. It may be doubtful whether the brilliant intellect, which, inspiring noble thoughts, leaves still the great thinker grovelling in the lowest vices and slave of his passions, without the self-command to keep them in sway, is superior to that which, knowing good and evil, grasps almost instinctively at the first. Such, in its uncorrupted nature, is woman's intellect—such her inspiration. While man *writes*, she *does;* while he imagines the hero-soul, she is often performing its task; while he is painting, she is acting. The heart, it is sometimes argued, and not the brain, is the priceless pearl of womanhood, "the oracular jewel, the Urim and Thummim, before which gross man can only inquire and adore."[40] This is fancy and not reasoning. The heart is known to be only a part of our anatomical system, regulating the currents of the blood, and nothing more. It has, by an allegory based upon exploded error, been allowed to stand for a certain class of feelings which every body now knows to be, equally with other classes, dependant upon the brain; and, in a serious argument, not the heart and the brain, but the difference of brain; not the feeling and the intellect, but the varieties of intellect, should be discussed. We consider, therefore, the question of pre-eminence as simply idle. We have already endeavoured to prove that, whatever the intellect of woman, it would have no influence in altering the relative position of the sexes; we now go farther, and maintain that the nature of her intellect confirms this position. The higher her intellect, the better is she suited to fulfil that heaviest task of life which makes her the "martyr to the pang without the palm."[41] If she suffers,—what is this but the fate of every higher grade of humanity, which rises in suffering as it rises in dignity? for, is not all intellect suffering?

We have, throughout this article, made no reference to the biblical argument, because, with those who receive it, it is too well known and too decisive to need farther comment. To those who reject it, it is of course no argument. We have endeavoured to prove that common sense, quite independently of revelation, marks the place of woman, and that while the Scriptures confirm, they are by no means necessary to decide the question.

The resolutions of the last Worcester Convention are taken so entirely (in many sentences verbatim) from the article in the Westminster, which we have been reviewing, that very evidently the same mind has inspired both, showing thus a systematizing of the subject, that proves, we fear, some truth in the assertion of the reviewer, that this movement is a political one, and "carried on in a form which denotes an intention to persevere."[42] A letter was read to the meeting from Miss Martineau, and put-

---

40. Kingsley, *Yeast*, p. 145.
41. Elizabeth Barrett Browning, "The Cry of the Children," line 44; the full text is, "They know the grief of man, without its wisdom / They sink in man's despair, without its calm; / Are slaves, without the liberty in Christdom / Are martyrs, by the pang without the palm."
42. Mill and Taylor, "Enfranchisement," p. 149.

Enfranchisement of Woman 355

ting two and two together, we conclude that Miss Martineau, was the *de facto* composer of these resolutions, in which morbid vanity, "that brawl-begotten child of struggling self-conceit and self-disgust," so painfully exhibits itself. Should we prove mistaken, we can only regret that there should be two women in the world capable of such a composition. The reviewer thinks, farther, that this move "is destined to inaugurate one of the most important of those movements towards political and social reform, which are the best characteristics of the present age."[43] When a grave periodical allows such sentiments to soil its pages, it is time for us to cease to laugh. It is time for man to open his eyes to the mischievous effects of a progressive system of reform, which allows, not illogically, such a bud to be grafted upon it. It is time for woman, in right earnest, to take up arms in her own cause, ere she be hurled by traitors of her own sex from the high pedestal where God has placed her. Let her wield those weapons of love, charity, affection, firmness, and fortitude, with which Nature arms her, and, though her path be through sorrow, even through sorrow climbs she to perfection. Richter somewhere compares a young bride to the sleeping child of *Carafola*, over which an angel holds a crown of thorns.[44] The angel of sorrow shall indeed wake her by pressing that crown upon her brow; but let her not shrink from the waking. "Life is real! Life is earnest!" and its duties are not to be shunned because our weakness relishes them not. Let woman make herself free, in the true sense of the word, by the working out of her mission. "Liberty is duty, not license;" and woman is freest when she is the truest woman; when she finds the fewest difficulties in the way of conforming herself to her nature.

"Not enjoyment, and not sorrow,
　Is our destined end or way,
But to live that each to-morrow
　Find us farther than to-day.

"Let us then be up and doing,
　With a heart for any fate,
Still achieving, still pursuing,
　Learn to labour and to wait."[45]

---

43. Ibid.
44. *Leben des Quintus Fixlein*, in Johann Paul Friedrich Richter, *Werke* (Munich, 1962), 4:33; it is interesting that the 1827 Carlyle translation of *Quintus Fixlein* does not contain this passage, so one infers McCord had recourse to the original, though there is no other evidence that she read German; "Carafola" should be "Garafola," in other words, Benvenuto Garafola, 1481–1559, a painter of the school of Raphael.
45. Longfellow, "A Psalm of Life," lines 9–12, 33–36; McCord has omitted five stanzas, and "to live" should be "to act."

Woman is not what she might be, not what she ought to be. Half persuaded, as she is, that her position is one of degradation and inferiority, she becomes, as a matter of necessity, degraded to that opinion, just in so far as she is convicted of its truth; and hence, too often, folly becomes her pleasure, vanity her pride. But this is man's blotting of God's fair work. Woman is neither man's equal nor inferior, but only his different. It would indeed be well if man, convinced of this, could, in his relations with her, "throw aside his instruments of torture," and aid rather than oppress her. Thus, we firmly believe, it will be, in the perfection of time, worked out by woman's endurance and patient labouring in her own sphere; but never, certainly, by her assumption of another, equally ill-adapted to her mental and her bodily faculties. For her it is (God's apostle of love) to pass through life with "the cross, that emblem of self-sacrifice, in her hand, while her pathway across the desert is marked by the flowers which spring beneath her steps." Life's devoted martyr she may be—man's ministering angel she may be; but, for heaven's sake, mesdames, the conventionists,—not Cuffee's rival candidate for the Presidency!

## 11.

*John Holmes Bocock*

"Emerson on History"[1]

John Holmes Bocock was one of those restless Presbyterians who were responsible for more square miles of print than almost any other Southern social group, who seem as omnipresent in the Old South mind as Methodists in the New South; earnest, indefatigable, wary, and cutting. He was a Virginian, born in Buckingham County in 1813 and dying in Lexington a little across the state in 1872.[2] If that suggests rootedness, the impression is erroneous. He was educated at Amherst College in Massachusetts, where he was contemporary to Henry Ward Beecher. Upon their graduation in 1835, Beecher is said to have remarked, "When next we meet it will be upon the topmost wave of controversy," which has the ring of Beecher complacency but is a remark almost too neat to be credible as a prophecy of both theological and sectional dissidence.[3] In 1836 Bocock entered the Union Theological Seminary in Prince Edward County, Virginia, and by the end of the decade had been licensed as an evangelist. For a few years he plied his indigent trade in and around Appomattox, until he resolved to try his fortune to the West. At Parkersburg in the mountains of western Virginia he preached for two years, but then pushed further on to become chaplain to a Louisiana planter and his slaves. But the steamy reaches of the Delta proved inimical to his health and he went, ill, on a steamer up the Mississippi as far as Cincinnati and staggered around the streets—or so his biographer reports—until a "Christian gentleman" took the saddlebags preacher into his restoring care. As Bocock said of his Western venture and the discontent that had occasioned it, "I

---

1. John Holmes Bocock, "Ralph Waldo Emerson—History," *SLM* 18 (April 1852): 247–55.
2. Clement R. Vaughn, "Biographical Sketch," in *Selections from the Religious and Literary Writings of John H. Bocock, D.D.*, ed. His Widow (Richmond, 1891), pp. ix–xxvii.
3. Ibid., p. x.

found that the desperate remedy I had sought for was worse than the disease."[4]

Back in Virginia, he was pastor for five years at the Providence Church in Louisa County before moving to another Presbytery at Harrisonburg in the Shenandoah valley. In 1856 he eventually reached a fashionable ministry, in the District of Columbia at Georgetown. There, balanced between North and South, he tried discretion on the touchy matters of slavery and sectionalism, though his temperament was far from neutral, but the war forced his hand and his resignation. Thereafter he tried to be chaplain to a Virginia regiment for six months, but his health was unequal to the rigors of campaign and he had to recuperate for a year before taking another church in Halifax. Again he sickened and moved to the mountains and a new ministry in Fincastle, and again his health failed, but fatally. A restless life, it found space and energy enough to fill a posthumous volume of over six hundred pages.

His widow gathered up his writings, quietly bowdlerized them, and found a clergyman friend to write a biographical preface.[5] Most of his pieces were theological: sermons, devotions, prayers, reflections upon the religion of others. He wrote a good deal for Thornwell's *Southern Presbyterian Review*, but also, as in this essay on Ralph Waldo Emerson, in secular mood for the *Southern Literary Messenger*. Bocock was committed to his region, but not blind to what he regretfully viewed as intellectual deficiencies. Indeed, his obituary essay on the antebellum Southern mind, written in 1869 as "Authorship at the South," anticipates the historiographical orthodoxy of recent years. Why is the South unimpressive in its literature? Bocock's answers will sound familiar to the reader, even if they were meant as pained apologia. "Our Southern states have usually been more intent upon the production of men than books"; "the predilection of Southern men for the bar and for political life"; "a habitual and deeply-seated fondness among our country gentlemen for English literature of the reign of Queen Anne"; "the sparseness of the population in the country at the South has been a great hindrance

---

4. Ibid., p. xii.
5. For example, his review of "Bledsoe's Theodicy," *Southern Presbyterian Review* 8 (April 1855): 517, has the remark, "Though the book is one of higher pretensions, and in some respects, of decidedly superior merits, to the common anti-Calvinistic tracts, in which our Methodist brethren take delight." In *Selections*, p. 331, the reference to Methodists has been deleted.

to literary pursuits"; "as literature is analytical and philosophic, the South could not addict herself freely and fully to its influence and spirit, as the highly developed consciousness of her Caucasian children would have prompted her to do, because that race had so much to do with the inferior servile race"; "the tranquillity of our career as independent States hitherto until recently; the barrenness of historical romance which has marked our localities."[6]

It was not likely that an Old School Presbyterian like Bocock would be sympathetic to Emerson. This essay is a spirited attack upon the silken reveries of Concord from the standpoint of a robust and sarcastic empiricism. Reid and Paley are ranged against Coleridge and Hegel. Emerson's provincial New England perception is mocked for its claim to represent Americanism. Bocock plays the old game of the conservative student of the classics, seeming to expose the apparently new as the obviously old. He drives wedges into the faint cracks of transcendental organicism. In one sense, Emerson and Bocock share a Romantic persuasion. For both, the recipe for an American literature is Wordsworthian in its rapt contemplation of nature. But Bocock's Romanticism is less fascinated in the nature of the contemplation, more inclined to grant that the thing seen is as real as the mind seeing, less disposed to vary the mythic interpretation of history. As an advocate of cultural particularisms, Bocock is perhaps the more Romantic. His charge that Emerson insufficiently appreciated the historical evolution and dynamic of human nature, the cultural variety of man in time and place, was an accusation from a historicist to an ahistoricist.

WE do not pretend to show a novelty, in setting at the head of our sheet the name of Emerson, the mystic essayist of Concord, Massachusetts. We believe it is some twelve or fifteen years since the first of these three volumes of Essays of his was issued from the Boston press.[7] There are

---

6. *Selections*, pp. 455–83; there is no evidence that Bocock directly influenced later opinion, although Jay B. Hubbell (by no means a devotee of the orthodoxy) mentions the essay in his *The South in American Literature, 1607–1900* (Durham, 1954), pp. 451, 893.

7. Ralph Waldo Emerson, *Essays* (Boston, 1841).

hardly any American books which are more inviting than they are, on the first glance. There may be readers to whom they have continued to be attractive long after the first glance. And we freely admit that the taste of such readers is as much entitled to respect, for its own sake, as is our own widely different taste. A few years before the advent of Emerson, the works of SAMUEL TAYLOR COLERIDGE made their appearance, in fair type and binding, in those departments of the booksellers' shops which are devoted to rich and rare novelties. These works were *The Friend*, *The Aids to Reflection*, and the *Statesman's Manual*.[8] They were admired in their early day by many ambitious schoolboys of the metaphysical turn of mind. They may have been admired by some grown men: we will not pretend to deny it. But we venture to surmise that the number of the admirers of Coleridge in the whole American Union, among full-grown men, did not much exceed the number of the present House of Representatives, that is, about one for every seventy thousand of the population of the country. The Coleridgeites said he was rejected because he was profound and the public taste was superficial or shallow. The No-Coleridgeites said he was muddy and obscure, and that his thoughts were, after all, not worth the trouble of the interpretation. The suit is yet pending. And we think that many epochs of New Constitutions will pass away, before a judge shall be found on the bench in the Republic of Letters, who shall have retained a due impartiality in the case, while he was acquiring the information necessary to decide it. In every nation of readers, there will always be some whose intellectual life is set, more or less, on the key of *omne ignotum pro mirifico*.[9] There will always be some whose appetites demand a seasoning so keen, that clearness, connexion, and sobriety of thought will seem but weary dulness. Things which are small things, or even nothings, when reduced to their adequate terms of expression, have often been made to appear great things, by being thrown loosely out, in florid, and mystic, and deep-sounding sentences, with a scrap of Greek in the frontispiece, after the manner of Coleridge and Bulwer,[10] or a few lines of wild, enigmatical English verse, after the manner of Waldo Emerson. There will always be some readers to whom what are called *suggestive* books are most acceptable; that is, books which do not *express* things, but lead their reader into gorgeous realms of bewilderment, and because his mind is not occupied with the thoughts of the author, he is thereby compelled by very intellectual hunger to shape out dreams and visions of his own.

Readers of this class liked Coleridge greatly. Readers of this class

---

8. Coleridge, *The Friend: A Series of Essays* (London, 1812); *Aids to Reflection* (London, 1825); *The Statesman's Manual* (London, 1816).

9. Tacitus, *Agricola*, 30.3: trans. whatever is unknown is supposed to be magnificent; "mirifico" should be "magnifico," though this sounds like a deliberate misquotation.

10. Edward Bulwer-Lytton, 1803–1873, the English novelist.

certainly, and it may be others too—we pretend not to say—will like the Essays of Ralph Waldo Emerson.

Mr. Emerson has attained to the honour of a laudatory review in Blackwood's Magazine, an honour to which very few American writers have attained. In that article, he is commended as being decidedly American in tone and spirit. "We are quite sure that no French or German critic could read the speculations of Emerson, without tracing in them the spirit of the nation to which this writer belongs." "The spirit of the New World, and of a self-confident democracy could not be more faithfully translated into the language of a high and abstract philosophy than it is here."[11] Such is the opinion of the foreign critic. And without the slightest intention of satire, we fully admit that an Englishman may be a better judge of what is American, in this respect, than we are. And yet in this case we venture to think that the English critic has widely erred as to the main spirit of Emerson's writings. We are at best no great admirer of that often heard phrase, *American Literature*. What does it mean? Does not all expression of human thought in an artistic manner, in true and fitting words, depend on the individual circumstances of a writer more than on his political condition? Climate, scenery, personal dependence or independence, joyousness or gloom, these have certainly much to do with the utterance of thought in written words. Yet there is no such intelligible thing as an American climate. The girdle of seasons, and the panorama of gorgeous, changing cloud and sky, which pass annually over Louisiana and Texas, are as much the American climate as are the grand artillery of winter, and the brief, bright summer days, around the shores of Lake Michigan. The face of nature looks very differently at Rockfish Gap on the Blue Ridge of mountains in Virginia, from what it does at Franconia in the Notch of the White Mountains in New Hampshire; and very differently at either of these places from what it does in some vast cypress plain in Louisiana, where the palmetto stands everywhere like giants' hands struggling up from the earth, and the thick-set cane is around you, and the wild birds enliven the whole air. And yet all who look closely into the subject tell us that these things have much to do with literature, and we respectfully suggest that a Northern literature, a Southern literature, a Western literature, an Atlantic literature, are much more intelligible expressions than an American literature. The latter expression seems to us totally "void for indefiniteness," with an exception which will be presently mentioned. And so it would be any where in a geographical area as large as ours. If a man who speaks good sense, speaks of European literature, he means an aggregate mass of intellectual productions, and certainly he does not mean any one definite

---

11. [William Henry Smith], "Emerson," *Blackwood's Magazine* 62 (December 1847): 644, 645.

thing. The writings of Hungarians, and the writings of Irishmen, would both be European literature; and might probably at this time, breathe much the same political spirit, and come from men not dissimilarly situated; yet they would be distinguishable productions. The literature of Russia, and that of Naples, would hardly be found similar, though both countries are in Europe, and both peoples are under the heel of despotism. French literature and English literature are far from being the same article, though nothing but "a narrow frith divides" the two nations.

But the writer in Blackwood seems to think that Emerson's writings are American in their spirit, because they breathe the spirit of "a self-confident democracy"—using the words in that broad sense in which our government is distinguished from the monarchies and despotisms of Europe, and not in the partisan sense in which they are employed here. Here we admit that there may be such a thing on the one hand, as a republican spirit in literature, and on the other hand, there may be such a thing as a monarchical and despotic spirit in literature. This we admit to be an exceptional case in which the phrase, "American literature," may have some definite meaning. In this case it may mean a literature breathing the spirit of republican liberty. In this sense the writings of Ralph Waldo Emerson may be very American. We had not discovered it. Very probably the writer in Blackwood had. Yet we do not believe that this is the best meaning, or probably the correct meaning, to attach to the indefinite phrase. By American literature our countrymen do not probably mean a literature which shall breathe the spirit of our government, so much as a literature which shall hallow the localities of our land, and throw the charm of genius around the spots where the ashes of our fathers sleep. A native literature ought to do for Massachusetts, or for Virginia, or for Louisiana, what Burns and Walter Scott have done for Scotland; Miss Edgeworth and Charles Lever for Ireland;[12] Shakspeare and Wordsworth for England; that is, cause every one whom its pages have charmed to desire to see, and incline to love and gloat over, the localities which came to the mental vision while the spell of genius was upon it. Writers who would do this for the American States, hallowing the country and producing a love of the local soil in the bosoms of the people, and stopping the tide of restless, roving emigration, ever thirsting for new scenes, and new lands, and new skies, would do what is worthy to be done, and what would deserve the name of native literature. Mr. Ralph Waldo Emerson is an idealist of the most transcendent wing and of the highest cloud. We do not intend to approach very near to the verge of the abyss of metaphysics to fetch thence the definition of an idealist. Emerson's panegyrist in Blackwood, says of him, that he "has denied the

---

12. Maria Edgeworth, 1767–1849, noted chiefly for *Castle Rackrent* (1800); Charles James Lever, 1806–1872, best known for *Harry Lorrequer* (1839).

substantial, independent existence of a material world, but he does not deny the existence of a phenomenal world."[13] He dreameth the dreams of Germany. He is the younger brother of Kant, and Fichte, and Schelling, and Hegel. They say that the German mind was so repulsed from outward things, by the civil despotism prevailing around it, that it flew inwards into its own dark depths, and entered thus upon these minute self-analyses and self-deifications. But these are not American dreams. We cannot expect that a mind thus involved, and believing that the material world is at best but an appearance, but a drama of successive phenomena, should encircle American scenery with halos of the enchantment of genius, or do much else to draw our hearts to the local objects of the land in which we live. Let the men of Prussia and of Austria dream thus. But why should an American? Is not the world of manly thought and healthy action open to him? We are not surprised when a prisoner, confined for long years in a dungeon, tames the flies and spiders, makes companions of the frogs and mice, and scrawls adages and ditties upon the stones of his prison-walls. But we are surprised at such things in one who has the clear, free sky above him, and the wide world around him.

We must beg the reader's indulgence for a few words on another point—not so much for the importance of its bearing on our estimate of Mr. Emerson, as for the intrinsic and substantive importance which it seems to us to possess. We have been speaking of American modes of thought. But is there not such a thing also as an American mode of expression? It seems to us that there is. We are by no means without excellent models of a style of expression in language, which is thoroughly American. Take the productions of John Randolph, of John Quincy Adams, of John Caldwell Calhoun, of Daniel Webster. The literary world knows, or ought to know, something of them all. The casts of their political opinions, the circumstances of their education, the places in which they were reared, were all different—some of them very widely different. We believe that if one phrase would comprehend them all on any subject whatever, it would be as to the style of their language. Nervous simplicity, directness, freshness, clearness, are terms which approach very near to comprehending them all. And from the circle of the meaning of those terms there are not many writers, of any age or land, who lie farther remote, as we humbly think, than Mr. Ralph Waldo Emerson. This, then, is our critical estimate of these volumes: Considered in reference to their subject matter, they might almost as well have borne on their title-page to have been written by *English* Coleridge, or by *German* Kant, or by *Jew* Spinoza, or by Erigena *Scotus*, or by Thomas *Aquinas*, as by Emerson, the *American*. Considered as to their style, very few, if any, books have ever been published on this side of the

13. Smith, "Emerson," p. 655.

Atlantic, which contained so much straining after the hot house wonders and paradoxes of expression peculiar to the mystical writers of Europe and of ancient ages. We never saw any books written in America, hardly excepting the "Key of Heaven," and the "Garden of the Soul," which to us savoured so decidedly of the monastery and of dream-life. We never saw any books, from any side of the Atlantic, except, probably, some of Coleridge's worst, and some of the most German of German books, which contained so little of that peculiar and pleasant mode of American expression, in which words stand flatly and clearly for things, for facts, for realities, and not for mere notions, visions, dreams, gleams, species, antitypes of meaning. Strict justice requires that it should be added, that we have seen few books of any description, from which, it seems to us, less that is really valuable may be derived.

The title of the first of these Essays is: HISTORY. On the first passage of the fly-leaf preceding it are the following words:

"There is no great and no small
To the soul that maketh all,
And where it cometh all things are;
And it cometh every where."

Happily we do not think the reader will hold us bound to tell him what these sybilline words mean. On the second page of the fly-leaf occur the following lines—

"I am owner of the sphere,
Of the seven stars and the solar year,
Of Caesar's hand, and Plato's brain.
Of Lord Christ's heart, and Shakspeare's strain."

These verses are attachés not of the volume, but of the essay on history, with which we have now more directly to do. And for that reason they are quoted just as they stand. There can be few readers of the Messenger upon whom the last four lines will not produce a decidedly unpleasant impression, and most justly. It may be that the peculiar and most singular views of the author, as developed further on, will excuse him from the wild and reckless, maniac vanity, which these words seem at first view to carry on their face. And we do not discuss the question now, further than to suggest that they are probably intended only as a bold, short expression of the philosophical opinion upon which he chiefly dwells in the succeeding essay. He makes a more distinct announcement of the philosophical principle on which he thinks history is to be studied, in the following sentence which introduces the essay itself:

"There is one mind common to all individual men. Every man is an inlet to the same and to all of the same. He that is once admitted to the right of reason is made a freeman of the whole estate. What Plato has thought he may think; what a saint has felt he may feel; what at any time has befallen any man he can understand. Who hath access to this universal mind is a party to all that is or can be done, for this is the only and sovereign agent. Of the works of this mind history is the record."[14]

It is especially necessary to my present purpose to put the reader in possession of Mr. Emerson's views of the nature of History as clearly as may be. Even to those who have before them his essay on the subject, the main point of his meaning may be almost as clearly conveyed, in the extracts now to be given, as in the whole piece itself. We do not look regularly at his meaning, but merely get glimpse after glimpse, as one standing in the front yard of some large and gloomy building might occasionally see one piece and another of its furniture, as a torch on the hearth by turns flamed up and yielded to darkness, and flamed up and yielded again. Much of the essay seems to us to be composed of the intervals of darkness when the torch shines not. The following passages seem, taken in connection with what have already been given, about as fully to convey his peculiar view of the relation between individual man and history as can be done in a limited space:

"A man is the whole encyclopedia of facts. The creation of a thousand forests is in one acorn, and Egypt, Greece, Rome, Gaul, Britain, America, lie folded already in the first man. Epoch after epoch, camp, kingdom, empire, republic, democracy, are merely the application of his manifold spirit to the manifold world."—p. 1.

"Of the universal mind each individual man is one more incarnation. All its properties consist in him. Each new fact in his private experience flashes a light on what great bodies of men have done, and the crises of his life refer to national crises." *Ibid.*

"Each new law and political movement has meaning for you. Stand before each of its tablets and say, 'Under this mask did my Proteus nature hide itself.'"—*p.* 5.

"All that Shakspeare says of a king, yonder slip of a boy that reads in a corner feels to be true of himself."—*p.* 6.

"I have no expectation that any man will read history aright, who thinks that what was done in a remote age, by men whose names have resounded far, has any deeper sense than what he is doing to-day. The world exists for the education of each man. There is no age or state of society or mode of action in history, to which there is not somewhat corresponding in his life."—*p.* 7.

"I can find Greece, Asia, Italy, Spain, and the Islands—the genius and creative principle of each and of all eras in my own mind."—*p.* 9.

14. Emerson, *Essays*, p. 3.

"Civil and natural history, the history of art and of literature, must be explained from an individual history, or must remain words. There is nothing but is related to us, nothing that does not interest us,—kingdom, college, tree, horse, or iron shoe, (!) the roots of all things are in man. Santa Croce and the Dome of St. Peters are lame copies after a divine model. Strasburg Cathedral is a material counterpart of the soul of Erwin of Steinbach. The true poem is the poet's mind; the true ship is the ship-builder."—p. 16.

"The primeval world—the Fore-World as the Germans say—I can dive to it in myself as well as grope for it with researching fingers in catacombs, libraries, and the broken reliefs and torsos of ruined villas."—p. 21.[15]

And the author proceeds in the latter part of the essay to give the meaning of several of the old Greek fables, and some even of more recent works of fiction, as interpreted in reference to individual man. The story of Prometheus, that of Antaeus, of Tantalus, of the Sphinx, and of Helen; and the romances of Perceforest, Amadis de Gaul, and the Bride of Lammermoor, (!) are then explained as symbols of things in man's individual life. And so history is to be understood! "All public facts are to be individualized, all private facts are to be generalized."[16]

In these extracts the observant reader will find some things of which he may be inclined to dispute the accuracy in point of fact. Other things he will see, whose claim to be admitted to the honors of sense and reason he will be strongly disposed to dispute. But Mr. Emerson is not a common man; he is an Idealist. Shall he be held subject to the laws which are made for and by such coarse and common spirits as a Locke, a Reid, or a Paley?[17] "Will a courser of the sun work softly in the harness of a dray-horse? His hoofs are of fire, and his path is through the heavens; will he lumber on mud highways, dragging ale for earthly appetites, from door to door?"

There is one thought, however, which can hardly be forborne to be indulged in reference to Mr. Emerson's principal maxim of philosophy, that there is "one mind common to all individual men." We do not see how he can gratulate himself that he is one and the same mind with Plato, with any more propriety than that with which he must lament that he is one and the same mind with that Herostratus who burnt the temple of Diana. Why should he follow his principles when they make him identical with the good and great, and not when they equally legitimately make him identical with others. If he is possessor of "Plato's brain," he is also on the same principle, possessor of the brain of Thersites.[18] If he has "Caesar's hand"

---

15. Ibid., pp. 4, 5, 6, 7, 8, 15, 18; Bocock has slightly misquoted here and there, without altering the substance.
16. Ibid., p. 18.
17. William Paley, 1743–1805, the English theologian, noted for his *Natural Theology: or, Evidences of the Existence and Attributes of the Deity* (1802).
18. A Greek at the siege of Troy who insulted Agamemnon and was killed by Achilles for mocking his grief for Penthesilea.

he has also the hand of Cinna the poor poet whom the mob killed for his bad verses. If he has "Shakspeare's strain," he is just as truly the singer of the songs of Bavius, of Mevius,[19] and of the mighty hero of the Dunciad. This is probably an oversight of Mr. Emerson. It is certainly an omission. To supply it we propose the following variation of the poetic lines we have quoted above, from the second page of the fly-leaf:

> I walk upon the very foot,
> Of the famous Lord John Bute;
> The very hand now on the paper,
> Once obeyed Sir William Draper;
> I have the very self-same ear,
> With which King George the Third did hear;
> I too possess the very skull,
> That once with Horne Tooke's brains was full;
> I have John Wilkes's thinking art,
> With Lord George Gordon's noble heart.

Truly, as Mr. Emerson says, "the transmigration of souls is no fable."[20]

One man is *like another as one apple or one peach is like another*. "As in water face answereth to face, so the heart of man to man."[21] But one man is not the *same* as another, nor does one man possess the moral or intellectual faculties of another, any more than one apple or one peach has the same saccharine juice, or the same seeds, as another. Human beings are all of a kindred nature with each other, and have therefore common resemblances, like the successive crops of apples which grow upon the same tree. From nice sympathies of nature which are set in harmony by the Divine Hand which made them, the impulses, motives, principles, and aspirations of one are intelligible to another. This is far, very far from being a new truth. Yet it is all we can make of the grand maxim, that "there is one mind common to all individual men."

But if not, if there be more in it than this poor residuum of ours, if Mr. Emerson, being an Idealist, has seen by the aid of "Plato's brain," what we, ungifted thus, and fettered to an earthly sphere, have not seen and

---

19. Bavius and Maevius were Augustan poets, known for their bitter attacks upon contemporaries like Horace and Vergil.

20. Lord John Stuart, 3d Earl of Bute, 1713–1792, the favorite of George III and prime minister, 1762–1763; Sir William Draper, 1721–1787, the defender of the Marquis of Granby against the Junius Letters; John Horne Tooke, 1736–1812, politican and philologist; John Wilkes, 1727–1797, opponent of Bute, eventual M.P., and pornographer; Lord George Gordon, 1751–1793, agitator and president of the Protestant Association for the repeal of the Relieving Act of 1778, instigator of the No-Popery Riots of 1780 (he later converted to Judaism); Emerson, *Essays*, p. 27.

21. Proverbs 27:19.

cannot see, then the star of Mesmer[22] must "pale its ineffectual fires" before the crescent of Emerson with its "lunar horns." Mesmer professed only to establish, by magnetic power, such a connection between two minds that the thoughts and senses of one were also the common property of the other. But that connection the seer of Concord discovers to have been long ago established, even from of old, between all human minds that ever were, or ever will be, without the aid of the magnetic fluid. How magnificent are the powers of an Idealist!

Our author's interpretations of the old mythological fables of Greece, as allegories which have meaning for individual life:—that the story of Antaeus means that both "the body and the mind of man are invigorated by habits of conversation with nature;" that the riddle of Orpheus shows the power of music to "unfix, and as it were to clap wings to solid nature;" that "Tantalus means the impossibility of drinking the waters of thought which are always gleaming and waving in sight of the soul"—are not novelties in the history of Grecian learning.[23] We suppose in fact that such a mode of interpretation has occurred to every thoughtful student, in his school days, as he has perused the notes, so rich in classic romance, which the learned Ludovicus Desprez has attached to the Delphin edition of Horace.[24] Whoever has at hand a copy of Anthon's Lempriere,[25] and will turn to the articles: PROMETHEUS, ALOIDES, IO, EUROPA, and twenty others, which might be mentioned if it was of any use to take the time to mention them, will see at once that this mode of interpretation was no unrevealed mystery at the time when that not very exhaustive, or very complete, or very accurate work was published. And whoever has gotten hold of *Creutzer's Symbolik*, a German book, of which Anthon makes, with great propriety, a good deal of use in that department of his work, will see that whole books have been written on the subject of the symbolical interpretation of the Greek fables.[26] We do not pretend to say that a book in so general circulation as Aesop's Fables, with the common Croxall appendage of a moral to each one, is a familiar instance of Mr. Emerson's discovery already in extensive use.[27] No less an authority, however, than Joseph Addison has spoken of them (in the Spectator, No. 133) as compositions of a

---

22. Friedrich Anton Mesmer, 1734–1815, the German physician and promoter of "mesmerism," later known as hypnotism.

23. Emerson, *Essays*, p. 26.

24. *Quinti Horatii Flacci Opera. Interpretatione et Notis Illustravit Ludovicus Desprez* (Paris, 1691).

25. Charles Anthon, *A Classical Dictionary* (New York, 1807): Anthon was building upon the Classical Dictionary of Lempriere.

26. Georg Friedrich Creuzer, *Symbolik und Mythologie der Alten Völker* (Leipzig, 1810–1823).

27. Samuel Croxall, *Fables of Aesop and Others* (London, 1722).

similar kind to the allegorical fables of the Greeks.[28] Yet they are not exactly fair instances in the present case, because the things spoken and done, of which they give account, have not always human agents, but agents belonging to the brute creation, as the Cock and Fox, the Cat and the Mice, the Country Mouse and the City Mouse, the Ass in the Lion's skin, the vain Jackdaw, besides numbers of ants, grasshoppers, geese, cranes, larks, kites, eagles, and heathen deities. Mr. Emerson's great maxim, that "all public facts are to be individualized, all private facts are to be generalized," and that he "can dive into himself and find the primeval world,"[29] does not therefore meet with an exact and full accomplishment in Aesop's Fables, because most of those fables are things said and done by the lower order of animals, and he seems to have intended that things said and done by man in history should be used as segments and revelations of the nature of individual men. This defence is made *for* our author. He could only make a moiety of it for himself, in consistency with another great truth which he has uttered on the 29th page of this same essay on History. "The transmigration of souls is no fable. I would it were; but men and women are only half human. Every animal of the barn-yard, the field, and the forest, of the earth and of the waters that are under the earth, has contrived to get a footing and to leave the print of its features and form in some one or other of these upright, heaven-facing speakers."[30] So it seems that the conversations which old Phrygian Aesop has reported, between animals of the barn-yard, and field, and forest are, at last, no so far out of the line of the application of Mr. Emerson's great principle as he himself interprets it. It would seem that, on principles of public utility, he would better advance the other moiety also, and make his principle fairly embrace the Fables of Aesop as well as those of Prometheus, and Orpheus and Tantalus. For it can hardly be questioned, that by so doing, he would comprehend a class of beautiful allegories, more useful and instructive, and strange as it may seem to him, teaching more of human nature than that class of very beautiful fables which he has applied himself more expressly to interpret. Nor are all of Aesop's Fables made up of the fabulous *res gestae* of the brute creatures. It is hard to see how Mr. E. can decline to admit that he has been fairly anticipated in the discovery of the symbolical interpretation of ancient fable, probably by the Athenians and Romans themselves, but certainly by Lestrange[31] and Dr. Croxall, in refer-

28. Number 183 (29 September 1711), in *The Spectator*, ed. D. F. Bond (Oxford, 1965), 1:219–23.
29. Emerson, *Essays*, pp. 18, 19.
30. Ibid., p. 27.
31. Sir Roger L'Estrange, *Fables of Aesop and Other Eminent Mythologists: with Morals and Reflexions* (London, 1692).

ence to such fables as Aesop at Play, Caesar and the Slave, the master and his scholar, the Travellers, the Trumpeter taken prisoner, and others, in which no beast, bird or fish speaks, and no impossible things are said or done. Some of the ancient critics, of whom Addison tells us, in the before cited paper of the Spectator, attempted to turn the whole Iliad and Odyssey of Homer into allegorical representations with application to individual men and the qualities of our personal nature, making Achilles represent anger, Pallas wisdom, and so of other characters. And it is certain that Mr. Emerson was anticipated in his principle of giving an allegorical interpretation to the Myths of the Greeks, by Prodicus, as early as 390 years before the christian era, who invented the famous fable of the choice of Hercules, and secured himself a welcome wherever he travelled among the cities of Greece, by the narration of it.[32]

With all this high authority for spoiling the romance of early Greece, we cannot see wherefore it is desirable. We shall speak presently of that mode of interpretating history with which it is attempted to be connected. If this mode of understanding the mythology be defended on the ground that it makes those early and beautiful conceptions of the Grecian mind more instructive, we reply, that it is very common-place instruction, and easily had in purer forms from other sources. Upon the whole the myth is injured by the interpretation; for it loses more in the beauty and clearness of its dramatic form than it gains in significancy. If the fact be brought forward that the Greeks themselves attached an allegorical meaning to some of their own beautiful romances, it may be replied that where they did so, we may do so, where they did not do so, we have no authority to do so. This seems to us to be the safe and clear principle of criticism on the whole subject. If this is not so, then one critic may make Prometheus and Orpheus and Tantalus mean one thing, and another critic may make them mean another thing, according to the higher or lower developments of Idealism in the minds of the critics. For ourselves we frankly confess we would rather have the old than the new. We would rather have Homer's Orpheus and Tantalus, with the dramatic interest of the scenery and the persons, and the grand, wild light of romance around them, than the Orpheus and Tantalus of Creutzer and of Emerson, representing qualities of one individual person. We would rather have Livy's Romulus and Remus than Niebuhr's Romulus and Remus, if he leaves such characters standing at all in the realms of probability. We would rather have Scott's Bride of Lammermoor, standing as nature and the author put it, representing a whole group of human characters, acting as men and women did act, or

---

32. Prodicus, fl. 400 B.C., a rhetorician of the island of Ceos and a contemporary of Gorgias; in his story of Hercules, the figures of Vice and Virtue, personified as women, appear to the hero and alternately offer him arduous tasks and sensual pleasures, with Hercules choosing the former. See Xenophon, *Memorabilia*, II, 1, 21–34.

might have acted, and may act again, than Emerson's Bride of Lammermoor, with Sir William Ashton standing for "vulgar temptation," and Lucy Ashton for "fidelity" and Ravenswood Castle for "proud poverty."[33]

The method of interpreting history propounded in this essay of Mr. E., is but a consistent carrying on of that by which he reads the riddles of the mythology, with the slight variation that, here, both the type in the historical event, and the antitype in man's mental nature, are supposed to be facts. History is but a grand drama of that spiritual nature which is in every man, which the events of the world are enacting before his face, to demonstrate to him what is within himself. "Of the universal mind each individual is one more incarnation. All its properties consist in him."[34] History is but a perpetual series of charades to exhibit faculties, principles, capacities and aspirations in each individual man. It is but the delineation of human nature in an eternal series of Mexican picture-writing. The rise and fall of empires, the discovery of new continents, all great acts of statesmen, all progress of arts, sciences, commerce and refinements, all battles and sieges, all revolutions and reactions, all heroism and all tyranny, are but as the flights of birds before the Roman augurs; they are but as the answers of Delphi and Dodona to the Greeks, telling the qualities of man's individual nature. There is much that is imposing in this theory, as there are not a few splendidly beautiful fragments in the language in which it is stated. Yet every one feels at once that there is a fallacy in it somewhere, and that of a sweeping extent. We believe that it lies palpably on the surface. All men have more or less of the kindred nature, of common resemblance, of family likeness. But with this family likeness, it is a fact as familiar as household words, that there are endless diversities both of body and mind. No two men are exactly alike in the face, and there are probably more numerous diversities of mind than of body. It is therefore not exactly sound to reason from Greek history to American history. The senators of a certain city of early Greece acted thus and thus, therefore the city-fathers of Concord, of Cambridge, of Boston, or of Salem, would do the same thing, is not exactly sound. Still less is it sound to reason from masses of men, whole cities and kingdoms, to individual human nature. Though Mr. Emerson says he can find Greece, Asia, Spain and Italy in his own mind, we hope and believe that he cannot find the revolt at Corcyra, the Jacquerie, the Massacre of St. Bartholomew, and the Reign of Terror, in his own mind, however deeply he may dive into it. It may be replied that these terrible chapters of history had their origin in human nature, that human nature is responsible for them, that they are pictures of human nature. True, but it is not the human nature of every individual man. Cir-

---

33. Emerson, *Essays*, p. 29.
34. Ibid., p. 4.

cumstances of birth, education and life, exert very great influence, no doubt, upon human character; but it is yet a truism, doubtless discussed warmly by most of us when Sophomores in college, and which will not be discussed here because it seems very little less than self-evident, that there are original, native differences between different individual men. So far then from any individual in the United States to-day being able to see himself depicted in Greek or Egyptian or Roman history, it is probable that no individual man can see himself accurately depicted in the biography of the man nearest in his circumstances of all that have lived, or in all biographies together which have ever been written. Idealism makes men mere bundles of qualities, successive incarnations of the same thing. God makes men living souls, complete persons, each like himself, and incommensurable by any earthly philosophy. The whole edifice of the theory seems to have been built upon a figure of speech. It is true that history exhibits the capabilities of human nature. But it is human nature in the aggregate. All human nature is not in every individual man. Every man is not Plato. Every woman is not Helen. Every man is not Robespierre. Every woman is not Lucretia Borgia. If these short plain propositions are true, then this theory of history is not true. It affirms of every man what is only true of all men taken together.

The Idealist method of interpreting history may be brought to a fair test in another way. If it be true that every man "dive into himself" and find a department of his nature corresponding to the Grecian period of history, and another department within himself corresponding to the Roman period of history, and another department corresponding to the French, and another to the English period of history, if each "man is the whole encyclopedia of facts," if each man "is the compend of time," if each "man is a bundle of relations, a knot of roots, whose flower and fruitage is the world"[35] as Mr. Emerson so repeatedly asserts, then a wise man, well skilled in reading himself ought to be able to certify us concerning those periods whose records are of doubtful authenticity. If, having the history given, he is so readily able to find within himself the correlative department of individual nature, then, on the other hand, having himself given, he ought also to be able to tell whether any supposed chapter of history is fabulous, or whether it is a veritable piece of that great image which all history draws of individual man. If the two things are so clearly correlative then a philosopher at least, if no other man, ought to be able to find out the history from his own nature, as well as to find out his own nature from the history.

M. Bailly, an accomplished historian of Astronomy, who was put to death by Robespierre, came to the conclusion from tracing the history

---

35. Ibid., pp. 29, 30; the phrase "the whole enyclopedia of facts" does not occur.

of that science among the Chaldeans, Egyptians, Persians, Indians, and Chinese at very early periods, that there must have been a very ancient and highly cultivated people of Asia long before historic Nineveh, of whose memory every trace is now extinct, who were the instructors of the nation around them in astronomy. It seemed to him very probable that the sun, moon and star worship of the Chaldeans was not the cause of their astronomical discoveries, but that their astronomy, or that of their ancestors, or that of some neighboring nation from whom they borrowed it, laid the foundation for their peculiar religion.[36] We are informed of the settlement of the valley of the Tigris and the Euphrates, and the erection of seven cities in that neighborhood, at a very early period of sacred history. There is then almost silence concerning that region of the world for about 1,500 years according to the common chronology; after which we are suddenly presented with the city of Nineveh as a very great and populous city, exhibiting marks of decline and age in the ripeness of the vices of luxury among its people. From the time of Nimrod the hunter to the time of Jonah the prophet, was a longer period of time than has elapsed from the Saxon conquest of England to the present day. From the slight incidental notices which we have of the east, in the meantime, showing some knowledge of the arts, from the going out of similar gigantic styles of architecture into Egypt and into India as if from some common centre, as well as from the traces of astronomy, there is some reason to believe that a civilized nation lived, and grew, and declined, and perished in that region, in this unwritten period of time, either around Nineveh or some other of the seven cities, as its centre and capital. Yet history is dumb in relation to the life of that nation. Even the recent discoveries of Mr. Layard, of hoary and grand antiquity as they are, extend back only to the epoch where that lost period terminates.[37] Can Mr. Emerson dive into himself and certify us whether the conjecture of Bailly, that there was a civilized nation there, whose records are lost, is true or false? Can he ascertain, from gazing into the mirror of his own pure and amiable ideal nature what was the nature of that lost history?—how that lost nationality differed from the recorded Assyrian or Egyptian or Grecian national life?

Again. Plato gives us (in his Timaeus) a tradition which he shows to have been regularly handed down to his day from Solon, and which Solon professed to have heard from the priests of Lais in Egypt, that there was once a very large island in the Atlantic ocean far west of the pillars of Hercules, and fronting the mouth of that strait; that this Atlantic Island was as large as Asia and Libya together; and that there was once a powerful league of kings upon it, reigning over people of considerable civiliza-

36. Jean Sylvan Bailly, *Histoire de l'astronomie ancienne, depuis son origine jusqu'à l'établissement de l'école d'Alexandrie* (Paris, 1775).
37. Austen Henry Layard, *Nineveh and Its Remains* (London, 1849).

tion and refinement, who pushed their conquests over the whole north of Africa and in Europe as far as Etruria. It is a well-known bone of contention among antiquarians. Some regard the whole story as a fable. Others have been inclined to accept it is true, and to regard it as a dim tradition of America, wafted across the ocean, like the floating canoes which long afterwards led Columbus to the New World. Can Mr. Emerson look into the "encyclopedia of facts" which he finds in his own ideal nature, and tell us whether or not there was once a high civilization in those Atlantic Isles, long before the time of the Athenian Solon, or whether the whole affair is but a fable of the Egyptian priests of Lais?

What advantage will the reading world gain by this theory of history? Suppose it to be accepted. Then George Washington, on the page of history will be but an anatomy of the integrity and firmness which each of us carried in his own bosom. The history of Alexander, of Caesar, of Cromwell, of Napoleon, will be but an ethical account of our ambition. The stories of Helen, of Cleopatra, and of Mary, Queen of Scots will become only elegant and allegorical ways of describing to fair ladies what the power of beauty is. The grand annals of Pericles, of Tully, of Richelieu, of Pitt, of Jefferson, of Webster, and of Calhoun, will be converted into ethical sections of individual statesmanship! Kid, Blue Beard and the Red Rover will be fierce and bold acquisitiveness set sailing upon the high seas. Othello will become African jealousy; Hamlet will be a fine but feeble soul overtasked by destiny; Antonio will mean the generosity which is in each of us; Bassanio, our success; and Shylock, our avarice. It is a retrograde process. It is a leap from Laputa into Lilliput. It is a transmutation of the philosopher's stone into dust and ashes. In what respect would the great dark volumes of ethical abstractions into which history would thus be turned, be more valuable, more instructive, more pleasing than the fresh, and clear, and living volumes that they now are?

Contrary to the socialist theory, on the one hand, man has an individual being, and nature has provided him with faculties adapted to it, and imposed on him duties incident to it. Not that we are to say to him, with Montaigne: "Cut loose from society, you and a companion are enough for each other, or you for yourself"[38]—but there ought to be a part of his life strictly sacred and individual. He has individual rights. He has individual wants. He has individual duties. He must learn them by his own practical sense, judging of the demands of his nature so far as it is not soiled, and by the records of the lives of other individuals.

But contrary to the Idealist theory on the other hand, man has also social rights, social wants and social duties. They do not interfere with his

---

38. Montaigne, *Oeuvres complètes*, ed. A. Thibaudet et Maurice Rat (Paris, 1962), p. 242, has: "vous et un compagnon estes assez suffisant theatre l'un à l'autre, ou vous à vous mesmes."

individual wants, rights and duties. A sound individualism is the only safe basis of a sound socialism. We mean simply to say that good citizenship is as far from monkery or idealism on the one hand as it is from the phalanx of the Fourierite on the other hand. And for fear of being charged by the good sense of the reader, with multiplying words to point out that middle way in which it is best and safest to go, when there are so few yet among us who doubt or object to it, we leave the point with this mere suggestion of the principle which seems to lie at the foundation of all well-organized society. Among those parts of human history which are social, and not individual, and can have little or no meaning when looked at in the light of the idealist parellelism, are the constitution of a state or, as we may say, the mode and principle of its legislation; then its legislation itself, or the way of declaring the will of the sovereign authority, including the established means of public education, the regulations of trade and commerce and all other municipal regulations; its treaty making power or its way of covenanting with other nations; and other things of the kind too obvious to be mentioned, which are builded on a foundation broader than individual man, which grow out of qualities in man that have no meaning except in society; and without which individual men could not enjoy sufficient liberty to do things worth recording, or to study the records of what others have done.

We have not pretended to much more, in the preceding pages, than to suggest some hints of the abundant and manifold argument by which this idealist scheme of interpreting history may be refuted, when its mystical darkness shall settle upon us, if that time should ever arrive, in a thicker cloud than it has yet done. Mr. Emerson has as yet not a great many followers in the United States. Practical thinking, contact with the realities of life, and nervous good sense will probably separate from his school some of those who now temporarily adhere to it. His views are said not always to have escaped, even in the streets of Boston, that good-humored sneer which is the natural appendix of an enthusiasm so transcendental that it soars out of common sight, so amiable that nobody could persecute it, and so grotesque that few are found to follow it. There are other peculiarities about the school of thought which he seems endeavoring to found, to which a future occasion may afford us the pleasure of a reference.

# 12.

*Richard Henry Nisbet*

## "American Authorship and Nathaniel Hawthorne"[1]

This essay is an example of an intelligent piece by an obscure amateur. It was merely signed, upon its appearance in 1853, by an "R.H.N. of Macon, Ga." Scurrying through census data, local history, and genealogical studies uncovers that this probably signified Richard Henry Nisbet, a young physician. Almost nothing is known of him, save that he was born in 1832 in Madison, Georgia, married a Martha Dennis in 1859 and had three children, served in the Civil War, and died in 1870.[2] Rather more is known of his father, Eugenius Aristides Nisbet, a prominent Georgian lawyer, politician, and occasional author. The elder Nisbet was educated at the South Carolina College and the University of Georgia, before studying law in Litchfield, Connecticut. He served in the Georgia legislature from the late 1820s for a decade, where he was a follower of the Troup faction, one associated with states rights doctrine. Latterly he became a Whig and was in Congress for two terms from 1840, before returning to become a justice of the newly created Georgia Supreme Court. He stayed on the bench until 1853, when he resumed a private law practice in Macon. In the 1850s he was a Know-Nothing. Though he went to the convention of 1861 a Unionist, he stayed to become a secessionist and, indeed, drafted the ordinance of severance. He ran for governor in 1861, but was defeated by Joseph E. Brown. What is perhaps most relevant for his son and this essay on Hawthorne, Eugenius Nisbet was known as a literary man, wrote

---

1. [Richard Henry Nisbet], "American Authorship—Hawthorne," *SQR* n.s. 7 (April 1853): 486–508.
2. The 1850 Federal Census for Georgia lists no "R.H.N." who was a head of household; Newton Alexander Nisbet, *Nisbet Narrations* (Charlotte, N.C., 1961), pp. 280–81, identifies a Richard Henry Nisbet.

for the periodicals (including the *Southern Quarterly Review*, for which his son wrote this), was a founding member of the Georgia Historical Society, and was once offered the chair of Belles Lettres at the University of Georgia. He also helped to establish Oglethorpe College, adherent to the Presbyterian Church of which he was an elder. So the Nisbet family provided a context that makes this precocious essay plausible.[3]

It is not a very learned piece. It has no snatches of Cicero, no allusions to Guizot, no encomia of Goethe, no matured reflection on politics or metaphysics. It pretends to a certain aged aloofness, in speaking with casual compliment of "our young American authors," and manages no small awareness of the literary squabbles of the Augustan age. But it is really just a young man, who had kept up with the literary fashions, in between pursuing a medical career, and thought it might be agreeable to set down his thoughts. It may be the only time he did it, or it may not. We do not know. The style is pell-mell and raw. But one can understand why William Gilmore Simms should have admitted it to the pages of his *Review*. Many of its themes are characteristically Simms: that letters should be a profession, that America needs to match the literary outpouring of Europe, that writing can and should be conscious of morality, that the American land itself could promote insight of a special kind. Some notes are more personal to Nisbet. Simms knew about the strength and weakness of the periodical, but Nisbet's awareness is more detached and conscious that too much American energy went into transitory magazines, that intelligence stood in danger of being "lost in the sands." As a criticism of Hawthorne, its appreciative tone is not as unusual as legend once had it. The New Englander was understood as more than a writer of children's stories by his contemporaries.[4] Nisbet softens Hawthorne more than recent criticism might allow, makes him more the reformer than that skeptic and ironist might have wished, but the estimate—free from any striking sectional animosity—stands lucid.

---

3. *Dictionary of American Biography* (New York, 1934), 7: 527–28; see [Eugenius A. Nisbet], "The State of Georgia—Its Duties and Destinies," *SQR* 8 (October 1845): 421–80; "Views on Female Education and Character," *Southern Lady's Book* 1 (June 1840): 321–22; on Nisbet and the Georgia Historical Society, see *Georgia Historical Quarterly* 4 (June–September 1920): 42.

4. Bernard A. Cohen, ed., *The Recognition of Nathaniel Hawthorne: Selected Criticism since 1828* (Ann Arbor, 1969), pp. 3–115.

AMERICAN authorship, like American politics, is fast becoming a trade. We should, perhaps, have nothing to say against the fact (for professional literature must always possess this character), if the commodity vended were, in all respects, worthy of the money paid for it, and were always what it is claimed to be. But, in this doubt lies the embarrassing difficulty which renders the trade in it of questionable propriety. The political demagogue, who drives a bargain with his constituency—who barters his conscience, his patriotism, and his constituency for the more substantial items of the loaves and fishes—is not, perhaps, more culpable that the writer who panders to the established tastes of his readers, as the most obvious method of ensuring success and patronage. The first to rail out against the utilitarian spirit of the age, he is the first to cast his sop to Cerberus also. Snugly ensconsed in his retiracy, amid ink-blots, periodicals and manuscripts, his heart warmed by the genial influence of his whiskey punch and glowing grate, he would repel, with scorn, the idea of *his* concocting improper viands for the craving appetites of the many. Nobody is more apt than himself to rate the demagogueism of the country; nobody prates morals with such an air of authority and sincerity. He is the censor of age and stage, and licenses no licenses but his own. Is he superior to the infirmities he denounces? Is he—to put the question more directly—is he superior to the tastes for which he undertakes to provide? for it is in this very superiority to the popular tastes, that the literary man is to ground his hope to survive his contemporaries, and justify his pretensions to position. Who will say that our American authors are more solicitous in this respect of this superiority, than the miserable creatures of party, who descend for present favours to the meanest tastes and passions of the multitude? It requires a rare strength of character, a wondrous native endowment, to rise above the general temptation, and to withstand those whom we yet solicit; and the melancholy conclusion is forced upon us, by a free perusal of our literature so-called, that there are precious few who contemplate anything beyond present pay and present audience. It is in the *degrading* sense of the word *trade*, that we censure and condemn what we regard as the evil in our literary professions. The author is too frequently of the same moral with the demogogue. His morals are cant; his pretension imposture; he is very much a humbug; he lectures to-night with discourse full of patriotism; he panders to-morrow to the same spirit which he denounces to-night. A single night's sleep makes a wonderful change in his dream. He has been particularly eloquent against the vices of the demagogue who sacrifices character and conscience upon the altars of party and a base public opinion; yet, never seems to suspect that he himself, in the volume he is about preparing for the press, is emulous of the same sort of success, precisely on the same conditions. He seeks his pay by pandering to vicious tastes, and the lowest standards of social judgment. He is a scandal-monger; he paints debaucheries; he elevates a sin into public interest; he decorates moral deformities in Christian and fanciful costume; he runs a-muck against all decorum, yet has no charity for him who plays the same game on a different stage. Would he enjoy a monopoly of the vices of cant, and slander, and specious frauds upon common sense and virtue, that he has no toleration for political sinners, who pursue the trade in politics which he pursues in letters? Let any one calmly review our literature, and he will find it marked by the very vices which distinguish our politics. It is insincere; it is a sham; it speaks not from itself, but from the people; it represents the people justly, but only in their worst attitudes—their inferior aims—their most pernicious excitements. It is characterized by a vulgar tone—by a deficient aim—by a want of all aim—by a lack of all the essentials of individuality and character. However painful it may be to confess a truth so humbling to our national self-esteem, we are yet constrained to admit that there is quite as much truth as malice in the sharp judgment of European criticism upon our literature. It is not wholly just; but whole justice we are scarcely to expect from Europe. Nor is the European critic quite capable of judging, since he does so from a partial knowledge only of our facts and performances. He sees really little more of our books than those which are pertinaciously sent him by writers and cliques, who labour only to bolster up and secure favourable foreign opinion in behalf of their own articles. But enough is seen by which to decide upon much more; and, with the reservation already suggested, we repeat that we cannot often gainsay the foreign judgment upon our labours. Our literature is full of vulnerable places; its armour is exceedingly frail and pervious to assault; and the shaft of the European critic may be well let fly, without his incurring much reproach, or even suspicion of malice, jealousy and all uncharitableness, in respect to the letters of the country.

Of the inferiority of our literature, we have spoken. To what is it ascribable? Clearly to the want of proper motive. Its appeal is too low; it does not seek the adequate tribunal; it works only for the present, which is a fatal error, and it works for money; it is simply a trade among us, looking to market profits and pecuniary recompense, rather than to the utterance of new truths and the prosecution of a divine mission. We are, of course, not insensible to the fact, that nearly all that is valuable in English literature, and, perhaps, in the literature of every country, is professional. It should be so. The labourer in every field, who labours honestly and with capacity, is worthy of his recompense. The world owes the author a living, no less than the statesman and mechanic. But this living is to be drawn from labours which are conducted with reference to the conditions upon which the literary man receives his endowment. His is a superior trust, a special mission, which he is to wage without regard to its results *to himself*, and with due heed only to its results upon humanity. As the highest of all teachers, he is to lift his people, not descend to them; or, to descend to their minds only so far as to enable him to lift them successfully. He is to descend to their understandings rather than their morals.

Something, it is true, may be urged in extenuation of our faults, our deficiencies and short-comings in literature. Our defence is in our social infancy as a people; and it is not justly pleaded when we say that our authors adapt their writings to our manners and the peculiarities of our people. If they did this, there would be the merit of truthfulness in the representation; and, though the portraiture failed to elevate us, it would yet have its merit in its historical resemblance. But this is what is *not* done; and very few of our writers, even the most successful, are American in their *atmosphere*. They are imitators of the European, and depict foreign rather than native characteristics in their pictures. But it is not enough to paint a people simply as they are, unless we place the better ideal in close proximity, by way of contrast, and rebuke our present, by such aspects of the future as shall show how we can immeasurable elevate the national moral. If we do more than cleverly and justly depict our existing moods and conditions, our literature will remain for long years in *statu quo*; and for a literature to become stationary, is to show deficient vitality. It will be a promulgation of the condemnatory decree, "Thus far, but no farther."[5] Are we satisfied to submit to this decree? We regret to think that there are many who believe we should. We have read the opinion expressed in grave reviews, like our own, that British literature is quite good enough for us at present. *Good* enough it may be; but, even to value justly a foreign literature, it is essential that we should have our own. No people enters with sympathy upon the enjoyment of a foreign treasure, until their own exercise is prepared to conduct them to the discovery of such as they should themselves possess. But there are some who go yet farther, and, regarding only the material progress of the country in arms and mechanical arts, they allege that we have quite enough literature of our own for the time we can devote to it. We can neither consume nor dispose of more; and in this statement we have the whole secret of our moral danger. It is clear that we do not value the things of life so much as the things of earth; that we do not seek so much the soul, and the triumphs which belong to its full development, as the gains and appetites of the creature. This is the lamentable difficulty in the way of our literature, which affects its professors

---

5. Job 38:11: "hitherto shalt thou come, but no further."

equally with the shop-man and the demagogue. The consequence is chiefly to be felt in the schools in which our young men are to be trained, and the inadequacy of the resources which have been provided for the public education. Our universities are such only in name. Our scientific academies are almost totally wanting in the apparatus of instruction. The passage through college exacts no devotion of the student, and requires little effort; and to graduate, we do not need to be thorough, but only not to expose ourselves and our professors. Here, at the outset, we find the evil influence upon our literature, of the unexacting nature of our people in such matters—of their easy faith in what they possess—of their indifference to the thing sought for—in short, of their low and debasing standards of an intellectual education. How shall our literature make a figure in any of the respects which require elaborate preparation, great research, and curious investigation, when we have scarce any public libraries of value? In Europe, there is not a state in which you may not find vast collections of books, coated with the dust of venerable centuries, supplying every want of the student, meeting every emergency, satisfying every doubt, reaching every difficulty. In their noble haunts of learning, which contain and breathe forth the whole great soul of the past in all its centuries, the student, perforce, drinks inspiration from the very atmosphere. In these sacred abodes and genius-guarded enclosures, the "growing thousands" are allowed to breathe the pure air of the noblest inspiration. Such glorious receptacles of learning—such time-honoured depositories of genius and intellect—are sufficient of themselves to compel, by sympathy and attraction alone, the progress of a great system of intellectual education, and to draw it onward to perfection. As long as British literature shall be mentioned within these moss-clad and holily endowed sanctuaries, it cannot but feel new life and new vigour with the progress of the years. As long as the present state approaches with devout bearing and humbled inquiry to the venerable past, there is certainty of present performance, and of the yearly birth of new, brave spirits in literature, worthy of their predecessors. The future finds its best guaranty in this continued progress and performance; and just so long as the American people shall reject these fountains of study and inspiration—shall forbear to make such great collections—shall fail to concentrate their patronage upon great central sources of learning in each state—shall refuse to cherish favourite schools, and to endow favourite universities—reject the past—degrade the present by present purposes only—just so long shall it be absurd to expect the highest and noblest fruits of literature from the hands of their sons, and just so long shall it continue to be a mere impertinence to offer a comparison between American and European letters. In the latter region, the great harvest is made; and the golden grain, which has required the sunshine of five hundred years to ripen, is now being reaped by the community. In the latter we have not planted—we refuse to plant; and how should we hope to reap? What is given to us of our own, is the spontaneous overflow of nature—green and flourishing, but rank, unpruned, with a wilderness of undergrowth to be stripped and cleared away—with time needed for mellowing, and sunshine for favourable growth—the dew and sun, and care of friendly patronage and reverent appreciation. These conditions given, and with the steady and flourishing promise of our literary growths already, we may reasonably count upon a glorious and plenteous harvest.

But we must have our nurseries of learning, where the tender plants may have proper care, cultivation and pruning—where experienced hands shall train, and whence authority may speak to a people, and compel their reverence for those things and thoughts which they now hold in disesteem. We have just compared our infant literature to the natural growth of our mighty forests. The comparison is true in most respects. Rank, dense, luxuriant, it wastes itself in excess of verdure, but bears few fruits. There are blossoms in abundance. How unlike that of our European sires, which may be said to resemble their well-ordered and highly-cultivated parks, where art becomes the handmaid of nature, and excess is rooted out—the wild, the unseemly, the hurtful—science and art ever at hand to reduce to order and to elevate to beauty. They do not lack luxuriance, but they know that an excess of it is hurtful to the tree. They do not lack a noble growth, for they possess stately and wide-spreading giants, hoar with the antiquity of a thousand years, and venerable with mossy honours. But they require the fruit as well as the foliage, and their art is addressed to the secret of so serving both as that neither shall be hurtful to the other.

In this teeming land, even liberty, from too much rankness and the absence of this training care, grows too much to weeds. The very excess of freedom threatens to endanger its fruits, and in no respect does it show itself more hurtfully than in the reckless march which it takes over the heads and necks of art, literature, good taste and all refining and conserving influences. Our enterprise is the strict result of our liberty; and the two go together hand in hand, so perfectly satisfied with one another, and with nothing else, that they threaten to extend their sway over an extent of empire, which, unhappily, appears likely to be as barren of the good, the permanent and noble, as it is boundless in extent. It is sad to think that liberty should ever make alliance with any power which should prompt her to despise the song of that poet who has always taught the love of liberty and so frequently won her victories. Our freemen are of a temper that disdain the pleading notes of the lyre, and though it sounds here and there throughout the land, who listens, of all the plodding, pushing, pressing thousands, to whom a civilized progress seems only a ceaseless march from territory to territory and from trade to trade. Shall we ever listen gratefully to that lyre, as the Scotch to the rustic lay of Burns? Will it ever possess a charm for our ears, a spell for our hearts, grovelling as we do in the most sordid cares, and with the most narrow notions of what belongs to the soul of a great nation? It is sad to feel that, under present conditions, the hope is idle; and to doubt, if ever, when Time shall have left his hoary foot-prints upon our homes and marts, our patriarchal fresh homes and lovely landscapes, and made them venerable with years, there shall be legendary songs to hallow them to the souls of our children, as they are hallowed by antiquity to the eye. To dream of a time when the music of our national lyres shall sound sweetly to the ears of our people, and win loving echoes from their hearts, we must assume a great change in the characteristics of popular mood, and a wondrous elevation of its mind. Shall we be required to wait until its physical energies are exhausted— until we shall see filled up with flourishing hamlets all the wilderness of space between the Atlantic and the Western waters, before we cherish the hope that the literature of our country shall rise to a glorious height of argument, and wave her virgin banner in triumph from the Apalachian summits? Were it not better to ask, if we may not effect a change in our policy, in our moral, by which we may anticipate results which are too precious to be left to time and chance; and which, if we rely only upon these, we shall probably fail always to accomplish. To effect this change of policy and moral, what is to be done? By what means serve the cause, and promote the efforts of native literature? Make it an honourable thing? Free it from its demogogueical characteristics? We have already indicated the first steps to this object; libraries, good schools, well conducted universities, where mind, set apart for sacred offices, relieved of its dependence upon the popular voice, may rise into the consciousness of authority, over the popular mood, and school its objects, and command its sympathies and elevate its aims.

This is a public duty. For the men of letters, themselves, and of their duties, apart from such as belong to the public, we are to say something. Contemplating the past and present of American letters, we have not ventured to contemplate their destiny. This will depend upon such changes as we do not foresee, but which we are not necessarily to suppose unlikely or impossible. We began by censuring our existing authorship as a thing of too much trade; as that which did not sufficiently look to the noble mission of the literary man, and made itself quite subservient to the vulgar and inferior aims of the ordinary citizen. We repeat the conviction, that but too many of our authors look simply to the consummation of a hireling's task in what they write; and, without reflection, nay, it would seem, even cheerfully sacrifice their hopes of fame, to the attainment of the easy object of pacifying the village critic, or pleasing the milliner's apprentice. There are others who work more worthily, and whose labours, if concentrated, and addressed to worthy ends, might give reputation to themselves, and the most wholesome tone to our literature. But these again waste themselves in vehicles of publication which are necessarily impermanent—gazettes and periodicals—poured out to waste, like the waters of an Eastern river, running out and lost in the sands. We are free to say, that much of the most genuine, truthful and heartiest literature of the country is thus issued in vain. It serves, no doubt, a useful present purpose; but what, if the writers were governed by motives which looked to a higher audience, and one of longer duration? Would it not be improved, and bettered as an inevitable consequence of the better aim? We think so. We hold it to be matter of serious regret that the damp and dirty sheets of the transitory newspaper and periodical should absorb so much of the best talent, taste and enthusiasm of American mind. Were the vehicle of another form and character, how many glorious and bright but fitful flashes of the national genius, might be concentrated into the broad, steady sun of literature, instead of glimmering upon us, as they brighten, with the momentary fervour of the summer lightning. How many pale and ineffectual gleams, such as we now behold in this unprofitable and unpromising sphere, would grow into beacon and directing lights, showing the way to posts of triumph and successful conquest, to those who now wander heedlessly and without aim on the uncertain seas! But, here again, the hope is baffled, and the desire, by that sole American idea of profit or cost. The newspaper, the periodical, yield present pay; and the popular ingenuity rules the genius of the popular author. The day's work, not the life's work, is the consideration. The author should have his "higher law," or he is nothing. If he will sacrifice his time, talent, genius, to Demus, what wonder that Demus requites him as he does his politicians,—flings him aside for other slaves with better shows of muscle, and of more impudent promise.

We must not now be understood as desiring to preach against periodical literature. We have admitted that it is very nigh the best we have. We know its uses. The most that is done for the popular enlightenment, perhaps, comes from this very source. It enlightens where it can, and when it can, in accordance with the fact, that it ministers, under ordinary standards, to the popular requisition. It conveys a certain amount of truth to the common mind, amidst a wilderness of exaggeration and absurdity. It finds its way to the cabin of labour, as well as to the marble palace of affluence. Science avails itself of its agency, and *progress* finds it a prime auxiliar. It is, in fact, the peculiar American medium of government and tuition; of politics and art; is not to be despised or neglected, and is destined to be still more powerful as an agent of moral power. We find in it a frequent, wholesome corrector of abuses, of profligacy as well as ignorance; a rebuke to mismanagement; a reformer of vice. It is, perhaps, more than politicians and schools, the foundation upon which the great experiment of self-government must rest. Wise heads find it our corner-stone, and we are the last to cry out against it, save as it occupies too exclusively and absorbingly the place of public guardian and teacher in the land.

For this, its hands are not sufficiently clean. It is not sufficiently scrupulous. It is partizan. It is the creature of the day. Its aims are selfish and for the present only. It sows tares with the wheat. It sacrifices principles to men and parties. Its vocation is not truth, but party; and it fluctuates with party, so that the doctrine which it denounces to-day it takes to its embrace to-morrow. Now, when the seeds of discord are scattered broadcast over the country, we begin to see the evil fruits of so vast a power in such irresponsible hands. The periodical press, of course including the newspaper, has much to do with the birth and growth of this baleful spirit among us. Politics and party have their vitality in this agency. The politics of Congress are all first originated by the popular press. Scarce a measure comes up before the Federal legislature that has not first been determined on by the journalists, one side or the other; and, as one of the most obvious modes of public tuition, we should not object, were the motives of the public press of a nobler sort, did it aim to serve the people only by a due service to humanity and intellect. But it is as the pander and not as the mentor, that it too much employs itself. It sinks to the service, not rises; and with a power which is resistless, the popular cause is almost entirely left to its control. Now, when the clouds gather, it behooves it to exert all of good which it possesses, to arrest the evils which have too much originated with itself. On literary grounds we deplore this power of the popular press. We lament that it has grown to such a mighty channel, so deep, so wide; that it absorbs the converging currents of our literature, and frequently for its debasement. That it swallows up its conservatism—that it makes it reckless, eager, headstrong and capricious. That it teaches to despise deliberation, aim, preparation, finish;—and so, necessarily detracts from what is inherently valuable, and might become most worthy, in American authorship.

That we have all the native elements of a pure, genuine and durable literature, with original material in abundance from which to fashion, and upon which to build, no thinking and observing person will deny. We can already point to a long catalogue of names, male and female, in all the departments of literary labour, whose works conclusively show our resources, though they also declare for our deficiences. We need not repeat the list, nor dwell upon the details of what they have severally done. Since, then, we are admitted to possess the endowments for the creation of a national literature, what is it prevents the consummation of an end so desirable? Perhaps we should sufficiently answer the question by saying that the popular mind does not think the matter so desirable—does not, indeed, think of the matter at all. And, no doubt, this was the case with every people that ever lived, at some period in their history. But this answer, while it may serve the people themselves, or the journalist, is not to satisfy the author. It is his very mission to create the taste and passion for his own labours, and to make them necessary to his race. It is our complaint that he does not feel or acknowledge this mission, and what he does is rather addressed to the people as they are, than to the people as they should be. Hence it is that our poets are mostly poetasters, our authors scribblers, our historians a mere cross of the declaimer upon the chronicler. Hence, fancy becomes the staple of the poet instead of his decoration; the lack of aim rendering unessential the agency of thought and imagination. Authorship is unappreciated by the people, and, therefore, it depreciates itself for the same people. It is unvalued by the crowd, and hence its toils to lessen, by every effort, its own value. The people do not patronize high gifts of literature, therefore we must lower them. In other words, we must toil not so much in our vocation, as for our inferiors; not for the glorious rewards of fame, but for the small profits and wretched earnings of the day.

It is one of the misfortunes of American literature that it has not yet arrived at the dignity of a profession. It is with most a relaxation rather than a labour. It does not contemplate the application of a life-time. It is rather the occasional exercise of a mind seeking relief from other employments. How should it task the best energies of heart and genius? Instead of the great field of struggle, the rewards of which are commensurate with the magnitude of the arena, and the multitude of the combatants, literature is only a sort of parade-ground for our men of talents. They have no idea that they are strong in the sight of assembled nations, or of growing generations. They think only of the small conquest in the sight of the parish, over parish rivals. What need of much preparation for such holiday tourneys? Will genius rouse itself to noble passions for such small game? And what need of toil and labour—toil of head and suffering of heart,—and weariless industry, such as marked the progress of stout, savage, dogged, determined, sleepless, study-loving and honest Sam Johnson,— buried to the eyes in bulk of folios—musty with the must of books,—his blear eyes, dimly lighted by farthing candles, peering into the antique realms of black letter. Yet without such self-sacrifice and such toils, how expect to achieve the permanent conquests of authorship? And Johnson's case is not an isolated one. Look at Dryden, Milton, Swift,—all, indeed, who are happily niched in the temple of literary immortality. The labour is the essential condition of success,—the genius and talent being of course assumed!—all other successes are passing, fleeting, however bright for the moment—mere flashes of a light that quickly goes out in utter darkness. And the labour can only result from the deliberate adoption of authorship as a profession—one of the most exacting as it is the most honourable in the world. We must have the profession in place of the trade in literature—the work, not the *relaxation*; and we may then hope for such a spirit in the land as shall not leave us long without such a constellation of worthies as will never let the national greatness perish. These are things to be hoped for, because these are things to be taught. When each priest of the muses shall approach the temple as clothed in a sacred mission which he cannot for the very life of him neglect;—when the poet shall pass into the circle, thick clad in mail of proof, fearless of the shafts of criticism, and prepared to do battle with all comers for the prize—meet rivalry face to face, and manfully engage in the struggle with the mightiest of earth;—when, trained for the course by penance, and patience, and long devotion, and master hands, he will rise to the emergency, and brave every opposition—asking the world for audience and umpire, and challenging the bravest of all the world's genius—then, only, can we hope to assert for our literature its perfect independence. When New-York, like London, shall become a great literary centre,—Boston like Edinburgh, New Orleans like Paris, and other places, with claims just as good, to relative position, shall possess the advantages of population, art, education and wealth commensurate—then may we look, but hardly till then, for the dawning of that bright day for which we yearn. But the conditions which we have indicated must first be fulfilled. The men of letters must raise the people, not sink with them; and their agencies must be found in their own higher aims; to promote which we must endow great libraries, establish the noblest retreats of learning, and discard all mere trading teachers and professors, even as we discard the trading poetaster and trafficking politician. Can this be done? May we hope that the children of our loins shall yet behold in our country an empire of art and song, and genius, such as shall be worthy of our ancestral nations?

And yet our people seem to recognize the necessity and uses of books, if not of literature. In the quantity if not the quality of our publications, we might almost lay claim to compare with the old English Elizabethan period, of which so much boast is made. Our age may be distinguished as the bookish, and America makes as perfect contributions to the mass as any other country. It seems to be the decree,—books *must* be made. Go ye all and make books. The voice which the prophet heard in Patmos[6] seems to be ringing forever in the ears of our youth—"Write!" and write they do, after some fashion, with a vengeance. They write to *order*, and here is the mischief. They write to suit the whim and caprice of the inconsistent multitude—write to *please* only. "How servile is the task to please alone!"[7]

6. Revelation 1:19: the prophet, Saint John the Divine, hearing God say, "I am Alpha and Omega, the first and the last."

In this inferiority of aim lies the secret of bad performance, and only temporary reputation. The taste changes, and the author is left behind by his old associates. They are trying other fashions in literature. They have a new hobby. At one moment they are Byronic, at another Wordsworthian; anon they change to Keats and Shelly, and pass with wonderful speed to Tannyson or Milnes.[8] None of these detain them long. In prose fiction, Miss Porter gives way to Sir Walter, Sir Walter to Bulwer Lytton, he to G. P. R. James, James to Harry Lorrequer, he to Eugene Sue,[9] Sue to Dickens, Dickens to Thackeray; and so on to the "crack of doom." That the American is content to follow in the path of either of these is fatal to his own claims. Yet the greater number do this, and the land is flooded not only with English reprints but English repetitions. Only the other day, Tennyson wrote a pretty but very fatiguing collection of small elegiac— "In memoriam"—upon a young friend.[10] On the instant, the whole swarm of American poetasters found that they had young friends to bewail, and wrote memorials. Such a lugubrious clamour in lugubrious verse never before annoyed the ears of the public. The notion was—Tennyson is popular. His quaintnesses take. His mysteries are so delicate. His affectations so tickle the young ladies. We have only to Tennysonize in order to share his popularity. The whole ambition, at the bottom of this philosophy, was that of winning the attention of "snug coterie and literary lady." What of value in any literature can spring from motives so paltry and ridiculous? What of merit can there be in any production which appeals to the merely social tastes, precisely as the tailor and mantua-maker appeals to the caprices of vanity in dress? Now we shall have high literary shirt collars; and now they shall be low. Now we shall have long blue skirts to our coats, and now we go for the literary Lamartine,[11] which is sack and swallow tail together.

The publishers have a great deal to do in influencing the writers of a country to these fluctuations and caprices in the forms and fashions of literature. It must be admitted that, to a large degree, they have always exercised this influence in every age and country; not, mark you, with the

---

7. Possibly an adaptation of Luke 10:40: "But Martha was cumbered about much serving, and came to him, and said, Lord, does thou not care that my sister hath left me to serve alone?"

8. Richard Monckton Milnes, 1809–1895, poet and biographer of Keats; he was also a friend of Tennyson.

9. Jane Porter, 1776–1850, a Scottish novelist known for *Thaddeus of Warsaw* (1803) and *Scottish Chiefs* (1810); George Payne Rainsford James, 1799–1860, a prolific popular English novelist who latterly lived in the United States; Harry Lorrequer, in other words, Charles Lever; Eugene Sue, 1804–1857, the French novelist, known for *The Mysteries of Paris* (1844) and *The Wandering Jew* (1845).

10. Tennyson, *In Memoriam* (London, 1850).

11. Alphonse Marie Louis de Lamartine, 1790–1869, French poet, novelist, historian, and politician.

master minds of literature, but with the scrub race, or with those who, having certain literary endowments, were yet the slaves of certain conventional tastes and appetites which kept them in a state of vassalage. With truly great authors, there was no intermediate influence acknowledged between themselves and the people. They spoke directly to the heart of humanity and have thus taken possession of it forever. But the greater number have always recognized the publisher as the great medium with the public, and Curll, Lintot and Murray,[12] prescribe to them the method by which to win a current reputation; and, more important still, the money compensation which follows it. Thus, Goldsmith obeys the order of the publisher, and compiles a Natural History without any knowledge of the subject, instead of writing, from himself, new Vicars of Wakefield, and fresh, sparkling comedies, of true British humour.[13] What is true of Britain, and other countries, and the authors thereof, is in still greater degree true of ours. An evil everywhere, the mischief is more than ever potent with us, where we have classes of readers which the old world does not possess, and where we lack the higher standards of social moral. Here, the publisher is autocrat. As he can procure any quantity of European books for nothing, it behooves our author to submit implicitly to his guidance, if he hopes for his help in delivering him of his progeny. Our publishers embody the wants and indicate the tastes of the people. It is they who declare what is good and worthy of republication from the foreign press, giving us, in nine cases out of ten, the worst instead of the best, writings of the day. They are even more absolute when they have to deal with the young American author. It behooves him to be made of very pliant material. He must be adaptable. Adaptation to the public, is the necessity—a necessity which, once acknowledged, in the case of a people whose tastes are even more capricious than the tastes of a people are proverbially said to be, must necessarily end in his utter overthrow after a single season. It is, accordingly, a regular see-saw with our authors. "Now we go up, up, up; and now we go down, down, downy." Now, we find books of travels all the go; and Stephens is the cry.[14] Nobody like Stephens. But suddenly Stephens subsides. There is no more said of Stephens. The very echoes forget him. Then Headley takes the field.[15] Publisher after publisher writes

12. Edmund Curll, 1675–1747, bookseller and publisher of Addison, Swift, and Pope, with whom he had a great quarrel for which he was repaid in *The Dunciad*; Barnaby Bernard Lintot, 1675–1736, publisher of Vanbrugh, Pope, Gay, and Steele; John Murray, 1778–1843, publisher of Byron, George Borrow, Charles Lyell, and the Tory *Quarterly Review*.
13. R. Brookes, *A New and Accurate System of Natural History*, 6 vols. (London, 1763–1764), to which Goldsmith wrote a preface and the introductions to vols. 1–4.
14. John Lloyd Stephens, 1805–1852, an American traveler and author chiefly of *Incidents of Travel in Egypt, Arabia, Petraea and the Holy Land* (1837) and *Incidents of Travel in Greece, Turkey, Russia and Poland* (1838).
15. Joel Tyler Headley, 1813–1897, the popular military historian.

to him:—Give us blood and battle—Napoleon and his Marshals—Washington and his Generals—Cromwell and his Massacres. The public cry aloud for blood. They snuff for it on every hand. So Headley triumphs, and finds heroes by the hundred, in the portly, well fed, beef-eating Generals of "Seventy-Six." But Headley suddenly sinks out of sight, as Stephens did before him, and in his place we have Ik Marvel; dreamy, delicate, fine contemplative Ik Marvel.[16] We want Ik Marvels, say the publishers. All the ladies cry out for Ik Marvels. This is the season of sweet sentiment—the season of reverie, and dreams, which blend nature and fashion so happily together, that one cannot well know which is which, and don't much care, indeed. Ik Marvel gives place to Mrs. Stowe, and the literature of the negro, from the abolition manufactures, awakens all hearts to the superior, but defrauded and denied genius of the African, and to his wonderful merits and persecutions as a Christian martyr. So the public prescribe through the publisher. The author mostly confirms, and suffers his thoughts to be moulded into all shapes, and his genius to take all colours, as the hands of the dyer, from the hands of the publisher. The damsel who would pass from the school-room to the parlour, is not made to pass through a more despotic or ridiculous ordeal, when she submits to milliner and mantua-maker, and is pressed and padded, remade, remoulded, remodelled, while shoes pinch and shoulders ache—in utter despite of nature, in defiance of her forms, and in contempt for all the most permanent and material laws. Not a charm is left where nature placed it, in damsel or author. Both are subject, not merely to fashion, but fashion as represented by a medium which knows just as little of her laws as of the laws of literature. The author submits to this despotism, because he has no adequate appreciation of his own profession. Who should better understand the wants of humanity than the author?—and the wants of humanity are more earnest and exacting than the demands of fashion. If there be one faculty, more than another, which distinguishes the writer of prose or poetic fiction, it is that of entering into the popular heart, and rousing up all its thousand emotions. Yet, regarding the publisher as having the only passport to the public he sinks his own independence and the individuality in which his genius consists. The publisher has but one test of merit. Will the book sell? He does not ask or care if it be good. He does not undertake the business of publishing that he may make good books—he only seeks for saleable ones. You see good Christians selling Dumas, and Reynolds, and Paul de Kock[17]—

16. The pseudonym of Donald Grant Mitchell, 1822–1908, author of *A Bachelor's Reverie* (1850) and *The Lorgnette* (1850).
17. George William McArthur Reynolds, 1814–1879, author of *Alfred de Rosann: or, The Adventures of a French Gentleman* (1839), *The Bronze Statue: or, The Virgin Kiss* (1850) and *Esther de Medina: or, The Crimes of London* (1848); Charles Paul de Kock, 1793–1871, a French novelist known for his portrayals of Parisian low life, notably in *Le Barbier de Paris* (1826) and *La Grande Ville, Paris* (1842).

very good Christians they are. It is in the way of trade. There have been
fierce contests between professing Christian publishers, as to which should
have the exclusive privilege of flooding the market with the vilest immo-
ralities of Eugene Sue. Success in sale, is the only idea of success which
the publisher entertains. To get a publisher is the first great necessity with
the author. What then? He must conform. In the long interview which he
has with the literary autocrat, he is examined as to whether he can be
made presentable or not. Can he write pro or anti-slavery stories? They
are all the go. Can he manufacture moral tales, or Christmas tales, upon
old proverbs? Can he—but no matter about the catalogue. The sum of the
inquiry is whether he can manufacture the sort of books which are just
then most in fashion. He must come to it if he hopes for publisher's favour.
This functionary must needs cut and trim, and rig him out, will he, nill he,
according to the fashion of the month and the requirements of customers.
Should the poor author's self-esteem or vanity take umbrage, he must go
elsewhere—go farther and fare worse. But, in too many cases, he submits.
He yields himself to the shaping hand of his *maker*, and suffers squeezing
and stretching, and binding and padding, without a murmur, and he wins
puffs and pennies, which, to his surprise, last only for a season. But, during this season, he fancies he has a foretaste of immortality. A host of
presses speak his name. He surpasses all his predecessors. Go where he
will, he sees his dainty volume in busy hand. In car and steamer, he travels
with the wind. Boarding-school damsels sigh over his pretty sentiments,
and young masters on the way to college, cry aloud—"He's a great fellow,
demme!" He feeds a certain small appetite, which, perhaps, can enjoy no
more wholesome fare. "Milk for babes," says the apostle, "but meat for
men."[18] We could wish to see better food provided, for the sake of feeder
as well as purveyor. An old author says—"In very truth, it grieveth me
that men, those especially who profess themselves to be Christians, should
be so taken with the sweet baits of literature, that they can endure to read
nothing but what gives them immediate gratification, no matter how low
or sensual it may be." This is what we have perpetually to lament in the
case of American readers. That the author himself should become a party
to their errors and ill practices is the special evil that we deplore. To be
merely popular is not to be successful. Here is the monstrous blunder.
Success is a thing to grow gradually like merit, since a people is not expected all at once to enter into the deeper thoughts of an original writer.
Shakspeare has been growing every year since his death, and is not done
growing yet, and will possibly never cease to grow in success, and the
common admiration, till the millennium. Let the writer know, once for all,
that the smallest part of his office is to amuse and to entertain. That he

18. Either Corinthians 3:1 or Hebrews 5:12; in either case, the apostle is Paul.

degrades himself when he condescends only to brush away the "dusky gnome of ennui."[19] His vocation is very far otherwise—is a very noble and commanding one. He is to teach, and teach with power—the passions as well as the understanding—the heart as well as the fancy—and school to great thoughts as well as good manners. We are as much at a loss, looking at the sort of books which infest the land like the frogs of Egypt, as were the querists of that Grecian school, who sought to know "what should be in it, that men should love lies, where they make neither for pleasure, as with the poets, nor for profit, as with the trader; but only for the lie's sake."[20] The only escape for authorship from this despotism of the publisher, is in the exercise of independence. This will require patience. But patience, where there is merit, will finally secure the audience; and the publisher, be it remembered, is only sought as a medium by which to effect this object. A firm determination on the part of the writer of genius, to write only as his heart moves him, as Philip Sidney counsels—"look into thy heart and write"[21]—or, in the more copious language of independence of George Wither, who sings bravely—snapping his fingers equally at critics and publishers—who are a sort of critics—

"For I will, for no man's pleasure,
Change a syllable or measure;
Pedants shall not tie my strains
To our antique poet's veins;
*Being born as free as these,*
I will sing as I shall please."[22]

A determination which speaks quite as much for the manly character—nay, the genius—of old George, as for his self-esteem. It is clear that he

19. Samuel Taylor Coleridge, *The Friend*, ed. B. E. Rooke (Princeton, 1969), 2:10.
20. This seems to be a reference to the sophists, often criticized by Plato and Aristotle, though not in this precise language.
21. Sir Philip Sidney, "Astrophil and Stella," line 14: "'Foole,' said my Muse to me, 'looke in thy heart and write.'"
22. "Faire-Virtue, The Mistresse of Philarete," in *Juvenilia: Poems of George Wither* (London, 1871), 3: 738-39: Nisbet has omitted six lines, and it should read:

"For, I will for no mans pleasure
Change a Syllable or measure:
Neither for their praises adde
Ought to mend what they thinke bad;
Since it never was my fashion
To make worke of Recreation.
 *Pedants* shall not tye my straines
To our Antique *Poets* vaines;
As if we, in latter dayes,
Knew to love, but not to praise.
Being born as free as these,
I will sing, as I shall please."

has no slavish disposition for the beaten track; that to please, simply, is with him, not the principal or proper object; that publishers shall never coerce his muse into their straight—or *loose*—jackets; that his avarice is not enlisted to look after the merely marketable commodity. In short, that he feels his mission, and knows that to work successfully in his vocation, he must work with a due regard to what his peculiar genius requires, and not what the capricious appetite of desultory readers may demand. This is what our authors must aim at—what they must arrive at—before they can take the position in the world's literature, which we humbly think may yet be assumed by the native talent of the country.

We have wandered on in these remarks, following our humour, rather than any fixed plan of criticism. It had been our object, to discuss the merits of more than one of those young authors of our country, who, happily, seem to incline to better things and to a more independent development of their peculiar endowments. But we must waive the analysis for the present, and content ourselves with a few words of compliment bestowed on Nathaniel Hawthorne. It is with some pleasure that we refer to this name, as that of one who entertains his own literary ideal, and who, in all his writings, aims steadily at its proper development. He has been several years before the public, and may be said to have fairly passed through his apprenticeship. His "Mosses from an old Manse," are among the first of his labours which attracted attention.[23] They were short stories or sketches, quiet, contemplative, thoughtful, genial; somewhat quaint of style, fanciful in costume, and with a dash of humour having the flavour of Isaac Walton.[24] His tales were followed by a series of novels of psychological character:—The Scarlet Letter, The House of the Seven Gables, The Blithedale Romance[25]—novellettes rather than novels, and of a narrative and descriptive, rather than a dramatic form. In all these productions, Hawthorne has distinguished himself by certain traits of delicacy, discrimination, a pleasing social philosophy, and a striking, though morbid characterization. This morbid element works, at times, injuriously in all his portraits. It disarms them, and takes from their truthfulness as well as symmetry. It is the "brown horror" in his landscape. It impairs the charm, even if it increases the occasional power of his story. In the *joinery* of his story, indeed, Hawthorne does not show any surprising skill. Invention is not his quality, which lies rather in the latent and the unobtrusive—the didactic, rather than the dramatic parts of his labours—and appeals to us much more by the profound, yet unstudied metaphysics in his moral musings, descriptive and dialogue, than in the action of his piece. His style is

---

23. Nathaniel Hawthorne, *Mosses from an Old Manse* (New York, 1846).
24. Izaak Walton, 1593–1683, author of *The Compleat Angler* (1653).
25. Hawthorne, *The Scarlet Letter, A Romance* (Boston, 1850); *The House of the Seven Gables* (Boston, 1851); *The Blithedale Romance* (Boston, 1852).

very happy, very correct, easy, graceful, frequently forcible, and always marked by a singular propriety. The word is always in the right place, just where the thought and sentiment equally require it. His manner declares for a superior refinement, for great delicacy of mood, for timid sensibilities, and an exquisite capacity for blending into harmonious tone all the conflicting hues of passion and society. While he reminds us of the writers of an early period of British literature, by his quaintnesses of fancy and manner, there is nothing servile, nothing imitative merely, in his writings. Hawthorne is one of those whom we can refer to as writing for, and from, himself. It is his good fortune that the people have so soon risen *from* themselves to his appreciation. Possibly, this might not so soon have been the case, but for the expression of British approbation, which very certainly anticipated our own. Hawthorne, like Irving, is a writer to conciliate European criticism. His style is good and pure, his manner pleasing and persuasive, his polish beyond question, and he offends by no Americanisms. He assails no national prejudices, like Cooper, and, challenging regard only to his story, put forth with no pretension; and in as good English as that of any of his foreign citics, the auspices were all favourable and friendly which welcomed him to the audience. The sectionality of Hawthorne's writings is only discernible in their atmosphere. He adopts no prejudices of section and fights for none. That he feels them, we may conjecture, but his personality is strictly kept out of his authorship. It is this that enables him, in his shorter stories, to become so frequently the essayist, and to discourse his own experiences. We confess to reading Hawthorne's writings with a pleasure which we feel in the company of few other American authors. He beguiles us so pleasantly along, with so much grace and sweetness, speaks in a tone so easy and frank, rises into contemplations so natural to our route, and, inartificial always, is yet so proper. We lay down his volumes with a sigh. They might all be longer. Purely American in his art, he owes his success with the American to his freedom of place. It is because he is natural and genuine that he charms; because he is thoughtful and truthful; because there is no disproportion in his thoughts, which rise properly to the situations of his persons, while these are made consistently to accord with their characterization. Peculiarly choice and careful in the management of his words, and the expression of his ideas, nothing yet can be more easy than his style. The reader unconsciously coincides with his conclusions, in consequence of the felicity with which he states them, and we do not care to investigate a proposition which is so lucidly indicated by such becoming language. In the delineation of character, we are not sure that he is always truthful, even in respect to the morbid cases which he himself adopts; but with so much art does he smooth down his transitions, that one is at a loss to decide upon the actual place where the artist has failed to catch the feature. His descriptions are vague and dreamy, yet they possess a beauty that seems to grow out of their very indistinctness. He has but little saliency, no prominent traits, perhaps, and hence, is undramatic; but his portraits are impressive, though sometimes offensive, and his events are painful or pathetic, even when we feel their extravagance and unreasonableness. Even when he errs and fails, nobody would ever dream of charging him with mediocrity and commonplace. In his characterization, as in his description, the vagueness constitutes an element of the success. They are portraits in the dusk, and so indistinct, yet exaggerated. But there is nothing vague or uncertain in his opinions. These are clear, well stated, direct and ingenious, if not always conclusive. They indicate equally the good writer and the profound thinker. His stories are all possessed of a lively interest. They are all tragic, and some of them need not have been so. To make Zenobia commit suicide was not necessary in her case, and positively conflicts with the moral of her portrait as well as of the story. The remedy for the case of such a woman was to have found a rival in the other extreme of character to Hollingsworth, and to marry her off. The catastrophe in this story, is simply shocking. But we are not less pleased to look at Zenobia, and we can study her apart from the tragic conclusions of the author. She is sufficiently real for that. So is Hollingsworth. So, in fact, are most of the persons, though they are all drawn in exaggerated outlines. In Blythedale, our author does not make much of the place itself, and in this he differs from his course in the "House of the Seven Gables." He makes us see that with sufficient distinctness, and invests his details with our sympathies. Its neglected gardenplat—its antiquated gables—its creaking shutters—its mysterious passages, and all the ruins, and moss over all—all fasten themselves upon memory. We cannot drive from our sight that spectral representative of the once happy household, as she wanders—a ruin amongst ruins, lonely, abandoned—through the hollow-sounding halls of the ancient homestead, old, ugly and full of bitterness as she naturally is, with "herself to think of only and her sufferings." She interests us with sympathy; she has mourned over the shadows of past joys and perished hopes; she walks as a stranger in a land where all are strange; she has seen the lovely and the beautiful depart; she lingers only among the dead ashes of the household, and her sorrows are human, and compel our sympathies, without respect to herself. Our author succeeds in such delineations of touching situation. The truthfulness of the situation, and the force of the painting, make us heedless of any imperfections in the character.

Hawthorne is genuine as a writer. He does not adopt an affectation and nurse it into a monster. He is serious mostly in his revelations, and has seen all, or thinks he has, that he offers to reveal to us. His exaggerations are such in consequence of the atmosphere through which he paints them. His fancy is that which produces the *fata morgana*. It is the bulk, and breadth, and length, not the proportions, that are monstrous. The proportions are good; but the fog and mist of early morning light, or cloudy sunset, in mountainous situations, lift the image into gigantic developments. The shady and the misty hang over all his fancies; but once recognize this fact of medium and atmosphere, and his truthfulness is unquestionable. His quaintnesses are not affectations. They belong to a shy life, perhaps—to a longer association with books than men. He has his eccentricities, no doubt; but these are due to the same source—the morbid activity of his imagination or fancy, under peculiar situations and conditions. They do not disparage his writings, but serve to give them a charm, and constitute a large part of the writer's individuality. He has his own way of inculcating his philosophies, as he has in setting forth his pictures, and knows how to employ that "little glooming light, most like a shade," which sets off admirably the portraits of those who labour with perverse moods or passions. His costume of thought is sometimes no less fantastic than rich, but he wears it so happily, that we do not the less feel the *truth*, and admire the dress in which he garbs it. If quaint, he is never obscure—a sufficient proof that he himself has always a clear notion of what he designs to say. Hawthorne addresses himself very equally to the head and the heart. There is pabulum sufficient for the thought—there is feeling sufficient for the sympathies. His philosophies co-operate happily with his incidents, and enforce their influence. They both lay siege to the gentle soul, and soon persuade it to surrender on terms, if not at discretion. Hawthorne, in his descriptions, leads us to suspect that he has drawn more from English authors, in this respect, than from nature. There is more of Arcadia in his scenes than New-England. His literary tastes are not of Yankee nurture. He has lived out of its marts, and drank the purer air of the closet. His models are not in his contemporaries of either country. It is his merit and his hope, that he has not succumbed to demagogueism in literature, though he has written a life of General Pierce.[26] We do not quarrel with him for this. Pierce is a good man, according to all accounts, and Hawthorne is his friend; and we see no reason why the literary man should not make some occasional sacrifices for his friend, as well as any other person. We give him absolution for this biography, and only trust that he will not allow himself to be enmeshed more deeply into the snares of politics than he has already gone. He will always make a better author than politician. Enough. We have not aimed at a criticism of Hawthorne, but a compliment. He is one of the few among our young American authors, to

---

26. Hawthorne, *Life of Franklin Pierce* (Boston, 1852).

whom we look with confidence for the creation of an American literature; he will prosecute his career with industry and success, and contribute largely, we are satisfied, to that reforming progress which we believe to have already begun, making his influence for the future to be felt wherever his works are read.

## 13.

*Basil Lanneau Gildersleeve*

"The Necessity of the Classics"[1]

The most important respondent to Jesse Harrison's call in 1831 for German standards of classical scholarship was born in that same year in Charleston. Basil Gildersleeve was to become the greatest classicist of his American day.[2] He was to found the *American Journal of Philology* in 1880, he led the classics seminar at Johns Hopkins University for nearly forty years, he was to the professional study of Greek and Latin what Herbert Baxter Adams was to history, Daniel Coit Gilman to graduate education, and Franklin Giddings to sociology. That Gildersleeve did these things and plied his trade of the Greek syntactician with a whimsical ear and eye, that he was— by his frequent admission—a *litterateur manqué*, owed not a little to his Charleston background.[3]

Gildersleeve's father, Benjamin, had been a Presbyterian evangelist and the editor of a religious weekly. He had also been a Northerner, but took to Southern causes, like Nullification, with an alacrity that permitted his son to dub him benignly "a passably good southerner." For his first thirteen years, Gildersleeve's education had been undertaken by his father in snatched moments between thumping sermons and manuscripts: an imprecise classicism, "a very tumultuous affair," based in obvious authors like Caesar and Cicero and upon the New Testament in Greek. Upon his own initiative,

---

1. Basil Lanneau Gildersleeve, "Necessity of the Classics," *SQR* n.s. 10 (July 1854): 145–67: a review of Von G. Bernhardy, *Grundriss der Griechischen Litteratur; mit einem vergleichenden Ueberblick der Römischen* (Halle, 1852). Gildersleeve seems to have been more than usually plagued by typographical errors in this piece, not surprisingly perhaps, in view of its allusiveness. In deference to his obvious scholarly standing, I have made corrections.

2. C. W. E. Miller, "Basil Lanneau Gildersleeve," *American Journal of Philology* 45 (January 1924): 97–100.

3. *Selections from the Brief Mention of Basil Lanneau Gildersleeve*, ed. C. W. E. Miller (Baltimore, 1930), p. 372.

there were smatterings of Corneille, Racine, and Molière.[4] Later Gildersleeve was handed over to a local classics teacher, William Bailey, before starting at the College of Charleston. In 1845 his father moved to Richmond, where the young Basil spent a year as his secretary, then a year at Jefferson College in Pennsylvania before two at Princeton. At the last of these, he graduated in 1849. Back in Richmond, he assumed the role of classics teacher at a private school. In 1850 he traveled to Germany for three years of serious study: a winter at the University of Berlin, two semesters at Göttingen, two at Bonn, and the final examination for the Ph.D. back at Göttingen. He returned to Charleston in 1853 for three years of free-lance writing and tutorials and became one of the literary set at Russell's bookshop. But in 1856 he was elected to a professorship at the University of Virginia and he was to stay in Charlottesville until 1876 took him to the new Johns Hopkins and national influence, a sojourn punctuated by the Civil War and a Spencer bullet in the back, which left him a permanent limp.

As a young man, Gildersleeve had two chief passions, Charleston and Germany. Long after he left the city, he kept a map of it upon his wall. Later he knew the loyalty had been provincial, that Charleston did not after all bestride the world. "We were," he said in 1891 with affection, "incredibly narrow. Charleston was the center." His strongest memory, relevant to this essay, was of an inherited Anglophobia fed by elders who recalled the War of 1812 and, more vivid, a maternal grandmother who remembered British insolence during the British occupation of Charleston during the Revolution. Germany was a natural counterpoint, though it was the writings of Carlyle—that Scottish distruster of England—who introduced Gildersleeve to a passion for Goethe, "the most important of all the teachers I ever had." "Goethe's aphorisms were my daily food. I committed my favorite passages to memory. I repeated them over and over to myself in my long solitary rambles, and Goethe was my mainstay at a time when my faith had suffered an eclipse. This was the era of my Teutomania, the time when I read German, wrote German, listened to German, and even talked German—to myself if I could not find any long-suffering German to submit to my experiments."[5]

---

4. Gildersleeve, "Formative Influences," *Forum* 10 (February 1891): 608, 611.
5. Ibid., pp. 607, 614–15.

This essay was written upon his return to Charleston, freshly garlanded by Göttingen, and was his critical debut. Many years later he commented upon it, in the manner of the old and accomplished to their youth, slightingly. "In my collectanea it is among the 'juvenilia,' and marked 'not to be reproduced,'" though he then proceeded to reproduce portions. "All this," he remarked, "is pitifully young." Later its strictures on English classical scholarship seemed overdrawn, his enthusiasm for German philology not misplaced but exaggerated. But Gildersleeve was arguing from an established Southern tradition. It was not an inappropriate symbolism that one of his companions at Göttingen had been the grandson of the historian David Ramsay, the celebrator of the revolution against the Crown.[6]

What is most important in this essay is precisely its youthful élan. Classicism was not, for Gildersleeve, a dusty Augustan legacy. The eighteenth-century English tradition, the massive exception of Richard Bentley aside, was precisely his bête noire. Gildersleeve's nineteenth century was supposed to annihilate the dust, revivify the classics, render the lines of Greece and Rome fresh and relevant by the preparatory care of close readings and subtle scholarship. Behind the quarrels over the digamma in Homer that were to lengthen in the late nineteenth century into tedious minutiae, there was the gleaming vision of a marbled white Athens under constantly blue skies that a Wolf or a Winckelmann had, with intoxication if not accuracy, bequeathed to generations of Germans and Americans. Sitting in Charleston and damning Charles Anthon for a fool, Basil Gildersleeve did not feel old-fashioned. He was, indeed, quite newfangled and pleased with himself for it.

HOWEVER slight the analogy may be between ancient and modern colonization, it is, notwithstanding, interesting to observe even the faint semblances of prototypes, which lie scattered throughout the range of history,

---

6. *Brief Mention of . . . Gildersleeve*, pp. 364–76; Gildersleeve, *The Creed of the Old South, 1865–1915* (Baltimore, 1915), p. 113; he must particularly have smiled, in retrospect, at his confident assertion that "the science of textual criticism may now be regarded as complete."

# Necessity of the Classics 401

and to recognize a foreshadowing of our own genesis in the foundation of states long extinct. Sybaris had been destroyed in one of those internecine wars which disfigure the annals of Lower Italy, and the beneficent genius of Athens prompted united Hellas to found a common colony on the ruins of the fairest city of Magna Graecia. Apollo was selected as the leader, and Thurii arose, celebrated on account of its origin and constitution.[7] We, too, are a common colony of united Europe; every nation has sent its contingent, and our origin and constitution are, like those of Thurii, unique. But who is the leader of our grand colony? Is it the Grecian Apollo or the Roman Mercury? A few more generations, and we shall be as little a colony of Europe as England is a colony of Hengist and Horsa.[8] The old colonists are dead, the old elements have become effete or have passed over into new forms, and, in this chaos, culture and lucre may well seem to the vulgar apprehension to be striving for the mastery. From all sides we hear outcries against the utilitarianism of our century and of our country. Plautus, the poet, is grinding at the mill.[9] Pegasus is impounded, and Castaly choked up.[10] Such declamations are useless. The greatest geniuses move but in and with their time, and "like the waves which, forced away by the passage of a ship, rush together immediately behind it, so doth error, when master-spirits have crowded it out and made room for themselves, close with natural rapidity in the rear." All that is not founded on the necessities of the age, is evanescent, and all attempts to revive a dead science can end, at best, in a momentary galvanization. Were it our purpose to repeat the story of the revival of learning, to fall into raptures over Plato the divine and Ovid the holy,[11] the judicious reader would do well to pause on the threshold. It might become a sanguine humanist like Poliphilus[12] to

---

7. [We avoid current quotations from the classics. See K. F. Hermann, Griech. Staatsalterhümer, 80, 22—(Political Antiquities of Greece). The dodecade of the φυλαί of Thurii is, according to Niebuhr—(Lectures on Ancient History, II, 137, Eng. trans.)—a multiple of the Ionic tetrad and the Doric triad.] Hermann's Lehrbuch der Griechischen Staatsalterhümer (Heidelberg, 1831) was translated as A Manual of the Political Antiquities of Greece (Oxford, 1836); φυλαί means tribes or clans; Thurii was founded, on the old site of Sybaris in Southern Italy, in 443 B.C. by Pericles: Herodotus and Lysias were said to have been among its colonists.
8. Said to have been the Jutish invaders of Britain, circa 449, and founders of Kent.
9. Plautus, 254–184 B.C., the Roman comedian.
10. The Castalian spring at Delphi.
11. [Coleridge, note to the Garden of Boccaccio.] As a note to his poem "The Garden of Boccaccio," Coleridge had observed, "I know few more striking or more interesting proofs of the overwhelming influence which the study of the Greek and Roman classics exercised on the judgments, feelings, and imaginations of the literati of Europe at the commencement of the restoration of literature, than the passage in the Filicopo of Boccaccio: where the sage instructor, Racheo, as soon as the young prince and the beautiful girl Biancofiore had learned their letters, sets them to study the Holy Book, Ovid's Art of Love."
12. [In his Hypnertomachia. See Wachler, Handbuch der Geschichte der Litteratur, b. III. s. 11; Comp. Goethe. Werke, b. III, s. 191.] [Francesco Colonna], Hypnertomachia Poliphili (Venice, 1499).

prove at length that, of all nations, the Greeks have dreamed the most beautiful life-dream, or a philosopher like Hegel to wish himself a Cecropiad of Athens' palmy days.[13] We have a far different task from that of dreaming and wishing. We must watch the chaos not as idle spectators, but as sentient participants.

There never has been an age so profoundly introspective as our own—none so zealous in giving itself an account of its own impulses. It is to this century that we owe the thousand and one essays on the "Genius of Christianity," "The Spirit of our Present Age," "Our Condition and Prospects." In this consciousness of our state, many have seen the symptoms of our unhealthiness. It has been fashionable for some years to speak of the unconsciousness of genius, to speak of self-analysis as the sure sign of sickliness and weakness, and every school-boy holds forth on the text furnished by Mr. Carlyle's "characteristics." The greatest poet of the two preceding generations inculcated this maxim with the utmost ardour; repeated it in every form. Not even the dullest reader ever arose from the perusal of Goethe without at least this one idea, that the great characteristic of genius is unconscious spontaneity.[14] "On the whole," says Carlyle, who has

---

13. Cecrops was the legendary founder and king of Athens, so this refers to an Athenian of noble lineage.

14. [To hedge in the assertion of the text with such limitations as readily suggest themselves, would be equivalent to cancelling it, and we must, therefore, "reserve the point." We subjoin a brace of quotations from Xenia:

"Ja, das ist das rechte Gleis,
Dass man nicht weiss
Was man denkt,
Wenn man denkt,
Alles ist als wie geschenkt."

And again—

"'Wie hast du's denn so weit gebracht?
Sie sagen, due habest es gut vollbracht?'
Mein kind! Ich hab' es klug genacht,
Ich habe nie uber das Denken gedacht."]

Trans.

Yes, that is the way,
One does not know
What one thinks,
When one thinks,
Everything is as a gift:

*Zahme Xenien*, in *Goethe's Sämmlichte Werke* (Stuttgart und Tübingen, 1854), 1:180.

How did you get so far?
They say you have succeeded.
My child! I have been clever,
I have never reflected on thought.

Ibid., 1:199. (The *Xenien* were satirical epigrams, composed by Goethe and Schiller in 1795–1796, in answer to their critics.)

adopted this principle and applied it in his peculiar manner, "genius is ever a secret to itself. Of this old truth we have, daily, new evidence. The Shakspeare takes no airs for writing *Hamlet* and the *Tempest*, understands not that it is anything surprising; Milton, again, is more conscious of his faculty, which is, accordingly, an inferior one."[15] What becomes, then, of Carlyles's great idol, Goethe himself, whose power of self-analysis is unparalleled? The ancients appear to us less conscious of their individual power than others, because our acquaintance with them is, after all, confined to a limited sphere. With the exception of Pindar and a few precious fragments, all the lyric poetry of Greece has perished. It is to this department that we must look for a display of self-consciousness; not to the Epos, which, in its antique form, is foreign to our culture; nor to the drama, for the individuality of the author is modified in the two great coryphaei, under whom the Attic tragedy reached its culmination, by the characters represented both in the dialogue and the chorus. It is in lyric poetry and the professedly personal parabasis of the old comedy, that we find as perfect a recognition of self, and as clear a statement of the principles of art, as can be found in any modern poet. Pindar and Simonides carried on a controversy in their odes, and evidently pursued different theories of art.[16] Pindar, as true and antique as a statue from the Parthenon, measured his own proportions as carefully as Phidias did those of his Pallas, and proudly asserted his own superiority in lines which strongly reminded us of Goethe's own self-exaltation.[17] How many men, in the whole range of literature, are secrets to themselves? Homer has escaped the charge of self-consciousness from the remoteness of his antiquity and the mystery of his origin, Shakspeare from the peculiar nature of the drama; and yet Homer and Shakspeare, if carefully studied with reference to this point, would evolve strange results.[18] We owe the erroneous impressions which are stamped on the

15. "Characteristics," in Carlyle, *Critical and Miscellaneous Essays* (London, 1887), 2: 196.
16. [Bernhardy, Gesch. der Gr. Litteratur, s. 511. More in Schneidewin's Prologomena to Simonides, p. xxx. Rauchenstein, Einleitung in Pindar's Siegeslieder, s. 66.] Gottfried Bernhardy, Rudolf Rauchenstein, and F. G. Schneidewin respectively.
17. [Pindar. Ol. II. 86 seqq.

μαθόντες δὲ λάβροι
παγγλωσσίᾳ, κόρακες ὥς, ἄκραντα γαρύετον
Διὸς πρὸς ὄρνιχα θεῖον.

Goethe in his Xenia—

Sollen die Dohlen dich nicht umschrein
Musst nicht Knopf auf dem Kirchthurm seyn.]

Trans. Those academic poets accustomed to loud-mouthed quarrels chatter in vain, like crows, against the godlike bird of Zeus. And, If you wish the jackdaws not to scream about you/You must not be the pinnacle of the church steeple. *Xenien*, in *Sämmtlichte Werke*, 1:191: it should read, "Sollen dich die Dohlen nicht. . . ."

18. [Coleridge has a few remarks tending to this point, in Biographia Literaria, chap. II.]

minds of our educated men, to the abuse of those two very convenient and fashionable words, *objective* and *subjective*. How much farther down these terms will go, how much more hackneyed they will become, it is not easy to conceive. Now, while we are writing, a plain matter-of-fact man is called "too objective," while another, properly termed an arrant liar, is pronounced "too subjective." It is, therefore, not without design, that we here briefly protest against ranging antiquity under the banner of objectivity, and modern literature under the flag of subjectivity. No sensible man will suppose that human nature is so essentially different in different ages and countries. Archilochus and Hipponax lampooned as fiercely and grumbled as savagely as any denizen of Grub-street.[19] It is not because ancient literature is severe and statuesque, that we urge the necessity of an instauration of the study. It is because it is the offspring of a healthy humanity, that we would hold its fair, firm features up to the gaze of our teeming present, as the ancients are said to have environed the future mother with none but beautiful objects.

The dominant authority of the two classic nations cannot be shaken. The projective power of the one and the receptivity of the other have exhausted all the categories of literature, and have left standing norms for production and reproduction. The history of Grecian literature is essentially organic—"First the blade, then the ear, then the full corn in the ear."[20] Poetry preceded prose. The Epos, which derived its material from without, was the forerunner of lyric poetry formed from within, while both were afterwards united in the artistic compass of the dramas, in which action supplemented narration and modulated the ideal flight of lyric poetry. In the field of prose, to which mature reflection led the Grecian mind, we find the Epos transmuted into history, while the perceptions of the seer, at first communicated in numbers, pass from lofty verse into unfettered language, and the orator—as true an ὑποκριτής[21] as another—narrates and reasons in dramatic monologue. Here, as in all highly organized existences, we find transitions, half-classes, connecting links. Where full development is wanting, the indicative rudiment is found. Here, as in all highly organized existences, we find a brief bloom preceded by a gradual development and followed by a gradual decline. As there were many heroes before Agamemnon, so there were many poets before Homer. Many philosophers came after Plato, many poets succeeded Sophocles. The great Aristotle spanned the chasm which separated the old world from the new, and the great Euripides planted one foot on the firm shore of antiquity and

---

19. Archilochus, fl. circa 700 B.C., the Greek iambic and elegiac poet; Hipponax, fl. 540 B.C., the Greek iambic poet.

20. Mark 4:28.

21. Hypokrites, which meant first an interpreter, latterly an actor.

the other on the troubled waters of our agitated times, which were even then eddying up against the land.

The Greeks solved the problem—the Romans verified the solution. The former produced the flower from within outward; the latter proceeded in their imitation from without inward. The Roman drama preceded the bloom of lyric poetry, and lyric poetry was followed by the Epos. The traces of Roman literature, like those of the Kine in well-known myth, are all backwards.[22] Intense consciousness marks every step. In Rome we have the strange, but by no means unaccountable phenomenon, of grammarians in advance of and parallel with classical literature. No people ever observed so closely the celebrated sentence of Schiller—

"The weakling is to be despised
Who ne'er hath weighed what he fulfils."[23]

Livius Andronicus, with whom the history of Roman literature begins, was a *grammaticus*, and divided his time between the Odyssey, with which the *plagosus Orbilius* tortured little Horace, and his private class of Roman gentlemen.[24] In Ennius we find an instance of that straight-forward perseverance so truly Roman, which would undertake alike the laying of an aqueduct and the alteration of a language.[25] Had Mr. Pinkerton and Frederic II. been Romans, the English and German languages might this day be tricked out in the cast-off finery of Italian terminations.[26] Ennius was fully determined to introduce the hexameter—the *versus longus*—into the Italian literature, and he achieved it against difficulties, the number and magnitude of which have been but recently disclosed. Many and many a struggle did it cost the trilingual Calabrian before he could force the stubborn materials into that superb causeway over which the numbers of Virgil march so firmly. Attius, the tragic poet, attempted to reform the

---

22. This refers to the myth of Cacus, a monster or brigand who lived in a cave on the Aventine: he stole some of the cattle of Geryon, when Hercules rested, by dragging them tail first into the cave.

23. [Den schlechten mann muss man verachten
Die nie bedacht, was er vollbringt.]
Schiller, "The Song of the Bell," lines 15–16.

24. Livius Andronicus, circa 284–204 B.C., a playwright, perhaps best known for translating the Odyssey into Latin Saturnians; "plagosus" means "fond of flogging": see Horace, *Epistles*, II, i, lines 70–71.

25. Quintus Ennius, 239–169 B.C., the so-called father of Roman poetry; he was trilingual in Greek, Latin, and his native Oscan.

26. John Pinkerton, 1758–1826, the Scottish antiquary and editor of Horace Walpole's Letters; on Frederick the Great's suggested reform of German, cf. Madame de Staël, *Germany* (London, 1814), 1: 161–62: "he composed a little work, in which he proposes, among other changes, to add a vowel at the end of every verb, to soften the Teutonic dialect. This German, in an Italian mask, would produce the most comic effect in the world."

spelling.²⁷ Lucilius devoted more than one book of his *Saturae* to the subject of orthography.²⁸ Hence it is not surprising to find Caesar writing a treatise on grammar, or Cicero making etymologies, which sound marvellously like bad puns.²⁹ Indeed, the history of Roman literature cannot be studied aright without constant reference to the parallelism of grammatical and literary systems. We must watch Ennius cautiously clipping the refractory long syllables, Attius doubling his letters, Horace breaking in the high-trotting hexameter to a gentle amble, and Ovid, that seemingly careless child of the Muses, deftly arranging the fall of his pentameters. The writers of Rome were, at once, the *demiurgi* of language and of literature. By reason of this intense consciousness, the Roman literature has been called a bridge to lead us to Hellenism, a law-giving school-master to bring us to the knowledge of that grand aesthetic revelation. This mission is well-nigh accomplished with regard to the world at large, and is continued chiefly in its bearing upon individuals. To speak with Bernhardy, "the Roman literature has totally exhausted its world-historic task, and will henceforward develope a propaedeutic power rather than enter into the thesaurus of our ideas or the movements of our culture."³⁰

As the Roman literature was based on reflection, it ceased when there was nothing left to analyze. Satire and history, where the peculiar merits of original Roman conception found ample scope, were the one narrowed down to the pasquill, the other attenuated into the gossiping chronicle. The iron age of Latinity lost itself in the dross of the middle ages, before the spirit of Hellenistic productiveness had been crushed, under the pomp of the Byzantine court, before Paulus Silentiarius hymned the pulpit, or Tzetzes broke up the artistic rhythm of Homer into the halting jumble of the *versus politicus*.³¹ The formative elements of Graeco-Roman literature continued to work through the lapse of centuries, though straightened and distorted in its modes of operation and manifestation. Aristotle reigned supreme, though robbed of the fine robe in which he clothed his subtle distinctions, as he did his delicate frame, and draped in the rags of an

---

27. [Ritschl, De Vocalibus geminatis deque Lucio Attio grammatico. Bonnae. 1852]; Lucius Accius (the more usual form now, though Attius was not uncommon in Gildersleeve's day), 170–circa 86 B.C., the Latin poet.

28. Gaius Lucilius, circa 180–circa 102 B.C., the founder of Roman satire; Book 9 of his *Saturae* discusses grammar, in part attacking the orthographical theories of Accius.

29. Caesar wrote the *De Analogia* upon a journey across the Alps in 55 or 54 B.C.: it is dedicated to Cicero; Cicero himself wrote nothing specific on etymology, but often discussed the matter in his speeches.

30. [Grundriss der Romischen Litteratur, s. 132.] The Hegelian tone of this quotation will be apparent.

31. Paulus Silentiarius was an official at the court of Justinian, circa 560, and wrote a poetical description upon the restored church of Santa Sophia; Tzetzes, circa 1110–circa 1180, a Byzantine who wrote a commentary on Homer, as well as a long poem in accentual verse upon miscellaneous literary and historical subjects, in which he quoted more than four hundred authors.

Necessity of the Classics 407

Arabic version woven into a texture of barbarous Latin. Virgil, the sorcerer, took the place of Virgil, the poet, and figured as a prototypical Dr. Faustus.[32] The heroic forms of antiquity, historic as well as mythical, the fair impersonations of its theology, formed the groundwork of much of the poetry on which Roman tri-literature is based. Venus, the enchantress, has still her mountains in Germany. Alexander figures in the western as well as eastern myth. The princes of England derived their origin from Brutus.[33] The siege of Troy attracted listening ears, which were strangers to the Latin or Hellenic tongue. The most sacred persons of our theology were commingled with the plastic forms of mythology, and the legend of many a saint meets the eye of the enquirer in a heathen garb. Diana and Minerva, or Artemis and Athene, furnish parallels for many an artistic conception and many a theological dogma, which are admired and revered down to the present day.[34] Around the magic cadences of our existence, the twin eternities of the Hebrew faith and the Hellenic imagination have buried themselves inextricably, and the one can be as little dispensed with in art as the other in morals. The grand revolution of the Reformation overturned the physical systems of antiquity, and opened the field of science, which, no longer fettered by the terminology and categories of the schools, entered boldly on the search for new truths. But before Aristotle had given way to Bacon, Ptolemy to Copernicus, Theophrastus to Linnaeus, a victory was gradually but completely achieved. The humanists conquered the obscurants, and while much of the science of antiquity was made obsolete, the form reappeared triumphant, like the line of Egyptian kings who went away into the wilderness and returned to rule. The thought of these men was a beautiful one. Like Petrarch, their great forerunner, they wished to ignore the dark and turbulent dream which had passed over the world, and to wake, like Socrates, after some classic symposium, not a whit the worse for their copious draughts. Hence, the return to the same

---

32. [Bernhardy, 1. c. p. 413. This subject has recently excited much attention. We cite, in addition to Bernhardy's authorities, Michel and Tappet. A French scholar has written an especial Essay on Virgile l'enchanteur.] I have only been able to locate Guillaume Michel, Les bucoliques de Virgille Maron (Paris, 1516), scarcely recent and so probably not the Michel whom Gildersleeve had in mind.

33. For the myth of Brutus and Britain, see the invention in Geoffrey of Monmouth, The History of the Kings of Britain, ed. Lewis Thorpe (London, 1969), pp. 35–55.

34. [We have found a trace of the Immaculate Conception in the myth of Erectheus or Erichthonius, Schwenck, Mythologie des Griechen, p. 79. The legend was preserved in the Ἑκάλη of Callimachus, according to the Schol. on II. B. v. 547.] In the myth of Erichthonius, Hephaestus wished to marry Athena, petitioned Zeus successfully, but Zeus simultaneously gave Athena leave to repulse Hephaestus' attentions. God and goddess struggled, his seed fell to earth, germinated, and became the boy Erichthonius, whom Athena then adopted; the Hecale of Callimachus (fl. 260 B.C.) is a poem, chiefly narrating Theseus' battle with the Bull of Marathon; Schwenck is Conrad Schwenk, who wrote extensively on mythology, notably in Die Mythologie der Asiatischen Völker, der Aegypter, Griechen, Römer, Germanen und Slaven (Frankfurt am Main, 1843–1853).

forms and to the same language. But nature must have her right. Melanchthon was Schwarzerd, and Erasmus, Gerard still.[35] Yet the native literature, which soon eclipsed the appropriated literature of the learned, was full of reverence for the antique, which was displayed in the abundant transfer of material, and the warmth of an inspired imitation. Between the exuberance of this spring-time, and the precise but ingenious formality of the age of Louis XIV., stands the proudest monument of classical study and enthusiasm—one, whose height and depth will be more appreciated by the individual student the further he advances in the knowledge of the great honours which regulated the impulses of Milton's supreme genius. The warmth of the Italian school of philosophy was cherished in his bosom like the sacred prytaneum-fire of the ancient colonists, and while at times remote allusions and far-fetched comparisons show that he was the contemporary of his overlearned antagonist, for whom the biting epitaph was written, *"Hic situs est Salmasius, vir immortalis memoriae, expectans judicium,"*[36] still his keen vision seems to have penetrated even to our times, and to have taken in at least a part of the whole fabric. The vitally defective French "classic" drama was based on a system of artificial laws derived from the misinterpretation of Aristotle, and operating under false conditions. A seductive rhetoric and the brilliant prestige of court favour gained an ascendency for a mutilated and starveling growth, which, like a western Bagoas,[37] ruled the court of a western *grand monarque*. A new spirit came with the Phrygian cap and would-be antique absurdities of the first French Revolution—the spirit of enfranchisement. The false idols of the preceding generations were attacked by a new race of iconoclasts. The new Batrachomyomachia[38] of the classicists and Romanticists is now over. The world has withdrawn from its noise and confusion. The smoke of the battle-field has cleared away, and we can see the results plainly. The Romanticists tried to revive a poetical literature, which cannot take root in our reflective eye. The classicists held fast to a formal literature, which lacked the deep feeling with which our reflection is combined. The followers of the Latin school laid down laws which they themselves did not follow, and Byron's judgment was at variance with his art. In France piebald

---

35. Schwarzerd and Gerard were the original German names of Melanchthon and Erasmus.

36. Trans. Here lies Salmasius, man of undying memory, awaiting judgment: Claudius Salmasius, 1588–1653, the French philologist and polymath, the successor of Scaliger at Leyden; he died at the court of Queen Christina of Sweden. He was famous for his great memory and ambition for a worshiping posterity, which is the burden of the pun *vir immortalis memoriae*.

37. The eunuch, Bagoas, vizier to Artaxerxes III, commander in chief of the Persians during the invasion of Egypt (343 B.C.); he latterly murdered Artaxerxes to put Arses on the throne, then murdered Arses and elevated Darius III. He was in turn murdered by Darius.

38. The Battle of the Frogs and Mice, the parody of an epic poem, once attributed to Homer but now thought to be of a later date.

eclectiveness has taken the place of a national literature. The Greens and the Blues have formed a coalition.[39] In Germany a truer conception of the nature of classicism prevailed during the whole conflict, and has come forth triumphant. Romanticism is cherished only by a faction of modern obscurants. Stories of the feudal times—ballads of knights and 'ladies'—are now standing themes for travesty and parody, and it is ludicrously provoking to see this Brummagem ware brought forward in our country, which, if the fervent prayer of the great German poet,[40] to whom we have already had, and, indeed, in every question of culture must have, frequent reference, had but been heard, would have escaped the infliction. The recent literature of the English language has been marked by a steady return to antique themes. The deeper apprehension and livelier conception of Grecian myths has given rise to a class of poetry of peculiar and exquisite beauty. A soft rose light is thrown on the classic statue, and it seems alive. We are not ready to admit with some, that Keats and Tennyson have seen deeper into the Eleusinian mysteries of antiquity than the ancients themselves. Impersonations and conceptions to us, these were entities and realities to them. Keats may be "as sublime as Aeschylus,"[41] but the chasm between them is impassable. Here, too, we find a contradiction, in fact, to the specious fallacy that poetry can only flourish in an unenlightened age. On the ruins of Roman history Macaulay has built his "Lays." The heroic character is now a different being from the Achilles of the time of Louis Quatorze, who talks the court language, calls Iphigenia 'madame,' and wears a horse-hair wig. No poet of our age would bid the *fearful Naiads* fly before "Louis, by the grace of God, king of France and Navarre, accompanied by his field-marshals," as Victor Hugo maliciously phrases it.[42] In short, clas-

39. The two popular factions of late Roman politics.
40. [Den vereinigten Staaten
    \*   \*   \*   \*   \*   \*   \*
Benutzt die Gegenwart mit Glück.
Und wenn nun eure Kinder dichten,
Bewahre sie ein gut Geschick
Von Ritter—Räuber—und Gespenstergeschichten. Goethe, 6, iii, s. 120].
Trans.
    To America . . . Use well the present and good luck to you
    And when your children begin writing poetry
    Let them guard well in all they do
    Against knight—robber—and ghost-story.
Goethe, *Sämmlichte Werke*, 1:197 (this is the Stephen Spender translation, in *The Permanent Goethe*, ed. Thomas Mann [New York, 1948], p. 655).
41. Byron, on Keats's *Hyperion*, a manuscript note dated 12 November 1821, quoted in *Keats: The Critical Heritage*, ed. G. M. Matthews (London, 1971), p. 128. Byron was usually scathing towards Keats's verse.
42. [Entrouvant fort ridicules les Néréides dont Camöeus obsède les compagnons de Gama, on désirerait, dans le célèbre *Passage du Rhin* de Boileau, voir autre chose que des naiades craintives fuir devant Louis, par la grâce de Dieu, roi de France et de Navarre, accompagné de ses marechaux-des-camps et-armées.] Preface, *Nouvelles Odes* (1824), in Victor Hugo, *Oeuvres complètes*, ed. Jean Massin (Paris, 1967), 2:474.

sical machinery is worn out, but classic inspiration remains as fresh as ever.

A sure index of the returning influence of the ancient classics is to be found in that department of literature which seems to be the most remote from the classic norm. The general reader knows that the modern novel, which completed its form in the last century, and has filled up the measure of its high importance in the present, was almost unknown to the ancients; that from the first writer of Milesian stories, down to Aristaenetus,[43] the history of the Greek romance, no genuine product of the Hellenic mind, but arising from Hellenized nations, exhibits nothing but a series of smooth descriptions—luscious pictures, theatrical incantations, wild and improbable adventures. The modern novel is the exhibition of the highest talent, and the expositor of weighty principles. Yet, on this very field, if we mistake not a law of ancient art is every day asserting itself. We learn from the archaeology of art, that the types of Zeus and Athene were fixed by Phidias, Apollo and Aphrodite, by Scopas and Praxiteles, Hephaestus by Alcamenes. From these no subsequent artist ventured to deviate. The ideal was found, and no word could be added to, or taken away from, the finished revelation. The same law prevailed in the statuesque drama. Not even Euripides dared change the ground-features of the heroes, whom he brought upon the stage. Our modern literature has never been content with types. It has vehemently sought to produce new creations. And how has it succeeded? Except Shakspeare, that miraculous Prometheus, who broke the moulds of all his persons, whose four-worded characters[44] have a life distinct from all the rest of mankind; and how many creations are there in English literature? How many that are not types are not shadows? Examine the works of Dickens, universally extolled as a creative mind, and how many creations will be found that are not monsters or abortions? Let any one ask himself, is Quilp a human being? Is Barkis anything but a sentence? Is Uriah Heep a possibility? Wherever Dickens has succeeded, it has been in the delineation of a class, in Dick Swiveller, Miss Trotwood, Mr. Pickwick, all of whom are our acquaintances, all of whom we can, to use a popular term, at once *locate*. The works of our older novelists, Fielding and Smollet, present us with characters closely imitated from nature. The types, which they have thus formed, are immortal,, while the nightmares of a heated imagination must pass away even in the narrating. The characters of Sterne live again in Bulwer, and if the novel of the Caxtons is not equal to Tristram Shandy, neither is the Medicean Ve-

---

43. Aristaenetus, fl. fifth century, the author of epistolary romances.
44. [It was Coleridge, we think, who maintained that the character James Gurney, in King John, was fully depicted in the four words assigned him, "Good leave, good Philip."] Coleridge, *Notes and Lectures on Shakespeare*, ed. Mrs. H. N. Coleridge (London, 1849), 1:166; Gildersleeve is reading a little too much into Coleridge's remarks.

nus equal to the Cnidian. In this connection, it is remarkable that Thackeray, who has been blamed for a similar tendency, defends the reappearance of his standing characters, by an olio of apologues, the most clearly typical of all representations.

We have thus endeavoured to demonstrate, or, at least, to indicate, that the classics are eternal norms and present facts, that we are drawn toward them by a two-fold necessity, a natural and historic. It would be easy to proceed a step farther, and evolve the connection between our literature and the Graeco-Roman, from their common linguistic elements. But from this wide and inviting field, we are debarred by the limits of our article—and we must, therefore, content ourselves with the repetition of the old maxim, "He who is not acquainted with a foreign language, knows nothing of his own," and with urging its peculiar application. The premises being thus settled by demonstration and admission, we proceed to the practical consideration of the condition of classical study in our country. In order to do this, we must first look abroad. Our achievements in this department have been, at best, reproductions, and we must, therefore, examine the original before we judge of the imitation. Two nations have given tone to the study of the classics in this country, the English and the German. The former element is decaying, the latter just springing into life.

To some of the secluded scholars of our Southern country, who devote much of their abundant leisure to the perusal of the classics, and collect Aldines, Juntines and Elzevirs with bibliomaniac zeal, England may still seem to be the Gilead whence the balm must come.[45] But England has never had a philology. The scholars who arose from her soil were of foreign seed. The dragon's teeth brought forth a strange race. Bentley lived a century too soon, and England laughed at the new Aristarchus as she cheered glory-and-shame Porson, not knowing what she did.[46] It is sad to look at the full-length caricature of Bentley, which Pope has drawn, with such malicious distortion, in his Dunciad, and to reflect upon the uniform fate of all those great men who have been sent to that ungrateful people. But a just punishment has overtaken them. Their philological worthies have no national existence and form no national school. The type of their educationists is Dr. Busby, and the type of their scholars Dr. Parr.[47] It is astonishing with what vehement obstinacy, so to speak, England prides

---

45. All editions of classical texts.

46. Richard Porson, 1759–1808, Regius Professor of Greek at Cambridge from 1792 and, like Bentley, a fellow of Trinity College; cf. Gildersleeve, "Formative Influences," p. 365: "Among the first philological books I owned was the well-known collection of Porsoniana in four volumes containing Porson's Preface to the Hecuba, his edition of the Plutus and his Photius."

47. Richard Busby, 1606–1695, headmaster of Westminster School from 1638 to 1695, published various classical school books; Samuel Parr, 1747–1825, the so-called Whig Johnson, classical scholar, controversialist, churchman to various benefices.

herself upon the mere negative merit of keeping her quantity void of offence. In no country on the globe has so much turmoil been made about the fact that scholars know the right hand from the left, and leave Priscian's head unbroken. The most earless nation on earth—a nation which has produced no music, except those simple strains which, like currents of electricity, run round the whole globe, which cannot show a single composer of real eminence—prides itself upon an accuracy for which there is no parallel save that of a deaf musician. The whole world must be pestered with the information, that the British Senate knew that the penult of *vectigal* is long, and that Cambridge was aware that the penult of *profugus* is short: and these stories are hawked about wherever the English language is spoken, and every lad in the rudiments learns to sneer at Paley's quantity and triumph over Pitt's short syllable in *labenti*.[48] Every article on America contains some gibe at our unfortunate proclivity to Polish perversions.[49] Even men who should know better, lay special stress on the mechanical accomplishment of making verses. The same Bulwer who, in Pelham, laughed at the facility with which he could turn off Latin verses, compared with his other deficiencies,[50] in "the Caxtons" throws a slur on German erudition by contrasting Dr. Herrmann's eulogy of Pisistratus' ode with the parody of Mr. Caxton.[51] Classical education in England has been, for long years, one huge polypus of verse-making, an exercise which, however useful, still stands, in a pedagogical point of view, far behind the exercise of writing prose, not so much on account of the disproportion in numbers between those who possess the faculty divine and those who do not, as because vapidity and inanity cannot conceal themselves so well on the plain ground of the *pedestris oratio*, as in the flight of an *anser inter olores*, nor loose syntax and careless construction shelter themselves behind the convenient plea of poetic license.[52] "Long reading and observing, copious invention and ripe judgment," may enable a Herrmann to repro-

---

48. [Macaulay's Essays. Art. Thackeray's Chatham.] Gildersleeve, *Brief Mention*, p. 368, has a footnote at this point: "The Paley meant here is, of course, the Natural Theology man, against whom I had a grievance. Pitt's lăbenti reminds me of 'labitur atque lăbetur,' which appeared on a medal struck in honor of the Philological Congress at Hamburg some years ago. My informant, an eminent British scholar, did not fail to point the moral."

49. [Nos Póloni non cúramus quantítatem syllábarum.] Trans. We Poles do not care about the quantity of syllables.

50. ["I could make twenty Latin verses in half-an-hour; I could construe *without* an English translation all the easy Latin authors, and many of the difficult ones *with it*; I could *read* Greek fluently, and even translate it, through the medium of a Latin version at the bottom of the page."] Edward Bulwer-Lytton, *Pelham: or, The Adventures of a Gentleman* (rev. ed., London, 1835), p. 5.

51. Lytton, *The Caxtons: A Family Picture* (New York, 1903), pp. 29–30.

52. *Pedestris oratio*: literally, a speech on foot, which came to mean, firstly, prose and, secondly, common and prosaic; *anser inter olores*, a goose among swans; Vergil, *Eclogues*, 9, lines 35–36, has "videor . . . argutos inter strepere anser olores," I seem to honk like a goose among melodious swans.

duce Schiller in Greek or a Ritschl to supply the *lacunae* in Plautus; but, as Milton concludes, "these are not matters to be wrung from poor striplings, like blood out of the nose or the plucking of untimely fruit."[53] And yet, after all their true British boasting, the schools of England must be very defective in the matter of classical training, if we may judge by recent disclosures.[54] Scholars, who ignore Greek accents and are unacquainted with the composition of words of frequent occurrence and evident structure, are strangely misnamed. We, for our part, would apply in their favour the educational observation of the worthy South: "Stripes and blows are the last and basest remedy, and scarce ever fit to be used but upon such as carry their brains in their backs, and have souls so dull and stupid as to serve for very little else but to keep their bodies from putrefaction."[55]

Reprints of American school books, translations of German works, editions prepared by Germans, for the English market, do not constitute a national philology; and we, therefore, pass over to a brief notice of the Neo-Hellenistic school, under the leadership of Prof. Blackie, who has recently entered upon his high career as Professor of Greek in the University of Edinburgh.[56] This distinguished scholar bids fair to furnish as long

53. Johann Gottfried Hermann, 1772–1848, the German classical scholar and philologist, professor at Leipzig, who held that linguistic studies were the only proper aim of classical studies; Friedrich Wilhelm Ritschl, 1806–1876, professor of Latin at Bonn, known for his study of Plautus and one of the founders, with Mommsen, of modern epigraphy; John Milton, "Of Education," in *The Works of John Milton* (New York, 1931), 4:278.

54. [We have especial reference to an article in the Westminster Review for October, 1853, from which we extract the following morsel. "On one occasion, when urging the importance of etymology on the attention of a principal of a most respectable school, we said that a boy ought not to pass through his Greek studies without knowing the derivation of such a word as *sarcasm* (the word which occurred to us at the moment). His answer was: 'I am not ashamed to confess that I myself do not know.' Yet he was a superior scholar, and a man of great intelligence. An eminent Hellenist, now dead, whom we knew, in like manner did not know the derivation of paraphernalia. How many classical scholars are there who cannot tell the real meaning of so common a word as *squirrel*, detect *cura* in *proxy*, or show that *galaxy* and *lettuce* are, at base, one word." The first two instances of *crassa ignorantia* are so crass, that were they related of any respectable teacher in our country, we would reply, if not by the *lie direct*, at least by the *reproof valiant*. To find γάλα in γαλαξίας and *lacte* in *lactuca*, requires no superhuman exertion. *Proxy* (a contraction for *procuracy*) is not a fair instance, while the etymology of the shadow-tailed squirrel (σκίουρος) is as celebrated in its way as those of *fox* and *cucumber* in theirs.] See [W. B. Hodgson], "The School Claims of Languages, Ancient and Modern," *Westminster Review* n.s. 4 (October 1853): 450–98 (quotation on p. 458): sarcasm comes from the Greek, meaning to strip the flesh off; paraphernalia is a combination of "para," meaning "beside" and "pherne," a dowry, and thus means that portion of a woman's property that did not pass to the husband's estate; squirrel is a combination of two Greek words, meaning "shade" and "tail"; galaxy comes from the Greek, meaning milk, hence the Milky Way, the definitive galaxy; while lettuce, *lactuca* in Latin, is derived from *lac*, the Latin word for milk; fox derives, according to some scholars, from the Sanskrit *puccha*, a tail; I can detect no particular subtlety in *cucumber*, which comes from the Latin *cucumis*, a cucumber.

55. "A Discourse upon the Virtous Education of Youth," in Robert South, *Twelve Sermons and Discourses on Several Subjects and Occasions* (London, 1717), 5:28.

56. John Stuart Blackie, 1809–1895, became professor of Greek at the University of Edinburgh in 1852.

a succession of "heads" as any philosophic school of Athens could boast. We are to look, forsooth, for a revival of the study and general diffusion of the literature of ancient Greece, from a more intimate acquaintance with the Sclavonic tribes, which inhabit the seats of the ancient Hellenes, and which have received the mantle of their great predecessors in tatters.[57] The name of this professor is mentioned with great deference in the Westminster Review, and a fervent follower of the new school has had the hardihood to publish, in the North British Review,[58] an article on the Literature and Language of Modern Greece, which savours strongly of Romaic anthologies, and which we shrewdly suspect to be the production of some Edinburgh or Glasgow student, who has spent six months in Greece, and has derived his limited knowledge of the ancient tongue in that short space of time, from some of the illustrious professors whom he delights to honour.[59] "Greek," they triumphantly maintain, "is not a dead language;" and point to this and that purely classic word. It would require a close observer to tell the difference between an empty nut and a full one, between bark growing on its tree and that which has been stripped off. The difference is in the continuance of organic life. Latin was not more certainly a dead language in the middle ages than Greek is now. The ancient spirit, and, consequently, the ancient syntax and constructive power, are gone forever. The language of modern Greece is essentially a modern language, its syntax is loose and shambling, its composite words are the laughing stock of educated Europe. Its sentences run into the straight channels of modern construction, and only here and there a classic idiom reappears, as a fossil relic of a dead antiquity. The absurdities of this system of learning ancient Greek are, indeed, so glaring, that it would be an insult to the intelligent reader to pursue the subject much farther. The Romaic language, it is true, is undergoing a process of reconstruction, and, in the course of time, an approach will, no doubt, be made to the external semblance of ancient Greeks. Words of foreign origin have been resolutely plucked out, and others derived from the ancient language, or composed of Greek elements, have been substituted. The time will come when the eye and taste will no longer be offended by a *lingua franca* in Greek characters. But, as yet, the struggle has been chiefly with the vocabulary. The next step will be to remodel the syntax, an undertaking which, we venture to say, is hopeless. Words, the symbols of ideas, may be exchanged with comparative ease. But to alter the syntax, to change the sequence of men's thoughts, with

---

57. [The boasts of our Greek friends never fail to remind us faithfully of Lessing's bitter fable, (b.1, fab. 16,) founded on the text of Aelian (de nat. animal. 1, 28,) "'Ἵππος ἐρριμμένος σφηκῶν γένεσίς ἐστιν.] Gottfried Ephraim Lessing, *Werke* (Zurich, 1965), 1:150; the Greek means, a horse's carcass is the breeding place of wasps.
58. [Nov., 1853]
59. It was, in fact, by Blackie himself.

the structure of their sentences and the connection of their words, is nothing short of raising up children unto Abraham from the stones of the causeway. A modern Greek philologian told the writer, that since his school-boy days at least a thousand words, which were then culled carefully from dictionaries and committed to memory, had found their way not only into the written, but also into the spoken language. A thousand years must elapse before the Greeks give up their νὰ for ἵνα,[60] or restore the dative to its full rights, and bring back the optative and infinitive. What little literary merit there is in Greece is modern in its cast, and must be read with modern eyes and modern feelings. When the ancient models are held up over against these modern productions, and the Hellenist is forced, as he is by these stony advocates of "living Greek," to compare them, the only emotion excited is that of disgust. A single wild ballad, which jumbles Hercules, Alexander the Great and Themistocles, into one category, is far more pleasing to us than all the would-be eloquent speeches of the wordy representatives of the Parliament of the Ionian Islands.

We have taken leave of our English school-masters and English sciolists with joy, and not with grief, recommending, as a motto for their future productions, the words of Sir Andrew Aguecheek—"I am a great eater of beef, and, I believe, that does harm to my wit."[61]

"The history of sciences," says Goethe, "is a grand fugue, in which the voices of the peoples come in one by one."[62] The Germans are now dominant in the science of classical philology, and we must harmonize with them or make a senseless discord. To characterize German philology at once, briefly and satisfactorily, is impossible. To understand its present state and influence, we must go back to the Alexandrians, and trace the history of the ancient *grammatica* in its genesis, developement, flower and decay. We must sympathize with the ardent enthusiasm of the Italian period, and admire both the varied condition of the French school, and the patient industry of the plodding Dutch, as they

"Stuffed the head
With all such reading as was never read."[63]

We must, also, take note of individuals, such as are called, in our day, "representative men," because they cannot find representatives;[64] we must mark Scaliger's genius and Bentley's method. For, as the last great German school of philosophy boasts that it has absorbed and appropriated all the essential elements of its predecessors, so does the last great school of

---

60. The modern contracted form, as against the ancient uncontracted form.
61. *Twelfth Night*, I. iii. 81.
62. Goethe, *Maximen und Reflexionen*, in *Berliner Ausgabe* (Berlin, 1972), 18:562.
63. Pope, *The Dunciad*, IV, lines 249–50.
64. Possibly an allusion to Emerson's *Representative Men* (1850).

philology embrace, in its universality, the warmth of the Italian period, the material knowledge of the French school, the geniality of Scaliger, the method of Bentley, the accumulative perseverance of the Dutch. The results lie plainly before us. The science of textual criticism may now be regarded as complete. The irregular and empirical, though, at times, surpassingly ingenious attempts of former schools, have given way to a systematic treatment. The mechanical collation of manuscripts has been succeeded by an intellectual classification. Nor has the science of Hermeneutics been neglected. Less attractive in its nature, and more chary of flattering rewards than its twin-science, it has, notwithstanding, received great and increasing attention. Under the influence of a more expanded philosophy, departments, once considered as the mere auxiliaries of classical learning, have been drawn into the circle of philological study, and subjected to the same searching investigation and acute analysis. The history of ancient literature has been raised to a higher power; and a closer scrutiny into the latter, and a deeper penetration into the spirit of history, in its wider sense, are the legitimate results of a more profound and intellectual criticism. Niebuhr is the consequence of Wolf.[65] The numerous shoots which classical philology has put forth, derived their vigour from the parent stem. The experience and the thought of centuries, go to aid the youthful sciences of comparative and oriental philology. Lachmann and Haupt are, alike, celebrated in the criticism of German and Latin authors.[66] An encyclopaedia of classical philology is now possible. The expansion of the study has contributed to its unity.

Until within a few years our philological, or rather pedagogical labours, were eclectical in their character, or rather want of character. The methods varied according to the individuality of the teacher. The Westminster Grammar was used in our country in times not beyond the memory of man, nor indeed beyond the memory of the writer. Adams is still extensively employed, and the Dauphin editions, with their corrupt texts, defective commentaries, and, strange to say, excellent indexes, are still in demand.[67] But, on the whole, we have shown a willingness to receive, and a readiness to apply, the teachings of Germany, which contrasts favourably with the obstinacy of the English. Unfortunately, however, this receptivity has been, thus far, confined to a wholesale appropriation of the results, instead of an adoption and application of the method. Piracy is no more a reproach among our editors, than it was among the ancient Greeks. An-

---

65. Christian von Wolf, 1679–1754, the systematizer and popularizer of Leibniz.

66. Karl K. R. W. Lachmann, 1793–1851, who taught at both Berlin and Königsberg, was noted for his study of both Homer and Lucretius; Moritz Haupt, 1808–1874, was Lachmann's successor at Berlin and his friend.

67. *A Latin Grammar for the Use of Westminster School* (London, 1832); probably John Adams, *Lectiones Selectae* (7th ed., London, 1810); "Dauphin" should presumably read "Delphin," an edition of the classics begun in the late seventeenth century, *ad usum Delphini*, that is, for the use of Louis de France (1661–1711), the Dauphin and only son of Louis XIV; the works were reprinted frequently.

thon is the great fugleman of all these literary fillibusters. This Review has always entered its protest against the blind admiration with which he was once regarded, and can, therefore, speak plainly, now that his reputation is declining, without fear of reprehension. In all that Anthon has translated, compiled and copied, for the quarter of a century over which his literary activity extends, there is not a single contribution of real worth. Not even one half-pennyworth of bread to this intolerable deal of sack. His most useful works are his compilations, and the composite parts of these are not always chosen from the proper authorities, or graduated according to a proper measure. His classical dictionary is a map, in which Rhode Island and Texas are of equal size.[68] Of the beauties of his style, we need remind no one who has read the dialogues between Henry and Dr. B., or looked at a page of his annotations to Virgil and Horace. The clearest exegesis becomes in his hands obscure, and the neatest emendation bungling. *Nil tetigit quod non foedavit.*[69] His Homer is a mere "poney;" his book in Latin versification swarms with false quantities. These we might forgive. His great sin is, that he knows nothing of the spirit and aims of classical philology—that he offers to act as a medium for thinking men without thinking himself. But, fortunately, all our philologists are not of this class. Some transfer from their sources with discrimination, elegance and due acknowledgment; and, while those who might have attained to eminence in this department have found it too barren, and have left it for the area of politics or the field of lighter literature, there are some who have given an earnest, and many who are giving promise of original American contributions to philological science. We, of the South, should take this specially to heart. Our Northern brethren have developed greater commercial activity, and, without being more literary, have produced a more comprehensive literature. Here is a harvest untouched by the sickle. The host of school-books published at the North, go for nothing in the philological account. We must wake to higher efforts, for which we are well adapted by the quick conceptions, love of classic form and instinctive rejection of extravagance, which are our birthright. Here, the wild political,

---

68. [The apparent completeness of this work should not be suffered to deceive the student. We notice the following glaring instances among a host of omissions:—Callinus, the elegiac poet; Clitarchus, the historian: Constantinus Porphyrogennetus, at whose instance the celebrated extracts were made (Excerpta Constantini de Virtutibus et Vitiis etc.); Crates of Mallos; Diogenianus, the lexicographer; Dionysius Thrax, the grammarian; Duris of Samos, the historian; Philochorus, known as one of the writers of Ἀτθίδες; Musonius Rufus, the philosopher; Telesilla, the virgin heroine and poetess of Argos; Tolmides, the Athenian strategus; Zenodotus, the first librarian of Alexandria and editor of Homer.] The Atthides were ethnographical and historical treatises on Attica, popular between circa 350 and 200 B.C.

69. Trans. He touched nothing that he did not befoul: an adaptation of "nullum quod tetigit non ornavit," part of Samuel Johnson's epitaph for Oliver Goldsmith in Westminster Abbey.

social and physical theories of our day, find no debateable ground between those who know too much and those who know too little. If united with vigorous action, this conscious self-possession would make us the arbiters of literary destiny. The sentences which we pass are confirmed by time, but they lack the weight which power confers. If we make the South, where the materials abound, the centre of classical learning, we must hold the balance. To create and perpetuate such a classical school, we must have an enlarged and elevative system of education, and the rising generation must be trained in a domestic institution, of a higher type than the out-door schools, whither so many of youth go, seeking knowledge, and finding a miserable succedaneum.[70]

Our reviewers are often like the Pharisees, and make broad their phylacteries at the head of their articles, without paying much attention to the contents of the text. We do not desire to treat Professor Bernhardy so cavalierly, by making his valuable work a stalking-horse to our own considerations.[71] We have merely reversed the order of our thought in tracing back the continuity of reflections which arose from the study of this book, by which we were led to the consideration of the pre-eminence of the German school of classical philology, and thence, by easy steps, to the general discussion which has given a name, if not a character, to the preceding remarks. The subject which was the first in our conception, becomes, necessarily, the last in execution.

To write a history of Greek literature, is, in our day, an undertaking for which a boldness is necessary, little short of audacity. The material has increased so much in the last half century, that a supplement might be written, which would outnumber the pages of Harless' edition of the mammoth Fabricius.[72] Almost every department has its especial students. Monographs have thrown individual rays of light on almost every author. Life and light go together, and every material acquisition aids in the spiritual reconstruction of antiquity. To unite these separate atoms—to fuse them into a living unity, demands the strength of no common mind. A mere reader would have the substance without the life. A mere theorist would produce the semblance of a spirit without the body in which the spirit must have its being. In Professor Bernhardy, both requisites—theoretic con-

---

70. [The able letter of President Thornwell to Gov. Manning, on Public Instruction in South Carolina, has given an impulse in the right direction. Amid the jar of contending sects, and the "solemn chatterings" of theorists, it is grateful, beyond expression, to listen to such excellent and temperate counsel.]

71. [The first volume of Prof. Bernhardy's Outlines, containing the Inner History of Grecian literature, appeared in 1836, and the second volume, in which the Outer History of Greek poetry is comprised, in 1845. Upon the present revised edition or "Bearbeitung" of the 1st volume, the third volume will no doubt follow, thus completing the whole.]

72. Johann Albert Fabricius, *Bibliotheca Graeca*, ed. G. C. Harles (Hamburg and Leipzig, 1790–1809).

structiveness and comprehensive reading—are united in a high and rare degree. We do not claim for him absolute infallibility in theory or statement. A phrase may have misled him, or an important fact may have escaped his notice. But these intervals of giddiness and sleepiness, if such there be, are exceedingly rare. Our author seeks no excuse in the Horatian allowance:

Operi longo fas est obrepere somnum.[73]

We find, in the work before us, clear perceptions of literary laws, phenomena significantly grouped, controversies luminously and succinctly unfolded and decided, hints of penetrating suggestiveness. His style is unfortunately rugged, at times positively obscure, at all times demanding, imperatively, an attentive and thoughtful reader. He cannot be read with the same placid attention as Müller, and many a passage will balk even those most conversant with the idiom.[74] By reason of this defect and his numerous excellencies, our public is not yet prepared for him. For the present, the English reader must be content with the elegant but incomplete history by Müller—the review articles of Mure,[75] and the recent *opus tesselatum* of Anthon,[76] that gigantic scholasticus, who builds his philosophical houses out of specimen-bricks.

Many have raised the hue-and-cry of Hegelianism against Bernhardy's works. Philologians are not wont to swear by the magistral words of any school, and this imputation is intended to diminish the authority of our author. We, for our part, have found nothing in this volume that requires the aid of the Hegelian system, or the Hegelian terminology. If his peculiar views were transferred into our literature, they would be at once admired, and readily appreciated by many a M. Jourdain, who would afterwards be astounded at the discovery, that he had been speaking the language of Hegel without knowing it.[77]

---

73. Horace, *Ars Poetica*, line 360: trans. It is permitted to nod off during a long work.

74. Karl Otfried Müller, 1797–1840, lectured at Göttingen and championed the view that classical studies were a division of cultural history; he died on a visit to Greece.

75. [Bernhardy notices "this first attempt of the English" in the following way: "This author, acquainted, but not agreeing with the investigations of the Germans, gives us a series of ratiocinations in the spirit of British aesthetics."] William Mure, *A Critical History of the Language and Literature of Ancient Greece* (London, 1850–1857).

76. Either Charles Anthon, *A Latin-English and English-Latin Dictionary* (New York, 1852), or *A Manual of Grecian Antiquities* (New York, 1852), or *A Manual of Roman Antiquities* (New York, 1851).

77. The main character in Molière's *Le Bourgeois Gentilhomme*, who, becoming unexpectedly wealthy, seeks education and is astonished to learn that he had been speaking prose for forty years without knowing it.

## 14.

*James Henley Thornwell*

"Memoir of Dr. Henry"[1]

James Henley Thornwell was the leading Presbyterian theologian of his day in the South and among its most influential educators.[2] For most of a life that ended prematurely in 1862, he was associated with the South Carolina College, as an undergraduate, professor, and latterly president. The link was occasionally broken, by graduate study at Andover Theological Seminary (briefly, because of its Unitarian tendencies) and Harvard, by ministries at various South Carolina churches, and, in his last days, by a professorship in the Columbia Theological Seminary. He would, indeed, have broken the link more often, but the College knew a good thing when it saw one, and on several occasions, frustrated his attempts to discard the drudgeries of administration and teaching. As an educator, he demanded that religion be represented even in secular institutions like the South Carolina College. As a churchman, he upheld the strictest version of Old School Presbyterianism, standing resolutely upon the Westminster Confession of Faith. As a South Carolinian, he opposed Nullification, was doubtful of separate secession in 1850, was enthusiastic about Manifest Destiny, was sympathetic to the Know-Nothings, supported slavery, and welcomed with sorrow the rupture of 1861. As a writer, he was indefatigable. His collected writings, though incomplete, compose four stout volumes. As an editor, he was best known for the *Southern Presbyterian Review*, but he also tended the *Southern Quarterly Review* in its last few dying years.

Thornwell was born to relative poverty in 1812. His biographer,

---

1. James Henley Thornwell, "Memoir of Dr. Henry," *SQR* 2, n.s. 1 (April 1856): 189–206, a review of Robert Henry, *Eulogy on the late Honourable John Caldwell Calhoun* (Columbia, S.C., 1850).
2. Benjamin Morgan Palmer, *The Life and Letters of James Henley Thornwell, D.D.* (Richmond, 1875).

Benjamin Morgan Palmer, friend and fellow Presbyterian, decorously described Thornwell's father as one of "that important and useful class, so necessary under the partially feudal system that has passed away, who managed the estates of others; serving as middle men between the proprietors, who were often absentees, and the baronial estates, which they managed as their representative"; which means, stripped of chivalric obfuscation, on overseer.[3] He had died by the time Thornwell was eight. The boy's local reputation as a prodigious student attracted the patronage of two local planters, and their indulgence assisted his rise. From the first, Thornwell was unnervingly proper but not so decidedly religious. When he first attended the South Carolina College his "idol" was the notoriously atheist and materialist Thomas Cooper, and his ambitions chiefly literary. He dallied particularly over the new pages of the *Southern Review*. He was "saved" partly by the object of this memorial essay, Robert Henry, then professor of Metaphysics and Moral Philosophy, but mostly by an incorrigibly religious temperament.

This is a generous piece about a man whose importance for South Carolinian thought should not be underestimated. As a pedagogue, Robert Henry helped to instill among the elite of South Carolina a respect for logic, a willingness to proceed from premise to conclusion, that is noticeable in the Secession Convention of 1860. As a writer, he was less weighty. When young, Henry had staked out his philosophical position, a version of Lockean sensationalism best amplified by Thomas Brown. In age, he grew out of sympathy with the younger generation. Thornwell himself was espousing a doctrine halfway between Locke and the German phenomenologists, after a fashion paralleled by Sir William Hamilton's assimilation of Kant to Scottish common-sense philosophy. But if Henry, as Thornwell explained, "could not be induced to read a line" of the younger Germans, it was not because he felt them to be too transcendental. A man who prized Berkeley would not feel so, and was often heard to say "that if he were compelled to adopt one side of the alternative, he would find it far easier to maintain the non-existence of matter than the non-existence of mind."

That Thornwell was a restless polemicist makes the gentleness of this essay the more striking. He had in his time crossed swords with the Roman Catholics of Charleston over Millenarianism. Some-

3. Ibid., p. 3.

one once found him, the Calvinist, with floor covered in volumes of the Jesuit, Suarez, the last of scholastics, so that he could repel Popish heresy.[4] He held the line doggedly against the New School of Presbyterians. He spent long hours wrestling with Fichte, Schelling, and Hegel, as is clear from his repeated attempts at rebuttal. As for German theology, he wrote to a friend in 1853, "I have read Bunsen's Hippolytus and rose from its perusal with a feeling of the deepest sadness. It is an elaborate effort to prove that the Christianity of the early Church was moulded in the type of Schelling's philosophy. Under the pretext of zeal for the cause of evangelical religion, it annihiliates every distinctive doctrine of the Reformed Church." That the need for rebuttal was domestic as well as external can be gauged by the fact that Bunsen's devoted admirer was James Warley Miles, the most prominent transcendentalist in Thornwell's line of fire.[5]

Thornwell softens his differences with Henry, as befits a collegial memoir, an éloge. He glides over the discontent that he himself had felt over Henry's incompetence as a president and disciplinarian.[6] He defends, less successfully, Henry's defection from the cause of Thomas Cooper, when the president came under the attack of religious sects. And this can be traced, perhaps, to Thornwell's share in the volte-face. Thornwell was a man capable of sarcasm, but one who thought it was vice. This is consciously restrained in its style, both for what Thornwell knew of Henry and of himself. But it is a good sample of the Thornwell manner, bare, functional, expository, precise.

4. Ibid., p. 53.
5. Thornwell to Thomas E. Peck, 15 April, 1853, quoted in Palmer, *Thornwell*, p. 373; the next sentences read, "It is in the same vein with ———. They have drunk from the same fountains, and if possible, is still more superficial." I strongly suspect this deletion by Palmer conceals Miles's name. See Thornwell, "The Philosophy of Schelling," *SQR* 2, n.s. 2 (February 1857): 370–92.
6. Thornwell even had to quell a riot, occasioned by Henry after the latter's death. In the ten days between Henry's expiration and funeral, classes were suspended, the students grew restless, and mayhem ensued. Thornwell stalked from the Theological Seminary with the cry of "College! College!" to sort out town and gown alike. See Daniel W. Hollis, *South Carolina College* (Columbia, S.C., 1951), pp. 195–99.

THIS was the last public effort of Dr. Henry, though the interval which elapsed betwixt its delivery and his death was too long to justify us in speaking of it as "the last voice of the swan, chanting its own monody"— illa tanquam cycnea fuit divini hominis vox et oratio.[7] Yet we contemplate it with the same melancholy interest with which the friends of Crassus went into the senate-house, and gazed upon the spot where the orator closed his splendid career. When the eulogy was first published, we admired it as a just and beautiful tribute to the character and services of its illustrious subject; we cherish it now, as reflecting on every page the lineaments and features of its gifted author. It is an accurate transcript of Dr. Henry's mind; so exact that those who are familiar with his habits of thought, will see, in peculiar turns of expression which occasionally occur, and in the general air of the whole composition, the person of the author so vividly depicted as to produce the illusion of an actual conversation, a momentary belief that they are not reading a production of his pen, but listening to a discourse from his lips. We do not allude to such general qualities as severity of taste and richness of classical allusion; these are not personal characteristics; they are the ornaments, but not the essence of thought. There was a compactness in Dr. Henry's mode of thinking, a tendency to consolidate the results of his reflection in brief and pregnant maxims, which always seemed to us the most striking feature of his mind. It was exactly the quality which gives a charm to the histories of Thucydides and Tacitus. He had caught their spirit from a long, patient, delighted study of their works; and while he abhorred all vague and barren generalities, which cheat the shallow with the show of wisdom without the substance, he freely expressed himself in sententious aphorisms, which, weighty as they were brief, commended themselves to every man's judgment. He seized at once upon the principle which pervaded the details of a subject, and the conciseness with which he announced it, was but a reflection of the energy with which he conceived it. The eulogy before us abounds in illustrations of the quality in question. The biography, even in its most minute and trifling details, is enlivened by the spirit of philosophy. There is no set effort to be profound, no attempt at abstruse reflection. All is natural and easy; and yet he who should be tempted to pronounce it superficial on account of its simplicity, or commonplace on account of the apparent obviousness of its thoughts, should be reminded that, as it is the highest accomplishment of art to conceal art, so it is the highest proof of genius to conceal the traces of labour in its production. In moral subjects, the true is always natural, and when properly presented, will always seem obvious.

7. Trans. That voice and that speech were the swan song of the godlike man: Cicero, *De Oratore*, III, 2.6: Cicero's meditation upon the death of the orator L. Crassus (140–91 B.C.) was widely imitated in antiquity, notably by Tacitus upon the death of his father-in-law, Agricola; cf. *Agricola*, 43–46.

Pascal's reflections are none the less rich and nonethe less profound, because they occasion in us surprise that we had not thought of them before. As a general rule, what costs the reader labour, costs the writer none; and what cost the writer labour, costs the reader none. Ease and grace, like the inspiration of true eloquence, "come to us after we have wrestled all night." They are nature, but nature richly and laboriously improved.

Our design, however, in placing the eulogy on Mr. Calhoun at the head of our article, is not to make it the subject of our criticism; the judgment of the public has long ago forestalled us; but to make it the occasion of presenting a brief memoir of the life and character of Dr. Henry himself. He is justly entitled to this tribute at our hands. He was not only the most eminent scholar in this State; he was one of the earliest and ablest contributors to this Review. His articles, together with those of Elliott, and Legare, and Nott,[8] gave it, when first established, the exalted position which was then universally conceded to it, as a literary journal. He had promised to become a contributor again, and, at the time of his death, was engaged in preparing an article on a very interesting point in the history of Greek philosophy. In addition to these public considerations, we shall not deny that a private motive has not been without its effect. Dr. Henry was our revered instructor, and to him more than to any other man, living or dead, we are indebted for the direction of our own studies, and for whatsoever culture—"quod sentio quam sit exiguum"—our mind has received.[9] Twenty-six years ago, we entered his lecture-room, a raw, inexperienced, but ardent pupil. He was then in the vigour of his days. We shall never forget the impression which his profound learning, his lofty bearing, and his intense enthusiasm produced on our minds. We saw, what we had never seen before, a *ripe scholar*. The effect was electric; we felt the power of a new life; and from that day to this, amid all the vicissitudes of his and our own history, we have never ceased to regard him with filial love and reverential gratitude.

Dr. Henry was born in the city of Charleston, on the 6th December, 1792. His father, Peter Henry, a native of Banffshire, in Scotland, was the son and only child of a respectable farmer. He manifested an early inclination to the church, and probably received, for that purpose, a liberal education; but, through the intervention of the Duchess of Gordon, his attention was turned into the channel of business. After the death of his parents, he emigrated from Scotland to the West Indies, where he became a very successful merchant. He was born on the 23d of July, 1752.

Dr. Henry's mother, whose maiden name was Anne Adelaide Schwiers,

---

8. Henry Junius Nott, 1797–1837, professor of logic at the South Carolina College, author of a comic collection, *Novelettes of a Traveller* (1834), and contributor to the *Southern Review*.

9. Trans. I realize how little it is: Cicero, *Pro Archia*, 1.1.

was the daughter and youngest child of a merchant of great piety and worth in the city of Bremen. Her brother, Rev. Conrad Schwiers, D. D., was minister of the Dutch Reformed Church, Austin Friars, London, and author of a grammar of the Dutch language. He seems to have been a man of learning, and his social position may be inferred from the circumstance that his son married the niece of the Governor of Demarara, and was subsequently appointed regent of the place, with the title of Honourable. Anne Adelaide, the mother of Dr. Henry, was born in Bremen, on the 5th of June, 1757. She removed, at an early age, with some of her relatives to the West Indies; there she married Mr. Angel, of the island of St. Croix. He died in little more than a year after their marriage, leaving her a widow, with an infant son, the late Mr. Justus Angel, of John's Island, near Charleston. In an excursion, which it was supposed would not occupy more than a few hours, she was blown off at sea, and after weeks of hardship and exposure, landed finally at Kingston, Jamaica. There she became acquainted with Mr. Henry, and married him. They resided in Jamaica a few years, then removed to the Bay of Honduras, and at length, settled in Charleston, S. C., in May 1792. Having selected this city as his home, he returned to the West Indies to adjust his business, and to collect the debts which were still due to him there. He had settled his affairs to his satisfaction, and was on his return to Charleston, with a large amount of money, when he was captured by a French privateer, robbed of all that he had collected, and so barbarously treated, that he died of the effects of the cruelty, in Savannah, Georgia, on the 2nd September, 1794. His son Robert was thus consigned to the sole care of his mother; and he could not have been left in wiser or safer hands. With the remnants of her husband's fortune that she was able to put together in Charleston, she opened a dry goods store, from the earnings of which she succeeded in supporting herself and educating her children, without drawing upon the aid or the sympathy of others. She was, in many respects, a remarkable woman. Familiar with the languages of western Europe, conversant with affairs, of sound and vigourous understanding, she was fully competent to direct and superintend the training of her son, and to her, under God, he owes all that he afterwards became. He always cherished her memory with the profoundest veneration. He was accustomed, particularly, to commend her solid sense and her enlightened piety; and her letters show that she happily combined tenderness with firmness in her treatment of her children, and ardour of zeal with exemption from asperity or bigotry in her relations to God. Amid all the trying vicissitudes of her history, her faith was unshaken and her serenity unbroken.

She was deterred by no narrow consideration of economy from seeking the best masters for her son, assigning as a reason—and it is a proof of her great good sense—that poor teaching, however cheap, is always costly; and good teaching, however costly, is always cheap; that the best, in other words, is always the cheapest. As soon, therefore, as Robert had mastered the alphabet, she put him under the care of Rev. Dr. Buist, who had recently come to Charleston, with a high reputation, from the University of Edinburgh, having been commended to the Scotch or First Presbyterian congregation in the most flattering terms, by Drs. Robertson and Blair.[10] With Dr. Buist he began the Latin, as we have heard from himself, at six years of age. His Ainsworth's School Dictionary has his name written in it, in his mother's hand, under date of August 28th, 1800, so that he had begun to construe and translate, before he had completed his eighth year.[11]

As it had been the purpose of his father to educate him in England, his mother took him there in May, 1803, and put him under the charge of a Mr. Johnston, with whom he appears to have remained only a few months. He was thence transferred to the school of James Lindsay, D. D., Grove Hall, Oldford Bow, near London. With Dr. Lindsay, in addition to the Latin and Greek classics, he studied the French language, as appears from a record made in his copy of Gil Blas, in September, 1804. He continued under the care of Dr. Lindsay until 1808, when, at the solicitation of his mother, he relinquished the prospects of academic life, and took a situation in the counting-house of Mr. Hernandus Vos, a merchant of London, who carried on an extensive trade with the Dutch colonies of Demerara, Berbice, and Surinam. Here it was that the exigencies of his employment forced upon him the acquisition of the Dutch language; and with the help of his uncle's grammar, and the constant use of the language in the business of the house, he acquired such skill in it that he spoke and wrote it with fluency and ease. Here also he must have made his first attainments in the German. His introduction to Mr. Vos was through a merchant of Bremen, for whom he always retained a strong affection, and whose brother subsequently married his only sister. It is certain that, in 1809, he corresponded occasionally with his mother in the German language. It is probable that he remained in the counting room only about a year, when he resumed his academic studies with reference to preparation for the ministry of the gospel. In 1811 he entered the University of Edinburgh, and graduated Master of Arts, June 15th, 1814. We find among his papers memoranda of his having attended, in 1813, the classes of Prof. Brunton in Hebrew, Dr. Ritchie in Divinity, Dr. Brown (the celebrated Thomas Brown, the successor of Dugald Stewart) in Moral Philosophy, and Dr.

---

10. William Robertson, 1721–1793, the historian of Charles V, Scotland, and the Spanish conquest of America, and formerly Moderator of the Church of Scotland; Hugh Blair, 1718–1800, who lectured in belles lettres and rhetoric at the University of Edinburgh and whose *Lectures in Rhetoric* (1783) were very influential.

11. Robert Ainsworth, *Thesaurae Linguae Latinae Compendarius* (London, 1746, rev. ed. 1773).

Meiklejohn in Church History. In April, 1814, he completed his course at the Divinity Hall; and we now have before us his examination exercises, which were sermons on John xvii. 15, for Church History, and critical dissertations on Romans v. 6, ix. 2, 3, for the Divinity Hall.[12] We have no memoranda of his studies in 1811 and 1812, except that, in a letter to his mother, dated August, 1812, he complains of the undue importance assigned to the mathematics in Edinburgh. His own tastes led him to languages and philosophy, and he regrets that the time which he was anxious to give to Hebrew and Arabic, he was compelled to share with the exact sciences, in order to maintain a respectable position. We sympathize with him in his troubles, and, though, we would not banish the mathematics from our schools and colleges, nor underrate their importance as useful sciences, we cannot withhold the opinion, that, as a discipline of the mind, they are comparatively worthless. We agree cordially with Sir William Hamilton in the estimate which he has put upon them, and, until his arguments shall have been answered, we shall regard the question as settled.[13] Among the manuscripts of Dr. Henry are two articles, addressed to the editor of the Classical Journal, and dated July, 1813, which indicate his interest in the critical study of the Greek. One is an expositon of a passage in the Iliad, and the other an exposition of two passages in the New Testament. Both indicate a sound judgment and ripe scholarship. His interpretation of 1 Cor. xi. 10 is particularly ingenious, and, we are inclined to think, entirely original.[14]

Young Henry left the University with rare accomplishments. He was well skilled in the ancient and modern languages, and thoroughly imbued, under the enthusiastic teachings of Brown, with the love of philosophy. That he made a strong impression upon those who were competent to judge of merit, may be inferred from the following anecdote. While in Edinburgh, probably at the close of his university course, he had the pleasure of meeting Sir William Hamilton, then a young man, with the honours of Oxford blooming fresh upon him, at the house of a friend. Their interview was brief; they parted, and never met again; and yet, more than forty years afterwards, Sir William Hamilton retained as vivid a recollection of the scene as if it has recently occurred. He narrated the circumstance to a young gentleman from the South Carolina College, two years ago, and inquired with affectionate interest into the subsequent history of the young Carolinian.

12. John 17: 15: "I pray that thou shouldest take them out of the world, but that thou shouldest keep them from the evil"; Romans 9:2, 3: "That I have great heaviness and continual sorrow in my heart / For I could wish that myself were accursed from Christ for my brethren, my kinsman according to my flesh."
13. In many places, including Sir William Hamilton, *Lectures on Metaphysics and Logic*, ed. H. L. Mansel and J. Veitch (Edinburgh, 1860), 4: 64–66.
14. Neither seems to have been published in the *Classical Journal*; I Corinthians 11:10: "For this cause ought the woman to have power on her head because of the angels."

Having received his degree, Dr. Henry returned to London, and spent some time, how long we cannot say, with his friends there. The war between England and the United States preventing his return to his own country, he turned his mercantile attainments to a good account, by accepting an agency which yielded him an adequate support without drawing largely upon his time, and which gave him the opportunity of spending the year 1815 upon the continent of Europe. His letters show, that, in selecting the ministry of the gospel as his calling, he had been impressed with the deepest conviction of its importance. He had not chosen it as a trade, but as an awful department of most solemn and responsible labour, in which he might benefit the souls of others and save his own. He unbosomed himself freely to his mother, and often expressed his regret that he had not access to the society of experienced Christians, that he might have a deeper and more practical knowledge of the things of God. It was during this year that he passed through a painful trial of his faith, which his friends apprehended might eventuate in the renunciation of his profession. At some seasons in their history, all earnest minds have been tortured with the agony of doubt. Intense conviction is rooted in the storms of spiritual conflict. He alone believes deeply who has doubted deeply; and he alone can estimate the preciousness of an assured faith, who has experienced the anguish of its birth. This was illustrated in the case of Dr. Henry. Devoted to truth, and incapable of anything like insincerity or deceit, he could not profess what he did not feel to be true. Doubts were excited in his mind in relation to the doctrines of predestination and the Trinity; he was beset with scruples; and, though he had completed the usual routine of theological study, and had been licensed to preach according to the forms of the Scottish Church, yet, when these doubts took possession of his mind, he determined to renounce theology, unless his difficulties should be obviated by a full persuasion of the doctrines of his church. Happily for himself, his perplexity was not of long continuance. His sense of the evil and demerit of sin, and of the necessity of a real and proper satisfaction in order to the pardon of the sinner, soon sealed upon his heart a practical conviction which no difficulties of the speculative understanding should be allowed to set aside. The atonement of Christ he never could forego, and he has often declared to us, that the government of God would, in his judgment, be altogether unworthy of the Divine Being, if He should receive a transgressor into favour without it. He was the first to call our attention to the passage inserted in the first edition of Smith's Theory of the Moral Sentiments, and omitted in the later ones, and referred to it as a proof of the unhappy ascendancy which Hume had acquired over the mind of Smith.[15]

---

15. In the first, and in the subsequent four editions, Adam Smith had a vivid passage in defense of the doctrine of the Atonement. It was omitted in the sixth in favor of the noncom-

How his doubts became resolved upon the doctrine of predestination, we do not know; but we have repeatedly heard him express his cordial agreement with Augustine in his doctrine of grace.

Early in 1816, he returned to Charleston. The first record of his preaching is "May 19th, Sunday morning, preached in the first Presbyterian Church." In the following June he was invited to supply the French Protestant Church, where he preached alternately in French and English, until he was elected to the College. On the 25th May, 1817, he was ordained, according to Presbyterian forms, by the old Presbytery of Charleston, which not long afterwards became extinct. We have heard it said that the ordination of Mr. Henry was its last official act.

On the 19th March, 1818, he was married to Elizabeth Henrietta Connors, Daughter of Charles Connors, Esq., of Clarendon, South Carolina, who was a native of St. Stephen's parish. This amiable and accomplished lady, a pattern of meek and unobtrusive virtue, now survives him, together with six children, the fruits of their union. In December, 1818, he was chosen to the professorship of Moral Philosophy and Logic in the South Carolina College; and as the circumstances of his election were highly creditable to him, and are not generally known, our readers will excuse us for reciting them. His name was suggested by Hon. Mitchell King to Mr. Pringle, the President of the Senate, and, ex officio, a member of the Borad.[16] Mr. King also transmitted to Mr. Pringle two essays of Dr. Henry on subjects connected with the department for which he was a candidate. When the board met, Dr. Henry was put in nomination by Mr. Pringle, and his claims earnestly espoused by Judge Cheves. Dr. Maxcy, the president of the college, and a man, deservedly, of commanding influence with the board, had his heart set upon the election of another candidate.[17] Dr. Henry's essays were submitted to the board, and Dr. Maxcy requested the favour of being allowed to take them home and read them at his leisure. His request was complied with, and upon the reassembling of the board, he pronounced a high encomium upon the essays in question, and not only withdrew his opposition, but gave his cordial support to Dr. Henry, who was unanimously elected. It is a pity that such an ordeal were not now exacted of a man's fitness for a professor's chair, before he is called to fill

---

mital statement: "In every religion, and in every superstition that the world has ever beheld, accordingly, there has been a Tartarus as well as an Elysium; a place provided for the punishment of the wicked, as well as one for the reward of the just." Smith's modern editors conclude, with Henry, that Smith's respect for David Hume influenced the excision and substitution. See Adam Smith, *The Theory of Moral Sentiments*, ed. D. D. Raphael and A. D. MacFie (Oxford, 1976), pp. 91–92, 383–401.

16. Mitchell King, 1783–1862, born in Scotland, a Spanish prisoner in 1805, later a Charleston lawyer, a trustee of the South Carolina College and president of the College of Charleston; John Julius Pringle, 1753–1843, lawyer and politician.

17. Jonathan Maxcy, 1768–1820, was the college's first president.

it. In every other profession there is usually demanded a trial of skill before a candidate is entitled to its privileges; and the universities, as anciently constituted, attached great importance to academic disputations. But merit, in these days and in this country, is ascertained upon easier terms; and learning and intellectual ability are not the items which enter most largely into it. We are now content to accept a teacher, if he has capacity to learn, and gives a reasonable promise of being able to keep ahead of his class.

The sphere of labour into which Dr. Henry was now introduced was, in all respects, congenial with the tastes and cherished habits of his life. Philosophy was his favourite pursuit. He loved the classics, and was critically conversant with the choicest monuments of antiquity. But philology with him was only the handmaid of a higher truth; and he never felt himself so perfectly at home, as when conversing with Socrates in the streets, Plato in the gardens of the Academy, Aristotle in the Lyceum, or "the budge doctors of the Stoic fur,"[18] in their chosen walks. Man was the theme on which he concentrated the powers of his mind—man in all his relations and in all the aspects of his being. He accordingly entered upon the duties of his chair with ardour and enthusiasm, and the consequence was that new life was infused into a department of inquiry which had, previously, somewhat languished. His residence at Edinburgh, his partialities for the Scottish philosophy, and his fondness for Locke, it might have been presumed, would have led him to underrate the importance of the scholastic logic. This, happily, was not the case. The respective provinces of syllogism and induction were clearly perceived by him, and while he united most cordially in the homage which was generally and justly paid to Bacon, he detracted nothing from the equal merits and the equal glory of Aristotle. He was the first man to give to logic its proper place in the South Carolina College. He was the first of those who undertook to teach it there, that really understood it. He had imbibed none of the prejudices which had so largely infected other disciples of the new organon; and in his zeal for mood and figure, and his earnest evolutions of the importance and significance of forms, which ignorance pronounced barren and indolence dry, one was tempted to think that ancient Oxford had removed to Columbia, or that Marck Duncan was revived in one of his countrymen.[19] Logic, henceforward, became a prominent study in the State; and this circumstance will explain the general tendencies of mind which the statesmen and scholars of the commonwealth have confessedly exhibited.

The only literary labour with which, during the first years of his pro-

18. Milton, *Comus*, line 707.
19. Marck Duncan, 1570?–1640, a Scot appointed professor of philosophy and later regent at Saumur by Henry IV, author of the *Institutiones Logicae* (1612).

fessorship, Dr. Henry favoured the public, was an eulogy, delivered at the request of the faculty of the college, on Dr. Edward D. Smith, who had been professor of chemistry and mineralogy there, and whose character had won for him golden opinions from his colleagues, the students, and the people at large. His death was universally lamented as a public calamity. The tribute paid to him was worthy alike of the author and the subject. It was delivered December 12th, 1819, but not published until 1822.

The 4th May, 1820, he experienced a severe affliction in the loss of his mother, who died after a painful and lingering illness, which she bore with Christian patience and resignation to the will of God. She had lived to see her labours and anxieties crowned with success, in the circumstances of her children. They had been her jewels; for them she had lived, and toiled, and prayed; and it is a noble incentive to exertion, that her work had not been in vain. Her eldest son, Mr. Justus Angel, the fruit of her first marriage, was adorning the social position which, of all others, is most esteemed in this State, by the accomplishments of mind which his education in England had given him. Her son Robert was precisely in the station which her own heart would most ardently have coveted for him; and her only daughter, who still survives, was all that she could wish a daughter to be. She looked upon the heritage which God had given her, and could sincerely rejoice that she was able to bequeath a noble legacy to the country and the world. His promise had not failed; He had been a husband to the widow, and a father to the fatherless; and she was permitted to close her eyes with every earthly desire fulfilled, and with the confident hope of a richer joy in heaven. She had attained a good old age, wanting only a month of being exactly sixty-three years old; and we cannot but feel that the prayer of Simeon was appropriate to her case, "Lord, now lettest thou thy servant depart in peace."[20]

The following December, Dr. Henry delivered an eulogy, at the request of the faculty, on Dr. Maxcy, the late president of the college. His appointment to discharge such duties, is a proof of the estimate in which he was held by his colleagues; and the ability with which he performed them sufficiently vindicates their perspicacity and confidence. An eulogy on Maxcy was a very delicate undertaking; it was hardly possible to come up to the measure of public expectation. That extraordinary man, whose memory is still fresh in the hearts of his pupils, and whose influence still lingers in the college, in the general type which he impressed upon its discipline, seems to have been born for the government and direction of the young. Distinguished by dignity of character, elevation of sentiment, and a communicative sympathy, he infused his own spirit, by the gentle

20. Luke 2:29.

inspiration of his matchless eloquence, into the minds of his pupils. He at once awed and attracted. An atmosphere of moral power surrounded him, and none could approach him without feeling its influence, and paying an involuntary homage to virtue. "His presence," says an admiring pupil, in a production which we do not hesitate to signalize as one of the most exquisite gems in the casket of our literature, "quelled every disorder. The most riotous offender shrunk from the reproof of that pale brow and intellectual eye. The reverence that attended him stilled the progress of disaffection; and to him belonged the rare power—exercised in the face of wondering Europe by Lamartine—of quelling by persuasion the spirit of revolt."[21] He justly looked upon the formation of character, by inducing the conscious exercise of principle, as the main end of college government; the measure of its success is the extent to which the subjects of it are led to think, and, by their own determinations, to govern themselves; and the secret of its power is the charm of eloquence, example, and advice, by which they are led to develope and apply the law contained in the structure of their own souls. To teach men, in other words, to be a law unto themselves, is the scope of wise and judicious discipline. This principle Dr. Maxcy kept steadily in view; he made the college a school of character, and the man within the breast his most effective police. Through all the changes of its history, the college has retained the impression which he gave it; and to this more than to any other cause, is due the lofty sentiment of honour which has always pervaded it. That there are evils which the predominance of this mode of government fails to repress, cannot be denied; and because they are obvious and palpable, some have thought it advisable to substitute a system of military rigour, in which the facility of detection and the certainty of punishment shall be the principal restraints from disorder. The change, we think, would be injurious. There would not be the same culture of principle, the same manly self-reliance, the self-respect and dignity which are the natural result of the maxims of Maxcy; and the loss of these qualities would be dearly purchased by an exemption from a class of disorders which, after all, are rather mischievous than wicked— the offspring of levity and thoughtless frivolity rather than of malice.

The eulogy was published in 1822, and is one of Dr. Henry's most finished productions. In comparing it with the beautiful sketch of Mr. Petigru, we were struck with the difference between a pupil and a colleague in their estimate of Dr. Maxcy's genius, and the predominant tendencies of his mind. One makes him aesthetic, the other metaphysical. Mr. Petigru affirms that he "was deeply imbued with classical learning," while Dr. Henry asserts: "I could never discover that he possessed a keen relish for the

21. James Louis Petigru, *Oration Delivered at the Semi-Centennial Celebration of the South Carolina College* (Charleston, 1855), quoted in James Petigru Carson, *Life, Letters and Speeches of James Louis Petigru* (Washington, 1920), p. 306.

classical authors of antiquity; and for philological pursuits, strictly so called, I know that he entertained no very great reverence."²² Upon all other points, the two accounts are in harmony, and perhaps even here the discrepancy is more in appearance than reality. Dr. Henry paid one other tribute to the memory of Dr. Maxcy—the inscription upon the monument, erected to this illustrious man by the Clariosophic Society, came from his pen.²³ There needs no other record of his accomplished scholarship; and it is an interesting circumstance that the same monument consecrates the memories of the two men who have exerted the greatest influence upon the history and fortunes of the college, and that in the respective aspects of their usefulness. Dr. Maxcy shaped its government, and Dr. Henry its studies; and it is precisely the discipline of the one and the learning of the other that are perpetuated.

After the death of Dr. Maxcy, metaphysics were taught by Dr. Henry as a labour of love, or by a private arrangement with the Board of Trustees, until 1824, when they were formally transferred to his chair, and logic, belles lettres, and criticism erected into a new and independent department, which was first filled by Henry Junius Nott, Esq., at that time a conspicuous member of the bar.

The publications of Dr. Henry from 1822 to 1832, were purely occasional. They were, 1. Two sermons on the Connection between Faith and Practice, and on the Co-operation of Reason with Grace; these appeared November, 1822. 2. A Thanksgiving Sermon, preached February 5th, 1823, and published at the request of the students. The subject was, Religion productive of National Prosperity. 3. A Discourse on Duelling, occasioned by the deaths of Edward P. Simons and Archy Mason; preached December 7th, 1823, and published at the request of the House of Representatives. 4. A Discourse on the Beneficial Results consequent on the Progress of Liberal Opinions in Politics, delivered in the College Chapel, July 4th, 1824, and published in 1827. 5. Contributions to the Southern Review, from 1828 to 1832, of articles on Niebuhr's Roman History, the Romances of the Baron La Motte Fouque, Goethe's Wilhelm Meister, and Waterhouse's Junius.²⁴ During this period, however, his labours in the college were prodigious, and his application to study so intense, that the bell for morning prayers not unfrequently found him in his library, unconscious that a night had elapsed, and that he had not closed his eyes in

22. Ibid.; Henry, *An Eulogy on Jonathan Maxcy, D.D., Late President of the South Carolina College* (Columbia, 1822), pp. 12–13.
23. It still can be found at the center of the University of South Carolina campus: the inscription is reproduced in Maximilian LaBorde, *History of the South Carolina College* (Columbia, S.C., 1859), p. 123.
24. *Southern Review* 1 (May 1828): 320–41; 3 (February 1829): 31–63; 3 (May 1829): 353–85; and 7 (August 1831): 486–517; Thornwell has omitted Henry, *Funeral Sermon . . . on the Hon. Charles Miller . . . and . . . George Butler* (Columbia, S.C., 1821).

sleep. He prepared, as a part of his appointed duties, in addition to the lectures he had been accustomed to deliver on moral philosophy, a full course on metaphysics, the new branch which had been assigned him. His instructions in political philosophy embraced, in connection with the topics of the text book, a masterly analysis and exposition of the constitution of the United States, which still exists in manuscript, and occasional discussions of the points usually embraced in political economy. He was fresh from Edinburgh, where the work of Smith and the labours of Stewart had given extraordinary popularity to this department of speculation, and he was the first to introduce the subject in collegiate instruction in this country. Beside these, he gave, at irregular hours, the attendance of the students being voluntary, a very complete view of the evidences of Christianity, and interesting sketches of the history of philosophy. His lectures upon these subjects were extempore, and only a few notes, which he used as memoranda, are found among his papers. His vindication of Christianity was not without effect. Many a young man who came in doubt went away convinced. One case deserves to be recorded, though we cannot mention the name of the individual. A youth from another State came to the college, attracted by Dr. Cooper's fame, and his guardian's sympathy with Dr. Cooper's opinions. His mind was full of prejudice against religion. He was drawn by curiosity to Dr. Henry's apologetic lectures, and the result was that he left college a confirmed believer, and subsequently became a preacher of the gospel. To these disinterested services, must be added his kindness and courtesy, as well as his zeal for the interests of the college, in relieving the aged Professor of Languages of the instruction of the upper classes in Greek. In the midst of this ceaseless toil, he redeemed time for general literature, and if his means had been commensurate with his aims, he would have left a work which would have linked his name in immortal union with the name of a scholar whose genius was only equalled by his learning. Soon after the appearance of Niebuhr's work on Roman history, he determined to translate it into English, if satisfactory arrangements could be made for publishing the translation. He began the work, and had proceeded nearly through the first volume, when he abandoned the enterprise, because no publisher could be found who would assume the risk.

In 1833, Dr. Cooper, who had succeeded Dr. Maxcy, resigned the presidency of the college. His religious opinions had rendered him so offensive to the religious people of the State, that it became clearly impossible for the college to answer the ends of its establishment, if he continued at the head of it. He was a man of eminent abilities, and of extensive and varied attainments. The benevolence of his nature, the frankness of his temper, and the natural simplicity of his manners, joined to his wide spread fame as a man of science, and a sufferer in the cause of liberty, gave, in his person, the fairest opportunity to liberal opinions to illustrate their boasted power of good. The result, according to the popular verdict, was a miserable failure. Public sentiment demanded a change. Religion and education had always been regarded as inseparable allies, and it was no longer to be tolerated that the South Carolina College should present them in the attitude of unnatural hostility. All parties united in doing justice to the integrity and talents of Dr. Cooper; it was not a personal opposition to the man, but to the religious sentiments of which he had become the representative. He yielded to the popular demand, and withdrew from public observation to the quiet walks of literary labour. Dr. Henry was appointed temporarily to fill his place, and during the year (1834) in which he discharged the duties of the presidency, in addition to the labours of his own department, he drew up and delivered a course of lectures on political economy, a branch which Dr. Cooper had taught for some years previously. The friends of Dr. Henry took it for granted that he would be chosen as the permanent successor of Dr. Cooper. To use a phrase of his own, "he was in the line of succession." Dr. Cooper had been elected over him by only a single vote, though at that time Dr. Henry was a very young man, and had been very recently connected with the college. The board of trustees would, no doubt, have tendered the office to him with the utmost cheerfulness, had it not been that public sentiment involved Dr. Henry in the same condemnation with his illustrious colleague. They had been associated so long and amicably together, that a common odium attached to them both, and it was felt to be unsafe, in the new organization, to give the slightest ground for suspicion as to the religious character which the institution was thenceforth to bear. Not long before the meeting of the board, Dr. Henry published a sermon designed to vindicate his name from the unjust imputations of indifference or skepticism which had been cast upon him. The sermon was entitled, The Mysteries of Religion worthy the Assent of the Human Understanding.[25] But prejudices, which had long been accumulating, were not to be subdued at once. The board took what seemed to be the safe side, and elected another president. They were, unwilling, however, to lose him from the college, and consequently retained him in his professorship, while they sufficiently indicated their own conviction of his piety and merits by granting him the degree of doctor of divinity. Indignant at what he felt to be the injustice that was done him, he withdrew from the college to a small farm which he owned in the neighbourhood of Columbia, where he lived in great retirement for nearly two years, with the exception of two visits to the west, made for the purpose of seeking better lands.

There never was a more unfounded charge than that Dr. Henry sympathized with the opinions of Dr. Cooper. On every important point of morals, philosophy, and religion, they were the poles apart. Dr. Cooper

---

25. Published in Columbia, S.C., in 1834, and preached in Charleston in December 1833.

was an avowed materialist; Dr. Henry's tendencies were all to idealism. Dr. Cooper looked upon utility as the criterion of right; Dr. Henry looked upon right as the criterion of utility. Moral rules, according to Dr. Cooper, were flexible and variable; according to Dr. Henry, eternal and immutable. Dr. Cooper was first a Socinian, and afterwards a Deist, in religion; Dr. Henry a thoroughgoing advocate of the Nicene creed, and of an external, authoritative standard of faith. Dr. Cooper was mortally opposed to an order of clergy; Dr. Henry regarded it as indispensable to the public good. We speak what we know. There was but one subject on which they thoroughly agreed, and that was politics. They were both the ardent friends of liberty, and the zealous advocates of the liberal opinions which political economy had demonstrated to be the true interest of States. But, unfortunately for himself, Dr. Henry had never proclaimed his opposition to the doctrines of his friend. They lived on such good terms as gentlemen and as officers of the college, that the people could not understand the spirit of toleration which enabled them to walk together without being agreed. From our own experience and observation, while a student in the college, we are satisfied that the influence of Dr. Henry, within the legitimate sphere of his duties, was efficiently exerted in counteracting the tendencies of Dr. Cooper's doctrines. He never let slip an opportunity of vindicating religion, and the records of the Christian faith. We ourselves are particularly indebted to him for the able and satisfactory reply which he gave to us in private, to Dr. Cooper's celebrated assault on the Pentateuch.[26]

Dr. Henry passed his life in comparative obscurity until December, 1839, when he was induced, by the urgent solicitations of his friends, to accept the invitation of the board, and return to the college as Professor of Metaphysics, Logic, and Belles Lettres. None of his old associates were there. Cooper, and Nott, and Park, and Wallace, were dead.[27] He came among strangers, except that the distinguished chaplain of the college was an old pupil. But his learning commanded respect, and in 1841, when President Barnwell was compelled to retire from the institution, on account of his health, Dr. Henry was chosen by his colleagues chairman of the faculty, and held that trust until December, 1842, when he was unanimously elected president of the college. It was during these years that he changed his ecclesiastical relations. He had always been an advocate of the doctrine that regular succession from the apostolic period was a mark of the true church. This may have been the key to his episcopacy. Be that, however, as it may, he was ordained a deacon of the Protestant Episcopal Church,

---

26. Thomas Cooper, *On the Connection Between Geology and the Pentateuch: In a Letter to Professor Silliman* (Columbia, S.C., 1833); this pamphlet helped to depose Cooper from the presidency of the South Carolina College.

27. Thomas Park, 1767–1844, professor of languages at the South Carolina College between 1806 and 1834; James Wallace, ?–1851, an Irishman, professor of mathematics at the South Carolina College and occasional contributor to the *Southern Review*.

by the Right Reverend Bishop Gadsden, on the 10th March, 1841, and a presbyter or priest by the same bishop, on the 25th September, 1842.

Soon after his return to the college, the extraordinary compliment was paid to him, of being elected by the two societies to deliver their annual oration. It is the only case, we believe, in which a professor has been chosen to this office. The address was delivered on the 8th of December, 1840, and published at the request of the societies. The subject was, The Cultivation of the Fine Arts favourable to the Perfection of Private Character and the Development of Public Prosperity. In December, 1845, his relations to the college, for reasons which it would be altogether indelicate to discuss, either in the way of censure or approval, were changed.[28] From that time till the period of his death, he gave instructions in Greek, without being required to participate in the government and discipline of the institution. He was released from an intolerable burden of care and anxiety, and his days, no doubt, protracted by the comparative quiet which he was permitted to enjoy. His academic labours were occasionally diversified by other occupations. He preached two sermons, one on the Greatness of God, November 24th, 1847, the other on the Goodness of God, June 30th, 1848, at the Pinckney Lecture, in Charleston, which were published according to the provisions of the foundation.

In 1848 or 1849, he was proposed, by some of his friends, for the episcopate of Mississippi. When consulted on the subject, he replied that it was an office which should neither be sought nor shunned; that, if he were elected, he should consider it a call of Providence to a more extended sphere of usefulness; if not, he had learned that man's happiness consisted in entire conformity to the will of God. He was, therefore, neither chagrined nor disappointed when the result of the election was announced to him.

An address on eloquence, delivered before the Clariosophic Society of the College, at the dedication of their new hall, February 10th, 1849, the eulogy on Mr. Calhoun, and a letter on co-operation, which appeared in the South Carolinian, February 10th, 1851, complete the list of his publications.

For several years before his death, his friends had noticed, with apprehension and anxiety, that his strength was failing; his step had lost its elasticity, and his gait its freedom; he himself was persuaded that he was approaching his end; but it came, after all, unexpectedly. He was congratulating himself, only a few days before his last illness, that his health was firmer, and his physical feelings more natural than they had been for years. In a long excursion which we made with him, and in which we discussed some of the principal doctrines of modern philosophy, he alluded to his reviving energies, and expressed the hope that his previous feebleness had

---

28. Henry was relieved of the presidency, mainly for failure to maintain discipline among the students: attendance at chapel was lax, and fighting had broken out between students and the town marshals.

been a penalty, which, at length, was satisfied, for his early habits of imprudent study. Alas! all was delusive! On Monday, the 3rd of February, he took to his bed; on Wednesday, the 5th, he lay a corpse. His malady seized him while engaged in prayer. He had retired to his library, and, according to his custom, was invoking the blessing of God upon his studies, when he received an intimation that his studies were over. As the last act of his health was prayer, his friends may cherish the hope, that the first act of his ransomed spirit was praise. He was sixty-three years and two months old, the day he died. His first connection with the college was for sixteen years precisely; his second, for sixteen years and a little more than a month; so that he had been upwards of thirty-two years engaged in the office of instruction.

Dr. Henry, in person, was of middle stature, with a well proportioned and compactly built frame, and an air of commanding dignity. His head was large, and his brain well developed; his features were regular and handsome; his countenance noble and frank, and his whole face beamed with intelligence. He bore in his aspect the marks of his pedigree. His expansive forehead, his clear complexion, and his light hair proclaimed a German origin, while the dogged resolution which was compressed in his lips and reflected from his eye betrayed the blood of the Cameronian and Covenanter. He inherited from both races the peculiarities of his mind, the fervid genius of the Scot and the patient industry of the German, united in a common zeal for the pursuits of philology and philosophy. His natural temper was irascible, but self-government was the study of his life. In his domestic relations he was a model of tenderness and affection. The most conspicuous feature of his character was his scrupulous regard to truth. He abhorred every appearance of prevarication and deceit, and no one could look upon his face without being impressed with his manly and noble ingenuousness. He could conceive of no circumstance under which a lie was admissible. The conventional evasion by which a visitor is turned from the door, under the plea of "not at home," he contemplated only with disgust. It is obviously an artifice of cowardice, to purchase an exemption from a disagreeable intrusion, without the risk or responsibility of offence. As to the pretext that it deceives no one, it may be confidently said that, if it does not deceive, it perplexes. The man is left in doubt; he knows not whether you are really from home, or only wish to be undisturbed by his company, and the effect is, that he must act upon the supposition of your absence, whether you were absent or not. He must *presume* the statement to be literally true, whatever reasons he may have for suspecting it to be false. The very design of the equivocation is to create this presumption, in order to avoid the imputation of rudeness. In morals, says Jeremy Taylor, our first thoughts are generally our best;[29] and we suspect that no one ever

---

29. *Doctor Dubitantium: or, The Rule of Conscience*, in *The Whole Works of the Right Reverend Jeremy Taylor, D.D.*, ed. A. Taylor (London, 1851), 9: 45–46.

employed this expedient for the first time without a violent shock to his moral sensibilities, and a forfeiture of something of his own self-respect.

We cannot conclude this memoir without adverting briefly to Dr. Henry's philosophical opinions. He had been, as we have seen, a pupil of Dr. Brown; and always retained an exalted estimate of Brown's metaphysical abilities. The general system of his master he cordially adopted. Reid's doctrine of an immediate perception of external objects he rejected, not by virtue of the principle that the relation of knowledge implies an analogy of existence, but because he was persuaded that the only facts given in consciousness were the successive changes in the states of our own being. The uniformity of these changes we were compelled to attribute to some permanent cause, but except as the unknown cause of known phenomena—an explanation which our constitution constrained us to receive as the only consistent explanation of a series of regular effects—he contended that we knew nothing of the existence or properties of matter. He was thus what Sir William Hamilton calls a cosmothetic idealist, or hypothetic realist. What Sir William Hamilton calls "the fact of consciousness in perception," he positively denied. The only difference betwixt these views and those of Berkley, was the admission of a mysterious something as the cause of intellectual phenomena, independent of mind. The affinity betwixt the systems is obvious at a glance, and, next to Dr. Brown, the philosopher whom Dr. Henry most prized was the Bishop of Cloyne. We have often heard him say, that if he were compelled to adopt one side of the alternative, he would find it far easier to maintain the non-existence of matter than the non-existence of mind. Thought we know directly and immediately, while matter is known to us only in its relations to thought. In his academic teachings, he was accustomed to begin with Locke, as being the point of departure of most of the modern schools. He took the aspect of Locke's theory, though fully sensible of its imperfect development in the hands of its master, which led to idealism, and he was saved from the consequences which Berkley fairly deduced, only by an appeal to a primitive belief, which guaranteed a transcendent reality beyond the sphere of consciousness. The authority of our primary beliefs he accordingly concurred with the whole Scottish school in receiving, but he was not partial to the phraseology by which Reid expressed them, nor satisfied with the reduction he had made of them. Though an accomplished German scholar, and well versed in German literature, he had no taste for the German philosophers. His estimate of Kant was precisely that of Dugald Stewart,[30] and as to Kant's successors, we do not believe that Dr. Henry could ever be induced to read a line of their writings.

In morals, though he excogitated a system of his own, and developed

---

30. For example, Dugald Stewart, *Dissertation: Exhibiting the Progress of Metaphysical, Ethical and Political Philosophy*, ed. Sir William Hamilton (Edinburgh, 1854), pp. 389–427.

it with great ingenuity, the leading hints were suggested by his favourite authors, Berkley and Brown. Assuming as a postulate, that society was the natural state of man, and the well-being of society the end of law, he deduced his moral rules from the a priori consideration of its nature, and the conditions indispensable to its conservatism and security. They were, consequently, the products of the understanding, and not the dictates of an original and special faculty. In the development of his scheme, he subjected social relations to an analysis from which he inferred the necessity of three great laws, into which, he supposed, all our moral duties might be finally resolved—truth, justice, benevolence. Conscience he regarded as belonging exclusively to the emotional part of our nature, and as having no other office than to operate as a sanction in reference to the rules which the understanding had elicited. It was in no sense a law; it was simply a motive to enforce the law. Hence, he contended, that to speak of an enlightened conscience was absurd; the light was not in it, but in the understanding; it was nothing but the feeling of approbation or disapprobation, consequent upon the contemplation of our conduct as in conformity or otherwise with the rule whose authority we acknowledged. The feeling of approbation, prospectively considered, was a sense of obligation; retrospectively considered, conviction of merit or ill desert—self-approbation or remorse. Moral truth, being the product of the understanding, from the contemplation of fixed and permanent relations, was itself immutable. The truth was *necessary*, if society were given, and no man could depart from it, upon any considerations whatever, without making himself an outlaw. Our duties to God he resolved, in the same way, into the personal relation we sustain to him. There was a species of society betwixt us. Communion was the highest form of religion, and communion was society intensified.

Such is a brief outline of the doctrine to which the students of the South Carolina College were inured for more than twenty years.

The death of Dr. Henry we regard as a great calamity to the college, not so much because it is deprived of his teachings, as deprived of his presence. The spectacle of a man of erudition is itself a stimulus to exertion. It operates powerfully on the young. They see what industry and application can accomplish, and have an example of successful effort. Besides this, they are led to perceive in what genuine scholarship consists. The distinction is kept before them between learning and pedantry—real merit and factitious pretension. Dr. Henry was on all hands confessed to be a man of extraordinary attainments. He walked the campus among able and learned professors, and all conspired to do him reverence; and, as he unfolded his stores before his pupils, the dullest were, for a moment, inspired with a gleam of literary ardour. We sincerely trust that his mantle may fall on worthy shoulders. It will take an Elisha to supply the place of Elijah.

# Acknowledgments

This book was planned when I was a Junior Fellow of the Michigan Society of Fellows, that intelligent institution, and its necessity considered with the advice, always informed and often right, of Mills Thornton; it was continued at the University of Cambridge and substantially completed at the Southern Studies Program of the University of South Carolina. To the patronage of that program and to the staff of the South Caroliniana Library, I am especially indebted. The home of Francis Lieber and the old campus of the South Carolina College was a fitting place to work upon such a book as this. To those who assisted, advised, and enlightened me in Columbia and Charleston, I must render my thanks: to Dianne Cox, Ann Fripp Hampton, Elizabeth Adams, Tony Owens, Allen Stokes, Anna Wells Rutledge, Lacy Ford, Gene Waddell, David Moltke-Hansen, George Rogers, and Clyde Wilson. James B. Meriwether offered not only the gift of a visiting professorship but also a home, sympathy, and scrutiny; help astonishing from so considerable a student of William Faulkner to so indifferent an admirer of Yoknapatawpha. Latterly at the University of Arkansas, I must thank those who helped to find a place for an unfashionably long manuscript: Willard Gatewood, John Guilds, and Miller Williams. Evan and Anita Bukey were kind enough to translate passages from Goethe with care and grace. Secretarial help was provided, always promptly and with good humor, by Jamie Lax, Lynn Burnett and Therese Luers. Portions of the introduction were read to seminars at the Universities of Oxford and Cambridge, where they benefited from the comments of John Thompson, Mark Kaplanoff, John Oldfield, William Dusinberre, Duncan McLeod, and Jack Pole; an abridged version has been published in the *Intellectual History Group Newsletter*, where Thomas Bender and William R. Taylor were helpfully critical. The publication of this book was made possible in part by a grant from The Arkansas Endowment for the Humanities.

My greatest debt is expressed by the dedication of this volume, in language fitting for a Tacitean. Richard Lounsbury helped with much of the Latin and all of the Greek, in the midst of his involuntary peregrinations. More, he has served for several years as the conscience of my prose, a bartering office, a matter beyond mere thanks.

M. O'B.
April 1982
Fayetteville, Arkansas

# Suggestions for Further Reading

## Primary Sources

Adger, John B., et al., eds. *The Collected Writings of James Henley Thornwell*. 1871. 4 vols. Edinburgh: The Banner of Truth Trust, 1974.

Bell, Malcolm, Jr. *Major Butler's Legacy: Five Generations of a Slaveholding Family*. Athens: University of Georgia Press, 1987.

Bleser, Carol, ed. *The Hammonds of Redcliffe*. New York: Oxford University Press, 1981.

———, ed. *Secret and Sacred: The Diaries of James Henry Hammond, a Southern Slaveholder*. New York: Oxford University Press, 1988.

Briggs, Ward W., Jr., ed. *The Letters of Basil Lanneau Gildersleeve*. Baltimore: Johns Hopkins University Press, 1987.

Burr, Virginia Ingraham, ed. *The Secret Eye: The Journal of Ella Gertrude Clanton Thomas, 1848–1889*. Chapel Hill: University of North Carolina Press, 1990.

Calhoun, Richard J., ed. *Witness to Sorrow: The Antebellum Autobiography of William J. Grayson*. Columbia: University of South Carolina Press, 1990.

Ceplair, Larry, ed. *The Public Years of Sarah and Angelina Grimké: Selected Writings, 1835–1839*. New York: Columbia University Press, 1989.

Clifton, James M., ed. *Life and Labor on Argyle Island: Letters and Documents of a Savannah River Rice Plantation, 1833–1867*. Savannah, Ga.: The Beehive Press, 1978.

Evans, Augusta Jane. *Beulah*. 1859. Edited by Elizabeth Fox-Genovese. Baton Rouge: Louisiana State University Press, 1992.

———. *Macaria; Or, Altars of Sacrifice*. 1864. Edited by Drew Gilpin Faust. Baton Rouge: Louisiana State University Press, 1992.

Garcia, Céline Frémaux. *Céline: Remembering Louisiana, 1850–1871*. Edited by Patrick J. Geary. Athens: University of Georgia Press, 1987.

Houzeau, Jean-Charles. *My Passage at the "New Orleans Tribune": A Memoir of the Civil War Era*. Edited by David C. Rankin. Translated by Gerard F. Denault. Baton Rouge: Louisiana State University Press, 1984.

Hubbs, G. Ward, ed. *Rowdy Tales from Early Alabama: The Humor of John Gorman Barr.* Tuscaloosa: University of Alabama Press, 1981.

Jacobs, Harriet A. *Incidents in the Life of a Slave Girl Written by Herself.* Edited by Jean Fagin Yellin. Cambridge: Harvard University Press, 1987.

Johnson, Michael P., and James L. Roark, eds. *No Chariot Let Down: Charleston's Free People of Color on the Eve of the Civil War.* Chapel Hill: University of North Carolina Press, 1984.

Kibler, James Everett, Jr., ed. *Selected Poems of William Gilmore Simms.* Athens: University of Georgia Press, 1990.

Lemmon, Sarah McCulloch, ed. *The Pettigrew Papers: Volume 1, 1685–1818.* Vol. 1 of *The Pettigrew Papers.* Raleigh, N.C.: State Department of Archives and History, 1971.

———, ed. *The Pettigrew Papers: Volume 2, 1819–1843.* Vol. 2 of *The Pettigrew Papers.* Raleigh: North Carolina Department of Cultural Resources, Division of Archives and History, 1988.

Lyman, Stanford M., ed. *Selected Writings of Henry Hughes: Antebellum Southerner, Slavocrat, Sociologist.* Jackson: University Press of Mississippi, 1985.

Meats, Stephen, and Edwin T. Arnold, eds. *The Writings of Benjamin F. Perry.* 3 vols. Spartanburg, S.C.: Reprint Company, 1980.

Meriwether, Robert L., et al., eds. *The Papers of John C. Calhoun.* 20 vols. to date. Columbia: University of South Carolina Press, 1959–.

Moore, Rayburn S., ed. *A Man of Letters in the Nineteenth-Century South: Selected Letters of Paul Hamilton Hayne.* Baton Rouge: Louisiana State University Press, 1982.

Paskoff, Paul F., and Daniel J. Wilson, eds. *The Cause of the South: Selections from "De Bow's Review," 1846–1867.* Baton Rouge: Louisiana State University Press, 1982.

Ramsay, David. *The History of the American Revolution.* 1789. Edited by Lester H. Cohen. 2 vols. Indianapolis: Liberty Fund, 1990.

Rosengarten, Theodore. *Tombee: Portrait of a Cotton Planter with the Plantation Journal of Thomas B. Chaplin, 1822–1890.* New York: William Morrow, 1986.

Ruffin, Edmund. *Incidents of My Life: Edmund Ruffin's Autobiographical Essays.* Edited by David F. Allmendinger. Charlottesville: University Press of Virginia, 1990.

Ruffner, Henry. *Judith Bensaddi, a Tale: And Seclusaval, or the Sequel to the Tale of Judith Bensaddi.* Edited by J. Michael Pemberton. Baton Rouge: Louisiana State University Press, 1984.

Simms, William Gilmore, ed. *The Charleston Book: A Miscellany in Prose and Verse.* 1845. Spartanburg, S.C.: Reprint Company, 1983.

Woodward, C. Vann, ed. *Mary Chesnut's Civil War.* New Haven: Yale University Press, 1981.
Woodward, C. Vann, and Elisabeth Muhlenfeld, eds. *The Private Mary Chesnut: The Unpublished Civil War Diaries.* New York: Oxford University Press, 1984.

*Secondary Works*

Allmendinger, David F. *Ruffin: Family and Reform in the Old South.* New York: Oxford University Press, 1990.
Ayers, Edward L. *Vengeance and Justice: Crime and Punishment in the 19th-Century American South.* New York: Oxford University Press, 1984.
Bakker, Jan. "Caroline Gilman and the Issue of Slavery in the Rose Magazines, 1832–1839." *Southern Studies* 24 (Fall 1985): 273–83.
———. *Pastoral in Antebellum Southern Romance.* Baton Rouge: Louisiana State University Press, 1989.
Bartley, Numan V., ed. *The Evolution of Southern Culture.* Athens: University of Georgia Press, 1988.
Bodenhamer, David J., and James W. Ely, Jr., eds. *Ambivalent Legacy: A Legal History of the South.* Jackson: University Press of Mississippi, 1984.
Boles, John B., and Evelyn Thomas Nolen, eds. *Interpreting Southern History: Historiographical Essays in Honor of Sanford W. Higginbotham.* Baton Rouge: Louisiana State University Press, 1987.
Briggs, Ward W., Jr., and Herbert W. Benario, eds. *Basil Lanneau Gildersleeve: An American Classicist:* Baltimore: Johns Hopkins University Press, 1986.
Bruce, Dickson D., Jr. *The Rhetoric of Conservatism: The Virginia Convention of 1829–30 and the Conservative Tradition in the South.* San Marino, Calif.: Huntington Library, 1982.
Cooper, William J., Jr., Michael F. Holt, and John McCardell, eds. *A Master's Due: Essays in Honor of David Herbert Donald.* Baton Rouge: Louisiana State University Press, 1985.
Corgan, Francis X., ed. *The Geological Sciences in the Antebellum South.* Tuscaloosa: University of Alabama Press, 1982.
Davis, David Brion. *Slavery and Human Progress.* New York: Oxford University Press, 1984.
D'Entremont, John. *Southern Emancipator: Moncure Conway, the American Years, 1832–1865.* New York: Oxford University Press, 1987.
Farmer, James Oscar, Jr. *The Metaphysical Confederacy: James Henley Thornwell and the Synthesis of Southern Values.* Macon, Ga.: Mercer University Press, 1986.

Faust, Drew Gilpin. *The Creation of Confederate Nationalism: Ideology and Identity in the Civil War South.* Baton Rouge: Louisiana State University Press, 1988.

———. *James Henry Hammond and the Old South: A Design for Mastery.* Baton Rouge: Louisiana State University Press, 1982.

Ford, Lacy K. "Republican Ideology in a Slave Society: The Political Economy of John C. Calhoun." *Journal of Southern History* 54 (August 1988): 405–24.

Fox-Genovese, Elizabeth. "The Fettered Mind: Time, Place, and the Literary Imagination of the Old South." *Georgia Historical Quarterly* 74 (Winter 1990): 622–50.

———. *Within the Plantation Household: Black and White Women in the Old South.* Chapel Hill: University of North Carolina Press, 1988.

Fox-Genovese, Elizabeth, and Eugene D. Genovese. "The Divine Sanction of Social Order: Religious Foundations of the Southern Slaveholders' World View." *Journal of the American Academy of Religion* 55 (1987): 211–33.

———. *Fruits of Merchant Capital: Slavery and Bourgeois Property in the Rise and Expansion of Capitalism.* New York: Oxford University Press, 1983.

Freehling, Alison Goodyear. *Drift Toward Dissolution: The Virginia Slavery Debate of 1831–1832.* Baton Rouge: Louisiana State University Press, 1982.

Freehling, William W. "James Henley Thornwell's Mysterious Antislavery Moment." *Journal of Southern History* 57 (August 1991): 383–406.

Friedman, Jean E. *The Enclosed Garden: Women and Community in the Evangelical South, 1830–1900.* Chapel Hill: University of North Carolina Press, 1985.

Gates, Henry Louis, Jr. *The Signifying Monkey: A Theory of African-American Literary Criticism.* New York: Oxford University Press, 1988.

Genovese, Eugene D. "Larry Tise's *Proslavery:* A Critique and Appreciation." *Georgia Historical Quarterly* 72 (Winter 1988): 670–83.

———. *The Slaveholders' Dilemma: Freedom and Progress in Southern Conservative Thought, 1820–1860.* Columbia: University of South Carolina Press, 1992.

———. "The Southern Slaveholders' View of the Middle Ages." In *Medievalism in American Culture*, edited by Bernard Rosenthal and Paul E. Szarmach, 31–52. Medieval & Renaissance Texts & Studies, vol. 55. Binghamton: State University of New York, 1989.

———. *Western Civilization Through Slaveholding Eyes: The Social and Historical Thought of Thomas Roderick Dew.* New Orleans: Graduate School of Tulane University, 1986.

Genovese, Eugene D., and Elizabeth Fox-Genovese. "The Religious Ideals of Southern Slave Society." *Georgia Historical Quarterly* 70 (Spring 1986): 1–16.

———. "Slavery, Economic Development, and the Law: The Dilemma of the Southern Political Economists, 1800–1860." *Washington and Lee Law Review* 41 (Winter 1984): 1–29.

Goen, C. C. *Broken Churches, Broken Nation: Denominational Schisms and the Coming of the Civil War.* Macon, Ga.: Mercer University Press, 1985.

Gray, Richard. *Writing the South: Ideas of an American Region.* Cambridge: Cambridge University Press, 1986.

Greenberg, Kenneth S. *Masters and Statesmen: The Political Culture of American Slavery.* Baltimore: Johns Hopkins University Press, 1985.

Guilds, John C., ed. *"Long Years of Neglect": The Work and Reputation of William Gilmore Simms.* Fayetteville: University of Arkansas Press, 1988.

Gwin, Minrose C. *Black and White Women of the Old South: The Peculiar Sisterhood in American Literature.* Knoxville: University of Tennessee Press, 1985.

Hall, Kermit L., and James W. Ely, Jr., eds. *An Uncertain Tradition: Constitutionalism and the History of the South.* Athens: University of Georgia Press, 1989.

Harrington, J. Drew. "Classical Antiquity and the Proslavery Argument." *Slavery & Abolition* 10 (May 1989): 60–72.

Havard, William C., and Walter Sullivan, eds. *A Band of Prophets: The Vanderbilt Agrarians After Fifty Years.* Baton Rouge: Louisiana State University Press, 1982.

Haygood, Tamara Miner. *Henry William Ravenel, 1814–1887: South Carolina Scientist in the Civil War Era.* Tuscaloosa: University of Alabama Press, 1987.

Hobson, Fred. "Surveyors and Boundaries: Southern Literature and Southern Literary Study After Mid-Century." *Southern Review* 27 (October 1991): 739–55.

———. *Tell About the South: The Southern Rage to Explain.* Baton Rouge: Louisiana State University Press, 1983.

Horsman, Reginald. *Josiah Nott of Mobile: Southerner, Physician, and Racial Theorist.* Baton Rouge: Louisiana State University Press, 1987.

———. *Race and Manifest Destiny: The Origins of American Racial Anglo-Saxonism.* Cambridge: Harvard University Press, 1981.

Humphries, Jefferson, ed. *Southern Literature and Literary Theory.* Athens: University of Georgia Press, 1990.

Johnson, Michael P., and James L. Roark. *Black Masters: A Free Family of Color in the Old South.* New York: W. W. Norton, 1984.

Jones, Anne Goodwyn. *Tomorrow is Another Day: The Woman Writer in*

*the South, 1859–1936.* Baton Rouge: Louisiana State University Press, 1981.
Kaufman, Allen. *Capitalism, Slavery, and Republican Values: American Political Economists, 1819–1848.* Austin: University of Texas Press, 1982.
Kennedy, J. Gerald, and Daniel Mark Fogel, eds. *American Letters and the Historical Consciousness: Essays in Honor of Lewis P. Simpson.* Baton Rouge: Louisiana State University Press, 1987.
Kohl, Lawrence Frederick. *The Politics of Individualism: Parties and the American Character in the Jacksonian Era.* New York: Oxford University Press, 1989.
Kousser, J. Morgan, and James M. McPherson, eds. *Region, Race, and Reconstruction: Essays in Honor of C. Vann Woodward.* New York: Oxford University Press, 1982.
Kreyling, Michael. *Figures of the Hero in Southern Narrative.* Baton Rouge: Louisiana State University Press, 1987.
———. "Southern Literature: Consensus and Dissensus." *American Literature* 60 (March 1988): 83–95.
Luker, Ralph. *A Southern Tradition in Theology and Social Criticism, 1830–1930: The Religious Liberalism and Social Conservatism of James Warley Miles, William Porcher DuBose and Edgar Gardner Murphy.* New York: Edwin Mellen Press, 1984.
McCash, William B. *Thomas R. R. Cobb: The Making of a Southern Nationalist.* Macon, Ga.: Mercer University Press, 1983.
McCoy, Drew R. *The Last of the Fathers: James Madison and the Republican Legacy.* Cambridge: Cambridge University Press, 1989.
McFeely, William S. *Frederick Douglass.* New York: W. W. Norton, 1991.
McLoughlin, William B. *Cherokee Renaissance in the New Republic.* Princeton: Princeton University Press, 1986.
Martin, Waldo E., Jr. *The Mind of Frederick Douglass.* Chapel Hill: University of North Carolina Press, 1984.
Miller, Randall M., and Jon L. Wakelyn, eds. *Catholics in the Old South: Essays on Church and Culture.* Macon, Ga.: Mercer University Press, 1983.
Mitchell, Betty L. *Edmund Ruffin: A Biography.* Bloomington: Indiana University Press, 1981.
Muhlenfeld, Elisabeth. *Mary Boykin Chesnut: A Biography.* Baton Rouge: Louisiana State University Press, 1981.
Newman, Stephen L. "Thomas Cooper, 1759–1839: The Political Odyssey of a Bourgeois Ideologue." *Southern Studies* 24 (Fall 1986): 295–305.
Numbers, Ronald L., and Todd L. Savitt, eds. *Science and Medicine in the Old South.* Baton Rouge: Louisiana State University Press, 1989.
Oakes, James. *The Ruling Race: A History of American Slaveholders.* New York: Alfred A. Knopf, 1982.

———. *Slavery and Freedom: An Interpretation of the Old South.* New York: Alfred A. Knopf, 1990.
O'Brien, Michael. "Biography and the Old South: A Review Essay." *Virginia Magazine of History and Biography* 93 (October 1985): 375–88.
———. *A Character of Hugh Legaré.* Knoxville: University of Tennessee Press, 1985.
———. *Rethinking the South: Essays in Intellectual History.* Baltimore: Johns Hopkins University Press, 1988.
———. "'A Sort of Cosmopolitan Dog': Francis Lieber in the South." *Southern Review* 25 (April 1989): 308–22.
———. "'The Water Rose in the Graves': Discontinuity and Localism in Nineteenth-Century Southern Thought." In *The United States South: Regionalism and Identity*, edited by Valeria Gennaro Lerda and Tjebbe Westendorp, 55–74. Rome: Bulzoni Editore, 1991.
O'Brien, Michael, and David Moltke-Hansen, eds. *Intellectual Life in Antebellum Charleston.* Knoxville: University of Tennessee Press, 1986.
Pease, William H., and Jane H. Pease. *The Web of Progress: Private Values and Public Styles in Boston and Charleston, 1828–1843.* New York: Oxford University Press, 1985. Reprint. Athens: University of Georgia Press, 1991.
Poesch, Jessie. *The Art of the Old South: Painting, Sculpture, Architecture & the Products of Craftsmen, 1560–1860.* New York: Alfred A. Knopf, 1983.
Riley, Sam G. *Index to Southern Periodicals.* Westport, Conn.: Greenwood Press, 1986.
———. *Magazines of the American South.* Westport, Conn.: Greenwood Press, 1986.
Rogers, James A. *Richard Furman: Life and Legacy.* Macon, Ga.: Mercer University Press, 1985.
Rubin, Louis D., Jr. *The Edge of the Swamp: A Study in the Literature and Society of the Old South.* Baton Rouge: Louisiana State University Press, 1989.
———. "The Way It Was with Southern Literary Study: A Reminiscence." *Mississippi Quarterly* 43 (Spring 1990): 47–63.
Scott, Patrick. "From Rhetoric to English: Nineteenth Century English Teaching at South Carolina College." *South Carolina Historical Magazine* 85 (July 1984): 233–43.
Severens, Kenneth. *Charleston Antebellum Architecture and Civic Destiny.* Knoxville: University of Tennessee Press, 1988.
Severens, Martha R., and Charles L. Wyrick, Jr., eds. *Charles Fraser of Charleston: Essays on the Man, His Art and His Times.* Charleston, S.C.: Carolina Art Association, 1983.

Shaffer, Arthur H. *To Be an American: David Ramsay and the Making of the American Consciousness.* Columbia: University of South Carolina Press, 1991.
Shalhope, Robert E. *John Taylor of Caroline, Pastoral Republican.* Columbia: University of South Carolina Press, 1980.
Shields, Johanna Nicol. "A Sadder Simon Suggs: Freedom and Slavery in the Humor of Johnson Hooper." *Journal of Southern History* 56 (November 1990): 641–64.
———. "A Social History of Antebellum Alabama Writers." *Alabama Review* 42 (July 1989): 163–91.
Shore, Laurence. *Southern Capitalists: The Ideological Leadership of an Elite, 1832–1885.* Chapel Hill: University of North Carolina Press, 1986.
Simpson, Lewis P. *The Brazen Face of History: Studies in the Literary Consciousness in America.* Baton Rouge: Louisiana State University Press, 1980.
———. "The Critics Who Made Us: Allen Tate." *Sewanee Review* 94 (Summer 1986): 471–85.
———. *Mind and the American Civil War: A Meditation on Lost Causes.* Baton Rouge: Louisiana State University Press, 1989.
———. "The State of Southern Literary Scholarship." *Southern Review* 24 (Spring 1988): 245–52.
Snay, Mitchell. "American Thought and Southern Distinctiveness: The Southern Clergy and the Sanctification of Slavery." *Civil War History* 35 (December 1989): 311–28.
Stephens, Lester D. *Joseph LeConte: Gentle Prophet of Evolution.* Baton Rouge: Louisiana State University Press, 1982.
Stowe, Steven M. *Intimacy and Power in the Old South: Ritual in the Lives of the Planters.* Baltimore: Johns Hopkins University Press, 1987.
———. "Singleton's Tooth: Thoughts on the Form and Meaning of Antebellum Southern Family Correspondence." *Southern Review* 25 (April 1989): 323–33.
Tise, Larry E. *Proslavery: A History of the Defense of Slavery in America, 1701–1840.* Athens: University of Georgia Press, 1987.
Watson, Ritchie Devon, Jr. *The Cavalier in Virginia Fiction.* Baton Rouge: Louisiana State University Press, 1985.
Wilson, Clyde N. *Carolina Cavalier: The Life and Mind of James Johnston Pettigrew.* Athens: University of Georgia Press, 1990.
Wimsatt, Mary Ann. *The Major Fiction of William Gilmore Simms.* Baton Rouge: Louisiana State University Press, 1989.
Woodward, C. Vann. *The Future of the Past.* New York: Oxford University Press, 1989.

Wyatt-Brown, Bertram. "God and Honor in the Old South." *Southern Review* 25 (April 1989): 283–96.

———. *Southern Honor: Ethics and Behavior in the Old South.* New York: Oxford University Press, 1982.

———. *Yankee Saints and Southern Sinners.* Baton Rouge: Louisiana State University Press, 1985.

# Index

## A

Abel, 199, 200
Accius, 405–6, 406
Achilles, 133, 320, 409
Adair, Robert, 99, 116
Adam, 198
Adams, Brooks, 2
Adams, Henry, 281
Adams, Herbert Baxter, 230, 398
Adams, Jasper, 23
Adams, John (classicist), 416
Adams, John (revolutionary), 135
Adams, John Quincy, 363
Adams, Samuel, 135
Addison, Joseph, 22, 24, 368–69, 370
Aelian, 414 n. 57
Aeschylus, 409
Aesop, 368, 369
Africa, 169
*African Repository and Colonial Journal*, 56
Agamemnon, 404
Ainsworth, Robert, 426
Aix-la-Chapelle, 92, 93–95, 104
Alaric, 162
Alcala, 147
Alcamenes, 410
Alcibiades, 157
Alexander of Macedon, 374, 407, 415
Algiers, 65
Alibert, J. L., 30
Alien and Sedition Laws, 150
Alison, Archibald, 126, 153 n. 44
Allston, Washington, 1, 330 n. 20
*Almanac de Gotha*, 85
Aloides, 368
Amadis of Gaul, 366
*American Journal of Philology*, 398
American Revolution, 105, 135, 149–51, 175–76, 228–62 passim, 332
American System, 47
Amherst, 357
Amiens, 290
Amiens, Treaty of, 61

Amphictyon, Council of, 158
Anaxagoras, 320
Ancillon, Johann Peter Friedrich, 91, 116–23 passim
Andover Theological Seminary, 420
Angel, Justus, 425, 431
Angel, Mr. (of St. Croix), 425
Anhalt, 108, 109
Anne (Queen of England), 136, 358
Antaeus, 366, 368
Anthon, Charles, 222 n. 62, 368, 400, 416–17, 419
Antigone, 320
Antonius, Marcus, 61, 61 n. 17
Antwerp, 92, 97, 110, 112–13
Aphrodite, 410
Apollo, 401, 410
Appomattox (Va.), 357
Aquinas, Thomas, 76, 155 n. 47, 363
Archilocus, 404
Argyll, Archibald Campbell, 2d duke of, 286, 287, 308 n. 33
Aristaenetus, 410
Aristarchus, 411
Aristophanes, 75
Aristotle: as inductionist, 77; *Poetics*, 101; Byzantium on, 158 concept of *accident*, 194; *Politics*, 201 n. 47; Gildersleeve on, 404, 406, 407; and French drama, 408; and Robert Henry, 430
Arminianism, 61
Armoricans, 222
Arnold, Benedict, 332
Arnold, Matthew, 1
Arnold, Thomas, 264, 265
Arrivabene, Giovanni, 98
Arses, 408 n. 37
Art: Harrison on, 68–72; Legare on, 112–13, 114, 115–16, 117–18; Porcher on, 310–36
Artaxerxes, 408 n. 37
Artemis, 407
Asia, 145, 174, 255, 256

453

## 454 Index

Athena, 407, 407 n. 34, 410
Athens, 173, 209, 402
Atlantis, 373-74
Attila, 162
Augusta, Princess of Prussia, 113
Augustine of Hippo, 181, 182, 202 n. 47
Augustus (Octavius), 130, 131-33,132 n. 12, 174 n. 71, 189, 314
Austen, Jane, 10
Austria, 60, 61, 62, 67, 68, 134 n. 19, 170 n. 66, 341, 363

### B

Babel, 203
Babylon, 39, 160
Bacon, Francis: Harrison on, 59, 75, 76, 77; on Henry VII, 153; style of, 181; and philosophy of history, 181-82; as scientist, 407; and Robert Henry, 430
Bacon, Nathaniel, 231
Bagoas, 408
Bailey, William, 399
Baillet, Comte Joseph de, 116, 117
Bailly, Jean Sylvan, 372-73
Balzac, Honoré de, 23, 114, 116, 280
Bancroft, George: translates Heeren, 80; in Germany, 91; as historicist, 229; on Virginia, 239, 241, 244, 251; on Gayarre, 281; Porcher on, 311.
Barnwell, Robert Woodward, 436
Bassano, Hugues-Bernard Maret, duc de, 114
Bastiat, Frédéric, 338
*Batrachomyomachia*, 408
Bavius, 367
Bayle, Pierre, 59
Beattie, James, 74
Beaufort (S.C.), 30
Beecher, Henry Ward, 357
Beerbohm, Max, 337
Bekker, Immanuel, 23, 104
Belgium, 64, 93, 102, 119
Bentham, Jeremy, 23
Bentinck, Lord William Cavendish, 62
Bentivoglio, Costanza Trotti, 98
Bentley, Richard, 80, 400, 411, 415, 416
Benton, Thomas Hart, 349
Béranger, Pierre Jean de, 23
Bercovitch, Sacvan, 14 n. 30
Bergé, M., 99
Bergheim, 95
Berkeley, George, 67, 421, 439, 440
Berkeley, William, 243, 244
Berlin, 91, 105, 112-23 passim, 264 n. 5, 399
Bernadotte, Jean Baptiste Jules, 63
Bernhardy, Gottfried, 403, 406, 418-19

Birmingham, 86
Bismarck, Otto von, 25
Biton, 320
Blackie, John Stuart, 413-14
Blacks: and intellectual history, 13-14; McCord on, 18-19, 341, 345, 346, 347, 348-49, 356; and Old South, 24-25; racial type, 58; and mulattoes, 99; and racism, 121; Dew on, 167-70; and civilization, 203-4, 205-6; in Virginia, 240-42, 245; and profitability of slavery, 255-58; and art, 330; and literature, 390
*Blackwoods Magazine*, 361
Blair, Hugh, 426
Blanche of Castile, 349
Bledsoe, Albert Taylor, 16, 358 n. 5
Boccaccio, Giovanni, 401 n. 11
Bocock, John Holmes: sketch of, 357-59; essay by, 359-75 Boileau-Despréaux, Nicolas, 133, 409 n. 42
Bologna, 327
Boniface VIII, 212
Bonn, 55, 91, 96, 97-104 passim, 399
Bordeaux, 147
Borgia, Lucrezia, 372
Borgo, Pozzo di, 98
Bossuet, Jacques Bénigne, 133, 182
Boston, 3, 56, 185, 329-30, 387
Böttiger, Karl August, 57, 70
Bourdon, Louis Pierre Marie, 80
Boyle, Robert, 75
Brazil, 64
Bremen, 425
Bremer, Fredrika, 265
Brewster, David, 75
Bronson, Oliver, 99
Brooks, Cleanth, 11
Brooks, Preston, 339
Brooks, Sidney, 98, 99, 101
Brougham, Henry, 84, 121
Brown, Joseph E., 376
Brown, Mather, 335 n. 25
Brown, Thomas, 126, 421, 426, 439, 440
Browning, Elizabeth Barrett, 182 n. 13, 354
Brugger, Robert, 2
Brunton, Mr., 426
Brussels, 91, 92, 96, 97, 103, 104, 307-8, 317, 287-88
Brutus, Marcus Junius, 131, 407
Buchanan, George, 321
Buckingham County (Va.), 357
Buist (schoolmaster), 426
Bunsen, Christian K. J., 278, 422
Burke, Edmund: *Reflections*, 72, 163; quoted, 87-88, 137; mentioned, 126, 135
Burns, Robert, 336, 362, 382
Burton, Robert, 82, 253 n. 17, 321

Busby, Richard, 411
Bute, John Stuart, 3d earl of, 367
Butler, Samuel (poet and satirist), 75
Buttman, Phillip Karl, 80
Byron, George Gordon, Lord: Legaré on, 13, 90; *Childe Harold's Pilgrimage*, 69, 191–92, 309; *Don Juan*, 81; *English Bards and Scotch Reviewers*, 83 n. 92; *Prophecy of Dante*, 131, 161; *The Age of Bronze*, 152; *Ode on Venice*, 160, 162; on Hazlitt, 208; as romantic, 408; on Keats, 409; mentioned, 24, 388
Byzantium, 158, 406

C

Cabanis, Pierre Jean Georges, 196
Cable, George Washington, 281 n. 5
Cacus, 405
Caesar, Gaius Julius: Napoleon compared to, 114; Emerson and, 364, 366; and mythology, 374; and Gildersleeve, 398; as grammarian, 406; mentioned, 120, 222
Cain, 198, 213
Calderón de la Barca, Pedro, 100, 146
Calhoun, John Caldwell: Parrington discusses, 8; and James H. Smith, 30; quoted, 125; statue of, 312, 328–36 passim; eulogy of, 424, 437; mentioned, 1, 363, 374
California, 178, 296
Caligula, 173 n. 69
Callimachus, 407 n. 34
Callinus, 417 n. 68
Calvin, John, 61, 218, 422
Cambacérès, Jean Jacques Regis de, 121
Cambridge, 412
Camoens, Luis de, 189 n. 26, 409 n. 42
Campbell, Charles, 233
Campbell, Lord Archibald (1682–1761), 286
Canada, 177, 290, 292
Canning, George, 63 n. 22, 65, 66, 66 n. 36, 67
Canova, Antonio, 71, 321, 322, 333, 335
Capet, Hugh, 52
Cardozo, Jacob, 31
Carlisle, George William Frederick, 7th earl of, 4 n. 7, 345
Carlists, 84, 116
Carlostadt, 217, 218
Carlyle, Thomas, 32, 229, 237, 399, 402–3
Carthage, 65
Caruthers, William Alexander, 8, 13 n. 26, 14
Cash, Wilbur J., 1, 2
Cassius (Gaius Cassius Longinus), 132 n. 12
Castlereagh, Robert Stewart, 2d viscount, 62, 64
Catherine II of Russia, 349

Catiline, 121
Cato the Younger, 132
Cecrops, 402
Celts, 313
Cervantes Saavedra, Miguel de, 113
Channing, William Ellery, 22
Chantrey, Francis Legatt, 71, 72, 333, 334, 335
Charlemagne, 93–94
Charles II, 243
Charles V, 97
Charleston (S.C.): Conversation Club, 3, 20; as literary center, 6, 27; New South and, 7; and political imagination, 12; College of, 20, 264, 311, 399; Trent on, 22; Library Society, 29, 312; and Miles, 263; Calhoun's statue in, 331; and Gildersleeve, 398, 399, 400; and Robert Henry, 424, 425, 426, 429, 437; mentioned, 31, 185, 265, 337
Chateaubriand, Francois Rene, vicomte de, 31, 127, 151, 198, 296
Chaucer, Geoffrey, 239 n. 14
Cheronea, 158
Chesnut, Mary, 19, 339
Cheves, Langdon, 19, 337, 338, 429
China, 141, 143, 191, 293
Chomenes, 321
Christ, Jesus, 213, 364
Christina, queen of Sweden, 408 n. 36
Cibber, Colley, 80–81
Cicero: and Verres, 61 n. 17; and common sense, 78–79; *Academicae Quaestiones*, 78 n. 76; and Catiline, 121; and oratory, 134, 150 n. 37; *De Officiis*, 191 n. 29; *De Republica*, 201; and Gildersleeve, 398; as etymologist, 406; *De Oratore*, 423; mentioned, 222, 321, 374, 377
Cid, 147 n. 34
Cincinnati, 357
Cinna, 367
Cities, 19–20, 21, 142, 200
Clarendon (S.C.), 429
Classical scholarship, 80, 100–1, 104, 113, 119–20, 143 n. 29, 398–419 passim
Claude Lorrain, 68, 321
Clay, Henry, 55, 56
Cleobis, 320
Cleombrotus, 320
Cleopatra, 374
Cockerel, John, 111
Coke, Sir Edward, 60 n. 12, 292
Coleridge, Samuel Taylor: concept of the clerisy, 2; and modernism, 12; *Biographia Literaria*, 74, 76, 77, 180 n. 81, 403 n. 18; as German, 80; *The Friend*, 182 n. 12, 360, 392; *Aids to Reflection*, 360; *Statesman's Manual*, 360; *The Garden of Boccaccio*, 401

n. 11; *Lectures on Shakespeare,* 410 n. 44; mentioned, 22, 27, 264, 359, 363, 364
Cologne, 91, 95, 97, 110, 315
Columbia (S.C.), 20, 337
Columbus, Christopher, 374
Commines, Philippe de, 79
Commodus, 138
Common sense philosophy: Harrison on, 72–81; and Bocock, 359, 366; and Thornwell, 421; and Robert Henry, 421, 430, 434, 439–40
Comte, Auguste, 178
Concord (Mass.), 359
Confucius, 143
Congaree River, 111
Constant, Benjamin, 55, 57, 99, 126
Constantine the Great, 130
Constantinople, 263
Constantinus Porphyrogennetus, 417 n. 68
Constitution of 1787, 149
Conti, 288, 300–1
Cooke, John Esten, 13 n. 26
Cooper, James Fenimore, 1, 55, 79, 330 n. 20, 394
Cooper, Thomas, 17, 21, 23, 37, 126, 179, 422, 434–36
Copernicus, 407
Copley, John Singleton, 335 n. 25
Corinth, 209
Corn Laws (G.B.), 45
Corneille, Pierre, 133, 144, 319, 399
Cornelia, 253
Correggio, 91
Cousin, Victor, 131, 182, 183, 184, 186, 264
Crafts, William, 8
Crassus, Lucius Lucinius, 423
Crates of Mallos, 417 n. 68
Crawford, 204 n. 49
Creuzer, Georg Freidrich, 23, 368, 370
Croly, George, 153 n. 44
Cromwell, Oliver, 243, 374, 390
Croxall, Samuel, 368, 369–70
Crozat, Anthony, 282, 283
Crozat, Marie Anne, 282
Crystal Palace, 327–28
Cuba, 62
Cunningham, Allan, 23, 72
Curll, Edmund, 389

### D

D'Abrantes, Laure Junot, duchesse, 114
Daedalus, 49
D'Aguesseau, Henri François, 13, 59
D'Angoulême, Marie Therese Charlotte, duchesse, 114
Dante Alighieri, 146
D'Aremberg, Auguste Marie Raymond, 95

D'Argenson, Marc Rene de Voyer, marquis, 288
Darius III, 408 n. 37
D'Arnin (Heinrich Friedrich von Arnim), 106, 116, 119, 120
D'Avenant, Sir William, 180
David, Jacques Louis, 324
Davis, Paulina, 349, 350
Davis, Richard Beale, 14 n. 30
Davy, Humphrey, 76
*De Bow's Review,* 3, 4, 18, 20
*Debrett's,* 85
Decatur (Ga.), 177
Declaration of Independence, 149
Dehon, Thomas, 101
Delphi, 401
Democrats (party), 280
Demosthenes, 13, 134, 150 n. 37
Denmark, 63, 71
Desmarets, Nicolas, 288
Desprez, Ludovicus, 368
Dew, Thomas Roderick: sketch of, 125–27; essay by, 127–76; mentioned, 17, 31, 228
Diana, 407
Dickens, Charles, 388, 410
Diderot, Denis, 126
Diehl, Carl, 24, 24 n. 51
Digby, Kenelm, 76
Diogenianus, 417 n. 68
Dionysius Thrax, 417 n. 68
Disraeli, Benjamin, 24, 178
D'Israeli, Isaac, 155 n. 47
Donne, John, 73 n. 56
Doughty, Thomas, 321
Draper, William, 367
Dresden, 55, 91, 109
Drummond, William, 78
Dryden, John, 115, 386
Dublin, 183, 185
DuBose, William, 311
Dumas, Alexander, *père*, 390
Duncan, Marck, 430
Dunlop, John, 150 n. 37
Dupin, Charles, 23, 60
Dura, 186
Durham, 177, 224
Duris of Samos, 417 n. 68
Düsseldorf, 91, 104
Dutens, Louis, 182

### E

Eaton, Clement, 16
Edgeworth, Maria, 362
Edinburgh: and John Law, 284, 285, 286, 299; and Robert Henry, 426–27, 430, 434; mentioned, 23, 185, 387
*Edinburgh Review,* 3, 5, 76 n. 66, 83 n. 92, 90

Editha, 110
Edwards, Bryan, 167 n. 61
Egypt, 141, 165, 209, 224, 365
Eichhorn, Johann Gottfried, 24
Elba, 63
Elberfeldt, 104, 106, 112, 121
*Elegant Extracts*, 310
Eliot, T. S., 11, 12
Elizabeth I of England, 67, 136, 327, 349, 350
Elliott, Stephen (the elder), 17, 29, 424
Elliott, Stephen (the younger), 29
Elliott, William, 10
Emerson, Ralph Waldo, 1, 6, 7, 17, 25, 358–75 passim, 415
Empson, William, 83 n. 92
Ennius, Quintus, 405, 406
Erasmus, 408
Erichthonius, 407 n. 34
Erigena, John Scotus, 363
Ernesti, Johann August, 78–79
Erwin of Steinbach, 366
Essex, Robert Devereaux, 2d earl of, 136, 350
Euripides, 100, 101, 404, 410
Europa, 368
Eustace, John Chetwood, 69
Eustace of Blois, 69 n. 46
Evain, Louis Auguste Frederique, 107
Everett, Alexander Hill, 99
Everett, Edward, 80, 99

F

Fabricius, Johann Albert, 418
Faulkner, William, 10, 11
Faust, Drew Gilpin, 2, 26
Faustus, 81, 318, 407
Fearon, Henry Bradshaw, 53, 54
*Federalist Papers*, 150
Fénelon, François de Salignac de la Mothe, 133, 153
Ferdinand VII, 63
Ferdusi, 146
Fiammingo, Dionisio (Denys Calvaert), 112
Fichte, Johann Gottlieb, 25, 265–66, 363, 422
Fielding, Henry, 410
Fiesoli, 68
Filmer, Robert, 126, 135
Fincastle (Va.), 358
Finland, 63
Fitch, John, 49
Fitzhugh, George, 13, 16, 32
Flanders, 314, 327
Flaxman, John, 333, 334
Florence, 16–62, 68, 69, 316, 333, 366
Foote, Henry Stuart, 349
Forsyth, Joseph, 68

Fouché, Joseph, 114
Fouqué, Friedrich Heinrich Karl, Baron de La Motte-, 433
Fourierism, 375
Fox, Charles James, 99, 135
Frankfurt am Main, 91
Franklin, Benjamin, 135
Fraser, Charles, 321
Frederick II of Prussia, 113, 405
Frederick III of Prussia, 124
Frederick William II of Prussia, 61 n. 18
Frederick William III of Prussia, 117
Frederick William IV of Prussia, 113
Fredrickson, George M., 13, 19
French Revolution of 1789: and British, 61; and Canning, 67; memoirs of, 114–15; Brougham on, 121–22; Dew on, 166; Holmes on, 225; McCord on, 350; mentioned, 93, 332
Frothingham, Octavius Brooks, 7
Fuller, Margaret, 328 n. 19
Fulton, Robert, 49

G

Gadsden (Bishop), 437
Gainsborough, Thomas, 321
Galilei, Galileo, 75
Garafola, Benvenuto, 355
Gates, Horatio, 332
Gayarré, Charles Étienne Arthur: sketch of, 280–83; essay by, 283–309; mentioned, 12, 20
Gelon, king of Syracuse, 65 n. 32
General Theological Seminary, 263
Geneva, 172 n. 68, 288
Genoa, 62
Genovese, Eugene, 13
Genseric, 162
Geoffrey of Monmouth, 407 n. 33
George I of England, 299 n. 26, 308
George III of England, 105, 367
Georgia, 376–77
Georgia Historical Society, 377
Georgia, University of, 376
Ghent, 65
Gibbon, Edward: and literature, 12; and the Grand Tour, 23; Harrison on, 78; on the Antonines, 137 n. 23; Holmes on, 195; mentioned, 59, 158 n. 45, 174, 178, 234, 310
Gibson, John, 71
Giddings, Franklin H., 398
*Gil Blas*, 426
Gildersleeve, Basil: sketch of, 398–400; essay by, 400–419
Gildersleeve, Benjamin, 398, 399
Gillespie, Neil, 17

## Index

Gilman, Daniel Coit, 398
Glasgow, 86
Goethe, Johann Wolfgang von: Harrison meets, 55, 57; *Faust*, 74, 80 n. 85, 110, 318–19; reviewed in *Edinburgh Review*, 83; *Werther*, 112; Porcher on, 318–19; Gildersleeve on, 401 n. 12, 403, 409; *Wilhelm Meister*, 433; minor writings, 409, 415; *Xenien*, 402 n. 14; mentioned, 22, 69, 77, 80, 377
Goldsmith, Oliver, 129, 316, 389, 412 n. 69
Gordon, Lord George, 367
Gothic art, 97, 109–10, 118, 224, 315–17
Goths, 159
Gott, Joseph, 71
Gottingen, 56, 147, 399, 400
Gourdin, Robert Newton, 264
Gower, Francis Leveson, 74, 80, 95
Gracchi, 253, 320, 337
Grayson, William John, 312
Greece, 71, 139–40, 145, 156–59, 165 n. 58, 212, 314, 398–419 passim
Greenough, Horatio, 329–30, 335
Gregory I, 80 n. 85
Gregory VII, 225, 226
Gregory XVI, 55
Grenville, George, 135
Greville, Charles, 95 n. 15
Greville, Lady Charlotte, 95
Grigsby, Hugh Blair, 17
Grimké, Thomas S., 23, 31
Grimm, Jakob Ludwig Karl, 23
Guiana, 177
Guizot, François, 23, 183, 184, 185, 186, 229, 235, 377
Gypsies, 203–4

### H

Haiti, 203, 205
Halifax (Va.), 358
Hall, Basil, 86
Hallam, Henry, 23
Hamburg, 111
Hamilton, Alexander, 23
Hamilton, George Baillie, 116, 117, 118, 122
Hamilton, Sir William, 421, 427, 439
Hammond, James Henry, 16, 35, 312
Hampden, John, 126, 135, 152
Hampden-Sydney College, 55
Hanover, 60, 84
Hanseatic League, 162
Harles, G. C., 418
Harris, James, 194 n. 33
Harrison, Jesse Burton: sketch of, 55–57; essay by, 57–88; mentioned, 91, 398
Harrison, Samuel Jordan, 55

Harrisonburg (Va.), 358
Harvard, 55, 56, 420
Hastings, Warren, 61
Haupt, Moritz, 416
Havre, 92
Hawthorne, Nathaniel, 1, 6, 371, 393–97 passim
Hayne, Paul Hamilton, 7
Hayne, Robert Young, 253
Hazlitt, William, 208
Headley, Joel Tyler, 389–90
Healy, George Peter Alexander, 334
Heeren, Arnold Hermann Ludwig, 23, 77, 80, 120, 126, 151 n. 38
Hegel, Georg Wilhelm Friedrich: Harrison and, 59; and Miles, 264; as Hellenist, 402; and Bernhardy, 406 n. 30; Gildersleeve on, 419; and Thornwell, 422; mentioned, 359, 363
Heidelberg, 121
Heineccius, Johann Gottlieb, 89
Helen of Troy, 366, 372, 374
Hélène of Mecklenberg, 117
Hengist, 401
Henry, Anne, 424–25
Henry, Elizabeth Connors, 429
Henry, Patrick, 135, 176, 239, 253, 261, 321, 424, 425
Henry, Robert, 17, 420–40 passim
Henry IV of France, 301
Henry VII of England, 153
Hentz, Caroline Lee, 13 n. 26
Hephaestus, 407 n. 34, 410
Hercules, 370, 415
Herder, Johann Gottfried von: and Holmes, 19; historical philosophy, 182–83, 195; Holmes on, 184, 224; and H. A. Washington, 230; mentioned, 22, 194, 214
Hermann, Johann Gottfried, 412–13
Hermann, Karl Friedrich, 401 n. 7
Herodotus, 119, 139, 157
Herostratus, 366
Hesse, 105
Hippolytus, 100
Hipponax, 404
Hobbes, Thomas, 126, 135, 230
Hodgson, W. B., 413 n. 54
Hogarth, William, 320, 321
Holifield, E. Brooks, 2
Holland, 64, 148, 162, 286, 327
Holland, Henry Richard Vassall Fox, 3d baron, 62
Holman, C. Hugh, 10, 12 n. 24
Holmes, George Frederick: on periodicals, 3–4, 5–6; biography of, 16, 17, 18; sketch of, 177–79; essay by, 179–227
Holmes, Oliver Wendell, 7 n. 11, 281 n. 5

# Index 459

Holy Alliance, 64, 66–67, 151
Homer: wrongly quoted, 113; Pope's translation, 115; *Odyssey*, 123; and Byzantium, 158; *Iliad*, 189, 202 n. 47; as literary model, 322, 325, 403; Anthon's edition of, 417; mentioned, 146, 250, 370, 400, 404, 406, 408 n. 38
Hooke, Robert, 181
Hooker, Richard, 67
Horace (Quintus Horatius Flaccus): Harrison on, 81; Dew on, 131, 132 n. 12; *Carmina*, 141, 192, 216; *Epodes*, 151 n. 37; *Satires*, 344; Delphin edition of, 368; *Epistles*, 405; versification, 406; Anthon's annotations to, 417; *Ars Poetica*, 419; mentioned, 22, 120
Horsa, 401
Houdon, Jean Antoine, 335
Houston, Samuel, 349
Howison, Robert Reid, 233, 234, 238–40
Hubbell, Jay B., 12 n. 24, 359 n. 6
Huger, Francis Kinloch, 109 n. 54
Hugo, Gustav von, 101
Hugo, Victor, 409 n. 42
Hume, David: and Dew, 126, 127; *Essays*, 128, 135, 142, 341 n. 13; cited on Italy, 162; and Adam Smith, 428–29; mentioned, 310
Hungary, 362

I

India, 24, 61, 128, 209, 255
Indians, 203–4, 295
Io, 368
Iphigenia, 409
Ireland, 362
Irving, Washington, 86, 394
Isabella of Castile and León, 349

J

Jackson, Andrew, 56
Jacksonianism, 27, 230
James, George Payne Rainsford, 388
James, Richard, 71
Jamestown (Va.), 232, 233
Jamison, David Flavel, 19, 178
Japan, 24
Jardine, George, 75, 76
Jefferson, Thomas: and Parrington, 9; as deist, 21; and Harrison, 55, 56; on the Gazette of Leyden, 83; and slavery, 127; papers of, 228; H. A. Washington on, 229; on early Virginia, 240–41; *Notes on Virginia*, 310; on Houdon's statue of Washington, 335 n. 25; and equality, 344; mentioned, 1, 23, 125, 126, 135, 176, 239, 253, 261, 374

Jefferson College, 399
Jeffrey, Francis, 4, 76 n. 66, 326
Jena, 147
Jerusalem, 213, 214
Jews, 212–15
Joan of Arc, 350
Job, 324, 380
John, Saint, the Divine, 387
John of Salisbury, 194 n. 33
John of Saxony, 124
Johns, John, 228
Johns Hopkins University, 230, 399
Johnson, Samuel, 115, 154 n. 45, 234, 386, 417 n. 69
Jomini, Antoine Henri, 23
Jonson, Ben, 144
Junius, 310, 433
Justinian, 58, 60, 143
Juvenal, 79, 120

K

Kant, Immanuel, 23, 30, 31, 265, 363, 421, 439
Kassel, 91, 105, 106
Keats, John, 66, 388, 409
Kennedy, John Pendleton, 8, 12
Kent, James, 65
Kepler, Johannes, 59, 75, 166
King, Grace, 280 n. 3
King, Mitchell, 90, 429
King George County (Va.), 229
Kingsley, Charles, 340 n. 12, 354
Klopstock, Friedrich Gottlieb, 23
Know-Nothings, 376, 420
Knox, John, 225
Kock, Paul de, 390
Korea, 241
Kossuth, Louis, 341

L

Lachmann, Karl K. R. W., 104, 416
Lafayette, Marie Joseph P. Y. R. G. du Motier, marquis de, 55, 109
La Fontaine, Jean de, 340, 344, 349
Lamartine, Alphonse Marie Louis de, 18, 23, 280, 388, 432
Lamb, Lady Caroline, 90
Landais, Napoleon, 189 n. 26
Landseer, Sir Edwin Henry, 321
La Rochelle, 290
Las Casas, Bartolomé de, 204
Latin America, 65, 66–67
La Tour, Madame Baillet de, 93
Law, John, 27, 280–309 passim
Law de Lauriston, 309
Lawrence, Mrs., 286

Layard, Austen Henry, 373
Laybach, Congress of, 64
Lee, Mary Elizabeth, 337
Legaré, Hugh Swinton: *Southern Literary Messenger* on, 6, 19; Hayne on, 7; Trent on, 8; and Parrington, 8; library on, 22, 23; and Harrison, 57; sketch of, 89–91; diaries of, 92–124; mentioned, 13, 17, 424
Legaré, Mary Swinton, 89, 96, 108
Leicester, Robert Dudley, earl of, 136
Leipzig, 91
Lempriere, John, 368
Leopold II of Austria, 61 n. 18
Lessing, Gotthold Ephraim, 80, 414 n. 57
L'Estrange, Sir Roger, 369
Lever, Charles, 362, 388
Leyden, 83, 148
*Library of Southern Literature*, 8
Lieber, Francis, 8, 59 n. 10
Liege, 92–93, 111
Lindsay, James, 426
Linnaeus, Carolus, 58, 407
Lintot, Barnaby Bernard, 389
Liverpool, 86
Livingston, Edward, 101
Livingston, Julia, 101
Livius Andronicus, 405
Livy (Titus Livius), 62 n. 19, 370
Locke, John: Harrison on, 74, 75; and Thornwell, 421; and Robert Henry, 430, 439; mentioned, 126, 135, 366
Lolme, Jean Louis de, 66
Lombardy, 159
London, 55, 56, 71, 92, 185, 285, 387, 425, 426, 428
Long, George, 56
Longfellow, Henry Wadsworth, 7 n. 11, 343, 355
Lorn, Marquis of, 286
Louis XI, 138
Louis XIII, 301
Louis XIV, 133, 189, 172 n. 68, 288, 408, 409
Louis XV, 283
Louis XVI, 61 n. 18
Louisa County (Va.), 358
Louisiana, 57, 280–304 passim, 357, 361, 362
*Louisiana Advertiser*, 57
Louisiana Historical Society, 57
*Louisiana Law Reports*, 57
Lowell, James Russell, 6, 7
Lowell (Mass.), 24
Lucan (Marcus Annaeus Lucanus), 132
Lucian, 182
Lucilius, Gaius, 406
Lucretius (Titus Lucretius Carus), 67
Luther, Martin, 123, 124, 217, 218, 225, 226, 314
Lycurgus, 168

Lynchburg (Va.), 55, 56
Lyons, 290
Lysias, 165 n. 58
Lytton, Edward Bulwer- (novelist), 23, 360, 388, 410–11, 412

M

Macaulay, Thomas Babington, 3, 55, 229, 321, 409, 412 n. 48
McCord, David James, 17, 338, 339
McCord, Louisa Susanna: on slave emancipation, 18–19; and city life, 20; sketch of, 337–39; essay by, 339–56; mentioned, 17
McCulloch, James, 126
McDuffied, George, 126
Macedon, 158
Machiavelli, Niccolo, 113
Mackintosh, Sir James, 23, 74 n. 60, 86, 99, 102, 133, 172 n. 68
Macon (Ga.), 177, 376
McVickar, John, 126
Madison, James, 55, 56, 126–27, 176, 239
Madison (Ga.), 376
Maecenas, Gaius, 130, 132 n. 12
Maevius, 367
Magdeburg, 91, 106–12 passim
Magna Carta, 230
Mai, Angelo, 202 n. 47
Maintenon, Françoise d'Aubigné, marquise de, 136
Maistre, Joseph de, 23
Malthus, Thomas, 47, 48, 51, 52, 53, 126
Manchester, 24, 168, 316
Manlius Torquatus, 320
Manzoni, Alessandro, 23
Maria Theresa, 349
Marlborough, Sarah Churchill, duchess of, 136
Marlowe, Christopher, 318
Marseilles, 147
Marshall, John, 239
Martignac, Jean Baptiste Sylvère Gay, vicomte de, 68
Martineau, Harriet, 341, 342, 347, 348, 352, 354, 355
Marx, Karl, 32
Mary, Queen of Scots, 374
Mason, Archy, 433
Mason, George, 176
Massachusetts, 232, 362
Maxcy, Jonathan, 429, 431–32, 433, 434
Mazzini, Guiseppe, 25
Melanchthon, Philip, 123, 124, 217, 408
Melville, Herman, 1
Memminger, Christopher Gustavus, 213 n. 53

Mencken, H. L., 8
Mengs, Anton Raphael, 69
Mercury, 401
Mesmer, Friedrich Anton, 368
Mesopotamia, 263
Methodism, 70, 358 n. 5
*Methodist Quarterly Review*, 17
Metternich, Clemens W. N. L., Fürst von, 115
Mezentius, 73
Michelangelo Buonarroti, 114, 316, 322, 333, 336
Michelet, Jules: and Holmes, 179; and Vico, 182, 194, 201 n. 46; untranslated, 186; and humanity, 189, 190, 215; Holmes on, 195–96, and Jews, 214; mentioned, 23, 25, 183, 184
Michigan, 361
Mickle, William J., 189 n. 26
Milan, 224
Miles, James Warley: J. S. Rhett on, 31, 265; sketch of, 263–66; essay by, 266–79; and Thornwell, 422; mentioned, 17
Mill, James, 98 n. 23, 126
Mill, John Stuart, 343–55 passim
Miller, Hugh, 316
Miller, Perry, 2, 6, 26
Milnes, Richard Monckton, 388
Milton, John: *Paradise Lost*, 76, 199; and Samuel Johnson, 115, 154 n. 45; *Paradise Regained*, 174; Porcher on, 317–18, 322; Carlyle on, 403; on education, 413; *Comus*, 430; mentioned, 386, 408
Minerva, 407
Mississippi, University of, 177
Missouri (state), 177
Mitchell, Donald Grant, 390
Mohammedanism, 61, 260
Molière, Jean Baptiste Poquelin, 115, 144, 169, 347, 399, 419
Monroe, James, 64, 66, 337
Monroe Doctrine, 66–67
Montaigne, Michel Eyquem, seigneur de, 374
Montesquieu, Charles Louis de Secondat, baron de Brède et de: and England, 60; *De l'esprit des lois*, 65, 84, 182; and liberalism, 66; as historian, 195; as environmentalist, 196, 220–21; mentioned, 17, 133, 134, 183, 194
Monticello, 55
Moore, Thomas, 22, 85
Morgan, Augustus de, 79–80
Morgan, Lady Sydney, 57, 82
Morpeth, Lord. *See* Carlisle, earl of
Mott, Lucretia Coffin, 349, 350
Mozart, Wolfgang Amadeus, 72, 116
Müller, Karl Otfried, 419
Munich, 91

Münzer, Thomas, 108, 217, 218
Mure, William, 419
Murray, John, 389
Musonius Rufus, 417 n. 68

N

Napier, McVey, 75–76
Naples, 60, 65, 67, 314, 321, 362
Napoleon, Louis, 341
Napoleon Bonaparte: in 1815, 63, 114–15; as adventurer, 93; and French Revolution, 114–15; and literature, 130–31; Croly on, 153 n. 44; mentioned, 109, 332, 347, 374
Nashville, 27
Nassaus (House of Orange), 93
Nassé, M. (physician), 103–4
Neander, Johann, 265
Nebuchadnezzar, 186
Nero Claudius Caesar, 132, 138, 173 n. 69
Nerva, Marcus Cocceius, 132
New Criticism, 11, 12
New England: and intellectual history, 6, 7, 14, 22; and Germany, 24; and tariff, 44; compared to Virginia, 243, 246, 251; and Emerson, 359; and Hawthorne, 396; mentioned, 2, 26
New Hampshire, 361
New Orleans, 6, 57, 280, 387
New South, 8, 15, 357
Newton, Isaac, 59, 75, 181, 347
New York, 184, 232, 387
Ney, Michel, 115
*Nibelungen*, 104
Nichophemus, 165 n. 58
Niebuhr, Barthold Georg: Schlegel on, 102; Byzantine histories of, 104; on France, 147; and Rome, 370; as heir of Wolf, 416; and Robert Henry, 433, 434; mentioned, 23, 77, 126, 195, 229
*Niles Weekly Register*, 31, 44
Nineveh, 373
Nisbet, Eugenius Aristides, 376–77
Nisbet, Richard Henry: sketch of, 376–77; essay by, 378–97
Noah, 201, 203
Nordhausen, 104, 106, 107
North, Frederick, 8th baron, 135
*North American Review*, 4, 23, 57, 99
North Carolina, 108
Norway, 63
Nott, Henry Junius, 17, 424, 433, 436
Nott, Josiah, 13
Nullification, 20, 30, 91, 398, 420

O

Oglethorpe College, 377

Ohio, 328, 340
Olympics, 139
Orangeburg (S.C.), 177, 263
Orleans, 290
Orleans, Ferdinand Philippe, duc d' (1810–1842), 117
Orleans, Philippe II, duc d' (1674–1723), 282, 288–308 passim
Orpheus, 368, 369, 370
Osterweis, Rollin G., 19
Otho, 110
Ovid (Publius Ovidius Naso), 119, 132, 401, 406
Owen, Robert, 126, 342
Oxford, 427
Oxford (Miss.), 177
Oxford Movement, 263

P

Paley, William, 23, 27, 359, 366, 412
Palgrave, Francis, 83 n. 92
Palmer, Benjamin Morgan, 420–21
Pandects, 58
Paris: Harrison in, 55, 56; Legaré in, 90; and Pradon, 100; and centralization, 141, 147; Miles in, 264; and Law, 280–309 passim; and women, 338; mentioned, 387
Park, Thomas, 436
Parkersburg (Va.), 357
Parr, Samuel, 411
Parrington, Vernon Louis, 8, 9
Pascal, Blaise, 424
Patterson, William B., 92
Paul, Saint, 391
Paulus Silentiarius, 406
Peel, Sir Robert, 31, 39 n. 23
Pegasus, 401
Pendleton, Edmund, 176
Perceforest, 366
Pericles, 82, 189, 314, 320, 374
Persia, 156, 256
Peter I of Russia, 124, 308 n. 32
Petigru, James Louis, 432
Petrarch (Francisco Petrarca), 407
Phidias, 321, 322, 323, 330, 336, 403, 410
Philadelphia, 185, 330, 337
Philip II of Macedon, 157–58
Philip II of Spain, 314
Philip IV of Spain, 100
Philochorus, 417 n. 68
Phoenicia, 222, 256
Pierce, Benjamin Franklin, 396
Pilnitz, 61
Pindar, 139, 158, 403
Pinkerton, John, 405
Pisistratus, 412

Pitt, William, 1st earl of Chatham, 3, 135, 321, 374, 412
Pius VIII, 55
Plato: Dialogues, 101; Byzantium on, 158; on history, 275; and Emerson, 364, 366, 367, 372; and Atlantis, 373; mentioned, 410, 404, 430
Plautus, 66 n. 33, 401, 413
Plutarch, 121 n. 94, 168 n. 63
Pocahantas, 231
Poe, Edgar Allan, 1, 2, 5, 8, 12, 18
Poland, 64, 93, 171, 175, 412
Polignac, Jules Armand, prince, 85
Poliphilus (Francesco Colonna), 401–2
Polybius, 113
Polynices, 320
Pomey, Antoine, 69 n. 45
Ponsonby, John, 64
Poor Law Reports, 23
Pope, Alexander, 22, 24, 115, 367, 411, 415
Porcher, Frederick Adolphus: and cities, 20; on James S. Rhett, 30; sketch of, 310–12; essay by, 312–36; mentioned, 17
Porphyry, 194 n. 33
Porson, Richard, 411
Porter, Jane, 388
Portugal, 64, 66
Potsdam, 110, 111, 124
Powers, Hiram, 328–36 passim
Powhatan, 251
Pradon, Nicholas, 100
Prague, 91
Praxiteles, 410
Presbyterianism, 225, 357, 377, 398, 420–22
Prescott, William Hickling, 281
Preston, William Campbell, 22, 23
Prince Edward County (Va.), 357
Princeton, 399
Pringle, John Julius, 429
Prior, Matthew, 286
Prodicus, 370
Prometheus, 366, 368, 369, 370
Propertius, Sextus, 131
Proteus, 141
Prussia, 62, 67, 91, 98, 111, 123, 124, 170 n. 66, 172 n. 68, 363
Ptolemy (Claudius Ptolemaeus), 407
Punic Wars, 222
Puritans, 219, 243, 246, 251

Q

Quedlinburg, 110
Quesnay, François, 126

R

Rabelais, François, 181 n. 9

Racine, Jean, 100, 133, 136, 140, 144, 146, 319, 399
Raleigh, Walter, 136, 282
Ramsay, David, 400
Randolph, Edmund, 176
Randolph, John, 363
Raphael Santi, 68, 77, 91
Rauchenstein, Rudolf, 403
Raymond, Daniel, 126
Raynal, Guillaime Thomas François, Abbé, 83, 133
Reconstruction, 264
Reformation, 123–24, 178, 217–19, 232, 314, 407
Reform Bill of 1832, 82
Reichard, Heinrich A. O., 114
Reid, Thomas, 74, 359, 366, 439
Remus, 370
Republicanism, 82–83, 100, 120–21, 125–76 passim
Retzsch, Friedrich August Moritz, 319, 336
Reynolds, George William McArthur, 390
Reynolds, Sir Joshua: on history, 282; as incubus, 320; on models, 322; on sculpture, 323, 324, 333, 334; mentioned, 71, 335
Rhett, James Smith. *See* James Hervey Smith
Rhett, Robert Barnwell, 29
Rhode Island, 417
Ricardo, David, 47, 48, 126
Richardson, Charles, 180 n. 26
Richelieu, Armand Jean du Plessis, duc de, 374
Richmond (Va.), 6, 12, 19, 177, 232 n. 9
Richter, Jean Paul, 355
Riego, Rafael de, y Nuñez, 64
Ritchie, Dr., 426
Ritschl, Friedrich Wilhelm, 413, 406 n. 27
Roane, John, 176
Robertson, William, 310, 426
Robespierre, Maximilien Marie Isidore, 372
Roederer, Pierre Louis, 121
Romagna, 159
Rome: Harrison in, 55, 56; art of, 71, 321, 327, 333, 366; idea of, 139–40; oratory of, 150 n. 37; decay of, 159; imperial, 160, 212, 230; religion of, 314; and Gildersleeve, 398–419 passim; mentioned, 209
Romulus, 370
Rousseau, Jean Jacques, 133, 134, 225
Rubens, Peter Paul, 112, 113
Rubin, Louis D., Jr., 10
Ruffin, Edmund, 16
Rumsey, James, 49
Ruskin, John, 312
Russell, Lord George William, 113, 117, 118, 121 n. 95

Russell, Lord William, 135, 152
*Russell's Magazine*, 264, 311
Russia, 62, 63, 64, 67, 83, 170 n. 66, 175, 177, 362
Ryder, Albert Pinkham, 1

S

Sacheveral, Henry, 85
Saint-Simon, Claude Henri de Rouvroy, comte de, 23
Saint-Simon, Louis de Rouvroy, duc de, 136, 290 n. 23, 299, 300
St. Trond, 93
Salic Law, 84
Salisbury, 224
Sallust (Gaius Sallustius Crispus), 119
Salmasius, Claudius, 408
Saluda (N.C.), 106
San Angelo, 55
San Jago de Compostella, 147
Sanskrit, 102
Sardinia, 62, 67, 170 n. 66, 172 n. 68
Savannah (Ga.), 425
Savigny, Friedrich Karl von, 23, 101, 120
Saxons, 74, 221, 222, 229, 230, 242, 251, 313
Saxony, 62
Say, Jean Baptiste, 126
Scaliger, Julius Caesar, 415, 416
Scarron, Paul, 136
Schelling, Friedrich Wilhelm Joseph von, 363, 422
Schiller, Johann Christoph Friedrich von, 22, 23, 77, 110, 402 n. 14, 405, 413
Schlegel, August Wilhelm von, 23, 55, 57, 80, 98–104 passim, 127
Schlegel, Friedrich von, 23, 77, 126, 132, 146, 177–227 passim
Schliermacher, Friedrich Daniel Ernst, 264
Schneidewin, Friedrich Wilhelm, 403
Schwenk, Conrad, 407 n. 32
Schwiers, Conrad, 425
Scopas, 410
Scotland, 47, 72, 110, 362
Scott, Sir Walter, 85, 90, 362, 366, 370–71, 388
Scythia, 157
Sejanus, Lucius Aelius, 130, 138
Seneca, Lucius Annaeus, 70
Seneca Falls (N.Y.), 346 n. 28
Senegal Company, 293
Senior, Nassau, 23, 98
Seth, 199, 200
Sévigné, Marie de Rabutin-Chantal, marquise de, 340 n. 12
Seymour, Emma, 114
Shakespeare, William: Italian plays, 10;

## Index

Macbeth, 73, 244, 340, 344; and Germans, 80–81, 146; *Henry V*, 84; and Samuel Johnson, 115; *Othello*, 144, 233, 374; *Pericles*, 144; *Merchant of Venice*, 297, 374; *Henry VIII*, 307; as Gothic writer, 317, 318, 319; *Tempest*, 318, 403; as Elizabethan, 327; *Measure for Measure*, 340; and Emerson, 364, 365; *Hamlet*, 374, 403; *King John*, 410; *Twelfth Night*, 415; mentioned, 353, 362
Shand, Peter J., 29, 30
Sheffield, 345
Shelley, Mary, 324
Shelley, Percy Bysshe, 388
Sheridan, Richard Brinsley, 61, 135, 152
Sidney, Algernon, 126, 135, 152, 230
Sidney, Sir Philip, 282, 392
Sieyès, Emmanuel Joseph, 120, 121–22
Silesia, 100
Simms, William Gilmore: as professional writer, 2; as editor, 4; and Morpeth, 4 n. 7; and Parrington, 8; literary theory of, 12; and intellectual history, 12; on Legaré, 6, 19; political imagination of, 20; as historian, 281; and Porcher, 311; and Nisbet, 377; mentioned, 1, 14
Simonides, 403
Simons, Edward P., 433
Simpson, Lewis P., 9, 11
Sismondi, Jean Charles Léonard Simonde de: Smith on, 24–54 passim; on Spain, 147 n. 34; on Italy, 159, 161 n. 51, 162 n. 55; mentioned, 126, 127
Sistine Chapel, 55
Skinner, Quentin, 16, 17
Slavery. *See* Blacks
Smith, Adam: *Wealth of Nations*, 33; Sismondi on, 33–34; on Europe, 38; *Theory of Moral Sentiments*, 428–29; mentioned, 126, 434
Smith, Edward D., 431
Smith, Henry Nash, 14
Smith, James Hervey: sketch of, 29–32; essay by, 32–54; on Miles, 231, 232
Smith, John Raphael, 71
Smithfield, 168
Smollett, Tobias George, 310, 410
Socinius, 218
Socrates, 77, 407, 430
Solfarata, 56
Somerset, James, 60
Somerset House, 72
Sophie Charlotte of Prussia, 117
Sophocles, 100, 404
South, Robert, 413
South Carolina, 6, 7, 10, 20, 27, 87, 253, 310
South Carolina College, 90, 263, 376, 420–40 passim

South Carolina Historical Society, 311
*Southern Agriculturalist*, 4
*Southern Lady's Book*, 337
*Southern Literary Messenger*, 4, 5, 6, 18, 19, 21, 178, 358
*Southern Presbyterian Review*, 358, 420
*Southern Quarterly Review*, 3, 4, 17, 18, 20, 21, 264, 311, 377, 420
*Southern Rose*, 337
*Southern Review*, 20, 21, 29, 30, 57, 90–91, 424, 433
Southey, Robert, 126
Spa, 111
Spain, 38, 60, 63–64, 65, 67, 147 n. 34, 157, 281, 327
Sparta, 83, 209
Spenser, Edmund, 239, 317
Spinoza, Baruch, 363
Staël, Anne Louise Germaine Necker, baronne de Staël-Holstein: *Considérations*, 60; and liberalism, 66, 131; and August von Schlegel, 98, 99; *Influence of Literature*, 133, 134, 149; *De L'Allemagne*, 145, 405 n. 26; and Necker, 337; and women, 338; mentioned, 57, 127
Starke, Mariana, 69
Stephens, Alexander Hill, 8
Stephens, John Lloyd, 389
Sterne, Laurence, 410
Stewart, Dugald, 23, 126, 153 n. 42, 166 n. 59, 426, 434, 439
Stoicism, 70
Stolberg, 106, 107
Stowe, Harriet Beecher, 338, 390
Strasburg, 224, 366
Strauss, David Friedrich, 276, 277
Stuarts, 243
Suarez, Francisco, 422
Sue, Eugène, 388, 391
Suetonius (Gaius Suetonius Tranquillus), 113, 174 n. 71
Sully, Maximilien de Béthune, duc de, 282, 299, 301–2
Sumner, Charles, 339
Sweden, 63
Swedenborg, Emanuel, 114
Swift, Jonathan, 374, 386
Switzerland, 162
Sybaris, 401

T

Tacitus, Cornelius, 119, 120, 222, 360, 423
Taglioni, Maria, 113
Talleyrand, Charles Maurice de, 55, 57, 62, 114, 121
Tantalus, 366, 368, 369, 370

Tasso, Torquato, 146
Tate, Allen, 9, 10, 11, 12, 19
Taylor, Harriet, 343–55 passim
Taylor, John, 8, 438
Taylor, William Cooke, 183, 184, 185, 186, 202–3, 206, 214
Taylor, William R., 13, 14, 22
Telesilla, 417 n. 68
Tencin, Abbé, 298
Tennyson, Alfred, Lord, 341, 388, 409
Texas, 361, 417
Thackeray, William Makepeace, 388, 411
Thebes, 160, 209
Themistocles, 157, 173, 415
Theocritus, 113
Theophrastus, 407
Thersites, 366
Theseus, 407 n. 34
Thierry, Augustin, 23
Thiers, Adolphe, 23
Thiersch, Berhardy, 80
Thiersch, Friedrich, 80
Thom, James, 336
Thoreau, Henry David, 1, 6, 17
Thornwell, James Henley: and religious orthodoxy, 21; and Bocock, 358; on education, 418 n. 70; sketch of, 420–22; essay by, 422–40; mentioned, 17
Thorwaldsen, Albert Bertel, 71, 330 n. 20
Thucydides, 82, 157, 423
Thurii, 401
Tiberius Julius Caesar Augustus, 1, 130, 138
Ticknor, George, 22, 23, 55, 56, 90, 91
Tieck, Christian Ludwig, 115
Tieck, Ludwig, 23, 80
Tilly, Johannes Tserklaes, count of, 110
Titian (Tiziano Vecellio), 118
Titus Flavius Sabinus Vespasianus, 132
Tocqueville, Alexis de, 23, 100, 120, 280
Tolmides, 417 n. 68
Tooke, Andrew, 69
Tooke, John Horne, 367
Tours, 290
Transcendentalism, 15, 357–75 passim
Trenck, Franz von der, 109
Trent, William Peterfield, 4, 8, 22
Tribonian, 60
Troppau, Congress of, 64, 65
Troup, George Michael, 376
Troy, 407
Trumbull, John, 335 n. 25
Tucker, Beverley, 8, 12, 13, 16, 17, 25, 125, 228
Tucker, Cynthia, 228
Tucker, George, 3, 12, 13, 16, 17
Turgot, Anne Robert Jacques, 182
Turin, 288

Turkey, 83, 85, 256
Tuscany, 159
Tyler, John, 89
Tzetzes, 406

U

Ulpian, 60
Union Theological Seminary, 357
Urihuela, 147
Utrecht, Treaty of, 65

V

Valckenaer, M. C. A., 196
Valencay, 63
Valla, Lorenzo, 202 n. 47
Vallambrosa, 68
Van Buren, Martin, 56
Vandyke, Sir Anthony, 112
Vaulx-Cernay, Pierre de, 339
Veblen, Thorstein, 50 n. 31
Vendôme, Louis Joseph, duc de, 288
Venice, 56, 71, 160, 308–9
Venus, 407
Vergil (Publius Vergilius Maro): Georgics, 38, 43; *Aeneid*, 73, 193; *Eclogues*, 151 n. 38, 174, 201, 412 n. 52; as Faustus, 407; and Anthon, 417; mentioned, 113, 131, 143, 322, 405
Verona, 64
Verres, Caius, 61
Vespasian (Titus Flavius Vespasianus), 132
Vico, Giambattista, 22, 179, 182, 189, 190, 191, 192, 193, 194, 195, 196, 201
Victor Amadeus, 288
Victoria, 84 n. 93
Vienna, 60, 62, 98, 134 n. 19, 185
Villèle, Jean Baptiste Séraphin Joseph, comte de, 67
Villemain, Abel François, 23, 220–21
Villers, Charles F. D. de, 23, 147
Vinci, Leonardo da, 69, 114
Virginia: and Harrison, 55–57; and England, 87; and Dew, 125, 126, 141, 175–76, 177; Washington on, 228–62; and Bocock, 357–59; mentioned, 6, 27, 362
Virginia, University of, 56, 177, 399
Virginia Historical Society, 126
Visconti, Guiseppe Arconati, 98–104 passim
Voltaire, François Marie Arouet de, 17, 60, 113, 124, 133, 134, 175, 182, 225
Vos, Hernandus, 426

W

Waddel, Moses, 90
Wale, Sir Charles, 94

Wallace, James, 436
Walpole, Horace, 405 n. 26
Washington, George, 23, 135, 175–76, 239, 253, 262, 332, 335, 374, 390
Washington, Henry Augustine: sketch of, 228–30; essay by, 231–62
Weber, M. (publisher), 104
Webster, Daniel, 23, 363, 374
Webster, Noah, 311
Weimar, 55
Weld, Angelina Grimké, 349, 350
Wellington, Arthur Wellesley, 1st duke of, 62, 63
West, Benjamin, 320–21, 335 n. 25
West Indies, 425
*Westminster Review*, 343
Westmoreland County (Va.), 228
Whateley, Richard, 264
Wheaton, Henry, 23, 121
Whiggery, 73, 81, 229, 280
Whitefoord, Mr., 29
Wilberforce, William, 348
Wilkes, John, 367
William and Mary, College of, 126, 177, 228
William I of Germany, 113
William I of Holland, 117, 119
William of Orange, 148
Willington Academy, 263
Willkie, Sir David, 321
Wilson, Edmund, 11

Wilson, Richard, 321
Winckelmann, Johann Joachim, 70, 400
Wirt, William, 8, 12, 13 n. 26
Wish, Harvey, 16
Wither, George, 392
Wittenberg, 123, 124, 314
Wolf, Friedrich August, 400, 416
Women, 169 n. 65, 259–60, 311, 337–56
Worcester Convention, 341, 343, 344, 346, 348, 354
Wordsworth, William, 58, 325–27, 359, 362, 388
Wright, Frances, 342
Wyatt, Richard James, 71
Wythe, George, 176

X

Xantippe, 352
Xenophon, 165 n. 58, 370 n. 32, 157

Y

Yale, 311
Young, Mrs. Thomas John, 265

Z

Zenodotus, 417 n. 68
Zeus, 407 n. 34, 410
Zwingli, Ulrich, 217

www.ingramcontent.com/pod-product-compliance
Lightning Source LLC
Chambersburg PA
CBHW021845300426
44115CB00005B/24